TENTH EDITION

FILM ART

AN INTRODUCTION

David Bordwell Kristin Thompson

University of Wisconsin—Madison

Mc
Graw
Hill

Connect
Learn
Succeed™

FILM ART: AN INTRODUCTION, 10TH EDITION

Published by McGraw-Hill, a business unit of The McGraw-Hill Companies, Inc., 1221 Avenue of the Americas, New York, NY, 10020. Copyright © 2013 by The McGraw-Hill Companies, Inc. All rights reserved. Printed in the United States of America. Previous editions © 2010, 2008, and 2004. No part of this publication may be reproduced or distributed in any form or by any means, or stored in a database or retrieval system, without the prior written consent of The McGraw-Hill Companies, Inc., including, but not limited to, in any network or other electronic storage or transmission, or broadcast for distance learning.

Some ancillaries, including electronic and print components, may not be available to customers outside the United States.

This book is printed on acid-free paper.

2 3 4 5 6 7 8 9 0 DOW/DOW 1 0 9 8 7 6 5 4 3

ISBN   978-0-07-353510-4
MHID   0-07-353510-9

Senior Vice President, Products & Markets:
   Kurt L. Strand
Vice President, General Manager:
   Michael J. Ryan
Vice President, Content Production
   & Technology Services: Kimberly
   Meriwether David
Managing Director: William R. Glass
Director: Christopher Freitag
Brand Manager: Laura Wilk
Director of Development: Rhona Robbin
Senior Development Editor: Kirstan A.
   Price
Editorial Coordinator: Jessica Holmes
Digital Product Analyst: Jay Gubernick

Director, Content Production: Terri Schiesl
Project Manager/Content Project Manager:
   Mel Valentin
Buyer: Susan K. Culbertson
Designer: Allister Fein/Margarite Reynolds
Cover and Interior Designer: Elise Lansdon
Cover Image: The Kobal Collection at
   Art Resource, NY
Content Licensing Specialist: Jeremy
   Cheshareck
Media Project Manager: Brent dela Cruz
Typeface: 10.5/12 Times Roman
Compositor: Thompson Type
Printer: RR Donnelly – Willard

All credits appearing on page or at the end of the book are considered to be an extension of the copyright page.

Library of Congress Cataloging-in-Publication Data
Bordwell, David.
   Film art : an introduction / David Bordwell, Kristin Thompson.—10th ed.
      p. cm.
   ISBN 978-0-07-353510-4 (acid-free paper)—ISBN 0-07-353510-9 (acid-free paper)
   1. Motion pictures—Aesthetics. I. Thompson, Kristin, 1950– II. Title.
PN1995.B617 2012
791.4301—dc23

                              2012021855

www.mhhe.com

ABOUT THE AUTHORS

David Bordwell is Jacques Ledoux Professor Emeritus of Film Studies at the University of Wisconsin–Madison. He holds a master's degree and a doctorate in film from the University of Iowa. His books include *The Films of Carl-Theodor Dreyer* (University of California Press, 1981), *Narration in the Fiction Film* (University of Wisconsin Press, 1985), *Ozu and the Poetics of Cinema* (Princeton University Press, 1988), *Making Meaning: Inference and Rhetoric in the Interpretation of Cinema* (Harvard University Press, 1989), *The Cinema of Eisenstein* (Harvard University Press, 1993), *On the History of Film Style* (Harvard University Press, 1997), *Planet Hong Kong: Popular Cinema and the Art of Entertainment* (Harvard University Press, 2000), *Figures Traced in Light: On Cinematic Staging* (University of California Press, 2005), *The Way Hollywood Tells It: Story and Style in Modern Movies* (University of California Press, 2006), *Poetics of Cinema* (Routledge, 2008), and *Pandora's Digital Box: Films, Files, and the Future of Movies* (Irvington Way Institute Press, 2012). He has won a University Distinguished Teaching Award and was awarded an honorary degree by the University of Copenhagen. His website is www.davidbordwell.net.

Kristin Thompson is an Honorary Fellow at the University of Wisconsin–Madison. She holds a master's degree in film from the University of Iowa and a doctorate in film from the University of Wisconsin–Madison. She has published *Eisenstein's Ivan the Terrible: A Neoformalist Analysis* (Princeton University Press, 1981), *Exporting Entertainment: America in the World Film Market 1907–1934* (British Film Institute, 1985), *Breaking the Glass Armor: Neoformalist Film Analysis* (Princeton University Press, 1988), *Wooster Proposes, Jeeves Disposes, or, Le Mot Juste* (James H. Heineman, 1992), *Storytelling in the New Hollywood: Understanding Classical Narrative Technique* (Harvard University Press, 1999), *Storytelling in Film and Television* (Harvard University Press, 2003), *Herr Lubitsch Goes To Hollywood: German and American Film After World War I* (Amsterdam University Press, 2005), and *The Frodo Franchise: The Lord of the Rings and Modern Hollywood* (University of California Press, 2007). She blogs with David at www.davidbordwell.net/blog, and is a contributor to TheOneRing.net. In her spare time, she studies Egyptology.

The authors have also collaborated on *Film History: An Introduction* (McGraw-Hill, 3rd. ed., 2010), *Minding Movies: Observations of the Art, Craft, and Business of Filmmaking* (University of Chicago Press, 2011), and, with Janet Staiger, on *The Classical Hollywood Cinema: Film Style and Mode of Production to 1960* (Columbia University Press, 1985).

To our parents,

Marjorie and Jay Bordwell

and Jean and Roger Thompson

EXPERIENCE *FILM ART* WITH CONNECT FILM

Studying the arts isn't just about learning the facts; that's why we emphasize the skills of watching and listening closely. Together with the Criterion Collection, we've developed CONNECT FILM to introduce students to the world of film and challenge them to develop the critical analysis skills necessary to become informed viewers.

CONNECT TO ACCESS
Film Clips

Partnership with the prestigious Criterion Collection provides author-created tutorials that guide students through key films clips, highlighting important aspects discussed in each chapter and modeling the critical viewing skills central to the course.

CONNECT TO PREPARE
for Film Analysis Assignments

Writing prompts featuring film stills and links to movie clips challenge students to practice analyzing the different aspects of the film to prepare them for their longer written assignments.

CONNECT TO MASTER
the Basics

Interactive film activities help students develop a fluency in the core vocabulary and concepts of the course by applying the content from each chapter to frames from contemporary and classic films.

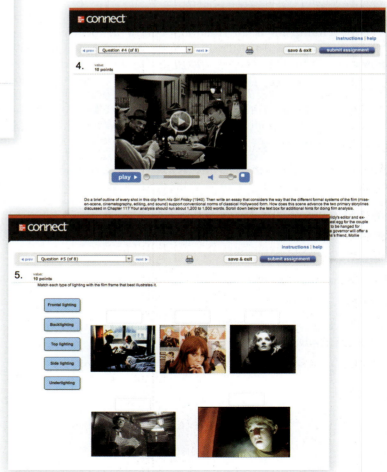

FILM ART + **The Criterion Collection = Connect Film**

Authors David Bordwell and Kristin Thompson partnered with the Criterion Collection to create brief video tutorials that clarify and reinforce key concepts and model the critical skills necessary to become informed viewers. The clips can be shown in class or assigned for students to view on their own, with brief optional follow-up quizzes.

Criterion Collection Selections

Film Lighting: Introduction

Light Sources in *Ashes and Diamonds* (1958)

Available Lighting in *Breathless* (1960)

Staging in Depth in *Mr. Hulot's Holiday* (1953)

Color Motifs in *The Spirit of the Beehive* (1973)

Lens and Camera Movement: Introduction

Tracking Shots Structure a Scene in *Ugetsu* (1953)

Tracking Shot to Reveal in *The 400 Blows* (1959)

Style Creates Parallelism in *Day of Wrath* (1943)

Staging and Camera Movement in a Long Take from *The Rules of the Game* (1939)

Editing with Graphic Matches in *Seven Samurai* (1954)

Shifting the Axis of Action in *Shaun of the Dead* (2004)

Crossing the Axis of Action in *Early Summer* (1951)

Crosscutting in *M* (1931)

Elliptical Editing in *Vagabond* (1985)

Jump Cuts in *Breathless* (1960)

Sound Mixing in *Seven Samurai* (1954)

Contrasting Rhythms of Sound and Image in *Mr. Hulot's Holiday* (1953)

Offscreen Sound in *M* (1931)

What Comes Out Must Go In: 2D Computer Animation

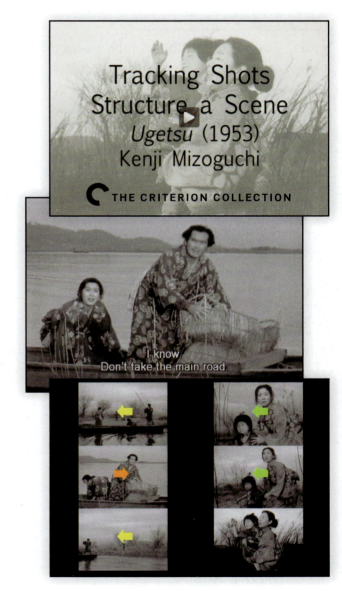

BRIEF CONTENTS

CONTENTS

CHAPTER 3   Narrative Form   72

PART 3 • Film Style

CHAPTER 4   The Shot: Mise-en-Scene   112

CHAPTER 5   The Shot: Cinematography   160

CHAPTER 6   The Relation of Shot to Shot: Editing   218

CHAPTER 7   Sound in Cinema   266

CHAPTER 8   Summary: Style and Film Form   308

PART 4 • Types of Films

CHAPTER 9   Film Genres   328

CHAPTER 10   Documentary, Experimental, and Animated Films   350

PART 5 • Critical Analysis of Films

CHAPTER 11   Film Criticism: Sample Analyses   402

PART 6 • Film Art and Film History

CHAPTER 12   Historical Changes in Film Art: Conventions and Choices, Tradition and Trends   458

PREFACE

Key Features and Learning Aids in the Tenth Edition

With a skills-centered approach, *Film Art* provides the respected scholarship and analytic tools students need to:

- **Understand** key vocabulary and concepts of film forms, techniques, and history
- **Appreciate** a wide variety of classic and contemporary films and the creative choices made by filmmakers to shape the experience of viewers
- **Analyze** films critically and systematically to enrich their understanding and appreciation of any film, in any genre

The text emphasizes the study of complete films, with an approach that examines how a film is created, how an entire film functions, and how the art of film has developed over time.

New "Creative Decision" Sections

CREATIVE DECISIONS

In-depth examples deepen students' appreciation for how creative choices by filmmakers affect how viewers respond. Discussions include performance and camera positioning in *The Social Network,* editing in *The Birds,* and overlapping dialogue cuts in *The Hunt for Red October.*

A Closer Look Boxes

Detailed examinations of issues of importance in contemporary cinema provide detailed looks at such topics as the use of computer generated imagery (CGI) in *The Lord of the Rings,* editing in *L.A. Confidential,* and motifs in *The Shining.*

Authors' Blog, "Observations on Film Art"

In what Roger Ebert calls "the most knowledgeable film blog on the web," David Bordwell and Kristin Thompson share their ideas and experiences with instructors and students (http://www.davidbordwell.net/blog). Throughout the text, "Connect to the Blog" references point to blog entries with relevant ideas, terms, and film examples, connecting ideas in *Film Art* to the current film scene in an accessible way.

Chapter Summary and Recommendations for DVD and Blu-ray Supplements

Each chapter includes suggestions for DVD and Blu-ray supplements that provide particularly effective resources related to key topics.

More Than 1,200 Frame Enlargements

The text is generously illustrated with frame enlargements rather than production stills, allowing students to study images that directly correspond to the finished films.

P.1 Production still

P.2 Frame enlargement

P.1, P.2 Production stills vs. frame enlargements. Both images have been used to illustrate discussions of Jean Renoir's *Rules of the Game*. In P.1, a production still, the actors have been posed for the most balanced composition and the clearest view of all three. In P.2, a frame enlargement from the film itself, the composition is looser than that shown in the production still. The frame enlargement also reveals that Renoir uses the central doorway to suggest action taking place in depth. Very often, a production still doesn't capture important features of the director's visual style.

New to the Tenth Edition

Chapter 1 Updated and expanded information on digital production, distribution, and exhibition, with information on computer-generated special effects in *Iron Man* and *Attack of the Clones*.

Chapter 2 New introductory section asking students to contrast the opening scenes of *Jurassic Park* and *Close Encounters of the Third Kind*.

Chapter 3 New introductory section asking students to construct the plot of a hypothetical romantic comedy. Additional examples of narrative principles in *Julie & Julia*, *Harry Potter and the Prisoner of Azkaban*, and *Lebanon*.

Chapter 4 New introductory section asking students to analyze a shot from *Inglourious Basterds*. A dedicated section analyzing a scene from *L'Avventura*; new information on performance capture, with *Avatar* and *Pirates of the Caribbean* as examples; and a new section about eye-scanning a shot from psychological research on *There Will Be Blood*. Other new examples from recent films include *A Prophet*, *Moon*, *Green Lantern*, and *Angels & Demons*.

Chapter 5 Expanded information on video cinematography, including a new box on digital 3D cinema. Additional examples from *Domino*, *Power and Water*, *The Mill and the Cross*, *Tron: Legacy*, *House of Wax*, *Avatar*, *127 Hours*, *The Social Network*, *The Departed*, *Secretariat*, *Laura*, *The Milk of Sorrow*, and *Hunger*.

Chapter 6 New introduction emphasizing students' own experiences with editing videos. A dedicated section on four shots from *The Birds*; and new examples from *Unstoppable*, *Winter's Bone*, *Contagion*, and *Matchstick Men*.

Chapter 7 New section asking students to imagine different uses of sound in a telephone conversation. New feature "Creative Decisions: To Overlap or Not to Overlap?" with a new example from *M*. Other new examples from *The Snake Pit*, *The King's Speech*, *127 Hours*, and *Chungking Express*.

Chapter 8 New sections on "Creative Decisions: Style and the Filmmaker" and "Watching and Listening: Style and the Viewer," plus an example from *Inception*.

Chapter 9 New section asking students to reconstruct conventions of romantic comedy. Fresh examples from *Serendipity*, *(500) Days of Summer*, *The Secret in Their Eyes*, *Paranormal Activity*, and *Stomp the Yard!*

Chapter 10 Extended film analyses of *Koyaanisqatsi* and *Dimensions of Dialogue* replace *A Movie* and *Fuji* from previous editions. New examples from *Harry Potter and the Deathly Hallows: Part I*, *Sita Sings the Blues*, *My Dog Tulip*, *Rivers & Tides*, *Grizzly Man*, *The War Tapes*, and *Inside Job*.

Chapter 12 New feature on "Creative Decisions—Film Form and Style across History." Expanded discussion of traditions and movements in film history, showing how they have influenced later filmmaking. New examples from *Trouble in Paradise*, *The Robe*, *Dust in the Wind*, *Suspense*, *Bye Bye Birdie*, *Down with Love*, *La petite fille et son chat*, *Tom, Tom the Piper's Son*, *Twilight Zone: The Movie*, *Apocalypse Now*, *Blue Velvet*, *The Two Minutes to Zero Trilogy*, *The Usual Suspects*, *Offside*, *The Idiots*, *Jaws*, *Goodbye Solo*, *The Sixth Sense*, and *Kill Bill: Volume 1*.

FROM THE AUTHORS

If you're in your late teens or early twenties, we have something in common with you. That was the age when we became curious about—some would say, obsessed with—film, cinema, movies.

What fueled our enthusiasm was a simple love of this medium and the great films we saw. For us, films that are classics today, from *Alphaville, 2001,* and *The Godfather* through *Jaws* and *Nashville* to *Pulp Fiction* and *Chungking Express,* were new movies. Over the years, we've watched film history unfold, and our excitement at new developments hasn't flagged.

Of course, we loved particular films and admired particular filmmakers. At the same time, we were entranced by the artistic possibilities of film as an art form. As teachers and writers, we roamed widely, trying to understand films from very different traditions—from silent avant-garde cinema to modern Hong Kong film, from Los Angeles to Paris to Tokyo. We've written about modern Hollywood, including *The Lord of the Rings,* and filmmakers working outside Hollywood—for example, Carl Dreyer, Sergei Eisenstein, and Yasujiro Ozu. In the last five years, we've extended our explorations to the Web, where we blog regularly about the many things that interest us in film.

Studying the arts isn't just about learning facts. That's why in *Film Art* we have always emphasized the skills of watching and listening closely. With the tenth edition of *Film Art* we are excited to announce a partnership with the prestigious Criterion Collection of DVDs and Blu-ray discs in our new CONNECT FILM digital program (see pp. iv–v). The Criterion Collection is dedicated to gathering many of the greatest classic and contemporary films from around the world. Criterion editions provide the highest technical quality and include award-winning supplements. They are a natural partner in introducing a new generation to cinema studies. We've created a series of clips that model the critical viewing skills that will help you become informed viewers.

This tenth edition of *Film Art* needed to be even more inclusive. We've written it during a time of major technological change. Digital technology has given many people access to filmmaking tools, and it has changed film distribution and exhibition. You can watch movies on your laptop or mobile phone, and films now arrive at theaters on hard drives rather than film reels. Because we focus on concepts, and because the techniques we study remain central to all sorts of moving-image media, much of what we studied in earlier editions remains valid. Still, we've expanded our discussion to include the creative choices opened up by digital cinema.

Studying the arts isn't only about learning facts and concepts either, although both are important. In addition, studying the arts broadens our tastes. In ten editions of *Film Art,* we've made reference to many well-known films but also to many that you've probably never heard of. This is part of our plan. We want to show that the world of cinema teems with a great many unexpected pleasures, and we hope to get you curious.

In surveying film art through such concepts as form, style, and genre, we aren't trying to wrap movies in abstractions. We're trying to show that there are principles that can shed light on a variety of films. We'd be happy if our ideas can help you to understand the films that you enjoy. And we hope that you'll seek out films that will stimulate your mind, your feelings, and your imagination in unpredictable ways. For us, this is what education is all about.

Acknowledgments

Over three decades, many people have aided us in the writing and revision of this book. We are grateful to Ernest R. Acevedo-Muñoz, David Allen, Rick Altman, George Angell, Tino Balio, Michael Barker of Sony Pictures Classics, Lucius Barre, John Belton, Joe Beres, Ralph Berets, Jake Black, Robin Blaetz, Les Blank, Vince Bohlinger, Eileen Bowser, Edward Branigan, Martin Bresnick, Ben Brewster, Michael Budd, Peter Bukalski, Colin Burnett, Elaine Burrows, Richard B. Byrne, Mary Carbine, Jerome Carolfi, Corbin Carnell, Jerry Carlson, Kent Carroll, Noël Carroll, Paolo Cherchi Usai, Jeffrey Chown, Gary Christenson, Anne Ciecko, Gabrielle Claes and the staff of the Cinémathèque Royale de Belgique, Bruce Conner, Kelley Conway, Mary Corliss of the Museum of Modern Art Film Stills Department, Susan Dalton, Robert E. Davis, Ethan De Seife, Dorothy Desmond, Marshall Deutelbaum, Kathleen Domenig, Suzanne Fedak, Susan Felleman, Maxine Fleckner-Ducey of the Wisconsin Center for Film and Theater Research, Don Fredericksen, Jon Gartenberg, Ernie Gehr, Kristi Gehring, Kathe Geist, Rocky Gersbach, Douglas Gomery, Claudia Gorbman, Ron Gottesman, Eric Gunneson, Debbie Hanson, Howard Harper, Dorinda Hartman, Denise Hartsough, Kevin Heffernan, Paul Helford, Linda Henzl, Rodney Hill, Michele Hilmes, Richard Hincha, Jan-Christopher Horak of the UCLA Film Archive, Lea Jacobs, Bruce Jenkins, Derek Johnson, Kathryn Kalinak, Charlie Keil, Vance Kepley, Christina King, Laura Kipnis, Barbara Klinger, Jim Kreul, Don Larsson, Jenny Lau, Thomas M. Leitch, Gary London, José Lopez, Patrick Loughney of the Library of Congress Motion Picture Division, Moya Luckett, Mike Maggiore of the Film Forum, Charles Maland, Mark McClelland, Roger L. Mayer, Norman McLaren, Donald Meckiffe, Jackie Morris of the National Film Archive, Charles Musser, James Naremore, Kazuto Ohira of Toho Films, David Popowski, Badia Rahman, Hema Ramachandran, Paul Rayton, Daniel Reynolds, Matt Rockwell, Jonathan Rosenbaum, Cynthia S. Runions, Leo Salzman, James Schamus of Focus Features, Ethan de Seife, Rob Silberman, Charles Silver of the Museum of Modern Art Film Study Center, John Simons, Ben Singer, Scott Sklenar, Joseph Evans Slate, Harry W. Smith, Jeff Smith, Michael Snow, Katerina Soukup, Katherine Spring, John C. Stubbs, Dan Talbot of New Yorker Films, Richard Terrill, Jim Udden, Edyth von Slyck, Susan White, Tona Williams, Beth Wintour, Chuck Wolfe, James Yates, and Andrew Yonda.

In preparing this edition, we're grateful to many of the above, as well as to Todd Berliner, Anna Brusutti, Leslie DeBauche, Eric Diensfrey, Jane Greene, Jim Healy, Patrick Keating, Sergio Andres Lobo-Navia, Christopher Lupke, Liza Palmer, John Powers, Dave Resha, Leo Rubinkowski, Benjamin Smith, Robert Spadoni, Mads Suldrup, and James Udden. We also appreciate the suggestions for revision and Connect content offered by Barbara L. Baker (University of Central Missouri), Heather Bigley (University of Florida), Michael Bliss (Virginia Polytechnic Institute and State University), Steve Gilliland (West Virginia State University), Michael B. Green (Arizona State University), Rodney Hill (Georgia Gwinnett College), Robert J. Hudson (Brigham Young University), Christopher P. Jacobs (University of North Dakota), Robert Mayer (Oklahoma State University), Nicholas Tanis (New York University), and Susan Tavernetti (De Anza College).

We owe special thanks to Erik Gunneson, producer and director of our video supplements; to Stew Fyfe, who prepared many of the frame enlargements for this edition; and to Petra Dominkova, whose eagle eye scanned our ninth edition for slips, misprints, and inconsistencies. Warm thanks as well go to Peter Becker and Kim Hendrickson of the Criterion Collection for their generosity in cooperating with us on the video extracts.

As ever, we're indebted to the McGraw-Hill publishing team, particularly Chris Freitag, Laura Wilk, Kirstan Price, Mel Valentin, Stacey C. Sawyer, and Betty Chen.

David Bordwell
Kristin Thompson

Teaching and Learning with *Film Art*

Online Learning Center (www.mhhe.com/filmart10e)

The Online Learning Center for *Film Art* includes a variety of helpful teaching resources:

- Instructor's manual
- Test bank
- PowerPoint presentations
- Image bank

McGraw-Hill Create (www.mcgrawhillcreate.com)

Design your own ideal course materials with McGraw-Hill's Create™. Rearrange or omit chapters, combine material from other sources, upload your syllabus or any other content you have written to make the perfect resource for your students. Search thousands of leading McGraw-Hill textbooks to find the best content for your students; then arrange it to fit your teaching style. You can even personalize your book's appearance by selecting the cover and adding your name, school, and course information. When you order a Create book, you receive a complimentary review copy. Get a printed copy in 3 to 5 business days or an electronic copy (e-Comp) via e-mail in about an hour. Register today at www.mcgrawhillcreate.com.

CourseSmart (www.coursesmart.com)

CourseSmart offers thousands of the most commonly adopted textbooks across hundreds of courses from a wide variety of higher education publishers. It is the only place for faculty to review and compare the full text of a book online, providing immediate access without the environmental impact of requesting a printed exam copy. At CourseSmart, students can save up to 50 percent off the cost of a printed book, reduce their impact on the environment, and gain access to powerful web tools for learning, including full text search, notes and highlighting, and e-mail tools for sharing notes among classmates. Visit coursesmart.com to learn more.

Tegrity Campus (http://tegritycampus.mhhe.com)

Tegrity is a service that makes class time available around the clock. It automatically captures every lecture in a searchable format for students to review when they study and complete assignments. With a simple one-click start-and-stop process, you capture all computer screens and corresponding audio. Students replay any part of any class with easy-to-use browser-based viewing on a PC or Mac. With Tegrity Campus, students quickly recall key moments by using Tegrity Campus's unique search feature, which lets them efficiently find what they need, when they need it, across an entire semester of class recordings. To learn more about Tegrity, watch a 2-minute Flash demo at http://tegritycampus.mhhe.com.

McGraw-Hill Campus™

McGraw-Hill Campus is a new one-stop teaching and learning experience available to users of any learning management system. This institutional service allows faculty and students to enjoy single sign-on (SSO) access to all McGraw-Hill Higher Education materials, including the award-winning McGraw-Hill Connect® platform, from directly within the institution's web site. McGraw-Hill Campus provides faculty with instant access to all McGraw-Hill Higher Education teaching materials (for example, eTextbooks, test banks, PowerPoint slides, animations and learning objects), allowing them to browse, search, and use any instructor ancillary content in our vast library at no additional cost. Students enjoy SSO access to a variety of free (for instance, quizzes, flash cards, narrated presentations) and subscription-based products (for example, McGraw-Hill Connect).

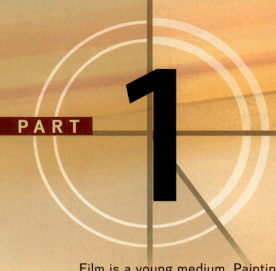

PART 1

Film is a young medium. Painting, literature, dance, and theater have existed for thousands of years, but film was invented only a little more than a century ago. Yet in its comparatively short span, the newcomer has established itself as an energetic and powerful art.

It's this art that we explore in this book. The chapters that follow show how creative people have used film to give us experiences that we value. We examine the principles and techniques that give film its power to tell stories, express emotions, and convey ideas.

But this art has some unusual features we should note from the start. More than most arts, film depends on complex technology. Without machines, movies wouldn't move. In addition, film art usually requires collaboration among many participants, people who follow well-proven work routines. Films are not only created but produced. Just as important, they are firmly tied to their social and economic context. Films are distributed and exhibited for audiences, and money matters at every step.

Film Art and Filmmaking

Chapter 1 surveys all these aspects of the filmmaking process. We examine the technology, the work practices, and the business side of cinema. All these components shape and sustain film as an art.

1

Film as Art: Creativity, Technology, and Business

Motion pictures are so much a part of our lives that it's hard to imagine a world without them. We enjoy them in theaters, at home, in offices, in cars and buses, and on airplanes. We carry films with us in our laptops, tablets, and cellphones. Press a button, and a machine conjures up movies for your pleasure.

Films communicate information and ideas, and they show us places and ways of life we might not otherwise know. Important as these benefits are, though, something more is at stake. Films offer us ways of seeing and feeling that we find deeply gratifying. They take us through experiences. The experiences are often driven by stories centering on characters we come to care about, but a film might also develop an idea or explore visual qualities or sound textures.

It doesn't happen by accident. Films are *designed* to create experiences for viewers. To gain an understanding of film as an art, we should ask why a film is designed the way it is. When a scene frightens or excites us, when an ending makes us laugh or cry, we can ask how the filmmakers have achieved those effects.

It helps to imagine that we're filmmakers, too. Throughout this book, we'll be asking you to put yourself in the filmmaker's shoes. This shouldn't be a great stretch. You've taken still photos with a camera or a mobile phone. Very likely you've made some videos, perhaps just to record a moment in your life—a party, a wedding, your cat creeping into a paper bag. And central to filmmaking is the act of choice. You may not have realized it at the moment, but every time you framed a shot, shifted your position, told people not to blink, or tried to keep up with a dog chasing a Frisbee, you were making choices.

You might take the next step and make a more ambitious, more controlled film. You might compile clips into a YouTube video, or document your friend's musical performance. Again, at every stage you make design decisions, based on how you think this image or that sound will affect your viewers' experience. What if you start your music video with a black screen that gradually brightens as the music fades in? That will have a different effect than starting it with a sudden cut to a bright screen and a blast of music.

At each instant, the filmmaker can't avoid making creative decisions about how viewers will respond. Every moviemaker is also a movie viewer, and the choices are considered from the standpoint of the end user. Filmmakers constantly ask themselves: *If I do this, as opposed to that, how will viewers react?*

The menu of filmmaking choices has developed over time. Late in the 19th century, moving pictures emerged as a public amusement. They succeeded because they spoke to the imaginative needs of a broad-based audience. All the traditions that emerged—telling fictional stories, recording actual events, animating objects or drawings, experimenting with pure form—aimed to give viewers experiences they couldn't get from other media. Men and women discovered that they could use cinema to shape those experiences in various ways. Suppose we center the actors so they command the frame space? Suppose we cut up a scene into several angles? Suppose we move the camera to follow the actors? Learning from one another, testing and refining new choices, filmmakers developed skills that became the basis of the art form we have today.

Thinking like a filmmaker is all very well, you might say, if you want a career in the business. What if you just want to enjoy movies? We think that you can appreciate films more fully if you're aware of how creative choices shape your experience. You've probably looked at some making-of bonuses on DVD versions of films you love, and some of those supplements have increased your enjoyment. We enhance our appreciation of *The Social Network* or *Inception* when we know something of the filmmakers' behind-the-scenes discussion of character motivation and specific line readings. We can always get more out of the films we see, and thinking about the filmmakers' choices helps us to understand why we respond as we do.

This is why we start our survey of film art by looking at the process of film production. Here we can see, in very tangible ways, the sorts of options available to people working in this medium. In every chapter that follows, we invoke what film artists have said about the ways they've chosen to solve creative problems.

Throughout this book, we focus on the two basic areas of choice and control in the art of film: form and style. **Form** is the overall patterning of a film, the ways its parts work together to create specific effects (Chapters 2 and 3). **Style** involves the film's use of cinematic techniques. Those techniques fall into four categories: mise-en-scene, or the arrangement of people, places, and objects to be filmed (Chapter 4); cinematography, the use of cameras and other machines to record images and sounds (Chapter 5); editing, the piecing together of individual shots (Chapter 6); and sound, the voices, effects, and music that blend on a film's audio track (Chapter 7). After examining the various techniques, Chapter 8 integrates them in an overview of film style. In more distant chapters, we discuss how form and style differ among genres and other types of films (Chapters 9–10). We consider how we can analyze films critically (Chapter 11) and how film form and style have changed across history, offering filmmakers different sets of creative choices (Chapter 12). In all, we'll see how through choice and control, film artists have created movies that entertain us, inform us, and engage our imaginations.

Art vs. Entertainment? Art vs. Business?

The term *art* might put some readers off. If cinema originated as a mass medium, should we even use the word? Are Hollywood directors "artists"? Some people would say that the blockbusters playing at the multiplex are merely "entertainment," whereas films for a narrower public—perhaps independent films, or foreign-language fare, or experimental works—are true art.

Usually the art/entertainment split rests on a value judgment: art is serious and worthy, whereas entertainment is superficial. Yet things aren't that simple. As we just indicated, many of the artistic resources of cinema were discovered by filmmakers working for the general public. During the 1910s and 1920s, for instance, many filmmakers who simply aimed to be entertaining pioneered new possibilities for film editing. As for the matter of value, it's clear that popular traditions can foster art of high quality. Just as Shakespeare and Dickens wrote for broad audiences, much of the greatest 20th-century music, including jazz and the blues, was rooted in popular traditions. Cinema is an art because it offers filmmakers ways to design experiences for viewers, and those experiences can be valuable regardless of their pedigree. Films for audiences both small and large belong to that very inclusive art we call film or cinema.

Sometimes, too, people consider film *art* to be opposed to film as a *business.* This split is related to the issue of entertainment, since entertainment generally is sold to a mass audience. Again, however, in most modern societies, no art floats free from economic ties. Novels good, bad, or indifferent are published because publishers expect to sell them. Painters hope that collectors and museums will acquire their work. True, some artworks are funded through subsidy or private donations, but that process, too, involves the artist in a financial transaction.

Films are no different. Some movies are made in the hope that consumers will pay to see them. Others are funded by patronage (an investor or organization wants to see the film made) or public money. (France, for instance, generously subsidizes film projects.) You might make short videos for YouTube or Vimeo at little cost, but if you hope to make a feature-length digital movie, you face the problem of paying for it. If you can't earn a little from it, you may still hope that the project will lead to a job.

The crucial point is that considerations of business don't necessarily make the artist less creative or the project less worthwhile. Money can corrupt any activity, but it doesn't have to. In Renaissance Italy, painters were commissioned by the Catholic church to illustrate events from the Bible. Michelangelo and Leonardo da Vinci worked for hire, but we revere their artistry.

In this book we won't assume that film art precludes entertainment. We won't take the opposite position either, claiming that only Hollywood mass-market movies are worth our attention. Similarly, we don't think that film art rises above commercial demands, but we also won't assume that money rules everything. Any art form offers a vast range of creative possibilities.

As an art, film offers experiences that viewers find worthwhile—diverting, provocative, puzzling, or rapturous. But how do films do that? To answer that question, we'll go back a step and ask: Where do movies come from?

They come from three places. They come from the imagination and hard work of the filmmakers who create them. They come from a complex set of machines that capture and transform images and sounds. And they come from companies or individuals that pay for the filmmakers and the technology. This chapter examines the artistic, technological, and business sides of how films come into being.

Creative Decisions in Filmmaking

In *Day for Night,* French filmmaker François Truffaut plays a director making a movie called *Meet Pamela.* Crew members bring set designs, wigs, cars, and prop pistols to him, and we hear his voice telling us his thoughts: "What is a director? A director is someone who is asked questions about everything."

Making a film can be seen as a long process of decision-making, not just by the director but by all the specialists who work on the production team. Screenwriters, producers, directors, performers, and technicians are constantly solving problems and making choices. Sometimes the decisions are practical ones that won't affect the look or sound of the final film, as when a source of electricity has to be found to power the lights on location. A great many decisions, though, do affect what we see and hear on the screen. There are business choices about the budget, marketing, distribution, and payments. Then there are artistic choices. What lighting will enhance the atmosphere of a love scene? Given the kind of story being told, would it be better to let the audience know what the central character is thinking or to keep her enigmatic? When a scene opens, what is the most economical way of letting the audience identify the time and place? We can see how decisions shape the process by looking in more detail at a single production.

To See into the Night in Collateral

Michael Mann's *Collateral,* released in 2004, is a visually striking psychological thriller set in Los Angeles in a single night. The mysterious Vincent (Tom Cruise) hires a cab driver, Max (Jamie Foxx), to drive him to several appointments. When Max learns that Vincent is a hired killer, he struggles to break their bargain and escape. But Vincent forces him to carry on as a getaway driver. In the course of the evening, the two men spar verbally and move toward a climactic chase and confrontation.

Mann and his crew made thousands of decisions during the making of *Collateral.* Here we look at five important choices: one that influenced the film's form and one each for our four categories of mise-en-scene, cinematography, editing, and sound.

Scriptwriter Stuart Beattie originally set *Collateral* in New York City. In the screenplay, Max was a loser, hiding from the world in his cab and getting little out of life. Vincent was to goad him about his failures until Max had finally had enough and stood up to him. Once Mann came on board as director, he altered the plot in several ways. The setting became Los Angeles. Max became less a loser and more a laid-back, intelligent man content to observe the world from behind a steering wheel, endlessly delaying his plans to start his own limousine service. This more appealing Max becomes our point-of-view figure for most of the film. For example, we don't see the first murder but stay with Max in the cab until the shocking moment when a body hurtles down onto his cab roof. The story largely consists of Max's conflict with Vincent, so Mann's decision to change Max's traits altered their confrontations as well. In the finished film, moments of reluctant mutual respect and even hints of friendship complicate the men's relationship. Such decisions as these reshaped the film's overall narrative form.

The switch to Los Angeles profoundly affected the film's style. For Mann, one of the attractions was that this tale of a random crossing of destinies took place almost entirely at night, from 6:04 P.M. to 4:20 A.M. He wanted to portray the atmospheric Los Angeles night, where haze and cloud cover reflect the city's lights back to the vast grid of streets. According to one of the cinematographers, Paul Cameron, "The goal was to make the L.A. night as much of a character in the story as Vincent and Max were."

This was a major decision that created the film's look. Mann was determined not to use more artificial light than was absolutely necessary. He relied to a considerable degree on street lights, neon signs, vehicle headlights, and other sources in the locations where filming took place. To achieve an eerie radiance, his team came up with a cutting-edge combination of technologies.

Digital Cinematography Certain choices about photographing *Collateral* were central to its final look and also dictated many other decisions. For example, traditional Hollywood productions employed cameras loaded with rolls of photographic film. Night scenes were shot using large banks of specialized spot- and floodlights. If the light was too weak, dark areas would tend to go a uniform black.

Mann and his cinematographers decided to shoot portions of *Collateral* on recently developed high-definition (HD) digital cameras. Those cameras could shoot on location with little or no light added to the scene **(1.1).** They could also capture the distinctive night glow of Los Angeles. As Mann put it, "Film doesn't record what our eyes can see at night. That's why I moved into shooting digital video in high definition—to see into the night, to see everything the naked eye can see and more. You see this moody landscape with hills and trees and strange light patterns. I wanted that to be the world that Vincent and Max are moving through."

1.1–1.3 Digital filming for *Collateral*. A digital camera shoots in a dim alley. As in many shots, the skyline of downtown Los Angeles figures prominently (1.1). An eerily glowing cityscape, with digital cinematography making a row of palm trees stand out against a dark sky (1.2). Vincent stalks one of his victims in a law library with huge windows overlooking the city (1.3). On regular photographic film, the streets and buildings would go uniformly dark, with only points of light visible.

1.1

1.2

1.3

Cinematographer Dion Beebe enthused, "The format's strong point is its incredible sensitivity to light. We were able to shoot Los Angeles at night and actually see silhouettes of palm trees against the night sky, which was very exciting" **(1.2).** In a particularly dark scene at the climax, the characters become visible only as black shapes outlined by the myriad lights behind them **(1.3).** The suspense is heightened as we strain to see the figures.

Custom-Made Lights Though digital cameras could pick up a great deal in dark situations, the audience needed to see the faces of the actors clearly. Much of the action takes place inside the taxi as Max and Vincent ride and talk. The actors' faces had to be lit, but the filmmakers wanted to avoid the sense that there was artificial light in the cab.

To create a soft, diffuse light, the filmmakers tried an innovative approach: electroluminescent display (ELD) panels. The technology had been used in digital watches and cell phones, but it had never been employed in filming. Flexible plastic panels of various sizes were custom-made, all with Velcro backings that would stick to the seats and ceiling of the cab **(1.4, 1.5).** These ELD panels could then be turned on in various combinations. Although they look bright in Figure 1.5, the effect on the screen was a soft glow on the actors. In a shot like Figure **1.6,** we might simply take it for granted that the light coming through the windows and the glow of the dashboard panel are all that shines on the characters. Such dim illumination on the faces allows the lights visible through the windows to be brighter than they are, helping to keeping the city "as much of a character in the story as Vincent and Max were."

Here's a case where an artistic decision led to new technology. Since *Collateral* was made, a similar lighting technology, the LED (light-emitting diode) has become common in flashlights, scoreboard displays, and computer monitors. Specially designed LED units have become central to film production. Mann's team solved a problem in mise-en-scene, and a new option was added to the menu available to other filmmakers.

1.4

1.5

1.6

1.4–1.6 Unobtrusive lighting. One of the ELD panels specially made for illuminating the cab interior (1.4). Several ELD panels were attached to the back of a seat to shine on Tom Cruise as Vincent (1.5). The units created a dim glow on the actors (1.6).

Seamless Editing *Collateral* contains several dynamic action scenes, including a spectacular car crash. The plan was for a cab going nearly 60 miles per hour to flip, then bounce and roll several times before coming to rest upside down. If we put ourselves in the filmmakers' place, we can imagine their options about how to show the crash.

Mann's team could have put the camera in a single spot and swiveled it to follow the car rolling past. That might have been a good idea if the scene showed us the crash through the eyes of an onlooker whose head turns to watch it. But there is no character witnessing the crash.

The filmmakers decided to generate excitement by showing several shots of the car rolling, each taken from a different point along the trajectory of the crash. One option would have been to use several cabs and execute numerous similar crashes, each time filmed by a single camera that would be moved between crashes from place to place to record the action from a new vantage point. Such a procedure would have been very expensive, however, and no two crashes would have taken place in exactly the same way. Splicing together shots from each crash might have created discrepancies in the car's position, resulting in poor "matches on action," as we'll term this technique in Chapter 6.

Instead, the team settled on a technique commonly used for big action scenes. Along the cab's path were stationed multiple cameras, all filming at once **(1.7)**. The economic benefits were that only one car had to be crashed and the high expense of keeping many crew members working on retakes was reduced. Artistically, the resulting footage allowed the editing team to choose portions of many shots and splice them together in precise ways **(1.8, 1.9)**. The result is an exciting stream of shots, each taken from farther along the taxi's path.

Music in Movements Composers are fond of saying that their music for a film should serve the story so well that the audience doesn't notice it. For *Collateral*, Mann wanted James Newton Howard to score the climax so as to not build up

1.7–1.9 **Editing a car crash.** On location after the execution of the car crash in *Collateral*, director Michael Mann surveys digital monitors displaying shots taken by multiple cameras covering the action (1.7). The result: A seamless continuation of the cab's movement. A shot taken from one camera shows the car flipping over, its hood flapping wildly (1.8) is followed by a cut to another shot, taken from a camera placed on the ground and continuing the same movement, now with the vehicle rolling toward the viewer (1.9). This particular camera was placed in a very thick metal case.

1.7

1.8

1.9

excitement too quickly. According to Howard, "Michael was very clear about the climax taking place in three movements." "Movements" as a term is usually applied to the parts of a symphony, a concerto, or a sonata. Thus the idea was that the score for this last part of the film should play a major role in shaping the progression and rhythm of the action.

At the climax, Vincent is trying to kill a character who is important to Max, while Max tries frantically to save both himself and the other character. Howard and Mann called the first musical movement "The Race to Warn," since Vincent gets ahead of Max in running to the building where the potential victim is located. Despite the fact that both men are running and the situation is suspenseful, Howard avoids rapid rhythms. He begins with long-held string chords over a deep, rumbling sound, then adds sustained brass chords with a strong beat accompanying them. The accompaniment is dynamic but doesn't reach a high pitch of excitement.

The second movement, "The Cat and Mouse," accompanies Vincent getting into the building, turning off the electricity, and stalking his victim in near darkness (1.3). Again, the chords are slow, with ominous undertones, dissonant glides, and, at a few points, fast, eerie high-string figures as Vincent nears his goal. During the most suspenseful moments in the scene, when Vincent and his prey are in the darkened room, strings and soft, clicking percussion accompany their cautious, hesitant movements.

Finally, there is a swift chase sequence, and here Howard's score is louder and faster, with driving tympani in very quick rhythm as the danger grows. Once the chase tapers off, the percussion ends, and slow, low strings accompany the final quiet shots.

These decisions and many others affect our experience of *Collateral*. Thanks to the digital imagery and innovative lighting, we have a sense of characters moving through an eerie, unfamiliar-looking world. The editing of the crash allows the taxi to come hurtling toward the camera several times. The music accompanying the fast-chase/slow-stalking/fast-chase climax helps heighten the suspense and build the excitement. Creative decision-making is central to every film, and *Collateral* stands out for making several unusual choices.

Mechanics of the Movies

Filmmaking relies on technology and financing. First, filmmakers need fairly complicated machines. Anyone with a pen and paper can write a novel, and a talented kid with a guitar can become a musician. Movies demand much more. Even the simplest home video camera is based on fiendishly complex technology. A major film involves elaborate cameras, lighting equipment, multitrack sound-mixing studios, sophisticated laboratories, and computer-generated special effects. Partly because of the technology, making a movie also involves businesses. Companies manufacture the equipment, other companies provide funding for the film, still others distribute it, and finally theaters and other venues present the result to an audience. In the rest of this chapter, we consider how these two sides of making movies—technology and business—shape film as an art.

Illusion Machines

Moving-image media such as film and video couldn't exist if human vision were perfect. Our eyes are very sensitive, but they can be tricked. As anyone who has paused a DVD knows, a film consists of a series of *frames,* or still pictures. Yet we don't perceive the separate frames. Instead, we see continuous light and movement. What creates this impression?

No one knows the full answer. For a long time people thought that the effect results from "persistence of vision," the tendency of an image to linger briefly on our retina. Yet if this were the cause, we'd see a bewildering blur of superimposed stills instead of smooth action. At present, researchers believe that two psychological processes are involved in cinematic motion: critical flicker fusion and apparent motion.

If you flash a light faster and faster, at a certain point (around 50 flashes per second), you see not a pulsating light but a continuous beam. A film is usually shot and projected at 24 still frames per second. The projector shutter breaks the light beam once as a new image is slid into place and once while it is held in place. Thus each frame is actually projected on the screen twice. This raises the number of flashes to 48, the threshold of what is called *critical flicker fusion.* Early silent films were shot at a lower rate (often 16 or 20 images per second), and projectors broke the beam only once per image. The picture had a pronounced flicker—hence an early slang term for movies, "flickers," which survives today when people call a film a "flick."

Apparent motion is a second factor in creating cinema's illusion. If a visual display is changed rapidly enough, our eye can be fooled into seeing movement. Neon advertising signs often seem to show a thrusting arrow, but that illusion is created simply by static lights flashing on and off at a particular rate. Certain cells in our eyes and brain are devoted to analyzing motion, and any stimulus resembling movement tricks those cells into sending the wrong message.

Apparent motion and critical flicker fusion are quirks in our visual system, and technology can exploit those quirks to produce illusions. Some moving-image machines predate the invention of film **(1.10, 1.11)**. Film as we know it came into being when photographic images were first imprinted on strips of flexible celluloid.

Making Films with Photographic Film

For over a century, movies have been made and displayed on photochemical media, varieties of photographic film. But in recent years, at an accelerating pace, movies have also been made and shown on digital media. In some respects the

1.10

1.11

1.10–1.11 Early moving-image gadgets. The Zoetrope, which dates back to 1834, spun its images on a strip of paper in a rotating drum (1.10). The Mutoscope, an early-20th-century entertainment, displayed images by flipping a row of cards in front of a peephole (1.11).

basic machines involved are similar, but there are enough differences to warrant us considering them separately. So let's look first at the earliest and still widely used format, films on film.

Physically, a photographically based film is a ribbon of still images, each one slightly different from its mates. That ribbon starts life as unexposed film stock in a camera. Eventually the finished movie is another strip of film run through a projector. Both the camera and the projector move the film strip one frame at a time past a light source. For a fraction of a second, the image is held in place before the next one replaces it. In a camera, the lens gathers light from the scene photographed, while a projector uses a light source to cast the images on the screen. In a sense, the projector is just an inverted camera (**1.12–1.13**).

In filming, the most common shooting rate is 24 frames per second (fps), and in projection the same rate is usually maintained. In the 35mm format, the film whizzes through the projector at 90 feet per minute, meaning that a two-hour feature will consist of about two miles of film. In the typical theater, the film print is mounted on one big platter, with another platter above or below to take it up after it has passed through the projector (**1.14**).

The film strip that emerges from the camera is usually a *negative*. That is, its colors and light values are the opposite of those in the original scene. For the images to be projected, a *positive* print must be made. This is done on another machine, the *printer,* which duplicates or modifies the footage from the camera. Like a projector, the printer controls the passage of light through film—in this case, a negative. Like a camera, it focuses light to form an image—in this case, on the unexposed roll of film (**1.15**). Although the filmmaker can create nonphotographic images on the filmstrip by drawing, painting, or scratching, most filmmakers have relied on the camera, the printer, and other photographic technology.

If you were to handle the film that runs through these machines, you'd notice several things. One side is much shinier than the other. Motion picture film consists of a transparent plastic *base* (the shiny side), which supports an *emulsion,* layers of gelatin containing light-sensitive materials. On a black-and-white filmstrip, the emulsion contains grains of silver halide. Color film emulsion adds layers of chemical dyes that react with the silver halide components. In both case, billions

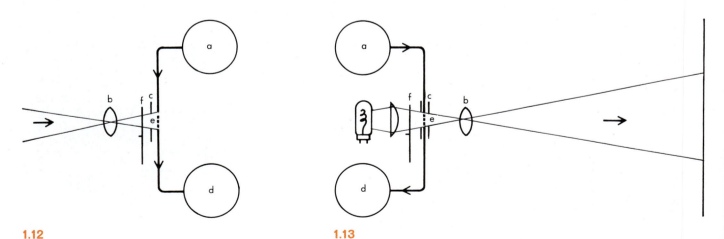

1.12   **1.13**

1.12–1.13 Moving the film: Camera and projector. In a light-tight chamber (1.12), a drive mechanism feeds the unexposed motion picture film from a reel (a) past a lens (b) and aperture © to a take-up reel (d). The lens focuses light reflected from a scene onto each frame of film (e). The mechanism moves the film intermittently, with a brief pause while each frame is held in the aperture. A shutter (f) admits light through the lens only when each frame is unmoving and ready for exposure. The projector is basically an inverted camera, with the light source inside the machine rather than in the world outside (1.13). A drive mechanism feeds the film from a reel (a) past a lens (b) and aperture © to a take-up reel (d). Light is beamed through the images (e) and magnified by the lens for projection on a screen. Again, a mechanism moves the film intermittently past the aperture, while a shutter (f) admits light only when each frame is pausing.

1.14 **Platter projection.** Multiscreen theaters use platter projection, which winds the film in long strips and feeds it to a projector (seen in the left rear). The film on the platters is an Imax 70mm print.

of microscopic particles form clusters of light, dark, and color corresponding to the scene photographed.

What enables film to run through a camera, a printer, and a projector? The strip is perforated along both edges, so that small teeth (called *sprockets*) in the machines can seize the perforations (sprocket holes) and pull the film at a uniform rate and smoothness. The strip also reserves space for a sound track.

The size and placement of the perforations and the area occupied by the sound track have been standardized around the world. So, too, has the width of the film strip, which is called the *gauge* and is measured in millimeters. Commercial theaters use 35mm film, but other gauges also have been standardized internationally: Super 8mm, 16mm, and 70mm (**1.16–1.20**).

Usually image quality increases with the width of the film because the greater picture area gives the images better definition and detail. All other things being equal, 35mm provides significantly better picture quality than does 16mm, and 70mm is superior to both. The finest photographic quality currently available for public screenings is that offered by the Imax system (**1.21**).

With the rise of digital filmmaking, 16mm has declined as an amateur gauge. If you take an introductory production course, you are more likely to shoot with a digital camera than a 16mm one. Yet a higher-quality version of the gauge, Super 16mm, still gets used in commercial films seeking to economize or to achieve a "documentary look." Recent films utilizing Super 16mm include *The Wrestler, The Hurt Locker, Lebanon,* and *Black Swan.* Super 8 film is still occasionally used in professional production, usually to simulate home movies or television images; *Super 8* used both Super 16 and Super 8 to present the amateur footage shot by its young protagonists. Imax and other cameras employing 65mm film have been used for fiction films, including some scenes in *The Dark Knight, Inception,* and *Mission Impossible: Ghost Protocol.*

The sound track runs down along the side of the filmstrip. Magnetic tracks, consisting of magnetic tape running along the film strip (1.20), have virtually vanished. Most films today have an optical sound track, which encodes sonic information in the form of patches of light and dark running down along the frames. During

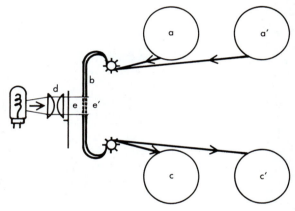

1.15 **Printing the film.** All printers are light-tight chambers that drive a negative or positive roll of film from a reel (a) past an aperture (b) to a take-up reel ©. At the same time, a roll of unexposed film (a', c') moves through the aperture (b), either intermittently or continuously. By means of a lens (d), light beamed through the aperture prints the image (e) on the unexposed film (e'). The two rolls of film may pass through the aperture simultaneously. A printer of this sort is called a *contact* printer. Contact printers are used for making work prints and release prints, as well as for various special effects.

1.17 16mm

1.20 70mm

1.19 35mm

1.16 Super 8mm   **1.18** 35mm

1.16–1.20 Film gauges. Super 8mm (1.16) has been a popular gauge for amateurs and experimental filmmakers. *Year of the Horse*, a concert film featuring Neil Young, was shot partly on Super 8. 16mm film (1.17) has been used for both amateur and professional film work. A variable-area optical sound track (p. 13) runs down the right side. 35mm film (1.18) is the standard theatrical film gauge. In this sample a variable-area sound track runs down the side of the strip. A 35mm strip from *Jurassic Park* (1.19) shows an optical (analog) stereophonic sound track (p. 13) on the left of the images, encoded as two parallel squiggles. The Morse code–like dots between the stereophonic track and the picture area are a timecode to sync the film with DTS files on a CD-ROM. 70mm film (1.20), another theatrical gauge, was used for historical spectacles and epic action films into the 1990s. In this strip from *The Hunt for Red October*, a stereophonic magnetic sound track runs along both edges of the filmstrip and between the edges of the picture and the sprocket holes, allowing for six discrete channels of sound.

1.21 Imax film. The Imax image is printed on 70mm film but runs horizontally along the strip, allowing each image to be 10 times larger than 35mm and triple the size of 70mm. The Imax film can be projected on a very large screen with no loss of detail.

production, electrical impulses from a microphone are translated into pulsations of light, which are photographically inscribed on the moving filmstrip. When the film is projected, the optical track produces varying intensities of light that are translated back into electrical impulses and then into sound waves. The optical sound track of 16mm film is on the right side (1.17), whereas 35mm puts an optical track on the left (1.18, 1.19). In each, the sound is usually encoded as *variable-area,* a wavy contour of black and white along the picture strip.

A film's sound track may be *monophonic* or *stereophonic.* The 16mm filmstrip (1.17) and the first 35mm film strip (1.18) have monophonic optical tracks. Stereophonic optical sound is registered as a pair of squiggles running down the left side (1.19). For digital sound, a string of dots and dashes running along the film's perforations, or between the perforations, or close to the very left edge of the frames provides the sound-track information. The projector scans these marks as if reading a bar code.

Films as Digital Media

Digital information technology gave filmmakers a set of new tools. Computers first came into use in editing and in special-effects processes, and eventually digital shooting and projection became feasible. The term "digital film" may seem contradictory, but almost immediately everyone understood it. Just as audio books and e-books were still called books, digital films counted as films, even though they never involved light hitting celluloid. Some people prefer to speak of "digital capture" rather than "digital filming," but most call digital image-creators "filmmakers." So will we.

Digital filming To some extent a professional digital motion picture camera functions in the same way as the 35mm camera. The camera operator uses a viewfinder to frame a scene. There are controls to manipulate exposure and the speed of recording. At the front, a lens gathers and focuses light reflected from the scene. A shutter-like mechanism breaks the input into frames, usually 24 per second. A professional digital camera also looks very much like a traditional 35mm camera (**1.22**). The design reflects manufacturers' effort to make the new device feel familiar to cinematographers. Some digital cameras can accept lenses used for 35mm machines.

1.22 Digital motion picture camera. In the Panavision Genesis camera, which has been used on such films as *Secretariat,* a recorder containing a digital tape cassette attaches to the rear or top. The tape can run for 50 minutes.

1.23 Combining digital video and film. In *julien donkey-boy,* pixels and grain yield a unique texture, and the high contrast exaggerates pure colors and shapes to create a hallucinatory image.

But instead of a strip of film whizzing through a gate behind the lens, the digital camera has a fixed sensor. The sensor is covered with a grid of millions of microscopic diodes, or photosites. Each of these diodes captures a bit of light. These create pixels (short for "picture elements") in the final image. The sensor converts these patterns of light into electrical impulses that are sent to a recording medium and registered as files of ones and zeroes. A similar process of sampling and digital conversion occurs while recording sound.

As with physical film, there are several formats of digital image recording. Just as a 35mm image would in most cases look sharper and richer in detail than a 16mm one, so the quality of digital images can vary. A film frame holds billions of crystalline specks carrying visual information. Pixels are much larger, so making digital imagery as finely detailed as 35mm film is a challenge. Digital image quality depends on several factors, including how many pixels the image contains and the types of compression applied to the files.

The first wave of digital cinema in the 1990s utilized the format known as DV (digital video). The images were quite low-resolution (about 350,000 pixels), but lit by an experienced cinematographer they could be attractive, as in Spike Lee's *Bamboozled,* shot by Ellen Kuras. Some filmmakers played up the pebbly textures of DV imagery. *Dancer in the Dark* uses saturated DV imagery to suggest the fantasy world of a young mother going blind, while *28 Days Later* fitted the rough-edged format to a horror film. Harmony Korine shot *julien donkey-boy* with mini-DV consumer cameras, transferred the footage to film, and reprinted it several times **(1.23).**

As digital photography improved in the 2000s, high-definition (HD) video emerged as a preferred choice for digital filmmaking, amateur or professional. Today HD video usually refers to digital formats of 720p and 1080p. The numbers refer to the number of horizontal lines in the display, and "p" stands for progressive scan, which refreshes each frame in the manner of a computer monitor; 720p images contain about 921,000 pixels, and 1080p images have nearly 2.1 million. Further innovations have led to much higher-resolution imagery—that is, images that are sharper, more detailed, and freer of artifacts. The newer formats, often known as "digital cinema," were standardized at 2K (usually rated at 2,048 pixels across, or about 3.2 million pixels in all) and 4K (4,096 pixels across, or over 12.7 million pixels). **Figure 1.24** schematically shows the relative number of pixels in these formats. Since the information carried on each image increases both vertically and horizontally, each step up multiplies the resolution: 4K carries not twice but four times the amount of information in 2K. Each format can produce images in different proportions, or aspect ratios, and these make the pixel count vary somewhat. (More on aspect ratios in Chapter 5.)

The images may be recorded to digital videotape, running through a magazine attached to the camera (1.22). Alternatively, the images may be stored on a hard drive or memory card. When the images are downloaded and backed up, the capture medium is wiped clean for reuse. The great advantage of this system is that digital media cost much less than raw film stock, an expensive component of a traditional film's budget. The downside is that such huge amounts of data require a lot of storage space. A finished feature film may consist of 10 to 12 terabytes (TB) of data, and the amount shot may consume 100 to 300 TB. For this reason, digital imagery is subjected to many compression and decompression processes from production through to final projection. A feature film projected at your local multiplex probably takes up no more than 32K megabytes (MB) on the hard drive file that is fed to the projector.

In the late 1990s, George Lucas commissioned Sony to make a high-quality digital camera, which he utilized on *Star Wars: Episode II—Attack of the Clones* (2002). It used the 1080p format. Michael Mann's digital camera on *Collateral* also

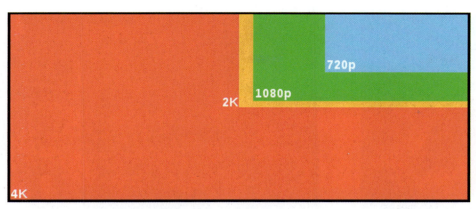

1.24 Resolution in four standard digital formats. The lowest-resolution digital moving image system in common use, 720p, contains 1,280 (width) by 720 (height), yielding 921,600 pixels (.92 megapixels). (A megapixel is a million pixels.) 720p is used primarily for U.S. broadcast and cable television and for internet video. The next step up is 1080 HD, with either progressive or interlaced scanning. HD commonly measures 1,920 by 1,080 pixels, for a total of 2,073,600 pixels (2.1 megapixels). The 2K format maximally supports 2,048 by 1,556 pixels, yielding 3,186,688 pixels (3.2 megapixels). Both 1080 HD and 2K are used for filming, with 2K the baseline standard for commercial theatrical projection. It might seem that 4K would have twice as many pixels as 2K, but the 4K file actually contains four times as many pixels. At a maximum it measures 4,096 by 3,112 pixels, yielding 1,263,472 pixels (12.6 megapixels).

delivered 2K-resolution images. More and more big-budget directors embraced HD digital formats, particularly for their price and convenience. Lucas claimed that apart from creating spectacular special effects, using HD for *Attack of the Clones* and *Revenge of the Sith* saved millions of dollars. A comparable system was employed on *Sin City,* which combined HD footage of the actors with graphic landscapes created in postproduction. Basing the entire project on digital technology allowed director Robert Rodriguez to edit, mix sound, and create special effects in his home studio in Austin, Texas.

Today many commercial films shot digitally employ the 2K format, and beginning in 2009, a few films, including *District 9, Che,* and *Knowing,* used 4K systems. Many have claimed that 4K images are the equal in visual quality to those of 35mm. Prestigious films such as David Fincher's *Zodiac* and *The Social Network* showed that high-resolution capture could in many respects rival 35mm film while harboring its own artistic possibilities.

Most professional cameras have two big advantages over lower-cost models. They employ minimal data compression, and they tend to have larger sensors, ones about the same size as a frame of 35mm film. Both factors make for higher image quality. But consumer and "prosumer" cameras have also found roles in professional production. Filmmakers working on low budgets have discovered that not only dedicated video cameras but digital single-lens reflex still cameras (DSLRs) can yield high-quality video imagery. Even some cellphone cameras have the capacity for 1080p recording. Park Chan-wook, the Korean director of *Oldboy,* shot a prize-winning short film on his iPhone. These paraprofessional tools have proved particularly valuable for documentary filmmakers, who need to shoot hours of footage cheaply.

Digital Projection   For some years, films shot on digital video were transferred to photographic film and sent to theatres as 35mm prints. After rather slow growth, digital projection exploded in 2010–2011 and was quickly replacing 35mm projection in most commercial venues around the world.

Digital theatrical projection is usually in either the 2K or 4K format. The most common projection hardware employs microscopic mirrors and is manufactured in

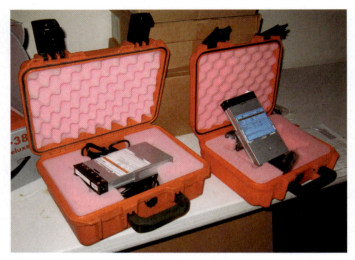

1.25

1.26

1.25–1.26 **Digital theatrical projection.** Films are shipped to theaters on hard drives (1.25). Compare 1.14, the preparation of a film for platter projection. Figure 1.26 shows a Sony digital projection system. The projector is run from a server that stores films and trailer files loaded from the Digital Cinema Package. The touch-screen monitor on the left allows the operator to control the screening through a playlist. The dual lenses on the upper right are used for 3D screenings.

CONNECT TO THE BLOG
www.davidbordwell.net/blog

We survey the development of digital projection in our series "Pandora's digital box."

" We don't shy away from all-digital filmmakers. We just happen to really, really love film. With artists who are passionate about image making, you don't hear, 'I want to make film look like digital!' You hear, 'I want digital to look like film.'"
—Paul Korver, head of the Cinelicious postproduction company, Hollywood

various designs by several companies. Running speeds are standardized at 24 fps and 48 fps. The film is encoded as a Digital Cinema Package (DCP), a set of files containing images, sound, subtitles, and other information. The DCP, delivered on a hard drive and heavily encrypted, provides a compressed version of the film **(1.25)**. The DCP loads into a server that feeds one or more projectors in a theater complex **(1.26).**

The new filmmaking and projection technology was given a boost by the resurgence of 3D films in the mid-2000s. Digital filming proved more reliable and efficient for stereoscopic movies, which were almost always projected digitally. (Imax retained some theatres that projected 3D on two strips of 70mm film.) James Cameron's colossal hit *Avatar* served as a showcase not just for 3D but for digital filmmaking in general.

Many directors remain loyal to shooting in 35mm, maintaining that film stock has photographic qualities that most HD video can't duplicate. Christopher Nolan shot parts of *The Dark Knight* on IMAX and parts of *Inception* on 65mm because "for me, production of a large-scale film is all about recording the best, highest-quality image possible." Nonetheless, the surge in digital projection has encouraged many directors to shift from 35mm film to HD formats, and most of those shooting on film have embraced digital tools for editing, special effects, and sound mixing.

Whether shooting on film or on video, the filmmaker faces comparable artistic choices. Now that we have a sense of the technical tools available, we can turn to the ways filmmakers work with them.

Making the Movie: Film Production

Important as technology is, films are part of social institutions as well. Sometimes the social context is very intimate, as when a family records their lives to show friends and relations. But films that aim at the public enter a wider range of institutions.

A movie typically goes through three phases: *production, distribution,* and *exhibition.* An individual, group, or company makes the film. A distribution company rents copies to theater chains, and theaters exhibit the film. Later, a DVD version is distributed to chain stores or rental shops, and it's exhibited on TV monitors, computer screens, or portable displays. For video on demand, streaming, and websites such as YouTube, the Internet serves as both a distribution and exhibition medium.

The whole system depends on having movies to circulate, so let's start by considering the process of production. Most films go through four distinct phases:

1. *Scriptwriting and funding.* The idea for the film is developed and a screenplay is written. The filmmakers also acquire financial support for the project.

2. *Preparation for filming.* Once a script is more or less complete and at least some funding is assured, the filmmakers plan the physical production.

3. *Shooting.* The filmmakers create the film's images and sounds.

4. *Assembly.* The images and sounds are combined in their final form. This involves cutting picture and sound, executing special effects, inserting music or extra dialogue, and adding titles.

The phases can overlap. Filmmakers may be scrambling for funding while shooting and assembling the film, and some assembly is usually taking place during filming. In addition, each stage modifies what went before. The idea for the film may be radically altered when the script is hammered out; the script's presentation of the action may be drastically changed in shooting; and the material that is shot takes on new significance in the process of assembly. As the French director Robert Bresson puts it: "A film is born in my head and I kill it on paper. It is brought back to life by the actors and then killed in the camera. It is then resurrected into a third and final life in the editing room where the dismembered pieces are assembled into their finished form."

These four phases include many particular jobs. Most theatrical releases result from dozens of specialized tasks carried out by hundreds of experts. This fine-grained division of labor has proved a reliable way to prepare, shoot, and assemble large-budget movies. On smaller productions, individuals perform several roles. A director might also edit the film, or the principal sound recordist on the set might also oversee the sound mixing. For *Tarnation,* a memoir of growing up in a troubled family, Jonathan Caouette assembled 19 years worth of photographs, audiotape, home movies, and videotape. Some of the footage was filmed by his parents, and some by him as a boy. Caouette shot new scenes, edited everything on iMovie, mixed the sound, and transferred the result to digital video. In making this personal documentary, Caouette executed virtually all the phases of film production himself.

The Scriptwriting and Funding Phase

Two roles are central in this phase: producer and screenwriter. The tasks of the *producer* are chiefly financial and organizational. She or he may be an "independent" producer, unearthing film projects and trying to convince production companies or distributors to finance the film. Or the producer may work for a distribution company and generate ideas for films. A studio may also hire a producer to put together a particular package.

The producer nurses the project through the scriptwriting process, obtains financial support, and arranges to hire the personnel who will work on the film. During shooting and assembly, the producer usually acts as the liaison between the writer or director and the company that is financing the film. After the film is completed, the producer often has the task of arranging the distribution, promotion, and marketing of the film. The producer is usually responsible as well for paying back the money invested in the production.

A single producer may take on all these tasks, but in the contemporary American film industry, the producer's work is further subdivided. The *executive producer* is often the person who arranged the financing for the project or obtained the literary. Once the production is under way, the *line producer* oversees the day-to-day activities of director, cast, and crew. The line producer is assisted by an *associate producer,* who acts as a liaison with laboratories or technical personnel.

> " A screenplay bears somewhat the same relationship to a movie as the musical score does to a symphonic performance. There are people who can read a musical score and 'hear' the symphony—but no two directors will see the same images when they read a movie script. The two-dimensional patterns of colored light involved are far more complex than the one-dimensional thread of sound."

—Arthur C. Clarke, co-screenwriter, *2001: A Space Odyssey*

 CONNECT TO THE BLOG
www.davidbordwell.net/blog

We consider the art of the screenwriter in two entries: "JCC" and "Scriptography"

The chief task of the *screenwriter* is to prepare the *screenplay* (or script). Sometimes the writer will compose an original screenplay and send it to an agent, who submits it to a production company. Or an experienced screenwriter meets with a producer in a "pitch session," where the writer can propose ideas for scripts. The first scene of Robert Altman's *The Player* mocks pitch sessions by showing screenwriters proposing strained ideas like "*Pretty Woman* meets *Out of Africa*." Alternatively, the producer may have an idea and hire a screenwriter to develop it. This approach is common if the producer has bought the rights to a novel or play and wants to adapt it for the screen.

The screenplay usually goes through several stages. These include a *treatment,* a synopsis of the action; then one or more full-length scripts; and a final version, the *shooting script.* Extensive rewriting is common, and writers often must revise their work several times.

If the producer or director finds one writer's screenplay unsatisfactory, other writers may be hired to revise it. Most Hollywood screenwriters earn their living by rewriting other writers' scripts. As you can imagine, this often leads to conflicts about which writer or writers deserve onscreen credit for the film. In the American film industry, these disputes are adjudicated by the Screen Writers' Guild.

Shooting scripts are constantly changed, too. Some directors allow actors to modify the dialogue, and problems on location or on a set may necessitate changes in the scene. In the assembly stage, script scenes that have been shot are often condensed, rearranged, or dropped entirely.

As the screenplay is being prepared, the producer is planning the film's finances. He or she has sought out a director and stars to make the package seem a promising investment. The producer must prepare a budget spelling out *above-the-line costs* (the costs of literary property, scriptwriter, director, and major cast) and *below-the-line costs* (the expenses allotted to the crew, secondary cast, the shooting and assembly phases, insurance, and publicity). The sum of above- and below-the-line costs is called the *negative cost* (that is, the total cost of producing the film's master negative). In 2007, the average Hollywood negative cost ran to about $70 million.

Some films don't follow a full-blown screenplay. Documentaries, for instance, are difficult to script fully in advance. In order to get funding, however, the projects typically require a summary or an outline, and some documentarists prefer to have a written plan even if they recognize that the film will evolve in the course of production. When compiling a documentary from existing footage, the filmmakers often write the final voice-over commentary after assembling most of the sequences.

The Preparation Phase

When funding is more or less secure and the script is solid enough to start filming, the filmmakers can prepare for the physical production. In commercial filmmaking, this stage of activity is called **preproduction.** The *director,* who may have come on board the project at an earlier point, plays a central role in this and later phases. The director coordinates the staff to create the film. Although the director's authority isn't absolute, he or she is usually considered the person most responsible for the final look and sound of the film.

At this point, the producer and the director hire crew and cast the roles, and scout locations for filming. They also prepare a daily schedule for shooting. This is done with an eye on the budget. The producer assumes that the separate shots will be made "out of continuity"—that is, in the most convenient order for production—and put in proper order in the editing room. Since transporting equipment and personnel to a location is a major expense, producers usually prefer to shoot all the scenes taking place in one location at one time. For *Jurassic Park,* the main characters' arrival on the island and their departure at the end of the film were both shot at the start of production, during the three weeks on location in Hawaii. A producer must also plan to shoot around actors who can't be on the set every day. Many producers try to schedule the most difficult scenes early, before cast and crew begin to tire. The complex prizefight sequences of *Raging Bull* were filmed first, with the dialogue scenes shot later. Keeping all such contingencies in mind, the producer comes up with a schedule that juggles cast, crew, locations, and even seasons most efficiently.

During preproduction, several things are happening at the same time under the supervision of the director and producer. A writer may be revising the screenplay while a casting supervisor is searching out actors. In large-scale production, the director orchestrates the contributions of specialists in several units. He or she works with the *set unit, or production design unit,* headed by a *production designer.* The production designer is in charge of visualizing the film's settings. This unit creates drawings and plans that determine the architecture and the color schemes of the sets. Under the production designer's supervision, an *art director* oversees the construction and painting of the sets. The *set decorator,* often someone with experience in interior decoration, modifies the sets for specific filming purposes, supervising workers who find props and a *set dresser* who arranges things on the set during shooting. The *costume designer* is in charge of planning and executing the wardrobe for the production.

Working with the production designer, a *graphic artist* may be assigned to produce a **storyboard,** a series of comic strip–like sketches of the shots in each scene, including notations about costume, lighting, and camera work **(1.27).** Most directors do not demand a storyboard for every scene, but action sequences and shots using special effects or complicated camera work tend to be storyboarded in detail. The storyboard gives the cinematography unit and the special-effects unit a preliminary sense of what the finished shots should look like. The storyboard images may be filmed, cut together, and played with sound to help visualize the scene. This is one form of *animatics.*

Computer graphics can take planning further. The process of *previsualization,* or "previs," reworks the storyboards into three-dimensional animation, complete with moving figures, dialogue, sound effects, and music. Contemporary software can create settings and characters reasonably close to what will be filmed, and textures and shading can be added. Previsualization animatics are most often used to plan complicated action scenes or special effects **(1.28),** but they can also help the

1.27

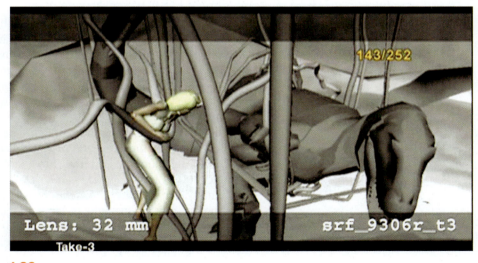

1.28

1.27–1.28 Planning the movie visually. A page from the storyboard for Hitchcock's *The Birds* (1.27). Animated previsualization from *King Kong* (1.28).

director to test options for staging scenes, moving cameras, and timing sequences. A substantial previs, complete with a temporary soundtrack, was made for *The Last Airbender.* Cinematographer Andrew Lesnie suggests how widely it was used from pre-planning to post-production: "It proved invaluable to the visual-effect, special-effects, stunt, lighting, production and art departments, and made the whole production a lot more cost efficient."

The Shooting Phase

Although the term *production* refers to the entire process of making a film, Hollywood filmmakers also use it to refer to the *shooting phase.* Shooting is also known as *principal photography.*

Units and Personnel

During shooting, the director supervises what is called the *director's crew,* consisting of these personnel:

- The *script supervisor,* known in the classic studio era as a "script girl." (Today one-fifth of Hollywood script supervisors are male.) The script supervisor is in charge of all details of *continuity* from shot to shot. The supervisor checks details of performers' appearances (in the last scene, was the character's coat buttoned or not), props, lighting, movement, camera position, and the running time of each shot.

- The *first assistant director (AD),* a jack-of-all-trades who, with the director, plans each day's shooting schedule. The AD sets up each shot for the director's approval while keeping track of the actors, monitoring safety conditions, and keeping the energy level high.

- The *second assistant director,* who is the liaison among the first AD, the camera crew, and the electricians' crew.

- The *third assistant director,* who serves as messenger for director and staff.

- The *dialogue coach,* who feeds performers their lines and speaks the lines of offscreen characters during shots of other performers.

- The *second unit director,* who films stunts, location footage, action scenes, and the like at a distance from where principal shooting is taking place.

The most visible group of workers is the *cast.* The cast may include *stars*—well-known players assigned to major roles and likely to attract audiences. The cast also includes *supporting players,* or performers in secondary roles; *minor players*; and *extras,* those anonymous persons who pass by in the street and occupy distant desks in large office sets. One of the director's major jobs is to elicit performances from the cast. The first AD usually works with the extras and takes charge of arranging crowd scenes.

On some productions, there are still more specialized roles. *Stunt artists* are supervised by a *stunt coordinator*; professional dancers work with a *choreographer.* If animals join the cast, they are handled by a *wrangler.* There have been pig wranglers (*Mad Max Beyond Thunder Dome*), snake wranglers (*Raiders of the Lost Ark*), and spider wranglers (*Arachnophobia*).

Another unit of specialized labor is the *photography unit.* The leader is the *cinematographer,* also known as the *director of photography* (or *DP*). The cinematographer is an expert on photographic processes, lighting, and camera technique. We have already seen how important Michael Mann's two DPs, Dion Beebe and Paul Cameron, were in achieving the desired look for *Collateral* (pp. 5–9). The cinematographer consults with the director on how each scene will be lit and filmed **(1.29).** The cinematographer supervises these workers:

- The *camera operator,* who runs the machine and who may also have assistants to load the camera, adjust and follow focus, push a dolly, and so on.

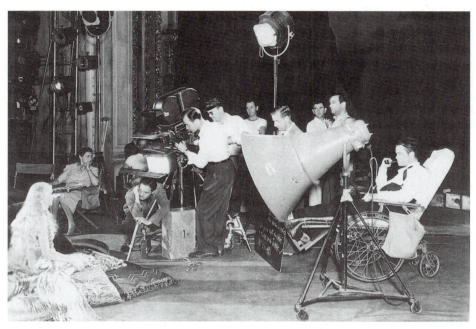

1.29 **Shooting phase of production.** On the set of *Citizen Kane,* Orson Welles directs from his wheelchair on the far right, cinematographer Gregg Toland crouches below the camera, and actress Dorothy Comingore kneels at the left. The script supervisor is seated in the left background.

- The *key grip,* who supervises the *grips.* These workers carry and arrange equipment, props, and elements of the setting and lighting.
- The *gaffer,* the head electrician who supervises the placement and rigging of the lights.

Parallel to the photography unit is the *sound unit.* This is headed by the *production recordist* (also called the *sound mixer*). The recordist's principal responsibility is to record dialogue during shooting. Typically, the recordist uses a tape or digital recorder, several sorts of microphones, and a console to balance and combine the inputs. The recordist also tries to capture some ambient sound when no actors are speaking. These bits of room tone are later inserted to fill pauses in the dialogue. The recordist's staff includes:

- The *boom operator,* who manipulates the boom microphone and conceals radio microphones on the actors.
- The *third man,* who places other microphones, lays sound cables, and is in charge of controlling ambient sound.

Some productions also have a *sound designer,* who enters the process during the preparation phase and who plans a sonic style appropriate for the entire film.

A *visual-effects unit,* overseen by the *visual-effects supervisor,* is charged with preparing and executing process shots, miniatures, matte work, computer-generated graphics, and other technical shots **(1.30).** During the planning phase, the director and the production designer have determined what effects are needed, and the supervisor consults with the director and the cinematographer on an ongoing basis. The visual-effects unit can number hundreds of workers, from puppet- and modelmakers to specialists in digital compositing.

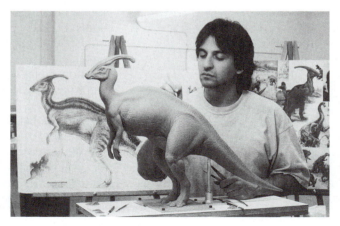

1.30 **Creating special effects.** Sculpting a model dinosaur for *Jurassic Park: The Lost World.* The model was scanned into a computer for digital manipulation.

1.31 Labeling takes. A slate shown at the beginning of a shot in Jean-Luc Godard's *La Chinoise*.

A miscellaneous unit includes a *makeup staff,* a *costume staff, hairdressers,* and *drivers,* who transport cast and crew. During shooting, the producer is represented by a unit called the *producer's crew.* Central here is the *line producer,* who manages daily organizational business, such as arranging for meals and accommodations. A *production accountant* (or *production auditor*) monitors expenditures, a *production secretary* coordinates telephone communications among units and with the producer, and *production assistants* (or *PAs*) run errands. Newcomers to the film industry often start out working as production assistants.

Scenes and Takes   All this coordinated effort results in many hours of footage and recorded sound. For each shot called for in the script or storyboard, the director usually does several *takes,* or versions. For instance, if the finished film requires one shot of an actor saying a line, the director may do several takes of that speech, each time asking the actor to vary the delivery. Only one take, or even one part of the take, becomes the shot included in the finished film. Left-over footage can be used in coming-attractions trailers and electronic press kits.

Because scenes seldom are filmed in plot order, the director and the crew must have some way of labeling each take. As soon as the camera starts, one of the cinematographer's staff holds up a *slate* before the lens. On the slate is written the production, scene, shot, and take. A hinged arm at the top, the clapboard, makes a sharp smack that allows the recordist to synchronize the sound track with the footage in the assembly phase **(1.31).** Thus every take is identified for future reference. There are also electronic slates that keep track of each take automatically and provide digital readouts.

In filming a scene, most directors and technicians follow an organized procedure. While crews set up the lighting and test the sound recording, the director rehearses the actors and instructs the cinematographer. The director then usually supervises the filming of a *master shot.* The master shot typically records the entire action and dialogue of the scene. There may be several takes of the master shot. Then portions of the scene are restaged and shot in closer views or from different angles. These shots are called *coverage,* and each one may require many takes. Today most directors shoot a great deal of coverage. The script supervisor checks to ensure that details are consistent within all these shots.

For most of film history, scenes were filmed with a single camera, which was moved to different points for different setups. More recently, under pressure to finish principal photography as quickly as possible, the director and the camera unit often use two or more cameras, even for routine coverage. Action scenes like the taxi smashup in *Collateral* are usually shot from several angles simultaneously, because chases, crashes, and explosions are difficult to repeat for retakes. The battle scenes in *Gladiator* were filmed by 7 cameras, whereas 13 cameras were used for stunts in *XXX.*

For dialogue scenes, a common tactic is to film with an A camera and a B camera, an arrangement that can capture two actors in alternating shots. Still, some directors prefer the single-camera method. The camera assistant on Quentin Tarantino's *Inglourious Basterds* sums up the artistic advantages: "You get such a hand-crafted movie. The actors know they're going to do a lot of setups because it's only one camera, but they get to perfect their craft. The camera rolls for as many takes as necessary to perfect each shot."

When special effects are to be included, the shooting phase must carefully plan for them. In many cases, actors will be filmed against blue or green backgrounds so that their figures can be inserted into computer-created settings. Or the director may film performers with the understanding that other material will be composited into the frame **(1.32).** If a moving person or animal needs to be created by computer, a specialized unit will use *motion capture.* Here small sensors are attached all over the body of the subject, and as that subject moves against a blank background or a set, a special camera records the movement **(1.33, 1.34).** Each

1.32 Combining actors and special effects. For the climax of *Jurassic Park*, the actors were shot in the set of the visitor's center, but the velociraptors and the *Tyrannosaurus rex* were computer-generated images added later.

1.33

1.34

1.33–1.34 Motion capture. For *Iron Man*, Robert Downey Jr. performed in a motion-capture suit covered with sensors (1.33). The same scene with a computer-animated suit partially added (1.34).

A CLOSER LOOK

Some Terms and Roles in Film Production

The rise of packaged productions, the use of free-lance workers, and other factors have led producers to credit everyone who worked on a film. Meanwhile, the specialization of large-scale filmmaking has created its own jargon. We have explained some of the most colorful terms in the text. Here are some other terms that you may see in a film's credits.

ACE: After the name of the editor; abbreviation for the American Cinema Editors, a professional association.

ASC: After the name of the director of photography; abbreviation for the American Society of Cinematographers, a professional association. The British equivalent is the BSC.

Additional photography: Crew shooting footage apart from the *principal photography,* typically supervised by the director of photography.

Best boy: Term from the classic studio years, originally applied to the gaffer's assistant. Today film credits may list both a *best boy electric* and a *best boy grip,* the assistant to the key grip.

Casting director: Member who searches for and auditions performers for the film, and suggests actors for *leading roles* (principal characters) and *character parts* (fairly standardized or stereotyped roles). She or he may also cast *extras* (background or nonspeaking roles).

Clapper boy: Crew member who operates the clapboard (slate) that identifies each take.

Concept artist: Designer who creates illustrations of the settings and costumes that the director has in mind for the film.

Dialogue editor: Sound editor specializing in making sure recorded speech is audible.

Digital image technician: Specialist who assists the cinematographer on image capture in digital formats. Also known as *video controller.*

Dolly grip: Crew member who pushes the dolly that carries the camera, either from one setup to another or during a take for moving camera shots.

Foley artist: Sound-effects specialist who creates sounds of movement by walking or by shifting materials across large trays of different substances (sand, earth, glass, and so on). Named for Jack Foley, a pioneer in postproduction sound.

---

sensor provides a point in a wire-frame figure on a computer. That image can then be animated and built up to a completely rendered person or animal to be inserted digitally into the film.

The Assembly Phase

Filmmakers call the assembly phase **postproduction.** Yet this phase doesn't begin after the shooting is finished. Typically, postproduction staff members work behind the scenes throughout shooting. Since the advent of digital postproduction tools, many filmmakers prefer to start editing, sound mixing, special effects, and other important tasks immediately after the first footage is shot.

Picture Editing   Before the shooting begins, the director or producer probably hires an *editor* (also known as the *supervising editor*). This person catalogues and assembles the takes produced during shooting. The editor also works with the director to make creative decisions about how the footage can best be cut together.

Because each shot usually exists in several takes, because the film is shot out of plot order, and because the master-shot/coverage approach yields so much footage, the editor's job can be a daunting one. A 100-minute feature, which amounts to about 9,000 feet of 35mm film, may have been carved out of 500,000 feet of raw footage. Shooting on video can also generate a huge amount of material to be edited. Over 286 hours of footage were sent to postproduction for *The Social Network.* For this reason, postproduction on major Hollywood pictures often takes up to seven months. Sometimes several editors and assistants are brought in.

> " A couple of guys in a coffee shop set out to write a gag; a couple of guys with a camera set out to film a gag; a couple of guys in an editing room set out to make sense of the trash that's been dumped on their desks."
>
> —David Mamet, director, *The Spanish Prisoner* and *Redbelt*

Greenery man: Crew member who chooses and maintains trees, shrubs, and grass in settings.

Lead man: Member of set crew responsible for tracking down various props and items of decor.

Loader: Member of photography unit who loads and unloads camera magazines, as well as logging the shots taken and sending the film to the laboratory.

Matte artist: Member of special-effects unit who paints backdrops that are then photographically or digitally incorporated into a shot to indicate a setting.

Model maker: (1) Member of production design unit who prepares architectural models for sets to be built. (2) Member of the special-effects unit who fabricates scale models of locales, vehicles, or characters to be filmed or scanned as substitutes for full-size ones.

Property master: Member of set crew who supervises the use of all props, or movable objects in the film.

Publicist, unit publicist: Member of producer's crew who creates promotional material regarding the production. The publicist may arrange for press and television interviews with the director and cast and for coverage of the production in the mass media.

Scenic artist: Member of set crew responsible for painting surfaces of set.

Still photographer: Member of crew who takes photographs of scenes and behind-the-scenes shots of cast members and others. These photographs may be used to check lighting or set design or color, and some will be used in publicizing the film.

Timer, color timer: Laboratory worker who inspects the negative film and adjusts the printer light to achieve consistency of color across the finished product. In digital postproduction, the timer is sometimes called the *colorist.*

Video assist: A video camera attached to the motion picture camera that allows immediate playback of a shot. This allows the director and cinematographer to check lighting, framing, or performances.

Typically, the editor receives filmed material as quickly as possible. This footage is known as the *dailies* or the *rushes.* The editor inspects the dailies, leaving it to the *assistant editor* to synchronize image and sound and to sort the takes by scene. The editor meets with the director to examine the dailies, or if the production is filming far away, the editor informs the director of how the footage looks. Since retaking shots is costly and troublesome, constant checking of the dailies is important for spotting any problems with focus, exposure, framing, or other visual factors. From the dailies, the director selects the best takes, and the editor records the choices. To save money, "digital dailies" are often shown to the producer and director, but since video playback on small monitors can conceal defects in the original footage, many editors prefer to check the shots on a big screen before.

As the footage accumulates, the editor assembles it into a *rough cut*—the shots loosely strung in sequence, without sound effects or music. Rough cuts tend to run long—the rough cut for *Apocalypse Now* ran 7½ hours. From the rough cut, the editor, in consultation with the director, builds toward a *fine cut* or *final cut.* The unused shots constitute the *outtakes.* While the final cut is being prepared, a *second unit* may be shooting *inserts,* footage to fill in at certain places. These are typically long shots of cities or airports or close-ups of objects. At this point, titles are prepared, and further laboratory work or special-effects work may be done.

Until the mid-1980s, editors cut and spliced the *work print,* footage printed from the camera negative. In trying out their options, editors were obliged to rearrange the shots physically. Now virtually all commercial films are edited digitally. The dailies are transferred first to tape or a hard drive. The editor enters notes on each take directly into a computer database. From these, the editor can call up any shot, join it to another shot, trim it, or junk it. Special effects and music can be tried out as well.

As the editing team puts the footage in order, other members of the team manipulate the look of the shots via computer. If the footage has been shot on film, it may be scanned frame by frame into computer files to create a *digital intermediate* (DI). The DI is manipulated in many ways, most importantly to change light levels and to alter colors. The purpose is to make sure that shots made at different times of day or in different locales can be cut together to create a consistent look throughout a scene. Such tasks are handled by *digital color grading,* and the job is done by the *colorist.* To some extent the colorist takes over tasks that a cinematographer and traditional grader would originally have performed in the photographic laboratory, and the two may work together on the DI. Nowadays if a problem arises on set, the filming continues, with the crew deciding, "we'll fix it in post." As we'll see in Chapter 5, digital tools can make precise changes in portions of the image.

Ironically, the use of digital intermediates has encouraged some filmmakers to continue working on 35mm photographic film stock. They believe that they can best exploit the visual richness of film by digital manipulation. Jacques Audiard's *A Prophet* was shot on 35mm, but after transfer to a DI it was shown at the Cannes Film Festival as a 2K version. Audiard was thrilled with the way it looked on the screen: "It's a miraculous hybrid that magnifies the beauty of 35mm." Many directors and cinematographers share Audiard's enthusiasm for this "hybrid" approach.

Special Effects   For special effects, filmmakers turn to computer-generated imagery (CGI). Their tasks may be as simple as deleting distracting background elements or building a crowd out of a few spectators. George Lucas has claimed that if an actor blinked at the wrong time, he just erased the blink digitally. CGI can also create imagery that would be virtually impossible with photographic film **(1.35)**. Computers can conjure up photorealistic characters such as Gollum in *The Lord of the Rings*. (See pp. 166–167.) Fantasy and science fiction have fostered the development of CGI, but all genres have benefited, from the comic multiplication of a single actor in *Charlie and the Chocolate Factory* to the grisly realism of the digitally enhanced Omaha Beach assault in *Saving Private Ryan*. In *The Curious Case of Benjamin Button*, CGI substituted for make-up, allowing Brad Pitt and Cate Blanchett to plausibly portray their characters through youth to old age.

Sound Editing   Once the shots are arranged in something approaching final form, the *sound editor* takes charge of building up the sound track. The director, the composer, the picture editor, and the sound editor view the film and agree on

1.35 Computer-generated imagery. In the chase through the airways of Coruscant in *Attack of the Clones,* the actor was shot against a blue or green screen, and the backgrounds and moving vehicles were created through CGI.

where music and effects will be placed, a process known as *spotting*. The sound editor may have a staff whose members specialize in mixing dialogue, music, or sound effects.

Surprisingly little of the sound recorded during filming winds up in the finished movie. Often half or more of the dialogue is rerecorded in postproduction, using a process known as *automated dialogue replacement (ADR)*. ADR usually yields better quality than location sound does. With the on-set recording serving as a *guide track,* the sound editor records actors in the studio speaking their lines (called *dubbing* or *looping*). Nonsynchronized dialogue such as the babble of a crowd (known in Hollywood as "walla") is added by ADR as well.

Similarly, very few of the noises we hear in a film were recorded during filming. A sound editor adds sound effects, drawing on a library of stock sounds or creating particular effects for the film. Sound editors routinely manufacture footsteps, car crashes, pistol shots, and fists thudding into flesh (often produced by whacking a watermelon with an axe). In *Terminator 2,* the sound of the T-1000 cyborg passing through jail cell bars is that of dog food sliding slowly out of a can. Sound-effects technicians have sensitive hearing. One veteran noted the differences among doors: "The bathroom door has a little air as opposed to the closet door. The front door has to sound solid; you have to hear the latch sound. . . . Don't just put in any door, make sure it's right."

Like picture editing, modern sound editing relies on computer technology. The editor can store recorded sounds in a database, classifying and rearranging them in any way desired. A sound's qualities can be modified digitally—clipping off high or low frequencies and changing pitch, reverberation, equalization, or speed. The boom and throb of underwater action in *The Hunt for Red October* were slowed down and reprocessed from such mundane sources as a diver plunging into a swimming pool, water bubbling from a garden hose, and the hum of Disneyland's air-conditioning plant. One technician on the film called digital sound editing "sound sculpting."

During the spotting of the sound track, the film's *composer* enters the assembly phase as well. The composer compiles cue sheets that mark exactly where the music will go and how long it should run. The composer writes the score, although she or he will probably not orchestrate it personally. While the composer is working, the rough cut is synchronized with a *temp dub*—accompaniment pulled from recorded songs or classical pieces. Musicians record the score with the aid of a *click track,* a taped series of metronome beats synchronized with the final cut.

Dialogue, effects, and music are recorded on separate tracks, and each type of sound, however minor, will occupy a separate track. During the mixing, for each scene, the image track is run over, once for each sound, to ensure proper synchronization. The specialist who performs the task is the *rerecording mixer,* usually supervising a team of mixers. Each scene may involve dozens of tracks of individual sounds, which are all mixed together. Equalization, filtering, and other adjustment take place at this stage. The director typically oversees some mixing sessions, particularly the one creating the final mix.

For a film-based project, the *camera negative,* which was the source of the dailies and the work print, is too precious to serve as the source for final prints. Traditionally, from the negative footage, the laboratory draws an *interpositive,* which in turn provides an *internegative.* The internegative is then assembled in accordance with the final cut, and it serves as the primary source of future prints. An alternative, as we've seen, is to create a digital intermediate that can be recorded back to film as an internegative.

Once the internegative has been created, the master sound track is synchronized with it. The first positive print, complete with picture and sound, is called the *answer print.* After the director, producer, and cinematographer have approved an answer print, *release prints* are made for distribution. Using a digital intermediate makes it possible to generate additional internegatives as old ones wear out, all without any wear on the original materials.

> " [ADR for *Apocalypse Now*] was tremendously wearing on the actors because the entire film is looped, and of course all of the sound for everything had to be redone. So the actors were locked in a room for days and days on end shouting. Either they're shouting over the noise of the helicopter, or they're shouting over the noise of the boat."
> —Walter Murch, sound designer

Films that are shot digitally may proceed through postproduction without ever being put on photochemical stock. The director and cinematographer approve a master tape version that will be converted to the Digital Cinema Packages released to theatres. Further conversions will turn out video versions for DVD, streaming, and other platforms. These transfers often demand new judgments about color quality and sound balance. The master tape of the finished film, along with all the footage and materials used in the creation of the movie, will be stored on files. Because digital media have a short life, most film studios arrange for the finished film and the most valuable supplementary footage to be saved on 35mm film as well.

Special Versions   The work of production does not end when the final theatrical version has been assembled. In consultation with the producer and director, the postproduction staff prepares airline and broadcast television versions. For a successful film, a director's cut or an extended edition may be released on DVD or the Internet. Different versions may be prepared for different countries. European prints of Stanley Kubrick's *Eyes Wide Shut* featured more nudity than did American ones, in which some naked couples were blocked by digital figures added to the foreground.

Many fictional films have dramatized processes of film production. Federico Fellini's *8½* concerns itself with the preproduction stage of a film that is abandoned before shooting starts. François Truffaut's *Day for Night*, David Mamet's *State and Main*, Christopher Guest's *For Your Consideration*, and Tom DiCillo's *Living in Oblivion* all center on the shooting phase. The action of Brian De Palma's *Blow Out* occurs while a low-budget thriller is in sound editing. *Singin' in the Rain* follows a single film through the entire process, with a gigantic advertising billboard filling the final shot.

Artistic Implications of the Production Process

Every artist works within constraints of time, money, and opportunity. Of all the arts, filmmaking is one of the most pressurized. Budgets must be maintained, deadlines must be met, weather and locations are unpredictable, and the coordination of any group of people involves unforeseeable twists and turns. Even a Hollywood blockbuster, which might seem to offer unlimited freedom, is actually confining on many levels. Big-budget filmmakers sometimes get tired of coordinating hundreds of staff and wrestling with million-dollar decisions, and they start to long for more relaxed productions. Steven Soderbergh swung between high-profile projects like the star-packed *Ocean's 11* franchise and smaller projects like *Bubble,* shot with nonprofessional actors on 1080p HD.

We appreciate films more when we realize that in production, every film is a compromise made within constraints. When Mark and Michael Polish conceived their independent film *Twin Falls Idaho,* they had planned for the story to unfold in several countries. But the cost of travel and location shooting forced them to rethink the film's plot: "We had to decide whether the film was about twins or travel." Similarly, the involvement of a powerful director can reshape the film at the screenplay stage. In the original screenplay of *Witness,* the protagonist was Rachel, the Amish widow with whom John Book falls in love. The romance and Rachel's confused feelings about Book formed the central plot line. But the director, Peter Weir, wanted to emphasize the clash between pacifism and violence. So William Kelley and Earl Wallace revised their screenplay to stress the mystery plot line and to center the action on Book and the introduction of urban crime into the peaceful Amish community. Given the new constraints, the screenwriters found a new form for *Witness.*

Some filmmakers struggle against their constraints, pushing the limits of what's considered possible. The production of a film we'll study in upcoming chapters, *Citizen Kane,* was highly innovative on many fronts. Yet even this project had to accept studio routines and the limits of current technology. More commonly, a filmmaker works with the same menu of choices available to others. In directing *Collateral,*

Michael Mann made creative choices about how to use digital cameras and low lighting levels. Other filmmakers working in 2004 could have taken the same risks, but Mann saw new ways of employing such techniques. The overall result was a visual style that no other film had achieved, though others soon imitated it.

Starting our study of film art with a survey of production allows us to understand some of the possibilities offered by images and sounds. It also helps put us in the filmmaker's shoes: we can see the decisions from the inside. We realize that everything in the finished movie springs from choices that we too would face. Later chapters will discuss the artistic consequences of decisions made in production—everything from storytelling strategies to techniques of staging, shooting, editing, and sound work. By choosing within production constraints, and sometimes pushing against them, filmmakers create film form and style.

Modes of Production

The scale and type of production varies—from large-scale studio filmmaking involving hundreds of people to do-it-yourself productions completed by a single filmmaker—and obviously shapes the final film.

Large-Scale Production

The fine-grained division of labor we've been describing is characteristic of *studio* filmmaking. A studio is a company in the business of creating films. The most famous studios flourished in Hollywood from the 1920s to the 1960s—Paramount, Warner Bros., Columbia, and so on. These companies owned equipment and extensive physical plants, and they retained most of their workers on long-term contracts. Each studio's central management planned all projects, then delegated authority to supervising producers, who in turn assembled casts and crews from the studio's pool of workers.

Organized as efficient businesses, the studios created a tradition of carefully tracking the entire process through paper records. At the start, there were versions of the script. During shooting, reports were written about camera footage, sound recording, special-effects work, and laboratory results. In the assembly phase, there were logs of shots catalogued in editing and a variety of cue sheets for music, mixing, looping, and title layout. This sort of record-keeping has remained a part of large-scale filmmaking, though now it is done mostly on computer.

Although studio production might seem to resemble a factory's assembly line, it was always more creative, collaborative, and chaotic than turning out cars or microchips is. Each film is a unique product, not a replica of a prototype. In studio filmmaking, skilled specialists collaborated to create such a product while still adhering to a "blueprint" prepared by management **(1.36)**.

The centralized production system has virtually disappeared. The giant studios of Hollywood's golden age have become distribution companies, although

1.36 Large-scale production. Studio production was characterized by a large number of highly specialized production roles. Here several units prepare a moving-camera shot for *Wells Fargo* (1937).

they may initiate, fund, and oversee the making of some of the films they distribute. The old studios had stars and staff under contract, so the same group of people might work together on film after film. Now each film is planned as a distinct package, with director, actors, staff, and technicians brought together for the project. The studio may provide its own soundstages, sets, and offices for the production, but in most cases, the producer arranges with outside firms to supply cameras, catering, locations, special effects, and anything else required.

Still, the detailed production stages remain similar to what they were in the heyday of studio production. Each phase of filmmaking has encompassed more and more specialized tasks in recent years, largely because of the expansion of production budgets and the growth of computer-based special effects. *Avatar* listed over 2,500 names in its final credits.

Exploitation, Independent Production, and DIY

Not all films using the division of labor we have outlined are big-budget projects financed by major companies. There are also low-budget *exploitation* products tailored to a particular market—in earlier decades, fringe theaters and drive-ins; now, video rentals and sales. Troma Films, maker of *The Toxic Avenger,* is probably the most famous exploitation company, turning out horror movies and teen sex comedies for $100,000 or less. Nonetheless, exploitation filmmakers usually divide the labor along studio lines. There is the producer's role, the director's role, and so on, and the production tasks are parceled out in ways that roughly conform to mass-production practices.

Exploitation production often forces people to double up on jobs. Robert Rodriguez made *El Mariachi* as an exploitation film for the Spanish-language video market. The 21-year-old director also functioned as producer, scriptwriter, cinematographer, camera operator, still photographer, and sound recordist and mixer. Rodriguez's friend Carlos Gallardo starred, coproduced, and coscripted; he also served as unit production manager and grip. Gallardo's mother fed the cast and crew. *El Mariachi* wound up costing only about $7,000.

Unlike *El Mariachi,* most exploitation films don't enter the theatrical market, but other low-budget productions, loosely known as *independent* films, may. Independent films are made for the theatrical market but usually without major distributor financing. Some independents are well-known directors, such as Spike Lee, David Cronenberg, and Joel and Ethan Coen, who prefer to work with budgets significantly below the industry norm. In such cases, the director usually initiates the project and partners with a producer to get it realized. Financing often comes from television firms, with major U.S. distributors buying the rights if the project seems to have good prospects. For example, David Lynch's low-budget *The Straight Story* was financed by French and British television before it was bought for distribution by Disney.

As we would expect, these industry-based independents organize production in ways close to the full-fledged studio mode. Nonetheless, because these projects require less financing, the directors can demand more control over the production process. For *Slumdog Millionaire,* a relatively low-cost project, director Danny Boyle had the freedom to shoot some of the film on 35mm and other portions on smaller 2K digital cameras, which were easier to maneuver in the crowded streets of Mumbai.

The category of independent production is a roomy one, and it also includes more modest projects by less well-known filmmakers. Examples are Victor Nuñez's *Ulee's Gold,* Phil Morrison's *Junebug,* and Miranda July's *Me and You and Everyone We Know.* Even though they are far less costly than studio projects, independent productions face many obstacles **(1.37).** Filmmakers may have to finance the project themselves, with the help of relatives and friendly investors; they must also find a distributor specializing in independent and low-budget films. Still, if you

> "Deep down inside, everybody in the United States has a desperate need to believe that some day, if the breaks fall their way, they can quit their jobs as claims adjusters, legal secretaries, certified public accountants, or mobsters, and go out and make their own low-budget movie. Otherwise, the future is just too bleak."
>
> —Joe Queenan, critic and independent filmmaker

CONNECT TO THE BLOG
www.davidbordwell.net/blog

Studio films and independent ones aren't always that far apart, as we suggest in "Independent film: How different?"

1.37 Independent production. In making *Just Another Girl on the IRT,* independent director Leslie Harris used locations and available lighting in order to shoot quickly. She finished filming in just 17 days.

were an independent filmmaker, you might believe the advantages outweigh the drawbacks. Independent production can treat subjects that large-scale studio production ignores. No film studios would probably have supported Kevin Smith's *Clerks* or Lena Dunham's *Tiny Furniture* or Ben and Joshua Safdie's *Go Get Some Rosemary.* Because the independent film does not need as large an audience to repay its costs, it can be more personal and controversial. And the production process, no matter how low the budget, still relies on the basic roles and phases established by the studio tradition.

Small-Scale Production

In large-scale and independent production, many people work on the film, each one a specialist in a particular task. But there's also a tradition of a single filmmaker assuming all or many of the roles: planning the film, financing it, performing in it, running the camera, recording the sound, and putting it all together. For his low-budget horror film *Monsters,* Gareth Edwards acted as writer, director, cinematographer, and special-effects supervisor. He did his own location scouting from his computer, using Google Earth to survey Mexico, Belize, and Guatemala.

Experimental and documentary traditions have given great weight to the film dominated by a single person's efforts. Consider Stan Brakhage, whose films are among the most directly personal ever made. Some, such as *Window Water Baby Moving,* are lyrical studies of his home and family **(1.38).** Others, such as *Dog Star Man,* are mythic treatments of nature; still others, such as *23rd Psalm Branch,* are quasi-documentary studies of war and death. Funded by grants and his personal finances, Brakhage prepared, shot, and edited his films virtually unaided. While he was working in a film laboratory, he also developed and printed his footage. With over 150 films to his credit, Brakhage proved that the individual filmmaker can become an artisan, executing all the basic production tasks.

The 16mm and less costly digital video formats are customary for small-scale production of this sort. Financial backing often comes from the filmmaker, from grants, and perhaps from obliging friends and relatives. There is very little division of labor: the filmmaker oversees every production task and performs many of them. Although technicians or performers may help out, the creative decisions rest with the filmmaker. Experimentalist Maya Deren's *Meshes of the Afternoon* was shot by her husband, Alexander Hammid, but she scripted, directed, and edited it and performed in the central role **(1.39).** Amos Poe made his lengthy, evocative experimental film *Empire II* by placing a small digital camera in a window of his Manhattan apartment and exposing single frames in bursts at intervals over an entire year **(1.40).** Poe edited the film himself, reworked the images digitally, and assembled the sound track from existing songs and original music.

Such small-scale production is common in documentary filmmaking as well. Jean Rouch, a French anthropologist, made several films alone or with a small crew in his efforts to record the lives of marginal people living in alien cultures. Rouch wrote, directed, and photographed *Les Maîtres fous* (1955), his first widely seen film. He examined the ceremonies of a Ghanaian cult whose members lived a double life: most of the time they worked as low-paid laborers, but in their rituals, they passed into a frenzied trance and assumed the identities of their colonial rulers.

Similarly, Barbara Kopple devoted four years to making *Harlan County, U.S.A.,* a record of Kentucky coal miners' struggles for union representation. After eventually obtaining funding from several foundations, she and a small crew spent 13 months living with miners during the workers' strike. During filming, Kopple acted as sound recordist, working with cameraman Hart Perry and sometimes also a lighting person. A large crew was ruled out not only by Kopple's budget but also by the need to fit naturally into the community. Like the miners, the filmmakers were constantly threatened with violence from strikebreakers **(1.41).**

1.38 Small-scale production. In *The Riddle of Lumen,* Stan Brakhage turns shadows and everyday objects into vivid patterns.

1.39

1.40

1.39–1.40 Handmade movies. In *Meshes of the Afternoon,* multiple versions of the protagonist were played by the filmmaker, Maya Deren (1.39). For *Empire II,* Amos Poe digitally manipulated this tantalizing glimpse of the Manhattan skyline (1.40).

1.41 Small-scale documentary filmmaking. In *Harlan County, U.S.A.*, the driver of a passing truck fires at the film crew. Working organically within the community, the filmmakers were threatened with violence similar to that experienced by the striking coal miners they were filming.

On rare occasions small-scale production becomes *collective* production. Here, instead of a single filmmaker shaping the project, several film workers participate equally. The group shares common goals and makes production decisions democratically. Roles may also be rotated: the sound recordist on one day may serve as cinematographer on the next. One instance is the Canadian film *Atanarjuat: The Fast Runner.* Three Inuits (Zacharias Kunuk, Paul Apak Angilirq, and Paul Qulitalik) and one New Yorker (Norman Cohn) composed a screenplay based on an oral tale about love, murder, and revenge. Cast and crew spent six months shooting in the Arctic, camping in tents and eating seal meat. "We don't have a hierarchy," Cohn explained. "There's no director, second, third or fourth assistant director. We have a team of people trying to figure out how to make this work." Because of the communal nature of Inuit life, the Igloolik team expanded the collective effort by bringing local people into the project. An early showcase for the strengths of digital video **(1.42),** *Atanarjuat: The Fast Runner* won a prize at the 2002 Cannes Film Festival. Collective production may be getting more popular, as YouTube and other media-sharing sites have encouraged high-school classes to make films together.

Small-scale production allows the filmmakers to retain tight control of the project. The rise of digital video formats has made small-scale production more visible. *The Gleaners and I* (see p. 175), *The Yes Men, Encounters at the End of the World, The Sweetest Sound, The Cove, Anvil! The Story of Anvil, Restrepo,* and other documentaries indicate that the theatrical market and festival circuit have room for works made by single filmmakers or small production units.

The introduction of consumer and prosumer digital cameras and affordable software for computer postproduction has led to the rise of "do it yourself" (DIY) filmmaking. Individuals or small groups of amateurs can make their own films and share them on YouTube, Vimeo, and other websites. An early instance was Arin Crumley and Susan Buice's *Four Eyed Monsters,* a filmed reenactment of the couple's unconventional romance that got some festival exposure before moving to a self-published DVD and YouTube.

Artistic Implications of Different Modes of Production

Production and Film Categories We sometimes categorize films on the basis of how they were made. We can distinguish a *fiction* film from a *documentary* on the basis of production phases. The fiction film is characterized by much more control over the preparation and shooting phases. By contrast, the documentary filmmaker usually controls only certain portions of preparation, shooting, and assembly. Some stages (such as script and rehearsal) may be omitted, whereas others (such as setting, lighting, and performance) are present but often uncontrolled. In interviewing an eyewitness to an event, the filmmaker typically controls camera work and editing but does not tell the witness what to say or how to act. For example, there was no script for the documentary *Manufacturing Consent: Noam Chomsky and the Media.* Filmmakers Mark Achbar and Peter Wintonick instead shot long interviews in which Chomsky explained his ideas.

1.42 Collective filmmaking. The hero of *Atanarjuat: The Fast Runner* pauses in his flight across the ice. "We made our film in an Inuit way," Norman Cohn explained, "through consensus and collaboration."

Similarly, a *compilation* film assembles existing images and sounds that provide historical evidence on a topic. The compilation filmmaker may minimize the shooting stage and create a story from archival footage. For *The Power of Nightmares,* Adam Curtis gathered newsreel and television footage, television commercials, and clips from fiction films to track the rise of fundamentalist politics and religion after World War II.

One more kind of film is distinguished by the way it's produced. The *animated* film is created frame by frame. Images may be drawn directly on the film strip, or the camera may photograph drawings or three-dimensional models, as in the *Wallace and Grommit* movies. *Corpse Bride* was created without using motion picture cameras; instead, each frame was registered by a digital still camera and transferred to film. Today most animated films, both for theater screens and for the Internet, are created directly on computer with imaging software.

Production and Authorship

Production practices have another implication for film as an art form. Who, it is often asked, is the "author," the person responsible for the film? In individual production, the author must be the solitary filmmaker—Stan Brakhage or perhaps you. Collective film production creates collective authorship: the author is the entire group. The question of authorship becomes difficult to answer only when asked about large-scale production, particularly in the studio mode.

Studio film production assigns tasks to so many individuals that it is often difficult to determine who controls or decides what. Is the producer the author? In the prime years of the Hollywood system, the producer might have had nothing to do with shooting. The writer? The writer's script might be completely transformed in shooting and editing. So is this situation like collective production, with group authorship? No, because there is a hierarchy in which a few main players make the key decisions.

Moreover, if we consider not only control and decision making but also individual style, it seems certain that some studio workers leave recognizable and unique traces on the films they make. Cinematographers such as Gregg Toland, set designers such as Hermann Warm, costumers such as Edith Head, choreographers such as Gene Kelly—the contributions of these people stand out within the films they made. So where does the studio-produced film leave the idea of authorship?

Most people who study cinema regard the director as the film's primary "author." Although the writer prepares a screenplay, later phases of production can modify it beyond recognition. And although the producer monitors the entire process, he or she seldom controls moment-by-moment activity on the set. It is the director who makes the crucial decisions about performance, staging, lighting, framing, cutting, and sound. On the whole, the director usually has most control over how a movie looks and sounds.

This doesn't mean that the director is an expert at every job or dictates every detail. The director can delegate tasks to trusted personnel, and directors often work habitually with certain actors, cinematographers, composers, and editors. In the days of studio filmmaking, directors learned how to blend the distinctive talents of cast and crew into the overall movie. Humphrey Bogart's unique talents were used very differently by Michael Curtiz in *Casablanca*, John Huston in *The Maltese Falcon*, and Howard Hawks in *The Big Sleep*. Gregg Toland's cinematography was pushed in different directions by Orson Welles (*Citizen Kane*) and William Wyler (*The Best Years of Our Lives*).

During the 1950s, young French critics applied the word *auteur* (author) to Hollywood directors who they felt had created a distinctive approach to filmmaking while working within the Hollywood studio system. Soon American critics picked up the "auteur theory," which remained a central idea for film academics and students. Now you will occasionally read reviews or see spots on television that use the term to refer to a respected and distinctive director.

Today well-established directors can control large-scale production to a remarkable degree. Until 2011, Steven Spielberg resisted using digital editing. The late Robert Altman disliked ADR and used much of the casual on-set dialogue in the finished film. In the days of Hollywood's studio system, some directors exercised power more indirectly. Most studios did not permit the director to supervise editing, but John Ford often made only one take of each shot. Precutting the film "in his head," Ford virtually forced the editor to put the shots together as he had planned.

Around the world, the director is generally recognized as the key player. In Europe, Asia, and South America, directors frequently initiate the film and work

> " The thing that makes me sad is that there's tons of kids that I meet all the time . . . who don't know anything about film history. . . . The number who couldn't say that Orson Welles directed *Citizen Kane* was staggering. . . . They were infatuated with the business and the glamour of the business, and not filmmaking."
> —Stacy Sher, producer, *Pulp Fiction* and *Erin Brockovich*

> " The times when [our job] is most satisfying are when you really are in sync with the director. It is almost like you are trying to crawl into their brain, and it is about fulfilling their vision, which is what everybody's role on a film is."
> —Ellen Lewis, casting director

CONNECT TO THE BLOG
www.davidbordwell.net/blog

Screenwriters often take issue with the idea of directorial authorship, but we defend it in "Who the devil wrote it? (Apologies to Peter Bogdanovich.)"

closely with scriptwriters. In Hollywood, directors usually operate on a freelance basis, and the top ones select their own projects. For the most part, it is the director who shapes the film's unique form and style, and these two components are central to cinema as an art.

Bringing the Film to the Audience: Distribution and Exhibition

We've spent some time considering film production because that is where film art begins. What of the other two phases of filmmaking? As in production, money plays a significant role in both distribution and exhibition. We'll see as well that these phases have effects on film art and viewers' experiences of particular films.

Distribution: The Center of Power

Distribution companies form the core of economic power in the commercial film industry. Filmmakers need them to circulate their work; exhibitors need them to supply their screens. Europe and Asia are home to some significant media companies, but six Hollywood firms remain the world's major distributors. The names are familiar: Warner Bros., Paramount, Walt Disney/Buena Vista, Universal, Sony/Columbia, and Twentieth Century Fox.

These firms provide mainstream entertainment to theaters around the world. The films they release account for 95 percent of ticket sales in the United States and Canada, and about half of overseas market. In world capitals, the majors maintain branch offices that advertise films, schedule releases, and arrange for prints to be made in local languages (either dubbing in the dialogue or adding subtitling). With vigorous marketing units in every region, the majors can distribute non-U.S. films as well as Hollywood titles. For example, Hayao Miyazaki's popular animated films (*Spirited Away, Howl's Moving Castle*) are distributed on video by Disney's Buena Vista arm, even in Miyazaki's homeland of Japan.

The major distributors have won such power because large companies can best endure the risks of theatrical moviemaking. Filmmaking is costly, and most films don't earn profits in theatrical release. Worldwide, the top 10 percent of all films released garner 50 percent of all box office receipts. The most popular 30 percent of films account for 80 percent of receipts. Distributors are in a position to move films smoothly from theatrical runs to cable TV, DVD and other platforms. Typically, a film breaks even or shows a profit only after it has been released in these ancillary markets.

In the United States, theater owners bid for each film a distributor releases, and in most states, they must be allowed to see the film before bidding. Elsewhere in the world, distributors may force exhibitors to rent a film without seeing it (called *blind booking*), perhaps even before it has been completed. Exhibitors may also be pressured to rent a package of films in order to get a few desirable items (*block booking*).

Once the exhibitor has contracted to screen the film, the distributor can demand stiff terms. The theater keeps a surprisingly small percentage of total box office receipts (known as the *gross* or *grosses*). One standard arrangement guarantees the distributor a minimum of 90 percent of the first week's gross, dropping gradually to 30 percent after several weeks. These terms aren't favorable to the exhibitor. A failure that closes quickly will yield almost nothing to the theater, and even a successful film will make most of its money in the first two or three weeks of release, when the exhibitor gets less of the revenue. Averaged out, a long-running success will likely yield no more than 50 percent of the gross to the theater. To make up for this drawback, the distributor allows the exhibitor to deduct from the gross the expenses of running the theater (a negotiated figure called the *house nut*).

In addition, the exhibitor gets all the cash from the concession stand, which may deliver up to 70 percent of the theater's profits. Without high-priced snacks, movie houses couldn't survive.

After the grosses are split with the exhibitor, the distribution company receives its share (the *rentals*) and divides it further. A major U.S. distributor typically takes 35 percent of the rentals as its distribution fee. If the distributor helped finance the film, it takes another percentage off the top. The costs of prints and advertising are deducted as well. What remains comes back to the filmmakers. Out of the proceeds, the producer must pay all *profit participants*—the directors, actors, executives, and investors who have negotiated a share of the rental returns.

For most films, the amount returned to the production company is relatively small. Once the salaried workers have been paid, the producer and other major players usually must wait to receive their share from video and other ancillary markets. Because of this delay, and the suspicion that the major distributors practice misleading accounting, powerful actors and directors may demand "first-dollar" participation. In that case, their share will derive from the earliest money the picture returns to the distributor.

Majors and Minors

The major distributors all belong to multinational corporations devoted to leisure activities. For example, Paramount Pictures, which produces and distributes films, is owned by Viacom, which controls Comedy Central, MTV, and other cable channels. Time Warner not only owns Warner Bros. but also has broadcast and cable services (CNN, HBO, Turner Classic Movies, and the Cartoon Network) along with publishing houses and magazines (*Time, Sports Illustrated, People,* and DC Comics). Twentieth Century Fox is a subsidiary of News Corp, which owns many newspapers, book publishers, cable news and sports channels, and half-interest in Australia's National Rugby League. Columbia Pictures is an arm of Sony, which has extensive holdings in electronics, recorded music, and mobile communications.

Independent and overseas filmmakers usually don't have access to direct funding from major distribution companies, so they try to presell distribution rights to finance production. Sometimes the distribution rights are sold in advance of production and provide some of the film's budget. Alternatively, once a film is finished, a producer may try to attract distributors' attention at film festivals. In 2005, the South African production *Tsotsi* won the People's Choice Award at the Toronto International Film Festival, and its North American rights were bought by Buena Vista. Similarly, after a successful screening at the Cannes Film Festival, Sony Pictures Classics bought the Argentine film *The Secret in Their Eyes* for U.S. distribution and it went on to win an Academy Award.

More specialized distributors, such as the New York firms Kino and Milestone, acquire rights to foreign and independent films for rental to art cinemas, colleges, and museums. As the audience for these films grew during the 1990s, major distributors sought to enter this market. The independent firm Miramax generated enough low-budget hits to be purchased by the Disney corporation. With the benefit of Disney's funding and wider distribution reach, Miramax movies such as *Pulp Fiction, Scream, Shakespeare in Love,* and *Hero* earned even bigger box-office receipts. Sony Pictures Classics funded art house fare that sometimes crossed over to the multiplexes, as *Crouching Tiger, Hidden Dragon* did.

By belonging to multinational conglomerates, film distributors gain access to private investors, bank financing, stock issues, and other sources of funding. Branch offices in major countries can carry a film into worldwide markets. Sony's global reach allowed it to release 11 different sound track CDs for *Spider-Man 2,* each one featuring artists famous in local territories. Just as important, media conglomerates can build *synergy*—focusing sectors of the company on promoting a single piece of content, usually one that is "branded." *Batman* and *The X-Files* are famous instances of how the film, television, publishing, and music wings of a firm could

1.43 **Product placement.** In *Lethal Weapon*, as Murtaugh and Riggs leave a hotdog stand, they pass in front of a movie theater. The shot provides advance publicity for *The Lost Boys*, another Warner Bros. film released four months after *Lethal Weapon*. The prominence of Pepsi-Cola in this shot is an example of *product placement*—featuring well-known brands in a film in exchange for payment or cross-promotional services.

reinforce one another. Every product promotes the others, and each wing of the parent company gets more business. One film can even advertise another within its story **(1.43).** Although synergy sometimes fails, multimedia giants are in the best position to take advantage of it.

Distributors arrange release dates, make prints, and launch advertising campaigns. For big companies, distribution can be efficient because the costs can be spread out over many units. One poster design can be used in several markets, and a distributor who orders a thousand prints from a laboratory will pay less per print than the filmmaker who orders one. Large companies are also in the best position to cope with the rise of distribution costs. Today, the average Hollywood film is estimated to cost at least $80 million to make and an additional $40 million to distribute.

Release Patterns   The risky nature of mass-market filmmaking has led the majors to two distribution strategies: *platforming* and *wide release*. With platforming, the film opens first in a few big cities. It then gradually expands to theaters around the country, although it may never play in every community. If the strategy is successful, anticipation for the film builds, and it remains a point of discussion for months. The major distributors tend to use platforming for unusual films, such as *Brokeback Mountain* and *The King's Speech,* which need time to accumulate critical support and positive word-of-mouth. Smaller distributors use platforming out of necessity, since they can't afford to make enough prints to open wide, but the gradual accumulation of buzz can work in their favor, too.

In wide release, a film opens at the same time in many cities and towns. In the United States, this requires that thousands of copies be shipped out, so wide release is available only to the deep-pocketed major distributors. Wide release is the typical strategy for mainstream films, with two or three new titles opening each weekend on 2,000–4,000 screens. A film in wide release may be a midbudget one—a comedy, an action picture, a horror or science fiction film, or a children's animated movie. Or it may be a very big-budget item, a *tentpole* picture such as *The Dark Knight* or the latest Harry Potter installment.

CONNECT TO THE BLOG
www.davidbordwell.net/blog

With help from some colleagues, we defend movie franchises in "Live with it! There'll always be movie sequels. Good thing, too."

Distributors hope that a wide opening signals a "must-see" film, the latest big thing. Just as important, opening wide helps to recoup costs faster, since the distributor gets a larger portion of box office receipts early in the run. Still, it's a gamble. If a film fails in its first weekend, it almost never recovers momentum and can lose money very quickly. Even successful films usually lose revenues by 40 percent or more every week they run. So when two high-budget films open wide the same weekend, the competition is harmful to all. Companies tend to plan their tentpole release dates to avoid head-to-head conflict. On the weekend in May 2005 when the final installment of Fox's *Star Wars* saga opened on nearly 3,700 U.S. screens, other distributors offered no wide releases at all. *Episode III—Revenge of the Sith* grossed nearly $160 million in four days.

Wide releasing has extended across the world. As video piracy has spread, distribution companies have realized the risks of opening wide in the United States and then waiting weeks or months before opening overseas. By then, illegal DVDs and Internet downloads would stifle the theatrical release. As a result, U.S. companies undertake *day-and-date* releasing for their biggest tentpole pictures. *Matrix: Revolutions* opened simultaneously on 8,000 screens in the United States and 10,000 screens in 107 other countries. In a stroke of showmanship, the first screening was synchronized to start at the same minute across all time zones.

Selling the Film   The distributor provides not only the movie but a publicity campaign. The theater is supplied with a *trailer,* a short preview of the upcoming film. Many executives believe that a trailer is the single most effective piece of advertising. Shown in theaters, it gets the attention of confirmed moviegoers. Posted on websites, a trailer gains mass viewership.

Publicists run press junkets, flying entertainment reporters to interview the stars and principal filmmakers. "Infotainment" coverage in print, broadcast media, and online builds audience awareness. A "making of" documentary, commissioned by the studio, may be shown on cable channels. A prominent film's premiere creates an occasion for further press coverage **(1.44).** For journalists, the distributor provides electronic press kits (EPKs), complete with photos, background information, star interviews, and clips of key scenes. Even a modestly budgeted production such as *Waiting to Exhale* had heavy promotion: five separate music videos, star visits to Oprah Winfrey, and displays in thousands of bookstores and beauty salons. *My Big Fat Greek Wedding* cost $5 million to produce, but the distributors spent over $10 million publicizing it.

In 1999, two young directors found their target audience by creating a website purporting to investigate sightings of the Blair Witch. "The movie was an extension of the website," noted a studio executive. When *The Blair Witch Project* earned over $130 million in the United States, distributors woke up to the power of the Internet. Now every film has a webpage, enticing viewers with plot information, star biographies, games, screen savers, and links to merchandise. Distributors have realized that Web surfers will eagerly create "viral marketing" if they're allowed to participate in getting the word out. Fan sites such as Harry Knowles's Ain't It Cool News publicize upcoming films through steady leaks and exclusive access. Online contests can harvest email addresses for promotion of products and

CONNECT TO THE BLOG
www.davidbordwell.net/blog

Fan events like ComicCon have become a new way for Hollywood distributors to promote popular films directly to moviegoers, as we discuss in "Comic-Con 2008, Part 2."

1.44 Publicity builds audience awareness. A press conference held at Te Papa Museum in Wellington, New Zealand, as part of the December 1, 2003, world premiere of *The Lord of the Rings: The Return of the King.*

other films. Every few days during the production of *King Kong,* Peter Jackson sent a total of 90 brief "Production Diaries" to a fan site; they were later released as an elaborate DVD boxed set. The industry soon embraced wireless publicity as well, offering trailers, cell phone downloads, and text-messaging campaigns.

Although TV ads and outdoor displays like billboards and bus-shelter posters eat up most film marketing costs, online publicity has grown hugely in importance. With free social-networking sites available, the cost is low. Traditional marketing for a single Hollywood film can run in the tens of millions of dollars, but as of 2011, a complete digital campaign could cost around $25,000. The down side is that social-networking sites need to be frequently updated to maintain fan interest. A British marketer sums it up: "We spent a huge amount of energy and time promoting and marketing *StreetDance 3D* on the social networks and lots of websites; we just didn't spend much actual money." For reasons of cost, independent filmmakers rely heavily on Internet marketing.

Individual websites used to be the core of a film's marketing, but Facebook is becoming the central clearing house. "The same assets we're putting online," explains one marketer, "are also being picked up and discussed by the social media communities we create. Our challenge is to keep them interested and engaged from the theatrical to the home entertainment release." Although Peter Jackson had posted his *King Kong* production shorts on a fan site, for *The Hobbit* he started a personal Facebook page where longer production featurettes were posted at wider intervals. The only official studio website for *The Hobbit,* "The Hobbit Blog," primarily posted links to the Facebook page.

Merchandising is a form of promotion that pays back its investment directly. Manufacturing companies buy the rights to use the film's characters, title, or images on products. These licensing fees defray production and distribution costs. If the merchandise catches on, it can provide the distributor with long-term income from an audience that might never have seen the film. Although *Tron* did poorly in theatrical release in 1982, the *Discs of Tron* video game became a popular arcade attraction. Today nearly all major motion pictures rely on merchandising, if only of a novelization or a sound track CD. Children's films tend to exploit the gamut of possibilities: toys, games, clothing, lunch boxes, and schoolbags. There were *Shrek* ring tones, bowling balls, and hospital scrubs. George Lucas's entertainment empire was built on his ownership of the licensing rights for *Star Wars* merchandise.

A similar tactic is *cross-promotion,* or *brand partnering,* which allows a film and a product line to be advertised simultaneously. The partner companies agree to spend a certain amount on ads, a practice that can shift tens of millions of dollars in publicity costs away from the studios. MGM arranged for the stars of the James Bond film *Tomorrow Never Dies* to appear in advertisements for Heineken, Smirnoff, BMW, Visa, and Ericsson. The five partner companies spent nearly $100 million on the campaign, which publicized the film around the world. As payback, the film included scenes prominently featuring the products. For *Shrek 2,* several companies committed to cobranded ads, including Burger King, Pepsi-Cola, General Mills, Hewlett-Packard, and Activision. Baskin-Robbins stores featured cardboard stand-up figures of Shrek, Donkey, and Puss-in-Boots grouped around a giant "Shrek's Hot Sludge Sundae." The U.S. Postal Service was drawn into the act, stamping billions of letters with a postmark featuring Shrek and Donkey.

Because blockbusters have come to rely on merchandising for ancillary income, the distributors have taken the initiative. In 2000, Disney established a franchise management team to help companies design the licensed toys, clothing, and other products. Other studios followed suit. A successful blockbuster can reap a merchandising bonanza. By 2011, the first *Cars* movie (2005) had generated over $10 billion in sales of licensed merchandise (not including DVDs)—many times the $462 million brought in from worldwide ticket sales.

Studios and merchandisers have discovered that they must target their products precisely. Surprisingly, toy sales tied to the early Harry Potter films were relatively

CONNECT TO THE BLOG
www.davidbordwell.net/blog

Internet sites don't guarantee success. We speculate on why in "Snakes, no, Borat, yes. Not all Internet publicity is the same."

disappointing. Given the aging population of Potter book readers and the darkening tone of the films, Warner Bros. concentrated on high-end collectibles, such as wool scarves and silk ties based on the characters' costumes. Reportedly, about 70 percent of Potter action figures are bought by college students.

Exhibition: Theatrical and Nontheatrical

We're most familiar with the exhibition phase of the business, the moment when we pay for a movie ticket or play a DVD or stream a movie. *Theatrical* exhibition involves screening to a public that pays admission, as in commercial movie houses. Other theatrical sites are city art centers, museums, film festivals, and cinema clubs. *Nontheatrical* exhibition includes all other presentations, such as home video, cable transmissions, Internet downloads, and screenings in schools and colleges.

Public movie exhibition centers on the commercial theater. Most theaters screen wide releases from the major distributors, while others specialize in foreign-language or independent films. In all, the theatrical moviegoing audience is not a colossal one. In the United States, admissions average around 30 million per week, which sounds like a huge number until we realize that the weekly television audience numbers about 200 million. Only about 10 percent of the U.S. population visits movie theaters once a month or more; about one-third never goes at all.

The most heavily patronized theaters belong to chains or circuits, and in most countries, these circuits are controlled by a few companies. Until the 1980s, most theaters housed only one screen, but exhibitors began to realize that several screens under one roof could reduce costs. The multiplex theater, containing up to fifteen or more screens, lured far bigger crowds than a single-screen cinema could. Centralized projection booths and concession stands also cut costs. The boom in building multiplexes allowed exhibitors to upgrade the presentation, offering stadium seating, digital sound, and in some cases Imax and 3D. Multiplexes can also devote occasional screenings to niche markets, as when live opera broadcasts are shown digitally. Multiplexes are now the norm in most of the world, with snacks adjusted to local tastes—popcorn and candy nearly everywhere, but also beer (in Europe) and dried squid (in Hong Kong).

The United States is the most lucrative theatrical market, contributing 30 percent of global box-office receipts. (See chart on next page.) By nation, Japan comes in second, chiefly because ticket prices are very high. Providing about 25 percent of the global box office, Western Europe (including the United Kingdom and the Nordic countries) is the most important regional market outside North America. For these reasons, filmmakers around the world aim for distribution in these prosperous countries.

Markets in Latin America, Eastern Europe, India, the Middle East, and Africa are still developing, but China is rapidly rising to the top tier. In 2010, over a third of a billion tickets were sold there. In China, as in other emerging territories, the growth was fostered by the multiplex strategy. Hollywood distributors see overseas multiplexes as a golden opportunity. By investing in theaters overseas, they are guaranteed an outlet for their product. (U.S. antitrust law blocks them from owning theaters at home.) Historically, Hollywood distributors have withheld films from countries in which ticket prices were too low to yield much profit. In 2000, the average ticket price in the Philippines hovered around $.70; in India, $.20. As developing countries expanded their middle class, comfortable multiplexes began to attract upscale viewers. By 2009, thanks largely to multiplex expansion, the global average ticket price was $4.61, an all-time high. Some of the rise was attributable to 3D showings, which were enormously popular outside the United States and allowed theaters to charge more.

In 1999, four of the 3,126 theaters in which *Star Wars: Episode I—The Phantom Menace* played had digital projectors. Conversion to digital projection was sluggish at first, but at the end of 2011, there were over 65,000 digital screens worldwide. Many were in developing markets such as China, Russia, Brazil, and India,

GUS VAN SANT: Your films have dominated the museum circuit in America—Minneapolis, Columbus . . .

DEREK JARMAN: Yes, Minneapolis in particular. That's where the films have actually had their life. They've crept into the student curriculum—which is a life. And now they go on through video. I never really feel shut out.

—Gus Van Sant, director, interviewing Derek Jarman, independent filmmaker

CONNECT TO THE BLOG
www.davidbordwell.net/blog

Have Hollywood films declined in popularity internationally? We don't think so, as we explain in "World rejects Hollywood blockbusters!?"

Movies on Screens: A 2010 Profile of International Theatrical Exhibition

Worldwide production of theatrical motion pictures: **5,669 features**
Worldwide attendance: **6.8 billion admissions**
Worldwide number of screens: **123,067 (36,200 digitally equipped)**
Worldwide box-office gross receipts: **$31.8 billion**

USA box-office receipts: **$9.6 billion**
Western Europe box-office receipts: **$8.4 billion**
Japan box-office receipts: **$2.5 billion**

Countries and Numbers of Screens

Highest: USA 39,547; India 10,020; China 7,831; France 5,478; Mexico 4,818; Germany 4,699; Spain 4,080; Italy 4,033; UK 3,741; Japan 3,412

Lowest: Honduras 26; Oman 23; Azerbaijan 20; Tunisia 16

Annual admissions

Highest: India 2.7 billion; USA 1.2 billion; China 376.7 million; France 206.0 million; Mexico 189.5 million; UK 164.2 million; Japan 175.1 million

Other: Brazil 134.4 million; Colombia 33.6 million; New Zealand 16.5 million; Iceland 1.7 million (highest per capita film attendance: 5.3 times per year)

Average Ticket Prices

Highest: Switzerland $14.84; Japan $14.42; Denmark $14.34; Norway $14.32

Lowest: Egypt $2.39; Venezuela $2.31; Philippines $1.87; India $0.50

Others: Australia $11.32; Canada $9.52; UK $9.19; France $8.16; USA $7.77; China $3.99

Source: *IHS Screen Digest*

where newly built multiplexes were wholly digital. European countries began to convert on a large scale, and in August 2011, Norway became the first country to go 100 percent digital in its commercial theaters. During 2012, the halfway point in digitizing theater screens worldwide was expected to be passed.

Although films are shown in such venues as museums, archives, and film clubs, the most important theatrical alternative to commercial movie houses has become the *film festival*. The first major annual film festival was held in Venice in 1932, and although it had to be suspended during World War II, it was revived afterward and endures today. Festivals were mounted in Cannes, Berlin, Karlovy Vary, Moscow, Edinburgh, and many other cities. Today there are thousands of festivals all over the world—some large and influential, such as the Toronto Film Festival, and others aimed primarily at bringing unusual films to local audiences. Some festivals promote specific genres, such as the Brussels International Festival of Fantastic Film, or specific subject matter, such as the New York Gay and Lesbian Film Festival.

Occasionally, festivals show major Hollywood films. In 2010, *Robin Hood* was the opening-night presentation at the Cannes International Film Festival. Usually, however, the focus is on less mainstream cinema. Some festivals, like those in Cannes and Pusan, South Korea, include markets where such films can find distributors. The International Film Festival Rotterdam even helps to finance films made in developing countries. Not all festivals award prizes, but the bigger ones that do—most notably Cannes, Venice, and Berlin—can draw attention to films that might otherwise get lost among the hundreds of movies circulating among festivals.

Festivals offer an outlet for films that might never be picked up for release beyond their country of origin. For example, during the mid-1980s, programmers showcased the films of Abbas Kiarostami, Mohsen Makhmalbaf, and other Iranian directors. By winning prizes and critical acclaim at festivals, Iranian films gained commercial distribution in Europe and North America.

Passing from festival to festival becomes a mode of distribution for many films, which are sometimes promoted by the stars or directors in question-and-answer sessions. If a film fails to find a theatrical distributor, it may go straight to DVD and to screenings on specialized cable channels, such as the Sundance Channel and the Independent Film Channel in the United States.

> ❝ I've come to realize that my festival run is my theatrical run."
> —Joe Swanberg, independent film director, *Hannah Takes the Stairs*

Ancillary Markets: Taking Movies beyond the Theater

When a film leaves theatrical distribution, it lives on. Home video creates a vast array of ancillary markets "downstream," and taken together these return more money than the theatrical release. Distributors carefully plan the timing of their video releases according to *windows* of scheduling. Typically the video version appears first on hotel pay-television systems, then on pay-per-view cable, then on DVD release, then on pay cable outlets like HBO, and eventually on network broadcast and basic cable. Thanks to greater Internet bandwidth, Video on Demand (VOD) has become an important window. Sometimes VOD becomes available after a film's theatrical release, sometimes during it, and sometimes even before it. Each window is delayed by a certain period from the initial release. For example, DVD/ Blu-ray releases become available three to six months after the film's theatrical opening. The windows strategy maximizes the income from consumers with different levels of interest. Video has proved a boon to smaller distributors, too. Foreign and independent films yield slim returns in theatrical release, but all the video markets can make these items profitable.

With only about one in ten Americans being regular moviegoers, television, in one form or another, has kept the theatrical market going. During the 1960s, the U.S. television networks began supporting Hollywood production by purchasing broadcast rights to the studios' output. Lower-budget filmmakers depended on sales to European television and U.S. cable outlets. Videocassette versions arrived in the 1980s, and surprisingly they didn't harm the theatrical side of the business. In 1997, when the DVD format was introduced, consumers embraced it as a substitute for VHS tape. In the United States, the Walmart chain became the main purveyor of DVDs, accounting for over a third of all sales.

The major U.S. studios set up home entertainment divisions to sell DVDs. Because the discs cost less than VHS tapes to create, the studios reaped huge rewards, and the broadcast aftermarket remained brisk as well. Currently a studio film earns only a quarter or less of its total income from theatrical screenings. All forms of home video yield about 70 percent, with the remainder coming from licensed merchandise and other income.

Despite the swift success of the DVD format, it caused distributors some worries as well. The discs were easy to copy and manufacture in bulk, so piracy took off worldwide. A bootleg DVD of a Hollywood movie could sell for as little as $.80 in China. Moreover, with nearly 60,000 DVD titles available at the end of 2005, shelf space was at a premium, so discount chains dumped slow-moving titles into bargain bins. DVD purchases stalled, and rentals became more popular with the rise of subscription services such as Netflix. The Blu-ray disc, which not only offered superior quality but also provided connectivity to the Web, was designed to replace the DVD, but sales didn't achieve the success of the earlier format.

The video market sustains most commercial filmmaking in the long run, but movie theatres remain central to the exhibition system. A theatrical screening focuses public interest. Critics review the film, television and the press publicize it, and people talk about it. The theatrical run usually determines how successful a movie will be in ancillary markets. Theatrical hits may account for as much as 80 percent of subsequent rentals.

Even though the worldwide theatrical audience grew during the 1990s, most of the growth was in developing countries. U.S. and European attendance showed signs of flattening or even declining. Multiplexes were competing with home theaters, video games, and Internet entertainment. Exhibitors tried various ways to keep audiences coming. One successful strategy involved building Imax screens in multiplexes and showing studio tentpole pictures in that immersive format. A second strategy focused on digital 3D. The push toward 3D production encouraged exhibitors to install digital projection systems faster than they probably would have otherwise. In turn, the major studios began tailoring their blockbusters to 3D. Both Imax and 3D screenings charged higher ticket prices, which benefited exhibitor and distributor alike.

The stupendous rise in usage of the Internet after 2000 transformed distribution and exhibition. As broadband access increased and more people acquired high-speed connections, films of any length could be made available online. For the major distributors, the Net offered a chance to resell their product, but without the problems of DVDs. Selling movies as downloads or renting them as streaming video eliminated the cost of making discs. Video on Demand promised huge profits, and encryption could prevent consumers from copying films. The new model would move away from buying or renting packaged media and toward purchasing a service. Online distribution efforts of this sort were launched by Netflix, Hulu (a consortium of studios), Apple's iTunes store, and many smaller companies. To make downloading more attractive, the majors and other media companies started planning ways of letting consumers store their purchased films in online lockers that could be accessed by many digital devices.

The major distributors were not the only beneficiaries of Web 2.0. The Net offers a far more level playing field than traditional distribution. Films that would never be shown in a multiplex can gain enormous audiences online. Judson Laipply's "Evolution of the Dance" (over 180 million views), "JK Wedding Entrance Dance" (nearly 70 million views), and innumerable pieces starring household pets showed that amateur videos, once limited to family or friends, could become Internet sensations. More carefully made films could get exposure on an unprecedented scale

1.45 **Distributing a film via the Web.** Johan Rijpma's graceful *Tape Generations*, an abstract animation choreographing rolls of transparent tape, was downloaded over half a million times in seventeen days.

(**1.45**). Rival high schools won millions of viewers with elaborate single-take lipdubs. YouTube and Vimeo revived the short-film format for a new generation, and hopeful filmmakers saw posting a film online as a way to bypass corporate gatekeepers.

Some filmmakers still want to show their work in theaters. To meet that desire, festivals of DIY films have arisen, including the DIY Film Festival, based in Los Angeles and traveling to other cities. Another started in 2001, when 10 small teams of filmmakers in Washington, D.C., accepted a challenge to make a short film in 48 hours. All the completed shorts would be screened as a program immediately after the deadline. The result was the 48 Hour Film Project, which has become popular in dozens of cities around the world. More informally, the Kino Kabaret movement began in 1999 in Montréal with the slogan "Do well with nothing, do better with little, and do it right now!" The movement consists of local "cells" in sixty cities around the world. These meet to screen their members' latest films.

DVDs and the Internet, videogame players and cell phones, laptops and tablet computers—all these have revolutionized film viewing. Today people can watch films, short or long, amateur or professional, virtually anywhere. Digital technology not only changed theatrical exhibition; it redefined nontheatrical distribution and exhibition.

Artistic Implications of Distribution and Exhibition

Grosses, synergy, ticket prices, and movies on game consoles might seem very remote from issues of film as an art. Yet film is a technological medium usually aimed at a broad public, so the ways in which movies are circulated and shown can affect viewers' experiences. Home video turns viewing into a small-group or individual activity, but seeing a film in a packed theater yields a different response. Comedies, most people feel, seem funnier in a theater, where infectious laughter can ripple through a crowd. Filmmakers are aware of this difference, so they preview comedies many times to test audience reactions.

Video distribution and exhibition have created new choices in the realm of storytelling. Until the 1980s, people couldn't rewatch a movie whenever they wished. With videotape and then DVDs viewers can pore over a film. Bonus materials encourage them to rerun the movie to spot things they missed. Some filmmakers have taken advantage of this opportunity by creating *puzzle films* such as *Memento, Donnie Darko,* and *Inception,* which fans scrutinize for clues to plot enigmas **(1.46, 1.47)**. Video versions can deviate from and complicate the theatrical release version, as the extra ending of *The Butterfly Effect* does. Some interactive DVD movies permit the viewers to choose how the plot develops. The DVD of Greg Marcks's *11:14* allows you to enter parallel story lines at various points, in effect recasting the film's overall form.

With the Internet as a major distribution platform, we should expect variations in narrative form. Short-form storytelling is already in full bloom online. Events

CONNECT TO THE BLOG
www.davidbordwell.net/blog

In this age of new media, have movies lost their importance to audiences? Some would say yes, but we argue against that idea in "Movies still matter."

CONNECT TO THE BLOG
www.davidbordwell.net/blog

Have DVDs radically changed the way movies tell their stories? Mostly not, we argue in "New media and old storytelling."

1.46

1.47

1.46–1.47 Planting clues for DVD re-watching. A viewer scrutinizing *Magnolia* on DVD would notice that the extraordinary meteorological event at the climax is predicted by the recurring numerals 82, referring to chapter and verse in the biblical book of Exodus (1.46). Elsewhere, the figure 82 appears as coils in the rooftop hose (1.47).

> *The Matrix* is entertainment for the age of media convergence, integrating multiple texts to create a narrative so large that it cannot be contained within a single medium."
>
> —Henry Jenkins, media analyst

> Not until seeing [*North by Northwest*] again on the big screen did I realize conclusively what a gigantic difference screen size does make. . . . This may be yet another reason why younger people have a hard time with older pictures: they've only seen them on the tube, and that reduces films' mystery and mythic impact."
>
> —Peter Bogdanovich, director, *The Last Picture Show* and *Mask*

like the festivals run by the 48 Hour Film Project also encourage the making of short films, especially given the assumption that most of the films will later be posted on the Internet. We're likely to find movies designed specifically for mobile phones; television series are already creating "mobisodes" branching off the broadcast story line. The Web is the logical place for interactive films that use hyperlinks to amplify or detour a line of action.

Marketing and merchandising can extend a theatrical film's story in intriguing ways. The *Star Wars* novels and video games give the characters more adventures and expand spectators' engagement with the movies. The *Memento* website hinted at ways to interpret the film. The *Matrix* video games supplied key information for the films' plots, while the second movie in the trilogy sneaked in hints for playing the games. As a story world shifts from platform to platform, a multimedia saga is created, and viewers' experiences will shift accordingly. *Matrix* viewers who have never played the games understand the story somewhat differently from those who have.

Even product placement offers some artistic opportunities. We're usually distracted when a Toyota truck or a box of Frosted Flakes pops up on the screen, but *Back to the Future* cleverly integrates brands into its story. Marty McFly is catapulted from 1985 to 1955. Trapped in a period when diet soda didn't exist, he asks for a Pepsi Free, but the counterman says he'll have to pay for it. Later, buying a bottle of Pepsi from a vending machine, Marty tries frantically to twist off the cap, but his father-to-be George McFly casually pops it off at the machine's built-in opener. Pepsi soft drinks weave through the movie, reasserting Marty's comic inability to adjust to his parents' era, and perhaps stirring some nostalgia in viewers who remember how teenage life has changed since their youth.

A filmmaker's stylistic choices can be affected by distribution and exhibition, too. Consider image size. From the 1920s through the 1950s, films were meant to be shown in large venues (**1.48**). A typical urban movie house seated 1,500 viewers and boasted a screen 50 feet wide. This scale gave the image great presence, and it allowed details to be seen easily. Directors could stage dialogue scenes showing several characters in the frame, all of whom would be quite visible (**1.49**). In a theater of that time, a tight close-up would have had a powerful impact.

When television became popular in the 1950s, its image was rather unclear and very small, in some cases only 10 inches diagonally. If you were a filmmaker obliged to fill this fuzzy little frame, you'd probably do what early TV directors did. They tended to rely on close shots, which could be read easily on the monitor (**1.50**). In the 1960s and 1970s, movie attendance dropped and big theaters were split into smaller auditoriums. As screens shrank, filmmakers began to rely more on close-ups in the TV manner. This tendency has continued until today. Modern multiplex screens can be quite large, but the ultimate destination for most films is the video monitor, which might be as small as a cellphone screen. As a result, it seems likely that commercial films will continue to treat conversation scenes in tight close-ups (**1.51**). In this respect, technology and exhibition circumstances have created stylistic constraints. Yet some contemporary filmmakers have stuck to the alternative option (**1.52**), designing their films for the scale of a theater screen.

There's also the matter of image proportions, and here again, television exhibition exercised some influence. Since the mid-1950s, virtually all theaters have shown films on screens that were wider than

1.48 Traditional large-screen movie house. The interior of the Paramount Theater in Portland, Oregon, built in 1928. Capacity was 3,000 seats, at a time when the city population was about 300,000. Note the elaborate decoration on the walls and ceilings, typical of the "picture palaces" of the era.

the traditional TV monitor. For decades, when movies were shown on television, the sides of the imager were cropped off, and the practice continues in the era of wide-screen television (**1.53, 1.54**). In response, some filmmakers chose to compose their shots by placing the key action in a spot that could fit snugly on the television screen. This created subtle differences in a shot's expressive effects (**1.55, 1.56**). Relying on the safe area often encouraged filmmakers to employ more *singles,* shots showing only one player. In a wide-screen frame, a single can compensate for the cropping that TV would demand (**1.57**).

To preserve the original proportions of a film, a DVD version will usually be *letterboxed.* Dark bands at the top and bottom of the screen approximate the theatrical proportions of the image. Nearly all filmmakers approve of this, but Stanley Kubrick preferred that video versions of some of his films be shown "full frame." This is why we've reproduced the shots from *The Shining* (2.12, 2.13) full-frame, even though nobody who watched the movie in a theater saw so much headroom. Almost no commercial theaters can show films full-frame today, but Jean-Luc Godard usually composes his shots for that format; you couldn't letterbox **1.58** without ruining the composition. In these instances, distribution and theatrical exhibition initially constrained the filmmakers' choices, but video versions expanded them.

The introduction of widescreen TV monitors has created a new problem for film images. Traditional television monitors had a 4:3 ratio, which was suitable for showing old films or TV programs shot on film. Widescreen TVs may suit recent

1.49

1.50

1.49–1.50 Shot scale adjusted for image display. On the large screen of a picture palace, all the figures and faces in this shot from *The Thin Man* (1934) would have been quite prominent (1.49). Early television relied heavily on close-ups because of the small screen size, as in this shot from a 1953 *Dragnet* episode (1.50).

1.51

1.52

CONNECT TO THE BLOG
www.davidbordwell.net/blog

We explore another peril of watching films on video—logos superimposed on films—in "Bugs: the secret history."

1.51–1.52 Close-up or long shot? Extreme close-ups of actors' faces are common in modern cinema, as in this shot from *Red Eye*. Filmmakers are adjusting their style to the fact that most viewing takes place on video formats (1.51). In *Flowers of Shanghai*, director Hou Hsiao-hsien builds every scene out of full shots of several characters. The result loses information on a small display and is best seen on a theater screen (1.52).

1.53

1.54

1.53–1.54 Changing compositions in video distribution. In *L4yer Cake*, a wide image in the original (1.54) is cropped to fit conventional TV monitors for a cable airing (1.54).

1.55

1.56

1.55–1.56 Expressive effects and video cropping. As Rose, the heroine of *Titanic*, feels the exhilaration of flying on the ship's prow, the strongly horizontal composition emphasizes her outstretched arms as wings against a wide horizon (1.55). In the side-cropped video version, nearly all sense of horizontal sweep has disappeared (1.56).

1.57 Adjusting composition for the television frame. As with many modern wide-screen films, the essential information on screen left in this shot from *Catch Me If You Can* would fit within a traditional television frame. Still, cropping out the right half would lose a secondary piece of information—the pile of take-out food cartons that implies that Agent Hanratty has been at his desk for days.

1.58 Full-frame composition. A very dense shot from the climax of Godard's *Detective*. Although Godard's films are sometimes cropped for theater screenings and DVD versions, the compositions show to best advantage in the older, squarer format.

1.59 Incorrect aspect ratio (4:3 stretched to 16:9). Here *Angel Face* (1952) is rendered on an incorrectly set widescreen television monitor. Many viewers do not know how to change a monitor's ratio, and some monitors make it difficult to correct the problem.

films, but older material can suffer. A widescreen TV image has an aspect ratio of 16:9, making it one-third wider than the standard one. Some monitors have controls to adjust the ratio and allow black bands on the sides to provide "windowboxing," the vertical equivalent of letterboxing. But if there's no windowboxing, the picture is stretched **(1.59).** Not all digital innovations work to the advantage of viewers—or filmmakers.

 CONNECT TO THE BLOG
www.davidbordwell.net/blog

Jean-Luc Godard's films present special challenges to the projectionist and DVD producer, as we show in "Godard comes in many shapes and sizes."

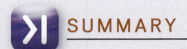 SUMMARY

The art of film depends on technology, from the earliest experiments in apparent motion to the most recent computer programs. It also depends on people who use that technology, who come together to make films, distribute them, and show them. As long as a film is aimed at an audience, however small, it enters into a social dynamic of production, distribution, and exhibition. Out of technology and work processes, filmmakers create an experience for their viewers. Along the way, they inevitably make choices about film form and style. What options are available to them? How might filmmakers organize the film? How might they draw on the techniques of the medium? The next two parts of this book survey the possibilities.

 RECOMMENDED DVD AND BLU-RAY SUPPLEMENTS

Before laser discs and DVDs, making-of documentaries weren't common, but some documentaries on older films have been put together using modern cast and crew interviews, finished footage, still photography, and other material. Excellent examples of these include "The Making of *American Graffiti*," "The Making of *Jaws*," "The Making of *Amadeus*," "Guns for Hire: The Making of *The Magnificent Seven*," and "Destination Hitchcock: The Making of *North by Northwest*." The supplements for *Alien* are grouped in "preproduction," "production," and "postproduction" sections, and a particularly good example of a screen test (Sigourney Weaver's) is included. "The Making of *20,000 Leagues Under the Sea*" is one of several supplements on the DVD for that film, making it an unusually thorough treatment of an older film (1954). The Criterion Collection's edition of *The Night of the Hunter* includes a two-hour documentary, "Charles Laughton Directs *The Night of the Hunter*." This includes takes of various shots of Laughton directing the performances of the child actors, including retakes.

Once the DVD age began, supplements came to be a part of the filmmaking process, with on-set footage and interviews planned in advance. A good early example is "The Making of *Jurassic Park*," with its accompanying supplements. As bonus materials became popular, longer and more systematic supplements were concocted. An outstanding example is "The Hundred Days" documentary for *Master and Commander.* The extended-edition DVDs for *The Lord of the Rings* raised the bar for in-depth coverage, with two supplemental discs for each entry in the trilogy. Though not going that far, the recent deluxe sets of the director's cut of *Blade Runner* include an unusually comprehensive three-and-a-half-hour making-of; it moves from initial conception through to the release of the film, and even covers the director's cut.

Supplements often include storyboard images as galleries. Director Ridley Scott trained in painting and design, and some of the impressive storyboard images that he created for *Alien* are displayed in its supplements. The "Story" section of *Toy Story*'s documentaries shows scenes of a storyboard artist explaining the action to the main filmmakers, with the sketches shown side-by-side with his presentation. Later the storyboard images are compared with the final images.

Some unusual supplements include an unconventional production diary for the independent film *Magnolia* and an evocative 8-minute compilation, "*T2*: On the Set," of footage from the shooting of *Terminator 2: Judgment Day.* "The Making of *My Own Private Idaho*" demonstrates well how cost-cutting can be done on a low-budget indie.

As previsualization becomes more common, DVD supplements are beginning to include selections: "Previsualization" on the *War of the Worlds* disc (where the animatics run in split screen, beside finished footage), animatics for each part of *The Lord of the Rings,* and the "Day 27: Previsualization" entry in *King Kong: Peter Jackson's Production Diaries,* as well as a featurette on previs, "The Making of a Shot: The T-Rex Fight" (including the scene in 1.28).

The marketing of a film seldom gets described on DVD, apart from the fact that trailers and posters come with most discs. There are rare cases of coverage of the still photographer making publicity shots on-set: "Taking Testimonial Pictures" (*A Hard Day's Night*) and "Day 127: Unit Photography" (*King Kong: Peter Jackson's Production Diaries*). The same two DVDs include "Dealing with 'The Men from the Press,'" an interview with the Beatles' publicist, and "Day 53: International Press Junket," where *King Kong*'s unit publicist squires a group of reporters around a working set.

In general, the *King Kong: Peter Jackson's Production Diaries* discs deal with many specifics of filmmaking and distribution that we mention in this chapter: "Day 25: Clapperboards," "Day 62: Cameras" (where camera operators working on-set open their machines to show how they work), "Day 113: Second Unit," and "Day 110: Global Partner Summit," on a distributors' junket.

Agnès Varda includes a superb film-essay on the making of *Vagabond* in the French DVD, which bears the original title *Sans toit ni loi.* (Both the film and the supplements have English subtitles.) Director Varda's charmingly personal making-of covers the production, marketing, and showcasing of *Vagabond* at international film festivals. Varda also prepared an affectionate making-of featurette about her husband Jacques Demy's 1967 *Young Girls of Rochefort,* which is available on the British Film Institute's DVD release.

Hellboy II: The Golden Army has a lengthy making-of documentary, "*Hellboy*: In Service of the Demon," that touches on most phases of production. *Pirates of the Caribbean: Dead Man's Chest* has two detailed, surprisingly candid supplements: "Charting the Return," on preproduction, and "According to Plan," on principal photography. *The Golden Compass* has a series of short documentaries that are more interesting than their bland titles suggest. "Finding Lyra Belacqua" traces the casting process rather than simply showing audition tapes; "The Launch" deals briefly with press junkets and even interviews a junket producer.

Some compact recent production supplements include "Climbing *Cold Mountain,*" a 14-minute film which includes footage on location scouting, set design and construction, rehearsals, editing, the musical score, and test screenings (including shots of preview-screening audiences answering questions). "Unholy War: Mounting the Siege," a 17-minute making-of, dealing specifically with the siege sequence of *Kingdom of Heaven,* covering planning and building the sets and the shooting process. Footage shows Ridley Scott questioning the production crew about what can and cannot be done and stressing the balance between the financial and creative sides of filmmaking. Other *Kingdom of Heaven* supplements also devote unusual attention to the marketing phase: "Press Junket Walkthrough," "Poster Explorations," and a collection of four trailers and forty TV spots. Other useful making-ofs are "Deciphering Zodiac" (*Zodiac*) and "I Am Iron Man" (*Iron Man*).

For more details on some of the supplements recommended here, see the "Beyond Praise" series on our blog: "Beyond praise: DVD supplements that really tell you something"; "Beyond praise 2: More DVD supplements that really tell you something"; "Beyond praise 3: Yet more DVD supplements that really tell you something"; and "Beyond praise 4: Even more DVD supplements that really tell you something."

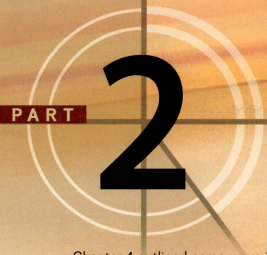

2

Chapter 1 outlined some ways in which people, working with technology, make films. Now we can ask more basic questions.

If you were to make a film, what would guide you in putting the whole thing together? How would you fit the various parts to one another? How would you try to shape the viewer's experience of the whole film? Thinking about these questions will help us understand how we respond to individual movies and how cinema works as an artistic medium.

The next two chapters explore questions like these. We assume that a film isn't a random assortment of things. If it were, viewers wouldn't care if they missed a movie's ending, or if scenes were shown out of order. But viewers do care. When you describe a book as hard to put down or a song as engaging, you're implying that a pattern exists there. The

Film Form

pattern is pulling you along. This overall pattern of relationships among parts is called *form.*

Chapter 2 examines form in film. This concept is one key to understanding cinema as an art. Filmmakers are thinking about a film's form at each stage of the production process, and formal matters demand creative decisions at every turn.

Although there are several ways of organizing films into formal wholes, the one that we most commonly encounter involves telling a story. Filmmakers are well aware that narrative form arouses our interest and impels us to follow a series of events from start to finish. Chapter 3 examines how certain principles allow a story to arouse and fulfill our expectations. We consider examples of non-narrative form in Chapter 10.

2

The Significance of Film Form

You are a filmmaker. How might you start your movie? With an exciting bit of action that grabs the viewer's interest? Or with something more slowly paced that gradually builds up involvement?

Steven Spielberg's *Jurassic Park* follows option one. Park workers nervously surround a shipping container housing an unseen, thrashing, roaring beast. Workers train their weapons on the case as it's opened to release the creature into the park. The gate slides open, but the heaving cage knocks a worker to the ground. Suddenly he's seized and dragged into the container **(2.1).** The guards fire at the creature, but the man slides into darkness.

The film doesn't present another dinosaur attack for an hour. In the meantime, we get background information about the park, its genetically bred inhabitants, and the characters who have been brought there. Conflicts build and schemes emerge. Yet before all this development of the drama, Spielberg and his screenwriters Michael Crichton and David Koepp have given us a taste of the suspense and physical action coming up later. Since the opening doesn't show us the velociraptor, we look forward to seeing the beast fully, and in action. The filmmakers' creative decisions have shaped our experience—teasing us with the promise of thrills but making us wait while the plot is filled in. Primed by this opening, we'll be vigilant for anything that would put the characters at risk. And of course the violence of the first scene gives the lie to the bland cuteness of the park's publicity rolled out in later scenes. We know, as the visiting scientists don't, that behind the family-friendly surface this is a dangerous place.

Spielberg's *Close Encounters of the Third Kind* begins in a far less aggressive way. During a desert sandstorm, men in goggles and protective suits meet a French scientist. They exchange greetings before pressing forward to check a fleet of vintage airplanes, reported missing in 1945. The man serving as a translator raises a flurry of questions: "Where's the crew? How did they get here?" **(2.2)** The investigative team finds an old man nearby. Although his face is badly sunburned, he's smiling. "He says the sun came out last night. He says it sang to him."

Instead of shocking us with violence, *Close Encounters'* opening poses a series of mysteries. Those will deepen in the scenes to come: a UFO swerves near a commercial jet, a little boy follows unseen home invaders into the night. The calmness of the opening, the friendly professionalism of the scientists, and the joyous reaction of the old man to what he's seen indicate that the film will be gentle, slow-moving, and concerned with characters trying to understand what is making extraordinary things happen. This will be an interplanetary mystery story, not a horror-action-adventure like *Jurassic Park*.

2.1

2.2

2.1–2.2 Hard and soft openings. Grabbing the audience in *Jurassic Park* (2.1) versus enticing the audience in *Close Encounters of the Third Kind* (2.2).

Either strategy for starting a movie, abrupt or gradual, can have a strong effect on the viewer. The choices come down to a matter of *form*—the way parts work together to create an overall effect. If you are a director or screenwriter, you face perpetual choices about form. As a viewer, you are responding to it at every moment.

The Concept of Form in Film

Form as Pattern

The arts offer us intensely involving experiences. We say that movies draw us in or immerse us. We can lose track of time when listening to music, and when we enjoy a novel, we may say, "I really got into it." All these ways of talking suggest that artworks involve us by engaging our senses, feelings, and mind in a *process.* That process sharpens our interest, focuses our attention, urges us forward. How does this happen?

Because the artist has created a pattern. Artists design their works—they give them form—so that we can have a structured experience. For this reason, form is of central importance in film.

> " I believe in soft openings for movies. . . . I think it's almost impossible to lose an audience in the first ten minutes. . . . It's not television. You don't have to grab them. In a movie with a very fast opening, you end up paying for it somewhere along the way—usually by having to explain what happened in the fast and furious action."
>
> —Robert Towne, screenwriter, *Chinatown*

"Screenplays are structure."
—William Goldman, screenwriter, *Butch Cassidy and the Sundance Kid*

"Because of my character, I have always been interested in the engineering of direction. I loved hearing about how [director] Mark Sandrich would draw charts of Fred Astaire's musicals to work out where to put the dance numbers. What do you want the audience to understand? How do you make things clear? How do you structure sequences within a film? Afterwards—what have you got away with?"
—Stephen Frears, director, *The Grifters*

Our minds are very good at finding patterns in things—faces in the clouds, a drumbeat in a downpour. Artworks rely on this dynamic, unifying effort of the human mind. Novels present a pattern of events that create suspense or surprise, while paintings expect that we'll be sensitive to composition and color. Artworks in all media ask us to pay attention, to anticipate upcoming events, to construct a whole out of parts, and to feel an emotional response to the pattern that we help create.

In similar ways, a film coaxes us to connect sequences into a larger whole. The savage attack at the start of *Jurassic Park* establishes the park's raptors as a force to be reckoned with later. We'd be disappointed if they never reappeared in the plot. Similarly, *Close Encounters* promises to reveal the fates of the missing World War II pilots and the runaway boy.

Even small details get linked in a pattern. Early in *Collateral*, the taxi driver Max is shown wiping down his cab's dashboard and steering wheel before setting out on his night shift. He then carefully clips a snapshot to his sun visor. For a moment, he simply gazes at the postcard view of a tropical island (**2.3**). These gestures prompt us to see Max's personality as neat and orderly. They also suggest that in the city's turmoil, he clears a quiet mental space for himself. The next scene's cues reinforce our judgment of Max's character (**2.4–2.5**). Small or large, local or far-ranging, the patterns we find engage our interest, our minds, and our emotions.

These instances suggest that a film is not simply a random batch of elements. Like all artworks, a film has **form.** By form, in its broadest sense, we mean the overall set of relationships among a film's parts.

This description of form is still very abstract, so let's draw some examples from one movie you've probably seen. In *The Wizard of Oz,* the viewer is expected to follow a story—that is, a pattern of *narrative* elements. These are events that involve the characters. Dorothy dreams that a tornado blows her to Oz. There she encounters other characters, and together they have adventures. Eventually Dorothy awakens from her dream to find herself home in Kansas. Alongside the story, we can also notice *stylistic* elements: the way the camera moves, the arrangements of color in the frame, the use of music, and other devices. Stylistic elements utilize the various film techniques we'll be considering in later chapters.

Because *The Wizard of Oz* is designed to give us a particular experience, we actively relate the elements within each set to one another. We know that the narrative elements form a pattern, a story. We see the tornado as causing Dorothy's trip to Oz, and her adventures there result from her desire to get home. Likewise, we identify the characters in Oz as similar to characters in Dorothy's Kansas life. Various stylistic elements also form patterns. We recognize the "We're Off to See the Wizard" tune whenever Dorothy picks up a new companion. Our experience of the film depends on our recognizing and anticipating how these broad patterns will develop.

Moreover, our minds tie these two sorts of patterning together. In *The Wizard of Oz,* the narrative development can be linked to the stylistic patterning. Colors identify story landmarks, such as Kansas (in black and white) and the Yellow Brick Road. Movements of the camera call our attention to story action. And the music serves to describe certain characters and situations. The relationships among all these elements make up the overall form of *The Wizard of Oz.*

"Form" Versus "Content"

Very often people think of "form" as the opposite of something called "content." This implies that a poem or a musical piece or a film is like a jug. An external shape, the jug, *contains* a liquid that could just as easily be held in a cup or a pail. Under this assumption, form becomes less important than whatever it's presumed to contain.

We don't accept this assumption. We think that every component functions as part of a pattern, big or small, that engages the viewer. So we'll treat as formal elements many things that some people consider content. From our standpoint, subject matter and abstract ideas all enter into the total form of the artwork. They may cue

2.3

2.4

2.5

2.3–2.5 Patterns create character. Max is introduced as able to tune out his environment, thanks to the island on his postcard (2.3). We're reminded of this when in the next scene, as the passengers quarrel, he tips down the visor and stares at the postcard, as if to shut out the unpleasantness in his back seat (2.4–2.5).

us to frame certain expectations or imagine certain possibilities. The viewer relates these elements to one another dynamically. Consequently, subject matter and ideas become somewhat different from what they might be outside the artwork.

Consider extraterrestrials and UFOs. In popular thinking, aliens can be either peaceful or hostile, but if you were going to make a film about UFOs, you'd have to decide how to treat the subject. That would be a decision about form. In *Independence Day,* presenting the aliens as an invading horde fits well with a story of Americans of all classes uniting to conquer a threat. By contrast, *Close Encounters of the Third Kind* treats alien visitors as spiritual teachers, creatures who restore people's sense of wonder and promise a better life. The aliens of *Mars Attacks!* pretend to be peaceful but then turn treacherous, and their cunning reveals the ineptitude of the people in power. This treatment suits the film's satire of modern politics and media. In each case, the filmmakers' choices about form have repurposed the basic subject matter of aliens. What we might call the content is governed by the film's formal context.

Formal Expectations

We're now in a better position to see how film form grabs and holds us. It creates expectations and sustains them over time. Suppose that *Jurassic Park* never revealed the raptors, or *Close Encounters* never explained its puzzles. We'd think that something important had been left out, to say the least. Once we're caught up in following the interrelations among elements, we want the patterns to develop and conclude.

Expectations color our everyday experiences. Psychological experiments have shown that if people are told that a cheap wine is expensive, they rate it as tasting better than if they're told its true price. Creating expectations is central to advertising any product. A film's title, its poster, its online promotion, and its trailers aim to set up particular expectations. You would not go to a film called *Eat Pray Love* anticipating a raunchy teen comedy.

Expectation pervades our experience of artworks. In reading a mystery, we expect that a solution will be offered at some point, usually the end. In listening to a piece of music, we expect repetition of a melody or a motif. In looking at a painting, we search for what we expect to be the most significant areas, then scan the less prominent portions. From beginning to end, our involvement with a work of art depends largely on expectations.

We can illustrate this with a little experiment. Assume that "A" is the first letter of a series. What follows?

AB

After seeing A, you probably thought that the next letters would run in alphabetical order. Your expectation was confirmed. What follows AB? Most people would say "C." But form doesn't always follow our initial expectation.

ABA

Here form takes us a little by surprise. If we are puzzled by a formal development, we readjust our expectations and try again. What follows ABA?

ABAC

Here the main possibilities were either ABAB or ABAC. (Note that your expectations limit possibilities as well as select them.) If you expected ABAC, your expectation was fulfilled, and you can confidently predict the next letter. If you expected ABAB, you still should be able to make a strong guess at the next letter:

ABACA

Simple as this game is, it illustrates the involving power of form. As a viewer or listener you don't simply let the parts parade past you. You enter into an active participation with them, creating and readjusting expectations as the pattern develops over time.

If you're a filmmaker, you want to arouse and shape viewers' expectations. This is what happens in the opening scenes of *Jurassic Park* and *Close Encounters*. Similarly, *The Wizard of Oz* begins with Dorothy running down a road with her dog Toto (**2.6**). Immediately, we form expectations. She seems to be fleeing from someone; will she be caught? Perhaps she will meet another character or arrive at her destination. Even such a simple action asks us to participate in the story's development by

CONNECT TO THE BLOG
www.davidbordwell.net/blog

Even at the very beginning of a film, the title can give us clues to its subjects, themes, and form—or baffle us. We consider various options in "Title wave."

2.6 What does the audience expect? Dorothy pauses while fleeing with Toto at the beginning of *The Wizard of Oz.*

adjusting our expectations about what may happen. Much later in the film, we come to expect that Dorothy will get her wish to return to Kansas. Indeed, the settings of the film give *The Wizard of Oz* a large-scale ABA form: Kansas-Oz-Kansas.

You probably noticed that the formal development of *The Wizard of Oz* didn't satisfy our expectations immediately, as our alphabet exercise did. What we normally call *suspense* involves a delay in fulfilling an established expectation. As the term implies, suspense leaves something suspended—not only the next element in a pattern but also our urge for completion. Both the opening raptor attack in *Jurassic Park* and the mysteries in *Close Encounters* leave a pattern uncompleted, and as a result they keep us in suspense.

Expectations may also be cheated, as when we expect ABC but get ABA. In general, *surprise* is a result of an expectation that is revealed to be incorrect. We don't expect that a gangster in 1930s Chicago will find a rocket ship in his garage; if he does, our reaction may require us to readjust our assumptions about what can happen in this story. This example suggests that comedy often depends on cheating expectations and creating surprise.

One more pattern of our expectations needs tracing. Sometimes an artwork will cue us to think about what might have come *before* a certain point. When Dorothy runs down the road at the beginning of *The Wizard of Oz,* we wonder not only where she is going but where she's been and what she's fleeing from. In other words, filmmakers can arouse *curiosity* about earlier events. As Chapter 3 will show, curiosity is an important factor in narrative form.

Already we have several possible ways in which filmmakers' creative decisions about form can engage us. The filmmaker can cue us to make expectations and then gratify them. The expectations may be gratified quickly, as when we soon learn why Dorothy is running down the road. Or the filmmaker may wait quite a while before fulfilling our expectations, as with the raptors' eventual reappearance in *Jurassic Park*. And the filmmaker may set up expectations only to undercut them, creating surprise.

At a limit, the filmmaker may choose to disturb our expectations. We often associate art with pleasure, but many artworks offer us conflict, tension, and shock. An artwork's form may even strike us as unpleasant because of its imbalances or contradictions. For example, experimental films may jar rather than soothe us. Viewers frequently feel puzzled or shocked by *Eat, Scorpio Rising,* and other avant-garde works (pp. 369–386). We'll encounter similar challenges when we examine the editing of Sergei Eisenstein's *October* (Chapter 6) and the style of Jean-Luc Godard's *Breathless* (Chapter 11).

Yet even when they disturb us, filmmakers still arouse and shape formal expectations. For example, on the basis of our experience of most movie stories, we expect that the main characters introduced in the first half of a film will be present in the second half. Yet Wong Kar-wai punctures this expectation in *Chungking Express* (pp. 425–429). When our expectations are thwarted, we may feel disoriented, but then we adjust them to look for other, more appropriate, ways of engaging with the film's form.

If we can adjust our expectations to a disorienting work, we may find it satisfying in a new way. Hollis Frampton's *Zorns Lemma,* for example, slowly trains the viewer to associate a series of images with the letters of the alphabet. Viewers often become quite absorbed in watching the series take shape as a cinematic picture puzzle. As *Chungking Express* and *Zorns Lemma* also suggest, a disturbing work can reveal to us our normal expectations about form. Such films can coax us to reflect on our taken-for-granted assumptions about how a movie must behave.

There is no limit to the number of ways in which a film can be organized. Some filmmakers will ask us to recast our expectations in drastic ways. Still, our enjoyment can increase if we welcome the unfamiliar experiences offered by formally challenging films.

" The idea of suspense is closely bound up with the idea of fiction. This is as it should be: to tell a story is to create suspense, and the art of the storyteller resides in this ability to make dull subjects sound entertaining and plots whose solution everyone knows in advance, exciting."
—Thomas Mann

CONNECT TO THE BLOG
www.davidbordwell.net/blog

Why is it that we feel suspense even if we're rewatching a film and know the outcome? We talk about how that happens in "This is your brain on movies, maybe."

" Now, if you're going to do action films, a certain amount of repetition, which certainly is a kind of straitjacket, is inevitable. You are going to have to deal with gunfights and chases. . . .

So it becomes a kind of game. The audience knows what the conclusion will be, but you still have to entertain them. So you are always walking on the edge of a precipice—trying to juggle the genre expectations. . . ."
—Walter Hill, director, *The Driver* and *The Warriors*

Conventions and Experience

Our ABAC example illustrates still another point. One guide to your expectations is your *prior experience.* Your knowledge of the English alphabet makes ABA an unlikely sequence. This fact suggests that artistic form is not a pure activity isolated from other experiences.

Artworks are human creations, and the artist lives in history and society. As a result, the artwork will relate, in some way, to other works and to aspects of the world. A tradition, a dominant style, a popular form—elements like these will be common to several different artworks. These common traits are usually called *conventions.*

For example, the first few scenes of a film often explain background information about the characters and the action; this sort of exposition is a narrative convention. *Genres,* as we will see in Chapter 9, depend heavily on conventions. Urban thrillers tend to feature spectacular car crashes, so Michael Mann's use of the device in *Collateral* (p. 000) accords with that genre convention. It's a convention of the musical film that characters sing and dance, as in *The Wizard of Oz.* It's one convention of narrative form that the conclusion solves the problems that the characters confront, and *Wizard* likewise accepts this convention by letting Dorothy return to Kansas.

If the filmmaker can't avoid connecting to both art and the larger world, neither can the audience. When we respond to cues in the film, we call on our experiences of life and other artworks. You were able to play the ABAC game because you had learned the alphabet. You may have learned it in everyday life (in a classroom or from your parents) or from an artwork (perhaps from a rhyming song or TV cartoons). Similarly, we're able to recognize the journey structure in *The Wizard of Oz* because we've taken trips ourselves. We've also read such books as Homer's *Odyssey* and Tolkien's *The Lord of the Rings,* and we've seen other films organized around the journey pattern.

In recognizing film form, then, the audience must be prepared to understand formal cues through knowledge of life and of other artworks. But what if the two principles come into conflict? In ordinary life, people don't simply start to sing and dance, as they do in *The Wizard of Oz.* Very often conventions demarcate art from life, saying implicitly, "In artworks of this sort, the laws of everyday reality don't operate. By the rules of *this* game, something 'unreal' *can* happen." All stylized art, from opera, ballet, and pantomime to slapstick comedy, depends on the audience's willingness to suspend the laws of ordinary experience and to accept particular conventions. Why do characters in musicals sing to one another? Why doesn't Buster Keaton smile? It's beside the point to ask such questions. Filmmakers assume that we're familiar with conventions and are willing to go along with the game. You probably haven't met a contract killer in real life, but the cues in the early scenes of *Collateral* prompt you to take Vincent as a movie version of a hit man.

Further, conventions can change. Very brief flashbacks to earlier events in the story are common in today's films, but they would have been considered unusual in the 1930s and 1940s. Similarly, conventions of earlier periods of film history can seem odd to us today. Filmmakers rely on existing conventions, but they also may try to create new ones. For example, some modern directors have deliberately made films that lack the quick turns of events we associate with Hollywood movies. Films like Béla Tarr's *Satan's Tango* move at a solemn pace and ask us to concentrate on details of setting and sound. In other words, we're being asked to summon up an unusual set of expectations. As Tarr's sort of filmmaking attracted interest, other filmmakers explored the approach, so that this trend created its own set of conventions.

Form and Feeling

Emotion plays a large role in our experience of form. To understand this role, let's distinguish between *emotions represented* in the artwork and an *emotional response* felt by the spectator. If an actor grimaces in agony, the emotion of pain is represented

CONNECT TO THE BLOG
www.davidbordwell.net/blog

Slumdog Millionaire uses some conventions in novel ways, as we show in "Slumdogged by the past."

> " To a story-teller a journey is a marvelous device. It provides a strong thread on which a multitude of things that he has in mind may be strung to make a new thing, various, unpredictable, and yet coherent. My chief reason for using this form was technical."
> —J. R. R. Tolkien

within the film. But that emotion might not be felt by us in the audience; if the movie is a comedy, we might laugh. Both types of emotion have formal implications.

Emotions represented within the film play particular roles in the film's overall form. The dinosaur wranglers in the opening of *Jurassic Park* are grim and tense; their emotional attitude fits Spielberg's effort to show the park as a dangerous place. But the little boy in the opening of *Close Encounters* reacts to the offscreen aliens ransacking the kitchen with a smile of delight. This prepares us to expect that in later scenes the visitors will be shown as benevolent.

Form shapes the spectator's emotional response, too. We have just seen how cues in the artwork interact with our prior experience, especially our experience of artistic conventions. Often form in artworks appeals to our ready-made emotional responses. All other things being equal, we tend to smile at a gurgling baby and recoil from acts of torture.

But form can create new responses instead of harping on old ones. An artwork may lead us to override or suspend our everyday emotional responses. No one wants to meet Freddy Kruger or Hannibal Lecter in real life, but as film characters they may become spellbinding. In the abstract, we might find the land of Oz a child's paradise. But because the film's developing plot leads us to sympathize with Dorothy in her desire to go home, we feel satisfaction when she finally returns to Kansas.

The dynamic aspect of form also engages our feelings. Expectation, for instance, spurs emotion. To wonder what will happen next is to invest some emotion in the situation. Delayed fulfillment of an expectation—suspense—may produce anxiety or sympathy. (Will the detective find the criminal? Will boy get girl? Will the melody return?) Gratified expectations may produce a feeling of satisfaction or relief. (The detective solves the mystery; boy does get girl; the melody returns one more time.) Cheated expectations and curiosity about past material may produce puzzlement or keener interest. (So he isn't the detective? This isn't a romance story? Has a second melody replaced the first one?)

Note that all of these possibilities *may* occur. No recipe can guarantee that the filmmaker will achieve a specific emotional response. It is all a matter of context—that is, of each artwork's overall form. All we can say for certain is that the emotion felt by the spectator will emerge from formal patterns that she or he perceives in the work. This is one reason why we should try to notice as many formal relations as possible in a film. The richer our perception, the deeper and more complex our response may become.

The death of a child is perhaps the most sorrowful event that can occur in people's lives. Most films would use this event to summon up the sadness we would also feel in life. But artistic form can alter the emotional tenor of even this unhappy situation. In Jean Renoir's *The Crime of M. Lange,* the cynical publisher Batala rapes and abandons Estelle, a young laundress. After Batala disappears, Estelle becomes integrated into the neighborhood and returns to her former fiancé. But Estelle is pregnant by Batala and bears his child.

The scene when Estelle's employer, Valentine, announces that the child was born dead is one of the most emotionally complex in cinema. The first reactions expressed by the characters are gravity and sorrow **(2.7).** Suddenly, Batala's cousin remarks, "Too bad. It was a relative." In the film's context, this is taken as a joke **(2.8).** The shift in the emotion represented in the film catches us off guard. Since these characters are not heartless, we must readjust our reaction to the death and respond as they do—with relief. Estelle's survival is far more important than the death of Batala's child. This is a daring, extreme example, but it dramatically illustrates how the emotions presented onscreen and aroused in us depend on the context created by form.

Form and Meaning

Like emotion, **meaning** is important to our experience of artworks. As viewers we are constantly testing the work for larger significance, for what it says or suggests.

CONNECT TO THE BLOG
www.davidbordwell.net/blog

Scholars have studied the ways in which we respond emotionally to movies. We discuss their lines of argument in "Now you see it, now you can't."

2.7

2.8

2.7–2.8 Context reshaping emotion. In *The Crime of M. Lange,* the neighbors initially display grief at the news of Batala and Estelle's baby (2.7). But in reaction to Batala's cousin's remark, everyone breaks out into smiles (2.8). The film's formal development has rendered appropriate a reaction that might be perverse in ordinary life.

And filmmakers often create movies to convey their ideas and opinions. They want us to grasp the meanings they've offered.

What sorts of things might filmmakers and spectators think of as meaningful? Let's look at four remarks we might make about the meaning of *The Wizard of Oz.*

1. **Referential meaning.** *During the Depression, a tornado takes a girl from her family's Kansas farm to the mythical land of Oz. After a series of adventures, she returns home.*

This is very concrete, close to a bare-bones plot summary. Here the meaning depends on the spectator's ability to identify specific items: the hard times of America in the 1930s and features of midwestern climate. A viewer unacquainted with such information would miss some of the meanings cued by the film. We can call such tangible meanings *referential,* since the film refers to things or places already invested with significance in the real world.

A film's subject matter—in *The Wizard of Oz,* American farm life in the 1930s—is often established through referential meaning. And, as you might expect, referential meaning plays a role within the film's overall form. Suppose that instead of having Dorothy live in flat, spare, rural Kansas, the film made Dorothy a child living in a posh section of Beverly Hills. When she got to Oz (transported there, perhaps, by a hillside flash flood), the contrast between the crowded opulence of Oz and her home would not have been nearly as sharp. Here the referential meanings of Kansas and the Great Depression play a definite role in the overall contrast of settings that the film's form creates.

2. **Explicit meaning.** *A girl dreams of leaving home to escape her troubles. Only after she leaves does she realize how much she loves her family and friends. Nothing she finds elsewhere can replace them.*

This assertion is still fairly concrete in the meaning it attributes to the film. If someone were to ask you the *point* of the film—what it seems to be trying to get across—you might answer with something like this. Perhaps you would also mention Dorothy's closing line, "There's no place like home," as a summary of what she has learned. Let's call this sort of openly asserted meaning an *explicit meaning.*

Like referential meanings, explicit meanings function within the film's overall form. They are controlled by context. For instance, we might want to take "There's no place like home" as a statement of the meaning of the entire film. But, first, *why* do we take that as a strongly meaningful line? In ordinary conversation, it's a cliché. In context, however, the line gains great force. It's uttered in close-up, it comes at the end of the film (a formally privileged moment), and it refers back to all of Dorothy's desires and ordeals, recalling the film's narrative movement toward her goal. It is the *form* of the film that gives the homily an unfamiliar weight.

This example suggests that we must examine how explicit meanings in a film interact with other elements of the overall form. Usually, we can't isolate a particularly significant moment and declare it to be *the* meaning of the whole film. Dorothy's "There's no place like home" does capture one meaningful element in *The Wizard of Oz.* But her remark is counterbalanced by the entire beguiling Oz fantasy. Oz is attractive but dangerous; home is drab but safe and loving.

In trying to see the meaningful parts within a larger whole, it's useful to set significant moments against one another. Thus Dorothy's final line could be juxtaposed to the scene of the characters getting spruced up after their arrival at the Emerald City. We can try to see the film as about not only Oz or only Kansas, but rather the relation of the two—the delight and risk of a fantasy world versus the comfort and stability of home. Thus the film's total system is larger than any one explicit meaning we can find in it. Instead of asking, "What is this film's meaning?" we can ask, "How do the various meanings relate to one another?"

3. **Implicit meaning.** *An adolescent who must soon face the adult world yearns for a return to the simplicity of childhood, but she eventually accepts the demands of growing up.*

This is more abstract than the first two remarks we've mentioned. This one suggests that *The Wizard of Oz* is about something general, the passage from childhood to adulthood. On this view, the film implies that, as they grow up, people may desire to return to the apparently uncomplicated world of childhood. Dorothy's frustration with her aunt and uncle and her urge to flee to a place "over the rainbow" become examples of a general conception of adolescence. Unlike the "no place like home" line, this meaning isn't stated directly. We can call this suggestion an *implicit meaning.* When perceivers ascribe implicit meanings to an artwork, they're usually said to be *interpreting* it.

Clearly, **interpretations** vary. One viewer might propose that *The Wizard of Oz* is really about adolescence. Another might suggest that it is really about courage and persistence, or that it is a satire on the adult world. One of the appeals of artworks is that they ask us to interpret them in several ways at once. Again, the filmmaker invites us to perform certain activities—here, building up implicit meanings, guided by the film's overall form.

Some filmmakers claim to avoid implicit meanings altogether. They leave them to viewers and critics. Of *There Will Be Blood*, director Paul Thomas Anderson said, "It's a slippery slope when you start thinking about something other than just a good battle between two guys. . . . Tell a nasty story and let the rest take care of itself." But other filmmakers try to steer viewers toward implicit meanings, sometimes called *subtexts.* Robert Zemeckis described his *Forrest Gump* as "a movie about grieving." Director Greg Mottola describes the friends' separation at the end of *Superbad* as having several possible subtexts: "It's homosexual panic or it's bravado or it's all these shades of what young men go through to try to appear a certain way to women and to their peers."

Once we identify a film's meaning, either explicit or implicit, we're often tempted to split up the film into the content portion (the meaning) and the form (the vehicle for the content). Explicit and implicit meanings suggest very broad concepts, often called *themes.* A film may have as its theme courage or the power of faithful love. Such descriptions have some value, but they are very general; hundreds of films fit them. To summarize *The Wizard of Oz* as being simply about the problems of adolescence does not do justice to the specific qualities of the film as an experience. We suggest that the search for implicit meanings should not leave behind the *particular* and *concrete* features of a film.

This isn't to say that we should avoid interpreting films. But we should strive to make our interpretations precise by seeing how each film's thematic meanings are suggested by the film's form. In a narrative film, both explicit and implicit meanings depend on the relations between story and style. In *The Wizard of Oz,* the Yellow Brick Road has no meaning in and of itself. But if we examine the functions it fulfills in relation to the narrative, the music, the colors, and so on, we can argue that the Yellow Brick Road does suggest meanings. Dorothy's strong desire to go home makes the road represent that desire. At the same time, because it's made of yellow bricks—rare in our everyday world—it partakes of some of the magical qualities of Oz. In a way, the road encapsulates the tension between Oz and Kansas that we see throughout the movie. We want Dorothy to be successful in getting to Oz and going back to Kansas. So the road can suggest the themes of Oz's attraction and the desirability of getting home.

Interpretation need not be an end in itself. It also helps in understanding the overall form of the film. Once we've noticed the Yellow Brick Road as a thematic element, we could analyze its functions in larger patterns. We could see that it gains narrative importance because Dorothy's indecision at a crossroads allows her to

> "Critics enable us to see how parts of an artwork serve larger designs. Often this requires that the critics offer interpretations or explications of the larger aims of the work, but these overviews are often introduced, in large measure, in order to explain why the works have the parts they do."
>
> —Noël Carroll, philosopher of art

meet the Scarecrow. We could work out a color scheme for the film, contrasting the yellow road, the red slippers, the green Emerald City, and so forth. In such ways, when we interpret a film we should try to harmonize the meanings we detect with the film's overall formal development.

4. **Symptomatic meaning.** *In a society in which human worth is measured by money, the home and the family may seem to be the last refuge of human values. This belief is especially strong in times of economic crisis, such as that in the United States in the 1930s.*

Like statement 3, this is abstract and general. It situates the film within a trend of thought that is assumed to be characteristic of American society during the 1930s. The claim could apply equally well to many other films, as well as to many novels, plays, poems, paintings, advertisements, radio shows, political speeches, and a host of cultural products of the period.

But something else is worth noticing about the statement. It treats an explicit meaning in *The Wizard of Oz* ("There's no place like home") as displaying a set of values characteristic of a whole society. We could treat implicit meanings the same way. If we say the film implies something about adolescence as a crucial time of transition, we could suggest that emphasis on adolescence as a special period of life is also a recurrent concern of American society. So, it's possible to understand a film's explicit or implicit meanings as bearing traces of a particular set of social values. We can call this *symptomatic meaning,* and the set of values that get revealed can be considered a social **ideology.**

Symptomatic meanings remind us that meaning of all sorts is largely a social phenomenon. Many meanings of films are ultimately ideological; that is, they spring from systems of culturally specific beliefs about the world. Religious beliefs, political opinions, conceptions of race or gender or social class, even our most deeply seated notions of life's values—all these constitute our ideological frame of reference. We're tempted to think that our beliefs are the best explanations of how the world is. But if we compare our own ideology with that of another culture or era we see how historically and socially shaped many of those views are. In other times and places, *home* and *adolescence* don't carry the meanings they carried in 1930s America. Some cultures don't have the idea of adolescence at all.

Films, like other artworks, can be examined for their symptomatic meanings. Again, however, the abstract and general quality of such meanings can lead us away from the film's concrete form. As in analyzing implicit meanings, we should ground symptomatic meanings in the film's specific aspects. A film *enacts* ideological meanings through its form. We'll see in Chapter 11 how the narrative and stylistic system of *Meet Me in St. Louis* and *Raging Bull* can be analyzed for ideological implications.

To sum up: Films have meaning because we attribute meanings to them. Sometimes the filmmaker guides us toward certain meanings; sometimes we find meanings the filmmaker didn't intend. If we're engaged by a film, we'll search for referential, explicit, implicit, and symptomatic meanings. But a film is a film, not a collection of themes. The filmmaker who wants to make a general statement or suggest implicit meanings will still have to work out the film in concrete terms, through particular choices about form and style. When we look closely at a film, we should keep the same balance in mind, not letting our urge for wider significance outweigh our focus on the film as a dynamic whole.

Evaluation: Good, Bad, or Indifferent?

In talking about an artwork, people often *evaluate* it. They make claims about its goodness or badness. Reviews in print media and on the Internet exist almost solely to tell us whether a film is worth seeing, and our friends often urge us to go to their latest favorite. But often we discover that a much-praised film seems mediocre to us. How, then, are we to evaluate films with any degree of objectivity?

We can start by realizing that there is a difference between *personal taste* and *evaluative judgment.* To say "I liked this film" or "I hated it" is not equal to saying, "It's a good film" or "It's wretched." Very few of us limit our enjoyment to the greatest works. Most people can enjoy a film they know is not particularly good. What critics call "guilty pleasures" are movies that are enjoyable despite being bad in some respects.

All this suggests that personal preference need not be the basis for judging a film's quality. Instead, the critic who wishes to make a relatively objective evaluation will use specific *criteria.* A criterion is a standard that can be applied in the judgment of many works. By using a criterion, the critic gains a basis for comparing films for relative quality.

There are many different criteria. Some people evaluate films on *realistic* criteria. Aficionados of military history might judge a film entirely on whether the battle scenes use historically accurate weaponry. Other people condemn films because they don't find the action plausible. They dismiss a scene by saying, "Who'd really believe that X would meet Y just at the right moment?" We have already seen, though, that artworks often violate laws of reality and operate by their own conventions and internal rules. Coincidental encounters, usually at embarrassing moments, are a convention of genres like comedy. So realism, then, isn't a criterion that we can apply in every case.

Viewers can also use *moral* criteria to evaluate films. Most narrowly, aspects of the film can be judged outside their context in the film. Some viewers might feel that any film with nudity or profanity or violence is bad, while other viewers might find just these aspects valuable because they provoke strong reactions. Likewise, some viewers might condemn Renoir's slightly humorous handling of the baby's death in *The Crime of M. Lange,* regardless of the scene's context. More broadly, viewers and critics may employ moral criteria to evaluate a film's overall significance, and here the film's complete formal system becomes pertinent. We can judge a film good because of its overall view of life, its willingness to show opposing points of view, or its emotional range.

While realistic and moral criteria are well suited to particular purposes, we should also recognize that there are criteria that assess films as artistic wholes. Such criteria allow us to take each film's form into account as much as possible. *Coherence* is one such criterion. This quality, often referred to as *unity,* has traditionally been held to be a positive feature of artworks. So, too, has *intensity of effect.* If an artwork is vivid, striking, and emotionally engaging, it may be considered more valuable.

Another criterion is *complexity.* We can argue that, all other things being equal, complex films are good. A complex film engages our interest on many levels, creates a multiplicity of relations among many separate formal elements, and tends to create intriguing patterns of feelings and meanings.

Yet another formal criterion is *originality.* Originality for its own sake is pointless, of course. Just because something is different doesn't mean that it is good. But if an artist takes a familiar convention and uses it in a way that gives viewers a fresh experience, then (all other things being equal) the resulting work may be considered good from an aesthetic standpoint.

Note that all these criteria are matters of degree. One film may be more complex than another. Moreover, there is often a give-and-take among the criteria. A film might be complex but lack coherence or intensity. Ninety minutes of a black screen would make for an original film but not a very complex one. A slasher movie may create great intensity in certain scenes but may be wholly unoriginal, as well as disorganized and simplistic. In applying the criteria, the analyst often must weigh one against another.

Evaluation can serve many useful ends. It can call attention to neglected artworks or make us rethink our attitudes toward accepted classics. But just as the discovery of meanings is not the only purpose of formal analysis, we suggest that evaluation is most fruitful when it is backed up by a close examination of the film. General statements ("*The Wizard of Oz* is a masterpiece") seldom enlighten us very much. Usually, an evaluation is helpful insofar as it points to aspects of the film and shows us relations and qualities we have missed. "*The Wizard of Oz* is more coherent than it looks at first. Look at all the parallels! Miss Gulch's written order to take Toto is echoed by the Wicked Witch's fiery skywriting addressed to the citizens of the Emerald City, 'Surrender Dorothy.'" Like interpretation, evaluation can usefully drive us back to the film's particular formal strategies, helping us to understand them better.

In reading this book, you'll find that we have generally minimized evaluation. We think that most of the films and sequences we analyze are good based on the artistic criteria we mentioned, but the purpose of this book is not to persuade you to accept a list of masterpieces. Instead, by considering how films create our experiences through form and style, you will have an informed basis for whatever evaluations you want to make.

Principles of Film Form

Form doesn't equal formula. Scientists discover powerful laws governing the physical world, but in the arts there are no laws of form that all artists must follow. Artists create within culture, so many principles of artistic form are matters of convention. An outer-space adventure such as Andrei Tarkovsky's *Solaris* isn't faulty because it doesn't follow the conventions at work in *Star Wars: Episode IV—A New Hope*. Still, there are some broad principles that artists, filmmakers included, draw on. These are ideas of function, similarity and repetition, difference and variation, development, and unity and disunity. We'll draw on *The Wizard of Oz* for our main examples.

Function

If form is a pattern of elements, we would expect that those elements fulfill functions. They *do* something in the larger whole. Of any element in a film we can ask, *What are its functions?*

We say "functions" in the plural, because most elements serve several purposes. Perhaps for some MGM executives, the song "Over the Rainbow" had the primary purpose of letting Judy Garland launch a hit tune. Still, the song fits the film because it fulfills certain narrative and stylistic functions. The lyrics establish Dorothy's desire to leave home, and the opening line's reference to the rainbow foreshadows her trip through the sky to colorful Oz. In fact, the "where" in the word "Somewhere" leaps a full octave, creating a musical equivalent of a trip to a distant land. In asking about formal function, therefore, we typically ask not, "How did this element get there?" but rather, "What is this element *doing* there?" and "How does it cue us to respond?"

In *The Wizard of Oz,* every major character fulfills several functions. For instance, Miss Gulch, the woman who wants to take Toto from Dorothy, frightens Dorothy into running away from home. In Oz she reappears as the wicked Witch who tries to seize the ruby slippers and keep Dorothy from going to the Emerald City and returning home. Even an element as apparently minor as the dog Toto serves many purposes. The dispute over Toto causes Dorothy to run away from home and to return too late to take shelter from the tornado. Later, when Dorothy is about to leave Oz, Toto's pursuit of a cat makes Dorothy jump out of the ascending balloon. Toto's gray color, set off against the brightness of Oz, recalls the black and white of the Kansas episodes at the film's beginning.

The story goes that when the actress Ingrid Bergman asked Alfred Hitchcock about her motivation in a particular scene, Hitchcock replied: "Your paycheck." But Hitchcock's joke deliberately confused the *actress's* reason for being in the movie (doing her job for pay) with the *character's* reason for doing what she does. Bergman's question can guide us in thinking about the functions of anything in a movie.

For Bergman, as for most actors, the word "motivation" applies the purposes of a character's actions. But the term doesn't apply only to performance matters. When we speak of *motivation* more generally, we're asking about what justifies anything being in the movie or taking the shape it does. If we see a man in beggar's clothes in the middle of an elegant society ball, we will ask why he's dressed in this way. Is he the victim of practical jokers who have told him that it's a masquerade party? Is he an eccentric millionaire? Such a scene does occur in *My Man Godfrey,* in which the young society people have been assigned to bring back a homeless man as part of a scavenger hunt **(2.9)**. The game motivates the presence of an inappropriately dressed character.

Motivation points to functions. Throughout *The Wizard of Oz,* one function Toto fulfills is to get Dorothy into scrapes. Since the plot requires that Dorothy run away from home, the screenwriters used her love of Toto to motivate her flight. When Toto jumps from the balloon to chase a cat, we motivate his action by appealing to notions of how dogs are likely to act when cats are around.

Motivation is so common in films that spectators take it for granted, but filmmakers must think about it often. A director may decide to let a character's wandering around a room motivate a camera movement. A cinematographer may have to choose between motivated and unmotivated lighting. Gabriel Beristain, who shot *Ring Two,* faced two options in shooting night scenes:

> You could go the straight route and motivate some sort of light through windows, which is the only logical source in play. Or you could decide not to worry about motivation and create chiaroscuro lighting that simulates darkness.

When we study principles of narrative form (Chapter 3) and various types of films (Chapters 9 and 10), we'll look more closely at how motivation gives elements specific functions.

Similarity and Repetition

In our example of the ABACA pattern, we saw how we were able to predict the next steps in the series. One reason for this was a regular pattern of repeated elements. Like beats in music or meter in poetry, the repetition of the A's in our pattern established and satisfied formal expectations. Similarity and repetition, then, constitute an important principle of film form.

If you were to make a film, you would rely on repetition constantly. You'd make sure that your main character reappeared often enough for him or her to be seen as central to the plot, and you'd probably have dialogue that reiterated main points about goals, conflicts, and themes. More subtly, you'd probably utilize what are called **motifs.** A motif is *any significant repeated element that contributes to the overall form.*

It may be an object, a color, a place, a person, a sound, or even a character trait. Max's tropical postcard is a motif signaled early in *Collateral.* In *Jurassic Park,* Dr. Alan Grant's dislike of children reappears as a motif—one that alters in the course of the adventure. A lighting scheme or camera position can become a motif. (See "A Closer Look," pp. 66–67.) Motifs often reappear at climaxes or highly emotional moments, as happens with the famous line from *Jerry Maguire,* "You complete me."

Motifs are fairly exact repetitions, but a film can chart broader similarities between its ingredients. To understand *The Wizard of Oz,* we must notice that the three Kansas farmhands have counterparts in the Scarecrow, the Tin Man, and the Cowardly Lion. We must notice additional echoes between characters in the frame

2.9 Motivation for formal elements. The heroine of *My Man Godfrey* studies her prize while the well-off crowd urges the unemployed Godfrey to make a speech. A scavenger hunt is the motivation for the homeless man's presence at the elegant society ball.

CONNECT TO THE BLOG
www.davidbordwell.net/blog

We discuss George Smiley's eyeglasses as a motif in *"Tinker Tailor:* A guide for the perplexed."

A CLOSER LOOK

Creative Decisions: Picking Out Patterns

In studying film as an art, you might sometimes wonder: Are all the patterns of form and style we notice really in the film? Do filmmakers actually put them there, or are we just reading them in?

When asked, filmmakers often say that their formal and stylistic choices aim to create specific effects. Hitchcock, a director who had an engineering bent, planned his stories carefully and chose techniques in full awareness of their possibilities. His film *Rope* confines the action to a single apartment and presents it in only eleven shots. *Rear Window* limits the action to what the hero can see from his apartment. In these and other films, Hitchcock deliberately set up constraints for himself, inviting his audience to enjoy the way he worked within them.

Filmmakers may work more intuitively than Hitchcock, but they still must choose one story development or another, one technique or another. The finished film can have an overall unity because the choices tend to mesh. Joel and Ethan Coen, the brothers who created *The Big Lebowski, Fargo,* and *True Grit,* don't set out with a particular style in mind. As Ethan puts it, "At the point of making the movie, it's just about making individual choices." Joel picks up the thread:

> . . . about the best way to tell the story, scene by scene. You make specific choices that you think are appropriate or compelling or interesting for that particular scene. Then, at the end of the day, you put it all together and somebody looks at it and, if there's some consistency to it, they say, "Well, that's their style."

Even if the Coens don't map out every option in advance, their films display distinctive patterns of form and style, and those definitely affect our response **(2.10–2.11)**.

Professionals pay attention to other filmmakers' creative decisions about form and style. While watching Stanley Kubrick's *The Shining,* Nicole Kidman pointed out how the composition of one shot had both an immediate point and a long-range story purpose **(2.12):**

> Here, in this scene, look at how there is this rack of knives hanging in the background over the boy's head. . . . It's important because it not only shows that the boy is in danger, but one of those very knives is used later in the story when Wendy takes it to protect herself from her husband **[2.13].**

> 〝 You can take a movie, for example, like *Angels with Dirty Faces,* where James Cagney is a child and says to his pal Pat O'Brien, 'What do you hear, what do you say?'—cocky kid—and then as a young rough on the way up when things are going great for him he says, 'What do you hear, what do you say?' Then when he is about to be executed in the electric chair and Pat O'Brien is there to hear his confession, he says, 'What do you hear, what do you say?' and the simple repetition of the last line of dialogue in three different places with the same characters brings home the dramatically changed circumstances much more than any extensive diatribe would."
>
> —Robert Towne, screenwriter, *Chinatown*

Kubrick told Kidman that a director had to repeat story information so that the audience could keep up. The knife pattern shaped viewers' experience, although they may not have been aware of it.

Kubrick's comment points up another reason we can have some confidence when we pick out patterns. A filmmaker doesn't create a movie from scratch. All films borrow ideas and storytelling strategies from other movies and other art forms. As we've seen, a lot that happens in films is governed by conventions. When Kubrick shows us the knives behind Danny, he's following a very old storytelling convention: prepare the audience for action that will come later. Similarly, *The Hudsucker Proxy* is a satirical comedy, and the steep perspective in 2.10 and 2.11 follows a convention of using exaggeration to create humor.

Very often, patterns in one film resemble patterns we've seen in other films. Even when filmmakers operate intuitively and don't tell us their trade secrets, we can notice how they treat familiar conventions of form and technique.

2.10

2.11

2.10–2.11 **Creating a film's style through compositional motifs.** In the *Hudsucker Proxy*, the boss dangles above the street in a very steep, centered-perspective composition (2.10). The same sort of composition is used to show the impersonal layout of desks in the Hudsucker company (2.11).

2.12

2.13

2.12–2.13 **Motifs anticipate action.** In *The Shining*, an early scene in the Hotel Overlook kitchen displays the telepathic rapport between Halloran and Danny, whose parents are caretaking the hotel for the winter. The knives are a natural part of the kitchen set but are aligned above Danny (2.12). Later Danny's mother, Wendy, goes to the same knife rack, seen from a different angle, to grab a weapon (2.13).

2.14

2.15

2.16

2.17

2.14–2.17 **Parallels between frame story and fantasy.** The itinerant Kansas fortune-teller, Professor Marvel (2.14), bears a striking resemblance to the old charlatan known as the Wizard of Oz (2.15). Miss Gulch's bicycle in the opening section (2.16) becomes the Witch's broom in Oz (2.17).

2.18

2.19

2.18–2.19 **Parallel compositions.** As the Lion describes his timidity, the characters are lined up (2.18) to form a mirror reversal of the earlier scene in which the others teased Zeke for being afraid of pigs (2.19).

story and in the fantasy **(2.14–2.17).** Such similarities are usually called *parallels.* Parallels cue us to compare two or more distinct elements by highlighting some similarity. For example, Dorothy says she feels that she has known the Scarecrow and the Tin Man before. At another point, the staging of a shot reinforces the parallels **(2.18, 2.19).**

Motifs can help create parallels among characters and situations. The viewer will notice, and even come to expect, that every time Dorothy meets a character in Oz, the scene will end with the song "We're Off to See the Wizard." This motif accentuates the broader similarities among Dorothy's encounters. Our recognition of parallelism provides part of our pleasure in watching a film, much as rhymes contribute to the power of poetry.

Difference and Variation

A filmmaker is unlikely to rely only on repetitions. AAAAAA is rather boring. There should also be some changes, or *variations,* however small. So difference, or variation, is another fundamental principle of film form. We've seen this principle at work already, when composer James Newton Howard provided three "movements" for the music accompanying the final scene of *Collateral* (pp. 7–8).

Differences among the elements are most apparent when characters clash. In *The Wizard of Oz,* Dorothy's desires are opposed, at various points, by the differing desires of Aunt Em, Miss Gulch, the Wicked Witch, and the Wizard, so that our experience of the film is engaged through dramatic conflict. But character conflict isn't the only way the formal principle of difference may appear.

If you were making a film, you'd seek out ways to contrast your characters and their environments. Perhaps you'd situate one character in nature and another in busy

2.20   **2.21**

2.20–2.21 Contrasting settings. Centered in the upper half of the frame, the Emerald City (2.20) creates a striking contrast to the similar composition showing the castle of the Wicked Witch of the West (2.21).

urban surroundings. You might stress contrasts of costume, or hairstyles, or color. *The Wizard of Oz* presents stark color oppositions: black-and-white Kansas versus colorful Oz; Dorothy in red, white, and blue versus the Witch in black. Settings are opposed as well—not only Oz versus Kansas but also the various locales within Oz **(2.20, 2.21).** Voice quality, musical tunes, and a host of other elements play off against one another, demonstrating that any motif may be opposed by any other motif.

Motifs will be repeated, but often not exactly. Variation will appear. In *The Wizard of Oz,* the three Kansas hands aren't identical to their counterparts in Oz. Parallelism thus requires a degree of difference as well as striking similarity. When Professor Marvel pretends to read Dorothy's future in a small crystal ball, we see no images in it (2.14). Dorothy's dream transforms the crystal into a large globe in the Witch's castle, where it displays frightening scenes **(2.22).** Similarly, Toto's disruption of a situation is a constant action motif, but it changes its function. In Kansas, he disturbs Miss Gulch and induces Dorothy to take Toto away from home, but in Oz, his disruption prevents Dorothy from returning home.

Not all differences come down to this-versus-that dualities. Dorothy's three Oz friends—the Scarecrow, the Tin Woodman, and the Lion—are distinguished by three things they lack (a brain, a heart, courage). Other films may rely on less sharp differences, suggesting a scale of gradations among the characters, as in Jean Renoir's *The Rules of the Game.* At the extreme, an abstract film may create minimal variations among its parts, such as in the slight changes that accompany each return of the same footage in J. J. Murphy's *Print Generation* (p. 376).

Repetition and variation are two sides of the same coin. To notice one is to be alert to the other. In thinking about films, we ought to look for similarities *and* differences. Shuttling between the two, we can point out motifs and contrast the changes they undergo, recognize parallelisms as repetition, and still spot crucial variations.

Development

One way to notice how similarity and difference operate in film form is to look for principles of *development* from part to part. Development places similar and different elements within a pattern of change. Our pattern ABACA is based not only on repetition (the recurring motif of A) and difference (the insertion of B and C) but also on a principle of *progression* that we could state as a rule: alternate A with successive letters in alphabetical order. Though simple, this is a principle of development, governing the form of the whole series.

Filmmakers often treat formal development as *a progression moving from beginning through middle to end.* The story of *The Wizard of Oz* shows development in many ways. It is, for one thing, a *journey:* from Kansas through Oz to Kansas.

CONNECT TO THE BLOG
www.davidbordwell.net/blog

One distinctive type of film form comes in the anthology film, combining short segments by several directors. It's a theme-and-variations approach that we discuss in "Can you spot all the auteurs in this picture?"

2.22 Similarity and difference. Through her crystal ball, the Wicked Witch mocks Dorothy. Contrast it with the earlier scene (2.14) in which the Kansas fortune-teller uses a smaller crystal ball.

2.23 Narrative development: Starting a journey. Dorothy puts her feet on the literal beginning of the Yellow Brick Road, as it widens out from a single point.

The good witch Glinda emphasizes this formal pattern by telling Dorothy that "It's always best to start at the beginning" **(2.23).** Many films possess such a journey plot. *The Wizard of Oz* is also a *search,* beginning with an initial separation from home, tracing a series of efforts to find a way home, and ending with home being found. Within the film, there is also a pattern of *mystery,* which usually has the same beginning-middle-end pattern. We begin with a question (Who is the Wizard of Oz?), pass through attempts to answer it, and conclude with the question answered. (The Wizard is a fraud.) *Close Encounters of the Third Kind* combines the patterns of journey, search, and mystery, adding the psychological change that occurs in protagonist Roy Neary. As these examples suggest, feature-length films often depend on several developmental patterns.

At some point in making a film, the filmmakers usually prepare a breakdown of its parts. This traces, in sketchy form, the film's pattern of development. When we want to analyze a finished film, we do the same thing. We make what's usually called a *segmentation*. A segmentation is simply a written outline of the film that breaks it into its major and minor parts, with the parts marked by consecutive numbers or letters. If a narrative film has 40 *scenes,* then we can label each scene with a number running from 1 to 40. It may be useful to divide some parts further (for example, scenes 6a and 6b). Segmenting a film enables us not only to notice similarities and differences among parts but also to plot the overall development. Following is a segmentation for *The Wizard of Oz* using an outline format. (In segmenting films, we label the opening credits with a "C," the end title with an "E," and all other segments with numbers.)

The Wizard of Oz: Plot Segmentation

C. Credits
1. Kansas
   a. Dorothy is at home, worried about Miss Gulch's threat to Toto.
   b. Running away, Dorothy meets Professor Marvel, who induces her to return home.
   c. A tornado lifts the house, with Dorothy and Toto, into the sky.
2. Munchkin City
   a. After Dorothy's house crashes to earth, she meets Glinda, and the Munchkins celebrate the death of the Wicked Witch of the East.
   b. The Wicked Witch of the West threatens Dorothy over the Ruby Slippers.
   c. Glinda sends Dorothy to seek the Wizard's help.
3. The Yellow Brick Road
   a. Dorothy meets the Scarecrow.
   b. Dorothy meets the Tin Man.
   c. Dorothy meets the Cowardly Lion.
4. The Emerald City
   a. The Witch creates a poppy field near the city, but Glinda rescues the travelers.
   b. The group is welcomed by the city's citizens.
   c. As they wait to see the Wizard, the Lion sings of being king.
   d. The terrifying Wizard agrees to help the group if they obtain the Wicked Witch's broomstick.
5. The Witch's castle and nearby woods
   a. In the woods, flying monkeys carry off Dorothy and Toto.
   b. The Witch realizes that she must kill Dorothy to get the ruby slippers.
   c. The Scarecrow, Tin Man, and Lion sneak into the Castle; in the ensuing chase, Dorothy kills the Witch.
6. The Emerald City
   a. Although revealed as a humbug, the Wizard grants the wishes of the Scarecrow, Tin Man, and Lion.

b. Dorothy fails to leave in the Wizard's hot-air balloon but is transported
    home by the ruby slippers.
7. **Kansas—Dorothy describes Oz to her family and friends**
E. **End credits**

Preparing a segmentation may look a little fussy, but in the course of this book,
we'll try to convince you that it can shed a lot of light on films. For now, just consider this comparison.

As you walk into a building, your experience develops over time. In many cathedrals, for example, the entryway is fairly narrow. But as you emerge into the
open area inside (the nave), space expands outward and upward, your sense of your
body seems to shrink, and your attention is directed toward the altar, centrally located in the distance. The somewhat cramped entryway makes you feel a contrast
when you enter the broad and soaring space. Your experience has been as carefully
planned as any theme park ride. Only by thinking back on it can you realize that the
planned progression of the building's different areas shaped your experience. If you
could study the builder's blueprints, you'd see the whole layout at a glance. It would
be very different from your moment-by-moment experience of it, but it would shed
light on how your experience was shaped.

A film works in a similar way. As we watch the film, we're in the thick of it.
We follow the formal development moment by moment, and we may get more and
more involved. But if we want to study the overall form, we need to stand back a bit.
Films don't come with blueprints, but by creating a plot segmentation, we can get a
comparable sense of the film's basic design. In a way, we're recovering the architecture of the movie. A segmentation lets us see the patterning that the filmmakers laid
out and that we felt intuitively while watching the film. In Chapters 3 and 10, we
consider how to segment different types of films, and several of our sample analyses in Chapter 11 use segmentations to show how the films work.

A quick way to size up how a film develops formally is to *compare the beginning with the ending*. By looking at the similarities and the differences between the
beginning and the ending, we can start to understand the overall pattern of the film.
We can test this advice on *The Wizard of Oz*. A comparison of the beginning and
the ending reveals that Dorothy's journey ends with her return home; the journey, a
search for an ideal place "over the rainbow," has turned into a search for a way back
to Kansas. The final scene repeats and develops the narrative elements of the opening. Stylistically, the beginning and ending are the only parts that use black-and-white film stock. This repetition supports the contrast the narrative creates between
the dreamland of Oz and the bleak landscape of Kansas.

At the film's end, Professor Marvel comes to visit Dorothy **(2.24),** reversing
the situation of her visit to him when she had tried to run away. At the beginning,
he had convinced her to return home; then, as the Wizard in the Oz section, he had
also represented her hopes of returning home. Finally, when she recognizes Professor Marvel and the farmhands as the basis of the characters in her dream, she
remembers how much she had wanted to come home from Oz.

Earlier, we suggested that film form engages our emotions and expectations in
a dynamic way. Now we're in a better position to see why. The constant interplay
between similarity and difference, and repetition and variation, leads the viewer to
an active engagement with the film's developing system. It may be handy to visualize a movie's development in static terms by segmenting it, but we ought not to forget that formal development is a *process*. Form shapes our experience of the film.

Unity and Disunity

When all the relationships we perceive within a film are clear and economically
interwoven, we say that the film has *unity*. We often call a unified film "tight," because there seem to be no gaps in its overall form. We feel that every element fulfills

CONNECT TO THE BLOG
www.davidbordwell.net/blog

If beginnings are important, then the very beginning is even more important, as "First shots" demonstrates.

2.24 Comparing beginning and ending. The visits of the final scene in *The Wizard of Oz* reverse events at the start of the film; Professor Marvel comes to visit Dorothy at her home, but at the start Dorothy met him after leaving home.

particular functions, that we understand the similarities and differences among elements, that the form develops logically, and that no element is superfluous. The film's overall unity can give our experience a sense of completeness and fulfillment.

But unity is a matter of degree. Very few films are perfectly tight. For example, at one point in *The Wizard of Oz,* the Witch refers to her having attacked Dorothy and her friends with insects, yet we have never seen them. What is the Witch referring to? In fact, a bee attack was originally shot but then cut from the finished film. The Witch's line about the insect attack now lacks motivation. More striking is a dangling element at the film's end: we never find out what happens to Miss Gulch. Presumably, she still has her legal order to take Toto away, but no one refers to this in the last scene. The viewer may be inclined to overlook this disunity, however, because Miss Gulch's parallel character, the Witch, has been killed off in the Oz fantasy, and we don't expect to see her alive again. Since perfect unity is scarcely ever achieved, we ought to expect that even a unified film may still contain a few unintegrated elements or unanswered questions.

If we look at unity as a criterion for evaluation, we may judge a film containing several unmotivated elements as a failure. But unity and disunity may be looked at nonevaluatively as well, as the results of particular formal conventions. For example, *Pulp Fiction* lacks a bit of closure in that it never reveals what is inside the briefcase that is at the center of the gangster plot. The contents, however, give off a golden glow, suggesting that they are of very great value (as well as evoking the "whatsit" in *Kiss Me Deadly,* a classic film noir). By not specifying the goods, the film invites us to compare characters' reactions to them—most notably, in the last scene in the diner, when Pumpkin gazes at it lustfully and the newly spiritual hit man Jules calmly insists that he will deliver it to his boss. In such ways, momentary disunities can fulfill particular purposes or suggest thematic meanings.

 ## SUMMARY

A filmmaker designs an experience for an audience by shaping the film's form, the overall pattern of parts. Things that are normally considered content—subject matter, or abstract ideas—take on particular functions within the overall form.

Our experience as viewers is shaped by the filmmaker's formal choices. Through the creative decisions they make, filmmakers nudge or thrust us in certain directions. Picking up cues in the work, we frame specific expectations that are aroused, guided, delayed, cheated, satisfied, or disturbed. We feel curiosity, suspense, and surprise. We compare the particular aspects of the artwork with things that we know from life and with conventions found in art.

The concrete context of the artwork expresses and stimulates emotions. It enables us to construct many types of meanings. And even when we apply general criteria in evaluating artworks, we ought to use those criteria to help us discriminate more, to probe more deeply into the particular aspects of the artwork. The rest of this book is devoted to studying these properties of artistic form in cinema.

We can summarize the principles of film form as a set of questions that you can ask about any film:

1. For any element in the film, what are its functions in the overall form? How is it motivated?

2. Are elements or patterns repeated throughout the film? If so, how and at what points? Are motifs and parallelisms asking us to compare elements?

3. How are elements contrasted and differentiated from one another? How are different elements opposed to one another?

4. What principles of progression or development are at work through the form of the film? Does a comparison of the beginning and ending point toward the film's overall form?

5. What degree of unity is present in the film's overall form?

In this chapter, we examined some major ways in which films as artworks can engage us as spectators. We also reviewed some broad principles of film form. Armed with these general principles, we can press on to distinguish more specific *types* of form that are central to understanding film art.

RECOMMENDED DVD AND BLU-RAY SUPPLEMENTS

The Warner Bros. two-disc special edition of *The Wizard of Oz* contains supplements documenting the film's production. See also Aljean Harmetz, *The Making of the Wizard of Oz* (New York: Limelight, 1984), and John Fricke, Jay Scarfone, and William Stillman, *The Wizard of Oz: The Official 50th Anniversary Pictorial History* (New York: Warner Books, 1989).

While the film was in postproduction, MGM executives quarreled about whether the song "Over the Rainbow" should be dropped. Some thought it was too long and slowed the pace; others suggested that singing in a barnyard was undignified. Producer Arthur Freed argued passionately for retaining the ballad, and he won. His reasoning was expressed in an early memo, and its wording shows that he was conscious of the song's role in motivating Dorothy's journey:

> The whole love story in *Snow White* is motivated by the song "Some Day My Prince Will Come" as Snow White is looking into the well. Dialogue could not have accomplished this half as well. I make this illustration for the purpose that we plant our *Wizard of Oz* script in a similar way through a musical sequence on the farm. Doing it musically takes all the triteness out of a straight plot scene. (Quoted in Fricke, Scarfone, and Stillman, *The Wizard of Oz,* p. 30)

DVD supplements tend to focus on behind-the-scenes production information and on exposing how techniques such as special effects and music were accomplished. Sometimes, though, such descriptions analyze formal aspects of the film. In "Sweet Sounds," the supplement on the music in *Charlie and the Chocolate Factory,* composer Danny Elfman discusses how the musical numbers that follow the disappearance of each of the obnoxious children created parallels among them and yet achieved variety by being derived from different styles of music.

"Their Production Will Be Second to None," on the *Hard Day's Night* DVD, includes an intelligent interview with director Richard Lester in which he talks about the overall form of the film. He remarks, for example, that in the first third, he deliberately used confined spaces and low ceilings to prepare for the extreme contrast of the open spaces into which the Beatles escape.

The "Production Design" supplement for *The Golden Compass* discusses motifs: circular elements in the sets and props associated with the heroine Lyra and the Oxford setting opposed to oval elements associated with the villainous Mrs. Coulter and the Magisterium. In portions of the director's and editor's commentary track for *Cold Mountain,* Anthony Minghella and Walter Murch discuss the structure of the film, including pacing and the adaptation of the novel.

3

Narrative Form

Stories surround us. In childhood, we learn fairy tales and myths. As we grow up, we read short stories, novels, history, and biography. The world's religions use stories to illustrate their doctrines. In court rooms juries hear different stories, all competing for recognition as the truth. Plays tell stories, as do films, television shows, comic books, paintings, dance, and many other cultural phenomena. In everyday life we tell each other tales—recalling our past, offering an anecdote, sharing a joke. We can't even escape by going to sleep, since we often experience our dreams as little narratives. Narrative is a fundamental way that humans make sense of the world.

The prevalence of stories in our lives is one reason that we need to take a close look at how films may embody **narrative form.** When we speak of "going to the movies," we almost always mean that we are going to see a narrative film—a film that tells a story. Likewise, a great many filmmakers choose narrative as the best way to express their ideas and feelings.

Principles of Narrative Form

Narrative form is most common in fictional films, but it can appear in all other basic types. The documentary *Super Size Me* chronicles the 30-day effort by a young man to eat only food from McDonald's, and it traces the effect of this diet on his body and mind. Many animated films, short cartoons or feature-length ones, tell stories. Some experimental and avant-garde films use narrative form, although the story or the way it is told may be quite unusual, as we shall see in Chapter 10.

Because stories are all around us, spectators approach a narrative film with definite expectations. We may know a great deal about the particular story the film will tell. Perhaps we've read the book that the film is based on, or this is a sequel to a movie we've seen. Even if we aren't already acquainted with the story's particular world, though, we have expectations that are characteristic of narrative form itself. We assume that there will be characters and that the actions they take will involve them with one another. We expect a series of incidents that will be connected in some way. We also probably expect that the problems or conflicts that arise will somehow be settled—either they will be resolved or, at least, a new light will be cast on them. A spectator comes prepared to make sense of a narrative film.

As the viewer watches the film, she or he picks up cues, recalls information, anticipates what will follow, and generally participates in the creation of the film's form. As we suggested in Chapter 2 (pp. 54–55), the film shapes our expectations by summoning up curiosity, suspense, surprise, and other emotional qualities. The ending has the task of satisfying or cheating the expectations prompted by the film as a whole. The ending may also activate memory by cueing the spectator to review earlier events, possibly considering them in a new light. When *The Sixth Sense* was released in 1999, many moviegoers were so intrigued by the surprise twist at the end that they returned to see the film again and trace how their expectations had been manipulated. Something similar happened with *The Prestige* (see pp. 298–306). As we examine narrative form, we need to recognize how it engages the viewer in a dynamic activity.

It's the filmmaker's task to create this engagement. How does this happen? We can start to understand the filmmaker's creative choices and the viewer's activity by looking a little more closely at what narrative is and does.

What Is Narrative?

We can consider a *narrative* to be *a chain of events linked by cause and effect and occurring in time and space.* A narrative is what we usually mean by the term *story,* although we'll be using *story* in a slightly different way later. Typically, a narrative begins with one situation; a series of changes occurs according to a pattern of cause and effect; finally, a new situation arises that brings about the end of the narrative. Our engagement with the story depends on our understanding of the pattern of change and stability, cause and effect, time and space.

A random string of events is hard to understand as a story. Consider the following actions: "A man tosses and turns, unable to sleep. A mirror breaks. A telephone rings." We have trouble grasping this as a narrative because we are unable to determine how the events are connected by causality or time or space.

Consider a new description of these same events: "A man has a fight with his boss. He tosses and turns that night, unable to sleep. In the morning, he is still so angry that he smashes the mirror while shaving. Then his telephone rings; his boss has called to apologize."

We now have a narrative, unexciting though it is. We can connect the events spatially. The man is in the office, then in his bed; the mirror is in the bathroom; the phone is somewhere else in his home. Time is important as well. The fight starts things off, and the sleepless night, the broken mirror, and the phone call occur one after the other. The action runs from one day to the following morning. Above all, we can understand that the three events are part of a pattern of causes and effects. The argument with the boss causes the sleeplessness and the broken mirror. The phone call from the boss resolves the conflict, so the narrative ends. The narrative develops from an initial situation of conflict between employee and boss, through a series of events caused by the conflict, to the resolution of the conflict. Simple and minimal as our example is, it shows how important causality, space, and time are to narrative form.

The fact that a narrative relies on causality, time, and space doesn't mean that other formal principles can't govern the film. For instance, a narrative may make use of parallelism. As Chapter 2 points out (pp. 65–66), parallelism points up a similarity among story elements. Our example was the way that *The Wizard of Oz* made the three Kansas farmhands parallel to Dorothy's three Oz companions.

A narrative may cue us to draw parallels among characters, settings, situations, times of day, or any other elements. *Julie & Julia* parallels two women, living in different periods, trying to juggle their marriages and their passion for cuisine **(3.1–3.2).** Julie never meets her idol Julia Child, but there is still a cause-effect link: Julie is inspired by the older woman's life. Sometimes a filmmaker goes further and doesn't link the parallel stories causally. Veřá Chytilová's *Something Different* alternates scenes from the life of a housewife and scenes from the career of a gymnast. Since the two women lead entirely separate lives, there are no causal connections between them. The parallel patterning encourages us to compare the women's life decisions.

CONNECT TO THE BLOG
www.davidbordwell.net/blog

When filmmakers create a prequel to an existing film story, they need to weave new patterns of cause and effect that lead to the story we already know. We discuss how prequels manage this task in "Originality and origin stories."

CONNECT TO THE BLOG
www.davidbordwell.net/blog

We analyze *Julie & Julia* in more depth, along with the parallel plot in *Enchantment,* in "Julie, Julia & the house that talked."

3.1

3.2

3.1–3.2 Narrative Parallels. *Julie & Julia:* Staging and composition emphasize similarities between the two women's stories.

The documentary *Hoop Dreams* makes a similar use of parallels. Two high school students from a black neighborhood in Chicago dream of becoming professional basketball players, and the film follows each one's pursuit of an athletic career. The film's form invites us to compare their personalities, the obstacles they face, and the choices they make. In addition, the film creates parallels between their high schools, their coaches, their parents, and older male relatives who vicariously pursue their own dreams of athletic glory. *Hoop Dreams,* like *Julie & Julia* and *Something Different,* remains a narrative film. Each of the parallel lines of action is organized by time, space, and causality. But parallelism allows the film to become more complex than it might have been had it concentrated on only one protagonist.

Telling the Story

We make sense of a narrative, then, by identifying its events and linking them by cause and effect, time, and space. We also look out for parallels that can shed light on the ongoing action. But there's a lot more to narrative than this bare-bones account. To dig deeper, let's again try to think like a filmmaker.

CREATIVE DECISIONS

How Would You Tell the Story?

You have a story. Let's say it's a romantic comedy following the development of a love affair. Your problem is: How to tell it?

For example, should you start at the beginning of the story, when the partners meet? You could trace the action chronologically from there, showing them falling in love, being separated, meeting other people, remeeting, and eventually being reunited as a couple in marriage. But you might consider another option. Suppose you break chronology and start your film with the couple's wedding day. Then you might flash back to the beginning, showing how they met, and then trace the love affair through its ups and downs.

But why stop your rearranging there? Why not start with the wedding day, flash back to the first meeting, then return to the wedding day, then flash back to the budding romance, then return to the wedding day, and so on? Instead of one long flashback framed by the wedding, you have several shorter ones that keep interrupting the wedding. Then you might ask: Who says the love-affair flashbacks have to be presented in chronological order? Maybe I can create more curiosity, or suspense, or surprise, or emotional engagement if I show the first meeting later in the film, out of chronological order. Perhaps just before the wedding, or just after their big bust-up? Although one event causes another, you don't have to respect 1-2-3 order.

While you're speculating about shuffling time periods, you might pause again. Wouldn't it be more engaging to start not with the wedding but with the couple's "darkest moment," the scene in which it seems they're never going to get together? Then flashing back to earlier, happier days could increase the suspense. Will they be reunited? That makes the wedding a sort of epilogue rather than the big event framing the overall action.

Each choice brings up further choices. If your flashbacks skip around a lot, you might worry about viewers' losing their bearings. So to help out, you might add superimposed titles identifying the time and place of the scene.

Time structure is only one of the storytelling choices you face. If you're planning the romantic comedy we sketched, from whose viewpoint will the tale be told? You could limit things to one character's standpoint, showing only what she or he knows about the unfolding action. *(500) Days of Summer* puts us firmly with the man who has fallen in love with the mysterious Summer. Alternatively, you could follow the more common convention of showing both members of the couple when they're alone or with other friends. You could mix in scenes of parents, coworkers, and the like. This asks your viewer to see the central relationship in a wider context.

Storytelling decisions about viewpoint involve what we'll be calling *narration.* Whatever the area of choice you face, you'll want to consider how the options affect the viewer. As we saw, presenting the story out of order could trigger curiosity or suspense. Confining us to what one character knows can enhance surprise, so that we learn new information only when he or she does.

■ ▪ ▪ ▪ ▪ ▪ ▪ ▪ ▪ ▪ ▫ ▫ ▫ ▫

Our romantic comedy is deeply unoriginal, but the point is just to show how filmmakers face choices in planning narrative form. Those choices involve time structure, narration, and other possibilities we'll examine.

Plot and Story

In our hypothetical movie, the love affair that runs from first meeting to wedding is what we'll be calling the **story.** The story is the chain of events in chronological order. But as we've seen, that story may be presented in various ways. If we use flashbacks instead of linear time, or if we decide to organize events around one character rather than another, or if we make other choices about presentation, we will be creating a different **plot.** As we've just seen, the same story can be presented in different ways—rendered as different plots—and each variant is likely to have different effects on the audience.

As viewers, we have direct access only to the plot that the filmmakers finally decided on. Yet eventually we arrive at an understanding of the underlying story. The filmmakers have built the plot from the story, but viewers build the story from the plot.

How do viewers do that? By making assumptions and inferences about what's presented. At the start of Alfred Hitchcock's *North by Northwest,* we know we are in Manhattan at rush hour. The cues stand out clearly: skyscrapers, bustling pedestrians, congested traffic **(3.3).** Then we watch Roger Thornhill as he leaves an elevator with his secretary, Maggie, and strides through the lobby, dictating memos **(3.4).** Already we can draw some conclusions. Thornhill is an executive who leads a busy life. We assume that before we saw Thornhill and Maggie, he was also dictating to her; we have come in on the middle of a string of events in time. We also assume that the dictating began in the office, before they got on the elevator. In other words, we infer causes, a temporal sequence, and another locale even though none of this information has been directly presented. We're probably not aware of making these inferences, but insofar as we understand what we see and hear, we are making them. The filmmaker has steered us to make them.

3.3

3.4

3.3–3.4 Depicted and inferred story events. Shots of hurrying Manhattan pedestrians in *North by Northwest* are followed by a shot introducing us to Roger Thornhill and his secretary. Viewers make inferences about the story and characters based on the information that is presented onscreen.

So the plot guides the viewer in building up a sense of all the relevant events, both the ones explicitly presented and those that must be inferred. In our *North by Northwest* example, the story would consist of at least two depicted events and two inferred ones. We can list them, putting the inferred events in parentheses:

(Roger Thornhill has a busy day at his office.)

Rush hour hits Manhattan.

(While dictating to his secretary, Maggie, Roger leaves the office, and they take the elevator.)

Still dictating, Roger gets off the elevator with Maggie and they stride through the lobby.

The total world of the story action is sometimes called the film's *diegesis* (the Greek word for "recounted story"). In the opening of *North by Northwest,* the traffic, streets, skyscrapers, and people we see, as well as the traffic, streets, skyscrapers, and people we assume to be offscreen, are all diegetic because they are assumed to exist in the world that the film depicts.

From the viewer's perspective, the *plot* consists of the action visibly and audibly present in the film before us. The plot includes, most centrally, all the story events that are directly depicted. In our *North by Northwest* example, only two story events are explicitly presented in the plot: rush hour and Roger Thornhill's dictating to Maggie as they leave the elevator. The plot also includes the information that characters may supply about earlier events in the story world, as when Roger mentions his many marriages.

Note, though, that the filmmaker may include material that lies *outside* the story world. For example, while the opening of *North by Northwest* is portraying rush hour in Manhattan, we also see the film's credits and hear orchestral music. Neither of these elements is diegetic, since they are brought in from outside the story world. The characters can't read the credits or hear the music. Credits and a film's score are thus *nondiegetic* elements. Similarly, in silent films, many of the intertitles don't report dialogue but rather comment on the characters or describe the location. These intertitles are nondiegetic. In Chapters 6 and 7, we consider how editing and sound can function nondiegetically.

Suppose Hitchcock had superimposed the words "New York City" over the traffic shots at the start of *North by Northwest,* in the way we considered adding dates to the scrambled scenes of our hypothetical rom-com. Such titles would be nondiegetic as well. (They aren't part of the story world; the characters couldn't read them.) Today superimposed titles are the most common sorts of nondiegetic inserts, but we can find more unusual ones. In *The Band Wagon,* we see the premiere of a hopelessly pretentious musical play. Through nondiegetic images, accompanied by a brooding chorus, the plot signals that the production bombed **(3.5–3.9).** The filmmakers have added nondiegetic material to the plot for comic effect.

From the standpoint of the filmmaker, the story is the sum total of all the events in the narrative. The storyteller can present some of these events directly (that is, display or mention them in the plot), can hint at events that are not presented, and can simply ignore other events. For instance, though we learn later in *North by Northwest* that Roger's mother is still close to him, we never learn what happened to his father. The filmmaker can also add nondiegetic material, as in the example from *The Band Wagon.* This is why we can say that the filmmaker makes a story into a plot.

The spectator's task is quite different. All we have before us is the plot—the arrangement of material in the film as it stands. We create the story in our minds, thanks to cues in the plot. And in telling someone about the movie we've just seen, we can summarize it in two ways: We can recap the story, or recap the plot.

We'll see that the story–plot distinction affects all three aspects of narrative: causality, time, and space. Each offers the filmmaker a huge array of choice for guiding the viewer's experience of the film.

3.5

3.6

3.7

3.8

3.9

3.5–3.9 Nondiegetic imagery in *The Band Wagon.* A hopeful investor in the play enters the theater (3.5), and the camera moves in on a poster predicting success for the musical (3.6). But three comic nondiegetic images reveal it to be a flop: ghostly figures on a boat (3.7), a skull in a desert (3.8), and an image referring to the slang expression that the play laid an egg (3.9).

Cause and Effect

If narrative depends so heavily on changes created by cause and effect, what kinds of things can function as causes in a narrative? Usually, the changes are brought about by characters. By triggering and reacting to events, characters play causal roles within the film's narrative form.

Characters as Causes   Most often, characters are persons, or at least entities like persons—Bugs Bunny or E.T. the extraterrestrial or the singing teapot in *Beauty and the Beast.* For our purposes here, Michael Moore is a character in *Roger and Me* no less than Roger Thornhill is in *North by Northwest,* even though Moore is a real person and Thornhill is fictional. In any narrative film, either fictional or documentary, characters create causes and register effects. Within the film's overall form, they make things happen and respond to events. Their actions and reactions contribute strongly to our engagement with the film.

Unlike characters in novels, film characters typically have a visible body. This is such a basic convention that we take it for granted, but it can be contested. Occasionally, a character is only a voice, as in *A Letter to Three Wives,* a film narrated by the woman who has sent a letter to three of her rivals. More disturbingly, in Luis Buñuel's *That Obscure Object of Desire,* one woman is portrayed by two actresses, and the physical differences between them may suggest different sides of her character. Todd Haynes takes this innovation further in *I'm Not There,* in which a folksinger is portrayed by actors of different ages, genders, and races.

Along with a body, a character has *traits:* attitudes, skills, habits, tastes, psychological drives, and any other qualities that distinguish him or her. Some characters, such as Mickey Mouse, may have only a few traits. When we say a character possesses several varying traits, some at odds with others, we tend to call that character complex, or three-dimensional, or well-developed. Sherlock Holmes, for instance, is a mass of traits. Some stem from his habits, such as his love of music or his addiction to cocaine, while others reflect his basic nature: his arrogance, his penetrating intelligence, his disdain for stupidity, his professional pride, his occasional gallantry.

As our love of gossip shows, we're curious about other humans, and we bring our people-watching skills to narratives. We're quick to assign traits to the characters onscreen, and usually the movie helps us out. Most characters wear their traits far more openly than people do in real life, and the plot presents situations that swiftly reveal them to us. The opening scene of *Raiders of the Lost Ark* throws Indiana Jones's personality into high relief. We see immediately that he's bold and resourceful, even a little impetuous. He's courageous, but he can feel fear. By unearthing ancient treasures for museums, he shows an admirable devotion to scientific knowledge. In a few minutes, his essential traits are presented straightforwardly, and we come to know and sympathize with him.

All the traits that Indiana Jones displays in the opening scene are relevant to later scenes in *Raiders*. In general, a character is given traits that will play causal roles in the overall story action. The second scene of Alfred Hitchcock's *The Man Who Knew Too Much* (1934) shows that the heroine, Jill, is an excellent shot with a rifle. For much of the film, this trait seems irrelevant to the action, but in the last scene, Jill is able to shoot one of the villains when a police marksman cannot manage it. Like most qualities assigned to characters, Jill's marksmanship serves a particular narrative function.

Not all causes and effects in narratives originate with characters. In the so-called disaster movies, an earthquake or tidal wave may precipitate a series of actions on the parts of the characters. The same principle holds when the shark in *Jaws* terrorizes a community. Still, once these natural occurrences set the situation up, human desires and goals usually enter the action to develop the narrative. In *Jaws,* the townspeople pursue a variety of strategies to deal with the shark, propelling the plot as they do so. The primary cause of the action in *Contagion* is a lethal virus spreading across the world, but the action concentrates on individual researchers struggling to find an antidote and on ordinary citizens trying to survive.

Hiding Causes, Hiding Effects   In general, the spectator actively seeks to connect events by means of cause and effect. Given an incident, we tend to imagine what might have caused it or what it might in turn cause. That is, we look for causal motivation. We have mentioned an instance of this in Chapter 2: In the scene from *My Man Godfrey,* a scavenger hunt serves as a cause that justifies the presence of a beggar at a society ball (see p. 63).

Causal motivation often involves the planting of information in advance of a scene, as we saw in the kitchen scene of *The Shining* (2.12, 2.13). In *L.A. Confidential,* the idealistic detective Exley confides in his cynical colleague Vincennes that the murder of his father had driven him to enter law enforcement. He had privately named the unknown killer "Rollo Tomasi," a name that he has turned into an emblem of all unpunished evil. This conversation may seem to offer only an insight into Exley's personality. Yet later, when the corrupt police chief Smith shoots Vincennes, the latter mutters "Rollo Tomasi" with his last breath. Later, the puzzled Smith asks Exley who Rollo Tomasi is. Exley's earlier conversation with Vincennes motivates his shocked realization that the dead Vincennes has fingered Smith as his killer. Near the end, when Smith is about to shoot Exley, Exley says that the chief is Rollo Tomasi. Thus an apparently minor detail returns as a major causal and thematic motif.

Most of what we have said about causality pertains to the plot's direct presentation of causes and effects. In *The Man Who Knew Too Much,* Jill is shown to be a good shot, and because of this, she can save her daughter. But the plot can also lead us to *infer* causes and effects, and thus build up a total story.

Consider the mystery story. A murder has been committed. That is, we know an effect but not the causes—the killer, the motive, and perhaps also the method. The mystery tale thus depends strongly on curiosity. We want to know about things that happened before the events that the plot presents to us. It's the detective's job to disclose, at the end, the missing causes—to name the killer, explain the motive, and reveal the method. That is, in the detective film, the climax of the plot (the action we see) is a revelation of prior incidents in the story (events we didn't see).

Although this pattern is most common in detective narratives, any film's plot can withhold causes and thus arouse our curiosity. Horror and science fiction films often leave us temporarily in the dark about what forces lurk behind certain events. Not until three-quarters of the way through *Alien* do we learn that the science officer Ash is a robot conspiring to protect the creature. In *Caché,* a married couple receives an anonymous videotape recording their daily lives. The film's plot shows them trying to discover who made it and why it was made. In general, whenever any film creates a mystery, the plot initially suppresses certain story causes and presents only enigmatic effects.

3.10 **Withholding story effects.** The final image of *The 400 Blows* leaves Antoine's future uncertain.

The plot may also present causes but withhold story *effects,* prompting suspense and uncertainty in the viewer. After Hannibal Lecter's attack on his guards in the Tennessee prison in *The Silence of the Lambs,* the police search of the building raises the possibility that a body lying on top of an elevator is the wounded Lecter. After an extended suspense scene, we learn that Lecter has switched clothes with a dead guard and escaped.

When a plot withholds crucial consequences at the ending, it can ask us to ponder possible outcomes. In the final moments of François Truffaut's *The 400 Blows,* the boy Antoine has escaped from a reformatory and runs to the seashore. The camera zooms in on his face, and the frame freezes **(3.10).** The plot does not reveal if Antoine is captured and brought back, leaving us to speculate on what might happen in his future. As in *Bicycle Thieves* (pp. 484–485), the story of *400 Blows* is, by the conventions of mainstream cinema, incomplete.

Time

Causes and their effects are basic to narrative, but they take place in time. Our story–plot distinction helps us to understand how filmmakers use narrative form to manipulate time.

As we watch a film, we construct story time on the basis of what the plot presents. For instance, a plot may present story events out of chronological order. In *Citizen Kane,* we see a man's death before we see his youth, and we must build up a chronological version of his life. Even if events are shown in chronological order, most plots don't show every detail from beginning to end. We assume that the characters spend uneventful time sleeping, eating, traveling, and so forth, so the periods containing such irrelevant action can be skipped over. Another possibility is to have the plot present the same story event more than once, as when a character recalls a traumatic incident. In John Woo's *The Killer,* an accident in the opening scene blinds a singer, and later we see the same event again and again as the protagonist regretfully thinks back to it.

In short, filmmakers must decide how the film's plot will treat chronological *order* and temporal *duration* and *frequency.* In turn, the viewer must actively pick up the cues about these time-based factors. Each one harbors important artistic possibilities.

Temporal Order: How Are Events Sequenced?   Filmmakers can choose to present events out of story **order.** A flashback, like the ones we proposed for our hypothetical romantic comedy, is simply a portion of the story that the plot presents out of chronological sequence. In *Edward Scissorhands,* we first see the Winona Ryder character as an old woman telling her granddaughter a bedtime story. Most of the film then shows events that occurred when the old lady was in high school. Likewise,

The Hangover starts at a point of crisis, when the bridegroom's buddies report that he's missing. The plot then flashes back to them assembling for their bachelor party.

Flashbacks usually don't confuse us, because we mentally rearrange the events into chronological order: teenage years precede old age, the hangover comes after a night of partying. If story events can be thought of as 1-2-3-4, then the plot that uses a *flashback* presents something like 2-1-3-4, or 3-1-2-4. The filmmaker can also shuffle story order by employing a *flashforward*. This pattern moves from present to future, then back to the present, and could be represented as 1-2-4-3. In either case, given the plot order we figure out story order.

Even a simple reordering of scenes can create complex effects. The plot of Quentin Tarantino's *Pulp Fiction* begins with a couple deciding to rob the diner they're sitting in. This scene actually takes place somewhat late in the story's chronology, but the viewer doesn't learn this until the final scene. At that point, the robbery interrupts a dialogue involving other, more central, characters eating in the same diner. Just by taking a scene that occurs late in the story and placing it at the start of the plot, Tarantino creates a surprise that maintains our interest through the film's last moments.

Tarantino was influenced by the film noir trend of the 1940s and 1950s, which exploited time ordering in ingenious ways. *D.O.A.* (1949) shows how flashbacks can shape the viewer's expectations across a whole film. A man strides into a police station to report a murder. "Who was murdered?" asks the officer. The man replies: "I was." As he starts to explain, we move into an extended flashback. The earliest story action in the past is rather innocuous and slowly paced. Had the plot presented the story in chronological order, viewers might have found these scenes flat. But knowing that the protagonist is dying makes us vigilant. Every encounter he has puts us on the alert: Is this what will kill him? Our anticipation wouldn't have been aroused so keenly if the story had been told in 1-2-3 order.

CONNECT TO THE BLOG
www.davidbordwell.net/blog

Mark Romanek learned the *D.O.A* lesson in directing *One Hour Photo*. "Creating suspense through film form" discusses how, after preview screenings fizzled, Romanek rearranged his plot to start late in the story action and to flash back to the beginning. "Now the audience is paying closer attention."

Temporal Duration: How Long Do the Events Take? The plot of *North by Northwest* presents four crowded days and nights in the life of Roger Thornhill. But the story stretches back far before that, indicated by the information about the past that is revealed in the course of the plot. The story events include Roger's past marriages, the U.S. Intelligence Agency's plot to create a false agent named George Kaplan, and the villain Van Damm's smuggling activities.

In general, a film's plot selects only certain stretches of story **duration.** The filmmakers might decide to concentrate on a short, relatively cohesive time span, as *North by Northwest* does. Or they might let their plot unfold across many years, highlighting significant stretches of time in that period. *Citizen Kane* shows us the protagonist in his youth, skips over some time to show him as a young man, skips over more time to show him middle-aged, and so forth. The sum of all these slices of *story* duration yields an overall *plot* duration.

But we need one more distinction. Watching a movie takes time—20 minutes or two hours or seven-plus hours (as Béla Tarr's *Satan's Tango* does). So there's a third duration involved in a narrative film, which we can call *screen* duration. The relationships among story duration, plot duration, and screen duration are complicated, but for our purposes, we can say this. The filmmaker can manipulate screen duration independently of the overall story duration and plot duration. For example, *North by Northwest* has an overall story duration of several years (including all relevant story events), an overall plot duration of four days and nights, and a screen duration of about 136 minutes.

Just as plot duration selects from story duration, so screen duration selects from overall plot duration. In *North by Northwest,* only portions of the plot's four days and nights are shown to us. An interesting counterexample is *Twelve Angry Men,* the story of a jury deliberating a murder case. The 95 minutes of the movie approximate the same stretch of time in its characters' lives.

At a more specific level, the filmmaker can use screen duration to override story time. For example, screen duration can *expand* story duration. A famous instance is that of the raising of the bridges in Sergei Eisenstein's *October.* Here an event that takes only a few moments in the story is stretched out to several minutes of screen time by means of the technique of film editing. As a result, this action gains a tremendous emphasis. The plot can also use screen duration to compress story time. A process taking hours or days is often condensed into a few swift shots. These examples suggest that film techniques play a central role in creating screen duration, and we'll see how in Chapters 5 and 6.

Temporal Frequency: How Often Do We See or Hear an Event?

Most commonly, a story event is presented only once in the plot. Occasionally, however, a single story event may appear twice or even more in the plot treatment. If we see an event early in a film's plot, and then, later in the plot, there is a flashback to that event, we see that same event twice. Some films use multiple narrators, each of whom describes the same event; again, we see it take place several times. This increased **frequency** may allow us to see the same action in several ways. Repetition can take place simply on the soundtrack. Sometimes only a single line of dialogue will reappear, haunting a character who can't escape the memory of that moment.

When a plot repeats a story event, the aim is often to provide new information. This occurs in *For a Few Dollars More,* in which the repeated scene gets expanded more fully each time that characters recall it. In *Amores Perros,* a traffic accident is shown three times, and each iteration traces how a different person is affected by the crash.

The manipulations of story order, duration, and frequency in the plot illustrate how we actively participate in making sense of the narrative film. The filmmaker designs the plot to prompt us about chronological sequence, the time span of the actions, and the number of times an event occurs. It's up to the viewer to make assumptions and inferences and to form expectations. Fortunately, we can usually put things together by appealing to our ordinary sense of time and cause and effect. A flashback, for instance, is often motivated as a character's memory. Other cues, such as clothing, age, settings, and the like can help us sort out a film's story time.

Still, some filmmakers have offered quite complicated time schemes. In *The Usual Suspects,* a petty criminal spins an elaborate tale of his gang's activities to an FBI agent. His recounting unfolds in many flashbacks, some of which repeat events we witnessed in the opening scene. Yet a final twist reveals that some of the flashbacks must have contained lies, and we must piece together both the chronology of events and the story's real cause–effect chain. Christopher Nolan's *Inception* creates several stories-within-stories, all unfolding simultaneously in dream-time, but the plot makes each one take place at a different rate. A second in one dream might last many minutes in another, so that we have several scales of plot duration. Through magic, *Harry Potter and the Prisoner of Azkaban* permits action we've already seen to run again, with different results **(3.11).**

> ❝ The multiple points of view replaced the linear story. Watching a repeated action or an intersection happen again and again . . . they hold the audience in the story. It's like watching a puzzle unfold."
>
> —Gus van Sant, director, on *Elephant*

3.11 Creating complex time schemes. In *Harry Potter and the Prisoner of Azkaban,* Harry and his friend Hermione use a magical device to go back in time. Here they watch themselves playing out the action from a scene we had witnessed earlier in the film.

Playing Games with Story Time

For both filmmakers and viewers, reconstructing story time on the basis of the plot might be seen as a sort of game. Most Hollywood films make this game fairly simple. Still, just as we enjoy learning the rules of new games, in unusual films, we can enjoy the challenge of unpredictable orderings of story events.

Pulp Fiction (1994) popularized "broken timelines" for a new generation of filmmakers and moviegoers. The film's plot begins and ends with stages of a restaurant holdup, seemingly a conventional frame situation in the present. Yet in fact the final event in the story, the flight of the Bruce Willis character and his girlfriend from Los Angeles, is not the final scene in the plot. The reordering of events is startling and confusing at first, but it becomes dramatically effective in forcing us to rethink scenes we have seen earlier.

The success of *Pulp Fiction* encouraged American filmmakers to play more freely with story time. *Go* (1999) presents the events of a single night three times, each time from a different character's point of view. We cannot figure out what happened until the end, since various events are withheld from the first version and shown in the second or third. Ten years later, audiences had become quite familiar with such "replay" plots. *Vantage Point* repeats an assassination and bombing, with each version clarifying a bit more of what actually happened in the story.

Replay plots can tease the viewer into fitting everything together. *Out of Sight* begins with an inept bank robber who falls in love with the FBI agent who pursues him. As their oddball romance proceeds, there is a string of flashbacks not motivated by any character's memory. These seem to involve a separate story line, and their purpose is puzzling until the film's second half. Then the last flashback, perhaps a character's recollection, loops back to the action that had begun the film and explains the main events. As often happens, the filmmaker uses cause-effect cues to help the viewer straighten out the broken timeline.

If replay films work to tease us with what happened in the past, filmmakers can use science fiction or fantasy premises to present alternative futures. These are sometimes called "what if?" narratives. Such films typically present a situation, then show how the story might proceed along different cause–effect chains if one factor is changed. *Sliding Doors* shows the heroine, Helen, fired from her job and heading home to her apartment, where her boyfriend is in bed with another woman. We see Helen entering the subway and catching her train, but then the action runs backward and she arrives on the platform again, this time bumping into a child on the stairs and missing the train. The rest of the film's plot moves between two alternative futures for Helen. By catching the train, Helen arrives in time to discover her boyfriend's affair and moves out. By missing the train, Helen arrives after the other woman has left and stays with her faithless lover. The plot shifts back and forth between these

alternative cause–effect chains before dovetailing them at the end.

Groundhog Day (1993) helped popularize what-if plots. On February 1, an obnoxious weatherman, Phil Connor, travels to Punxsutawney to cover the famous Groundhog Day ceremonies. He then finds himself trapped in February 2, which repeats over and over. The variants depend on how Phil acts—some days behaving frivolously, some days breaking laws **(3.12–3.13)**, and later trying to improve himself. Only after many such days does he become an admirable character, and the repetitions mysteriously stop.

Neither *Sliding Doors* nor *Groundhog Day* provides any explanation for the forking of its protagonist's life into various paths. We simply must assume that some higher power has intervened to improve the character's situation. Other films motivate the alternative futures by a piece of technology. The three *Back to the Future* films (1985, 1989, 1990) posit that Marty's friend Doc has invented a time-travel machine, and this gadget permits complicated crisscrossings

3.12

3.13

3.12–3.13 "What if?" narrative—replaying the same day. During one repetition of February 2 in *Groundhog Day*, Phil tests whether he can commit crimes. He's tossed in jail in the evening (3.12), only to wake up, as on other Groundhog Days, back at the bed-and-breakfast inn (3.13).

of cause and effect. In the first film, the machine accidentally transports Marty back to 1955. By accidentally thwarting his parents' romance, Marty endangers his own existence in 1985. Eventually, Marty induces his parents to fall in love and returns safely to 1985, where his life has been improved as a result of his first time trip.

But in the second *Back to the Future* installment, events in Marty's life in 2015 have effects in 1955. The villain Biff uses the time machine to travel back and change what happened then. In the process he wreaks harm on Doc and Marty's family. Marty must again travel back to 1955 to stop Biff from changing events. At the end of Part II, Marty becomes trapped in 1955, while Doc is accidentally sent back to 1885. Marty joins him there in Part III for another set of threatened changes to the future. Although the films maintain a unified cause–effect chain, the story becomes so convoluted that at one point Doc diagrams events for Marty (and us) on a blackboard. Variations on Doc's time-machine device for creating alternative futures can be found in *The Jacket, Déjà vu,* and *Source Code.*

The game of what-if emerged outside the United States as well. In 1981, Polish director Krzysztof Kieslowski made *Blind Chance,* which showed three sets of consequences depending on whether the protagonist caught a train at the beginning or not. Unlike *Sliding Doors,* however, *Blind Chance* presents these alternative futures as self-contained stories, one after the other. The same approach appears in *Run Lola Run.* Here the heroine's desperate attempts to replace a large sum that her inept boyfriend owes to drug dealers are shown as three alternative stories. Each one ends very differently because of small changes of action on Lola's part.

Although what-if premises make it more difficult for us to piece story events together, filmmakers usually give us enough clues along the way to keep us from frustration. Usually, the film does not provide a huge number of alternative futures—perhaps only two or three. Within these futures, the cause–effect chain remains linear, so we can piece it together. Characters sometimes point out the events that have changed their lives, as with Doc's blackboard explanation in *Back to the Future II.* In *Sliding Doors,* Helen remarks: "If only I had just caught that bloody train, it'd never have happened." The characters and settings tend to remain quite consistent for all the

CONNECT TO THE BLOG
www.davidbordwell.net/blog

We examine a recent what-if narrative in "Forking tracks: *Source Code.*" *Inception* presents a complex plot involving dreams within dreams. We look at its exposition, motivation, and embedded plotlines in "*Inception*: Dream a little dream within a dream with me" and a follow-up, "Revisiting *Inception.*"

alternative story lines—though often differences of appearance are introduced to help us keep track of events (**3.14, 3.15**). Moreover, the individual story lines tend to parallel one another. In all three presentations of events in *Run Lola Run,* the goal of getting money is the same, even though the progression and outcomes are different. The final version of events tends to give us the impression of being the

3.14

3.15

3.14–3.15 Cues for alternative futures in *Sliding Doors.* In one story line Helen gets her hair cut short (3.14). This helps distinguish her from the Helen of the other story line, who keeps her hair long (3.15). Before the haircut, a forehead bandage was a crucial cue.

definitive one, and so what-if films usually achieve a sense of closure.

Replay and what-if films appeal to the way we think in ordinary life. Our minds sometimes revisit certain events, and we speculate about how our lives would have changed if a single moment had been different. We easily understand the sort of game that these films proffer, and we're willing to play it.

More and more, however, *puzzle films* have denied us this degree of unity and clarity. Here filmmakers create perplexing patterns of story time or causality, trusting that viewers will search for clues by rewatching the movie. An example is *Memento,* which presents the hero's investigation along two time tracks. Brief black-and-white scenes show an ongoing present, with story action moving forward chronologically. The more extensive scenes, which are in color, move *backward* through time, so the first plot event we see is the final story event, the second plot event is the next-to-last story event, and so on. This tactic reflects the hero's loss of short-term memory, but it also challenges viewers to piece everything together. At the same time, there are enough uncertainties about the hero's memories to lead viewers to speculate that some mysteries remain unresolved at the close.

The DVD format, which allows random access to scenes, encouraged filmmakers along this path. So did the Internet. Websites still buzz with speculations about what really happened in *Donnie Darko, Identity, Primer, The Butterfly Effect,* and *Inception.* Like other films that twist or break up story time, puzzle movies seek to engross us in the dynamic game of narrative form.

Space

In film narrative, space is usually an important factor. Events occur in particular locales, such as Kansas or Oz; the Flint, Michigan, of *Roger and Me;* or the Manhattan of *North by Northwest.* We'll consider setting in more detail when we examine mise-en-scene in Chapter 4, but we ought briefly to note how plot and story can manipulate space.

Normally, the locale of the story action is also that of the plot, but sometimes the plot leads us to imagine story spaces that are never shown. In Otto Preminger's *Exodus,* one scene is devoted to Dov Landau's interrogation by a terrorist organization he wants to join. Dov reluctantly tells his questioners of his duties in a Nazi concentration camp (**3.16**). Although the film never shows this locale through a flashback, much of the scene's emotional power depends on our using our imagination to fill in Dov's sketchy description of how he survived.

Further, we can introduce an idea akin to the concept of screen duration. Besides story space and plot space, cinema employs screen space: the visible space within the frame. Just as screen duration selects certain plot spans for presentation, so screen space selects portions of plot space. We'll consider screen space and offscreen space when we analyze framing in Chapter 5.

3.16 **Imagining offscreen locales.** In *Exodus,* Dov Landau recounts his traumatic stay in a concentration camp. Instead of presenting this through a flashback, the narration dwells on his face, leaving us to visualize his ordeal.

Openings, Closings, and Patterns of Development

Our early experiment in romantic-comedy plotting began with beginnings and endings: How will you start your film? How will you conclude it? This echoed our discussion of formal development in Chapter 2, where we suggested that it's often useful to compare beginnings and endings. A narrative usually presents a series of changes from an initial situation to a final situation, and by considering how that pattern works, we can better understand the film.

Openings   A film does not just start, it *begins*. The opening provides a basis for what is to come and initiates us into the narrative. It raises our expectations by setting up a specific range of possible causes for what we see. Indeed, the first quarter or so of a film's plot is sometimes referred to as the *setup*.

Very often, the film begins by telling us about the characters and their situations before any major actions occur. Alternatively, the plot may seek to arouse curiosity by bringing us into a series of actions that has already started. (This is called opening *in medias res,* a Latin phrase meaning "in the middle of things.") The viewer speculates on possible causes of the events presented. *Close Encounters of the Third Kind* begins with investigators arriving in the desert to study World War II airplanes. An *in medias res* opening grabs our interest, but as Robert Towne notes (p. 51), sooner or later the filmmaker has to explain what led up to these events.

In either case, some of the actions that took place before the plot started—often called the *backstory*—will be stated or suggested so that we can understand what's coming later. The portion of the plot that lays out the backstory and the initial situation is called the *exposition*. Usually exposition takes place early in the film, but the filmmaker may postpone chunks of exposition for the sake of suspense and more immediate impact. James Cameron and Gale Anne Hurd did this in their screenplay for *The Terminator*. For nearly 40 minutes the plot provides chases, gunplay, and glimpses of a war-torn future before the fighter Reese explains what has caused the plight that he and Sarah Connor are in.

> " No exposition except under heat, and break it up at that."
> —Raymond Chandler, novelist and screenwriter for *Double Indemnity*

Development Sections   As a film's plot proceeds, the causes and effects create patterns of development. Some patterns are quite common. Change is essential to narrative, and a common pattern traces a *change in knowledge*. Very often, a character learns something in the course of the action, with the most crucial knowledge coming at the final turning point of the plot. In *Witness*, when John Book, hiding out on an Amish farm, learns that his partner has been killed and his boss has betrayed him, his rage leads to a climactic shoot-out.

Another common pattern of development is the *goal-oriented* plot, in which a character takes steps to achieve an object or condition. Plots based on *searches* would be instances of the goal plot. In *Raiders of the Lost Ark,* the protagonists try to find the Ark of the Covenant; in *North by Northwest,* Roger Thornhill looks for George Kaplan. Another variation on the goal-oriented plot pattern is the *investigation,* itself a kind of search. Here the protagonist's goal is not an object, but information, usually about mysterious causes.

Time may also provide plot patterns. A framing situation in the present may initiate a series of flashbacks showing how events led up to the present situation, as in *The Usual Suspects'* flashbacks. *Hoop Dreams* is organized around the two main characters' high school careers, with each part of the film devoted to a year of their lives. The plot may also create a specific duration for the action—a *deadline*. In *Back to the Future,* the hero must synchronize his time machine with a bolt of lightning at a specific moment in order to return to 1985. This creates a goal toward which he must struggle. Space can structure plot development, too, particularly when the action is confined to a single locale, such as a home (*Long Day's Journey into Night*). The film *Lebanon* confines its action to the interior of a military tank.

3.17 Time and space in plot patterning. In *Mr. Hulot's Holiday,* Hulot's aged, noisy car has a flat tire that breaks up a funeral—consistent with a comic pattern in which the vacationing Mr. Hulot repeatedly disturbs townspeople and other guests.

CONNECT TO THE BLOG
www.davidbordwell.net/blog

How do we learn to recognize that an ending is coming? Starting from an anecdote about a three-year-old watching *Snow White and the Seven Dwarfs,* we speculate on this subject in "Molly wanted more."

Any particular plot may combine these patterns. Many films built around a journey, such as *The Wizard of Oz* or *North by Northwest,* also involve deadlines. Jacques Tati's *Mr. Hulot's Holiday* uses both spatial and temporal patterns to structure its comic plot. The plot confines itself to a beachside resort and its neighboring areas, and it consumes one week of a summer vacation. Each day certain routines recur: morning exercise, lunch, afternoon outings, dinner, evening entertainment. Much of the film's humor relies on the way that Mr. Hulot alienates the other guests and the townspeople by disrupting their ingrained habits **(3.17).** Although cause and effect still operate in *Mr. Hulot's Holiday,* time and space are central to the plot's formal patterning.

Any pattern of development will encourage the viewer to create specific expectations. As the film trains the viewer in its particular form, these expectations become more and more precise. Dorothy's trip through Oz is hardly a sightseeing tour. Once we understand her desire to go home, each step of her journey (to the Emerald City, to the Witch's castle, to the Emerald City again) is seen as delaying or furthering her goal.

In any film, the middle portion may delay an expected outcome. When Dorothy at last reaches the Wizard, he sets up a new obstacle for her by demanding the Witch's broom. *North by Northwest*'s journey plot constantly postpones Roger Thornhill's discovery of the Kaplan hoax, and this, too, creates suspense. The pattern of development may also create surprise, the cheating of an expectation, as when Dorothy discovers that the Wizard is a fraud or when Thornhill sees the minion Leonard fire point-blank at his boss Van Damm. Patterns of development encourage the spectator to form long-term expectations that can be delayed, cheated, or gratified.

Climaxes and Closings   A film doesn't simply stop; it *ends.* The plot will typically resolve its causal issues by bringing the development to a high point, or *climax.* In the climax, the action is presented as having a narrow range of possible outcomes. At the climax of *North by Northwest,* Roger and Eve are dangling off Mount Rushmore, and there are only two possibilities: they will fall, or they will be saved.

Because the climax focuses possible outcomes so narrowly, it typically serves to settle the causal issues that have run through the film. In the documentary *Primary,* the climax takes place on election night; both Kennedy and Humphrey await the voters' verdict and finally learn the winner. In *Jaws,* battles with the shark climax in the destruction of the boat, the death of Captain Quint, the apparent death of Hooper, and Brody's final victory. In such films, the ending resolves, or closes off, the chains of cause and effect.

Emotionally, the climax aims to lift the viewer to a high degree of tension. Since the viewer knows that there are relatively few ways the action can be resolved, she or he can hope for a fairly specific outcome. When Brody slays the shark and discovers that Hooper has survived, their relief echoes ours. In the climax of many films, formal resolution coincides with an emotional satisfaction.

A few narratives, however, are deliberately anticlimactic. After creating expectations about how the cause–effect chain will be resolved, the film scotches them by refusing to settle things definitely. One famous example is the last shot of *The 400 Blows* (p. 81). In Michelangelo Antonioni's *L'Eclisse* ("The Eclipse"), the two lovers vow to meet for a final reconciliation but aren't shown doing so. When the filmmaker has chosen to let the ending remain open, the plot leaves us uncertain about the final consequences of the story events. The absence of a clear-cut climax and resolution may encourage us to imagine what might happen next or to reflect on other ways in which our expectations might have been fulfilled.

Narration: The Flow of Story Information

In looking at how a filmmaker tells a story, we've emphasized matters of plot structure: how the parts, from beginning to end, are fitted together to shape the viewer's experience. Filmic storytelling involves decisions about another sort of plot organization. Back when we were sketching alternatives for a romantic comedy (p. 75), we also faced the question of whether to build the scenes around one member of the couple, both members, or the couple and other characters around them. We could tell the same story from different characters' perspectives. The story of Little Red Riding Hood will be very different depending on whether we attach ourselves to the girl or to the wolf.

This means deciding what information to give the spectator, and when to supply it. Should we restrict the viewer just to what the character knows? Or should we give the viewer more information than the character has? In a stalking scene, should we show just the person being pursued, watching and listening for a threat we never see? Or should we show both the victim shrinking away and the stalker in pursuit? There is no right or wrong answer. The choice depends on the effect the filmmaker wants to achieve. What is clear is that the filmmaker can't avoid choosing how much information to reveal and when to reveal it.

Similarly, we might ask how objective or subjective our scene should be. Should we show only how characters behave, without any attempt to get inside their heads? Or should we add voice-over monologues that expose what they're thinking, or point-of-view shots that show what they can see? Should we try to dramatize their dreams, fantasies, or hallucinations? Again, it's a forced choice, and again we can imagine presenting the same story in a plot that is deeply subjective or one that is more objective.

These decisions involve **narration,** the plot's way of distributing story information in order to achieve specific effects. Narration is the moment-by-moment process that guides us in building the story out of the plot. Many factors enter into narration, but the most important ones for our purposes involve the factors we've just sketched out: the *range* and the *depth* of story information that the plot presents.

Range of Story Information: Restricted or Unrestricted?

D. W. Griffith's *The Birth of a Nation* begins by recounting how slaves were brought to America and how people debated the need to free them. The plot then shows two families, the northern Stoneman family and the southern Camerons. The plot also dwells on political matters, including Lincoln's hope of averting civil war. From the start, then, our range of knowledge is very broad. The plot takes us across historical periods, regions of the country, and various groups of characters. This breadth of story information continues throughout the film. When Ben Cameron founds the Ku Klux Klan, we know about it at the moment the idea strikes him, long before the other characters learn of it. At the climax, we know that the Klan is riding to rescue several characters besieged in a cabin, but the besieged people do not know this. On the whole, in *The Birth of a Nation,* the narration is very *unrestricted*. We know more, we see and hear more, than any of the characters can. Such extremely knowledgeable narration is often called *omniscient* ("all-knowing") narration.

Now consider the plot of Howard Hawks's *The Big Sleep*. The film begins with the detective Philip Marlowe visiting General Sternwood, who wants to hire him. We learn about the case as Marlowe does. Throughout the rest of the film, he is present in every scene. With hardly any exceptions, we don't see or hear anything that he can't see and hear. The narration is *restricted* to what Marlowe knows.

Each alternative offers certain advantages. *The Birth of a Nation* seeks to present a panoramic vision of a period in American history (based on a racist ideology).

CONNECT TO THE BLOG
www.davidbordwell.net/blog

We examine the idea of restricting the narration to what one character knows in "Alignment, allegiance, and murder."

> **"** In the first section [of *Reservoir Dogs*], up until Mr. Orange shoots Mr. Blonde, the characters have far more information about what's going on than you have—and they have conflicting information. Then the Mr. Orange sequence happens and that's a great leveler. You start getting caught up with exactly what's going on, and in the third part, when you go back into the warehouse for the climax you are totally ahead of everybody—you know far more than any one of the characters."
>
> —Quentin Tarantino, director

CONNECT TO THE BLOG
www.davidbordwell.net/blog

Cloverfield uses an unusually restricted narration, confining itself to a video recording shot by the main characters. See our analysis, "A behemoth from the Dead Zone."

Omniscient narration is thus essential to creating the sense of many destinies intertwined with the fate of the country. Had Griffith restricted narration the way *The Big Sleep* does, we would have learned story information solely through one character—say, Ben Cameron. We could not witness the prologue scene, or the scenes in Lincoln's office, or most of the battle episodes, or the scene of Lincoln's assassination, since Ben is present at none of these events. The plot would now concentrate on one man's experience of the Civil War and Reconstruction.

Similarly, *The Big Sleep* benefits from its restricted narration. By limiting us to Marlowe's range of knowledge, the film can create curiosity and surprise. Restricted narration is important to mystery films, since such films engage our interest by hiding important causes. Confining the plot to an investigator's range of knowledge plausibly motivates concealing important story information. *The Big Sleep* could have been less restricted if the screenwriter had alternated scenes of Marlowe's investigation with scenes that show the gambling boss, Eddie Mars, planning his crimes. But this would have given away some of the mystery. In both *The Birth of a Nation* and *The Big Sleep,* the narration's range of knowledge functions to elicit particular reactions from the viewer.

Range of Knowledge: A Matter of Degree

Unrestricted narration and restricted narration aren't watertight categories but rather two ends of a continuum. A film may present a broader range of knowledge than does *The Big Sleep* and still not attain the omniscience of *The Birth of a Nation.*

Early scenes of *North by Northwest,* for instance, confine us pretty much to what Roger Thornhill sees and knows. After he flees from the United Nations building, however, the plot takes us to Washington, where the members of the U.S. Intelligence Agency discuss the situation. Here the viewer learns something that Roger won't learn for some time: the man he seeks, George Kaplan, doesn't exist. From then on, we have a greater range of knowledge than Roger does. And we know a bit more than the Agency's staff: we know exactly how the mix-up took place. But we still don't know many other things that the narration could have divulged in the scene in Washington. For instance, the Agency's staff members don't identify the secret agent they have working under Van Damm's nose.

This oscillation between restricted and unrestricted narration is common in films. Typically the plot shifts from character to character, giving us a little more than any one character knows while still withholding some crucial items from us. Even if the plot is focused on a single protagonist, the narration usually includes a few scenes that the character isn't present to witness. *Tootsie*'s narration remains almost entirely attached to actor Michael Dorsey, but a few shots show his acquaintances shopping or watching him on television.

Lebanon, set during the June 1982 Israeli-Lebanese war, comes very close to purely restricted narration. Apart from the beginning and ending, the entire film is set inside a tank, where we are limited to what the four team members know. Usually films with such strong attachments to characters cheat a little by cutting to action taking place outside. Here there is no violation of the setting **(3.18, 3.19).** Necessary information from outside comes via radio communications. Director Samuel Moaz has said that his goal was to make audience members experience young soldiers' sense of the horror of war and their oppressive confinement. "You see only what they see. You know only what they know." Yet there are still moments when one soldier's reactions aren't noticed by the others, so we gain a slightly wider range of knowledge than any one character has.

Analyzing Range of Narration

An easy way to analyze the range of narration is to ask, *Who knows what when?* This question applies to the characters and the spectator as well. At any given moment, we can ask if we the audience knows more than, less than, or as much as the characters do. Sometimes we may get information that *no* character possesses. We shall see this happen at the end of *Citizen Kane.*

3.18

3.19

3.18–3.19 **Severely restricted range of knowledge.** In *Lebanon,* we see the world outside a tank as the characters do, through a gunner's crosshairs (3.18) or when the hatch is briefly opened (3.19).

Filmmakers can achieve powerful effects by manipulating the range of story information. Restricted narration tends to create greater curiosity and surprise for the viewer. For instance, if a character is exploring a sinister house, and we see and hear no more than the character does, a sudden revelation of a hand thrusting out from a doorway will startle us.

In contrast, as Hitchcock pointed out, a dose of unrestricted narration helps to build suspense. He explained it this way to François Truffaut:

> We are now having a very innocent little chat. Let us suppose that there is a bomb underneath this table between us. Nothing happens, and then all of a sudden, "Boom!" There is an explosion. The public is surprised, but prior to this surprise, it has seen an absolutely ordinary scene, of no special consequence. Now, let us take a suspense situation. The bomb is underneath the table and the public knows it, probably because they have seen the anarchist place it there. The public is aware that the bomb is going to explode at one o'clock and there is a clock in the decor. The public can see that it is a quarter to one. In these conditions this innocuous conversation

" Narrative tension is primarily about withholding information."
—Ian McEwan, novelist

becomes fascinating because the public is participating in the scene. The audience is longing to warn the characters on the screen: "You shouldn't be talking about such trivial matters. There's a bomb beneath you and it's about to explode!"

In the first case we have given the public fifteen seconds of surprise at the moment of the explosion. In the second case we have provided them with fifteen minutes of suspense. The conclusion is that whenever possible the public must be informed.

Hitchcock put his theory into practice. In *Psycho,* Lila Crane explores the Bates mansion in much the same way as our hypothetical character is doing above. There are isolated moments of surprise as she discovers odd information about Norman and his mother. But the overall effect of the sequence is built on suspense because we know, as Lila does not, that Mrs. Bates is in the house. (Actually, as in *North by Northwest,* our knowledge isn't completely accurate, but during Lila's investigation, we believe it to be.) As in Hitchcock's anecdote, our greater range of knowledge creates suspense because we can anticipate events that the character cannot. Once more, the filmmaker guides the viewer's expectations.

Depth of Story Information: Objective or Subjective?

A film's narration manipulates not only the range of knowledge but also the depth of our knowledge. The filmmaker must decide how far to plunge into a character's psychological states. As with restricted and unrestricted narration, there is a spectrum between objectivity and subjectivity.

A plot might confine us wholly to information about what characters say and do. Here the narration is relatively *objective.* Or a film's plot may give us access to what characters see and hear. The filmmaker might give us shots taken from a character's optical standpoint, the **point-of-view (POV) shot.** For instance, in *North by Northwest,* point-of-view editing is used as we see Roger Thornhill crawl up to Van Damm's window **(3.20–3.22).** Or we might hear sounds as the character would hear

3.20

3.21

3.22

3.20–3.22 Perceptual subjectivity in *North by Northwest.* Roger Thornhill looks in Van Damm's window (objective narration; 3.20), and an optical point-of-view shot follows (perceptual subjectivity; 3.21). This is followed by another shot of Roger looking (objectivity again; 3.22).

them, what sound recordists call *sound perspective*. In short, through either sight or sound, the filmmaker gives us what we might call *perceptual subjectivity*.

The filmmaker can go deeper, beyond the character's senses and into her or his mind. We can call this *mental subjectivity*. We might hear an internal voice reporting the character's thoughts, or we might see the character's inner images, representing memory, fantasy, dreams, or hallucinations. In *Slumdog Millionaire*, the hero is a contestant on a quiz show, but his concentration is often interrupted by brief shots showing his memories, particularly one image of the woman he loves **(3.23–3.24).** Here Jamal's memory motivates flashbacks to earlier story events.

Either sort of subjectivity may be signaled through particular film techniques. If a character is drunk, or drugged, the filmmakers may render those perceptual states through slow motion, blurred imagery, or distorted sound. Similar techniques may suggest a dream or hallucination.

But some imaginary actions may not be so strongly marked. Another scene in *Slumdog Millionaire* shows Jamal reuniting with his gangster brother Salim atop a skyscraper under construction. Jamal hurls himself at Salim, and we see shots of both falling from the building **(3.25–3.26).** But the next shot presents Jamal still on the skyscraper, glaring at Salim **(3.27).** Now we realize that the images of the falling men

3.23

3.24

3.23–3.24 Memories motivate flashbacks. Early in *Slumdog Millionaire*, it's established that during the quiz show (3.23) Jamal recalls his past—most often, his glimpse of Latika at the train station (3.24).

3.25

3.26

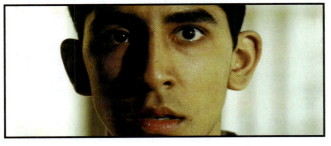

3.27

3.25–3.27 Suppressed cues for subjectivity in *Slumdog Millionaire.* Furious with Salim, Jamal grabs him and rushes toward the edge of the building (3.25). Several shots present their fall (3.26), but then the narration cuts back to Jamal, glaring at Salim (3.27). This shot reveals that he only imagined killing both of them.

were purely mental, representing Jamal's rage. Because the shots weren't marked as subjective, we briefly thought that their fall was really taking place.

Typically, moments of perceptual and mental subjectivity come in bursts. They tend to be embedded in a framework of objective narration. Point-of-view shots, like those assigned to Roger Thornhill in *North by Northwest,* and flashbacks or fantasies are bracketed by more objective shots. We are able to understand Jamal's memory of Latika and his urge to kill Salim because those images are framed by shots of actions that are really happening in the plot. Other sorts of films, however, may avoid this convention. Fellini's *8½,* Luis Buñuel's *Belle de Jour,* Peter Haneke's *Caché,* and *Memento* mix objectivity and subjectivity in ambiguous ways. *Inception* doesn't signal its dreams with the usual special effects, so that often we're not sure whether we're in reality or a dream (or a dream nested inside another dream).

If a filmmaker restricts our knowledge to a single character, does that restriction create greater subjective depth? Not necessarily. *The Big Sleep* is quite restricted in its range of knowledge, as we've seen. But we very seldom see or hear things from Marlowe's perceptual vantage point, and we never get direct access to his mind. *The Big Sleep* uses almost completely objective narration. The omniscient narration of *The Birth of a Nation,* however, plunges to considerable psychological depth with optical point-of-view shots, flashbacks, and the hero's final fantasy vision of a world without war. To maximize suspense, Hitchcock's films may give us slightly greater knowledge than his characters have. But at certain moments, he confines us to their perceptual subjectivity (usually relying on point-of-view shots). For the filmmaker, range and depth of knowledge are independent variables. These examples show that for the filmmaker, choices about the range of knowledge can be made independently of choices about depth of knowledge.

Incidentally, this is one reason why the term *point of view* is ambiguous. It can refer to range of knowledge (as when a critic speaks of an "omniscient point of view") or to depth (as when speaking of "subjective point of view"). In the rest of this book, we'll use "point of view" only to refer to perceptual subjectivity, as in the phrase "optical point-of-view shot," or POV shot.

Why would a filmmaker manipulate depth of knowledge? Plunging into mental subjectivity can increase our sympathy for a character and can cue stable expectations about what the characters will later say or do. The memory sequences in Alain Resnais's *Hiroshima mon amour* and the fantasy sequences in Federico Fellini's *8½* yield information about the protagonists' traits and possible future actions that would be less vivid if presented objectively. A subjectively motivated flashback can create parallels among characters, as does the flashback shared by mother and son in Kenji Mizoguchi's *Sansho the Bailiff* (**3.28–3.31**). A plot can create curiosity about a character's motives and then use some degree of subjectivity—for example, inner commentary or subjective flashback—to explain what caused the behavior. In *The Sixth Sense,* the child psychologist's odd estrangement from his wife begins to make sense when we hear his inner recollection of something his young patient had told him much earlier.

On the other hand, objectivity can be an effective way of withholding information. One reason that *The Big Sleep* does not treat Marlowe subjectively is that the detective genre demands that the investigator's reasoning be concealed from the viewer. The mystery is more mysterious if we do not know the investigator's hunches and conclusions before he reveals them at the end.

A film need not be in the mystery genre to exploit objective and restricted narration. Julia Loktev's *Day Night Day Night* follows a young woman who has been recruited as a suicide bomber. We see her accepted into the group, awaiting orders, and eventually embarking on the mission. One scene utilizes optical point of view extensively, while another does so briefly. There are a few moments of auditory subjectivity, when the noises of street traffic drop out. Yet these flashes of subjective depth stand out against an overwhelmingly objective presentation. For nearly the entire film, we have to assess the woman's state of mind purely through her physical

CONNECT TO THE BLOG
www.davidbordwell.net/blog

For more on the distinction between perceptual and mental subjectivity in narration see "Categorical coherence: A closer look at character subjectivity."

3.28

3.29

3.30

3.31

3.28–3.31 Characters sharing memories. One of the early flashbacks in *Sansho the Bailiff* starts with the mother, now living in exile with her children, kneeling by a stream (3.28). Her image is replaced by a shot of her husband in the past, about to summon his son Zushio (3.29). At the climax of the scene in the past, the father gives Zushio an image of the goddess of mercy and admonishes him always to show kindness to others (3.30). Normal procedure would come out of the flashback showing the mother again, emphasizing it as her memory. Instead, we return to the present with a shot of Zushio, bearing the goddess's image (3.31). It is as if he and his mother have shared the memory of the father's gift.

behavior. Moreover, our information about the story action is very limited. We are never told what political group has recruited her or why she has volunteered for the task. The woman herself does not know the plan, the members of the terrorist group, or the reasons she was picked. In fact, we know less than she does, because we get only hints about her past life. The impersonal, tightly restricted narration of *Day Night Day Night* not only creates suspense about her mission but also encourages curiosity about a rather large number of story events. These responses make judging her decisions difficult, and they lead us to reflect on why someone would volunteer for a suicide mission.

At any moment in a film, we can ask, "How deeply do I know the characters' perceptions, feelings, and thoughts?" The answer will point directly to how the filmmaker has chosen to present or withhold story information. We can then ask about what effects the narration has on us, the viewers.

The Narrator

Narration, then, is the process by which the plot presents story information to the spectator. The filmmaker may shift between restricted and unrestricted ranges of knowledge and varying degrees of objectivity and subjectivity. The filmmaker may also use a *narrator,* some specific agent who purports to be telling us the story.

The narrator may be a character in the story. We are familiar with this convention from literature, as when Huck Finn or Jane Eyre recounts a novel's action. In *D.O.A,* the dying man tells his story in flashbacks, addressing the information to inquiring policemen. In the documentary *Roger and Me,* Michael Moore frankly acknowledges his role as a character narrator. He starts the film with his reminiscences of growing up in Flint, Michigan, and he appears on camera in interviews with workers and in confrontations with General Motors security staff.

The narrator needn't be a character in the story. Non-character narrators are common in documentaries. We never learn who belongs to the anonymous "voice

When the Lights Go Down, the Narration Starts

When we open a novel, we don't expect the story action to start on the copyright page. Nor do we expect to find the story's last scene on the book's back cover. But filmmakers can start giving us narrative information during the credit sequences, and the process can continue to the very last moments we're in the theater.

Credit sequences are nondiegetic material, but they can assist our understanding of the story. Long ago filmmakers realized that credits could be enlivened by drawings and paintings keyed to the action **(3.32)**. Since the 1920s, the credits' graphic design and musical accompaniment have often conjured up the story's time and place **(3.33)**. The breezy credits of Truffaut's *Jules and Jim* offer glimpses of scenes to come while firmly establishing the two young men's friendship in 1910s Paris.

The film can set a mood simply by the music playing over simple titles, as in nervous score for *The Exorcist*, but the credits can take a more active role through type fonts, color, or movement. Saul Bass, a celebrated designer of corporate logos, gave Alfred Hitchcock's and Otto Preminger's films dynamic geometrical designs **(3.34)**. Rainer Werner Fassbinder was famous for his imaginative credit sequences, some in homage to the 1950s Hollywood melodramas he admired. In a similar vein, the brash collages in Pedro Almodóvar's credit sequences lead us to expect sexy irreverence **(3.35)**.

3.32 Incorporating illustration. An early example of illustrated credits for the 1917 comedy *Reaching for the Moon*.

3.35 Setting expectations of tone. A collage design suggesting sophistication and glamorous lifestyles (*Women on the Verge of a Nervous Breakdown*).

3.33 Evoking locations. *Raw Deal*, a crime film from 1948, begins in prison, and the credit sequence suggests the locale before the action begins.

3.36 Anticipating scenes. Some of the stick-figure credits in *Bringing Up Baby* anticipate scenes that will take place in the story action.

3.34 Hinting at actions and themes. Saul Bass's elegantly simple credits for *Advise and Consent* hint that the story will lift the lid off Washington scandals.

Plot elements can be announced quite specifically. Illustrations can anticipate particular scenes **(3.36)**. *Goldfinger*'s credits present a key motif, the gold-skinned woman, and anticipate several later scenes **(3.37)**. The plot premises of *Catch Me If You Can* are previewed in the title sequence, which pays affectionate homage to the animated credits of the film's period **(3.38)**. *Se7en*'s scratchy glimpses of cutting, stitching, and defacement launched a cycle of nightmarish credit sequences showing violation and dismemberment. Less overtly, the opening of *The Thomas Crown Affair* hints at the hero's scheme for stealing a painting.

Films often end their plot with an epilogue that celebrates the stable state that the characters have achieved, and that situation can be presented during the credits **(3.39)**. Sometimes key scenes will be replayed under the final credits, or new plot action will be shown. *Airplane!* began a fashion for weaving running gags into its final credits.

Occasionally, the filmmaker fools us. We think the plot has ended, and a long list of personnel crawls upward. But then the film tacks an image on the very end **(3.40)**. These "credit cookies" remind us that an enterprising filmmaker may exploit every moment of the film's running time to engage our narrative expectations.

3.37 Introducing motifs.
Goldfinger: The gilded woman will reappear in the film, while other scenes to come, including visions of the villain, are projected on areas of her body.

3.38 Evoking a time period and previewing a story. The streamlined animation of *Catch Me If You Can* evokes 1960s credit sequences while previewing story action and settings. Here the Tom Hanks character starts to trail Leonardo DiCaprio, who plays an impostor pretending to be an airline pilot.

3.39 Presenting an epilogue. In *Slumdog Millionaire,* the dance epilogue in the railway station is intercut with the major credits, which recall scenes from the film.

3.40 Credit cookies. Takeshi Kitano's *Sonatine* follows its final credit sequence with desolate images of a beach, wistfully reminding us of earlier scenes showing childish gangsters at play.

of God" we hear in *The River, Primary,* or *Hoop Dreams.* A fictional film may employ this device as well. *Amélie*'s cozy commentator adds a touch of fantasy, while the urgent voice-over we hear during *The Naked City* suggests that the film has a documentary authenticity.

Either sort of narrator may give us any range or depth of knowledge. A character narrator is not necessarily restricted and very often tells of events that she or he did not witness. This happens in *The Quiet Man,* when the relatively minor figure of the village priest recounts the action. Likewise, a non-character narrator might not be omniscient and could confine the commentary to what a single character knows. A character narrator might be highly subjective, telling us details of his or her inner life, or might be objective, confining the information strictly to externals. A non-character narrator might give us access to subjective depths, as in *Jules and Jim,* or might stick simply to surface events, as does the impersonal voice-over commentator in *The Killing.* In any case, the viewer's process of picking up cues, developing expectations, and constructing an ongoing story out of the plot will be partially shaped by what the narrator tells or doesn't tell.

CREATIVE DECISIONS

Choices about Narration in Storytelling

The Road Warrior (also known as *Mad Max 2*) offers a neat summary of how narration contributes to a film's overall effect. At certain points in the film, director George Miller and writers Terry Hayes and Brian Hannant chose to supply information that builds expectations and help us grasp the story. At other points, they decided to withhold information for the sake of surprise.

The plot opens with a voiceover commentary by an elderly male narrator who recalls "the warrior Max." After presenting exposition that tells of the worldwide wars that led society to degenerate into gangs of scavengers, the narrator falls silent. The question of his identity is left unanswered.

The rest of the plot is organized around Max's encounter with a group of peaceful desert settlers. They want to flee to the coast with the gasoline they have refined, but they're under siege by a gang of vicious marauders. The plot action involves Max's agreement to work for the settlers in exchange for gasoline. Later, after a brush with the gang leaves him wounded, his dog dead, and his car demolished, Max commits himself to helping the settlers flee their compound. The struggle against the encircling gang comes to its climax in Max's attempt to escape with a tanker truck.

Max is the protagonist; his goals and conflicts propel the developing action. After the anonymous narrator's prologue, most of the film is restricted to Max's range of knowledge. Like Philip Marlowe in *The Big Sleep,* Max is present in every scene, and almost everything we learn gets funneled through him. The narration also gives us a degree of subjectivity, again focused on Max. We get optical point-of-view shots as Max drives his car (**3.41**) or watches a skirmish through a telescope. When he is rescued after his car crash, his delirium is rendered as perceptual subjectivity, using the conventional cues of slow motion, superimposed imagery, and slowed-down sound (**3.42**). All of these narrational choices encourage us to sympathize with Max.

At certain points, however, the narration becomes more unrestricted. This occurs principally during chases and battle scenes, when we witness events Max does not know about. In such scenes, unrestricted narration builds up suspense by showing both pursuers and pursued or different aspects of the battle. At the climax, Max's truck successfully draws the gang away from the desert people, who escape to the south. But when his truck overturns, Max—and we—learn that the truck holds only sand. It has been a decoy. Thus our restriction to Max's range of knowledge creates a surprise.

> " The whole art of movies and plays is in the control of the flow of information to the audience . . . : how much information, when, how fast it comes. Certain things maybe have to be there three times."
>
> —Tom Stoppard, playwright and screenwriter of *Shakespeare in Love*

3.41

3.42

3.41–3.42 Narration in *The Road Warrior*: Optical point of view and perceptual subjectivity. The narration provides a point-of-view shot as Max drives up to an apparently abandoned gyrocopter (3.41). The injured Max's dizzy view of his rescuer uses double exposure to present his delirium as perceptual subjectivity (3.42).

3.43 Mental and perceptual subjectivity. As the camera tracks away from Max, we hear the narrator's voice: "And the Road Warrior? That was the last we ever saw of him. He lives now only in my memories."

There is still more to learn, however. At the very end, the elderly narrator's voice returns to tell us that he was the feral child whom Max had befriended. The settlers drive off, and Max is left alone in the middle of the highway. The film's final image—a shot of the solitary Max receding into the distance as we pull back **(3.43)**—suggests both a perceptual subjectivity (the boy's point of view as he rides away from Max) and a mental subjectivity (the memory of Max dimming for the dying narrator).

The narrative form of *The Road Warrior,* then, rests on decisions about both plot and narration. The plot organizes causality, time, and space through an extended flashback, and it gains further coherence through consistent choices about narration. The main portion of the film channels our expectations through an attachment to Max, alternating with briefer, more unrestricted portions. This main section is in turn framed by the mysterious narrator who puts all the events into the distant past. The narrator's presence at the opening leads us to expect him to return at the end, perhaps explaining who he is. The filmmakers' creative choices have organized narration in order to give us a unified experience.

The Classical Hollywood Cinema

Perhaps you've decided to try your hand at writing a screenplay and you've investigated books and websites that offer advice. *Make sure your main character wants something. Emphasize conflict. Take your character on an emotional journey. Be sure that your ending resolves the initial situation.* Suggestions like these can be valuable, but we need to recognize that they reflect only one tradition. This tradition has often been called that of "classical Hollywood" filmmaking.

The tradition is called "classical" because it has been influential since about 1920 and "Hollywood" because the tradition assumed its most elaborate shape in American studio films. The same mode, however, governs narrative films made in other countries. For example, *The Road Warrior,* although an Australian film, is constructed along classical Hollywood lines. And many documentaries, such as *Primary* or *Super Size Me* rely on conventions derived from Hollywood's fictional narratives.

This model of narrative form tends to present individual characters making things happen. Large-scale events such as floods, earthquakes, and wars may affect the action, but the story centers on personal psychological causes: decisions, choices, and traits of character.

Typically the plot focuses on one or two central characters who want something. Characters' desires set up a *goal,* and the course of the narrative's development will most likely involve the process of achieving that goal. In *The Wizard of Oz,* Dorothy has a series of goals; at first she wants to save Toto from Miss Gulch, and later she seeks to get home from Oz. Her desire to get home creates short-term goals along the way, such as getting to the Emerald City and then killing the Witch.

If this desire to reach a goal were the only element present, there would be nothing to stop the character from moving quickly to achieve it. But in the classical narrative there's a blocking element: an opposition that creates conflict. Typically, the protagonist comes up against a character with opposing traits and goals. As a result, the protagonist must overcome the opposition. Dorothy's desire to return to Kansas is opposed by the Wicked Witch, whose goal is to obtain the Ruby Slippers. Dorothy must eventually eliminate the Witch before she is able to use the slippers to go home. We shall see in *His Girl Friday* how the two main characters' goals conflict until the final resolution (pp. 403–406).

The classical plot traces a process of change. Often characters achieve their goals by changing their situation—perhaps they gain fame or money or just survival—but they also change their attitudes or values. At the end of *Jerry Maguire,* the hero has found a measure of professional success but also has learned the value of friendship and a loving family.

But don't all narratives tell stories of this sort? Actually, no. In 1920s Soviet films, such as Sergei Eisenstein's *Potemkin, October,* and *Strike,* no individual serves as protagonist. In films by Eisenstein and Yasujiro Ozu, many events are seen as caused not by characters but by larger forces (social dynamics in the former, an overarching rhythm of life in the latter). In narrative films such as Michelangelo Antonioni's *L'Avventura,* the protagonists are not active but rather passive. So a filmmaker need not put the striving, goal-oriented protagonist at the center of a film's story.

Classical Hollywood filmmakers tend to let psychological causes motivate most events. Throughout, motivation in the classical narrative film strives to be as clear and complete as possible—even in the fanciful genre of the musical, in which song-and-dance numbers express the characters' emotions or display stage shows featuring the characters. When there are discontinuities of character traits, those need explaining. In one scene of *Hannah and Her Sisters,* Mickey (played by Woody Allen) is in a suicidal depression. When we next see him several scenes later, he is bubbly and cheerful. What caused the abrupt change? Mickey explains via a flashback that he achieved a serene attitude toward life while watching a Marx Brothers film. Now the cause-effect pattern is clear.

In creating a classical film, the filmmakers adjust time to fit the cause-effect progress of the story. Every instant shows something that contributes to the flow of the story, and stretches of time that don't contribute are skipped over. The hours Dorothy and her entourage spend walking on the Yellow Brick Road are omitted, but the plot dwells on the moments during which she meets a new character. Specific devices such as *appointments* and *deadlines* make plot time depend on the story's

> " Movies to me are about wanting something, a character wanting something that you as the audience desperately want him to have. You, the writer, keep him from getting it for as long as possible, and then, through whatever effort he makes, he gets it."
>
> —Bruce Joel Rubin, screenwriter, *Ghost*

CONNECT TO THE BLOG
www.davidbordwell.net/blog

For a discussion of how characters' goals can be crucial to major transitions in the plot, see "Times go by turns."

cause–effect chain as well. When characters agree to meet and then we see them meeting, the stretch of time between the plan and the meeting becomes insignificant. Similarly, a deadline forces the action to reach a certain stage at a specific time.

Filmmakers working in the classical tradition have a range of choices about narration, but most tend to present the action objectively, in the way discussed on pages 90–92. The film will usually present an objective story reality, against which various degrees of perceptual or mental subjectivity can be measured. Classical filmmakers also tend toward fairly unrestricted narration. Even if we follow a single character, there are portions of the film giving us access to things the character does not see, hear, or know. *North by Northwest* and *The Road Warrior* remain good examples of this tendency. This weighting is overridden only in genres that depend heavily on mystery, such as the detective film, with its reliance on the sort of restrictiveness we saw at work in *The Big Sleep*.

Finally, most classical filmmakers prefer a strong degree of *closure* at the end. Leaving few loose ends unresolved, the films seek to wrap things clearly. We usually learn the fate of each character, the answer to each mystery, and the outcome of each conflict.

Again, none of these features is a law of narrative form in general. There is nothing to prevent a filmmaker from presenting the dead time, or narratively unmotivated intervals between more significant events. Jean-Luc Godard, Carl Dreyer, and Andy Warhol do this frequently, in different ways. The filmmaker's plot can also reorder story chronology to make the causal chain more perplexing. Jean-Marie Straub and Danièle Huillet's *Not Reconciled* moves back and forth among three widely different time periods without clearly signaling the shifts. *Love Affair, or the Case of the Missing Switchboard Operator* uses flashforwards interspersed with the main plot action; only gradually do we come to understand the causal relations of these flash-forwards to the present-time events. More recently, puzzle films (p. 86) tease the audience to find clues to enigmatic presentation of story events.

The filmmaker can also include material that is unmotivated by narrative cause and effect, such as the chance meetings in Truffaut's films, the political monologues and interviews in Godard's films, the intellectual montage sequences in Eisenstein's films, and the transitional shots in Ozu's work. Narration may be unexpectedly subjective, as in *The Cabinet of Dr. Caligari,* or it may hover ambiguously between objectivity and subjectivity, as in *Last Year at Marienbad.* Finally, the filmmaker need not resolve all of the action at the end; films made outside the classical tradition sometimes have open endings like that of *The 400 Blows* (p. 79).

Great films have been made within the classical tradition. Yet it remains only one way of using narrative form. If we want to gain a wider appreciation of all types of cinema, we can't demand that every movie conform to Hollywood conventions.

CONNECT TO THE BLOG
www.davidbordwell.net/blog

Coincidences supposedly have no place in tight storytelling, but they are more common than you might think. We talk about how filmmakers get away with them in "No coincidence, no story."

CONNECT TO THE BLOG
www.davidbordwell.net/blog

The classical approach to narrative is still very much alive, as we show in "Your trash, my treasure," devoted to *National Treasure.*

Narrative Form in *Citizen Kane*

Citizen Kane is one of the most original films to come out of Hollywood. It has won praise on many counts, not least its subtle approach to storytelling. Director Orson Welles and screenwriter Herman Mankiewicz made creative choices that continue to influence how films are made today. *Kane* is an ideal occasion to test how principles of film narrative can work in both familiar and fresh ways.

Overall Narrative Expectations in *Citizen Kane*

We saw in Chapter 2 that our experience of a film depends heavily on the expectations we bring to it. Before you saw *Citizen Kane,* you may have known only that it is regarded as a film classic. A 1941 audience would have had a keener sense of anticipation. For one thing, the film was rumored to be a disguised version of the life of the newspaper publisher William Randolph Hearst, a businessman as famous as Steve Jobs became. Spectators would thus be looking for events and references keyed to Hearst's life.

Several minutes into the film, the viewer can form more specific expectations about the relevant genre conventions. The early "News on the March" sequence suggests that this film may be a fictional biography, and this hint is confirmed once the reporter, Thompson, begins his inquiry into Kane's life. In this genre, the plot typically traces an individual's life and dramatizes certain episodes. The most prominent fictional biography released before *Kane* would include *Anthony Adverse* (1936) and *The Power and the Glory* (1933), about a somewhat Kane-like tycoon.

The viewer can also spot the conventions of the newspaper reporter genre. Thompson's colleagues resemble the wisecracking reporters in *Five Star Final* (1931), *Picture Snatcher* (1933), and *His Girl Friday* (1940). In this genre, the action usually depends on a reporter's dogged pursuit of a story against great odds. We therefore expect not only Thompson's investigation but also his triumphant exposure of the truth. In the scenes devoted to Susan, there are also some conventions typical of the musical film: frantic rehearsals, backstage preparations, and, most specifically, the montage of her opera career, which parodies the conventional montage of singing success in such films as *Maytime* (1937; p. 255). More broadly, the film evidently owes something to the detective genre, since Thompson is aiming to solve a mystery (Who or what is Rosebud?), and his interviews resemble those of a detective questioning suspects.

Note, however, that *Kane*'s use of genre conventions is somewhat equivocal. Unlike many biographical films, *Kane* is more concerned with psychological states and relationships than with the hero's public deeds or adventures. As a newspaper film, *Kane* is unusual in that the reporter fails to get his story. And *Kane* is not exactly a standard mystery, since it answers some questions but leaves others unanswered. *Citizen Kane* is a good example of a film that relies on genre conventions but often thwarts the expectations they arouse.

The same sort of equivocal qualities can be found in *Kane*'s relation to the classical Hollywood storytelling tradition. Even without specific prior knowledge about this film, we expect that, as an American studio product of 1941, it will follow that tradition. In most ways, it does. We'll see that characters' desires propel the narrative, causality is defined around traits and goals, conflicts lead to consequences, time is motivated by plot necessity, and narration is mostly objective and mixes restricted and unrestricted passages. We'll also see some ways in which *Citizen Kane* is more ambiguous than most films in the classical tradition. Desires, traits, and goals are not always spelled out; the conflicts sometimes have an uncertain outcome; at the end, the narration's omniscience is emphasized to a rare degree. The ending in particular doesn't provide the degree of closure we would expect in a classical film. *Citizen Kane* draws on Hollywood narrative conventions but also violates some of the expectations that we bring to a Hollywood film.

Plot and Story in *Citizen Kane*

After Welles and Mankiewicz decided to tell the life story of a fictional newspaper magnate, Charles Foster Kane, they faced a choice that's familiar to you by now. They could have presented Kane's life story chronologically, letting their plot present incidents in story order as most fictional biographies do. They chose another option. They decided to trace Kane's life through flashbacks, recalled by people who knew him. But Welles and Mankiewicz needed something to motivate the characters' flashbacks. They hit upon the idea of having a media reporter seek the meaning of Kane's dying word, "Rosebud." This generates a second line of action, the reporter Thompson's investigation of Kane's life. The result is a film that creates an unusual relation of plot to story.

We can start to understand this by outlining a segmentation like the one we made for *The Wizard of Oz*. The basic segments are typically scenes, and they form part of a larger section of the film. In the outline below, numerals refer to major parts, some of which are only one scene long. In most cases, however, the major parts consist of several scenes, and each of these is identified by a lowercase letter.

Citizen Kane: Plot Segmentation

C. Credit title

1. Xanadu: Kane dies

2. Projection room:
    a. "News on the March"
    b. Reporters discuss "Rosebud"

3. El Rancho nightclub: Thompson tries to interview Susan

4. Thatcher library:
    a. Thompson enters and reads Thatcher's manuscript
    b. Kane's mother sends the boy off with Thatcher
    c. Kane grows up and buys the *Inquirer*
    d. Kane launches the *Inquirer*'s attack on big business
    e. The Depression: Kane sells Thatcher his newspaper chain
    f. Thompson leaves the library

First flashback — b–e

5. Bernstein's office:
    a. Thompson visits Bernstein
    b. Kane takes over the *Inquirer*
    c. Montage: the *Inquirer*'s growth
    d. Party: the *Inquirer* celebrates getting the *Chronicle* staff
    e. Leland and Bernstein discuss Kane's trip abroad
    f. Kane returns with his fiancée Emily
    g. Bernstein concludes his reminiscence

Second flashback — b–f

6. Nursing home:
    a. Thompson talks with Leland
    b. Breakfast table montage: Kane's marriage deteriorates
    c. Leland continues his recollections
    d. Kane meets Susan and goes to her room
    e. Kane's political campaign culminates in his speech
    f. Kane confronts Gettys, Emily, and Susan
    g. Kane loses the election, and Leland asks to be transferred
    h. Kane marries Susan
    i. Susan has her opera premiere
    j. Because Leland is drunk, Kane finishes Leland's review
    k. Leland concludes his reminiscence

Third flashback — b
Third flashback — d–f
Third flashback (cont.) — g–j

7. El Rancho nightclub:
    a. Thompson talks with Susan
    b. Susan rehearses her singing
    c. Susan has her opera premiere
    d. Kane insists that Susan go on singing
    e. Montage: Susan's opera career
    f. Susan attempts suicide, and Kane promises she can quit singing
    g. Xanadu: Susan is bored
    h. Montage: Susan plays with jigsaw puzzles
    i. Xanadu: Kane proposes a picnic
    j. Picnic: Kane slaps Susan
    k. Xanadu: Susan leaves Kane
    l. Susan concludes her reminiscence

Fourth flashback — b–k

8. Xanadu:

Fifth flashback
- **a.** Thompson talks with Raymond
- **b.** Kane destroys Susan's room and picks up a paperweight, murmuring "Rosebud"
- **c.** Raymond concludes his reminiscence; Thompson talks with the other reporters; all leave
- **d.** Survey of Kane's possessions leads to a revelation of Rosebud; exterior of gate and of castle; the end

E. End credits

This sort of outline lets us recover the film's overall architecture. Our segmentation lets us see at a glance the major divisions of the plot and how scenes are organized within them. It also helps us notice how the plot organizes story causality and story time.

Citizen Kane's Causality

Citizen Kane's plot has two main lines of action, but the chain of causality in each one is somewhat unusual. Welles and Mankiewicz give us an investigation—one not conducted by detectives but by reporters. A media company has made a newsreel about tycoon Charles Foster Kane, and that newsreel is already completed when the plot introduces the reporters. But the newsreel fails to satisfy the boss, Rawlston, and his desire to revise the newsreel gets the search for Rosebud under way. He assigns the reporter Thompson a goal, which sets him digging into Kane's past.

Another line of action, Kane's life, has already taken place when the plot begins. Many years before, a poverty-stricken boarder at Kane's mother's boardinghouse has paid her with a deed to a gold mine. Thanks to these new-found riches, Mrs. Kane appoints Thatcher as young Charles's guardian. Thatcher's guardianship results in Kane's growing up into a spoiled, rebellious young man.

Usually an investigator searches for an object or a concealed set of facts. In this respect, Thompson's mission is straightforward: Who or what was Rosebud? But Thompson is also looking for a set of character traits. Rawlston's order is clear: "It isn't enough to tell us what a man did, you've got to tell us who he was." So finding the meaning of Rosebud promises to reveal something about Kane's personality. Kane, a rather complex character, has many traits that influence other characters' actions. But, as we'll see, *Citizen Kane*'s narrative leaves some of Kane's character traits uncertain.

Thompson has a goal, then. So does Kane, although his is less well-defined. At various times of his life he seems to be searching for fame, friendship, social justice, or a woman's love. But part of the point of the film is that his real goals are uncertain. At several points, characters speculate that Rosebud was something that Kane lost or was never able to get. Such vagueness about a major character's goal makes this an unusual narrative for the Hollywood tradition.

Thompson and Kane are the prime movers of the action in their plot lines. In Kane's life, other characters come into conflict with him, and he changes their lives. In Thompson's plot line, however, these characters serve to provide information about Kane. Thatcher knew him as a child. Bernstein, his manager, knew his business dealings. His best friend, Leland, had access to his personal life, his first marriage in particular. Susan Alexander, his second wife, knew him in middle age. The butler, Raymond, managed Kane's affairs during his last years. Without these witnesses, Thompson couldn't pursue Rosebud. These secondary characters help us, too, as we reconstruct the progression of story events.

The use of testimony spanning Kane's life solves a major storytelling problem Welles and Mankiewicz faced. But as we've seen, one creative choice often demands others. The film's story includes Kane's wife Emily and his son, so shouldn't they be given a chance to share their impressions of the great man? The problem is that their recollections would largely duplicate what we learn from Leland. Welles and Mankiewicz solve this problem in a simple way. They kill Emily and her son off in an auto accident, which occurs well before Thompson's investigation starts.

Time in *Citizen Kane*

Citizen Kane reshapes time in complex ways, and this gives the film much of its originality, particularly in the Hollywood of 1941.

Duration and Frequency

The most conventional aspect of narrative time in the film involves duration. We know that Kane is 75 years old at his death in 1941, and the earliest scene shows him at around age 10. Thus the plot covers roughly 65 years of his life, plus the week of Thompson's investigation. The only earlier story event is Mrs. Kane's acquisition of the mine deed in 1868, which probably took place shortly before she turned her son over to Thatcher. So the story runs a bit longer than the plot—roughly 73 years. This time span is presented in a screen duration of almost 120 minutes.

Like most films, *Citizen Kane* uses ellipses. The plot skips over years of story time, as well as many hours of Thompson's week of investigations. But plot duration also compresses time through *montage sequences,* such as those showing the *Inquirer*'s campaign against big business (4d), the growth of the paper's circulation (5c), Susan's opera career (7e), and Susan's bored playing with jigsaw puzzles (7h). Montage sequences became conventions of classical Hollywood cinema in the 1920s, and here they have their traditional function of condensing story duration in a comprehensible way. We'll discuss montage sequences in more detail in Chapter 8.

Kane is a little more unusual in its treatment of temporal frequency. One specific story event appears twice in the plot. In their respective flashbacks, both Leland and Susan describe her debut in the Chicago premiere of *Salammbo.* Watching Leland's account (6i), we see the performance from the front; we witness the audience reacting with distaste. Susan's version (7c) shows us the performance from behind and on the stage, emphasizing her humiliation. The plot's repeated presentation of Susan's debut doesn't confuse us, for we understand the two scenes as depicting the same story event. ("News on the March" has also referred to Susan's opera career, in parts G and H.) By repeating scenes of her embarrassment, the plot makes vivid the pain that Kane forces her to undergo.

Chronology and Flashbacks

Kane presents an unusual ordering of story events. The central structural decision, that of using Thompson's investigation to motivate a series of flashbacks, asks us to put things in chronological order. For example, the earliest *story* event is Mrs. Kane's acquisition of a deed to a valuable mine. We get this information during the newsreel, in the second sequence. But the first event we encounter in the *plot* is Kane's death.

To illustrate the maneuvers that Welles and Mankiewicz ask us to execute, in building up the film's story, let's assume that Kane's life consists of these phases:

Boyhood

Youthful newspaper editing

Life as a newlywed

Middle age

Old age

At first the plot doesn't present these story phases in chronological order. The early portions of the film boldly jump back and forth over many phases of Kane's life. The "News on the March" sequence (2a) gives us glimpses of all periods, and

CONNECT TO THE BLOG
www.davidbordwell.net/blog

Flashbacks were part of filmmaking tradition before *Citizen Kane.* For analysis of flashbacks in Hollywood films during the 1930s, and especially *The Power and the Glory,* which influenced Orson Welles, see "Grandmaster flashback."

Thatcher's manuscript (4) shows us Kane in boyhood, youth, and middle age. In the first flashback, Thatcher's diary tells of a scene in which Kane loses control of his newspapers during the Depression (4e). By this time, Kane is a middle-aged man. Yet in the second flashback, Bernstein describes young Kane's arrival at the *Inquirer* office and his engagement to Emily (5b, 5f). The plot demands that we sort these events into chronological story order.

The film becomes less demanding as it goes along, however. Later portions of the plot tend to concentrate on particular periods, and the flashbacks respect chronological order. Bernstein's recollections (5) concentrate on episodes showing Kane as newspaper editor and fiancé of Emily. Leland's flashbacks (6) run from newlywed life to middle age. Susan (7) tells of Kane as a middle-aged and an old man. Raymond's brief but significant anecdote (8b) concentrates on Kane in old age.

By getting more linear, the plot helps us grasp the story. If every character's flashback skipped around Kane's life as much as the newsreel and Thatcher's account do, the story would be much harder to reconstruct. As it is, the early portions of the plot show us the results of events we have not seen, while the later portions confirm or modify the expectations that we formed in the more nonlinear scenes. For instance, we know that Kane will lose his newspapers to Thatcher, and that knowledge lends a certain poignancy to Kane's "Declaration of Principles" in which he pledges to fight for the common man.

By arranging story events out of order, the plot cues us to form specific anticipations. In the beginning, with Kane's death and the newsreel version of his life, the plot creates strong curiosity about two issues. What does "Rosebud" mean? And what could have happened to make so powerful a man die alone and, apparently, unmourned?

There is also a degree of suspense. When the plot goes back to the past, we already have quite firm knowledge. We know that neither of Kane's marriages will last and that his friends will drift away. The plot encourages us to focus our interest on *how and when* a particular thing will happen. What will break Leland's friendship with Kane? What will trigger Susan's decision to walk out on him? As Hitchcock pointed out (p. 89), giving us more knowledge than the characters have can promote suspense.

"News on the March" as a Map of the Plot

In 1941, one of the most original sequences of the film was the "News on the March" newsreel. By looking over our segmentation, we can see that the newsreel is not only daring but very helpful. The very first sequence in Xanadu disorients us, for it shows the death of a character about whom we so far know almost nothing. But the newsreel quickly supplies a great deal of information about this mysterious figure. Moreover, by reviewing Kane's life, the newsreel makes it much easier to rearrange the plot events we'll see into linear story order. Here is an outline of "News on the March."

A. Shots of Xanadu

B. Funeral; headlines announcing Kane's death

C. Growth of financial empire

D. Gold mine and Mrs. Kane's boardinghouse

E. Thatcher testimony at congressional committee

F. Political career

G. Private life; weddings, divorces

H. Opera house and Xanadu

I. Political campaign

J. The Depression

K. 1935: Kane's old age

L. Isolation of Xanadu

M. Death announced

Now we can see that the newsreel offers us a capsule preview of the film's over-all plot. "News on the March" begins by emphasizing Kane as "Xanadu's Land-lord"; a short segment (A) presents shots of the house and the compound. This is a variation on the opening of the whole film (1), which consisted of a series of shots of the grounds, moving progressively closer to the house. That opening sequence had ended with Kane's death; now the newsreel follows the shots of the house with Kane's funeral (B). Next comes a series of newspaper headlines announcing Kane's death. If we compare this portion with the segmentation of the entire film's plot, we see that these headlines occupy the approximate formal position of the whole newsreel itself (2a). Even the title card that follows the headlines ("To forty-four million U.S. news buyers, more newsworthy than the names in his own headlines was Kane himself. . . .") is a brief parallel to the scene in the projection room, in which the reporters decide that Thompson should continue to investigate Kane's "newsworthy" life.

The order of the newsreel's presentation of Kane's life roughly parallels the order of scenes in the flashbacks told to Thompson. "News on the March" moves from Kane's death to a summary of the building of Kane's newspaper empire (C), with a description of the boarding-house deed and the mine (including an old photo-graph of Charles with his mother, as well as the first mention of the boy's sled). This bit parallels the first flashback (4), which tells how Thatcher took over the young Kane's guardianship from his mother and how Kane first attempted to run the *In-quirer*. The rough parallels continue: The newsreel tells of Kane's political ambitions (F), his marriages (G), his building of the opera house (H), his political campaign (I), and so on. In the main plot, Thatcher's flashback describes his own clashes with Kane on political matters. Leland's flashback (6) covers the first marriage, the affair with Susan, the political campaign, and the premiere of the opera *Salammbo*.

We haven't charted all of the similarities between the newsreel and the overall film. You can tease out many more by comparing the two closely. The crucial point is that the newsreel provides us with a map for the investigation of Kane's life. As we watch scenes in the flashbacks, we already expect certain events and have a rough chronological basis for fitting them into our story reconstruction.

CONNECT TO THE BLOG
www.davidbordwell.net/blog

Citizen Kane helped popularize flashback-based narratives in the 1940s. We look at some less familiar but equally interesting examples in "Chinese boxes, Russian dolls, and Hollywood movies." For more on flashbacks in movies old and new, see "Puppetry and ventriloquism."

Motivation in *Citizen Kane*

Citizen Kane follows classical Hollywood tradition in motivating the causes and effects that push the story forward. Even small details are justified causally. Why did Welles and Mankiewicz decide to make Thatcher a prosperous businessman? Their script could have had Mrs. Kane turn her son over to a kindly but poor family, one that wouldn't treat him as cruelly as apparently his father has. But Thatcher's social position motivates important events. By giving her son to Thatcher, Charles' mother catapults him into a wealthy circle, where he will wield the power we wit-ness across the film. Thatcher's elite standing also makes it easy for Thompson to pursue his initial research on Kane's life. Thatcher is influential enough to testify at a congressional hearing, so he can appear in the newsreel (the first time we encoun-ter him). As a self-important tycoon, he has chronicled his life in a journal, which Thompson can scan for information about Kane's childhood.

A striking instance of motivation involves Thompson's visit to Susan, Kane's second wife at the El Rancho nightclub (3). It's plausible that Thompson would start his search with Kane's ex-wife, presumably the surviving person closest to him. But let's think like a screenwriter. In the story, the young Kane is an audacious editor, thumbing his nose at the stuffed-shirt Thatcher and taking up the cause of the poor.

But Susan didn't know Kane then. If she had been given the first flashback, it would have dwelt on Kane's old age, a period in which he was pompous and self-centered. If Susan had told her story first, showing the elderly Kane, we would not sense his character change gradually. By delaying her flashback, the plot lets Thatcher, Bernstein, and Leland fill in Kane's early, rambunctious years. By then we're prepared to appreciate, from Susan's testimony, how he has decayed into a selfish, aggressive old man.

So the creative problem was find a way to prevent Susan from telling her story. The solution that Mankiewicz and Welles chose was to make Susan drunk and angry during Thompson's visit. Her refusal to speak to him motivates postponing her flashback. It also enhances the mystery around Kane—why won't she go on the record?—while her alcoholic haze suggests that he has damaged the people closest to him.

Some critics have argued that the search for Rosebud is a flaw in *Citizen Kane,* because the revelation of the boy's sled is an oversimplification. Does all this come down to the fact that Kane just longs for his lost childhood and his mother's love? If we assume that the point of the plot is simply to identify Rosebud, this charge might be valid. But in fact, Rosebud serves a very important motivating function. It creates Thompson's goal and thus focuses our attention on his digging into the lives of Kane and his associates. *Citizen Kane* becomes a mystery story; but instead of investigating a crime, the reporter investigates a character.

Furthermore, it's not clear that the plot lets us conclude that Rosebud is the final answer to the quest. In the final scene, Thompson gives up the search. He doubts that "any word can explain a man's life." Moreover, in the scene in the newsreel projection room, Rawlston suggests that "maybe he told us all about himself on his deathbed." Immediately, one of the reporters says, "Yeah, and maybe he didn't." Already the suggestion is planted that Rosebud may not provide any adequate answers about Kane. Later Leland scornfully dismisses the Rosebud issue and goes on to talk of other things. Characters' skepticism about the Rosebud clue helps justify Thompson's pessimistic attitude in the final sequence.

Linked to the uncertainties around Rosebud is a degree of ambiguity about psychological motivations. These relate primarily to Kane's character. The characters' varying portraits of Kane don't neatly tally. Bernstein still looks on Kane with sympathy and affection, whereas Leland is cynical about his own relationship with Kane. Likewise, the reasons for some of Kane's actions remain unclear. Does he send Leland the $25,000 check in firing him because of a lingering sentiment over their old friendship or from a proud desire to prove himself more generous than Leland? Why does he insist on stuffing Xanadu with hundreds of artworks that he never even unpacks? By leaving these questions open, the film invites us to speculate on various facets of Kane's personality. The ambiguities around Rosebud and Kane's character are unusual for the classical Hollywood tradition, which usually prefers more clear-cut explanations of character psychology.

Citizen Kane's Parallelism

Parallelism doesn't provide a major principle of development in *Citizen Kane*'s narrative form, but it crops up more locally. We've already seen important formal parallels between the newsreel and the film's plot as a whole. There is as well a parallel between the two major lines of action: Kane's life and Thompson's search. Both men are searching for Rosebud. Rosebud serves as a summary of the things Kane strives for through his adult life. We see him repeatedly fail to find love and friendship, living alone at Xanadu in the end. His inability to find happiness parallels Thompson's failure to locate the significance of the word "Rosebud."

Another narrative parallel juxtaposes Kane's campaign for the governorship with his attempt to build up Susan's career as an opera star. In each case, he seeks to inflate his reputation by influencing public opinion. In trying to achieve success for Susan, Kane forces his newspaper employees to write favorable reviews of her performances. This parallels the moment when he loses the election and the *Inquirer* automatically proclaims a fraud at the polls. In both cases, Kane fails to realize that his power over the public is not great enough to hide the flaws in his projects: first his affair with Susan, which ruins his campaign; then her lack of singing ability, which Kane refuses to admit. The parallels show that Kane continues to make the same kinds of mistakes throughout his life.

Patterns of Plot Development in *Citizen Kane*

The order of Thompson's visits to Kane's acquaintances allows the series of flashbacks to have a clear progression. Thanks to the delay in presenting Susan's flashback, Thompson moves from people who knew Kane early in his life to those who knew him as an old man. Moreover, each flashback contains a distinct type of information about Kane. Bernstein gives an account of the newspaper's growth, and then Leland traces Kane's changing political views. Both men provide the background to Kane's early success and lead into stories of Kane's personal life. Here we get the first real indications of Kane's failure. Susan continues to trace his decline by explaining how he ruled her life. Finally, in Raymond's flashback, Kane becomes a pitiable old man. Thompson's present-day inquiry has its own pattern of development, that of a search. By the ending, this search has failed, as Kane's own search for happiness or personal success had failed.

Because of Thompson's failure, the ending of *Citizen Kane* remains somewhat more open than was the rule in Hollywood in 1941. True, Thompson does resolve the question of Rosebud for himself by saying that it would not have explained Kane's life. To this extent, we have the common pattern showing the protagonist gaining greater knowledge. Still, in most classical narrative films, the main character reaches his or her initial goal, and Thompson, the main character of this line of action, fails to achieve his aim.

The line of action involving Kane himself has even less closure. Not only does Kane apparently not reach his goal, but the film never specifies what that goal is to start with. Most classical narratives create a situation of conflict. The character must struggle with a problem and solve it by the ending. Kane begins his adult life in a highly successful position, happily running the *Inquirer,* and then gradually falls into a barren solitude. His chief conflicts are with his wives and friends; his clash with a political boss rates only one scene. We are invited to speculate about exactly what, if anything, would have made Kane happy. *Citizen Kane*'s lack of closure in this biographical line of action made it a very unusual narrative for its day.

Still, the search for Rosebud does lead to a certain resolution. We the audience discover what Rosebud was. The ending of the film, which follows this discovery, strongly echoes the beginning. The beginning moved past fences toward the mansion. Now a series of shots takes us away from the house and back outside the fences, with the "No Trespassing" sign and large K insignia.

But even at this point, when we learn the answer to Thompson's question, a degree of uncertainty remains. Just because we have learned what Kane's dying word referred to, do we now have the key to his entire character? Or is Thompson's final statement correct—that no one word can explain a person's life? Perhaps the final shot of the "No Trespassing" sign hints that neither Thompson nor we should have expected to know Kane's mind fully. It is tempting to declare that all of Kane's problems arose from the loss of his sled and his childhood home life, but the film also suggests that this is too easy a solution. It is the kind of solution that the slick editor Rawlston would pounce on as an angle for his newsreel.

For years critics have debated whether the Rosebud solution does give us a key that resolves the entire narrative. This debate itself suggests the ambiguity at work in *Citizen Kane.* The film provides much evidence for both views and hence avoids complete closure. We can contrast this somewhat open ending with those of *His*

" Kane, we are told, loved only his mother—only his newspaper—only his second wife—only himself. Maybe he loved all of these, or none. It is for the audience to judge. Kane was selfish and selfless, an idealist, a scoundrel, a very big man and a very little one. It depends on who's talking about him. He is never judged with the objectivity of an author, and the point of the picture is not so much the solution of the problem as its presentation."

—Orson Welles, director

Girl Friday and *North by Northwest,* as well as with another open-ended film, *Do the Right Thing.* All are discussed in Chapter 11.

Narration in *Citizen Kane*

In analyzing how *Kane*'s plot manipulates the moment-by-moment flow of story information, it's useful to consider a remarkable fact. The only time we see Kane directly and in the present is when he dies. On all other occasions, he is presented at one remove—in the newsreel or in various characters' memories. This unusual treatment makes the film something of a portrait, a study of a man seen from different perspectives.

The film employs five character narrators, the people whom Thompson tracks down: Thatcher (whose account is in writing), Bernstein, Leland, Susan, and the butler, Raymond. The plot motivates a series of views of Kane that are more or less restricted in their range of knowledge. In Thatcher's account (4b–4e), we see only scenes at which he is present. Even Kane's newspaper crusade is rendered as Thatcher learns of it, through buying copies of the *Inquirer.* In Bernstein's flashback (5b–5f), there is some deviation from what Bernstein witnesses, but in general his range of knowledge is respected. For example, we never see Kane in Europe; we merely hear the contents of Kane's telegram, which Bernstein delivers to Leland.

Leland's flashbacks (6b, 6d–6j) deviate most markedly from the narrator's allotted range of knowledge. Here we see Kane and Emily at a series of morning breakfasts, Kane's meeting with Susan, and the confrontation of Kane with Boss Gettys at Susan's apartment. In scene 6j, Leland is present but in a drunken stupor most of the time. (The plot motivates Leland's knowledge of Kane's affair by having Leland suggest that Kane told him about it, but the scenes present detailed knowledge that Leland probably didn't possess.) By the time we get to Susan's flashback (7b–7k), however, the range of knowledge again fits the character more snugly. (In one scene, 7f, Susan is unconscious for part of the action.) The last flashback (8b) is recounted by Raymond and plausibly accords with his range of knowledge; he is standing in the hallway as Kane wrecks Susan's room.

Using different narrators to transmit story information fulfills several functions. It offers a plausible depiction of the process of investigation, since we expect any reporter to hunt down information through interviews. More deeply, the plot's portrayal of Kane himself becomes more complex by showing somewhat different sides of him, depending on who's talking about him. Moreover, the multiple narrators make the film resemble one of Susan's jigsaw puzzles. We must put things together piece by piece. The pattern of gradual revelation enhances curiosity—what is it in Kane's past that he associates with Rosebud?—and suspense—how will he lose his friends and his wives?

This strategy has important implications for film form. While Thompson uses the various witnesses to gather data, the plot uses the narrators both to furnish story information and to *conceal* information. The narration can motivate gaps in knowledge about Kane by appealing to the fact that nobody can know everything about anyone else. If we were able to enter Kane's consciousness, we might discover the meaning of Rosebud much sooner. But Kane is dead. The multiple-narrator format motivates the withholding of key pieces of information, and this in turn arouses curiosity and suspense.

Although each narrator's account is mostly restricted to his or her range of knowledge, the plot doesn't treat each flashback in much subjective depth. Most of the flashbacks are rendered objectively. Some transitions from the framing episodes use a voice-over commentary to lead us into the flashbacks, but these don't represent the narrators' subjective states. Only in Susan's flashbacks are there some attempts to render subjectivity. In scene 7c, we see Leland as if from her optical point of view on stage, and the phantasmagoric montage of her career (7e) reveals her fatigue and frustration. These scenes help make her the most sympathetic narrator, reinforcing our sense that Kane has cruelly forced her to pursue a singing career.

Against the five character narrators, the film's plot sets another source of knowledge, the "News on the March" short. We've already seen the crucial function of the newsreel in introducing us to *Kane*'s plot construction, with the newsreel's sections previewing the parts of the film as a whole. The newsreel also gives us a broad sketch of Kane's life and death that will be filled in by the more restricted behind-the-scenes accounts offered by the narrators. The newsreel is also highly objective, even more so than the rest of the film; it reveals nothing about Kane's inner life. Rawlston's assigns Thompson to add depth to the newsreel's superficial version of Kane.

Yet we still aren't through with the narrational manipulations in this complex and daring film. For one thing, all the localized sources of knowledge—"News on the March" and the five narrators—are linked together by the shadowy reporter Thompson. To some extent, he is our surrogate in the film, gathering and assembling the puzzle pieces.

It's very striking, especially for a film made over seventy years ago, that Thompson is barely characterized. We can't even identify his face. This, as usual, has a function. If we saw him clearly, if the plot gave him more traits or a background or a past, he would become the central protagonist, as reporters tend to be in the journalism genre. But *Citizen Kane* is less about Thompson the man than about his *search*. The plot's handling of Thompson makes him a neutral channel for the story information that he gathers, even though his conclusion at the end—"I don't think any word can explain a man's life"—suggests that he has been changed by his investigation.

Thompson is not, however, a perfect surrogate for us. That's because the film's narration inserts the newsreel, the narrators, and Thompson within a still broader range of knowledge. The flashback portions are predominantly restricted, but there are other passages that reveal an overall narrational omniscience.

From the very start, we are given a god's-eye view of the action. We move into a mysterious setting that we later learn is Kane's estate, Xanadu. We might have learned about this locale through a character's journey, the way we acquaint ourselves with Oz by means of Dorothy's trip. Here, however, an omniscient narration conducts the tour. Eventually, we enter a darkened bedroom. A hand holds a paperweight, and over this is superimposed a flurry of snow (3.44)

The image teases us. Is the narration making a lyrical comment on the action? Or is the image subjective, a glimpse into the dying man's mind or vision? In either case, the narration reveals its ability to command a great deal of story information. Our sense of omniscience is enhanced when, after the man dies, a nurse bustles into the room. Apparently, no character knows what we know.

At other points in the film, the omniscient narration calls attention to itself. During Susan's opera debut in Leland's flashback (6i), we see stagehands high above reacting to her performance. Most vivid is the omniscient narration at the end of the film. Thompson and the other reporters leave, never having learned the meaning of Rosebud. But we linger in the vast storeroom of Xanadu. And, thanks to the narration, we learn that Rosebud is the name of Kane's childhood sled. We can now associate the opening's emphasis on the snowy cottage with the closing scene's revelation of the sled.

This framing narration is truly omniscient. It withholds a key piece of story information at the outset, teases us with hints (the snow, the tiny cottage in the paperweight), and finally reveals at least part of the answer to the initial question. A return to the "No Trespassing" sign reminds us of our point of entry into the film. The film derives its unity not only from systematic choices about causality and time but also from a patterned narration that arouses curiosity and suspense and yields a surprise at the very end.

3.44 Narrational omniscience in *Citizen Kane*. The elusive image of the paperweight in *Citizen Kane*—seen by film viewers but not by any characters in the film.

SUMMARY

Not every analysis of a narrative film runs through all the categories we have covered here. Our purpose was as much to illustrate these concepts as to analyze *Citizen Kane*. With practice, you can become more familiar with these analytical tools and can use them flexibly, suiting your approach to the specific film at hand and the things that intrigue you about it. Should you become a filmmaker, all these matters, from cause-effect patterns to narrational organization, will confront you with a cascade of decisions. You may make your choices intuitively or through lots of thought and soul-searching, but these remain essential dimensions of storytelling. In looking at any narrative film, then, asking these questions will help you understand it better:

1. Which story events are directly presented to us in the plot, and which must we assume or infer? Is there any nondiegetic material given in the plot?

2. What is the earliest story event of which we learn? How does it relate to later events through a series of causes and effects?

3. How are story events connected in time? Have the filmmakers manipulated order, frequency, and duration in the plot so as to affect our understanding of events?

4. Does the closing reflect a clear-cut pattern of development that relates it to the opening? Do all narrative lines achieve closure, or are some left open?

5. How does the narration present story information to us? Is it restricted to one or a few characters' knowledge, or does it range freely among the characters in different spaces? Does it give us considerable depth of story information by exploring the characters' mental states?

6. How closely does the film follow the conventions of the classical Hollywood cinema? If it departs significantly from those conventions, what formal principle does it use instead?

Most films that we see employ narrative form, and the great majority of theatrical movies stick to the premises of Hollywood storytelling. Still, there are other formal possibilities. We consider aspects of nonnarrative form in Chapter 10.

In the meantime, other matters will occupy us. In discussing form, we've been examining how we as viewers engage with the film's overall patterning. A film, however, also presents a complex blend of images and sounds. Like the architecture of film form, the finer grain of cinematic techniques involves the filmmaker in creative problem-solving and decision-making. Our experience of the film is shaped by the filmmaker's choice and control and patterning of those techniques. Part Three shows how this all happens.

RECOMMENDED DVD AND BLU-RAY SUPPLEMENTS

Discussions of narrative form are rare in DVD supplements. In "Making of *Titus*," director Julie Taymor talks about such narrative elements as motifs, point of view, tone, and emotional impact, as well as the functions of film techniques such as music, setting, editing, cinematography, and lighting. In an unusual supplement for *The Godfather*, "Francis Coppola's Notebook," the director shows how he worked by making detailed annotations in his copy of Mario Puzo's original novel. Coppola discusses rhythm, emphasis, and the narrative functions of various techniques. The "Star Beast: Developing the Story" section of *Alien*'s supplements traces the story as it went through a series of very different versions.

The Editor's Commentary Track for *Kingdom of Heaven* includes some discussion of narrative form. After about the 50-minute mark, Dody Dorn discusses the cause-and-effect structure of the siege sequence. Throughout she discusses the functions of scenes. She mentions such additions as a close-up of one character to create a parallel with a close-up of another character in a similar scene. In general, Dorn conveys how an editor approaches the creation of a film narrative.

"Filmmakers' Journey Part One," a supplement for *The Da Vinci Code*, discusses character, timing, and rhythm. One passage that is particularly good for showing how filmmakers think about narrative form comes in a segment on the introduction of a major new character (Sir Lee Teabing) fully halfway through the film. There is also discussion of the film's series of journeys: "There was this sort of classic structure that we were working with."

The Warner Bros. DVD of *Citizen Kane* offers a remastered print of the film with commentary tracks by Roger Ebert and Peter Bogdanovich. A second disc contains a two-hour documentary, *The Battle over Citizen Kane*, exploring William Randolph Hearst's efforts to force RKO to destroy the film.

PART 3

We are still trying to understand how a movie creates an absorbing experience for the viewer. Chapter 2 showed that the concept of form offers a way to grasp the film as a whole. Chapter 3 examined how narrative form can shape a film and our response to it. Later we'll see that film-makers have employed other types of form in documentaries and experimental films.

When we see a film, though, we don't engage only with its overall form. We experience a *film*—not a painting or a novel. A painter knows how to manipulate color, shape, and composition. A novelist lives intimately with language. Likewise, filmmakers work with a distinct medium.

You're already somewhat aware of the creative choices available in the film medium. As a viewer you probably notice performance and color design. If you've made videos, you've become more aware of framing and composition, editing and sound. If you've tried your hand at making a fictional piece, you've already faced problems of staging and acting.

Film Style

Part Three of this book gives you a chance to learn about film techniques in a systematic way. We look at two techniques governing the shot, mise-en-scene and cinematography. Then we consider the technique that relates shot to shot, editing. Then we consider the role that sound plays in relation to film images. A wrapup chapter returns to *Citizen Kane* and examines how it coordinates all these techniques with its narrative form.

Each chapter introduces a single technique, surveying the choices it offers to the film-maker. We survey how various filmmakers have used the techniques. Several key questions will guide us: How can a technique shape the viewer's expectations? How may it furnish motifs for the film? How may a technique support the film's overall form—its story/plot relations or its narrational patterning? How may it direct our attention, clarify or emphasize meanings, and shape our emotional response?

The chapters that follow also explore how a film can organize its chosen techniques in consistent ways. This pattern of technical choices we call *style*. Style is what creates a movie's "look and feel." Late in each chapter, we focus on one or two particular films to show how the technique we're studying helps establish a distinctive style.

4

The Shot: Mise-en-Scene

Of all film techniques, **mise-en-scene** is the one that viewers notice most. After seeing a film, we may not recall the cutting or the camera movements, the dissolves or the offscreen sound. But we do remember the costumes in *Gone with the Wind* and the bleak, chilly lighting in Charles Foster Kane's Xanadu. We retain vivid impressions of the misty streets in *The Big Sleep* and the labyrinthine, fluorescent-lit lair of Buffalo Bill in *The Silence of the Lambs*. We recall Harpo Marx clambering over Edgar Kennedy's lemonade stand (*Duck Soup*) and Michael J. Fox escaping high-school bullies on an improvised skateboard (*Back to the Future*). Many of our most vivid memories of movies stem from mise-en-scene.

What Is Mise-en-Scene?

Consider this image from Quentin Tarantino's *Inglourious Basterds* (4.1). Aldo Raine, a U.S. soldier on a mission to assassinate Hitler, has been captured by SS Colonel Hans Landa. The shot seems a simple one, but if you're starting to think like a filmmaker, you'll notice how Tarantino has shaped the image to accentuate the action and engage our attention.

The shot presents the two men facing each other behind a movie theater. The alley is rendered minimally, in dark colors and subdued lighting. By playing down the setting, Tarantino obliges us to concentrate on the confrontation.

Although both men are positioned in profile, the image doesn't give equal weight to each one. The cowl masks Aldo's face. This costume choice encourages us to concentrate on the face that we can see. The lighting is important as well. A

4.1 What attracts your eye? Elements of mise-en-scene accentuate action and engage attention in this scene from *Inglourious Basterds*, in which Aldo Raine is captured by Colonel Landa.

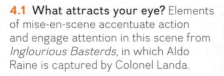

thread of illumination picks out the edge of Raine's cowl; without it, it would merge into the background. Again, however, it is Landa's face that gets greater emphasis. Strong lighting from above and left sharply outlines his profile, and a less powerful light (what filmmakers call *fill*) reveals his features.

Landa is emphasized in another way, through the actor's dialogue and facial expression. As Landa speaks, he shows delight in the capture of his quarry. His satisfaction bursts out when he chortles: "Alas, you're now in the hands of the SS—my hands, to be exact!" Letting the actor's hands fly up into the center of the frame and emphasizing them by the dialogue, Tarantino reminds us of the officer's florid self-assurance. This hand gesture will be developed when Landa playfully taps Raine's head with a forefinger: "I've been waiting a long time to touch you."

Although Tarantino has made many creative choices in this shot (notably the decision to film in a relatively close framing), certain techniques stand out. Setting, costume, lighting, and performance have all been coordinated to highlight Landa's gloating and remind us that he enjoys his cat-and-mouse interrogation tactics. Tarantino has shaped our experience of this story action by his decisions about mise-en-scene.

In the original French, *mise en scène* (pronounced meez-ahn-sen) means "putting into the scene," and it was first applied to the practice of directing plays. Film scholars, extending the term to film direction, use the term to signify the director's control over what appears in the film frame. As you would expect, mise-en-scene includes those aspects of film that overlap with the art of the theater: setting, lighting, costume and makeup, and staging and performance.

As the *Inglourious Basterds* shot suggests, mise-en-scene usually involves planning in advance. But the filmmaker may seize on unplanned events as well. An actor may add a line on the set, or an unexpected change in lighting may enhance a dramatic effect. While filming a cavalry procession through Monument Valley for *She Wore a Yellow Ribbon,* John Ford took advantage of an approaching lightning storm to create a dramatic backdrop for the action **(4.2).** The storm remains part of the film's mise-en-scene even though Ford neither planned it nor controlled it; it was a lucky accident that helped create one of the film's most affecting passages. Jean Renoir, Robert Altman, and other directors have allowed their actors to improvise their performances, making the films' mise-en-scene more spontaneous and unpredictable.

4.2 Unplanned events and mise-en-scene. While filming *She Wore a Yellow Ribbon,* John Ford took advantage of a thunderstorm in Monument Valley.

The Power of Mise-en-Scene

Filmmakers can use mise-en-scene to achieve realism, giving settings an authentic look or letting actors perform as naturally as possible. Throughout film history, however, audiences have also been attracted to fantasy, and mise-en-scene has often been used for this purpose. This attraction is evident in the work of cinema's first master of the technique, Georges Méliès. Méliès used highly original mise-en-scene to create an imaginary world on film.

A caricaturist and stage magician, Méliès became fascinated by the Lumière brothers' demonstration of their short films in 1895. (For more on the Lumières, see p. 178.) After building a camera based on an English projector, Méliès began filming unstaged street scenes and moments of passing daily life. One day, the story goes, he was filming at the Place de l'Opéra, but his camera jammed as a bus was passing. By the time he could resume filming, the bus had gone and a hearse was

CONNECT TO THE BLOG
www.davidbordwell.net/blog

For more on Méliès and his last years, visit our entry "Hugo: Scorsese's birthday present to Georges Méliès."

> When Buñuel was preparing *The Discreet Charm of the Bourgeoisie,* he chose a tree-lined avenue for the recurring shot of his characters traipsing endlessly down it. The avenue was strangely stranded in open country and it perfectly suggested the idea of these people coming from nowhere and going nowhere. Buñuel's assistant said, 'You can't use that road. It's been used in at least ten other movies.' 'Ten other movies?' said Buñuel, impressed. 'Then it must be good.'"

in front of his lens. When Méliès screened the film, he discovered something unexpected: a moving bus seemed to transform instantly into a hearse. Whether or not the anecdote is true, it at least illustrates Méliès's recognition of the magical powers of mise-en-scene. He would devote most of his efforts to cinematic conjuring.

To do so would require preparation, since Méliès could not count on lucky accidents like the bus–hearse transformation. He would have to plan and stage action for the camera. Drawing on his theatrical experience, Méliès built one of the first film studios—a small, crammed affair bristling with balconies, trapdoors, and sliding backdrops. Such control was necessary to create the fantasy world he envisioned **(4.3–4.6).** He drew shots beforehand, designed sets and costumes, and devised elaborate special effects. As if this were not enough, Méliès starred in his own films **(4.6).**

Méliès's "Star-Film" studio made hundreds of short fantasy and trick films based on a strict control over every element in the frame, and the first master of mise-en-scene demonstrated the resources of the technique. The legacy of Méliès's magic is a delightfully unreal world wholly obedient to the whims of the imagination.

4.3

4.4

4.5

4.6

4.3–4.6 Méliès and mise-en-scene. Méliès made detailed plans for his shots, as seen in the drawing and final version of the rocket-launching scene in *A Trip to the Moon* (4.3–4.4). For *The Mermaid* (4.5) he summoned up an undersea world by placing a fish tank between the camera and an actress, some backdrops, and "carts for monsters." In *La Lune à une mètre* (4.6) Melies plays an astronomer. His study and its furnishings, including telescope, globe, and blackboard, are all painted cut-outs.

Components of Mise-en-Scene

Mise-en-scene offers the filmmaker four general areas of choice and control: setting, costumes and makeup, lighting, and staging (which includes acting and movement in the shot).

Setting

Since the earliest days of cinema, critics and audiences have understood that setting plays a more active role in cinema than it usually does in the theater. André Bazin writes:

> The human being is all-important in the theatre. The drama on the screen can exist without actors. A banging door, a leaf in the wind, waves beating on the shore can heighten the dramatic effect. Some film masterpieces use man only as an accessory, like an extra, or in counterpoint to nature, which is the true leading character.

4.7 **Setting creates narrative expectations.** The railway yard at the opening of *Wendy and Lucy* is a setting that will take on significance later in the film.

In a film, the setting can come to the forefront; it need not be only a container for human events but can dynamically enter the narrative action. Kelly Reichardt's *Wendy and Lucy* begins with shots of a railroad yard as trains pass through (**4.7**). But we don't see any people. Wendy, who is making her way across the United States by car, is later seen walking her dog Lucy in a park. The opening shots of the rail yard suggest the sort of neighborhoods where she must stay. At later points in the film, the roar and whistle of rail traffic will increase suspense, but not until the ending will we come to understand why the opening emphasized the trains.

The filmmaker may select an existing locale for the action. The very early short comedy *L'Arroseur arrosé* ("The Waterer Watered," **4.8**) was filmed in a garden. At the close of World War II, Roberto Rossellini shot *Germany Year Zero* in the rubble of Berlin (**4.9**). Alternatively, the filmmaker may construct the setting. Méliès understood that shooting in a studio increased his control, and many filmmakers followed his lead. In France, Germany, and especially the United States, commercial filmmaking became centered on studio facilities in which every aspect of mise-en-scene could be manipulated.

Some directors have emphasized authenticity even in purpose-built settings. For example, Erich von Stroheim prided himself on meticulous research into details of locale for the sets of *Greed* (**4.10**). *All the President's Men* (1976) took a similar tack, seeking to duplicate the *Washington Post* office on a sound stage (**4.11**). Other films have been less committed to accuracy. Though D. W. Griffith studied the various historical periods presented in *Intolerance,* his Babylon constitutes a personal image of that city (**4.12**). Similarly, in *Ivan the Terrible,* Sergei Eisenstein freely stylized the decor of the czar's palace to harmonize with the lighting, costume, and figure movement, so that characters crawl through doorways that resemble mouse-holes and stand frozen before allegorical murals (**4.13**).

Setting can overwhelm the actors, as in Wim Wender's *Wings of Desire* (**4.14**), or it can be reduced to almost nothing, as in Francis Ford Coppola's *Bram Stoker's Dracula* (**4.15**). The overall design of a setting can shape how we understand story action. In Louis Feuillade's silent crime serial *The Vampires,* a criminal gang has killed a courier on his way to a bank. The gang's confederate, Irma Vep, is also a bank employee, and just as she tells her superior that the courier has vanished, an imposter, in beard and bowler hat, strolls in behind them (**4.16**). They turn away from us in surprise as he comes forward (**4.17**). Working in a period when cutting to closer shots was rare in a French film, Feuillade draws our attention to the man by centering him in the doorway.

But suppose a filmmaker is using a more crowded locale. How can a compact setting yield smooth drama? The heroine of Juzo Itami's *Tampopo* is a widow who

4.8

4.9

4.8–4.9 **Actual locations used as setting.** Although Louis Lumière's cameramen were famous for documentary filming, they also made short narratives such as the 1895 *Arroseur arrosé* (4.8). Roberto Rossellini's *Germany Year Zero* (4.9) maintained the tradition of staging fictional stories in actual locations.

4.10   **4.11**

4.10–4.11 Authenticity in constructed settings. Details such as hanging flypaper and posters create a tavern scene in *Greed* (4.10). To replicate an actual newsroom in *All the President's Men* (4.11), even wastepaper from the actual office was scattered around the set.

4.12   **4.13**

4.12–4.13 Stylized settings. The Babylonian sequences of *Intolerance* (4.12) combined influences from Assyrian history, 19th-century biblical illustration, and modern dance. In *Ivan the Terrible,* Part 2, the décor (4.13) dominates the characters.

4.14   **4.15**

4.14–4.15 The interplay of setting and actors. In *Wings of Desire,* busy, colorful graffiti draw attention away from the man lying on the ground (4.14). In contrast, in *Bram Stoker's Dracula,* apart from the candles, the setting of this scene has been obliterated by darkness (4.15).

is trying to improve the food she serves in her restaurant. In one scene, a cowboy-hatted truck driver takes her to another noodle shop to watch professionals do business. Itami has staged the scene so that the kitchen and the counter serve as two arenas for the action. At first, the widow watches the noodle-man take orders, sitting by her mentor on the edge of the kitchen (**4.18**). Quickly, the counter fills with customers calling out orders. The truck driver challenges her to match the orders with the customers, and she steps closer to the center of the kitchen (**4.19**). After she calls out the orders correctly, she turns her back to us, and our interest shifts to the customers, who applaud her (**4.20**).

As the *Tampopo* example shows, color can be an important component of settings. The dark colors of the kitchen surfaces make the widow's red dress stand out. Robert Bresson's *L'Argent* parallels its settings by drab green backgrounds and cold blue props and costumes (**4.21–4.23**). In contrast, Jacques Tati's *Play Time* displays sharply changing color schemes. In the first portion of *Play Time*, the settings and costumes are mostly gray, brown, and black—cold, steely colors. Later in the film, however, beginning in the restaurant scene, the settings start to sport cheery reds, pinks, and greens. This change in the settings' colors supports a narrative development that shows an inhuman city landscape that is transformed by vitality and spontaneity.

A full-size setting need not always be built. Through much of the history of the cinema, filmmakers have used miniature buildings to create fantasy scenes or simply to economize. Parts of settings could also be rendered as paintings and combined photographically with full-sized sections of the space. Now, digital special effects can conjure up settings in comparable ways. When the makers of *Angels & Demons* were refused permission to shoot in Vatican City, they built partial sets of St. Peter's Square and the Pantheon, then filled in the missing stretches (**4.24–4.25**).

In manipulating a shot's setting, the filmmaker may use a *prop,* short for *property.* This is another term borrowed from theatrical mise-en-scene. When an object

4.16

4.17

4.16–4.17 Setting guides attention. In *Les Vampires,* a background frame created by a large doorway emphasizes the importance of an entering character.

4.18

4.20

4.19

4.18–4.20 Activating areas of a setting. In *Tampopo,* at the start of the scene (4.18), the noodle counter, with only two customers, occupies the center of the action. The widow and her truck driver mentor stand inconspicuously at the left. After the counter is full (4.19), the dramatic emphasis shifts to the kitchen when the widow rises and takes the challenge to name the customers' orders. Her red dress helps draw attention to her. When she has triumphantly matched the orders, she gets a round of applause (4.20). By turning her away from us, Itami once more emphasizes the rear counter.

4.21

4.22

4.23

4.21–4.23 Color creates parallels among settings. Color links the affluent home in *L'Argent* (4.21) to the prison (4.22) and later to the old woman's home (4.23).

original plate

4.24

final composite

4.25

4.24–4.25 Digital set replacement. Only a portion of the buildings lining St. Peter's Square were built for *Angels & Demons*. The remainder of the set was covered with greenscreens during filming. Digital matte paintings were added to create major elements like the colonnades at the sides and the tops of the background buildings.

in the setting has a function within the ongoing action, we can call it a prop. Films teem with examples: the snowstorm paperweight that shatters at the beginning of *Citizen Kane,* the little girl's balloon in *M,* the cactus rose in *The Man Who Shot Liberty Valance,* Sarah Connor's hospital bed turned exercise machine in *Terminator 2: Judgment Day.* Comedies often use props to create gags **(4.26).**

Over the course of a narrative, a prop may become a motif. In Alexander Payne's *Election,* the fussy, frustrated high-school teacher is shown cleaning out spoiled food and hallway litter, and these actions prepare for the climactic moment when he crumples a ballot and secretly disposes of it **(4.27–4.29).** Payne calls this the motif of trash, "of throwing things away, since that's in fact the climax of the film. . . . So we establish it early on." Color may help props become motifs. In some scenes of *Finye* (*The Wind*), the recurrent use of orange creates a cluster of nature motifs **(4.30–4.32).** When we look at *Our Hospitality* later in the chapter, we'll examine how elements of setting, particularly props, can weave through a film to create motifs.

Costume and Makeup

If you were planning a film, you'd probably give as much attention to what your actors wear as you pay to their surroundings. Like setting, costume can have a great variety of specific functions in the film's overall form.

Costumes can play causal roles in film plots. In the runaway bus section of *Speed,* Annie's outfit provides the clue that allows Jack to outwit the bomber Howard. During a phone conversation Howard refers to Annie as a "Wildcat." Noticing Annie's University of Arizona sweater, Jack realizes that Howard must have hidden a video camera on the bus. Less obviously, costumes can become motifs, enhancing characterization and tracing changes in attitude **(4.33–4.36).**

In other films, costumes can be used for their purely graphic qualities. Throughout *Ivan the Terrible,* robes and capes are orchestrated with one another in their colors, their textures, and even the way they flow **(4.37).** *Freak Orlando* boldly uses costumes to display primary colors with maximum intensity **(4.38).**

In these last examples, as well as in *Tampopo* (4.18–4.20) and *L'Argent* (4.21–4.23), costume is coordinated with setting. Since the filmmaker usually wants to emphasize the human figures, setting may provide a more or less neutral background, while costume helps pick out the characters. Color design is particularly important

4.26 Comic use of props. The irresponsible protagonist of *Groundhog Day* eats an enormous breakfast; all the dishes serve as props in the diner setting.

> " The best sets are the simplest, most 'decent' ones; everything should contribute to the feeling of the story and anything that does not do this has no place. Reality is usually too complicated. Real locations contain too much that is extreme or contradictory and always require some simplifying: taking things away, unifying colors, etc. This strength through simplicity is much easier to achieve on a built set than in an existing location."
>
> —Stuart Craig, art director, *Notting Hill*

4.27

4.28

4.29

4.27–4.29 Props as motifs in *Election*. As he discards spoiled leftovers, the teacher is suspiciously watched by the custodian—who will play an important role in his downfall (4.27). He tosses a scrap of paper into the corridor trash bin (4.28). The motif culminates in a close-up of the teacher's hand discarding the crucial vote for student council president (4.29).

4.30

4.31

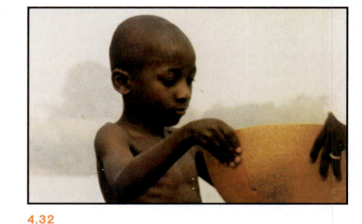

4.32

4.30–4.32 Color as a motif. Souleymane Cissé's *Finye* begins with a woman carrying an orange calabash as the wind rustles through foliage (4.30). Later, the vengeful grandfather prepares to stalk his grandson's persecutor by dressing in orange and making magic before a fire (4.31). At the end, the little boy passes his bowl to someone offscreen (4.32)—possibly a couple seen earlier in the film.

4.33

4.34

4.33–4.34 Costume and character. In a poignant moment in Griffith's *The Birth of a Nation*, the Little Sister decorates her shabby dress with "ermine" made of cotton dotted with spots of soot (4.33). The image suggests both her effort to be elegant and her realization of her poverty. In Fellini's *8½,* the film director Guido persistently uses his dark glasses (4.34) to shield himself from the world.

> The costume is a very important thing. It speaks before you do. You know what you're looking at. You get a reference and it gives context about the other characters and their relationships."
>
> —Harrison Ford, actor

here. The *Freak Orlando* costumes (4.38) stand out boldly against the neutral gray background of an artificial lake. In *The Night of the Shooting Stars,* luminous wheat fields set off the hard black-and-blue costumes of the fascists and the peasants **(4.39).** The director may instead choose to match the color values of setting and costume more closely **(4.40).** This "bleeding" of the costume into the setting is carried to a kind of limit in the prison scene of *THX 1138,* in which George Lucas strips both locale and clothing to stark white on white **(4.41).**

4.35

4.36

4.35–4.36 Costume and character change. When Hildy Johnson, in *His Girl Friday*, switches from her role of aspiring housewife to that of reporter, her hats change as well— from a stylish number with a low-dipping brim (4.35) to a more "masculine" hat with its brim pushed up, journalist-style (4.36).

4.37

4.38

4.37–4.38 Graphic qualities of costumes. In *Ivan the Terrible*, the sweeping folds of a priest's lightweight black robe contrast with the heavy cloak and train of the czar's finery (4.37). In *Freak Orlando*, stylized costumes with intense, primary colors are featured (4.38). The director, Ulrike Ottinger, is a professional costume designer.

Women in Love affords a clear example of how costume and setting can contribute to a film's narrative progression. The opening scenes portray the characters' shallow middle-class life by means of saturated primary and complementary colors in costume and setting **(4.42)**. In the middle portions of the film, as the characters discover love on a country estate, pale pastels predominate **(4.43)**. The last section of *Women in Love* takes place around the Matterhorn, and the characters' ardor has cooled. Now the colors have almost disappeared, and scenes are dominated by pure black and white **(4.44).** By combining with setting, costumes may reinforce narrative and thematic patterns.

Computer technology has been used to graft virtual costumes onto fully computer-generated characters, like Gollum in *The Lord of the Rings* or the many extras in the backgrounds of big crowd scenes. Entirely digital costumes for human actors are less common, but fantasy and science-fiction films have begun using them **(4.45).**

Many of these points about costume apply equally to a closely related area of mise-en-scene, the actors' makeup. In the early days of cinema, makeup was

4.39 Color contrast of costume and setting. In the climactic skirmish of *The Night of the Shooting Stars*, the dark costumes stand out starkly against the more neutral background.

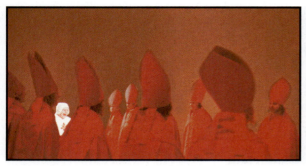

4.40

4.41

4.40–4.41 Color coordinates costume and setting. Fellini's *Casanova* creates a color gradation that runs from bright red costumes to paler red walls (4.40), the whole composition capped by a small white accent in the distance. In *THX 1138*, heads seem to float in space as white costumes blend into white settings (4.41).

4.42

4.43

4.44

4.42–4.44 Costume, setting, and narrative. Bright colors in an early scene of *Women in Love* (4.42) give way to the softer hues of trees and fields (4.43) and finally to a predominantly white-and-black scheme (4.44), contributing to the progression of the story.

4.45 Virtual costume. In making *Green Lantern*, Ryan Reynolds wore a plain gray outfit, and his tight green superhero costume was generated digitally.

necessary because actors' faces would not register well on film stocks. Over the course of film history, a wide range of possibilities emerged. Dreyer's *La Passion de Jeanne d'Arc* was famous for its complete avoidance of makeup **(4.46)**. For *Ivan the Terrible,* however, Nikolai Cherkasov plays the czar wearing a wig and a false beard, nose, and eyebrows **(4.47)**. Changing actors to look like historical personages has been one common function of makeup.

Today makeup usually tries to pass unnoticed, but it also accentuates expressive qualities of the actor's face. Since the camera may record cruel details that we wouldn't notice in ordinary life, unsuitable blemishes, wrinkles, and sagging skin will have to be hidden. The makeup artist can sculpt the face, making it seem narrower or broader by applying blush and shadow. Viewers expect that female performers will wear lipstick and other cosmetics, but the male actors are usually wearing makeup as well **(4.48, 4.49)**.

Film actors rely on their eyes to a very great extent (see A Closer Look, p. 138), and makeup artists can often enhance eye behavior. Eyeliner and mascara can draw attention to the eyes and emphasize the direction of a glance. Nearly every actor will also have expressively shaped eyebrows. Lengthened eyebrows can enlarge the face, while shorter brows make it seem more compact. Eyebrows plucked in a slightly rising curve add gaiety to the face, while slightly sloping ones hint at sadness. Thick, straight brows, commonly applied to men, reinforce the impression of a hard, serious gaze. In such ways eye makeup can assist the actor's performance **(4.50, 4.51)**.

4.46 Plain faces. Pale backgrounds focus attention on the actors' faces in many shots of *La Passion de Jeanne d'Arc.* The actors wore no makeup, and the director, Carl Dreyer, relied on close-ups and tiny facial changes to create an intense religious drama.

4.47 Makeup interprets a historical figure. In *Ivan the Terrible,* Part 1, makeup shapes the eyebrows and hollows the eye sockets to emphasize Ivan's piercing gaze, a central feature in director Sergei Eisenstein's conception of the all-knowing czar.

4.48

4.49

4.48–4.49 Creative choices in makeup. In *Heat* (4.48), Al Pacino's makeup gives him slightly rounded eyebrows and, with the help of the lighting, minimizes the bags under his eyes. In *The Godfather Part III,* made five years before *Heat,* Pacino looks older (4.49). Not only has his hair been whitened, but the makeup, again assisted by the lighting, gives him more sunken and baggy eyes, more hollow cheeks, and a longer, flatter chin.

4.50

4.51

4.50–4.51 Makeup: Man and woman. In *Speed,* Sandra Bullock's eyeliner, shadow, and arched brows make her eyes vivid and give her an alert expression (4.50). For the same scene, the eyeliner on Keanu Reeves makes the upper edges of his eyes stand out (4.51). Note the somewhat fierce slope of the eyebrows, accentuating his slight frown.

4.52 Horror makeup. Jeff Goldblum is nearly unrecognizable under grotesque makeup during his transformation into *The Fly.*

4.53

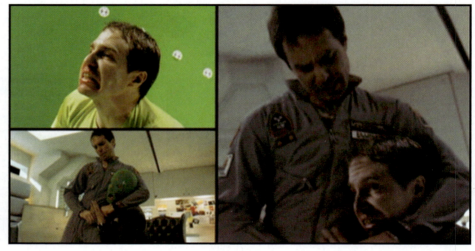

4.54

4.53–4.54 Digital makeup. In *Harry Potter and the Goblet of Fire*, Ralph Fiennes's nose was removed and replaced with nostrils appropriate to the snake-like Lord Voldemort (4.53). When two clones of the same man get into a fight in *Moon,* a stunt man wearing a green hood with motion-capture dots played one of the clones (4.54). Actor Sam Rockwell's head was shot separately and then inserted into the scene.

In recent decades, the craft of makeup has developed in response to the popularity of horror and science fiction genres. Rubber and plasticine compounds create bumps, bulges, extra organs, and layers of artificial skin **(4.52).** In such contexts, makeup, like costume, becomes important in creating character traits or motivating plot action.

Although most makeup continues to be physically applied to actors' faces, digital technology can be used as well. Minor clean-ups remove flaws or shadows from faces. More drastically, a villain can lose a nose, or, via head replacement, an actor can play two roles in the same shot **(4.53–4.54).** CGI has extended the importance of makeup, because now the filmmaker can sculpt entire bodies, not just faces. Gary Sinese's legs were removed so that he could play an amputee in *Forrest Gump,* and a muscular actor was made to look thin and weak before becoming a superhero in *Captain America: The First Avenger.*

Lighting

If you've shot videos with your cellphone or camera, you may not have thought much about manipulating lighting. Modern digital capture can produce a legible

> " Light is everything. It expresses ideology, emotion, colour, depth, style. It can efface, narrate, describe. With the right lighting, the ugliest face, the most idiotic expression can radiate with beauty or intelligence."
>
> —Federico Fellini, director

image in bright or dark situations, and for many purposes, all that matters is that the subject be visible. But the practiced filmmaker wants more than legibility. The image should have pictorial impact, and for that it's vital to control the lighting. Not many actual situations would yield the delicate edge lighting or facial fill light we saw in our shot from *Inglourious Basterds* (4.1).

In artistic filmmaking, lighting is more than just illumination that permits us to see the action. Lighter and darker areas within the frame help create the overall composition of each shot and guide our attention to certain objects and actions. A brightly illuminated patch may draw our eye to a key gesture, while a shadow may conceal a detail or build up suspense about what may be present. Lighting can also articulate textures: the curve of a face, the grain of a piece of wood, the tracery of a spider's web, the sparkle of a gem.

Highlights and Shadows   Lighting shapes objects by creating highlights and shadows. A highlight is a patch of relative brightness on a surface. The man's face in **4.55** and the edge of the fingers in **4.56** display highlights. Highlights provide important cues to the texture of the surface. If the surface is smooth, like glass or chrome, the highlights tend to gleam or sparkle; a rougher surface, like a coarse stone facing, yields more diffuse highlights. Shadows likewise do the same, allowing objects to have portions of darkness (called *shading*) or to cast their shadows onto something else. Thus the fingers in 4.56 are visible partly because they are shaded, while the stark vertical shadows of 4.55 imply prison bars offscreen.

Lighting creates not only textures but also overall shape. If a ball is lit straight on from the front, it appears round. If the same ball is lit from the side, we see it as a half-circle. Hollis Frampton's short film *Lemon* consists primarily of light moving around a lemon, and the shifting shadows and shading create dramatically changing patterns of yellow and black. This film almost seems designed to prove the truth of a remark made by Josef von Sternberg: "The proper use of light can embellish and dramatize every object."

Lighting joins with setting in controlling our sense of a scene's space. In 4.55, a few shadows imply an entire prison cell. Lighting also shapes a shot's overall composition. One image from John Huston's *Asphalt Jungle* welds the gang members into a unit by the pool of light cast by a hanging lamp. At the same time, the lighting sets up a scale of importance, emphasizing the protagonist by making him the most frontal and clearly lit figure (**4.57**).

Quality   For our purposes, we can say that filmmakers exploit and explore four major aspects of lighting: its quality, direction, source, and color. Lighting *quality*

> " Every light has a point where it is brightest and a point toward which it wanders to lose itself completely. . . . The journey of rays from that central core to the outposts of blackness is the adventure and drama of light."
> —Josef von Sternberg

4.55   **4.56**   **4.57**

4.55–4.57 Highlights and shadows. In Cecil B. DeMille's *The Cheat*, the man's face and body display highlights (4.55), while the cast shadows suggest the unseen bars of a jail cell. In Robert Bresson's *Pickpocket*, the edge of the fingers display highlights (4.56), while the hand is subtly modeled by shading. Shadows on faces create a dramatic composition in John Huston's *Asphalt Jungle* (4.57).

4.58

4.59

4.58–4.59 Hard versus soft lighting. In Satyajit Ray's *Aparajito,* Apu's mother and the globe she holds are emphasized by hard lighting (4.58). In another shot from the same film (4.59), softer lighting blurs contours and textures and makes for more diffusion and gentler contrasts between light and shade.

4.60 Frontal lighting. In Jean-Luc Godard's *La Chinoise,* frontal lighting eliminates most surface shading and makes the actress's shadow fall directly behind her, where we cannot see it.

4.61 Side lighting. In *Touch of Evil,* directed by Orson Welles, light from the left creates sharp shading of the character's nose, cheek, and lips.

4.62 Backlighting. In Godard's *Passion,* the lamp and window provide backlighting that presents the woman almost entirely in silhouette.

refers to the relative intensity of the illumination. *Hard* lighting creates clearly defined shadows, crisp textures, and sharp edges, whereas *soft* lighting creates a diffused illumination. In nature, the noonday sun creates hard light, while an overcast sky creates soft light. The terms are relative, and many lighting situations will fall between the extremes, but we can usually recognize the differences **(4.58, 4.59).**

Direction   The *direction* of lighting in a shot refers to the path of light from its source or sources to the object lit. For convenience we can distinguish among frontal lighting, sidelighting, backlighting, underlighting, and top lighting.

   Frontal lighting can be recognized by its tendency to eliminate shadows. In **4.60,** from Jean-Luc Godard's *La Chinoise,* the result of such frontal lighting is a fairly flat-looking image. Contrast **4.61,** in which a hard **sidelight** (also called a *crosslight*) sculpt's the character's features.

   Backlighting, as the name suggests, comes from behind the subject. The light can be positioned at many angles: high above the figure, at various angles off to the side, pointing straight at the camera, or from below. Used with no other sources of light, backlighting tends to create silhouettes, as in **4.62.** Combined with more frontal sources of light, the technique can create a subtle contour, as we saw with Raine's black cowl in *Inglourious Basterds* (4.1). This use of backlighting is called *edge lighting* or *rim lighting* **(4.63).**

   As its name implies, **underlighting** suggests that the light comes from below the subject. Since underlighting tends to distort features, it is often used to create dramatic horror effects, but it may also simply indicate a realistic light source, such as a fireplace, or, as in **4.64,** a flashlight. As usual, a particular technique can function differently according to context.

   Top lighting is exemplified by **4.65,** where the spotlight shines down from almost directly above Marlene Dietrich's face. Here top lighting creates a glamorous image. In our earlier example from *Asphalt Jungle* (4.57), the light from above is harder, in keeping with the conventional harshness of crime films. Director Jacques Audiard chose to use top lighting with very little fill in his prison drama *A Prophet*: "It's a matter of realism—everything is not visible all the time" **(4.66).**

Source   Lighting has a quality, and it has direction. It can also be characterized by its *source*. In making a documentary, the filmmaker may be obliged to shoot with whatever light is available. Most fictional films, however, use extra light

4.63 Edge, or rim, lighting. Edge lighting makes the outline of each actor's
body stand out from the background.
This shot from *Wings* shows edge lighting on many parts of the frame, especially along the actors' faces and hair
and on the edge of the porch.

4.64 Underlighting. In *The Sixth Sense*, a flashlight lights the boy's face from
below, enhancing our empathy with his fright as he feels the presence of a ghost.

sources to obtain greater control of the image's look. Typically the table lamps and
streetlights you see in a set aren't strong or varied enough to create a powerful image. Still, the filmmaker will usually create a lighting design that seems consistent
with the sources in the setting. The pattern of illumination is motivated by the visible sources. (See p. 63.)

Look back at Figure 4.1, the confrontation in *Inglourious Basterds.* The pattern
of light we see is roughly consistent with the source in the shot, the street lamp in
the alley. But that lamp at that distance could not produce the hard light on Landa's
head or the fill light that reveals his features. In **4.67,** from *The Miracle Worker,* the
window in the rear and the lantern in the right foreground appear to be the sources
of illumination, but many studio lights supplemented them.

Directors and cinematographers manipulating the lighting of the scene typically decide on two primary sources: a **key light** and a **fill light.** The key light is
the primary source, providing the brightest illumination and casting the strongest
shadows. The key light is the most directional light, and it is usually suggested by a
light source in the setting. A fill is a less intense illumination that "fills in," soften-
ing or eliminating shadows cast by the key light. By combining key and fill, and by
adding other sources, lighting can be controlled quite exactly.

The key lighting source may be aimed at the subject from any angle, as we've
seen. In our shot from *The Sixth Sense* (4.64), underlighting may be the key source,
while a softer and dimmer fill falls on the setting in the background. Lights from
various directions are often combined (**4.68**).

Classical Hollywood filmmaking developed the custom of using at least three
light sources per shot: key light, fill light, and backlight. The most basic arrangement
of these lights on a single figure is shown in **4.69.** The *backlight* typically comes
from behind and above the figure, the *key light* comes diagonally from the front,
and a *fill light* comes from a position near the camera. The key will usually be closer
to the figure or brighter than the fill. Typically, each major character in a scene will
have his or her own key light, fill light, and backlight. If another actor is added (the
dotted figure in 4.69), the key light for one can be altered slightly to form the backlight for the other, and vice versa, with a fill light on either side of the camera.

In **4.70,** the Bette Davis character in *Jezebel* is the most important figure, and
the **three-point lighting** centers attention on her. The key light is off left, making
her right arm brightly illuminated. A fill light comes from just to the right of the
camera. It is less bright than the key. This balanced lighting creates mild shading,
modeling Davis's face to suggest volume rather than flatness. (A slight shadow is
cast by her nose.) A bright backlight from the rear upper right highlights her hair

4.65 Top lighting for glamour.
Director Josef Von Sternberg frequently
used a high frontal light to bring out the
cheekbones of his star, as shown here in
Shanghai Express.

4.66 Top lighting for realism. Since
actors' eyes are crucial to their performances, most filmmakers light scenes to
make the eyes visible. But in the prison
cells of *A Prophet*, harsh single-source
lighting from above often renders the
eyes as dark patches, making the characters more sinister and inscrutable.

CONNECT TO THE BLOG
www.davidbordwell.net/blog

We discuss a lecture on lighting by master cinematographer Steven Poster (*Donnie Darko*) in "Light is a law."

4.67 Motivating light sources. In this shot from *The Miracle Worker,* motivated light from the window and lantern is enhanced by offscreen studio lights. If you look closely, you can see the extra sources reflected in the lantern.

4.68 Combining light sources and directions. In this frame from Eisenstein's *Bezhin Meadow,* the key light falling on the figures comes from the left side. It is hard on the face of the old woman in the foreground, but a fill light from the right softens the illumination on the man's face.

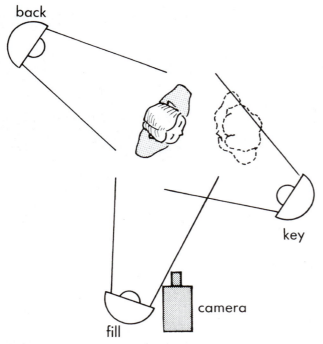

4.69 Three-point lighting, one of the basic techniques of Hollywood cinema.

4.70 Three-point lighting as it looks on the screen. In this frame from *Jezebel,* Betty Davis's character is the most important, and the lighting concentrates on her.

4.71 Three-point lighting in high key. In *Amélie,* the lighthearted romantic tone is enhanced by high-key, three-point lighting. Its layout of sources is similar to that shown in 4.69.

and edge-lights her left arm. Davis's backlight and key light also illuminate the woman behind her at the right, but less prominently. Other fill lights, called *background* or *set lighting,* fall on the setting and on the crowd at the left rear. Three-point lighting emerged during the studio era of Hollywood filmmaking, and it is still widely used, as in **4.71.**

We've referred to key, fill, and backlight as separate sources, but in production there will often be many lighting units providing each of those. Several lamps, for instance, might be recruited to provide a strong key light. Moreover, you've probably already realized that this three-point lighting system demands that the lamps be rearranged virtually every time the camera shifts to a new framing. In spite of the great cost involved, most commercial filmmakers choose to adjust lighting for each camera position. Changing light sources this way isn't very realistic, but it does enable filmmakers to create strong compositions for each shot.

Three-point lighting was particularly well suited for the high-key lighting used in classical Hollywood cinema and other filmmaking traditions. **High-key lighting** refers to an overall lighting design that uses fill light and backlight to create relatively low contrast between brighter and darker areas. Usually, the light quality is soft, making shadow areas fairly transparent. The frames from *Jezebel* (4.70) and *Amélie* (4.71) exemplify high-key lighting. Hollywood directors and cinematographers have chosen this pattern for comedies and most dramas.

High-key lighting is not used simply to render a brightly lit situation, such as a dazzling ballroom or a sunny afternoon. High-key lighting is an overall approach to illumination that can suggest different lighting conditions or times of day. Consider, for example, two frames from *Back to the Future*. The first shot **(4.72)** uses high-key illumination matched to daylight and a brightly lit malt shop. The second frame **(4.73)** is from a scene set in a room at night, but it still uses the high-key approach, as can be seen from the lighting's softness, its low contrast, and its detail in shadow areas.

Low-key lighting creates stronger contrasts and sharper, darker shadows. Often the lighting is hard, and fill light is lessened or eliminated altogether. The effect is of *chiaroscuro,* or extremely dark and light regions within the image. An example is **4.74,** from *Kanal.* Here the fill light and background light are less intense than in high-key technique. As a result, shadow areas on the left third of the screen remain hard and fairly opaque. In **4.75,** a low-key shot from Leos Carax's *Mauvais sang,* the key light is hard and comes from the left side. Carax eliminates both fill and background illumination, creating very sharp shadows and a dark void around the characters.

As our examples indicate, low-key lighting is often applied to somber, threatening, or mysterious scenes. It was common in horror films of the 1930s and *films noirs* (dark films) of the 1940s and 1950s. The low-key approach was revived in the 1980s in such films as *Blade Runner* and *Rumble Fish* and continued in the 1990s in films noirs like *Se7en* and *The Usual Suspects.* In *El Sur,* Victor Erice's low-key lighting yields dramatic chiaroscuro effects **(4.76).**

When the actors change position, the director faces another forced choice: to alter the lighting or not. Surprisingly often, directors decide to maintain a constant lighting on the actors as they walk, even though that's quite unrealistic. By

> "When taking close-ups in a colour picture, there is too much visual information in the background, which tends to draw attention away from the face. That is why the faces of the actresses in the old black and white pictures are so vividly remembered. Even now, movie fans nostalgically recall Dietrich . . . Garbo . . . Lamarr . . . Why? Filmed in black and white, those figures looked as if they were lit from within. When a face appeared on the screen overexposed—the high-key technique, which also erased imperfections— it was as if a bright object was emerging from the screen."
> —Nestor Almendros, cinematographer

> "When I started watching films in the 1940s and 1950s, Indian cinematography was completely under the influence of Hollywood aesthetics, which mostly insisted on the 'ideal light' for the face, using heavy diffusion and strong backlight. I came to resent the complete disregard of the actual source of light and the clichéd use of backlight. Using backlight all the time is like using chili powder in whatever you cook."
> —Subrata Mitra, cinematographer

4.72

4.73

4.72–4.73 High-key lighting for different times and settings. *Back to the Future*: A brightly lit malt shop in daytime (4.72) and Doc's laboratory at night (4.73) both get the high-key treatment.

4.74

4.75

4.74–4.76 **Low-key lighting.** In Andrzej Wajda's *Kanal,* low-key lighting creates a harsh highlight on one side of the woman's face, a deep shadow on the other (4.74). In *Mauvais sang,* a single key light without any fill on the actress's face leaves her expression nearly invisible (4.75). In *El Sur,* low-key lighting suggests that the child views the adult world as full of mystery and danger (4.76).

4.76

4.77

4.78

4.79

4.77–4.79 **Light, constant or changing?** At the end of Fellini's *Nights of Cabiria,* the heroine moves diagonally toward us, accompanied by a band of young street musicians (4.77). As she walks, the lighting on her face does not vary, enabling us to notice slight changes in her expression (4.78). By contrast, the sword fight in *Rashomon* is intensified by the contrast between the ferocious combat and the cheerfully dappled lighting pouring into the glade (4.79).

overlapping several different key-lighting units, the filmmaker can maintain a constant intensity on moving actors. As a result, distracting shadows and highlights do not flit across them **(4.77, 4.78).** Alternatively, the filmmaker may prefer to have the players move through shifting patches of light and shade **(4.79).**

In today's big-budget films, there are often three or more cameras covering scenes in large settings. To avoid lengthy rearrangement of dozens of lamps, the cinematographer will often opt for a soft, bright top-light covering the entire scene. Wherever the cameras are placed, the lighting units will not be visible on camera. In *The Wolfman* (2010), a nighttime forest scene had many lights nested in big translucent boxes hung on cranes above the location.

Color   We tend to think of film lighting as limited to two colors, the white of sunlight or the soft yellow of incandescent room lamps. In practice, filmmakers who choose to control lighting typically work with as purely white a light as they can. With filters placed in front of the light source, the film-maker can color the onscreen illumination in any fashion.

There may be a realistic source in the scene to moti-vate colored light (**4.80**). Alternatively, colored light can also be unrealistic. In Eisenstein's *Ivan the Terrible*, Part 2, a blue light suddenly bursts upon the actor without any diegetic source. In the context of the scene, the abrupt light-ing change expresses the character's terror and uncertainty (**4.81, 4.82**). Using lighting instead of acting to convey an emotion makes the scene more vivid and surprising.

Most film lighting is arranged as part of preparation for live-action filmmaking. But what if the settings and figures are created with a computer? Scanning a model or motion-capturing a figure does not record the light falling on it, and the resulting image is a neutral gray. Animators add simulated light to a scene using dedicated programs. Watch the credits for any special-effects-heavy film, and you will see long lists of names of people dealing with light and shade.

In *The Golden Compass,* the vicious combat between two armored polar bears was created entirely digitally. The fight takes place with a bright sun low in the sky, coming from off right. The icy clearing contains shadows of the surrounding crags (**4.83**). Simulated light is also used in digital animation. Pixar's *Cars* experimented with rendering the look of colored lights reflected on metal and glass (**4.84**).

We are used to ignoring the illumination of our everyday surroundings, so film lighting is easy to take for granted. Yet the power of a shot is centrally controlled by light quality, direction, source, and color. The filmmaker can manipulate and combine these factors to shape the viewer's experience in a great many ways. No component of mise-en-scene is more important than what Sternberg called "the drama and adventure of light."

Staging: Movement and Performance

When we think of a film director, we usually think of someone directing perform-ers. The director is the person who says, "Stand over there," "Walk toward the cam-era," or "Show that you're holding back tears." In such ways, the director controls a major component of mise-en-scene: the figures we see onscreen. Typically the fig-ure is a person, but it could be an animal (Lassie the collie, Balthasar the donkey), a robot, an object (**4.85**), or even a pure shape (**4.86**). Mise-en-scene allows all these entities to express feelings and thoughts; it can also dynamize them to create kinetic patterns (**4.87–4.88**).

Cinema gains great freedom from the fact that here expression and movement aren't restricted to human figures. Puppets may be manipulated frame by frame through the technique of *stop-action* or *stop-motion* (**4.89**). In science-fiction and fantasy movies, robots and fabulous monsters created as models can be scanned and movement added via computer manipulation (1.27). The filmmaker can breathe life into two-dimensional characters like Shrek or Daffy Duck. Even if the figures are fantastical, however, the filmmaker is obliged to stage their actions and con-struct their performances.

Acting and Actuality   Although abstract shapes and animated figures can be-come important in the mise-en-scene, the most familiar cases of figure expression and movement involve actors performing roles. An actor's performance consists of visual elements (appearance, gestures, facial expressions) and sound (voice, effects).

4.80 Filtered lighting. An orange filter suggests that all the light in this scene from *The Green Room* comes from candles.

4.81

4.82

4.81–4.82 Lighting without a mo-tivated source. In *Ivan the Terrible,* a character's fear registers on his face (4.81), and this is underscored by a blue light that bursts onto him (4.82).

CONNECT TO THE BLOG
www.davidbordwell.net/blog

Our entry on "The Cross" talks about a kind of staging largely forgotten in this era of rapid cutting and close framing. We discuss how scenic de-tails can be integrated into staging in "You are my density."

4.83

4.84

4.83–4.84 **Digitally simulated lighting.** In *The Golden Compass*, stark arctic sunshine from offscreen right falls as sidelight on the snow and the fighting bears (4.83). Simulated fill light was added to the onlookers and in areas of shading on the foreground bears. *Cars* puts on a virtuoso display of computer-simulated lighting, with neon signs reflecting in shiny surfaces as the cars cruise through their small-town street (4.84).

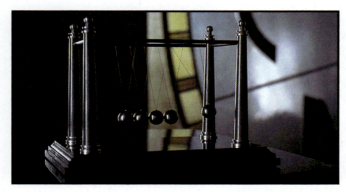

4.85

4.86

4.85–4.86 **Controlling figure movement.** In *The Hudsucker Proxy*, when the mailboy Norville proposes his new toy idea, the clicking balls on his boss's desktop inexplicably stop (4.85). The abstract film *Parabola* uses lighting and a pure background to emphasize shifting sculptural forms (4.86).

4.87

4.88

4.89 **Stop-motion animation.** Ladislav Starevich's puppet film *The Mascot* includes a conversation between a devil and a thief, with subtle facial expressions and gestures created through animation.

4.87–4.88 **Stasis and violence in figure movement.** In *Seven Samurai*, the samurai have won the battle with the bandits (4.87). Virtually the only movement in the frame is the driving rain, but the slouching postures of the men leaning on their spears express their tense weariness. By contrast, in *White Heat*, explosive movements and ferocious facial expressions present an image of psychotic rage as Cody Jarrett (James Cagney) learns of his mother's death (4.88).

At times, of course, an actor may contribute only visual aspects, as in silent movies. In rare cases, an actor's performance may exist only on the sound track of the film. In *A Letter to Three Wives*, Celeste Holm's character, Addie Ross, speaks a narration over the images but never appears on the screen.

Acting is often approached as a question of realism. But concepts of realistic acting have changed over film history. Today we may think that Hilary Swank in *Boys Don't Cry* and Heath Ledger and Jake Gyllenhaal in *Brokeback Mountain* give performances that are close to natural behavior. Yet in the early 1950s, the New York Actors Studio style, as exemplified by Marlon Brando's performances in *On the Waterfront* and *A Streetcar Named Desire*, was also thought to be extremely realistic. Fine though we may still find Brando's work, today his portrayals seem deliberate, heightened, and fairly unrealistic. Going back farther, post–World War II Italian Neorealist films were hailed as almost documentary depictions of Italian life (p. 488). But many of their performances now look as polished as those in Hollywood films. Already, major naturalistic performances of the 1970s, such as Robert De Niro's protagonist in *Taxi Driver*, seem quite stylized. Who can say what the acting in *Boys Don't Cry, Brokeback Mountain, Frozen River, The King's Speech*, and other films will look like in a few decades?

There's another reason to be cautious in appealing to realism. Not all films try to achieve it. Since the performance an actor creates is part of the overall mise-en-scene, films contain a wide variety of acting styles. Instead of assuming that acting must be realistic, we should try to understand what kind of acting style the film is aiming at. If the film is best served by a nonrealistic performance, the skillful actor will strive to deliver that.

For example, comedy seldom strives for surface realism. In *All of Me* Steve Martin portrays a man whose body is suddenly inhabited on the right side by the soul of a woman who has just died. Martin used sudden changes of voice, along with acrobatic pantomime, to suggest a split body, half-male and half-female. The performance doesn't conform to realism, since the plot situation couldn't exist in the real world. In a comedy, however, Martin's performance was completely appropriate, and hilarious.

It isn't only comedies that encourage stylized performance. Fantasy films do, too, as we see in certain parts of *The Wizard of Oz*. (How would a real Wicked Witch behave?) In melodramas and action films from Hollywood, India, Hong Kong, and other traditions, exaggerated performances are a crucial source of the audience's pleasure. Viewers do not expect narrowly realistic acting from martial-arts stars Jet Li and Jackie Chan.

CONNECT TO THE BLOG
www.davidbordwell.net/blog

How can we analyze film acting? We make some suggestions, especially about silent-film performance, in "Acting up." The entry "Faces behind Facebook" considers actors' performances in *The Social Network*.

❝I get impatient with many Hollywood films because there's this assumption that meaning or emotion is contained in those few square inches of an actor's face and I just don't see it that way at all. I think there's a power in withholding information, revealing things gradually. Letting the audience discover things within the frame in time, in the way they stand.❞
—Alison Maclean, director, *Crush*

We might think that the most important task facing an actor is speaking dialogue in a convincing and stirring way. Certainly, voice and delivery are very important in cinema, but considered in terms of mise-en-scene, the actor is always part of the overall visual design. Many film scenes contain little or no dialogue, but at every moment onscreen, the actor must be in character. The actor and director shape the performance pictorially.

Most of the time, film actors use their faces. This was most evident before movies had sound, and theorists of the silent film were full of praise for the subtle facial acting of Charlie Chaplin, Greta Garbo, and Lillian Gish. Since some happiness, fear, anger, and other facial expressions are understood easily across cultures, silent films could become popular around the world. Today, with mainstream films using many close-ups (see p. 45), actors' faces are hugely enlarged, and the performers must control their expressions minutely.

The most expressive parts of the face are the mouth, eyebrows, and eyes. All work together to signal how the character is responding to the dramatic situation. In *Jerry Maguire*, the accountant Dorothy Boyd accidentally meets Jerry at an airport baggage conveyor. She has a crush on him, partly because she admires the courageous mission statement he has issued to the sports agency that they work for. As he starts to back off from the statement, she eagerly quotes it from memory; Renée Zellwegger's earnest smile and admiring gaze suggest that she takes the issues more seriously than Jerry does **(4.90)**. This impression is confirmed when Jerry says, "Uh-huh" and studies her skeptically, his fixed smile signaling social politeness rather than genuine pride **(4.91)**. This encounter sets up one premise of the film—that Jerry's idealistic impulses will need constant shoring up, for he might at any moment slip back into being "a shark in a suit."

The eyes hold a special place in film. In any scene, crucial story information is conveyed by the direction of a character's glance, the use of the eyelids, and the shape of the eyebrows. One of Chaplin's most heart-rending moments comes in *City Lights,* when the blind flower girl, now sighted, suddenly realizes that he's her benefactor and we must find signs of hope in his eyes **(4.92)**.

Normally, we don't stare intently at the people we talk with. We glance away about half the time to gather our thoughts, and we blink 10–12 times a minute. But actors must learn to look directly at each other, locking eyes and seldom blinking. If an actor glances away from the partner in the conversation, it suggests distraction or evasion. If an actor blinks, it suggests a reaction to what is happening in the scene (surprise, or anxiety). Actors playing forceful characters often stare fixedly. Anthony Hopkins said this of playing Hannibal Lecter: "If you don't blink you can keep the audience mesmerized." (See 8.7, 8.9.) In our *Jerry Maguire* scene, the protagonists watch each other fixedly. When Jerry closes his eyes in response to Dorothy's praise, it indicates his nervousness about confronting the issues that his mission statement raised.

Thanks to facial expressions—eyes plus eyebrows plus mouth—actors can develop their characterizations across the film. *The Social Network* centers on two college friends, Mark Zuckerberg and Eduardo Savarin, who collaborate to create Facebook. Throughout the film Jesse Eisenberg plays Mark with knitted brows, squinting eyes, and a grimly set mouth, all suggesting his fierce concentration and competitiveness **(4.93)**. By contrast Andrew Garfield portrays the more trusting Eduardo with wide eyes, raised brows, and slightly bowed head **(4.94)**. In their climactic confrontation, during a deposition for the suit that Eduardo has filed against Mark, Eduardo's facial behavior has changed to a direct, frowning challenge **(4.95)**. This causes Mark to lower his head in embarrassment, an unusual reaction for the aggressive entrepreneur we've seen so far **(4.96)**.

4.90   **4.91**

4.90–4.91 Facial expressiveness in close-ups. Perky and sincere, Dorothy pledges allegiance to Jerry Maguire's idealistic memo (4.90). Jerry smiles politely, but his sideways glance and raised brows suggest that he is a bit put off by her earnestness (4.91).

4.92 Acting with the eyes. In the climax of *City Lights*, Chaplin nervously twirls a flower, so we can't see the shape of his mouth. We must read yearning in his brows and rapt, dark gaze.

4.93

4.94

4.95

4.96

4.93–4.96 Character domination through actors' expressions. Early in *The Social Network*, Mark insists that Eduardo invest more in Facebook. The actors' expressions establish Mark as a tough, demanding leader and Eduardo as more submissive (4.93–4.94). During the climactic deposition, Eduardo fights back facially, and Mark submits (4.95–4.96).

4.97

4.98

4.99

4.97–4.99 Extroverted acting for extravagant suffering. In *Tigre Reale*, Menichelli's right hand seizes her hair, as if pulling her head back in agony; but her body still expresses defiance, thrust forward and standing firm as the left hand grips her waist (4.97). As Menichelli begins to feel shame, she retreats toward the fireplace, turning from us and slumping in a way that suggests regret (4.98). She keeps her back to the camera as she withdraws, now a pathetic figure (4.99).

Actors act with their bodies as well as their faces. How a character walks, stands, or sits conveys a great deal about personality and attitude. In fact, during the 18th and 19th centuries, *attitude* was used to refer to the way a person stood. Stage acting gave early film a repertoire of postures that could express a character's state of mind. In the 1916 Italian film *Tigre Reale* (*The Royal Tigress*), the diva Pina Menichelli plays a countess with a shady past. At one point, she confesses this in a florid attitude that expresses noble suffering **(4.97).** While few actors today would resort to

this stylized posture, early film audiences would have accepted it as vividly expressive, like a movement in dance. Menichelli plays the rest of the scene more quietly, but she still employs expressive attitudes **(4.98, 4.99).**

Chaplin's and Menichelli's gestures show that hands are important tools of the film actor. Hands are to the body what eyes are to the face: They focus our attention and evoke the character's thoughts and feelings. Actress Maureen O'Hara said of Henry Fonda, "All he had to do was wag his little finger and he could steal a scene from anybody." A good example can be seen in the doomsday thriller *Fail-Safe*. Henry Fonda plays the U.S. president, who has learned that an American warplane has been accidentally sent to bomb the Soviet Union. Fonda stands erect at the phone as he hears distressing news about the plane's

progress, and he hangs up with his left hand **(4.100–4.103)**. By keeping most of the shot still and bare, director Sidney Lumet has given Fonda's fingers the main role, letting them express the president's measured prudence but also suggesting the strain of the crisis.

4.100

4.101

4.102

4.103

4.100–4.103 **Acting as finger exercise.** In *Fail-Safe*, the president stands erect at the phone as he hears distressing news about the plane's progress, and he hangs up with his left hand (4.100). The president pauses and rubs his fingers together thoughtfully (4.101), then he taps into the intercom with his right hand (4.102). As he waits, for a brief moment his left fingers waggle anxiously, betraying his nervous concern (4.103).

CONNECT TO THE BLOG
www.davidbordwell.net/blog

For more on how actors use their hands, see "Hand jive."

Finally, when we watch any fictional film, we are to some degree aware that the performances are the result of the actors' skills and decisions. (See "A Closer Look.") When we use the phrase "larger than life" to describe an effective performance, we seem to be acknowledging the actor's craft. In analyzing a particular film, we usually must go beyond assumptions about realism and consider the purposes that the actor's craft serves. How appropriate, we can ask, is the performance to the context established by the genre, the film's narrative, and the overall mise-en-scene? A performance, realistic or not, should be examined according to its function in the film's overall formal design.

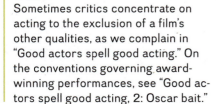

CONNECT TO THE BLOG
www.davidbordwell.net/blog

Sometimes critics concentrate on acting to the exclusion of a film's other qualities, as we complain in "Good actors spell good acting." On the conventions governing award-winning performances, see "Good actors spell good acting, 2: Oscar bait."

Acting: Functions and Motivation We can consider performance along two dimensions. A performance will be more or less *individualized,* and it will be more or less *stylized.* Often we have both in mind when we think of a realistic performance: it creates a unique character, and it does not seem too exaggerated or too underplayed. Marlon Brando's portrayal of Don Vito Corleone in *The Godfather* is quite individualized. Brando gives the Godfather a complex psychology, a distinctive appearance and voice, and a string of facial expressions and gestures that make him significantly different from the standard image of a gang boss. As for styliza-tion, Brando keeps Don Vito in the middle range. His performance is neither flat nor flamboyant. He isn't impassive, but he doesn't chew the scenery either.

Yet this middle range, which we often identify with realistic performance, isn't the only option. On the individuality scale, films may create broader, more anonymous *types*. Classical Hollywood narrative was built on ideologically stereo-typed roles: the Irish cop on the beat, the black servant, the Jewish pawnbroker, the wisecracking waitress or showgirl. Through *typecasting,* actors were selected and directed to conform to what audiences expected. Often, however, skillful perform-ers gave these conventions a freshness and vividness. The 1920s Soviet filmmakers adapted this principle, which they called *typage.* Here the actor was expected to por-tray a typical representative of a social class or historical movement **(4.104, 4.105).**

Whether more or less typed, the performance can also be located on a con-tinuum of stylization. A long tradition of film acting strives for an expressive natu-ralness, with actors speaking their lines with slightly more clarity and emotion than we usually find in everyday life. The director and the performer may choose to enhance this streamlined naturalness by adding specific physical actions. Frequent gestures and movements by the actors add plausibility to the humor of Woody Al-len's films **(4.106).**

The actor is usually obliged to express emotion, but emotions come in many colors. Some are intense and burst out violently **(4.107).** Other emotions are masked, as when jealousy and suspicion are covered by excessive politeness **(4.108).** Some-times emotional expression is broad and sweeping, almost operatic **(4.109).** And the same film may combine different degrees of emotional stylization. *Amadeus* contrasts a grotesque, giggling performance by Tom Hulce as Mozart with Murray Abraham's suave Salieri. The two acting styles sharpen the contrast between the older composer's decorous but dull music and the young man's offensive genius. In every film, the actor needs to blend the performance with the genre, the narrative, and the overall formal patterning.

Films like *Ivan the Terrible* and *Amadeus* create stylized performances through extroversion and exaggeration. The director can also explore the possibilities of very muted performances. Compared to normal practice, highly restrained acting can seem quite stylized. Robert Bresson is noted for such restrained performances. Using nonprofessional actors and drilling them in the de-tails of the characters' physical actions, Bresson makes his actors nearly flat by conventional standards **(4.110, 4.111).** Although these performances may upset our expectations, we soon realize that such restraint focuses our attention on details of action we never notice in most movies.

Motion and Performance Capture   Since the cre-ation of digitally generated characters Jar Jar Binks in *Star Wars: Episode 1—The Phantom Menace* in 1999 and Gol-lum in *The Lord of the Rings: The Two Towers* (2002), actors have had to learn new skills. In these early films, perform-ers in special suits covered with dots were filmed digitally to form the basis for characters' movements. Soon CGI (computer-generated imagery) programs allowed more dense arrays of dots to capture smaller details of facial movement **(4.112).** The addition of tiny cameras attached to the actors' heads permitted even subtler capture of expressions.

Now a distinction is made between *motion capture,* where the whole body is filmed, and *performance cap-ture,* which concentrates on the face **(4.113, 4.114).** Motion capture can also be used on animals. Thanks to capture

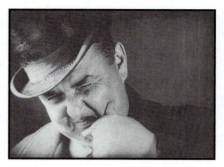

4.104

4.105

4.104–105 A range of acting styles in the same film. The opening of Eisenstein's *Strike* presents the cartoon-ish cliché of the top-hatted capitalist (4.104), while in contrast the workers are presented as earnest and resolute (4.105).

4.106 Expressive naturalness in acting style. In *Hannah and Her Sisters,* Mia Farrow as Hannah, Diane Wiest as her sister Holly, and Carrie Fisher as their friend April set a table, chatting about the other guests as they do so.

4.107   **4.108**   **4.109**

4.107–4.109 Stylized acting and emotion. In *Winchester 73*, James Stewart's mild manner occasionally erupts into vengeful anger, revealing him as on the brink of psychosis (4.107). The exaggerated smiles and gestures in *Trouble in Paradise* are amusing because we know that the women, competing for the same man, are only pretending to be friends (4.108). Nikolai Cherkasov's dramatically raised arm and thrown-back head are appropriate to *Ivan the Terrible,* which creates a larger-than-life portrait of its hero (4.109).

4.110   **4.111**

4.110–4.111 Restrained acting. Playing the heroine of *Au Hasard Balthasar,* Anna Wiazemsky looks without expression at her would-be seducer, who wants her to get in his car (4.110). She glances downward, still without registering her thoughts, before sliding in (4.111).

dots, ordinary horses can be transformed into fantastical creatures, as when the six-legged Direhorses were created for *Avatar. The Polar Express, Beowulf, The Adventures of Tintin,* and other animated films used motion and performance capture for both human and nonhuman creatures.

In predigital days, actors would play fantasy characters with heavy prosthetics and ample makeup. Motion capture and performance capture make it easier for the actor to concentrate on the performance. As James Cameron explained:

> Actors have said to me, half jokingly but a little nervously, "Are you trying to replace actors?" And of course, the answer is no, we love actors. This whole thing is about acting. It's about creating these fantasy characters through the process of acting. What we're replacing is five hours in the makeup chair, having rubber glued all over your face.

4.112 Digital capture of detailed facial movements. For his role as Davy Jones in *Pirates of the Caribbean: Dead Man's Chest,* actor Bill Nighy had white motion-capture dots applied to his face. His expressions were used to create virtual makeup, including a beard made of writhing tentacles.

Acting in the Context of Other Techniques   By examining how an actor's performance functions within the overall film, we can also notice how acting blends with other film techniques. For instance, the actor is always a graphic element in the film, but some films underline this fact. In *The Cabinet*

4.113

4.114

4.113–4.114 Motion and performance capture. In the high-tech studio used for *Avatar*, actors wear full-body motion-capture suits (4.113). For performance capture of Sam Worthington, green dots cover the most expressive areas of the face (4.114). A miniature camera, with rows of small LED bulbs trained on his face, adds extra light as it records his shifting expressions.

4.115

4.116

4.115–4.116 The actor as graphic element. In *The Cabinet of Dr. Caligari*, Cesare's body echoes the tilted tree trunks (4.115), his arms and hands their branches and leaves. In *Breathless*, Jean Seberg's face is linked to a Renoir painting (4.116). Does she give an inexpressive performance or an enigmatic one?

CONNECT TO THE BLOG
www.davidbordwell.net/blog

When digital technology is involved, where does the actor's performance leave off and the special effects begin? We consider the question in "Motion-capturing an Oscar."

of Dr. Caligari, Conrad Veidt's dancelike portrayal of the somnambulist Cesare makes him blend in with the graphic elements of the setting **(4.115)**. The graphic design of this scene in *Caligari* typifies the systematic distortion characteristic of German Expressionism (pp. 473–476).

In *Breathless*, director Jean-Luc Godard juxtaposes Jean Seberg's face with a print of a Renoir painting **(4.116)**. We might think that Seberg is giving a bland performance here, for she simply poses in the frame and turns her head. Indeed, her acting in the entire film may seem somewhat inexpressive. Yet her face and demeanor are appropriate for her role, a capricious American woman unfathomable to her Parisian boyfriend.

A performance may be shaped by editing as well. Because a film is shot over a period of time, actors perform in bits, with separate shots recording different portions of a scene. This process can work to the filmmaker's advantage. If there are alternate takes of each shot, the editor can select the best gestures and expressions and create a composite performance better than any sustained performance is likely to be. By adding sound and other shots, the filmmaker can build up the performance still further. Sometimes a performance will be created almost wholly in postproduction. The director may simply tell an actor to stare offscreen, wide-eyed. If the next shot shows a hand with a gun, we are likely to think the actor is depicting fear effectively.

4.117

4.118

4.117–4.118 Performance in long shot and close-up. *The Spider's Stratagem*: In long shot, the actors' manner of walking helps characterize them (4.117). The stiff, upright way in which the heroine holds her parasol is one of the main facets of Alida Valli's performance. In a closer framing, her performance displays detailed eye and lip movements (4.118).

4.119 Editing to create a performance. In *Aliens*, editing makes it seem that Jonesy is reacting angrily to something in the scene.

Camera techniques also create a controlling context for acting. Film acting, as you know, differs from theatrical acting. In a theater, we are usually at a considerable distance from the actor on the stage. We certainly can never get as close to the theater actor as the camera can put us in a film. For that reason, we're inclined to think that the film actor must always underplay—that is, act in a more restrained fashion than stage acting would require. But recall that the camera can be at *any* distance from the figure. Filmed from very far away, the actor is a dot on the screen—much smaller than an actor on stage seen from the back of the balcony. Filmed from very close, the actor's tiniest eye movement may be revealed.

Thus the film actor must behave differently than the stage actor does, but not always by being more restrained. Rather, she or he must be able to *adjust to each type of camera distance*. If the actor is far from the camera, he or she may have to gesture broadly or move around to be seen as acting at all. But if the camera and actor are inches apart, a twitch of a mouth muscle will come across clearly. Between these extremes, there is a whole range of adjustments to be made.

Often a shot will concentrate on either the actor's facial expression or on bodily movement. In most close shots, the face will be emphasized, and so the actor will have to control eyes, brows, and mouth quite precisely. But if the camera is farther back, or the actor is turned away from us, gestures and body language become the center of attention. In all, both the staging of the action and the camera's distance from the action control how we understand the performances (**4.117–4.118**).

Matters of context are particularly important when the performers are not actors, or even human beings. Framing, editing, and other film techniques can make trained animals give appropriate performances. Jonesy, the cat in *Aliens,* seems threatening because his hissing movement has been emphasized by lighting, framing, editing, and the sound track. (**4.119**).

As with every element of a film, acting offers an unlimited range of creative choices. It cannot be judged on a universal scale outside the context of the entire film's form.

Putting It All Together: Mise-en-Scene in Space and Time

Back in Chapter 2, we argued that viewers try to blend what they see and hear into a larger pattern (p. 54). This process starts at the level of the shot, when we have to assemble information into a coherent space and time. And creating that coherence requires that the filmmaker guide us to certain areas of the frame.

How do we know that viewers scan the frame for important information? The psychologist Tim Smith asked viewers to wear lightweight glasses that could track their eye movements and then showed them a scene from *There Will Be Blood*. The eye movements were recorded by computers and mapped onto the film sequence, so Smith could study how the viewers' attention shifted within the scene. There was remarkable agreement among the subjects about where to look at any moment. The primary points of attention were, as we might expect, items crucial to building up a story: faces and hand gestures (**4.120–4.121**). The characters' dialogue was important, too; the scan-paths revealed that people tend to look at the person speaking in the shot.

Before viewers can follow the story, recognize the emotional tenor of the scene, respond with their own emotions, and reflect on possible meanings, they must notice certain things in the frame. In setting up a shot, the filmmaker makes some things more salient than others. We noticed this happening when we examined how Tarantino nudged us to watch Colonel Landa in the scene from *Inglourious Basterds*. Thinking like a filmmaker means, to a large extent, finding ways to guide the viewer's eye. In other words, directors direct attention.

4.120

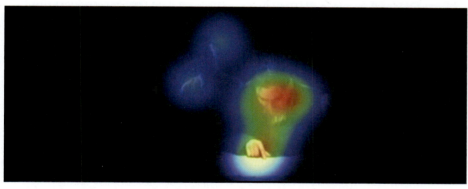

4.121

4.120–4.121 Scanning the shot. Tim Smith and his colleagues tracked several subjects' eye movements during a single shot of *There Will Be Blood*. Here is one frame from the sequence, as the characters examine a map (4.120). Smith's "peekthrough heatmap" graphically indicates the areas of interest for the eight viewers watching at that moment (4.121). The black surround represents areas not watched by anyone. Areas of attention are lit up, and the hotter the color, the more viewers are looking at that spot. At this instant, most viewers were concentrating on Sunday's face and hand, with two viewers looking at the man facing front behind him. As we might expect, faces, hands, and dialogue have commanded viewers' attention.

> "You can ask a bear to do something like, let's say, 'Stand up,' and the bear stands up. But you cannot say to a bear, 'Look astonished.' So you have him standing up, but then you have to astonish him. I would bang two saucepans, or get a chicken from a cage, then shake it so it squawked, and the bear would think, 'What was that?' and 'click' I'd have that expression."
> —Jean-Jacques Annaud, director, *The Bear*

> "The audience is only going to look at the most overriding thing in the frame. You must take charge of and direct their attention. It's also the principle of magic: what is the single important thing? Make it easy for them to see it, and you're doing your job."
> —David Mamet, director

CREATIVE DECISIONS

Mise-en-Scene in a Sequence from *L'Avventura*

To get a sense of the filmmaker's creative options in guiding our eye, let's look at another sequence. In Michelangelo Antonioni's *L'Avventura*, Sandro and Claudia are searching for Anna, who has mysteriously vanished. Anna is Claudia's friend and Sandro's lover, but during their search, they've begun to drift from their goal of finding her. They've also begun a love affair. In the town of Noto, they stand on a church rooftop near the bells, and Sandro says he regrets giving up architectural design. Claudia is encouraging him to return to his profession when he suddenly asks her to marry him.

She's startled and confused, and Sandro comes toward her. She is turned away from us. At first, only Sandro's expression is visible as he reacts grimly to her plea, "Why can't things be simpler?" **(4.122).** Claudia twists her arms around the bell rope, then turns away from him, toward us, grasping the rope and fluttering her hand. Now we can see that she's quite distraught. Sandro, a bit uneasy, turns away as she says anxiously, "I'd like to see things clearly" **(4.123).**

Brief though it is, this exchange shows how the tools of mise-en-scene—setting, costume, lighting, performance, and staging—can work together smoothly. We've considered them separately in order to examine the contribution each one makes, but in any shot, they mesh. They unfold on the screen in space and time, fulfilling several functions.

Most basically, the filmmaker has to guide the audience's attention to the important areas of the image. The filmmaker also wants to build up our interest by

4.122

4.123

4.122–4.123 **Frontality gets attention.** In *L'Avventura*, first Claudia has her back to the camera (4.122), and then Sandro does (4.123). Each shift is timed to show us a crucial facial reaction.

arousing curiosity and suspense. And the filmmaker tries to add expressive qualities, giving the shot an emotional coloration. Mise-en-scene helps the filmmaker achieve all these purposes.

How did Antonioni guide our attention in the Claudia–Sandro exchange? First, we're watching the figures, not the railing behind them. Based on the story so far, we expect Sandro and Claudia to be the objects of interest. At other points in the film, Antonioni makes them tiny figures in massive urban or seaside landscapes. Here, however, his mise-en-scene keeps their intimate interchange foremost in our minds.

Consider the first image merely as a two-dimensional picture. Both Sandro and Claudia stand out against the pale sky and the darker railing. They're also mostly curved shapes—heads and shoulders—and so they contrast with the geometrical regularity of the balcony. In the first frame, light strikes Sandro's face and suit from the right, picking him out against the rails. His dark hair is well positioned to make his head stand out against the sky. Claudia, a blonde, stands out against the railing and sky less vividly, but her polka-dot blouse creates a distinctive pattern. And considered only as a picture, the shot roughly balances the two figures, Sandro in the left half and Claudia in the right.

It's hard to think of the shot as simply two-dimensional, though. We instinctively see it as portraying a space that we could move around in. Claudia seems closer to us because her body masks things farther away, a spatial cue called *overlap*. She's also somewhat larger in the frame than Sandro, which reinforces our sense that she's closer. The rope slices across the bottom third of the frame, separating the couple (overlap again). Sandro himself overlaps the railing, which in turn overlaps the sky and the town beyond. We get a sense of distinct planes of space, layers lying closer to or farther from us. Costume, lighting, setting, and figure placement create this sense of a three-dimensional arena for the action.

Antonioni has used mise-en-scene to emphasize his characters and their interaction. But that interaction unfolds in time, and it gives him an opportunity to guide our attention while building up suspense and expressing emotion. Claudia is turned away from us when Sandro presses her to marry him, and the rope is taut between them (4.120). How will she respond?

Antonioni starts by giving Claudia a bit of business. She twists the rope around her arms and slips it over her back. This could be a hint that she's drawn to Sandro's proposal. At the same time, she hesitates. For as soon as he presses her, she turns away from him (4.121).

We know that faces give us access to characters' thoughts and emotions. Another filmmaker might have had Claudia already facing us when Sandro asked, so we'd see her response immediately. Antonioni instead makes things uncertain for a moment. He conceals Claudia's reaction and then lets her turn toward us. To make sure that we watch her and not Sandro at this moment, Antonioni has him turn away when she gestures and speaks ("I'd like to see things clearly"). Our attention is riveted on Claudia.

Soon enough, Sandro turns back toward the camera, so we can see his reaction, but already Claudia's anxiety has flashed out at us. Her complex relation to Sandro—attraction (sliding under the bell rope) and uncertainty (turning away tensely)—has been presented to us concretely.

This is only one moment in a complex scene, but it shows how various elements of mise-en-scene can cooperate to create a specific effect: the delayed revelation of a character's emotion. That revelation depended on the director's choices about what to show us at particular points. Once we've been guided to notice certain things, we can build up larger meanings and particular feelings. Let's now look at some specific options for using mise-en-scene to shape our sense of a film's space and time.

Space

Screen Space   In many respects, a film shot resembles a painting. It presents a flat array of colors and shapes. Before we even start to understand the image as a three-dimensional space, mise-en-scene offers many cues for guiding our attention and emphasizing elements in the frame.

Take something as simple as balancing the shot. Filmmakers often try to distribute various points of interest evenly around the frame. They assume that viewers will concentrate more on the upper half of the frame, probably because that's where we tend to find characters' faces. Since the film frame is a horizontal rectangle, the director usually tries to balance the right and left halves. The extreme type of such balancing is *bilateral symmetry*. In the battle scene in *Life on a String,* Chen Kaige stages one shot symmetrically **(4.124).**

More common than such near-perfect symmetry is a loose balancing of the shot's left and right regions. The simplest way to achieve compositional balance is to center the frame on the human body. Filmmakers often place a single figure at the center of the frame and minimize distracting elements at the sides, as in **4.125.** Many of our earlier illustrations display this flexible balance. Other shots may counterweight two or more elements, encouraging our eye to move back and forth, as in **4.126** and our *L'Avventura* dialogue (4.122, 4.123).

4.124 Symmetrical framing. A limited palette emphasizes this symmetrical composition in *Life on a String*.

Balanced composition is the norm, but unbalanced shots can also create strong effects. In *Bicycle Thieves,* the composition emphasizes the father's new job by massing most of the figures on the right **(4.127).** A more drastic example occurs in Michelangelo Antonioni's *Il Grido* **(4.128),** where two strong elements, the hero and a tree trunk, are grouped on the right side of the shot. The shot creates a powerful urge for the audience to see the woman's hidden face.

Sometimes the filmmaker will leave the shots a little unbalanced, in order to prime our expectation that something will change position in the frame. The cinema of the 1910s offers

4.125

4.126

4.125–4.126 Balancing the frame. *Mars Attacks!:* centering a single character (4.125) and balancing two (4.126).

5

The Shot: Cinematography

In controlling mise-en-scene, the filmmaker stages an event to be filmed. But what happens in front of the camera isn't the whole story. That event has to be captured, on a strip of film or in a digital format. The recording process opens up a new area of choice and control: cinematography.

Even if you're casually shooting a bit of video, you're making decisions about cinematography. (You might be letting the camera's automatic settings make some of them for you, but that's a decision too.) You're choosing the photographic qualities of the shot, such as exposure and frame rate. You're also choosing how to frame the shot, and whether to move the camera. And you're deciding how long the shot should run. These areas of choice are the same ones that filmmakers consider carefully. Just as nothing could be left to chance in lighting a shot like the one from *Inglourious Basterds* (4.1), so all the filmmaker's decisions about camerawork are shaped by a single concern: How will this creative choice affect the viewer?

The Photographic Image

Cinematography (literally, "writing in movement") depends to a large extent on *photography* ("writing in light"). Some filmmakers, working with 16mm or 35mm stock, have abandoned the camera to work directly on the material itself. But even the filmmaker who draws, paints, or scratches on film is creating patterns of light on celluloid. Most often, the filmmaker uses a camera to regulate how light from some object will be registered on the medium—sensitized photographic film or a video camera's computer chip. In either case, the filmmaker can select the range of tonalities, manipulate the speed of motion, and transform perspective.

The Range of Tonalities

You've probably noticed that it's rather hard to take a picture of a person lit by a sunny window. If Aunt Grace is well-exposed, her garden outside the window is too bright. (The technical jargon is "blown-out.") If you expose for the garden, Aunt Grace falls into shadow. This disparity is only one example of a broader area of choice in cinematography: the control of the image's range of tones and shades. Tonality is a matter of considering how the light registers on the film. Lighting, as we've seen, is a factor in mise-en-scene, but it's intimately connected with cinematography too. In production the cinematographer is almost always the person who arranges the lighting, so he or she is in the best position to control a shot's tonality.

Contrast   Let's start with one area of tonal control, the degree of contrast. **Contrast** refers to the comparative difference between the darkest and lightest areas of the frame. As we saw in Chapter 4, our eyes are highly sensitive to differences of color, shape, texture, and other aspects of a picture. Contrasts in the image help filmmakers to guide the viewer's eye to important parts of the frame and to give the shot an emotionally expressive quality—somber, cheerful, or whatever.

Most professional cinematography strives for a middle range of contrast: pure blacks, pure whites, and a large range in between, either grays (in black-and-white filming) or hues (in color filming). A higher-contrast image displays bright white highlights, stark black areas, and a narrow range of shades in between. A low-contrast image displays many intermediate grays or color shades with no true white or black areas **(5.1–5.6).** High-contrast images can seem stark and dramatic, while low-contrast ones suggest more muted emotional states.

Many factors are used to control contrast, including lighting, filters, choice of film stock, laboratory processing, and postproduction work. Historically, photochemical filmmaking relied on photographic stocks with various degrees of sensitivity to light. Some black-and-white films gathered more light than others, and so

5.1

5.2

5.1–5.6 Tonal contrast in black-and-white and color. Most black-and-white films employ a balance of grays, blacks, and whites, as in this shot from *Casablanca* (5.1). The dream sequence early in Ingmar Bergman's *Wild Strawberries* relies on high-contrast imagery, with almost no grays (5.2). Many shots in Michelangelo Antonioni's *Red Desert* have unusually low contrast, enhanced by the flat lighting and limited palette in the color design (5.3). Some contemporary films emphasize deep, rich blacks and push toward a high-contrast look, as in *Domino* (5.4). You can see the different degrees of contrast more clearly if we drain the color out of the original shots (5.5, 5.6).

5.3

5.4

5.5

5.6

5.7   5,8   5.9

5.7–5.9 **Color film and tonal range.** Technicolor became famous for its sharp, saturated hues, as seen in the trolley scene of *Meet Me in St. Louis* (5.7). Soviet filmmakers used a domestically made stock that tended to lower contrast and give the image a murky greenish-blue cast. Andrei Tarkovsky stressed these qualities in the monochromatic color design of his shadowy *Stalker* (5.8). Len Lye's abstract *Rainbow Dance* exploited the English stock Gasparcolor to create pure, saturated silhouettes that split and recombine (5.9).

> Why is *Who's Afraid of Virginia Woolf?* in black and white? "The words. The dialogue would have played differently in color."
> —Ernest Lehman, screenwriter

were suited for filming news events in actual conditions. Others gave a richer, wider contrast range, and these were used for most of the studio films of the 1920s through the 1960s, where lighting could be controlled exactly. Similarly, by picking different color film stocks, cinematographers could vary the image's color contrast **(5.7–5.9).**

Exposure   A crucial way to alter the tonalities in the image is through **exposure.** Exposure regulates how much light passes through the camera lens. Often we notice exposure only when an image seems too dark (underexposed) or too bright (overexposed). We expect that filmmakers will try for a balanced exposure. Sometimes, though, that's difficult to achieve and trade-offs must be made. Filmmakers constantly face the choice between the blown-out window and the silhouetted Aunt Grace in our amateur snapshot **(5.10, 5.11).**

Sometimes a filmmaker wants unbalanced exposure. American film noir cinematography of the 1940s underexposed shadowy regions of the image in keeping with low-key lighting techniques. Likewise, overexposure can create expressive effects **(5.12).** In addition, images shot with correct exposure can be overexposed or underexposed in developing, printing, or digital postproduction **(5.13).**

Exposure can be affected by **filters**—slices of glass or gelatin put in front of the lens of the camera or printer to reduce certain frequencies of light reaching

5.10   5,11

5.10–5.11 **Exposure levels.** For *Kasba*, Indian director Kumar Shahani decided to expose for the shop interior in one scene and let the countryside behind blow out (5.10). In another scene he exposed for the background and created silhouetted window frames (5.11). The first shot displays the vibrant colors of the shop's wares, while the second emphasizes the difference between the market activities outside and the mysterious interior.

5.12

5.13

5.12–5.13 Overexposure. In *Vidas Secas*, Nelson Pereira dos Santos overexposes the windows of the prison cell to sharpen the contrast between the prisoner's confinement and the world of freedom outside (5.12). *The Lord of the Rings: The Fellowship of the Ring* used digital grading to simulate photographic overexposure in the Moria sequence. In 5.13 the overexposure of the wizard's staff makes the Fellowship a bright island threatened by countless orcs in the darkness.

the film. Filters can alter the range of tonalities in radical ways. Hollywood cinematographers since the 1920s have sought to add glamour to close-ups, especially of women, by means of diffusion filters, along with gels or silks placed over light sources **(5.14)**. Before modern improvements in film stocks and lighting made it practical to shoot most outdoor night scenes at night, filmmakers routinely made such scenes by using blue filters in sunlight—a technique called *day for night* **(5.15)**.

Changing Tonality after Filming   Filmmakers have often manipulated the image's tonalities after filming. For instance, films could be printed on stocks that yielded different tonal values. Avant-garde directors have explored unusual ways of altering images after they came from the camera **(5.16, 5.17)**.

One of the most common adjustments in the silent-film era involved adding color to black-and-white images through tinting and toning. *Tinting* is accomplished by dipping the already developed film into a bath of dye. The dark areas remain black and gray, while the lighter areas pick up the color **(5.18)**. *Toning* worked in an opposite fashion. The dye was added during the developing of the positive print. As a result, darker areas are colored, while the lighter portions of the frame remain

5.14

5.15

5.14–5.15 Filters shape tonality. Studio films like *A Farewell to Arms* often employed diffusion filters, along with soft and high-key lighting, to create romantic images of women (5.14). For *The Searchers*, this scene of the protagonists spying on an Indian camp at night was shot in sunlight using day-for-night filters (5.15).

5.16

5.17

5.16–5.17 Experimental manipulation after filming. Throughout *Power and Water*, Pat O'Neill creates spectacular imagery by use of optical printing, matte work, and other special effects (5.16). By scratching the emulsion, Stan Brakhage emphasizes the eye motif that runs through *Reflections on Black* (5.17).

white or only faintly colored **(5.19)**. More ambitious and rare was hand-coloring, which filled certain parts of the shot with an appropriate color **(5.20)**. Later film-makers occasionally revived silent-film processes **(5.21)**.

For photochemically based filmmaking, the tonality of the finished film could be adjusted in laboratory work. The staff member assigned the role of *color timer* or *grader* has a wide choice about the color range of a print. A red patch in the image may be printed as crimson, pink, or almost any shade in between. Often the timer consults with the director to select a key tone that will serve as a reference point for color relations throughout the film.

Analog color grading became rare when digital grading achieved a comparable level of quality. If the footage has been shot on 35mm film, a scanner converts all the frames to digital files, creating a digital intermediate (DI) file. That is then adjusted with software. The graded footage is then scanned back onto 35mm negative stock to create the final master negative. If the project originates digitally, the

5.18

5.19

5.20

5.21

5.18–5.21 Adding color to black and white. Tinting creates a brownish color across the entire frame in the 1914 film *The Wrath of the Gods* (5.18). The color suggests the heat of an erupting volcano. In *Cenere* ("Ashes," 1916) the deep blue of the dark areas and the nearly white patches are characteristic of toning (5.19). Night scenes like this were often colored blue. Firelight was frequently red, while interiors were commonly amber. Hand-colorists used stencils laid over each frame to create vibrant imagery, as in Albert Capellani's 1906 *Aladdin, or the Wonderful Lamp* (5.20). For her experimental film *Daisies*, Vera Chytilová employs a crimson toning (5.21).

DI becomes the basis for the files sent to theaters on hard drives (1.25). Some cinematographers work with a digital imaging technician on the set to make grading decisions and determine the look of the DI.

Laboratory-based analog grading limited the filmmaker's choices about color and lighting, but DIs offered a greater range of control. With analog color grading, any change made to a shot affected the entire frame area, but digital programs allow the colorist to alter specific portions of a frame (**5.22**) and maintain the adjustment even if the item shifts in the course of a shot.

Likewise, scenes are still shot day-for-night, but the scene will be darkened in the digital intermediate. For the climactic night sequence in *Winter's Bone,* two women take the heroine to a pond. Some shots were taken in bright daylight, others were taken at dusk, and the close views of the women in the boat were shot at night, with lamps providing dim illumination. Through digital grading, all the shots were blended into a uniformly dark sequence. *Julie & Julia,* a romantic comedy, used the opposite technique, adding sunlight to scenes that had been shot on overcast days.

Digital postproduction has reshaped every area of technique, from mise-en-scene and cinematography to editing and sound. (See "A Closer Look," pp. 168–169.) With more opportunities, however, come more forced decisions. One editor, musing on the possibility that digital postproduction offers too many alternatives, says, "I still generally feel, if you don't have it [in shooting], it wasn't meant to be. You can't manipulate everything like that or we might as well all be in animation."

5.22 Selective digital grading. In this close-up from *The Lord of the Rings: The Fellowship of the Ring,* the oval on the actor's face indicates the area within which the colorist wants to change the lighting or the color.

> ❝ I have a hard enough time making up my mind about things without going into a DI suite; I don't think I'd ever get out of there. The process creates too many options."
> —Paul Thomas Anderson, director, *There Will Be Blood*

Speed of Motion

A gymnast's performance seen in slow motion, ordinary action accelerated to comic speed, a tennis serve stopped in a freeze-frame—our films and videos are full of such effects. We don't often reflect on the fact that they depend on a photographic power unique to cinema: control over the speed of movement seen on the screen.

The speed of the motion presented onscreen depends on the relation between the rate at which the film was shot and the rate of projection. Both **rates** are calculated in frames per second. The standard rate for film-based shooting, established when synchronized-sound movies came in at the end of the 1920s, was 24 frames per second (fps). Today's 35mm cameras commonly offer the filmmaker a choice of anything between 8 and 64 fps, with specialized cameras offering a wider range of choice. Professional HD cameras, typically standardized at around 24, 25, and 30 fps, offer a comparable menu of frame rates.

If the movement is to look accurate on the screen, the rate of shooting should correspond to the rate of projection. This is what normally happens with modern films, although as you know, playback equipment can be adjusted to run the film or video more slowly or more quickly. The main problem comes with silent films, which are sometimes shown speeded up from their original frame rates. Before the filming rate was standardized at 24 fps, films were taken at anywhere from 16 to 22 fps, and so they look jerky when screened at 24 fps. Projected at the correct speed, silent films look as smooth as movies made today.

As the silent films indicate, if a film is exposed at fewer frames per second than the projection rate, the screen action will look speeded up. This is the *fast-motion* effect sometimes seen in comedies. But fast motion has long been used for other purposes. In F. W. Murnau's *Nosferatu,* the vampire's coach rushes skittishly

A CLOSER LOOK

FROM MONSTERS TO THE MUNDANE
Computer-Generated Imagery in The Lord of the Rings

The films adapted from J. R. R. Tolkien's trilogy *The Lord of the Rings* (*The Fellowship of the Ring*, *The Two Towers*, and *The Return of the King*) show how CGI can be used for huge battle scenes, plausible monsters, and magical events. The films also illustrate how CGI shapes less spectacular, more mundane areas of production.

CGI was used at every stage of production. In preproduction, a sort of animated storyboard (a *previs*, for "previsualization") was made, consisting of *animatics*, or rough, computer-generated versions of the scenes. Each installment's previs was about as long as the finished film and coordinated the work of the huge staff involved in both digital and physical tasks.

During production of the three films, CGI helped create the mise-en-scene. Many shots digitally stitched together disparate elements, blending full-size settings, miniature sets, and matte paintings (5.60). A total of 68 miniature sets were built, and computer manipulation was required in each case to make them appear real or to allow camera movements through them. Computer paint programs could generate matte paintings for the sky, clouds, distant cliffs, and forests that appeared behind the miniatures.

Rings also drew on the rapidly developing capacity of CGI to create characters. The war scenes were staged with a small number of actual actors in costumes, but CGI added vast crowds of soldiers alongside them. As happens often nowadays, the *Rings* project demanded new software programs. A crucial program was Massive (for "Multiple Agent Simulation System in Virtual Environment"). Using motion-capture on a few *agents* (costumed actors), the team could build a number of different military maneuvers, assigning all of them to the thousands of crude, digitally generated figures. By giving each figure a rudimentary artificial intelligence—such as the ability to see an approaching soldier and identify it as friend or foe—Massive could generate a scene in which figures scattered or gathered in unpredictable ways **(5.23).**

The monsters encountered by the characters during their quest were more elaborately designed than the troops. A detailed three-dimensional model of each crea-

ture was captured with a scanning wand that could read into recesses and folds. A new software system, Character Mapper, captured motion from an actor and then adjusted the mass and musculature to imaginary skeletons. In the cave-troll sequence, the large, squat creature swings its limbs and flexes its muscles in a believable fashion.

The skeletal Gollum was created with a combination of motion-capture and CGI, but regular actors didn't escape the CGI process. The main characters were given digital look-alikes who replaced stunt doubles, executing dangerous or difficult movements. The action demanded that full-size actors play three-feet-tall hobbits who interact with characters considerably taller than them. The size difference was often created during filming by using small doubles or by placing the hobbits farther from the camera in false-perspective sets.

Cinematography also depended on CGI. For the cave-troll scene, director Peter Jackson donned a virtual-reality helmet and planned camera positions by moving around a virtual set and facing a virtual troll. The camera positions were motion-captured and reproduced in the actual filming of the sequence—which has a rough, handheld style quite different from the rest of the scenes.

In postproduction, animators erased telephone poles in location shots and helicopter blades dipping into the aerial shots of the Fellowship's voyage across mountains. Specialized programs added details, such as the ripples in the water in the Mirror of Galadriel.

Perhaps most important, digital grading altered the color of shots, giving each major location a distinctive look. Rivendell's scenes are in autumnal tones, while the early scenes in the Shire were given a yellow glow that enhanced the sunshine and green fields. The grading also utilized an innovative program that permitted adjusting the color values of individual elements within a shot. When Galadriel shows Frodo her mirror, she glows bright white, contrasting with the deep blue tones of Frodo's figure and setting **(5.24).** Thanks to digital grading, CGI techniques can do more than create crowds and creatures: it can shape the visual style of an entire film.

5.23

5.24

5.23–5.24 Mise-en-scene and cinematography controlled by digital postproduction. Vast crowds of soldiers with individualized movements were generated by the Massive software program for *The Two Towers* (5.23). In *The Fellowship of the Ring*, selective digital color grading makes one figure bright white while the rest of the scene has a muted tone (5.24).

5.25 **Fast motion.** Cars become blurs of light in *Koyaanisqatsi.*

across the landscape, suggesting his supernatural power. In Godfrey Reggio's *Koyaanisqatsi,* delirious fast motion renders the hectic rhythms of urban life **(5.25).** More recent films have used fast motion to grab our attention and accelerate the pace, whisking us through a setting to the heart of the action.

The more frames per second shot, the slower the screen action will appear. The resulting *slow-motion* effect is used notably in Dziga Vertov's *Man with a Movie Camera* to render sports events in detail, a function that continues to be important today. The technique can also be used for expressive purposes. In Rouben Mamoulian's *Love Me Tonight,* the members of a hunt decide to ride quietly home to avoid waking the sleeping deer; their ride is filmed in slow motion to create a comic depiction of noiseless movement.

Today slow-motion footage often functions to suggest that the action takes place in a dream or fantasy. It can also be used to convey enormous power, as in a martial-arts or superhero film. Slow motion is also used for emphasis, becoming a way of dwelling on a moment of spectacle or high drama. Slow-motion scenes of a couple walking add a lyrical rhythm to Wong Kar-wai's *In the Mood for Love,* suggesting that they are unwittingly dancing with each other.

To enhance expressive effects, filmmakers can change the speed of motion in the course of a shot. Often the change of speed helps create special effects. In *Die Hard* a fireball bursts up an elevator shaft toward the camera. During the filming, the fire at the bottom of the shaft was filmed at 100 fps, slowing down its progress, and then shot at faster speeds as it erupted upward, giving the impression of an explosive acceleration.

The *Die Hard* sequence creates a realistic-looking explosion, but sometimes filmmakers choose to call our attention to changes in the speed of capturing the action. The technique, which varies the frame rate during shooting, is called *ramping.* Since ramping alters exposure, lighting levels on the set have to be coordinated with the frame rate. For the fight scenes in *Sherlock Holmes,* the Phantom, a specialized digital camera used to create slow motion, was ramped from 24 fps to 800 fps and then back to 24 fps. During the passage of slow motion, a burst of light kept the exposure constant.

Ramping is sometimes used as a one-off effect to emphasize a bit of action, as in the *Sherlock Holmes* scene. But it can also function as a motif and create parallels. In an early scene of Michael Mann's *The Insider,* researcher Jeffrey Wigand leaves the tobacco company that has just fired him. As he crosses the lobby toward a revolving door, his brisk walk suddenly slows to a dreamlike drifting. The point of this striking stylistic choice becomes apparent only in the film's last shot. Lowell Bergman, the TV producer who has helped Wigand reveal that addictive substances are added to cigarettes, has been dismissed from CBS. Bergman strides across the lobby, and as he passes through the revolving door, his movement glides into extreme slow motion. The repetition of the technique compares two men who have lost their livelihoods as a result of telling the truth: two insiders who have become outsiders.

There are more extreme forms of fast and slow motion. *Time-lapse* cinematography permits us to see the sun set in seconds or a flower sprout, bud, and bloom in a minute. For this, a very low shooting speed is required—perhaps one frame per minute, hour, or even day. For *high-speed* cinematography, such as recording a bullet shattering glass, the camera may expose hundreds or thousands of frames per second. Most cameras can be used for time-lapse shooting, but high-speed cinematography requires specially designed cameras.

After filming, the filmmaker can still control the speed of movement on the screen. Until the early 1990s, the most common tool for this was the optical printer. This device rephotographs a film, copying all or part of each original frame onto another reel of film. The optical printer can reverse the action, accelerate it by skipping frames, slow the action by reprinting frames (*stretch printing*), or freeze the action by printing the same frame over and over. Today digital postproduction permits the same manipulations that were pioneered on the optical printer.

Many experimental films have played with the possibilities of altering the speed of original footage. With the help of an optical printer, Ken Jacobs's *Tom Tom the Piper's Son* explores the images of an early silent film by pausing the shots and enlarging portions of them. More mainstream films have also exploited the freeze-frame effect. It can underscore a piece of action or a line of dialogue, or suggest a character's memory. At the end of the film a freeze-frame can linger on a situation, imprinting it on the viewer's mind. It can also suggest that the story action hasn't quite resolved **(5.26)**.

5.26 Freeze-frame for a closing shot. In *A Moment of Innocence,* the final freeze frame lets us contemplate what the gestures imply about the young men's attitudes toward the woman. Another example of an irresolute final freeze frame is 3.10.

Perspective

You are standing on railroad tracks, looking toward the horizon. The tracks seem to meet in the distance, and the track ties get steadily smaller as they recede. You know that the tracks are in fact parallel, and the ties are of uniform size. What is happening?

Your eye gathers light reflected from the scene and creates an image of space and the things in it. The objects in the scene have some regular relation to one another. The tracks converge and the ties get smaller. Your vision, in other words, shows a *perspective* view of the scene: a set of spatial relations organized around a viewing point.

The **lens** of a photographic camera does roughly what your eye does. Located at a specific point, it gathers light from the scene and transmits that light onto the flat surface of the film or video chip to form an image that represents size, depth, and other dimensions of the scene. So a camera lens also creates a perspective image.

One difference between the eye and the camera, though, is that photographic lenses may be changed, and each type of lens will render perspective in different ways. If two different lenses photograph the same scene, the perspective relations in the resulting images can be drastically different. As we'll see, a wide-angle lens could exaggerate the depth you see down the track or could make the foreground trees and buildings seem to bulge. A telephoto lens could drastically reduce the depth, making the trees seem very close together and nearly the same size.

The Lens: Focal Length   Filmmakers think carefully about the perspective of an image. The main area of choice involves the **focal length** of the lens. In technical terms, the focal length is the distance from the center of the lens to the point where light rays converge to a point of focus on the film. The focal length alters the size and proportions of the things we see, as well as how much depth we perceive in the image.

We can distinguish three general sorts of lenses, based on their focal lengths and the ways they present perspective. We'll use 35mm film as our reference point, although the three types of lenses hold good for digital formats as well.

1. *The short-focal-length* (wide-angle) *lens*

In 35mm-gauge cinematography, a lens of less than 35mm in focal length is considered a wide-angle lens. It's called that because it takes in a relatively wide field of view. But in capturing the wider field, these lenses tend to distort straight lines lying near the edges of the frame, bulging them outward **(5.27–5.29)**. Less obviously, a short focal-length lens exaggerates depth, making figures in the foreground seem bigger and those in the distance seem farther away **(Fig. 5.30)**. As a result, when

> " I'm standing around waiting to see where the 50mm is going to be, or what size lens they're putting on, and in that unwritten book in my brain, I said, 'Don't ever let them shoot you full face, on a wide-angle lens, you'll end up looking like Dumbo.'"
>
> —Tony Curtis, actor

5.27–5.30 Wide-angle and perspective. In *Don't Look Now*, as the camera swivels to follow John Baxter, the wide-angle lens makes a street lamp he passes appear to lean to the right (5.27), and then to the left (5.28). Wide-angle close shots risk distortion, as with the young woman's hand in Mikhail Kalatozov's *The Cranes Are Flying* (5.29). In *The Little Foxes*, the lens makes the characters seem relatively far from one another, even though they're within a small area of the parlor (5.30).

5.27

5.28

5.29

5.30

figures move toward or away from the camera, a wide-angle lens makes them seem to cover ground more rapidly.

2. *The middle-focal-length* (medium) *lens*

A common length for a medium lens, in 35mm and high-end digital cinematography, is 50mm **(5.31).** This lens seeks to avoid noticeable perspective distortion. With a medium lens, horizontal and vertical lines are rendered as straight and perpendicular. (Compare the bulging effect of the wide-angle lens.) Parallel lines should recede to distant vanishing points, as in our railroad tracks example. Foreground and background should seem neither stretched apart (as with the wide-angle lens) nor squashed together (as with the telephoto lens).

3. *The long-focal-length* (telephoto) *lens*

Wide-angle lenses stretch space along the frame edges, but longer lenses flatten the space along the camera axis. Cues for depth and volume are reduced. The planes seem squashed together, much as when you look through a telescope or binoculars **(5.32).** (For this reason, long lenses are also called telephoto lenses.) Long lenses take in a narrower angle of vision than wide-angle or normal lenses do. As you'd expect, the effect of movement with a long lens is the opposite of what happens with the wide angle. A person moving toward the camera takes more time to cover what seems to be a small distance.

5.31 The medium focal-length lens. A shot made with a medium lens in *His Girl Friday*. Contrast the sense of distance among the actors seen in 5.30.

Today long lenses are typically 100mm or greater in length. You'll often see them at work in televised sports events, since they magnify action at a distance. In a baseball game, there will invariably be shots taken from almost directly behind the pitcher, using a camera located beyond the center field wall. You've probably noticed that such shots make the umpire, catcher, batter, and pitcher look unnaturally close to one another. In other contexts, the effect of a very long lens can be otherworldly **(5.33).**

Lens length can distinctly affect the spectator's experience. For example, expressive qualities can be suggested by lenses that distort objects or characters. A

5.32

5.33

5.32–5.33 Long lenses and perspective. In 5.32, from Chen Kaige's *Life on a String*, the long lens squashes the crowd members almost to a single plane. It also makes the rapids behind the men virtually a two-dimensional backdrop. In *Koyaanisqatsi*, an airport is filmed from a great distance, and an exceptionally long-focal-length makes the plane seem to land on a highway (5.33).

decision about lens length can make a character or object blend into the setting **(5.34–5.36)** or stand out in sharp relief **(5.37).** Filmmakers may exploit the flattening effects of the long-focal-length lens to create solid masses of space as in an abstract painting **(5.38).** A director can use the distortions of lens lengths for surprise effects as well **(5.39, 5.40).**

In taking snapshots you've probably used a **zoom lens** to enlarge some part of a shot. You may not have noticed that the lens changes focal length as well as framing, but that's what a zoom is—a lens designed to provide variable focal length. So the zoom not only resizes what's shown; it also changes the image's perspective. The zoom combines the wide-angle, medium, and telephoto options we've already looked at.

Fixed focal-length lenses can't change perspective relations while the camera is running, but the zoom can. Zoom lenses were originally used for documentary

> " In *New York, New York*, we shot only with a 32mm lens, the whole movie. We tried to equate the old style of framing, the old style meaning 1946–53."
> —Martin Scorsese, director

5.34

5.35

5.36

5.34–5.36 Long lenses and movement. In *Tootsie*, Dorothy becomes visible among the crowd at a considerable distance from the camera (5.34). After taking 20 steps, "she" seems only slightly closer (5.35). Finally, after taking 36 steps, Dorothy seems somewhat closer (5.36). The shot is held long enough for us to absorb Michael's makeover and to recognize that the masquerade is successful: He can merge into the crowd.

5.37

5.38

5.37–5.38 Lens length for expressive effect. In Ilya Trauberg's *China Express*, wide-angle distortion makes the man's hand more threatening (5.37). In *Eternity and a Day*, a long lens turns the beach and sea into two vertical blocks behind the character (5.38).

5.39

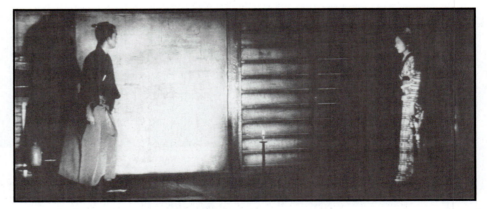

5.40

5.39–5.40 Focal length for surprise and suspense. In Kurosawa's *Red Beard*, when the mad patient comes into the intern's room, a long-focal-length lens makes her seem close and threatening (5.39). But a cut to a more perpendicular angle shows that they're actually several feet apart and that he is not yet in danger (5.40).

5.41

5.42

5.43

5.41–5.43 The zoom at work. The opening of *The Conversation* presents one of the most famous zoom shots in cinema. A long, slow zoom-in arouses considerable uncertainty about its target (5.42, 5.43), until it finally centers on a mime and our protagonist, surveillance technician Harry Caul (5.43). You can see how the varied focal lengths change perspective: In 5.41, the street tapers into the distance, but at longer lengths (5.42, 5.43), the pavement's grid doesn't recede.

shooting. Most filmmakers didn't try to zoom during filming, because they worried that the rapid warping or flattening of the image would be distracting. But in the late 1950s, filmmakers began zooming while shooting.

Since then, the zoom has sometimes been used to substitute for moving the camera forward or backward. During a zoom, the camera remains stationary, while the zoom shot magnifies or demagnifies the objects filmed **(5.41–5.43).** It can also create intriguing deformations of depth and scale, as we'll see when we examine *Wavelength*.

If you're not yet convinced that the choice of focal length matters, consider Ernie Gehr's abstract experimental film *Serene Velocity*. The scene is an empty corridor. Gehr shot the setting with a zoom lens, but in a very unusual way.

> [I] divided the mm range of the zoom lens in half and starting from the middle I recorded changes in mm positions. . . . The camera was not moved at all. The zoom lens was not moved during recording either. Each frame was recorded individually as a still. Four frames to each position. To give an example: I shot the first four frames at 50mm. The next four frames I shot at 55mm. And then, for a certain duration, approximately 60 feet, I went back and forth, four frames at 50mm, four frames at 55mm; four frames at 50mm, four frames at 55mm; etc. . . . for about 60 feet. Then I went to 45–60 [mm] and did the same for about 60 feet. Then to 40–65, and so on.

Onscreen, we see an image whose perspective relations pop in and out at us rhythmically—first with little difference, but gradually with greater tension between a telephoto image and a wide-angle image **(5.44).** In *Serene Velocity* Gehr engages us sheerly through formal patterning of focal lengths.

> " I tend to rely on only two kinds of lenses to compose my frames: very wide angle and extreme telephoto. I use the wide angle because when I want to see something, I want to see it completely, with the most detail possible. As for the telephoto, I use it for close-ups because I find it creates a real 'encounter' with the actor. If you shoot someone's face with a 200-millimeter lens, the audience will feel like the actor is really standing in front of them. It gives presence to the shot. So I like extremes. Anything in between is of no interest to me."
>
> —John Woo, director, *A Better Tomorrow* and *Hard Boiled*

5.44 Formal experiment with lens length. In *Serene Velocity*, telephoto shots of a hallway are juxtaposed to wide-angle shots taken from the same spot, creating a pulsating rhythm and an abstract play of rectangular shapes.

5.46

5.47

5.46–5.47 Depth of field yields selective focus. As often happens with selective focus, the main point of interest in this shot from Agnès Varda's *Vagabond* (*Sans toi ni loi*) is kept in focus, while the background is out of focus (5.46). More unusual is Léos Carax's decision in *Boy Meets Girl* to show his protagonist in the background, fascinated by the neck of the woman in the foreground (5.47).

5.45 Focal length in action. The opening shot of *Simple Men* focuses on the robber and the security guard in the middle ground. The yellow railing in the foreground is out of focus. In the distant background stands the female robber's partner, who is out of focus too. The lens's depth of field has determined what areas of the camera's view will be in focus.

The Lens: Depth of Field and Focus   You're well aware that a photograph or a movie scene can show some things in **focus** and let other things get fuzzy. That effect is, once more, due to the lens's focal length.

Every lens has a specific **depth of field:** a range of distances within which objects can be photographed in sharp focus, given a certain exposure setting. For example, suppose you are shooting with a 50mm lens and your subject is ten feet away. At one common exposure level, focusing the lens at 10 feet will render everything between 8½ and 12 feet away in acceptable focus. Outside that zone, either closer to the lens or farther way, objects will fall off.

All other things being equal, a wide-angle lens has a relatively greater depth of field than does a telephoto lens. A 32mm lens focused at 10 feet yields an acceptable focal range of about 6 to 25 feet. The opening shot of *Simple Men* shows depth of field at work (**5.45**).

Depth of field isn't the same as deep space, discussed in Chapter 4. *Deep space* is a term for the way the filmmaker has staged the action on several different planes, *regardless of whether all of these planes are in focus.* In the case of *Our Hospitality,* those planes usually are in sharp focus, but in other films, not every plane of deep space is in focus. In the *Simple Men* shot (5.45), we can see three planes of depth, but they aren't all in focus. Deep space is a matter of mise-en-scène, involving how the scene is arranged. Depth of field depends on the camera, with the lens determining what layers of a deep-space staging are in focus.

If depth of field controls perspective relations by determining which planes will be in focus, what choices are open to the filmmaker? He or she may opt for what is usually called *selective focus*—choosing to focus on only one plane and letting the other planes blur. As the *Simple Men* example suggests, selective focus guides the viewer's eye: we tend to pay attention to what is most clearly visible. Often this involves focusing on the main character and throwing the surroundings out of focus (**5.46**). Alternatively the director may choose to put an unexpected plane in focus and let the rest blur (**5.47**).

In Hollywood during the 1940s, partly because of the influence of *Citizen Kane,* filmmakers began using lenses of shorter focal length, along with more sensitive film stock and higher light levels, to yield a greater depth of field (**5.48**). This practice came to be called **deep focus.** Combined with deep-space staging, it became a major stylistic option in the 1940s and 1950s (**5.49**). The technique was even imitated in cartoons.

5.48   **5.49**

5.48–5.49 The golden age of deep-focus cinematography. In the famous contract-signing scene from *Citizen Kane*, everything is in sharp focus from one plane near the lens (Bernstein's head), through several planes in the middle ground, to the wall far in the distance (5.48). A similar example of deep-space staging combined with deep-focus cinematography is Anthony Mann's *The Tall Target* (5.49).

(See 4.144.) During the 1970s and 1980s, younger directors like Steven Spielberg and Brian De Palma revived deep-focus cinematography **(5.50).** Early HD cameras had small sensors, which kept all planes in focus **(Fig. 5.51).** As larger sensors were developed, cinematographers could more easily create selective, shallow-focus images.

Selective focus automatically steers our attention to a single important part of the shot. But deep focus tends to make several areas equally visible. So the filmmaker's choice of deep focus creates another set of options for guiding our eye. Those options include sound (we tend to watch who's speaking), elements of mise-en-scene, such as lighting and staging (p. 144), and aspects of framing and composition.

Just as a zoom lens lets the filmmaker change focal length while filming, focus can be altered within a shot by **racking focus,** or *pulling focus*. This is commonly used to switch our attention between foreground and background **(5.52–5.53),** making one plane blurred and another sharp.

Special Effects   The image's perspective relations can be shaped by **special effects.** The most unrealistic sort is **superimposition.** Here images are laid over one another, creating multiple perspectives within the frame. Superimpositions were originally created by double exposure either in the camera or in laboratory printing. For decades filmmakers presented dreams, visions, or memories superimposed over a character's face **(5.54).** Today, as you'd expect, superimpositions are created in digital postproduction.

Filmmakers working for American and European studios in the 1920s and 1930s devised other ways of manipulating perspective relations. Suppose you want to play a piece of action in the studio but persuade the viewer that it's taking place on location. The trick was to create a *composite*, in which separately photographed images are blended in a single composition.

> " If I made big-budget films, I would do what the filmmakers of twenty years ago did: use 35, 40, and 50mm [lenses] with lots of light so I could have that depth of field, because it plays upon the effect of surprise. It can give you a whole series of little tricks, little hiding places, little hooks in the image where you can hang surprises, places where they can suddenly appear, just like that, within the frame itself."
>
> —Benoît Jacquot, director, *A Single Girl*

5.50   **5.51**

5.50–5.51 Deep focus in film and video. In *The Untouchables*, a conversation scene is played in the foreground while setting and distant figures are also kept in focus (5.50). This shot uses a special split-focus lens that can render extreme depth, but a comparable effect is more easily achieved in digital video, where a small chip can yield extreme depth of field. If this shot, from Agnès Varda's *The Gleaners and I*, had been made on film, either Varda's hand or the truck would have been far more out of focus (5.51).

5.52

5.53

5.52–5.53 **Racking focus.** In this shot from *Last Tango in Paris*, Jeanne, the bench, and the wall in the distance are in focus, while Tom in the foreground is not (5.52). After the camera racks focus, Tom becomes sharp and the background is blurred (5.53).

5.54 **Superimposition.** In the opening of Quentin Tarantino's *Kill Bill, Vol. 1,* the Bride sees the first victim of her revenge, and her memory of a violent struggle is superimposed over a tight framing of her eyes.

One solution was to simply project footage of a setting onto a screen, then film actors in front of it. The whole ensemble could then be filmed from the front **(5.55).** This was called, logically enough, **rear projection** (or *process work*), and it was very widely used. You'll see it in many classic Hollywood films. When people are shown inside moving vehicles, the scenery whizzes by in rear projection. To modern eyes, rear projection seldom creates very convincing depth cues **(5.56).** A later modification, **front projection,** used angled mirrors to summon up more realistic-looking backgrounds. The results were showcased in the Dawn of Man sequence in *2001: A Space Odyssey.* For the train crash in *The Fugitive,* front and rear projection were used simultaneously within certain shots.

A more complicated approach to composite filming, also developed in the classical studio system, was **matte work.** A *matte* is a portion of the setting photographed on a strip of film, usually with a part of the frame empty. Through laboratory printing, the matte is joined with another strip of film containing the actors. It was common to have expert artists paint an image of the setting, and the painting was then filmed, leaving a blank space in the frame. The footage was combined with footage of action, filmed to fit the blank area. Several long shots in *The Wizard of Oz* exemplify classic matte painting (Fig. 2.20).

With a matte painting, the actor can't move into the painted portions of the frame without seeming to disappear. To solve this problem, filmmakers used a *traveling matte.* Here the actor was photographed against a blank, usually blue, background. In laboratory printing, a background was prepared and a moving outline of the actor was cut out of it. Then the shot of the actor was jigsawed into the moving gap in the background footage. Traveling mattes could present persuasive images of space adventure or show cartoon characters interacting with humans **(5.57, 5.58).**

5.55

5.56

5.55–5.56 Movies inside movies. Behind the scenes (5.55): Rear projection for *Boom Town* (1940). In Hitchcock's *Vertigo*, the seascape in the rear plane was shot separately and used as a back-projected setting for an embrace filmed under studio lighting (5.56). From the 1920s through the 1950s, rear projection was easier than taking cast and crew on location.

5.57

5.57–5.59 Traveling mattes. In *Star Wars: Episode IV—A New Hope*, the take-off of the *Millennium Falcon* was filmed as a model against a blue screen and matted into a shot of a building with imperial troopers firing upward (5.57). The animated figures in *Who Framed Roger Rabbit* were matted into live-action footage shot separately (5.58). For *Rumble Fish*, a black-and-white film, Francis Ford Coppola uses traveling mattes to color the fish in an aquarium—recalling early film's experiments with hand-coloring (5.59).

5.58

5.59

Like any technique, however, traveling mattes can also generate a stylized, deliberately unrealistic image **(5.59)**.

Now that filmmakers have software to do compositing, it might seem that rear projection and matte work are hopelessly outdated. But today's digital techniques mimic the special effects created by analog cinematography and lab work. Rear projection is still used, although usually with digitally shot footage. Digital special effects still require that the action be shot in front of a screen, either blue or green. The backgrounds, often digital matte paintings, are added later, as in traditional

5.60 Merging special effects. The digital composite from *The Fellowship of the Ring* integrates a partial but full-size set with an actor at the left, a miniature set in the middle ground, a matte painting of the background elements, and computer-animated waterfalls and falling leaves.

CONNECT TO THE BLOG
www.davidbordwell.net/blog

CGI can create spectacle, and some critics claim that the special effects make the story unimportant. We argue the opposite and talk about a film historian who agrees in "Classical cinema lives! New evidence for old norms."

compositing. Likewise, today's merging of several digital effects within a frame **(5.60)** resembles predigital practice. In *2001, Blade Runner* and other classic science-fiction films, a single shot might include animated miniatures or models, traveling mattes to render their movements, and ray bursts added in superimposition—all against a matte-painted background.

Most filmmakers choose to present tonality, speed of motion, and perspective in realistic ways. Like other film techniques, though, photographic manipulations of the shot needn't be used for realism. For instance, most movie shots don't want to confuse you about the positions or sizes of the characters. But Chytilová's *Daisies* presents a comic optical illusion **(5.61)**. Similarly, most CGI shots aim at a seamless integration that persuades us that we're seeing a realistic space. But in *The Mill & the Cross*, digital images of Brueghel's painting "The Way to Calvary" are stitched together with foreground scenes shot with actors **(5.62)**. The result tricks our eye by combining painterly and filmic perspectives. Like mise-en-scene, visual perspective can be stylized, imaginative, and blatantly unrealistic if the filmmaker chooses that path. It all depends on how the stylistic choices function in the pattern of the overall film.

Framing

You're very aware of **framing** when you take a photo or shoot a video. You don't usually want to cut off people's heads. Like tonality, speed of motion, and perspective, framing is carefully considered by filmmakers of all sorts. It's one of the most powerful cinematographic techniques.

Framing was crucial for the first major filmmaker in history, Louis Lumière. An inventor and businessman, Lumière and his brother Auguste devised one of the first practical cinema cameras **(5.63)**. The Lumière camera, the most flexible of its day, weighed only 12 pounds. This was the camera that Melies used for his cinematic trickery, but Louis Lumière's earliest films presented simple events—workers leaving his father's factory, a game of cards, a family meal. But even at so early a stage of film history, Lumière was able to use framing to transform everyday reality into a cinematic event.

Consider one of the most famous Lumière films, *The Arrival of a Train at La Ciotat Station* (1897). Lumière might have framed the shot by setting the camera

5.61

5.61–5.62 Playing with perspective.
In *Daisies*, Vera Chytilová uses setting, character position, and deep focus to make a comic point about the two women's amused deflation of men (5.61). Lech Majewski's *The Mill and the Cross* combines the flat canvas with the real locations and figures in the foreground, inviting us into a world that is half-painting, half three-dimensional landscape (5.62).

5.62

perpendicular to the platform, letting the train enter the frame from the right. Instead, Lumière stationed the camera at an oblique angle. The result is a dynamic composition, with the train arriving from the distance on a diagonal **(5.64).** If the scene had been shot perpendicularly, we would have seen only a string of passengers' backs climbing aboard. Lumière's oblique angle lets us see people's expressions and watch the ways they walk. There is also deep space: some figures move into the foreground and others can be glimpsed in the distance.

Simple as it is, this single-shot film, less than a minute long, shows that camera position shapes the way we perceive the filmed event. The same thing happens on a more intimate scale with another Lumière short, *Baby's Meal* (1895). A long shot would have situated the family in its garden, perhaps showing off their wealth. Instead, Lumière framed the figures at a medium distance, which emphasizes the family's gestures and facial expressions **(5.65).** The frame's sizing of the event has guided our understanding of the event itself.

5.63

5.64

5.65

5.63–5.65 Louis Lumière, early master of framing. In an era in which a camera might be the size of an office desk, the Lumière camera was portable and could be set up on a tripod quickly (5.63). For *The Arrival of a Train at La Ciotat Station*, Lumière's diagonal framing supplied a dynamic composition and considerable depth (5.64). For *Baby's Meal* (5.65), the framing is more frontal and intimate, excluding the garden in order to concentrate on the family.

5.86

5.87

5.88

5.86–5.88 **Changing compositional shape.** In *La Roue,* Gance employs a variety of circular and oval masks (5.86). In one shot of Griffith's *Intolerance,* most of the frame is boldly blocked out to leave only a thin vertical slice, emphasizing the soldier's fall from the rampart (5.87). Orson Welles used an iris to close a scene in *The Magnificent Ambersons* (5.88). The old-fashioned device adds a nostalgic note to the sequence, the last moment of shared happiness among the characters.

Masks and Multiple Images   The rectangular frame hasn't prevented some filmmakers from embedding other image shapes in it. This has usually been done by attaching **masks** over either the camera's or the printer's lens to block the passage of light. Masks were quite common in the silent cinema **(5.86, 5.87).** A moving circular mask that opens to reveal or closes to conceal a scene is called an **iris.** A number of directors in the sound cinema have revived the use of irises and masks **(5.88).**

We also should mention experiments with *multiple-frame,* or *split-screen,* imagery. In this process, two or more images, each with its own frame dimensions and shape, appear within the larger frame. Gance's *Napoleon* tried it on an epic scale (5.70), but it was used earlier, often to present scenes of telephone conversations. Modern filmmakers have turned to multiple-frame imagery to build suspense; we gain a godlike omniscience as we watch different story actions at exactly the same moment **(5.89).** The technique can be used subjectively as well **(5.90).**

5.89

5.90

5.89–5.90 **Multiple-frame imagery.** Split-screen shots often present two or more events taking place at the same time. The opening sequence of *The Thomas Crown Affair* (1968) shows men converging to commit a robbery (5.89). In *127 Hours,* the hero is trapped in a remote canyon, and Danny Boyle uses multiple frames to convey his perceptions and imaginings (5.90).

Choices about aspect ratio and embedded imagery shape the spectator's experience in important ways. Graphic factors such as masses, edges, and movement gain their impact in relation to frame width. Just as important, frame size and shape guides the spectator's eye. The filmmaker can concentrate our attention through masking or composition, or shift our attention across the frame by creating different points of interest. The same possibilities exist with multiple-frame imagery, which must be carefully coordinated either to focus the viewer's attention or to send it ricocheting from one image to another.

Onscreen and Offscreen Space

Whatever its shape, the frame limits the image with a boundary. Our eyes have a very wide field of view, somewhat over 180 degrees, but a camera lens shows a much smaller slice of the world. Is this a disadvantage?

No. The frame shapes our experience, calling attention to what the filmmaker wants us to see. Every act of framing, as Lumière intuitively realized, creates relationships among the things we see. In Figure 5.64, the train forms a diagonal, and the people move toward us. Framing the scene differently would have created different visual patterns, different relationships between the train and the travelers. Moreover, the fact that the frame carves out only a little from the overall visual field means that filmmakers can creatively exploit the space *offscreen,* the areas not shown inside the frame.

As viewers we help the filmmaker with this task, because we know that what's in the frame is part of a continuous world. If the camera moves away from a person to frame someone else, we assume that the first person is still there, outside the frame. Even in an abstract film, we can't resist the sense that the shapes and patterns that burst into the frame come from somewhere. So the filmmaker can imply the presence of things out of frame. You can have a character look or gesture at something offscreen. As we'll see in Chapter 7, sound can offer potent clues about offscreen space. And something from offscreen can come into the frame.

We're most aware of offscreen space when it creates suspense or surprise. A shadow from an unknown person outside the frame may slide across the shot and build up our expectations of a threat. Likewise, moments when a monster bursts into the frame are conventional in horror films, as we've seen in the 3D *House of Wax* (5.68). But any genre can employ incursions from offscreen. During a party scene in *Jezebel,* the heroine is the main focus of attention until a man's hand comes abruptly into the frame **(5.91–5.94).** Director William Wyler has used the selective powers of the frame to exclude something of great importance and then introduce it with startling effect. More systematically, D. W. Griffith's *Musketeers of Pig Alley* makes use of sudden intrusions into the frame as a motif developing across the whole film **(5.95, 5.96).**

These examples exploit areas lying beyond the four frame edges. There's also offscreen space behind parts of the setting, as when we see a mysterious door and hear sounds from inside it. The filmmaker can activate yet another offscreen zone, that of the camera and the area around it. In a thriller, a moving camera may represent the optical viewpoint of a stalker who isn't shown directly. The zone around the camera is used more imaginatively in Abbas Kiarostami's *Through the Olive*

5.91

5.92

5.93

5.94

5.91–5.94 Offscreen space revealed. In *Jezebel,* the heroine, Julie, greets some friends in medium shot (5.91). Suddenly a fist holding a glass appears in the left foreground (5.92). Julie notices and comes forward flirtatiously (5.93), and the camera retreats slightly to frame her with the man who toasted her (5.94). It's an attention-getting way to introduce Julie's new suitor.

Height   We may not think as much about camera height as we do angle and horizontal balance, but it's another area of choice for the filmmaker. Height is related to camera angle, since some angles demand that you position the camera higher or lower than the subject. But if the angle is kept straight-in, crouching to take a snapshot creates a different composition than taking it from eye-level. For instance, the Japanese filmmaker Yasujiro Ozu films from a low height but uses a straight-on angle (4.153, 6.142–6.145). This choice gives his shots a distinctive visual style.

Distance   The framing of the image stations us relatively close to the subject or farther away. This aspect of framing is usually called *camera distance*. The terms for camera distance are approximate, and they're usually derived from the scale of human bodies in the shot. Our examples are all from *The Third Man*.

In the **extreme long shot,** the human figure is lost or tiny **(5.105).** This is the framing for landscapes, bird's-eye views of cities, and other vistas. In the **long shot,** figures are more prominent, but the background still dominates **(5.106).** Shots in which the human figure is framed from about the knees up are called **medium long shots (5.107).** These are common, since they permit a nice balance of figure and surroundings.

The **medium shot** frames the human body from the waist up **(5.108).** Gesture and expression now become more visible. The **medium close-up** frames the body from the chest up **(5.109).** The **close-up** is traditionally the shot showing just the head, hands, feet, or a small object. It emphasizes facial expression, the details of a gesture, or a significant object **(5.110).** The **extreme close-up** singles out a portion of the face or isolates and magnifies an object **(5.111).**

5.105 Extreme long shot

5.106 Long shot

5.107 Medium long shot

5.108 Medium shot

5.109 Medium close-up

5.110 Close-up

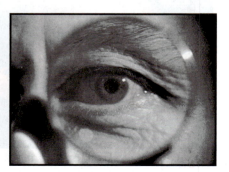
5.111 Extreme close-up

Note that the size of the photographed material within the frame is as important as any real camera distance. From the same camera distance, you could film a long shot of a person or a close-up of King Kong's elbow. We would not call the shot in **5.112** (from *La Passion de Jeanne d'Arc*) a close-up just because only Jeanne's head appears in the frame. In judging camera distance, the relative scale of the view determines how we label the shot.

Categories of framing are obviously matters of degree. No precise cutoff point distinguishes between a long shot and an extreme long shot. Filmmakers and film researchers find these terms useful, and they're usually clear enough for descriptive purposes.

Functions of Framing
Sometimes we're tempted to assign absolute meanings to angles, distances, and other qualities of framing. Does filming from a low angle automatically present a character as powerful? Does framing from a high angle always render the character as dwarfed and defeated? Verbal analogies are especially seductive. Does a canted frame mean that "the world is out of kilter"?

Making and watching movies would be a lot simpler if framings carried such hard-and-fast meanings. But the individual films would lose their uniqueness and richness. In fact, framings don't carry absolute or general meanings. In *some* films, angles and distance imply the meanings as mentioned above, but in other films—probably most films—they don't. To rely on formulas is to forget that meaning and effect always stem from the film's overall form and the immediate context.

For instance, at many points in *Citizen Kane*, low-angle shots of Kane do suggest his looming power. Interestingly, however, the film's lowest camera positions occur at the point of Kane's most humiliating defeat—his miscarried gubernatorial campaign (**5.113**). Here the low angle functions to isolate Kane and Leland. Similarly, the world is hardly out of kilter in the shot from Eisenstein's *October* shown in **5.114**. The canted frame dynamizes the effort of pushing the cannon. If the cliché about high-angle framings were correct, **5.115,** a shot from *North by Northwest*, would express the powerlessness of Van Damm and Leonard. In fact, the angle of Hitchcock's shot wittily prophesies how they plan to carry out a murder.

These three examples indicate that we can't reduce the richness of cinema to a few recipes. We must, as usual, look for the *functions* the technique performs in the particular *context* of the total film.

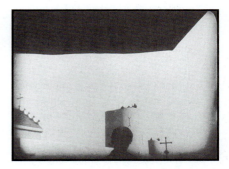

5.112 **Shot scale versus camera position.** In *La Passion de Jeanne d'Arc*, the framing is that of a rather long shot even though Jeanne's head is all we see of her. If the framing were simply adjusted downward, her whole body would be visible, along with much of the castle.

5.113

5.114

5.115

5.113–5.115 **Context controls framing.** In *Citizen Kane*, the protagonist is seen from below during his greatest defeat. By setting the figures against the ceiling and an abandoned campaign headquarters, the low angle suggests that Kane is increasingly isolated (5.113). A canted framing, as in Eisenstein's *October*, can create a dynamic composition and suggest a powerful force moving against gravity (5.114). As Van Damm reflects on pushing his mistress out of a plane, and the camera rises above him, he says, "I think that this is a matter best disposed of from a great height" (5.115).

CREATIVE DECISIONS

Camera Position in a Shot from The Social Network

> "I don't like close-ups unless you can get a kick out of them, unless you need them. If you can get away with attitudes and positions that show the feeling of the scene, I think you're better off using the close-up only for absolute punctuation—that's the reason you do it. And you save it— not like TV where they do everything in close-up."
>
> —Howard Hawks, director, *His Girl Friday*

One of the most important matters a director decides is the placement of the camera. "There's only one right spot for the camera in each shot," the adage goes, "and it's my job to find it."

Consider a shot from *The Social Network*. Throughout the film Mark Zuckerberg has been characterized as a driven hacker. We've seen that his scowling face can seem aggressive, especially in contrast to that of his friend Eduardo (4.93–4.96). Mark's rare smiles are somewhat twisted and self-regarding. But at the moment when he has just auditioned new programmers for Facebook, he seems to wear a grin of genuine joy. Instead of supplying a close-up of this expression, though, director David Fincher frames Mark in long shot **(5.116).** This is consistent with the narrational weight of the scene, as our range of knowledge has been restricted to Eduardo's. But the camera position also cools down any admiration we might be feeling for Mark. A closer view might have made him more sympathetic.

5.116 Camera distance and sympathy. There are plenty of close shots of Mark elsewhere in *The Social Network*. Yet at his moment of triumph, the framing (from Eduardo's optical point of view) plays down an expression that could humanize him a bit. Perhaps the somber lighting, not shared with the background characters, even gives his smile a sinister edge.

For filmmakers working with narrative form, camera placement is central to visual storytelling. A framing can stress a narratively important detail **(5.117, 5.118).** Camera distance specifies where characters are and how they respond to each other. Orchestrated by editing, as we'll see in the next chapter, distances and angles form patterns that guide us in building up the story.

Framing also can put us in a character's place. In Chapter 3, we saw that a film's narration may present story information with some psychological depth (p. 87). One option is perceptual subjectivity, the attempt to render what a character sees or hears. A shot's distance and angle may prompt us to take it as seen through a character's eyes, creating a *point-of-view (POV)* shot **(5.119, 5.120).** (See also p. 90.)

5.117

5.118

5.117–5.118 Camera distance as emphasis. The tears of Henriette in *A Day in the Country* are visible in extreme close-up (5.117). In *Day for Night*, a close framing emphasizes how carefully the film director arranges an actor's hands (5.118).

5.119

5.120

5.119–5.120 Subjective framings. In *Fury*, the hero in his jail cell is seen through the bars from a slightly low angle (5.119). The next shot, a high angle through the window toward the street outside, shows us what he sees, from his point of view (5.120).

Framings may serve the narrative in yet other ways. Across an entire film, the repetitions of certain framings may associate themselves with a character or situation. That is, framings may become motifs unifying the film **(5.121).** Alternatively, certain framings in a film may stand out by virtue of their rarity. In a film composed primarily of long shots and medium shots, an extreme close-up will have considerable force. The early scenes of Ridley Scott's *Alien* present few shots depicting any character's point of view. But when Kane approaches the alien egg, we see close views of it as if through his eyes, and the creature leaps straight out at us. The POV shot provides a sudden shock and marks a major turning point in the plot.

Apart from their narrative significance, framings can add a visual interest of their own. Close-ups can give hands and feet a weight they wouldn't have if we were just attending to dialogue and facial expression **(5.122).** Long shots can permit us to explore vistas. Much of the visual delight of Westerns, of David Lynch's *The Straight Story,* and other films rendering landscapes arises from long shots that make huge spaces manifest **(5.123).** By including a range of information, the long-shot framing encourages us to search for details or discover abstract patterns **(5.124).**

In both narrative and non-narrative films, our eye also enjoys the formal play presented by unusual angles on familiar objects **(5.125, 5.126).** "By reproducing the object from an unusual and striking angle," writes Rudolf Arnheim, "the artist forces the spectator to take a keener interest, which goes beyond mere noticing or acceptance. The object thus photographed sometimes gains in reality, and the impression it makes is livelier and more arresting."

The filmmaker may find ways to use framing for comic effect. You'll recall that in *Our Hospitality* Keaton stages many gags in depth. Now we can see that well-chosen camera angles and distances are also vital to the gags' success. If you turn back to p. 160, you'll notice that the railroad scene shown in 4.173 couldn't

5.121 Camera angle as a motif. In *The Maltese Falcon,* Kasper Gutman is frequently photographed from a low angle, emphasizing his obesity.

CONNECT TO THE BLOG
www.davidbordwell.net/blog

One way to add visual interest is to shoot straight into the rear plane of the setting, as we explain in "Shot-consciousness."

5.122

5.122–5.124 Camera distance for intricacy and scope. The close shots of thieves' surreptitious gestures have a narrative function in Robert Bresson's *Pickpocket,* but they also create a dazzling ballet of fingers and wrists (5.122). Helicopter shots in *Lessons of Darkness* give the desolate burning oilfields of Kuwait an eerie, horrifying grandeur (5.123). In Hou Hsiao-hsien's *Summer at Grandpa's,* the boy from the city visits his disgraced uncle, and the neighborhood is presented as a welter of rooftops sheltering a spot of bright red (5.124).

5.123

5.124

5.125–5.126 Seeing differently. René Clair in *Entr'acte* frames a ballerina from straight below, transforming the figure into a pulsating flower (5.125). In *La Passion de Jeanne d'Arc,* the upside-down framings are not motivated as a character's point of view; they build up to the frenzy of the soldiers' massacre of the crowd witnessing Jeanne's death (5.126).

5.125

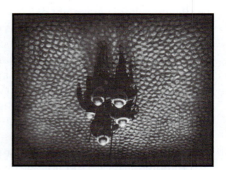

5.126

be as effective if it were filmed from the side and in extreme long shot. That way, we wouldn't clearly see that the two parts of the train are on parallel tracks. And we wouldn't see the engineer's unconcerned posture, which indicates his failure to realize what has happened. Like Lumière at the train station, Keaton chose depth staging and a diagonal camera position. The result creates a composition that highlights certain relations between things.

Similarly, offscreen space is vital to the gag shown in 4.182–4.184. Here Keaton lays out the comedy in time rather than space. Willie tugs on the rope. Then

5.127 Framing creates a visual joke. In *Play Time*, M. Hulot reacts with a start when he notices that a guard locking a door seems suddenly to have sprouted horns—the door handles.

an unseen effect of that tug becomes visible as the Canfield son hurtles past and disappears. Finally, Willie reacts and is dragged down into the abyss below the frameline. Keaton could have framed this moment in a different way—say, from a low angle that showed both Willie and the Canfield boy in the same frame. But that would have sacrificed the suspense of waiting for Canfield to plummet through the shot. Throughout *Our Hospitality* our reaction to Keaton's humor depends on his careful combination of mise-en-scene and framing.

In Tati's *Play Time*, mise-en-scene and camera position cooperate to create pictorial jokes. In **5.127**, a visual pun issues from the precisely chosen camera angle and distance, as well as from the mise-en-scene: the man's stooping posture and the door handles make him look like a goat. Tati maintained the approach of silent comedy within the sound cinema. As with other filmmakers, his choice of framing was governed by imagining how it would affect the viewer.

The Mobile Frame

Cinema isn't the only visual medium that employs framing. Most still images, of any type, possess aspect ratios, imply things happening outside the frame, and present an implied vantage point on the scene. But there is one resource of framing that is specific to films, either photochemical or digital. In cinema, the frame can *move* with respect to what it shows us.

In cinematography, *mobile framing* allows the filmmaker to change the camera angle, level, height, or distance *during* the shot. Just as important, the movement of the frame often persuades us that we're moving, too.

Types of Mobile Framing   We usually refer to the ability of the frame to be mobile as *camera movement*. In live-action filming, mobile framing is usually achieved by moving the camera physically during production. There are several kinds of camera movement, each with a specific effect onscreen.

The **pan** (short for *panorama*) movement swivels the camera on a vertical axis. The camera as a whole does not move to a new position. Onscreen, the pan scans space horizontally, as if the camera is "turning its head" right or left (**5.128, 5.129**). The **tilt** movement rotates the camera on a horizontal axis. It is as if the camera's head were swiveling up or down. Onscreen, the tilt movement yields the impression of unrolling a space from top to bottom or bottom to top (**5.130, 5.131**).

CONNECT TO THE BLOG
www.davidbordwell.net/blog

We analyze subtleties of framing in films by two masters, William Wyler and Kenji Mizoguchi, in "Sleeves."

5.128

5.129

5.130

5.131

5.128–5.131 **Panning and tilting the camera.** During a shot in Dreyer's *Ordet*, the camera pans right to keep the figures in frame as they cross a room (5.128, 5.129). François Truffaut's *The Bride Wore Black* begins with a tilt down a church spire to the church door (5.130, 5.131).

> " I realized that if I could just get to the really good scripts, I could approach it the way I approach literature—why the camera moves this way because of this motif—and then it became fascinating."
> —Jodie Foster, director, *Little Man Tate*

In the **tracking** or **dolly shot,** the camera as a whole changes position, traveling in any direction along the ground—forward, backward, diagonally, in circles, or from side to side **(5.132, 5.133).** In the **crane shot,** the camera moves above ground level. Typically, it rises or descends, often thanks to a mechanical arm that lifts and lowers it. A crane shot may move vertically, like an elevator **(5.134, 5.135),** or at some angle forward or back **(5.136, 5.137).** Variations of the crane shot are helicopter and airplane shots.

Sometimes the camera movement we see is simulated—that is, no camera actually moved in production. The main examples are seen in animation. With cel animation, which photographs one frame at a time, the actual camera stays in one

5.132

5.133

5.132–5.133 **The camera moves through space.** During this lateral tracking shot in Erich von Stroheim's *Greed*, the camera moves rightward along with the two characters (5.132, 5.133). Note how the figures remain in the same basic relationship to the frame as they stroll along a sidewalk, while the front of the house that they hope to buy remains visible behind them.

5.134

5.135

5.136

5.137

5.134–5.137 Craning down, craning up. In *Ivan the Terrible,* from a high-angle view of Anastasia's bier (5.134), the camera descends to end on a straight-on framing of Ivan slumped at its base (5.135). At the end of Karel Reisz's *Morgan!* the camera cranes diagonally up and back to reveal that the hero's apparently innocuous flower garden proclaims his Communist sympathies (5.136, 5.137).

5.138

5.139

5.140

5.138–5.140 Frame mobility without a moving camera. In *Peter Pan* cel animation imitates a pan shot.

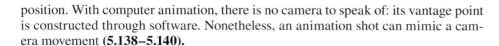

position. With computer animation, there is no camera to speak of: its vantage point is constructed through software. Nonetheless, an animation shot can mimic a camera movement (**5.138–5.140**).

Movement and Machinery For many decades, camera movements in live-action production depended on putting the camera on a dolly, a heavy cart. The dolly can usually move on its own wheels, but it is often mounted on rails, hence the term *tracking* (**5.141**). Tracking shots are also made with cranes, even if the camera position doesn't rise or fall as in the usual crane shot. Suspended from a jib arm, the camera can glide over rough terrain. *The Thin Red Line* employed a 72-foot crane arm that let the camera slither over hills of tall grass during battle scenes. "The whole idea of using that crane was to not make it feel like a crane," says cinematographer John Toll. "We wanted it to look like the most continuous, smooth dolly that had ever been built."

Body-mounted camera units are common as well. These devices allow the camera operator to steer the camera while walking. Servo mechanisms adjust for imbalances and jerkiness, so the camera seems to glide or float. The prototype of the body-worn camera stabilizer is the Steadicam, initially used on *Bound for*

> “ It's a compulsion of mine to move the camera, and I now know why. It enhances three-dimensionality. It puts you in the space, and if you move the camera the audience becomes aware of the space."
> —George Miller, director, *The Road Warrior*

5.141 **Tracking on rails.** The camera crew must push the dolly on the tracks to capture the shot. (Compare 1.36.) The 360° tracking shot has become a common technique in modern cinema. The shot, being prepared for *The Departed*, was omitted from the final film.

Glory, Rocky, and *The Shining.* Now many consumer video cameras have comparable image-stabilization systems.

A body-worn camera can go places that would be difficult for a dolly. The operator can smoothly follow actors climbing stairs, riding vehicles, and walking great distances **(5.142, 5.143)**. Some directors have taken advantage of the Steadicam to create lengthy shots moving through many locales, as in the opening scenes of Brian De Palma's *Bonfire of the Vanities* and Paul Thomas Anderson's *Boogie Nights*.

Sometimes the filmmaker does not want smooth camera movements and prefers a bumpy image. Commonly, this sort of shot is created by the **handheld camera.** Instead of anchoring the camera on some support like a dolly or a stabilizer, the operator simply walks with the camera braced on the shoulder. This sort of camera movement became common in the late 1950s, with the growth of the *cinéma vérité* documentary trend **(5.144, 5.145).**

5.142

5.143

5.142–5.143 **Steadicam tracking shot.** In Martin Scorsese's *Raging Bull,* the Steadicam follows the protagonist out of his dressing room and through a crowd up to the boxing ring.

5.144

5.145

5.144–5.145 **The handheld camera and documentary.** Don Pennebaker hand-holds the camera while filming his *Keep on Rockin'* (5.144). For the documentary *Primary,* a cameraman lifted the camera above his head and followed John F. Kennedy through a milling crowd (5.145).

Modern lightweight cameras, particularly digital models, allow cinematographers to improvise unusual camera mounts **(5.146).** For a large battle scene on a beach, the makers of *Robin Hood* (2010) mounted a camera on a Jet Ski, which could maneuver among several landing craft. For a scene in *There Be Dragons,* the operator wore a Steadicam and filmed moving shots from a Segway.

5.146 **Other camera supports.** *Secretariat's* race scenes involved mounting a miniature camera on the end of a broomstick.

The Zoom and the Mobile Frame   We've already seen that a zoom lens provides a continuous range of focal lengths. When the camera operator zooms during filming, the result is a mobile framing—even though the camera stays in one spot (5.41–5.43). Some viewers have trouble distinguishing a zoom-in from a forward tracking shot, or a zoom-out from a reverse tracking shot. But filmmakers know very well that there are major differences. The choice that the director and the cinematographer make can subtly shape how the viewer responds.

The zoom lens reduces or blows up some portion of the image. Although a tracking shot and a crane shot also enlarge or reduce areas of the frame, this is not all that they do. In the genuine camera movement, static objects in different planes pass one another at different rates. We see different sides of objects, and backgrounds gain volume and depth **(5.147, 5.148).** By contrast, a zoom enlargement doesn't alter the aspects or positions of the objects we see. Our vantage point is the same at the end of the shot as at the beginning **(5.149, 5.150).** When the camera moves, we sense our own movement through the space. In a zoom, a bit of the space gets steadily magnified or demagnified.

We've pinpointed these sorts of mobile framings as isolated options. But filmmakers frequently combine them within a single shot. The camera may track and pan at the same time or crane up while zooming out. In *Vertigo,* an especially

5.147

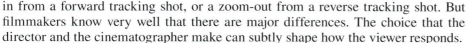

5.148

5.149

5.150

5.147–5.150 **Tracking shot versus zoom.** In Alain Resnais's *La Guerre est finie,* a tracking shot gives the objects considerable volume (5.147, 5.148). The wall has lost none of its solidity, and objects pass as if we were walking toward the sign. In Theo Angelopoulos's *Ulysses' Gaze,* a zoom shot simply blows up one area of the shot (5.149–5.150), as if we were adjusting a telescope. As the zoom occurs, the space looks flatter—the mark of a long-lens, or telephoto, framing.

tricky combination track-*out* and zoom-*in* plastically distorts the shot's perspective and conveys the protagonist's dizziness. The device reappears in Spielberg's *Jaws,* when Sheriff Brody at the beach suddenly realizes that the shark has attacked a child. Simultaneously tracking and zooming in opposite directions has become common in modern Hollywood filmmaking to express a character's sense of confusion or astonishment (what director Sam Raimi calls the "warp-o cam"). The combinations are endless.

Frame Mobility: Functions   Camera movements have held an appeal for filmmakers and audiences since the beginnings of cinema. Some of the earliest films made by Lumière cameramen were shots from trains or Venetian gondolas, and even today these films have a mesmeric power. Why?

For one thing, camera movements can increase information about the space of the image. Pan and tilt shots present new areas of the setting, and tracking shots and crane shots supply continually changing perspectives on it. As the camera shifts its point of view, objects or figures are usually revealed, so frame mobility can create a flow of new information for the viewer. Camera movement can as well make objects seem sharper and more vivid than in stationary framings. Certain camera movements give onscreen elements greater volume and solidity. This is apparently one reason modern directors like to circle around the action (5.141), as in the opening scene of *Reservoir Dogs.*

What's more, we tend to see camera movement as a substitute for *our* movement. When we see a forward tracking shot, we feel that we're approaching something or backing away. A crane shot that pulls away from something at ground level makes us feel a little weightless. We aren't completely fooled, of course. We never forget that we're watching a film in a theater. But camera movement provides several convincing cues for movement through space. Indeed, so powerful are these cues that filmmakers often make camera movements subjective—motivated narratively to represent what a moving character sees. Camera movement can be a powerful cue for a point-of-view shot.

When we walk through the world, our eyes see a somewhat bouncy view, but our optical system compensates for the jerkiness and creates a sense of stable motion. This sense of smooth movement can be captured by a traveling shot made with a dolly, a jib arm, or a Steadicam. Sometimes, however, handheld shots are used to suggest subjective point of view **(5.151).** Alternatively, the handheld shot can simply create a sense of anxious movement, as if the action were glimpsed on the fly **(5.152).**

5.151

5.152

5.151–5.152 **Handheld impressions.** In Samuel Fuller's *The Naked Kiss,* a handheld POV shot heightens the impact of a fight (5.151). As the protagonist of *julien donkey-boy* walks, we don't get a POV shot, but Harmony Korine's bouncy, mini-DV cameras follow him shuffling through his neighborhood (5.152). The handheld camera's jerky pace complements the explosions of color created by printing video up to 35mm.

5.153   **5.154**   **5.155**

5.153–5.155 Reframing. In *His Girl Friday*, director Howard Hawks strives to balance his compositions through reframing. When Hildy crosses from the left (5.153) to sit on the desk, the camera pans right to reframe her (5.154). This reframing is more noticeable than the next one: As Walter swivels his chair to face her, the camera reframes very slightly leftward (5.155).

Frame Mobility and Space   We can get a little more specific about the purposes and effects of mobile framings if we consider some functions they have—in relation to cinematic space and time, in relation to the overall form of the film.

Camera movement creates an interplay of onscreen and offscreen space. If you track the camera in, you exclude more space from the shot (5.147, 5.148). If you track back, as in our example from *Jezebel* (5.91–5.94), you reveal some space that was previously offscreen. The mobile frame also continually affects the angle, level, height, or distance of the framing. A crane up may change the angle from a low one to a high one; a track-in may change the shot scale from long shot to close-up.

As usual, one choice leads to others. For instance, just as filmmakers must decide how to motivate story actions or whether to motivate lighting sources, they must consider whether to motivate camera movement. Should you make the frame's changing space depend on the movement in the shot? Usually, the answer is yes. A panning movement may keep a racing car centered, a tracking shot may follow a character from room to room, or a crane shot may pursue a rising balloon. Sometimes the camera movement is quite minimal, as with **reframing.** If a character moves in relation to another character, often the frame will slightly pan or tilt to adjust to the movement (**5.153–5.155**). Because reframing movements are usually slight and motivated by the figures' movement, we seldom notice them.

The framing can move independently of the figures, too. Sometimes the camera drifts away from the characters to reveal something of narrative importance; the mobile frame is motivated not by figure movement but by the demands of the narration. In Jean Renoir's *Crime of M. Lange,* the protagonist sits at his desk writing Wild West stories, but the camera pans away to show cowboy gear cluttering his room, establishing that Lange lives in a fantasy world. Similarly, an independent camera movement can point out an overlooked clue, a sign that comments on the action, or an imminent threat. The camera can thus be relatively unrestricted in its range of knowledge, as in 5.136–5.137 when it reveals Morgan's hammer-and-sickle flower bed.

Filmmakers are especially fond of solo camera movements at the beginning of a scene or the entire film. A tracking shot can establish a locale and then smoothly let the characters enter the space (**5.156–5.159**). A camera movement can even foreshadow action to come. In the opening scene of *The Milk of Sorrow,* Fausta, a woman who is terrified of the world outside her home, tends her dying mother. Cinematographer Natasha Braier describes the purpose of a tracking shot (**5.160, 5.161**) early in the film: "The whole idea of this shot was to represent what is going to happen in the film. At the beginning of the story, Fausta is living with her mother in a hermetic world, and now that her mother is dead, she will have to venture outside,

> "I kept wondering, 'Can people talk this much in a feature film and anybody care?' And so I had to go through every moment in those dialogue scenes and look for the little events I would treat as large events. Like the ringing of a phone or the blinds being opened. . . . I had to treat those as fairly major events and have the moves of the camera be motivated by them, so that it would be organic to the scene yet still visually interesting."
>
> —John Patrick Shanley, writer and director, *Doubt*

CONNECT TO THE BLOG
www.davidbordwell.net/blog

One common function of tracking shots is to follow actors in conversation, as we discuss in "Walk the talk."

5.156–5.159 **Camera movement independent of the figures.** At the start of Otto Preminger's *Laura*, the camera glides through Waldo Lydecker's sitting room (5.156, 5.157), establishing him as a man of wealth and refinement, before revealing the detective McPherson (5.158). The framing then becomes motivated by figure movement, with the camera following McPherson's drift to a wall of masks (5.159).

5.156

5.157

5.158

5.159

5.160

5.161

5.160–5.161 **Camera movement anticipates story action.** In the opening scene of *The Milk of Sorrow*, an initial framing shows the protagonist in the room where she has spent so much time (5.160). A slow track forward nearly eliminates the window frame, framing her against the outside world that she will now have to confront (5.161).

and because of the way we frame her at the end of that shot, she actually appears to be outside."

Whether dependent on figure movement or independent of it, the mobile frame can profoundly affect how we perceive the space of the action. Different sorts of camera movements create different treatments of space. In *Last Year at Marienbad*, Resnais often tracks down corridors and through doorways, turning a fashionable resort hotel into a maze. For *Young and Innocent*, Hitchcock (a virtuoso of camera movement) devised a shot that moves from a high-angle long shot of a ballroom over the heads of the dancers to an extreme close-up of a drummer's blinking eyes. In such films as *The Red and the White*, Miklós Jancsó specialized in lengthy camera movements that roam among groups of people moving across a plain. His shots use all of the resources of tracking, panning, craning, zooming, and racking focus to sculpt plastic, ever-changing spatial relations.

When we see any mobile framing, we can ask: What particular trajectory does the camera pursue? How does it function to reveal or conceal offscreen space? Does the frame mobility depend on figure movement or is it independent, drawing our attention to other things?

Frame Mobility and Time   Mobile framing involves time as well as space, and filmmakers have realized that our sense of duration and rhythm is affected by the mobile frame. Since a camera movement consumes time on screen, it can create an arc of expectation and fulfillment. If the camera pans quickly from an event, we may be prompted to wonder what has happened. If the camera abruptly tracks back to show us something in the foreground that we had not expected, as in our earlier *Jezebel* example (5.91–5.94), we're taken by surprise. If the camera slowly moves in on a detail, gradually enlarging it but delaying the fulfillment of our expectations, the camera movement has contributed to suspense. In the pan shot across M. Lange's study mentioned earlier, Renoir makes us wonder why the camera strays from the main character and then answers the question by revealing Lange's fascination with cowboys.

The velocity of frame mobility is important, too. A zoom or a camera movement may be relatively slow or fast. Richard Lester's *A Hard Day's Night* and *Help!* started a fad in the 1960s for very fast zoom-ins and -outs. In comparison, one of the most impressive early camera movements, D. W. Griffith's monumental crane shot in Belshazzar's feast in *Intolerance,* gains majesty and suspense through its inexorably slow descent toward the immense Babylonian set (4.12).

Sometimes the speed of the mobile framing functions rhythmically, as in musical films. During the "Broadway Rhythm" number in *Singin' in the Rain,* the camera cranes quickly back from Gene Kelly several times, and the speed of the movement is timed to accentuate the lyrics. Frame velocity can also create expressive qualities—a camera movement can be fluid, staccato, hesitant, and so forth. *Cloverfield* is presented as an amateur video record of a monster's attack on Manhattan. At many points, the operator whips the camera around to capture a shocking incident, and our anxiety is intensified by the sudden speed of the panning movement (**5.162, 5.163**). By choosing the duration and speed of camera movements, the filmmaker can pace our understanding of the plot action.

Larger Patterns of Frame Mobility   While shaping time and space, mobile framings can become motifs across a film. In Carl Dreyer's *Day of Wrath,* the camera circles a shadowy chamber, surveying church officials who torture an old woman accused of being a witch. She tells her inquisitor that his death is imminent. Later in the film, her accuser lies on his deathbed, and a similar camera movement recalls her curse.

We see a more long-range motif in Hitchcock's *Psycho,* which begins and ends with a forward movement of the frame. During the film's first three shots, the camera pans right and zooms in on a nondescript building (**5.164**).

> " You really need to know why you are doing one of these moves. . . . If you pan on a long lens, it's a very different look than tracking with somebody; there's a very different feel to it."
> —Roger Deakins, cinematographer, *No Country for Old Men*

> " One thing I hate in films is when the camera starts circling characters. If three people are sitting at a table talking, you'll often see the camera circling them. I can't explain why, but I find it totally fake."
> —Takeshi Kitano, director, *Sonatine*

5.162

5.163

5.162–5.163 Speed of camera movement accentuates shock. In *Cloverfield* the video camera records an explosion in the street, and a whip pan to the right blurs the action (5.162). When the framing becomes stable again, we realize that the blurry movement was trying to follow the head of the Statue of Liberty rolling down the street (5.163).

5.164

5.165

5.166

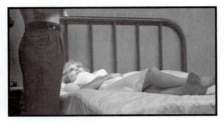

5.167

5.168

5.169

5.164–5.169 **Camera movement as a motif.** The opening of *Psycho*: The camera pans right and zooms in on a building in a cityscape (5.164). The camera moves toward a window to reveal the heroine and her boyfriend sharing a lunchtime tryst (5.165–5.167). The film's next-to-last shot begins at a distance from Norman (5.168) and moves in so that we see his expression as we hear his thoughts (5.169).

Camera movements carry us under a window blind and into the darkness of a cheap hotel room (**5.165–5.167**). The camera's movement inward, the penetration of an interior, is repeated throughout the film, often motivated as a subjective point of view when various characters move deeper and deeper into Norman Bates's mansion. The next-to-last shot of the film shows Norman sitting against a blank white wall, while we hear his interior monologue (**5.168**). The camera again moves forward into a close-up of his face (**5.169**). This shot is the climax of the forward movement initiated at the start of the film; the film has traced a movement into Norman's mind. Another film that relies heavily on a pattern of forward, penetrating movements is *Citizen Kane,* which depicts the same inexorable drive toward the revelation of a character's secret.

The filmmaker can develop other sorts of patterns. In Michael Snow's ←→ (usually called *Back and Forth*), the constant panning to and fro across a classroom, Ping-Pong fashion, determines the basic formal pattern of the film. It comes as a surprise when, near the very end, the movement suddenly becomes a repeated tilting up and down. As with lighting, color, and other techniques, cinematographic choices can develop in the course of the movie.

CREATIVE DECISIONS

Mobile Framing and Film Form in Grand Illusion and Wavelength

Two quite different films let us sum up ways in which the director can integrate the mobile frame into an overall form. One film uses the mobile frame in order to strengthen and support the plot's presentation of the story. The other film explores frame mobility in its own right and makes storytelling secondary—in fact, nearly nonexistent.

Jean Renoir's *Grand Illusion* is a war film in which we almost never see the war. Heroic charges and doomed battalions, the staple of the genre, are absent. World War I remains obstinately offscreen. Instead, Renoir concentrates on life in a German prisoner-of-war camp to suggest how relations between nations and social

5.170 A can used as a warning signal is sitting on a shelf.

5.171 It's pulled over, but it lands on a pillow and so makes no sound.

5.172 The camera pans left to reveal that the characters haven't noticed it.

5.170–5.172 *Grand Illusion*: Unrestricted narration

classes are affected by war. The prisoners Maréchal and Boeldieu are both French; Rauffenstein is a German officer. Yet the aristocrat Boeldieu has more in common with Rauffenstein than with the mechanic Maréchal. The film's plot traces the death of the Boeldieu-Rauffenstein upper class and the precarious survival of Maréchal and his pal Rosenthal. They escape the camp and take refuge in Elsa's farm, where they enjoy an interlude of peace. Eventually, however, they must flee across the border, back to France and presumably back to the war. Within this plot, Renoir has given camera movement several functions, all directly supportive of the narrative.

As we might expect, the camera will often follow the figures to keep our attention on them. The camera tracks with Maréchal and Rosenthal walking together after their escape; it tracks back when the prisoners are drawn to the window by the sound of marching Germans below. But the camera movements *independent* of character action make the film more unusual.

When the camera moves on its own in *Grand Illusion,* we are conscious of it actively interpreting the action, creating suspense or giving us information that the characters don't have. In one scene, a prisoner is digging in an escape tunnel and tugs a string signaling that he needs to be pulled out **(5.170)**. An independent camera movement builds suspense by showing that the other characters have missed the signal and do not realize that he is suffocating **(5.171, 5.172)**. Here camera movement creates a somewhat unrestricted narration.

The independent camera movements in *Grand Illusion* sometimes become motifs. For example, camera movements repeatedly link characters with details of their environment. Often a sequence begins with a close-up of some detail, and the camera draws back to anchor this detail in its larger context **(5.173, 5.174)**. More complicated is the scene of the Christmas celebration at Elsa's that begins with a close-up of the crèche and tracks back to show, in several stages, the interplay of reactions among the characters. Such camera movements are not simply decoration; beginning on a scenic detail before moving to the larger context makes story points economically. The opening detail not only establishes a new locale but highlights a thematic point, as with the squirrel cage. So does a track-in to a detail at the *end* of a scene, as when after Boeldieu's death, Rauffenstein cuts the geranium, the one flower in the prison **(5.175, 5.176)**. Other directors would have emphasized the detail by cutting to a close-up, but Renoir keeps the film's style consistent by using a camera movement.

Characters are tied to their environment by even more ambitious moving-camera shots. These stress important narrative parallels. For example, tracking shots compare actions in two officers' bars—one French **(5.177–5.179)**, one German **(5.180–5.182)**. Through his camera movements, Renoir indicates a similarity between the two warring sides, blurring their national differences and stressing common desires.

5.173–5.176 Tracking shots and details of setting in *Grand Illusion* ▶

5.173 Renoir begins the scene by framing a close-up of a caged squirrel.

5.174 Creating a narrative parallel, the camera tracks back to reveal Boeldieu and Maréchal discussing their escape plans.

5.175 As Rauffenstein moves to the geranium in the window . . .

5.176 . . . Renoir tracks in to a close shot of the flower as he cuts it. Earlier Boeldieu had admired the geranium.

5.177–5.182 Parallel camera movements in *Grand Illusion* ▼

5.177 In the first scene, as Maréchal leaves the French officers' bar . . .

5.178 . . . Renoir pans and tracks left from the door to reveal pin-ups (just coming into the frame at the right) . . .

5.179 . . . and a poster.

5.180 One scene later, in the German officers' bar, a similar camera movement, this time toward the right, leaves the characters . . .

5.181 . . . and explores on its own . . .

5.182 . . . discovering some similar decorations.

5.183 One of the most elaborate camera movements in the film starts on a crucifix.

5.184 The camera tilts down to a military portrait on an altar, underlining the irony of a chapel commandeered as an officer's quarters.

5.185 The camera tracks past whips, spurs, and swords . . .

5.186 . . . to an orderly who is preparing Rauffenstein's gloves.

5.187 The orderly then walks away from the camera to close a window before returning . . .

5.188 . . . to the foreground. The camera pans left and tracks back to reveal . . .

5.189 . . . a tidy table . . .

5.190 . . . at which Rauffenstein is revealed to be sitting, ready for breakfast. For aristocratic warriors, the comforts of home aren't interrupted by war.

5.183–5.190 Prison camp: Military elegance in *Grand Illusion*

Or consider how two moments of camera movement compare the war of the aristocrats and the war of the lower-class people. We are introduced to Rauffenstein's new position as commander of a POW camp through a lengthy tracking shot **(5.183–5.190)**. During this movement, Renoir presents, wordlessly, the military mystique of grace on the battlefield that characterizes the aristocrat's war. Late in the film, however, a parallel shot criticizes this one **(5.191–5.193)**. Elsa's war has none of Rauffenstein's glory, and our sense of that is conveyed chiefly through a parallel created by the repeated camera movement. Moreover, these camera movements work together with mise-en-scene, as the narrative parallel is reinforced by

5.191 This shot, set inside Elsa's farmhouse, also begins on an object, a photograph of her dead husband.

5.192 The camera tracks left past Elsa, who remarks, "Now the table is too large."

5.193 The camera continues, revealing the kitchen table, where her daughter sits alone. The chairs upended on the table reinforce the solitude of Elsa's life in the midst of war.

5.191–5.193 Farmhouse: War's cost in *Grand Illusion*

the subtle use of objects as motifs—the crucifixes in 5.173 and 5.183, the photographs in 5.174 and 5.181, and the tables that end both shots.

Moving the camera independently of figure movement also links characters with one another. Again and again in the POW camp, the camera shifts to join one man to his comrades, spatially indicating their shared condition. As the prisoners ransack the collection of women's clothes, one man decides to dress up in them. When he appears in drag, a stillness falls over the men. Renoir tracks silently over the prisoners' faces, each one registering a reticent longing for a world they have left behind.

A more elaborate linking movement occurs in the scene of the prison vaudeville show, when the men learn that the French have recaptured a city. Renoir presents the shot as a celebration of spatial unity, with the camera moving among the men as they begin defiantly to sing the "Marseillaise" (**5.194–5.200**). This complex camera movement circulates freely among the prisoners, suggesting their patriotic courage and unified defiance of their captors.

In Elsa's cottage as well, camera movement links characters. After feeding a cow, Maréchal enters the house, and a pan with him reveals Elsa scrubbing the floor. The culmination of the linking movements comes near the film's end, when Renoir pans from the Germans on one side of the border (**5.201**) to the distant French escapees on the other (**5.202, 5.203**). Even on this scale, Renoir's camera refuses to honor national divisions.

The French film critic André Bazin remarked: "Jean Renoir found a way to reveal the hidden meaning of people and things without destroying the unity that is natural to them." Renoir's precisely choreographed camera movements go beyond simply enabling us to grasp the story. By providing information at a certain pace, by placing emphasis and by making comparisons, the mobile frame in *Grand Illusion* becomes as important as the mise-en-scène.

Michael Snow's experimental film *Wavelength* gives the mobile frame a different role. Instead of helping us construct a story, the camera style blocks that effort. Instead Snow asks us to concentrate our attention on how frame mobility creates patterns in its own right. Like Gehr's *Serene Velocity* (p. 174), the film becomes an experiment in cinematography.

The film begins with a long-shot framing of a loft apartment, facing one wall and window (**5.204**). The camera zooms in abruptly a short distance and then holds that framing. It zooms in a bit more and then holds that (**5.205**). And so it goes throughout the film's 45-minute length. By the end, a photograph of ocean waves on the distant wall fills the frame in close-up.

Wavelength is structured primarily around a single kind of frame mobility, the zoom-in. The film's progression concentrates on how changing lens lengths transform the space of the loft. The sudden zooms create frequent abrupt shifts of perspective. In excluding parts of the room, the zoom-in also magnifies and flattens what we see; every change of focal length gives us a new set of spatial relations. As the film goes on, the zoom pushes more and more space offscreen. The sound track, for the most part, reinforces the basic formal development by emitting a single humming tone that rises consistently in pitch as the zoom magnifies the space.

Within *Wavelength*'s overall form, though, there are two contrasting patterns. The first is a series of filtered tints that plays across the image as abstract fields of color. These tints often work against the depth represented in the shot of the loft. A second pattern suggests a sketchy narrative. At various intervals, characters enter the loft and talk, listen to the radio, make phone calls, and perform other ordinary actions. There's even a mysterious death: a body is glimpsed on the floor (**5.206**). But these events remain unexplained in cause–effect terms and inconclusive as to closure (although at the film's end we do hear a sound that resembles a police siren). Furthermore, none of these actions swerves the mobile framing from its predetermined course. The jerkily shifting and halting zoom continues, even when it frames out important narrative information. *Wavelength* pulls in bits and pieces of narrative action, but they remain secondary; they're less important than the progression of the zoom.

5.194 As the lead "female" singer whips off his wig and requests the "Marseillaise" from the musicians . . .

5.195 . . . the camera moves right and the singer turns toward the audience.

5.196 The camera tracks farther right as others onstage sing along.

5.197 A tilt down shows two worried German guards in the foreground.

5.198 A track back to the left reveals a row of French prisoners in the audience on their feet, singing.

5.199 The camera tracks forward past them to the musicians and singer again . . .

5.200 . . . then pans quickly left to reveal the assembled prisoners again, this time declaring their patriotism directly to the camera.

5.194–5.200 *Grand Illusion*: Camera movement as prisoner solidarity

As an experimental film, *Wavelength*'s use of frame mobility arouses, delays, and gratifies unusual expectations. The fragmentary plot briefly arouses curiosity (What are the people up to? What has led to the man's death, if he does die?) and surprise (the apparent murder). But in general, a story-centered suspense is replaced by a *stylistic* suspense. The zoom is the only sign of development, so we're curious about what it will eventually reveal. But the revelation is delayed by the colored tints, the bits of plot, and the spasmodic qualities of the zoom itself. When the zoom finally reveals its target, our stylistic anticipations find fulfillment. The film's title stands revealed as a multiple pun, referring not only to the steadily rising pitch of the sound track but also to the distance that the zoom had to cross in order to re-veal the photo—a "wave length." This revelation is secondary to the experience of

5.201 The Germans realize that Maréchal and Rosenthal have crossed over into Switzerland.

5.202 Renoir pans to the right across the invisible border . . .

5.203 . . . to reveal the two escapees, tiny dots in the huge landscape.

5.201–5.203 Border crossing in *Grand Illusion*

5.204

5.206

5.204–5.206 The spasmodic space of *Wavelength*. Early in the film, much of the apartment is visible (5.204). Near the end, the abrupt zoom-ins have made the distant wall visible (5.205). A fallen body can be glimpsed at the bottom of the frame, but the zoom-ins will soon eliminate it from the frame (5.206).

watching the halting zoom change the space of the room, and watching a stylistic pattern curb our narrative appetite.

Grand Illusion and *Wavelength* illustrate, in different ways, how frame mobility can shape our perception of a film's space and time. Renoir motivated his style of frame mobility by narrative form, while Snow made the technique the principal formal concern, motivating other aspects of the film.

Duration of the Image: The Long Take

Throughout this chapter, we've seen that the decisions that filmmakers make about cinematography affect both space and time. The range of photographic tonalities, the shot's perspective relations, and the position of the camera are largely matters of space. But other possibilities, like speed of motion and mobile framing, have consequences for time, too. The last area of choice and control we consider involves time in an especially intriguing way.

One popular YouTube genre is the so-called lipdub, in which a group of performers, usually students, lip-sync a pop song. Usually these videos feature lengthy camera movements within a single shot. There is a certain pride in choreographing all the "singers" with the moving camera in the two or three minutes that the song takes. Cutting would be easier, but there'd be less sense of virtuosity, less of a wow factor.

The lipdub phenomenon reflects one constant factor across the history of film art: the idea that there's something to be gained by letting a shot run long. But how long,

CONNECT TO THE BLOG
www.davidbordwell.net/blog

We connect the video genre of the lipdub to traditions of long-take filming in "2-4-6-8, whose lipdub do we appreciate?"

and why? Jean-Luc Godard asks the question explicitly. "The only great problem with cinema seems to me, more and more with each film, when and why to start a shot and when and why to end it." What guides a director in deciding how long to let a shot last?

Real Time Is . . . What?

When people talk about filming something in "real time," they often imply that the shot is recording actual duration. Usually it is. If we film a runner taking three seconds to clear a hurdle, our projected film will typically consume three seconds. But the filmmaker can choose to override real duration. As we've already seen, that can be manipulated through slow or fast motion. Less obviously, narrative films don't always let us equate screen duration with story duration, even within a single shot.

As Chapter 3 pointed out (p. 80), story duration usually differs from plot duration, and both are affected by film techniques that shape screen time. You can compress story duration within a single shot. Here's an example from Yasajiro Ozu's *The Only Son*. It is well past midnight, and we have just seen a family awake and talking. The shot shows a dim corner of the family's apartment, but eventually the light changes. By the end of the shot, morning has come (**5.207, 5.208**). This transitional shot consumes about a minute of screen time, but that plainly isn't the "real time" of the story action. The story action takes at least five hours. Thanks to cues of lighting, setting, and sound, the sustained shot has condensed a story duration of several hours into a minute or so on the screen.

Other films use tracking movements to compress longer passages of time in a continuous shot. This sort of condensation has become easier with digital postproduction (**5.209, 5.210**). The final shot of *Signs* moves away from an autumn view through a window and through a room, to reveal a winter landscape outside another window. Months of story time have passed during the tracking movement.

5.207

5.208

5.207–5.208 Compressing screen duration within a single shot. A shot in *The Only Son* moves from night (5.207) to morning (5.208).

Functions of the Long Take

Shot durations have varied somewhat over history. Early cinema (1895–1905) tended to rely on shots of fairly long duration, since each film often consisted of only one shot. With the emergence of continuity editing in the period 1905–1916, shots became shorter. From the late 1910s to the early 1920s, an American film would have an average shot length of about 5 seconds. After the coming of sound, the average stretched to about 10 seconds. But in the mid-1930s, directors in several countries began to experiment with very lengthy shots. The intricate camera movements in *Grand Illusion,* from 1935, are good examples. Renoir and his peers showed that unusually lengthy shots—**long takes,** as they're called—represented a powerful creative resource.

A *long take* is not the same as a *long shot,* which refers to the apparent distance between camera and object. As we saw in examining film production (pp. 22–23),

5.209

5.210

5.209–5.210 Camera movement through the seasons. In Roger Michell's *Notting Hill,* the protagonist's walk through the Portobello street market moves through autumn (5.209), then winter (5.210). Eventually the shot ends with spring.

5.211 The long take and narrative form. A long take in *My Hustler* captures the seductive exchange of two gay men as they groom themselves in a bathroom.

a *take* is one run of the camera that records a single shot. To prevent ambiguity, we call a protracted shot a long take rather than a long shot.

In the films of Jean Renoir, Kenji Mizoguchi, Orson Welles, Carl Dreyer, Miklós Jancsó, Hou Hsiao-hsien, and Bèla Tarr, a shot may go on for several minutes. One shot in Andy Warhol's *My Hustler* runs for about 30 minutes and constitutes much of the film's second half **(5.211).** It would be impossible to appreciate the artistry of these films without considering what the long take contributes to form and style.

Usually, we can regard the long take as an alternative to a series of shots. The director may choose between presenting a scene in long takes and presenting it in several shorter shots. When an entire scene is rendered in only one shot, the long take is sometimes called a *sequence shot,* a translation of the French term *plan-séquence.* In any film, most filmmakers mix edited scenes with scenes handled in long takes. This allows the filmmaker to bring out specific values in particular scenes, or to associate certain aspects of narrative or non-narrative form with the different stylistic options.

A vivid instance occurs in Steve McQueen's *Hunger,* based on a hunger strike in a prison in Northern Ireland. Most of the scenes, including violent confrontations between prisoners and guards, consist of several shots. At this point, Bobby Sands, the main character, seems only one prisoner among many. Roughly halfway through the film, the plot starts to focus on him and we begin to understand his motives and plans. The key scene begins with a shot lasting nearly 18 minutes, a balanced view of Sands and an old friend who visits him **(5.212).** There is no camera movement. The effect is to rivet the viewer on the character's dialogue during a turning point in the action.

Alternatively, the filmmaker may decide to build the entire film out of long takes. Hitchcock's *Rope* is famous for containing only 11 shots, most running between 4 and 10 minutes. Similarly, each scene in *Winterwind, Red Psalm,* and other films by Miklós Jancsó consists of a single shot. In such cases, the long take becomes a large-scale part of a film.

In a long-take movie, editing can have great force. After a seven- or eight-minute shot, an elliptical cut can prove quite disorienting. Gus van Sant's *Elephant* traces events around a high-school shooting rampage, and it presents most scenes in very long takes following students through the hallways. Moreover, *Elephant*'s plot doesn't present the events in chronological order. The narration flashes back to show other school days, the boys' lives at home, and their preparations for the killings. So when a cut interrupts a long take, the audience must reflect for a moment to determine how the new shot fits into story chronology. The effect of the editing is unusually harsh, because the cuts tend to break the smooth rhythm of the sustained traveling shots **(5.213–5.215).**

Could a feature-length movie consist of one long take? Many directors have dreamed of it, but the lengths of film reels have been a constraint. A 35mm camera reel typically runs for only 11 minutes, so Hitchcock sought to hide some of *Rope*'s obligatory cuts. Extended 16mm reels of the type Warhol used in *My Hustler* (5.211) can run up to 30 minutes. With digital video, however, it is possible to shoot for hours on a single tape or file, and the Russian director Aleksander Sokurov seized this opportunity in *Russian Ark.* The film consists of a single shot nearly 90 minutes long, as the camera follows over 2,000 actors in period costume through St. Petersburg's immense Winter Palace. *Russian Ark* takes us through several eras of Russian history, culminating in a stupendous ballroom dance and a crowd drifting off into a wintry night **(5.216–5.218).**

5.212 The long take to mark a turning point. Backlighting and a lengthy, static shot in *Hunger* place us at a distance from Bobby Sands and his visitor. The director's stylistic choice allows us to concentrate on their words, which provide important exposition about the planned hunger strike.

The Long Take and the Mobile Frame

The static long take in *Hunger* is unusual; most long takes, like those in *Elephant* and *Russian Ark* (and in DIY lipdubs), rely on camera movement. Panning, tracking, craning, or

5.213

5.214

5.215

5.213–5.215 Discontinuous editing interrupts a long take. In a shot lasting two minutes, the camera follows Michelle into the library, where she starts reshelving books (5.123). Many of the long takes in *Elephant* frame the walking characters from behind. This conceals their facial expressions from us and emphasizes the school environment. Michelle turns as we hear a rifle being cocked (5.214). We expect a reverse shot to reveal the shooter. Instead, we get a flashback to earlier that day when the two boys showered together before going to school on their deadly mission (5.215).

5.216

5.217

5.218

5.216–5.218 *Russian Ark* **and the long take.** In *Russian Ark*, one episode takes place in the palace theater, with Catherine the Great pronouncing the rehearsal satisfactory (5.216). An hour or so later, still within the same shot, hundreds of aristocrats and officers descend a staircase toward the impending devastation of the Russian Revolution (5.217). Crew members moved through the Hermitage Museum, filming with a digital camera mounted on a Steadicam (218). Sokurov rehearsed *Russian Ark* for several months and completed the take used in the film on the fourth try.

zooming can be used to present continually changing vantage points that are comparable in some ways to the shifts of view supplied by editing.

Very often, frame mobility breaks the long-take shot into smaller units. In Mizoguchi's *Sisters of Gion*, one long take shows a young woman, Omocha, luring a businessman into becoming her patron **(5.219–5.224).** Though there is no cutting, the camera and figure movements demarcate important stages of the scene's action.

5.219 The long take begins with Omocha and the businessman seated. The camera follows her as . . .

5.220 . . . she moves to the opposite end of the room . . .

5.221 . . . and sits at a small table facing him.

5.222 A second phase of the shot begins as she begins to appeal to his sympathy and he moves to the table . . .

5.223 . . . and sits down to console her.

5.224 Finally, the camera moves into a tighter shot as she sits beside him and he succumbs to her advances.

5.219–5.224 *Sisters of Gion*: The long take marks stages of the action

CONNECT TO THE BLOG
www.davidbordwell.net/blog

Both *There Will Be Blood* and *The Most Beautiful* contain subtle staging in two unmoving long takes. We compare them in "Hands (and faces) across the table."

As in this example, long takes tend to be framed in medium or long shots rather than close-ups. The camera takes us through a fairly dense visual field, and the spectator has more opportunity to scan the shot for particular points of interest. This is recognized by Steven Spielberg, a director who has occasionally exploited lengthy takes:

> I'd love to see directors start trusting the audience to be the film editor with their eyes, the way you are sometimes with a stage play, where the audience selects who they would choose to look at while a scene is being played. . . . There's so much cutting and so many close-ups being shot today I think directly as an influence from television.

As we saw in the previous chapter, the arrangement of the mise-en-scene can guide our scanning of the frame. Accordingly, a director may choose to put editing aside and let a gradually unfolding long take steer us from one information-packed frame to another.

The example from *Sisters of Gion* illustrates another important feature of the long take. Mizoguchi's shot reveals a complete internal logic—a beginning, middle, and end. As a part of a film, the long take can have its own formal pattern, its own development, its own trajectory and shape. Suspense may develop; we start to ask how the shot will continue and when it will end.

The classic example of how the long take can constitute a formal pattern in its own right is the opening sequence of Welles's *Touch of Evil* **(5.225–5.236).** This opening shot makes plain crucial features of the long take. It offers an alternative to building the sequence out of many shots, and it stresses the cut that finally comes (occurring at the sound of the explosion of the car).

5.225 The opening shot begins with a close-up of a hand setting the timer of a bomb.

5.226 The camera tracks immediately right to follow first the shadow . . .

5.227 . . . and then the figure of an unknown assassin planting the bomb in a car.

5.228 The camera then cranes up to a high angle as the assassin flees and the victims arrive and set out in the car.

5.229 As the camera rounds the corner, it rejoins the car. A reverse tracking shot keeps it in frame.

5.230 The car passes Vargas and his wife, Susan, and the camera starts to follow them, losing the car and tracking diagonally backward with the couple through the crowd.

5.231 The camera tracks backward until both the occupants of the car and Susan and Vargas meet again.

5.232 The camera remains in one place to let the brief scene with the border guard play out.

5.233 After tracking left with the car, the camera catches up with Susan and Vargas and tracks forward toward them . . .

5.234 . . . bringing them into medium shot as they begin to kiss.

5.235 Their embrace is interrupted by the offscreen sound of an explosion, and they turn to look leftward.

5.236 The next shot zooms in to show the car in flames.

5.225–5.236 *Touch of Evil:* The virtuoso moving long take

Most important, the shot has its own internal pattern of development. We expect that the bomb shown at the beginning will explode at some point, and we wait for that explosion through the duration of the long take. The shot establishes the geography of the scene (the border between Mexico and the United States). The camera movement, alternately picking up the car and the walking couple, weaves together two lines of narrative cause and effect that intersect at the border station. Vargas and Susan are thus drawn into the action involving the bombing. Our expectation is fulfilled when the end of the shot coincides with the explosion (offscreen) of the bomb. The shot has guided our response by taking us through a suspenseful development.

The long take can present, in a single chunk of time, a complex pattern of events moving toward a goal, and this ability shows that shot duration can be as important to the image as photographic qualities and framing are.

SUMMARY

The film shot is a very complex unit. By controlling mise-en-scene, the filmmaker fills the image with material, arranging setting, lighting, costume, and staging within the formal context of the total film. Similarly, the shot is shaped by the cinematographic options we've been examining.

Those options bear on photographic qualities: tonality, speed of motion, and the varieties of perspective created by lens lengths, depth of field, and special effects. The filmmaker can also reckon in the aspect ratio and decide how the image is framed. Other creative choices involve varying camera placement—the angle, level, height, and distance at which we see the subject. The filmmaker can decide to move the frame in a host of ways, and can choose to exploit the long take with or without camera movement.

The array of choices is dazzling, and as with mise-en-scene, decision-making is at the center of film artistry. Forced to choose, the filmmaker pursues options that will give the viewer a specific experience—and perhaps also challenge the filmmaker's craft skills. In turn, the choices that are made can coalesce into a pattern, the style of that particular film.

You can sensitize yourself to cinematographic options in much the same way that you worked on mise-en-scene. Trace the progress of a single technique, such as camera distance, through an entire scene. Notice when a shot begins and ends, observing how a long take may function to shape the film's form. Watch for camera movements, especially those that follow the action (since those are usually the hardest to notice). Once you notice cinematographic qualities, you can move to an understanding of their various functions within the sequence and the film as a whole.

Film art offers still other possibilities for choice and control. Chapter 4 and this chapter focused on the shot. The filmmaker may also juxtapose one shot with another through editing, and that's the subject of Chapter 6.

RECOMMENDED DVD AND BLU-RAY SUPPLEMENTS

Two feature-length documentaries have been devoted to cinematography. *Visions of Light: The Art of Cinematography* includes many clips and interviews. *Cameraman: The Life & Work of Jack Cardiff,* contains witty and informative interviews with this great cinematographer and his collaborators on *The African Queen, The Red Shoes, Pandora and the Flying Dutchman,* and *Death on the Nile.* Cardiff talks about his use of Technicolor in *Black Narcissus* in "Painting with Light,"

Some DVD versions of films incorporate information about cinematography. The Criterion release of *Days of Heaven* features comments by John Bailey and Haskell Wexler. Criterion's DVD of *The Ice Storm* contains Frederick Elmes's "visual essay" explaining the decisions behind shooting several scenes. "Conversation with Barry Sonnenfeld" on the *Miller's Crossing* disc considers the effects of lens lengths on the film's style. Criterion's disc of *The Sweet Smell of Success* includes a 1973 documentary, *James Wong Howe: Cinematographer,* which surveys Howe's career from the 1920s. In one segment he demonstrates lighting setups for daytime, sunset, and nighttime scenes. Haskell Wexler's commentary for *Who's Afraid of Virginia Woolf?* contains considerable technical information.

On widescreen formats, *Oklahoma!*'s disc contains a very good comparison featurette, "CinemaScope vs. Todd-AO," as well as a short originally shown in theaters to introduce the new widescreen process, "The Miracle of Todd-AO." Raoul Coutard discusses anamorphic widescreen and color processes in an interview on the Criterion *Contempt* DVD (which also includes a "Widescreen vs. Full-Frame Demonstration").

Laboratory work is demonstrated in "Day 66: Journey of a Roll of Film," in *King Kong: Peter Jackson's Production Diaries,* which shows a Telecine machine making a digital intermediate. The process of selective digital grading, which we discuss on page 169, is explained in "Digital Grading," on the *Lord of the Rings: The Fellowship of the Ring* supplements.

Perspective and depth cues receive fascinating coverage in "Little People, Big Effects," a supplement to the *Darby O'Gill and the Little People* DVD. It includes footage of matte paintings for this film and for *Treasure Island.* There is a section on forced perspective, a technique employed 40 years later in *The Lord of the Rings,* and emphasis on achieving deep focus.

The third disc of the *Avatar* DVD and Blu-ray sets includes "The 3D Fusion Camera," a short chapter explaining how 3D works.

The "Outward Bound" chapter on the *Alien* disc demonstrates how models were shot to look realistic in the predigital era. *Speed*'s "Visual Effects" track covers motion control, the digital matte work and other tricks showing the bus jumping the freeway gap, and a huge miniature used for the final train crash. The "Special Effects Vignettes" for *Cast Away* trace the various layers built into CGI shots. "Visual FX: MTA Train" gives a brief but informative look at green-screen work in *Collateral*'s train scene. It shows how special effects vary colors and lights seen through the windows as the mood of the scene shifts. "Designing the Enemy: Tripods and Aliens" (*War of the Worlds*) show how software can help design digital figures. Each of the *Lord of the Rings* DVD sets contains extensive special-effects descriptions, and *The Return of the King* supplements include a segment on a very complex CGI scene: "Visual Effects Demonstration: 'The Mûmakil Battle.'"

"No Fate but What We Make," a *Terminator 2: Judgment Day* supplement, offers an excellent account of digital special effects in *The Abyss* and *Terminator 2,* and includes director James Cameron discussing perspective. "The Making of *Jurassic Park*" covers some of the same material but discusses how CGI moved beyond the rendering of shiny surfaces and began creating the rough textures of dinosaur skin.

More recent developments in computer effects are dealt with in "Meet Davy Jones," a supplement on the *Pirates of the Caribbean: Dead Man's Chest* DVD; it demonstrates important advances in motion-capture technology. Good making-ofs for other effects-heavy films are "Wired: The Visual Effects of *Iron Man*" and "Daemons" and "Armoured Bears" in the *Golden Compass* supplements. The use of CGI to create less noticeable effects, such as realistic settings and erasure of unwanted elements, is demonstrated in "The Visual Effects of *Zodiac*"; the "New York, New Zealand" section of *King Kong: Peter Jackson's Production Diaries*; and "In Camera: *The Dark Knight*."

The Dark Knight's supplement "Shooting Outside the Box," discusses the challenges of shooting sequences in the Imax format.

Now that multiple-camera shooting is common for many films, DVD supplements sometimes include sequences juxtaposing the different camera viewpoints. These tend not to provide much information about the process, but the "Interactive Multi-Angle Battle Scene Studies" for *Master and Commander* provide readouts of lens length and shooting speed (revealing how common it has become for shots of violent action to be done with varying degrees of slow motion). Similarly, *Speed*'s "Action Sequences: Multi-angle Stunts," provides a frames-per-second readout in its demonstration. *Dancer in the Dark*'s extreme use of multiple-camera shooting for the music numbers is explained in "100 Cameras: Capturing Lars von Trier's Vision."

The ultimate supplement dealing with long takes is "In One Breath," which documents the filming of the single elaborate shot that makes up *Russian Ark.*

6

The Relation of Shot to Shot: Editing

Since the 1920s, when film theorists began to realize what **editing** can achieve, it has been the most widely discussed film technique. This hasn't been all to the good. Some writers have mistakenly found in editing the key to good cinema (or even *all* cinema). Yet many film scenes don't use editing extensively. As we saw in the last chapter, some films consist of very few shots. Some major films from the 1910s, such as Victor Sjöström's *Ingeborg Holm,* consist largely of single-take scenes; these shape our experience by subtle manipulations of mise-en-scene. Other films, such as *Touch of Evil,* use long takes with camera movements to guide our moment-by-moment understanding of the action. Films relying on long takes aren't necessarily less "cinematic" than films that break down scenes into many shots.

Still, we can see why editing has exercised such an enormous fascination. It's very powerful. The ride of the Klan in *The Birth of a Nation,* the Odessa Steps sequence in *Potemkin,* the hunt sequence in *The Rules of the Game,* the shower murder in *Psycho,* Clarice Starling's discovery of the killer's lair in *The Silence of the Lambs,* the reconstruction of the Dallas assassination in *JFK,* the quickfire shifts among dream layers in *Inception*—these and many other screen moments derive their impact from editing. No wonder that cutting plays a huge role in mass-market filmmaking. Today's Hollywood movie typically contains between 1,000 and 2,000 shots; an action movie can have 3,000 or more.

Editing decisions can also build the film's overall form. The nested segments we found in *Citizen Kane* (pp. 101–102) are defined by editing transitions. In long-take films, shot changes usually mark out scenes or sequences. Warhol's *My Hustler* contains only three cuts, but they give the film four large-scale parts. By tying shot to shot and segment to segment, editing can shape our responses to individual scenes and the entire movie.

This powerful, pervasive technique confronts the filmmaker with a huge number of choices. Cut here or there? Put this shot before or after that one? Does this string of shots make sense? The options are multiplied in digital filmmaking, with its power to redo shots in postproduction. James Cameron comments:

> You can almost get buried by possibilities. In a normal editing situation, depending on the material, you might end up just selecting the performance that has the least number of deficits to it. But with what we've created, anything can be in focus, anything can be out of focus, or lit differently at any time. You can do virtual camera work on a performance that was shot six months earlier. . . . There's always the risk of getting bogged down. You find yourself asking, "Why?" a whole lot more than you normally

might. "Why am I on this angle? Why am I on a close-up on this actor when a wide shot might work better?" In a way, it puts you back to basics as an editor.

Even without the CGI resources of *Avatar,* a filmmaker must think constantly about editing.

What Is Editing?

You already know something about editing. As a viewer, you notice when the cutting is very fast, during a chase scene or a fight. If you've made some videos, you've probably done some editing, assembling various shots in your preferred order and trimming them until they seem the right length. You're aware that editing lets the filmmaker decide what shots to include and how they will be arranged.

These sorts of decisions are multiplied vastly in professional filmmaking. Just the matter of selection can be daunting. An editor on the typical feature-length film is faced with a mountain of footage. *The Social Network* in finished form ran two hours, but 286 hours of material were shot—not an unusual amount for such a project.

To ease the task, most fiction filmmakers plan for the editing phase during the preparation and shooting phases. Scripts, storyboards, and previsualizations allow shots to be imagined in advance. Documentary filmmakers often shoot extra footage of settings, documents, or significant objects. These can be useful in cutting together material caught on the fly. For *Paradise Lost: The Child Murders at Robin Hood Hills,* the directors filmed aerial shots of the neighborhood that was central to the crime. These serve as transitions linking sections of the film that follows.

Once the material is selected, the editor joins the shots, the end of one to the beginning of another. The most common join is the **cut.** A cut provides an instantaneous change from one shot to another. Other methods of joining shots produce more gradual changes. A **fade-out** gradually darkens the end of a shot to black, and a **fade-in** lightens a shot from black. A **dissolve** briefly superimposes the end of shot A and the beginning of shot B **(6.1–6.3).** In a **wipe,** shot B replaces shot A by means of a boundary line moving across the screen **(6.4).** Here both images are briefly on the screen at the same time, but they do not blend, as in a dissolve. Before the rise of digital editing in the 1990s, a cut was usually made by splicing two shots together with film cement or tape. Fades, dissolves, and wipes were executed with optical printers or in the laboratory. In computer editing, all types of edits are created with the software.

Although everyone is somewhat aware of editing, we can understand the filmmaker's creative choices more fully if we look at the technique systematically. In this chapter, we show how editing allows the filmmaker to manipulate time, space, and pictorial qualities in ways that shape the viewer's experience of the film.

> " Editing is the basic creative force, by power of which the soulless photographs (the separate shots) are engineered into living, cinematographic form."
> —V. I. Pudovkin, director

> " You can definitely help performances in the cutting room, by intercutting reaction, maybe re-recording lines, adding lines over reaction shots. And you can help a film's structure by moving sequences about and dropping scenes that hold up pacing. And sometimes you can use bits and pieces from different takes, which also helps a lot. What you can do in the editing room to help a film is amazing!"
> —Jodie Foster, actor and director

6.1

6.2

6.3

6.4

6.1–6.4 **Linking shots with optical devices.** The first shot of *The Maltese Falcon* (6.1) ends with a dissolve (6.2) to the second shot (6.3). In *Seven Samurai,* a wipe joins the last shot of one scene with the first of the next.

6.5 Shot 1

6.6 Shot 2

6.7 Shot 3

6.8 Shot 4

6.5–6.8 Editing for timing and impact: Four shots from *The Birds*.

Why Cut? Four Shots from The Birds

Here's a portion of the attack on the Bodega Bay waterfront in Alfred Hitchcock's *The Birds* (**6.5–6.8**).

1. *Medium shot, straight-on angle.* Melanie, Mitch, and the fisherman are standing by the restaurant window talking. Melanie is on the extreme right, the bartender is in the background (6.5).

2. *Medium close-up.* Melanie is standing by the fisherman's shoulder. She looks to right (out offscreen window) and up, as if following with her eyes. Pan right with her as she turns to window and looks out (6.6).

3. *Extreme long shot.* Melanie's point of view: The gas station across street, with the phone booth in the left foreground. Birds dive-bomb the attendant, swooping right to left (6.7).

4. *Medium close-up.* Melanie, in profile. The fisherman moves right into the frame, blocking out the bartender. Mitch moves right into the extreme foreground. All three in profile look out the window (6.8).

Each of these four shots presents a different bit of time and space and a different array of graphic qualities. The first shot shows the characters talking (6.5). A cut shifts us to a medium close-up shot of Melanie. Here space has changed (Melanie is isolated and larger in the frame), time is continuous, and the graphic configurations have changed (the arrangements of the shapes and colors vary). Another cut takes us instantly to what she sees (6.6). The gas station shot (6.7) presents a different space, another bit of time, and a different graphic configuration. Another cut returns us to Melanie (6.8), and again we are shifted instantly to another space, the next slice of time, and a different graphic configuration. The four shots are joined by three cuts.

Hitchcock could have presented the *Birds* scene without editing. Using deep-space staging, he might have created a deep-focus composition like those in Figures 5.48 and 5.49. He could have placed Mitch and the fisherman in the foreground, Melanie and the window in the middle ground, and the gull attack in the distance, visible through the window. The scene could now be played in one shot, for we would have no abrupt change of time or space or graphics.

But editing gives Hitchcock control of timing and impact. At a certain moment he can fasten our attention on Melanie alone, not the men: shot 2 demands that we notice her response. Similarly, shot 3 obliges us to watch the bird attack as she sees it, with nothing else in the frame to distract us. Editing allows Hitchcock to march us in step with the action, locking our reaction to the pace of the images.

We've seen that through mise-en-scene and cinematography the filmmaker can create a shot containing many points of interest. Tim Smith's experiment in eye-tracking (4.120–4.121) shows that a director can subtly guide our attention to a single area of a shot. Why didn't Hitchcock take that option? Because his cuts do more than simply isolate parts of the action: they *emphasize* them. The cut-in to Melanie enlarges her suddenly, creating a little punch. The same thing happens with the bird attack. If we watched it through a window in the distance, it would be a tiny part of the image. As an enlarged view of the gas station, it gains in significance.

In addition, if Hitchcock had presented all the action in a single shot, he wouldn't have engaged our minds in quite the same way. When he cuts from shot 2, of Melanie looking, to shot 3, the gull's swooping, we have to think a little. We have to infer that shot 3 is what Melanie sees. We've known this convention for most of our lives, but it still calls on us to use our imagination to connect the shots.

So a deep-space, deep-focus shot would have a rather different effect. But there was another option, you might say. What if Hitchcock used a continuous shot but moved his camera? Imagine that the camera frames the people talking, tracks in and rightward to Melanie as she turns, pans right to the window to show the dive-bombing gull, and pans back left to catch the group's expressions. This would constitute one complicated shot, somewhat like the *Grand Illusion* example we considered in the previous chapter (5.194–5.200). The varied framing would provide emphasis, picking out some parts of the scene while leaving out others. But camera movements, no matter how fast, would not present the *sudden* breaks that the cuts produce. Again, it's a matter of timing and heightened impact. In the *Grand Illusion* scene, the panning and tracking movements gradually reveal the reaction of the German officers to the prisoners' show. Cutting enables Hitchcock to make the bird attack more abrupt and startling—a quality that suits the story action at that point.

In all, editing allows Hitchcock to isolate and magnify each bit of action and to control the pace of our uptake. We must surrender to the swift, sharp flow of shots, but we also devote a bit of mental energy to figuring out how they fit together. When filmmakers want to pattern our experience so precisely, editing becomes an attractive stylistic option.

Dimensions of Film Editing

Editing offers the filmmaker four basic areas of choice and control:

1. Graphic relations between shot A and shot B
2. Rhythmic relations between shot A and shot B
3. Spatial relations between shot A and shot B
4. Temporal relations between shot A and shot B

Let's trace the range of choice and control in each area.

Graphic Relations between Shot A and Shot B

The four shots from *The Birds* show the time and space of the scene, but we can see them purely as graphic configurations as well. They display patterns of light and dark, line and shape, volumes and depths, movement and stasis. And we can compare these qualities across shots.

For instance, Hitchcock didn't drastically alter the overall brightness from shot to shot, because the scene takes place during the day. If the scene had been set at night, he could have cut from the fairly bright second shot in the bar (6.6, Melanie turning to the window) to a shot of the gas station swathed in darkness. That would have created a stronger contrast. Moreover, Hitchcock usually keeps the most important part of the composition roughly in the center of the frame. (Compare Melanie's position in the frame with that of the gas station in 6.7.) He could, however, have cut from a shot in which Melanie was in, say, upper frame left to a shot locating the gas station in the lower right of the frame. Again, there would have been a sense of less graphic continuity.

We've already seen that pictorial contrasts can be powerful in guiding our attention (p. 148), and Hitchcock's editing does work a bit on them. Melanie's hair and outfit make her a predominantly yellow and green figure, but the shot of the gas station is dominated by drab grays set off by touches of red in the gas pumps. Alternatively, Hitchcock could have chosen to cut from Melanie to another figure composed of similar colors. Furthermore, the action in Melanie's shot—her turning to the window—doesn't blend into the movements of either the attendant or the gull in the next shot. But Hitchcock could have echoed Melanie's movement by some motion in the shot that followed.

The implication is simple but powerful. If you put any two shots together, you'll create some interaction between the *purely pictorial* qualities of those two shots.

CONNECT TO THE BLOG
www.davidbordwell.net/blog

We discuss graphic matching in more detail in "Graphic content ahead."

6.9–6.13 Graphic matching, static and dynamic. A shot from *True Stories* showing the Texas horizon midway up the frame (6.9) is graphically matched with a shot showing the waterline of ancient seas in the same position (6.10). *Seven Samurai:* The first three (6.11–6.13) of six shots of running samurai. Kurosawa matches the shots through composition, lighting, setting, figure movement, and the panning camera movement.

6.9

6.10

6.11

6.12

6.13

The four aspects of mise-en-scene (lighting, setting, costume, and the movement of the figures) and most cinematographic qualities (photography, framing, and camera mobility) all furnish graphic elements. Every shot provides possibilities for purely graphic editing, and every cut creates some sort of graphic relationship between two shots.

Graphic Editing: Matches and Clashes   Graphics may be edited to achieve smooth continuity or abrupt contrast. The filmmaker may link shots by close graphic similarities, thus making a **graphic match.** Shapes, colors, overall composition, or movement in shot A may be picked up in the composition of shot B. A minimal instance is the cut that joins the first two shots of David Byrne's *True Stories* **(6.9, 6.10).** More dynamic graphic matches appear in Akira Kurosawa's *Seven Samurai.* After the samurai have first arrived at the village, an alarm sounds and they race to discover its source. Kurosawa cuts together six shots of different running samurai, all very brief and graphically matched **(6.11–6.13).** Filmmakers sometimes call attention to graphic matches at transitional moments **(6.14–6.16).**

6.14

6.15

6.16

6.14–6.16 Graphic matching in a transition. In *Aliens,* the curved outline of Ripley's sleeping face (6.15) is graphically matched by means of a dissolve (6.16) to the outline of the earth (6.16).

6.17

6.18

6.17–6.18 **Graphic matching: A matter of degree.** The woman and her friend, the cowboy truck driver (6.17), confront the enraged cook and his assistants. (6.18) Although the shots aren't precisely matched graphically, the key characters are placed in the same area of each shot.

Such precise graphic matching is rare. A looser graphic continuity from shot A to shot B is typical of most narrative cinema, as in the *Birds* shots. The director will usually strive to keep the main point of interest roughly constant across the cut, to maintain the overall lighting level, and to avoid strong color clashes from shot to shot. In Juzo Itami's *Tampopo,* an aspiring cook is trying to learn the secret of good noodles, and she questions a successful cook. Alternating shots keep each main character's face in the right center of each frame **(6.17, 6.18).**

Editing need not be graphically continuous. Filmmakers working in a wide-screen format often create mild graphic discontinuities when they frame characters facing one another. A scene from *Pulp Fiction* places the two hit men opposite each other in a restaurant booth, each framed distinctly off-center **(6.19, 6.20).** Compared to the *Tampopo* example, the cut here creates greater graphic discontinuity. Yet the overall effect is one of symmetry and balance, with each man filling the space left empty in the other shot.

Graphically discontinuous editing can be more noticeable. Orson Welles frequently sought a clash from shot to shot. In *Citizen Kane* a direct cut from the dark long shot of Kane's bedroom gives way to the bright opening title of "News on the March." Welles does something similar during a transition in *Touch of Evil* **(6.21, 6.22).** Alain Resnais's *Night and Fog* created a convention by utilizing an extreme graphic conflict between past and present. Resnais cut together color footage of an abandoned concentration camp today with black-and-white newsreel shots of the camps in the period 1942–1945.

6.19

6.20

6.19–6.20 **Graphic discontinuity yields editing symmetry.** *Pulp Fiction:* Vincent (6.20) and Jules (6.21) are at opposite ends of the screen in each shot, but the cutting creates an overall balance. It also offers our attention a predictable, left-right trajectory to follow.

6.21

6.22

6.21–6.22 **Graphic discontinuity in a transition.** In *Touch of Evil*, Welles dissolves from a shot of Menzies looking out a window on frame right (6.21) to a shot of Susan Vargas looking out a different window on frame left (6.22). The clash is emphasized by the contrasting screen positions of the window reflections.

Graphic Contrast in *The Birds*

Later in the *Birds* sequence, Hitchcock exploits a stronger conflict of graphic qualities. Gasoline spurting from the pump has flowed across the street to a parking lot. Melanie, along with several other people at the restaurant window, has seen a man accidentally set the gasoline alight. His car ignites, and an explosion of flame engulfs him. Melanie must watch helplessly as the flame races along the trail of gas toward the station. Hitchcock cuts the shots as shown in **6.23–6.33**:

Shot 30	(Long shot)	High angle. Melanie's POV. Flaming car, spreading flames (6.23).	73 frames
Shot 31	(Medium close-up)	Straight-on angle. Melanie, immobile, looking off left, mouth open (6.24).	20 frames
Shot 32	(Medium shot)	High angle. Melanie's POV. Pan with flames moving from lower right to upper left of trail of gasoline (6.25).	18 frames
Shot 33	(Medium close-up)	As 31. Melanie, immobile, staring down left center (6.26).	16 frames
Shot 34	(Medium shot)	High angle. Melanie's POV. Pan with flames moving from lower right to upper left (6.27).	14 frames
Shot 35	(Medium close-up)	As 31. Melanie, immobile, looking off right, staring aghast (6.28).	12 frames
Shot 36	(Long shot)	Melanie's POV. Gas station. Flames rush in from right. Mitch, sheriff, and attendant run out left (6.29).	10 frames
Shot 37	(Medium close-up)	As 31. Melanie, immobile, stares off extreme right (6.30).	8 frames
Shot 38	(Long shot)	As 36. Melanie's POV. Cars at station explode (6.31).	34 frames
Shot 39	(Medium close-up)	As 31. Melanie covers her face with her hands (6.32).	33 frames
Shot 40	(Extreme long shot)	Extreme high angle on city, flaming trail in center. Gulls fly into shot (6.33).	

6.23 Shot 30

6.24 Shot 31

6.25 Shot 32

6.26 Shot 33

6.27 Shot 34

6.28 Shot 35.

6.29 Shot 36

6.30 Shot 37

6.31 Shot 38

6.32 Shot 39

6.33 Shot 40

6.23–6.33 Editing for graphic contrast in *The Birds*. Hitchcock employs two types of contrast. First, his cutting contrasts the movement of Melanie's head with the trail of flames. A second contrast is between movement and stillness. The shots of the flames show movement of both the subject and the camera, while the shots of Melanie's head are completely static.

In graphic terms, Hitchcock has exploited two types of contrast. First, although each shot's composition centers the action (Melanie's head, the flaming trail), the movements thrust in different directions. In shot 31, Melanie looks to the lower left, but in shot 32, the fire moves to the upper left. In shot 33, Melanie is looking down center, but in shot 34, the flames still move to the upper left, and so on.

More important—and what makes the sequence impossible to recapture on the printed page—is the bold contrast between motion and stasis. The shots of the flames present plenty of movement: the flames rush along the trail of gasoline, and the camera pans to follow them. But the shots of Melanie could be still photographs, since each one is absolutely static. She doesn't turn her head in any shot, and the camera doesn't track in or away from her. Instead we get snapshots of her changing attention. By making movement conflict with counter-movement and with stillness, Hitchcock has powerfully exploited the graphic possibilities of editing.

Rhythmic Relations between Shot A and Shot B

Every shot is of a certain length, with its series of frames consuming a certain amount of time onscreen. Modern film, as we've seen (p. 10) typically runs 24 or 25 frames per second. Modern video formats run at approximately 24, 25, 30 or 48 frames per second. A shot can be as short as a single frame, or it may be thousands of frames long, running for many minutes when projected. The filmmaker can adjust the lengths of any shot in relation to the shots around it. That choice taps into the *rhythmic* potential of editing. Other film techniques, notably the soundtrack, contribute to the overall rhythm of the film, as you'd expect. But the patterning of shot lengths contributes considerably to what we intuitively recognize as a film's rhythm.

Flash Frames   Sometimes the filmmaker will use shot duration to stress a single moment. In one sequence of *The Road Warrior,* a ferocious gang member head-butts his victim. At the instant of contact, director George Miller cuts in a few frames of pure white. The result is a sudden flash that suggests violent impact. Such *flash-frames* have become conventions of action films. In any genre, flash-frames may mark transitions between segments or signal flashbacks or subjective sequences.

Flash-frames usually provide one-off accents. More commonly, the rhythmic possibilities of editing emerge when several shots in a series form a pattern. By making all the shots more or less the same length, the filmmaker can create a steady beat. Gradually lengthening shots can slow the rhythm, while shorter and shorter shots can accelerate it.

Rhythmic Cutting in *The Birds*   Hitchcock's editing builds a distinct rhythm during the gas-station attack we examined earlier. Since *The Birds* was shot on film, our chart provides frame counts based on a 35mm print.

The first shot, the medium shot of Melanie and the men talking (6.5), consumes almost a thousand frames, or about 41 seconds. But the second shot (6.6), which shows Melanie looking out the window, is much shorter—309 frames (about 13 seconds). Even shorter is shot 3 (6.7), which lasts only 55 frames (about 2⅓ seconds). The fourth shot (6.8), showing Melanie joined by Mitch and the fisherman, lasts only 35 frames (about 1½ seconds). Clearly, Hitchcock is accelerating the pace at the beginning of what will be a tense sequence. This arc of excitement could probably not have been achieved if Hitchcock had handled the action in a single shot.

In what follows, Hitchcock makes the shots fairly short but subordinates the length of the shot to the rhythm of the dialogue and the movement in the images. As a result, shots 5–29 (not shown here) have no fixed pattern of lengths. But once the essential components of the scene have been established, Hitchcock returns to strongly accelerating cutting.

In presenting Melanie's horrified realization of the flames racing from the parking lot to the gas station, shots 30–40 (6.23–6.33) climax the rhythmic intensification of the sequence. As the description on page 228 shows, after the shot of the spreading flames (shot 30, 6.23), each shot decreases in length by 2 frames, from 20 frames (5/6 of a second) to 8 frames—just one-third of a second! Two shots, 38 and 39, then punctuate the sequence with almost identical durations (a little less than 1½ seconds apiece). Shot 40 (6.33), an extreme long shot that lasts over 600 frames, functions as both a pause and a suspenseful preparation for the new attack. The scene's variations in rhythm alternate between rendering the savagery of the attack and generating suspense as we await the next onslaught.

We've had the luxury of counting frames on the actual strip of film. In the movie theater, we can't do this, but as viewers we do feel the shifting tempo that's

CONNECT TO THE BLOG
www.davidbordwell.net/blog

On the problems of frame-counting video versions, see "My name is David, and I'm a frame-counter."

> **"**I noticed a softening in American cinema over the last twenty years, and I think it's a direct influence of TV. I would even say that if you want to make movies today, you'd be better off studying television than film because that's the market. Television has diminished the audience's attention span. It's hard to make a slow, quiet film today. Not that I would want to make a slow, quiet film anyway!"
>
> —Oliver Stone, director

created by the changing shot durations. In general, by controlling editing rhythm, the filmmaker controls the amount of time we have to grasp and reflect on what we see. A series of rapid shots leaves us little time to think about what we're watching. In the *Birds* sequence, Hitchcock's editing impels the viewer's perception to move at a faster and faster pace. Very quickly we have to grasp the progress of the fire and Melanie's changes in position, and the acceleration builds rising excitement in the scene. Whipping up the spectator through rhythmic editing remains central to action scenes in movies today.

Spatial Relations between Shot A and Shot B

Editing can control graphics and rhythm, but it can also construct film space. When early filmmakers discovered this, they seemed giddy with their godlike power. "I am builder," wrote Soviet documentarist Dziga Vertov. "I have placed you . . . in an extraordinary room which did not exist until just now when I also created it. In this room there are twelve walls, shot by me in various parts of the world. In bringing together shots of walls and details, I've managed to arrange them in an order that is pleasing."

We can understand why Vertov was elated. Editing permits the filmmaker to juxtapose *any* two points in space and suggest some kind of relationship between them.

Establishing and Manipulating Space   If you're the director, you might start with a shot that establishes a spatial whole and follow this with a shot of a part of this space. This is what Hitchcock does in shot 1 and shot 2 of the *Birds* sequence (6.5, 6.6): a medium shot of the group of people followed by a medium close-up shot of only one, Melanie. Such analytical breakdown is a very common editing pattern.

Alternatively, you could construct a whole space out of component parts. Hitchcock does this in the *Birds* sequence, too. Note that in 6.5–6.8 and in shots 30–39 (6.23–6.32), we don't see an establishing shot including Melanie *and* the gas station. In production, the restaurant window need not have been across from the station at all; they could have been filmed in different towns or even countries. Yet the cutting, along with hints in the staging and on the soundtrack, compels us to believe that Melanie is across the street from the gas station.

Spatial manipulation of this sort is fairly common. In documentaries compiled from newsreel footage, for example, one shot might show a cannon firing, and another shot might show a shell hitting its target. We infer that the cannon fired the shell, though the shots may show entirely different battles. If a shot of a speaker is followed by a shot of a cheering crowd, we assume that they're in the same locale.

Today's editors can also alter space through *intra-frame editing.* Digital filmmaking makes it easy to combine parts of different shots into a single shot. In 35mm film-based production, this effect was accomplished during filming or during laboratory work, as with traveling mattes (p. 176). Now elements from different shots may be blended in editing. A character can be extracted from one shot and seamlessly pasted into another one. Vertov, who was fond of layering his images, would have found this software irresistible for creating tricks and lyrical effects (pp. 430–431), but most mainstream filmmakers use intra-frame editing to generate shots that look like normally photographed ones.

Constructive Editing: The Kuleshov Effect   Practicing filmmakers sometimes reflect on their tools and their craft. Take Lev Kuleshov, a master of silent cinema. As a teenager, he had worked as an actor and set designer for one of Russia's greatest directors, Yevgenii Bauer. Bauer relied on skillful staging and long takes (pp. 125–128), but when Kuleshov directed his first film at age 21, he modeled it on the faster-cut American films he admired. At the same time, Kuleshov wanted to study filmmaking scientifically, so in 1921 he conducted some informal experiments. His findings decisively demonstrated editing's power over the viewer's sense of space.

> " [In editing *The Dark Knight* for both Imax and 35mm presentation], we needed to extensively test to ensure that the cuts were not so quick that the audience would get disoriented, looking at that Imax screen, and at the same time not interfere with the pace of the standard cinema version."
> —Lee Smith, editor

CONNECT TO THE BLOG
www.davidbordwell.net/blog

For more on the Kuleshov effect in both older and more recent films, see "What happens between shots happens between your ears."

In one experiment Kuleshov intercut neutral shots of an actor's face with other shots. When the face was intercut with a bowl of soup, viewers reportedly said the man looked hungry. When the same facial shot was intercut with a dead woman, he was taken to look mournful. Kuleshov claimed that the editing made viewers assume that the actor's expression changed, so that the cutting actually created the performance. In addition, the editing pattern strongly suggested the man was reacting to nearby things that he could see. Similarly, Kuleshov cut together shots of actors "looking at each other" but on Moscow streets miles apart, then meeting and strolling together—and turning to look at the White House in Washington.

Although filmmakers had already discovered this editing tactic, film historians called the idea behind it the *Kuleshov effect.* In general, that term refers to cutting together portions of a space in a way that prompts the spectator to assume a spatial whole that isn't shown onscreen. Most often, this happens because the filmmaker has decided to withhold an establishing shot.

The Kuleshov effect has both practical and artistic advantages. For a hospital scene in *Contagion,* Steven Soderbergh did not have to spend time and money shooting an entire emergency room. He suggests the locale with simple close shots of the husband staring as his wife goes into convulsions **(6.34–6.35).** We never see the faces of the medical staff, and we don't even see the actors together in the frame. The artistic benefit of Soderbergh's creative choice is that he carries us quickly to the heart of the crisis facing the couple.

Once you start to watch for the Kuleshov effect, you'll find that it's quite common. Sometimes it's used to create almost impossible feats. In Corey Yuen Kwai's *Legend of Fong Sai-Yuk,* a martial-arts bout between the hero and an adept woman begins on a platform but then bursts into their audience. The two warriors fight while balancing on the heads and shoulders of people in the crowd. Most of the shots are rapidly edited and rely on the Kuleshov effect **(6.36– 6.37).**

More radically, the editing can present spatial relations as being ambiguous and uncertain. In Carl Dreyer's *La Passion de Jeanne d'Arc,* for instance, we know only that Jeanne and the priests are in the same room. Because the neutral white backgrounds and the numerous close-ups provide no orientation to the entire space, we can seldom tell how far apart the characters are or precisely who is beside whom. We'll see later how films can create even more extreme spatial discontinuities.

The viewer doesn't normally notice the Kuleshov effect, but a few films call attention to it. Carl Reiner's *Dead Men Don't Wear Plaid* mixes shots filmed in the present with shots from Hollywood movies of the 1940s. Thanks to the Kuleshov effect, *Dead Men* creates unified scenes in which Steve Martin converses with characters from other films. In *A Movie,* experimentalist Bruce Conner turns the Kuleshov effect into a visual joke by linking shots scavenged from very different sources **(6.38–6.39).**

Temporal Relations between Shot A and Shot B

Like other film techniques, editing can control the time of the action presented in the film. In a narrative film especially, editing usually contributes to the plot's manipulation of story time. Back in Chapter 3 we pointed out three areas in which plot time can cue the spectator to construct the story time: order, duration, and frequency. Our *Birds* example (6.5–6.8) shows how editing reinforces all three areas of control.

Editing Shapes Chronology
First, there is the *order* of presentation of events. The men talk, then Melanie turns away, then she sees the gull swoop, then she responds. Hitchcock's editing presents these story events in the 1-2-3-4 order of his shots. But he could have shuffled the shots into any order at all, even reverse (4-3-2-1). This is to say that the filmmaker may control story chronology through the editing.

6.34

6.35

6.36

6.37

6.38

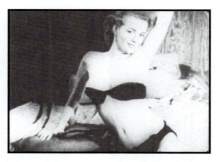

6.39

6.34–6.39 The Kuleshov effect enhances drama, stunts, and jokes. In *Contagion*, a husband (6.34) watches his wife dying (6.35), with no wide view establishing the ER. In *The Legend of Fong Sai-Yuk*, a shot of the woman's upper body (6.36) is followed by a shot of her legs and feet, supported by unwilling bystanders (6.37). In production, shots of the feet were made while the combatants were suspended above the crowd. The upper-body shots were filmed while the actors stood on some support below the frameline. In the found-footage film *A Movie*, one sequence cuts from a submarine captain peering through a periscope (6.38) to a woman gazing at the camera, as if they could see each other (6.39).

Controlling chronology can affect story–plot relations. We are most familiar with such manipulations in *flashbacks*, which present one or more shots out of their presumed story order. In *Hiroshima mon amour*, Resnais uses the protagonist's memory to motivate a violation of 1-2-3 order. Three shots (**6.40–6.42**) suggest visually that the position of her current lover's hand triggers a recollection of another lover's death years before. In contemporary cinema, brief flashbacks to key events may brutally interrupt present-time action. *The Fugitive* uses this technique to return obsessively to the murder of Dr. Kimble's wife, the event that initiated the story's action.

A much rarer option for reordering story events is the **flashforward.** Here the editing moves from the present to a future event and then returns to the present. A small-scale instance occurs in *The Godfather*. Don Vito Corleone talks with his sons Tom and Sonny about their upcoming meeting with Sollozzo, the gangster

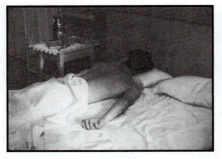
6.40

6.41

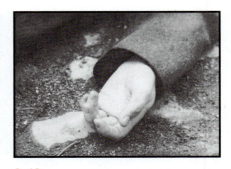
6.42

6.40–6.42 **Editing creates a flashback.** In *Hiroshima mon amour,* an optical point-of-view shot shows the protagonist's Japanese lover asleep (6.40). This is followed by a shot of her looking at him (6.41) and then a jump back into her past: a similar view of the hand of her dead German lover (6.42).

who is asking them to finance his narcotics traffic. As the Corleones talk, shots of their conversation in the present are interspersed with shots of Sollozzo going to the meeting in the future **(6.43–6.45).** The editing is used to provide exposition about Sollozzo while also moving quickly to the Don's announcement, at the gangsters' meeting, that he will not involve the family in the drug trade.

Filmmakers may use flashforwards to tease the viewer with glimpses of the eventual outcome of the story action. The end of *They Shoot Horses, Don't They?* is hinted at in brief shots that periodically interrupt scenes in the present. Such flash-forwards create a sense of a narration with a powerful range of story knowledge.

6.43

6.44

6.43–6.45 **Editing creates a flashforward.** In *The Godfather,* the Corleones discuss their upcoming meeting with Sollozzo (6.43). Jump ahead in time: Sollozzo arrives at the meeting, greeted by Sonny (6.44). The next few shots return us to the family conversation, where Don Vito ponders what he will tell Sollozzo (6.45). As they talk, more flashforwards to the meeting are inserted.

6.45

Editing Condenses or Expands Duration Filmmakers overwhelmingly present their shots in chronological order, but they are more likely to use editing to alter the *duration* of story events. **Elliptical editing** presents an action in such a way that it consumes less time on the screen than it does in the story. The filmmaker can create an *ellipsis* in three principal ways.

Suppose you want to show a man climbing a flight of stairs but you don't want to show every second of his climb. You could simply cut from a shot of him starting up the stairs to a shot of him reaching the top. If you feel that's a little too bumpy for your viewer, you could use a dissolve or some other punctuation that signals that some time has been omitted. This was a common option in world cinema before the 1960s. Devices like dissolves, fades, and wipes conventionally signaled an ellipsis in the action.

Alternatively, you could show the man at the bottom of the staircase, let him walk up out of the frame, hold briefly on the empty frame, then cut to an empty frame of the top of the stairs and let the man enter the frame. The *empty frames* on either side of the cut cover the elided time.

As a third option, you could create an ellipsis by means of a *cutaway* or *insert*. This is a shot of another event elsewhere that will not last as long as the elided action. In our example, you might start with the man climbing but then cut away to a woman in her apartment. You could then cut back to the man much farther along in his climb.

If you start to watch for them, you'll see that ellipses are fairly common in editing. Less common are shot-changes that *expand* story time. If the action from the end of one shot is partly repeated at the beginning of the next, we have **overlapping editing.** This prolongs the action, stretching it out past its story duration. The Russian filmmakers of the 1920s made frequent use of temporal expansion through overlapping editing, and no one mastered it more thoroughly than Sergei Eisenstein. In *Strike,* when factory workers bowl over a foreman with a large wheel hanging from a crane, two shots expand the action **(6.46–6.48).** In *October,* Eisenstein overlaps several shots of rising bridges in order to stress the significance of the moment.

Editing Can Repeat Story Actions We're accustomed to seeing a scene present action only once. Occasionally, however, a filmmaker may go beyond expanding an action to repeat it in its entirety. The very rarity of this technique may make it a powerful editing resource. In Bruce Conner's *Report,* there is a newsreel shot of John and Jacqueline Kennedy riding a limousine down a Dallas street. The shot is systematically repeated, in part or in whole, over and over, building up tension as the event seems to move by tiny increments closer to the inevitable

> " I saw *Toto the Hero,* the first film of the Belgian ex-circus clown Jaco van Dormael. What a brilliant debut. He tells the story with the camera. His compression and ellipses and clever visual transitions make it one of the most cinematic movies in a long time. The story spans a lifetime and kaleidoscopic events with such a lightness and grace that you want to get up and cheer."
>
> —John Boorman, director

> " [In editing James Bond films], we also evolved a technique that jumped continuity by simple editing devices. Bond would take a half-step towards a door and you would pick him up stepping into the next scene. We also used inserts cleverly to speed up a scene."
>
> —John Glen, editor and director

6.46

6.47

6.48

6.46–6.48 Expanding duration through cutting. In *Strike,* a wheel swings toward the foreman (6.46). From another angle we see it swing toward him again (6.47), and then again before striking him (6.48).

6.49

6.50

6.51

6.49–6.51 **Editing and the replay.** In *Police Story,* chasing the gangsters through a shopping mall, Jackie Chan leaps onto a pole several stories above them (6.49). He slides down in a shower of exploding lights (6.50). Cut to a new angle: Jackie leaps again, leading to an instant replay of the risky stunt (6.51). While the *Strike* sequence (6.46–6.48) briefly repeats bits of an action to extend a moment, this sequence from *Police Story* plays out an entire action several times.

CONNECT TO THE BLOG
www.davidbordwell.net/blog

Sit in on an editing session for Johnnie To's *The Mad Detective* and see why certain cuts were chosen in "Truly madly cinematically."

CONNECT TO THE BLOG
www.davidbordwell.net/blog

We discuss the emergence of continuity editing in many entries, particularly "John Ford, Silent Man," "Back to the vaults, and over the edge," "Looking different today?" A young filmmaker's multi-screen study of early editing is discussed in "A variation on a sunbeam: Exploring a Griffith Biograph film."

assassination. Occasionally in *Do The Right Thing,* Spike Lee cuts together two takes of the same action, as when we twice see a garbage can fly through the air and break the pizzeria window at the start of the riot. Jackie Chan often shows his most virtuoso stunts three or four times in a row from different angles to allow the audience to marvel at his daring **(6.49–6.51).**

Graphics, rhythm, space, and time are at the service of the filmmaker through the technique of editing. They offer potentially unlimited creative possibilities, which is to say they offer a vast menu of choices. Yet most films we see make use of a particular set of editing possibilities. This menu of choices is called **continuity editing,** and it has dominated film history for nearly a hundred years. We look at that next. Still, the most familiar way to edit a film isn't the only way to edit a film, and so we'll go on to consider some alternatives to this tradition.

Continuity Editing

Around 1900–1910, as filmmakers started to explore editing, they tried to arrange their shots so as to tell a story clearly. They developed an approach to editing, supported by specific strategies of cinematography and mise-en-scene, that was based on *narrative continuity.* Their explorations coalesced into a consistent style at the end of the 1910s, and it was embraced by filmmakers around the world. If you were to become a director, a cinematographer, a performer, or an editor, you'd need an intimate understanding of continuity editing.

We've seen that when a film technique is chosen and patterned to fulfill certain functions, a style emerges. Continuity editing offers a good example. It's a patterned use of a technique, based on filmmakers' decisions, that's designed to have particular effects on viewers. As its name implies, the continuity style aims to transmit narrative information smoothly and clearly over a series of shots. This makes the editing play a role in narration, the moment-by-moment flow of story information. All the dimensions of editing play a role in the continuity style. First, filmmakers usually keep graphic qualities roughly continuous from shot to shot. The figures are balanced and symmetrically deployed in the frame; the overall lighting tonality remains constant; the action occupies the central zones of the screen.

Second, filmmakers usually adjust the rhythm of the cutting to the scale of the shots. Long shots are left on the screen longer than medium shots, and medium shots are left on longer than close-ups. This gives the spectator more time to take in the broader views, which contain more details. By contrast, scenes of accelerated editing like the fire in *The Birds* favor closer views that can be absorbed quickly.

Above all, since the continuity style seeks to present a story clearly and forcefully, the filmmakers' editing choices shape space and time in particular ways.

Spatial Continuity: The 180° System

When working in the continuity style, the filmmaker builds the scene's space around what is called the **axis of action,** the *center line,* or the *180° line.* Any action—a person walking, two people conversing, a car racing along a road—can be thought of as occurring along a line or vector. This axis of action determines a half-circle, or 180° area, where the camera can be placed to present the action. The filmmaker will plan, stage, shoot, and edit the shots so as to maintain the axis of action from shot to shot.

The **180° system** can be imagined as the bird's-eye view in **6.52.** A girl and a boy are talking. The axis of action is the imaginary line connecting them. Under the continuity system, the director would arrange the mise-en-scene and camera placement so as to establish and sustain this line. A typical series of shots for continuity editing of the scene would be these:

1. A medium shot of the girl and the boy.
2. A shot over the girl's shoulder, favoring the boy.
3. A shot over the boy's shoulder, favoring the girl.

So far, so simple. But the choices are limited. To cut to a shot from camera position X, or from any position within the tinted area, would be considered a violation of the system because it *crosses* the axis of action. Indeed, some handbooks of

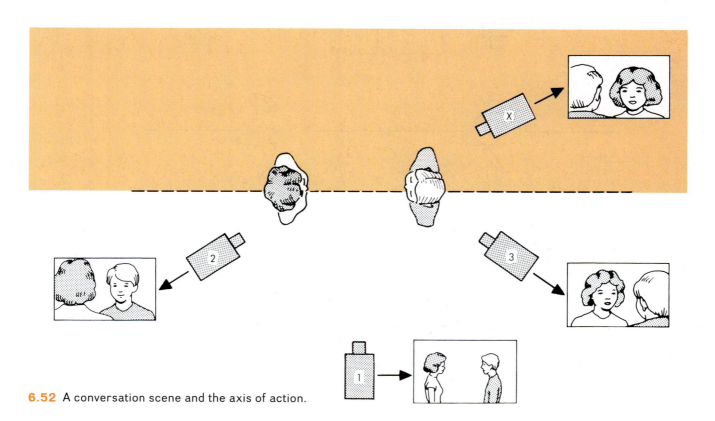

6.52 A conversation scene and the axis of action.

film directing call shot X flatly wrong. To see why, we need to examine what happens when a filmmaker follows the 180° system.

The 180° system ensures that relative positions in the frame remain consistent. In the shots taken from camera positions 1, 2, and 3, the characters occupy the same areas of the frame relative to each other. Even though we see them from different angles, the girl is always on the left and the boy is always on the right. But if we cut to shot X, the characters will switch positions in the frame. An advocate of traditional continuity would claim that shot X confuses us: Have the two characters somehow swiveled around each other?

The 180° system ensures consistent eyelines. If maintaining the axis of action keeps the figures facing in consistent directions, that has implications for the characters' gazes. In shots 1, 2, and 3, the girl is looking right and the boy is looking left. Shot X violates this pattern by making the girl look to the left.

The 180° system ensures consistent screen direction. Now imagine that the girl is walking left to right; her path constitutes the axis of action. As long as our shots do not cross this axis, cutting them together will keep the **screen direction** of the girl's movement constant, from left to right. But if we *cross* the axis and film a shot from the other side, the girl will now appear on the screen as moving from right to left. Such a cut could be disorienting.

Visualize the situation in 6.50, a standard scene of two cowboys meeting for a shootout on a town street **(6.53).** Cowboy A and cowboy B form the 180° line. But here A is walking from left to right and B is approaching from right to left, both seen in the shot taken from camera position 1. A closer view, from camera position 2, shows B still moving from right to left. A third shot, from camera position 3, shows A walking, as he had been in the first shot, from left to right.

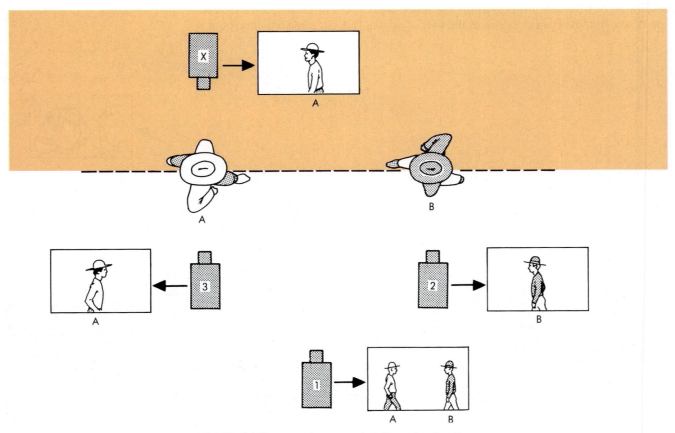

6.53 A Western shootout and the axis of action.

Now imagine that the third shot was instead taken from position X, on the opposite side of the line. A is now seen as moving from right to left. Has he lost his nerve and turned around while the second shot, of B, was on the screen? The filmmakers may want us to think that he is still walking toward his adversary, but the change in screen directions could make us think just the opposite. A cut to a shot taken from any point in the colored area would create this change in direction. Such breaks in continuity can be confusing.

It would be even more disorienting to cross the line as the scene's action is starting. In our shootout, suppose we didn't include an establishing shot but simply started with shot X, showing cowboy A walking from right to left. Suppose we follow that with shot 2, presenting B (from the other side of the line) also walking right to left. The two cowboys would seem to be walking in the same direction, as if one were following the other. We would very likely be startled if they suddenly came face to face within the framing of setup 1. This suggests that the Kuleshov effect, which omits an establishing shot, works best when it respects a consistent axis of action.

The 180° system prides itself on delineating space clearly. The viewer should always know *where the characters are* in relation to one another and to the setting. More important, the viewer always knows *where he or she is* with respect to the story action. The space of the scene, clearly and unambiguously unfolded, does not jar or disorient us. Most filmmakers believe that any disorientation will distract us from the unfolding plot action. We can't build up the story in our minds if we don't understand where characters are in space.

Continuity Editing in *The Maltese Falcon*

Thanks to the 180° principle, filmmakers have employed continuity editing to build up a smoothly flowing space that presents narrative action crisply and clearly. Let's consider a concrete example: the opening of John Huston's *The Maltese Falcon*.

Who's There? Where Are They?

The scene begins in the office of detective Sam Spade. In the first two shots, this space is established in several ways. First, there is the office window (shot 1a, **6.54**). The camera tilts down to reveal Spade (shot 1b, **6.55**) rolling a cigarette. As Spade says, "Yes, sweetheart?" shot 2 (**6.56**) appears.

This is important in several respects. It serves as an **establishing shot,** delineating the overall space of the office: the door, the intervening area, the desk, and Spade's position. Note also that shot 2 establishes a 180° line between Spade and his secretary, Effie. Effie could be the girl in 6.52, and Spade could be the boy. The first phase of this scene will be built around staying on the same side of this 180° line.

After Huston lays out the space for us in the first two shots, he analyzes it. Shots 3 (**6.57**) and 4 (**6.58**) show Effie and Spade talking. Because the 180° line established at the outset is adhered to (each shot presents the two from the same side), we know their location and spatial relationships. In cutting together medium shots of the two, however, Huston relies on two other common tactics within the 180° system.

> " I saw David Lynch and asked him: 'What's this about crossing the axis?' And he burst out laughing and said, 'That always gets me.' And I asked if you could do it, and he gave me this startled look and said, 'Stephen, you can do anything. You're a director.' Then he paused and said, 'But it doesn't cut together.'"
>
> —Stephen King, novelist, on directing his first film, *Maximum Overdrive*

CONNECT TO THE BLOG
www.davidbordwell.net/blog

How do you edit a simple action like entering a room? We survey some options in "Come in and sit down" and "Alignment, allegiance, and murder."

6.54 *The Maltese Falcon:* shot 1a

6.55 *The Maltese Falcon:* shot 1b

6.56 *The Maltese Falcon:* shot 2

6.57 *The Maltese Falcon:* shot 3

6.58 *The Maltese Falcon:* shot 4

CONNECT TO THE BLOG
www.davidbordwell.net/blog

For thoughts on the importance of eyeline directions in a very different art form, see "The eyeline match goes way, way back."

The first tactic is the **shot/reverse-shot** pattern. Once the 180° line has been established, we can show first one end point of the line, then the other. Here we cut back and forth from Effie to Spade.

A reverse shot is not literally the reverse of the first framing. It's simply a shot of the opposite end of the axis of action, usually showing a three-quarters view of the subject. In our bird's-eye view diagram (6.52), shots 2 and 3 form a shot/reverse-shot pattern, as 6.55 and 6.56 do here. We've seen examples of shot/reverse-shot cutting earlier in this chapter (Figures 6.17; 6.19, 6.20; and 6.34, 6.35).

The second tactic Huston uses here is the **eyeline match.** This occurs when shot A presents someone looking at something offscreen and shot B shows us what is being looked at. In neither shot are *both* looker and object present. In the *Maltese Falcon* opening, the cut from the shot of Effie (shot 3, 6.57) to the shot of Spade at his desk (shot 4, 6.58) is an eyeline match. The shots from *The Birds* of Melanie watching the bird attack and fire also create eyeline matches. So do the examples in which editing balances frame compositions (6.17, 6.18 and 6.19, 6.20).

Note that shot/reverse-shot editing need not employ eyeline matches. You could film both ends of the axis in a shot/reverse-shot pattern without showing the characters looking at each other. (In 6.58, Spade isn't looking at Effie.) On the whole, however, most shot/reverse-shot cuts also utilize the eyeline match.

The eyeline match is a simple idea but a powerful one, since the *directional* quality of the eyeline creates a strong spatial continuity. To be looked at, an object must be near the looker. The eyeline match often helped Kuleshov create false spaces through editing. His expressionless actor seems to be looking at whatever we see in the next shot, and the audience assumes that the performer is reacting accordingly.

Within the 180° system, the eyeline match, like constant screen direction, can stabilize space. Note how in shot 3, Effie's glance off right confirms Spade's position even though he is not onscreen. And though Spade does not look up after the cut to shot 4, the camera position remains on the same side of the axis of action (indeed, the position is virtually identical to that in shot 1b). We know that Effie is offscreen left. The breakdown of the scene's space is consistent. Thanks to the shot/reverse-shot pattern and the eyeline match, we understand the characters' locations even when they aren't in the same frame.

As we'd expect, the purpose is to make the shots clarify the cause-effect flow of the narrative. Shot 1 has suggested the locale and emphasized the protagonist by linking him to the window sign. The noise of the door and Spade's "Yes, sweetheart?" motivate the cut to shot 2. This establishing shot firmly anchors shot 1 spatially. It also introduces the source of the offscreen sound—the new character, Effie. The shot changes at precisely the moment when Effie enters, so we're unlikely to notice the cut. Our expectations lead us to want to see what happens next.

Shots 3 and 4 present the conversation between Spade and Effie, and the shot/reverse shot and the eyeline match reassure us as to the characters' locations. We may not even notice the cutting, since the style works to emphasize what Effie says and how Spade reacts. In shot 5, the overall view of the office is presented again, precisely at the moment when a new character enters the scene, and this in turn situates her firmly in the space. By adhering to the 180° system, Huston has emphasized the most important narrative elements—the dialogue and the entrance of new characters. The editing subordinates space to action.

The Client's Case: Developing the Spatial Layout   The overall coherence of the space we see is reaffirmed in shot 5, which presents the same framing as we saw in shot 2. The office is shown again (shot 5a, **6.59**), when the new character, Brigid O'Shaughnessy, enters. Spade stands to greet her, and the camera reframes his movement by a slight tilt upward (shot 5b, **6.60**). Shot 5 is a **reestablishing shot,** since it reestablishes the overall space that was analyzed into shots 3 and 4. The pattern, then, has been *establishment/breakdown/reestablishment*—one of the most common patterns of spatial editing in the classical continuity style.

After Brigid has walked toward Spade in shot 5, shot 6 presents a reverse angle on the two of them (shot 6a, **6.61**). She sits down alongside his desk (shot 6b, **6.62**). Up to this point, the 180° line has run between Spade and the doorway. Now the axis of action runs from Spade to the client's chair by his desk. Once established, this new line will not be violated.

A new tactic for ensuring spatial continuity has been introduced in this passage—the **match on action,** a very powerful device. This is simply a matter of carrying a single movement across a cut. As Brigid approaches Spade's desk at the end of shot 5 (6.60), her movement continues into the beginning of shot 6 (6.61). Again, the 180° system aids in concealing the match, since it keeps screen direction constant: Brigid moves from left to right in both shots. As you'd expect, the match on action is a tool of narrative continuity. So powerful is our desire to follow the action flowing across the cut that we ignore the cut itself.

Making a match on action requires skill. Given two shots of the same action, the editor must decide at what point to interrupt it; choosing the wrong point can make the cut bumpy. Moreover, if a piece of action isn't filmed by two cameras at once, it's likely that the first shot, in which the movement starts, will be filmed much earlier or later than the second. The risk of continuity errors—changes of position, or lighting, or props—is considerable.

After the match on action, the rest of the *Maltese Falcon* scene uses the same editing tactics we've already seen. When Brigid sits down, a new axis of action is established (shot 6b, 6.62). This enables Huston to break down the space into closer shots (shots 7–13, **6.63–6.69**). All these shots use the shot/reverse-shot tactic: the camera frames, at an oblique angle, one end point of the 180° line, then frames the other. (Note the shoulders in the foreground of shots 7, 8, and 10—6.63, 6.64, and 6.66.) Here again, the editing of space presents the dialogue action simply and unambiguously.

Beginning with shot 12, Huston's cuts also create eyeline matches. Spade looks off left at Brigid (shot 12, 6.68). She looks off left as the door is heard opening (shot 13, 6.69). Archer, just coming in, looks off right at them (shot 14, **6.70**), and they both look off at him (shot 15, **6.71**). The 180° rule permits us always to know who is looking at whom.

Huston could have played the entire conversation in one long take, remaining with shot 6b (6.62). Why has he broken the conversation into seven shots? As with the gas-station attack in *The Birds,* the cutting controls timing and emphasis. We'll look at Brigid or Spade at exactly the moment Huston wants us to. In a long take and a more distant framing, Huston would have to channel our attention in other ways, perhaps through staging or sound.

Furthermore, the shot/reverse-shot pattern stresses the development of Brigid's story and Spade's reaction to it. As she gets into details, the cutting moves from over-the-shoulder shots (6.63, 6.64) to framings that isolate Brigid (6.65 and 6.67) and eventually one that isolates Spade (6.68). These shots come at the point when Brigid, in an artificially shy manner, tells her story, and the medium close-ups arouse our curiosity

6.59 *The Maltese Falcon:* shot 5a

6.60 *The Maltese Falcon:* shot 5b

CONNECT TO THE BLOG
www.davidbordwell.net/blog

Hong Kong combat scenes are fine places to study precise continuity editing. See our entries, "Bond vs. Chan: Jackie shows how it's done" and "*Planet Hong Kong*: The dragon dances."

6.61 *The Maltese Falcon:* shot 6a

6.62 *The Maltese Falcon:* shot 6b

6.63 *The Maltese Falcon:* shot 7

6.64 *The Maltese Falcon:* shot 8

6.65 *The Maltese Falcon:* shot 9

6.66 *The Maltese Falcon:* shot 10

6.67 *The Maltese Falcon:* shot 11

6.68 *The Maltese Falcon:* shot 12

6.69 *The Maltese Falcon:* shot 13

6.70 *The Maltese Falcon:* shot 14

6.71 *The Maltese Falcon:* shot 15

CONNECT TO THE BLOG
www.davidbordwell.net/blog

Shots showing characters' reactions are crucial to a film. We talk about this in "They're looking for us."

about whether she's telling the truth. The shot of Spade's reaction (6.68) suggests that he's skeptical. The editing cooperates with framing and figure behavior to focus our attention on Brigid's tale, to let us study her demeanor, and to hint at Spade's response.

When Archer enters, the breakdown into close views stops for a moment, and Huston reestablishes the locale. Archer is integrated into the action by a rightward pan shot (shots 16a and 16b, **6.72** and **6.73**). His path is consistent with the scene's first axis of action, that running between Spade and the doorway. Moreover, the framing on him is similar to that used for Brigid's entrance earlier. (Compare shot 16b with 6a, figures 6.73 and 6.61.) Such repetitions allow the viewer to concentrate on the new information, not the manner in which it is presented.

Now firmly established as part of the scene, Archer hitches himself up onto Spade's desk. His position puts him at Spade's end of the axis of action (shot 17, **6.74**). During the rest of the scene, Huston's editing analyzes this new set of relationships without ever breaking the 180° line.

The viewer isn't supposed to notice all the things that we've analyzed. Throughout, the shots present space to emphasize the cause–effect flow—the characters' movements, words, and facial reactions. The editing has created spatial continuity in order to present continuity of story action.

6.72 *The Maltese Falcon:* shot 16a

6.73 *The Maltese Falcon:* shot 16b

6.74 *The Maltese Falcon:* shot 17

Continuity Editing: Some Fine Points

The continuity system, largely unchanged, remains in force today. Most narrative films still draw on 180° principles **(6.75, 6.76)**. But the system can be refined in various ways.

Characters in a Circle, Shifting the Axis   If a director arranges several characters in a circular pattern—say, sitting around a dinner table—then the axis of action will probably run between the characters of greatest importance at the moment. In **6.77** and **6.78,** from Howard Hawks's *Bringing Up Baby,* the important dialogue is occurring between the two men, so we can cut to positions around Aunt Elizabeth (in the foreground) to get consistent shot/reverse shots. When David Huxley leaves the table, however, the new arrangement of characters creates a new axis of action running between the two women **(6.79, 6.80).**

Both the *Maltese Falcon* and the *Bringing Up Baby* examples show that in the course of a scene the 180° line may shift as the characters move around the setting. In some cases, the filmmaker may create a new axis of action that allows the camera to take up a position that would have crossed the line in an earlier phase of the scene.

Deleting the Establishing Shot   The power of the axis of action and the eyelines it can create is so great that the filmmaker may be able to eliminate an establishing shot, thus relying on the Kuleshov effect. In Spike Lee's *She's Gotta Have It,* Nola Darling holds a Thanksgiving dinner for her three male friends. Lee never presents a shot showing all four in the same frame. Instead, he uses medium long shots including all the men (for example, **6.81**), over-the-shoulder shot/reverse

> " The way [Howard] Hawks constructs a continuity of space is remarkable, and generally holds you 'inside' it. There is no possible way of escape, unless the film decides to provide you with one. My theory is that his films are captivating because they build a sense of continuity which is so strong that it allows the complete participation of the audience."
>
> —Slobodan Sijan, director

6.75

6.76

6.75–6.76 Continuity editing in today's cinema. A train conversation in Duncan Jones' *Source Code* obeys the 180° system, with eyeline matches and foreground shoulders confirming our position on one side of the axis. The arrangement is similar to the one we show in 6.52, and to the staging and cutting in the *Maltese Falcon* scene.

6.77–6.80 **Continuity around the dinner table.** In *Bringing Up Baby,* shot/reverse-shot cutting puts the distracted David Huxley on the right (6.77) and Major Applegate on the left (6.78). After David leaves the table, a new axis is established along the length of the table. This permits a shot/reverse-shot exchange favoring first Aunt Elizabeth (6.79) and then Susan (6.80).

6.77

6.78

6.79

6.80

6.81

6.82

6.83

6.84

6.85

6.86

6.81–6.86 **Around the table with the Kuleshov effect:** *She's Gotta Have It.* The first shot, more or less from Nola's point of view, lays out the men's position at the table (6.81). Sometimes a momentary axis of action is established between the men (6.82). Nola is never shown in the same frame with her suitors, but her eyelines always tells us whom she's looking at (6.83). When the men look at her, each one's eyeline is consistent with their initial position at the table (6.84–6.85). In the last frame shown (6.86), we get an optical POV from Nola's position, as Greer addresses her directly.

shots among them (for example, **6.82**), and eyeline-matched medium close-ups of them. Nola is given her own medium close-ups (**6.83**).

Through eyelines and body orientations, Lee's editing keeps the spatial relations completely consistent. For example, each man looks in a different direction when addressing Nola (**6.84, 6.85, 6.86**). This cutting pattern enhances the dramatic action by making all the men equal competitors for her. They are clustered at one end of the table, and none is shown in the same frame with her. By organizing the scene around her orientation to the action Lee keeps Nola the pivotal character. The men are on display, and Nola is coolly judging each one's behavior.

Cheating with Cuts   Another felicity in the 180° system is the **cheat cut.** Sometimes a director may not have perfect continuity from shot to shot because each shot was composed for specific reasons. Must the two shots match perfectly? Again, narrative motivation decides the matter. If we're paying attention to the unfolding action and the 180° relations are kept reasonably constant, the director has some freedom to "cheat" mise-en-scene from shot to shot—that is, to slightly mismatch the positions of characters or objects.

Consider two shots from William Wyler's *Jezebel*. Neither Julie nor Pres moves during the shots, but Wyler has blatantly cheated the position of Julie **(6.87, 6.88).** Yet most viewers would not notice the discrepancy since it's the dialogue that is paramount in the scene. The shots are consistent with the axis of action, and the change from a straight-on angle to a slightly high angle helps hide the cheat. There is, in fact, a cheat in the *Maltese Falcon* scene, too, between shots 6b and 7. In 6b (6.62), as Spade leans forward, the back of his chair is not near him. Yet in shot 7 (6.63), it has been cheated to be just behind his left arm. Here again, the narrative flow overrides the cheat cut.

Crossing the Axis   Most continuity-based filmmakers prefer not to cross the axis of action. They would rather move the actors around the setting and create a new axis, as we saw in *The Maltese Falcon*. Still, can you ever legitimately cut to the other side of an established axis of action?

Yes, sometimes. A scene occurring in a doorway, on a staircase, or in other symmetrical settings may occasionally break the line. More often, filmmakers get across the axis by taking one shot *on the line itself* and using it as a transition. This strategy is rare in dialogue sequences, but it's common in chase scenes. By filming on the axis, the filmmaker presents the action as moving directly toward the camera (a *head-on* shot) or away from it (a *tail-on* shot). The climactic chase of *The Road Warrior* offers several examples. As marauding road gangs try to board a fleeing gasoline truck, George Miller uses many head-on and tail-on shots of the vehicles **(6.89–6.93).**

Filmmakers occasionally violate screen direction without confusing the viewer. They can do this most easily when a scene's physical layout is very well defined. During a chase in John Ford's *Stagecoach,* no confusion arises when the Ringo Kid leaps from the coach to the horses **(6.94, 6.95).** We aren't likely to think that the coach had swiveled to face in the opposite direction, as in the possible misinterpretation of the two cowboys' shootout (6.53).

CONNECT TO THE BLOG
www.davidbordwell.net/blog

Another refinement: What happens if a reverse shot is withheld? We show some examples and discuss their functions in "Angles and perceptions."

6.87

6.88

6.87–6.88 **The cheat cut.** In this shot from *Jezebel,* the top of Julie's head is even with Pres's chin (6.87), but in the second shot (6.88) she seems to have grown.

6.89

6.90

6.91

6.92

6.89–6.93 Crossing the axis of action. Near the climax of the chase in *The Road Warrior*, Max is driving the tanker left to right (6.89). In later shots he is still driving toward the right. An attacking thug perched on the front of the truck turns and looks off right in horror (6.90). The chieftain's vehicle, moving right to left, is coming toward them on a collision course (6.91). The crash is shown in several quick shots facing head-on to the vehicles (6.92). These head-on shots provide a transition to cross the axis, so that a long shot can now show Max's truck plowing through the wreckage from right to left (6.93)—opposite to the direction we've seen in earlier shots.

6.93

6.94   **6.95**

6.94–6.95 Breaking the axis successfully. In *Stagecoach*, in a long shot where all movement is toward the right, the hero begins leaping from the driver's seat down onto the horse team (6.94). In the next shot both he and the coach are moving leftward (6.95).

On the Axis: The POV Shot There's one more fine point with respect to spatial continuity, and it's especially relevant to a film's narration. We have already seen that a camera framing can strongly indicate a character's optical point of view, making the narration subjective. We saw this in our earlier example from *Fury* (p. 193). That example presents a cut from the person looking (5.119) to what he sees (5.120). We have also seen an instance of POV cutting in the *Birds* sequence (pp. 220–221).

Now we're in a position to see how optical POV is consistent with continuity editing, creating the type of eyeline-match editing known as *point-of-view cutting*.

Are You Looking at Me? Point-of-View Cutting in Rear Window

The eyeline match shows a person looking in one shot, followed by a shot showing what the person sees. Most eyeline matches, however, don't show the object of the look from the person's vantage point. When Effie looks at Sam Spade (6.57–6.58) or when Brigid looks off at Archer (6.69–6.70), the followup shot doesn't represent the character's point of view. By contrast, POV cutting gives us an eyeline match that presents something as seen by the person looking. The shot is more or less optically subjective. This option doesn't violate the 180° system because the subjective shot is taken from a position presumed to be right *on* the axis of action.

Again Alfred Hitchcock provides clear examples. *Rear Window* is built on a Peeping Tom situation. The photojournalist Jeff is laid up with a broken leg, so he watches life across the courtyard behind his apartment. He starts to wonder if his neighbor has murdered his wife, but he can't go over to investigate. He's confined to whatever clues he can spot from his window.

Throughout the film Hitchcock uses a standard eyeline-match pattern, cutting from a shot of Jeff looking **(6.96)** to a shot of what he sees **(6.97)**. Since there is no establishing shot that shows both Jeff and the opposite apartment, the Kuleshov effect operates here: our mind connects the two parts of space, as in our *Birds* POV sequences. More specifically, the second shot represents Jeff's optical viewpoint, and this is filmed from a position on his end of the axis of action **(6.98)**. The camera has not crossed the line. Through POV editing, the narration restricts us to what Jeff sees and hears.

Hitchcock is so interested in exploiting subjective cutting that he varies the POV shots as *Rear Window* goes on. Eager to solve the mystery, Jeff begins to use binoculars and a photographic telephoto lens to magnify his view. By using shots

6.96

6.97

6.96–6.97 POV cutting in *Rear Window.* Jeff looks out his window (6.96). The next shot shows what he sees from his optical POV (6.97).

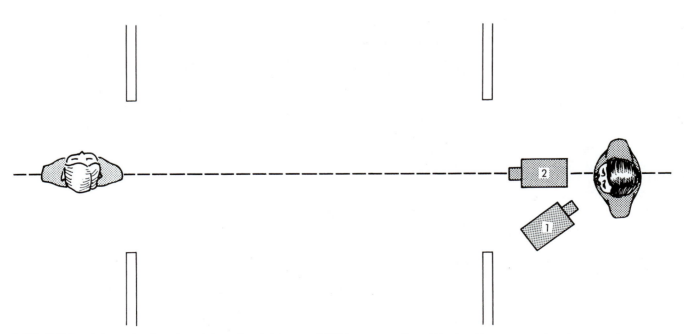

6.98 **POV and the axis of action.** An overhead diagram of POV cutting in *Rear Window.* You can see that the second camera setup doesn't cross the axis of action.

CONNECT TO THE BLOG
www.davidbordwell.net/blog

For more examples of point-of-view editing and an analysis of a scene, see "Three nights of a dreamer."

taken with lenses of different focal lengths, Hitchcock shows how each new optical tool enlarges what Jeff can see **(6.99–6.102).** As the suspense grows, we get to see more clues to a possible murder.

6.99

6.100

6.101

6.102

6.99–6.102 Magnifying POV. When Jeff looks through his binoculars (6.99), we see a telephoto POV shot of his neighbor (6.100). When he employs a powerful photographic lens (6.101), the POV shot enlarges his neighbor's activities even more (6.102).

Hitchcock's gradual enlargement of POV framings in *Rear Window* shows that a filmmaker can tweak standardized editing patterns in fresh ways. But in other respects the *Rear Window* scenes, like the gas-pump explosion in *The Birds,* are traditional. For instance, both films present a POV pattern consisting of three shots. We see a shot of the person looking, a shot of what's looked at (seen from a subjective angle), and a return to a shot of the person looking. This ABA scheme anchors the subjective shot in an objective framework and tells us clearly that someone is seeing something.

But what if you delete the first shot in the trio, the shot of someone looking? You can create a small surprise by concealing the fact that someone is being watched. This was the choice made by Debra Granik in one scene in *Winter's Bone* **(6.103–6.106).** Note that even though we lack the usual first shot of Ree looking, the POV shot remains on the 180-degree line, and the following cut to her remains consistent with that.

For *Halloween,* John Carpenter selected a very unusual pattern of POV cutting, one that has strong implications for narration in this slasher horror film **(6.107–6.110).** He created an uncertainty: Does Laurie actually see Michael Myers in the yard? Or is he a figment of her imagination? Or does the character have the supernatural power to disappear? The uncertainty plays into the film's larger mystery about whether the indestructible Michael is indeed "the boogyman." POV cutting is a fairly standardized technique, but it still offers many creative choices to the director inclined to experiment.

6.103

6.104

6.105

6.106

6.103–6.106 **Retroactive POV.** One scene in *Winter's Bone* ends with a telephoto shot of Ree walking her sister and brother to school (6.103). Cut to the sister in class, apparently seen from an objective standpoint (6.104). But soon she lifts her eyes to stare straight at the camera (6.105). Another cut reveals that we've been seeing the girl through Ree's eyes (6.106).

6.107

6.108

6.109

6.110

6.107–6.110 **POV cutting for uncertainty.** Laurie looks out her bedroom window (6.107). Cut to a shot, approximating her viewpoint, of Michael Myers in his mask (6.108). This seems a conventional POV shot, and the return to Laurie (6.109) suggests the standard ABA cutting pattern. But the next shot of the laundry line shows that Michael is now gone (6.110). It's very unusual to conceal such a drastic change in the POV area during a shot of the person looking. Did Laurie imagine that Michael was there? Or does he have the power to vanish? But if he can disappear, why doesn't she seem surprised?

Crosscutting

The continuity system shows that editing can endow the film's narration with a great range of knowledge. A cut can take us to any point on the correct side of the axis of action. Editing can even create omniscience, that godlike knowledge of things happening to people in many places. The outstanding technical device here is *crosscutting,* first extensively explored by D. W. Griffith in his last-minute rescue scenes. In *The Battle at Elderbush Gulch,* a cavalry troop is riding to rescue some settlers trapped in a cabin and battling the Indians outside **(6.111–6.114).** After 11 additional shots of the cavalry, various parts of the cabin interior, and the Indians outdoors, a 12th shot shows the cavalry riding in from the distance behind the cabin.

Crosscutting gives us a comparatively unrestricted knowledge of story information. It does this by alternating shots of events in one location with shots of events in other places. Crosscutting risks introducing some spatial discontinuity, but it binds the action together by creating a sense of cause and effect and simultaneous time. By setting one action against another in a short time span, it can build tension. In *Jerry Maguire,* for example, crosscutting interweaves the action of sports agent Jerry and his rival racing to phone the same clients **(6.115–6.118).**

Fritz Lang's *M* goes further, crosscutting three lines of action across the whole film. The police seek the child murderer, gangsters prowl the streets looking for him, and we occasionally see the murderer himself. Crosscutting ties together the different lines of action, bringing out a temporal simultaneity and the twists and turns of the pursuit. The crosscutting also gives us a range of knowledge greater than that of any one character. We know that the gangsters are after the murderer, but he and the police don't. Crosscutting also builds up suspense, as we form expectations that are only gradually fulfilled. It may create parallels as well, and Lang exploits this possibility by suggesting analogies between the police and the crooks.

6.111

6.112

6.113

6.114

6.111–6.114 **Crosscutting for a last-minute rescue.** In *The Battle of Elderbush Gulch,* Griffith cuts from a shot of the cavalry (6.111) to a view inside the besieged cabin (6.112). He cuts back to the cavalry (6.113) and then back to the cabin (6.114). The technique gives us an unrestricted range of knowledge and summons up suspense: Will the rescuers arrive in time?

6.115

6.116

6.117

6.118

6.115–6.118 Crosscutting for tension. Jerry is in a race to secure his clients' loyalty before his arrogant rival gets to them. A shot of Jerry seething (6.115) is followed by a cut to the rival and his assistant (6.116). As Jerry tries to reach his clients on the phone (6.117) we cut to his rival doing the same (6.118).

By maintaining spatial continuity, filmmakers draw the viewer into the active process of understanding a scene. We assume that setting, character movement, and character position will be consistent and coherent. We make inferences on the basis of cues, so that when Brigid and Spade look off left, we infer that someone is entering the room, and we expect to see a shot of that person. We also form expectations about what shot will follow the one we're seeing.

We have learned the continuity style so well that we aren't usually aware of how it shapes our responses. Filmmakers know how familiar we are with the spatial continuity system, and they can alter it, as long as the variations don't violate its basic principles. (See "A Closer Look.")

Temporal Continuity: Order, Frequency, and Duration

As we've seen in Chapter 3, in narrative form, the plot's presentation of the story action usually involves manipulating time. Continuity editing offers the filmmaker many choices about presenting story time. Those options involve the dimensions we've already charted: order, frequency, and duration.

Order and Frequency Continuity editing typically presents the story events in a 1-2-3 order. Spade rolls a cigarette in one shot, Effie enters in another shot, and so on. The most common violation of 1-2-3 order is a flashback, signaled by a cut or dissolve. As for frequency, classical continuity editing also often presents only *once* what happens *once* in the story. Within this tradition, it would be a gross mistake for Huston to repeat the shot of, say, Brigid sitting down (6.60). So chronological
(continued on page 253)

Intensified Continuity: *Unstoppable, L.A. Confidential,* and Contemporary Editing

By the 1930s, most of the world's commercial filmmakers had embraced the continuity editing system. But it underwent changes over the years. Today's editing practices abide by the principles of continuity but amplify them in certain ways. We can call this newer style *intensified continuity.*

A straightforward example comes from *Unstoppable* **(6.119–6.122).** This scene obeys the 180° system, but some of director Tony Scott's choices wouldn't have been made by Huston in *The Maltese Falcon* or Hitchcock in *Rear Window.* For one thing, the cutting is very fast. The conversation, which takes 28 seconds, is shown in 15 shots, an average of less than 2 seconds per shot. At one point, a single line of dialogue is broken into 3 shots.

Between 1930 and 1960, a film typically consisted of 300–800 shots. Things changed from the sixties onward, and today a 2-hour film might contain 3,000 shots or more. (*Unstoppable* has over 3,200.) The average shot in *The Bourne Ultimatum* lasts about 2 seconds. Hitchcock could cut action scenes quickly, as we saw in *The Birds'* gull attack, but his dialogue scenes were more slowly paced. By contrast, intensified continuity cuts conversations quickly as well. "You always hear things like, 'We need to put more energy into this scene,'" says Tim Streeto, editor of *Greenberg.* "That can translate into quick editing, where you go back and forth between two characters like a ping-pong match."

Partly because filmmakers have chosen faster editing, they tend to build their scenes out of fairly close views of individual characters, rather than fuller, longer-held shots. As we've seen, the viewer can absorb close views more quickly than long shots. As filmmakers have concentrated more on faces, they have opted for fewer establishing shots, and those may come late in the scene's action rather than near the start.

Moreover, many of the close shots are taken with telephoto lenses. Nearly all the shots in the *Unstoppable* scene

> " Now nobody trusts the actor's performance. If an actor has a scene where they are sitting in the distance, everybody says, 'What are you shooting? It has to be close-up!' This is ridiculous. You have the position of the hand, the whole body—this is the feeling of a movie. I hate movies where everybody has big close-ups all the time. . . . This is television. I have talking heads on my television set in my home all the time."
>
> —Miroslav Ondříček, cinematographer

6.119

6.120

6.121

6.122

6.119–6.122 **The persistence of classical continuity editing.** In *Unstoppable,* two railyard workers come to Connie, their supervisor, and report that an unmanned train is running free. The scene is treated through conventional continuity, with an establishing shot (6.119), reverse angles (6.120), eyeline matches (6.121), and over-the-shoulder framings (6.122). The axis of action is respected throughout, as is the balancing between decentered reverse shot (see 6.19–6.20).

are captured by long focal-length lenses, which can create fairly tight framings (6.120, 6.121). Because modern screen formats are wide, we may find two or more facial close-ups filling the screen. We also find more frame mobility. The *Unstoppable* scene includes many reframings, a tracking shot, and no fewer than five quick zooms.

These creative decisions create a faster, more concentrated version of classic continuity. We can analyze this style in a bit more detail by examining a scene from *L. A. Confidential*. After arresting three black suspects, Lieutenant Ed Exley prepares to bully a confession from them. The scene takes less than a minute but employs nine shots, two with significant camera movement. Director Curtis Hanson shifts the emphasis among several key characters by co-ordinating his editing with anamorphic widescreen compositions, staging in depth, tight framings, rack-focus, and camera movement **(6.123–6.134)**. Interestingly, the actors make little expressive use of their hands or bodies; the performances are almost completely facial.

The persistence of the continuity system may seem surprising, since modern films may feel rougher-textured than classic studio products. Mismatches on actions or eyelines are a bit more common now, but they're often used as an accent within a series of correctly matched cuts. A chase or a fight can be spiced up by a shift in screen direction or a jerkily matched movement. As Chris Lebenzon, an editor on *Unstoppable*, puts it: "In the action world, sometimes what used to be called a 'bad cut' is actually kind of a good one because it jars you in a way that's more appropriate to the scene."

Why did this intensified form of continuity become so common? It was encouraged by many factors, including computer-based editing, but television was a major influence. Since the 1950s, many television directors favored

CONNECT TO THE BLOG
www.davidbordwell.net/blog

After you've read about *L.A. Confidential*, you might visit our blog entries on the *Bourne* trilogy: "Unsteadicam chronicles," "[insert your favorite Bourne pun here]," and "I broke everything new again." The entry titled "Intensified continuity revisited" compares a scene in *The Shop Around the Corner* with the same one in the remake, *You've Got Mail*. For thoughts on multiple-camera shooting and continuity, see "Cutting remarks: On *The Good German*, classical style, and the Police Tactical Unit."

close-ups, fast cutting, and considerable camera movement. On small screens, closer views look better than long shots, which tend to lose detail, while rapid cutting and camera movement constantly refresh the image and might keep the viewer from switching channels. In the 1960s and 1970s, filmmakers realized that the movies they were making for theaters would find their ultimate audience on the home screen. Accordingly, many directors "shot for the box." Later generations of directors, such as Ridley Scott and David Fincher, began their careers in commercials and music videos, so they were already adept in the quick pace of modern television. Today intensified continuity is well adapted to being watched on laptop computers, tablets, and smartphones.

6.123 Shot 1: The scene begins by presenting only a portion of the space, a suspect in the interrogation room. A reflection shows Exley waiting and his colleagues milling about outside the room. This image singles out the core dramatic action to come—Exley's brutal confrontation with the suspects.

6.132 Shot 9a: A cut back to the two-shot supplies Smith's satisfied reaction.

6.133 Shot 9 continues: Exley turns away. The lens shifts focus to catch his grim face in the foreground, preparing us for the brutality he will display.

6.134 Shot 9 continues as Exley walks out of frame, revealing with a rack-focus Vincennes's skeptical expression. The telephoto lens, supported by the rack-focus, has supplied facial views of Smith, then Exley, and then Vincennes all in a single shot.

sequence and one-for-one frequency are the standard methods of handling order and frequency within the continuity style of editing. There are occasional exceptions, as we saw in our examples from *Hiroshima mon amour, The Godfather,* and *Police Story* (pp. 230–232).

Duration: Continuous or Elided   Duration offers more unusual editing possibilities. In the classical continuity system, story duration is seldom expanded by editing. Admittedly, overlapping cutting (p. 231) sometimes stretches out an action. But usually duration is presented continuously (plot time and screen time equaling story time) or is elided (story time being greater than plot time and screen time). Dialogue scenes are the most common examples; they're typically played out in their story duration.

Let's first consider *temporal continuity,* the most common possibility. Here a scene occupying, say, five minutes in the story also occupies five minutes when projected on the screen. We can pick out three ways to achieve temporal continuity, all of them present in the first scene of *The Maltese Falcon.*

First, the narrative progression of the scene has no gaps. Every movement by the characters and every line of dialogue are presented. Second, there's the sound track. Sound issuing from the story space (what is called *diegetic* sound) is a standard indicator of temporal continuity, especially when, as in this scene, the sound bleeds over each cut. Third, there's the match on action between shots 5 and 6. So powerful is the match on action that it creates both spatial *and* temporal continuity. The reason is obvious: if an action carries across the cut, the space and time are assumed to be continuous from shot to shot. Continuous story action, diegetic sound overlapping the cuts, and matching on action are three primary indicators that the duration of the scene is continuous.

The filmmaker may not want complete continuity of duration. Just as a novelist sometimes condenses a scene to its high points, a filmmaker may want to skip over some less important moments. That will demand editing that creates temporal ellipsis. An ellipsis is something that has been omitted, and thanks to cutting a filmmaker may skip over seconds, minutes, hours, days, years, or centuries. Let's say you want to show a character getting ready for work in the morning. If you're making a classically constructed film, you might reduce this process to a few shots of the character going into the shower, putting on shoes, and frying an egg. As we saw on p. 235, the classical approach to editing may use empty frames, cutaways, or optical devices like dissolves to cover short temporal ellipses.

Elliding time offers a good example of how cinematic conventions have changed. In films made before the 1960s, dissolves, fades, or wipes are typically used to indicate an ellipsis between shots, usually the end of one scene and the beginning of the next. The Hollywood rule was that a dissolve indicates a brief time lapse and a fade indicates a much longer one.

Contemporary filmmakers usually employ a cut for such transitions. For example, in *2001,* Stanley Kubrick cuts directly from a bone spinning in the air to a space station orbiting the earth, one of the boldest graphic matches in narrative cinema. The cut eliminates millions of years of story time. Less drastically, most contemporary films indicate the passage of time through direct cuts. Changes in lighting, locale, or character position cue us that story time has passed (**6.135–6.137**).

The dissolve and fade have made a comeback in the age of digital video. For one thing, editing programs provide them, along with many varieties of wipes, so these optical effects are easy to incorporate. In addition, many online documentaries employ dissolves in the older manner, to indicate a passage of time. When the maker of a YouTube video wants to skip over the boring stretches of a cat fighting with a paper bag, a gentle dissolve may do the trick.

Montage Sequences   One form of ellipsis has persisted from the 1920s to the present. Sometimes the filmmaker wants to show a large-scale process or a lengthy

6.135

6.136

6.137

6.135–6.137 Elliptical cuts in *Wendy and Lucy.* Arrested for shoplifting, Wendy is worried about having left her dog Lucy at the supermarket. As she's fingerprinted, Wendy glances up, and an eyeline match shows the clock (6.135). A cut to the next shot shows Wendy in a cell, indicating that some minutes have elapsed (6.136). The clock shot functioned as a cutaway to cover a time gap. In the cell, another cut shows Wendy in a different position (6.137). This suggests that still more time has passed. An older film would have implied the passage of time through dissolves, but here the abrupt changes of locale and character position suggest the same thing. A later shot of the clock will show that Wendy has been held for at least two hours.

period—a city waking up in the morning, a war, a child growing up. Here the filmmaker can pick another device from the menu: the **montage sequence.** (This should not be confused with the concept of *montage* in Sergei Eisenstein's film theory.) Brief portions of a process, informative titles (for example, "1865" or "San Francisco"), stereotyped images (such as the Eiffel Tower), newsreel footage, newspaper headlines, and the like can be joined by dissolves and music to create a quick, regular rhythm and to compress a lengthy series of actions into a few moments.

American studio films of the 1930s established some montage clichés—calendar pages fluttering away, newspaper presses pounding out an Extra—but in the hands of deft editors, such sequences became small virtuoso pieces. The driving pace of gangster films like *Scarface* and *The Roaring Twenties* owes a lot to dynamic montage sequences. Slavko Vorkapich, an experimental filmmaker, created somewhat abstract, almost delirious summaries of wide-ranging actions such as stock market crashes, political campaigns, and an opera singer's career **(6.138).**

Montage sequences have been a mainstay of narrative filmmaking ever since. *Jaws* employs montage to summarize the start of tourist season through brief shots of vacationers arriving at the beach. A montage sequence in *Spider-Man* shows Peter Parker sketching his superhero costume, inspired by visions of the girl he loves **(6.139, 6.140).** All these instances remind us that because montage sequences usually lack dialogue, they tend to come wrapped in music. In *Tootsie,* a song accompanies a series of magazine covers showing the hero's rise to success as a TV star.

As with space, the filmmaker who employs the continuity style uses cinematic time primarily to advance the narrative. Like graphics, rhythm, and space, time is organized to unfold cause and effect and arouse curiosity, suspense, and surprise. In turn, we viewers who know the conventions pick up the cues and engage with the ways in which time is presented. We expect the editing to present story events in chronological order, with perhaps occasional rearrangement through flashbacks.

6.138

6.138–6.140 **Montage sequences old and new.** *Maytime* uses superimpositions (here, the singer, sheet music, and a curtain rising) and rapid editing to summarize an opera singer's triumphs (6.138). *Citizen Kane* ironically refers to this passage in the montage sequences showing Susan Alexander's failures. For a montage sequence in *Spider-Man*, CGI technique creates a split image, showing both Peter's expression and a close-up of the costume he's designing (6.139). The *Spider-Man* sequence also uses a more traditional linking device, a dissolve that briefly superimposes two shots (6.140).

6.139

6.140

We expect that editing will usually respect the frequency of story events: If something happens once, we see it only once. And we assume that the actions that don't matter to story causality will be dropped or trimmed by judicious ellipses. All these expectations allow the viewer to follow the story with minimal effort.

But there are many alternatives to the continuity style of editing, and these are worth a look.

Alternatives to Continuity Editing

Powerful and widespread as it is, the continuity tradition remains only one approach to editing. As you'd expect, some filmmakers have explored other possibilities.

Graphic and Rhythmic Possibilities

Films using abstract or associational form have emphasized the graphic and rhythmic dimensions of editing. Instead of joining shot 1 to shot 2 to present a story, you could join them on the basis of purely graphic or rhythmic qualities, independent of the time and space they represent. In films such as *Anticipation of the Night, Scenes from Under Childhood,* and *Western History,* experimentalist Stan Brakhage uses purely graphic means of joining shot to shot. Continuities and contrasts of light, texture, and shape motivate the editing. Similarly, parts of Bruce Conner's *Cosmic Ray, A Movie,* and *Report* cut together newsreel footage, old film clips, film leader, and black frames on the basis of graphic patterns of movement, direction, and speed.

6.142

6.143

6.144

6.145

6.142–6.145 Graphic matching in narrative cinema. In *An Autumn Afternoon,* Ozu cuts from one man drinking sake (6.142) to another in a very similar costume doing the same thing (6.143). In *Ohayo,* Ozu creates a playful graphic match by cutting from a clothesline with a bright red sweater in the upper left (6.144) to an interior with a red lampshade in the same position (6.145).

6.141 Single-frame filming. This strip of film shows the one-frame shots in Breer's *Fist Fight.* Onscreen, they create a pulsating flicker of barely discernible images.

CONNECT TO THE BLOG
www.davidbordwell.net/blog

Early Japanese swordplay movies display some daring rhythmic editing, as we demonstrate in "Bando on the run."

Many nonnarrative films have emphasized editing rhythm over the images themselves. *Single-frame films* (in which each shot is only one frame long) are the most extreme examples of this concentration on rhythm. Two famous examples are Peter Kubelka's *Schwechater* and Robert Breer's *Fist Fight* **(6.141).** Other avant-garde experiments coordinate editing rhythm with abstract graphics, as we'll see with *Ballet mécanique* in Chapter 10.

The graphic and rhythmic possibilities of editing haven't been neglected in narrative film, either. In Busby Berkeley's elaborate dance numbers in *42nd Street, Gold Diggers of 1933, Footlight Parade, Gold Diggers of 1935,* and *Dames,* the story periodically grinds to a halt, and the film presents intricate choreography that highlights geometrical configurations of dancers and background (4.146, from *42nd Street*). More complex is the graphic editing of Yasujiro Ozu. Ozu's cutting is often dictated by a much more precise graphic continuity than we find in the classical continuity style. He playfully created close graphic matches on movement, position, and color **(6.142–6.145).**

Some silent filmmakers experimented with vigorous rhythmic cutting. In such films as Abel Gance's *La Roue,* Jean Epstein's *Coeur fidèle* and *La Glace à trois faces,* and Alexandre Volkoff's *Kean,* accelerated editing renders the tempo of an onrushing train, a whirling carousel, a racing automobile, and a drunken dance. We can find strong passages of rhythmic editing in sound cinema, too, from 1930s films such as Rouben Mamoulian's *Love Me Tonight* and René Clair's *Le Million* to later films—for example, *Assault on Precinct 13* and *The Terminator.* Pulsating rhythmic editing is prominent in films influenced by music videos, such as *Moulin Rouge.*

6.146

6.147

6.148

6.146–6.148 **Mixing continuity cues and discontinuity.** At one point in *Mon Oncle d'Amérique*, René's pesky office mate calls to him (6.146). Resnais cuts to a shot of Jean Gabin (René's favorite star) in an older film, turning in reverse shot (6.147), as if he were replying to the man. Only then does Resnais supply a shot of René turning to meet his questioner (6.148). The film doesn't definitely present the Gabin shot as a fantasy image. We can't tell whether René imagines himself as his favorite star, or whether the film's narration draws the comparison independent of René's state of mind.

Spatial and Temporal Discontinuity

How might you tell a story without adhering to the continuity rules? One option is to use spatial continuity in ambiguous ways. In *Mon Oncle d'Amérique*, Alain Resnais interrupts the stories of his three main characters with shots of each character's favorite movie star, taken from French films of the 1940s. In some scenes, the cutting relies on continuity cues but uses them to create a discontinuity that arouses some uncertainty in the viewer (**6.146–6.148**).

More drastically, a filmmaker may violate or ignore the 180° system. The editing choices of filmmakers Jacques Tati and Yasujiro Ozu are based on what we might call 360° space. Instead of an axis of action that dictates that the camera be placed within an imaginary semicircle, these filmmakers work as if the action were not a line but a point at the center of a circle and as if the camera could be placed at any point on the circumference. In *Mr. Hulot's Holiday, Play Time,* and *Traffic,* Tati systematically films from almost every side; edited together, the shots present multiple spatial perspectives on a single event. Similarly, Ozu's scenes construct a 360° space that produces what the continuity style would consider grave editing errors. Ozu's films often do not yield consistent relative positions, eyeline matches, and screen directions (**6.149, 6.150**).

6.149

6.150

6.149–6.150 **Ozu's 360° editing system.** One of the gravest sins in the classical continuity style is to match on action while breaking the line, yet Ozu does this comfortably in *Early Summer.* He cuts on the grandfather's gesture of drinking (6.149) to a view from the opposite side (6.150).

Are such cuts confusing? Defenders of the standard continuity system would say yes. But anyone who has seen films by Ozu or Tati can testify that their stories don't become unintelligible. These and other directors have found ways to keep the plot developments clear while also recalibrating our perception of space and time. Historically the continuity system offers one effective way to tell a story, but artistically, it isn't a necessity.

Apart from breaking or ignoring the 180° system, there are two other major tactics of discontinuity. One is the **jump cut.** Though this term is used in various ways, one primary meaning is this. When you cut together two shots of the same subject, if the shots differ only slightly in angle or composition, there will be a noticeable jump on the screen. Instead of appearing as two shots of the subject, the result looks as if some frames have been cut out of a single shot (**6.151, 6.152**). Many filmmakers believe that jump cuts can be avoided by shifting the camera at least 30 degrees from shot to shot (the so-called *30° rule*).

Even though jump cuts skip over some moments, they remain different from more common elliptical cuts. We saw an instance earlier, in the shots showing Wendy sitting in two positions on her cell bunk (6.136, 6.137). Those shots present two distinct angles on the subject, respecting the 30° rule. A jump cut, however, shows the action from one angle or two very similar ones.

Jump cuts are quite noticeable and were long considered amateurish mistakes. But audiences eventually accepted them, although not in the doses that Godard supplied. Filmmakers now may use jump cuts in montage sequences and during moments of surprise, violence, or psychological disturbance (**6.153, 6.154**).

6.151

6.152

6.153

6.154

6.151–6.154 Jump cuts then and now. Jean-Luc Godard's *Breathless* used jump cuts freely. A cut from this shot of Patricia (6.151) to the next one (6.152), creates a jarring effect, as if some frames had been dropped. From the first sequence onward, Ridley Scott's *Matchstick Men* uses jump cuts to suggest the neuroses that plague a swindler during everyday tasks like washing the dishes (6.153–6.154).

6.155

6.156

6.157

6.158

6.159

6.155–6.159 Nondiegetic editing. In *Fury,* Lang cuts from housewives gossiping (6.155) to clucking hens (6.156). A diegetic shot of Henri in *La Chinoise* (6.157) is followed by nondiegetic shots of the lion bed of King Tutankhamen (6.158) and his golden mask (6.159). Do the relics corroborate or challenge what Henri says?

A second sort of continuity disruption is created by the **nondiegetic insert.** Here the filmmaker cuts from the scene to a metaphorical or symbolic shot that doesn't belong to the space and time of the narrative **(6.155, 6.156)**. In Sergei Eisenstein's *Strike,* the massacre of workers is intercut with the slaughter of a bull. In Godard's *La Chinoise,* Henri tells an anecdote about ancient Egyptians, who thought that "their language was the language of the gods." As he says this **(6.157),** Godard cuts in two close-ups of relics from the tomb of King Tutankhamen **(6.158, 6.159)**. As nondiegetic inserts, coming from outside the story world, these prompt the spectator to search for implicit meanings and ask if the relics corroborate what Henri says.

There are still other alternatives to classical continuity, especially with respect to time. Although the classical approach to order and frequency of story events may seem the best option, it's only the most familiar. Story events don't have to be edited in 1-2-3 order.

Modern audiences have become accustomed to scenes that are interrupted by brief flashbacks. But some editing choices trigger greater uncertainty about exactly when something is taking place. Resnais's *La Guerre est finie* interrupts scenes cut in conventional continuity by images that may represent flashbacks, or fantasy episodes, or even future events. In Michael Haneke's *Caché* after a shot of a building, we see a boy looking out a window. This recalls the POV shots of Jeff looking at his neighbors in *Rear Window* (6.96, 6.97, 6.99–6.102). But in *Caché* the apparently logical connection is revealed to be false **(6.160, 6.161)**.

We've seen that editing can replay past scenes or Jackie Chan stunts (6.49–6.51). But filmmakers can repeat events to more disruptive effect. In *La Guerre est finie,* a future funeral is depicted in alternative ways, with the protagonist either present or absent. The escape sequence in Godard's *Pierrot le fou* not only scrambles the order of the shots but also plays with frequency by repeating one movement, Ferdinand jumping into the car (and showing it differently each time) **(6.162–6.165)**. These editing choices block our normal expectations about story action and force us to concentrate on piecing together the film's narrative.

6.160

6.161

6.160–6.161 **Ambiguous POV editing.** *Caché* repeatedly shows a luxurious apartment building seen from across the street. After one nighttime view (6.160), there is a two-second shot of a boy watching, also at night (6.161). Later we'll learn that the editing has misled us severely.

6.162

6.163

6.164

6.165

6.162–6.165 **Juggling temporal order and frequency.** In *Pierrot le fou,* Ferdinand jumps into the car as Marianne pulls away (6.162), but the next shot flashes back to them fleeing their apartment (6.163). After they seem to have escaped (6.164), earlier phases of the action are repeated, including Ferdinand's jump into the car (6.165).

The editing may take liberties with story duration as well. Although complete continuity and ellipsis are the most common ways of rendering duration, expansion—stretching a moment out, making screen time greater than story time—remains a distinct possibility. François Truffaut uses such expansions in *Jules and Jim* to underscore narrative turning points, as when the heroine Catherine lifts her veil or jumps off an embankment into a river.

Filmmakers have reworked some of the most basic tenets of the continuity system. We've indicated, for example, that a match on action strongly suggests that time continues across the cut. Yet Alain Resnais creates an impossible continuity of motion in *Last Year at Marienbad* (**6.166–6.167**). The smooth match on action,

6.166

6.167

6.166–6.167 **The impossible match on action.** In *Last Year at Marienbad,* small groups of guests are standing around the hotel lobby. A medium shot frames a blonde woman beginning to turn away from the camera (6.166). In the middle of her turn, there is a cut to her, still turning but in a different setting (6.167).

along with the woman's graphically matched position in the frame, implies that her head turns continuously, yet the change of setting contradicts this impression. As we'll see in Chapter 10, experimental films push ambiguous or contradictory editing even further.

Over time, audiences can become accustomed to discontinuities in narrative contexts. But with the jump cut, the nondiegetic insert, and the inconsistent match on action, temporal dislocations can push away from traditional notions of storytelling and create ambiguous relations among shots. These ambiguities needn't confuse us: they can stir our imaginations. Sergei Eisenstein's classic *October* provides many good examples.

CONNECT TO THE BLOG
www.davidbordwell.net/blog

We visit some striking editing decisions in "Some cuts I have known and loved."

CREATIVE DECISIONS

Discontinuity Editing in October

For many Soviet filmmakers of the 1920s, editing didn't simply serve the narrative progression, as in the continuity system that Kuleshov so much admired. Editing could be a tool for organizing the entire form of the film. Eisenstein's *Strike, Potemkin, October,* and *Old and New* were all built on the basis of certain editing devices—sometimes recruited to advance a plot, but at other times serving to comment on the action and suggest implicit meanings.

Eisenstein understood the continuity system quite well, but he sought to go beyond it. He believed that all sorts of clashes from shot to shot would prod the spectator to engage more actively with the film. Discontinuities of space and time could stir the spectator's senses by creating a sharp impact. They could arouse feelings, as viewers began to see the emotional connections among shots. And certain kinds of discontinuities could spur the spectator to reflect on the themes that Eisenstein sought to communicate.

No longer bound by conventional dramaturgy, Eisenstein's films roam freely through time and space. Crosscutting, eyeline cuts, and other devices of the continuity system are pushed in new directions, plunging us into a realm that could only exist on film. A short passage from *October* can illustrate how he uses editing discontinuities.

The sequence is the third one in the film (and comprises over 125 shots!). The story action is simple. The Provisional Government has taken power in Russia after the February Revolution, but instead of withdrawing from World War I, the government has kept its troops on the front. This maneuver has left the Russian people no better off than under the czar they deposed. In classical Hollywood cinema, this story might have been shown through a montage sequence of newspaper headlines smoothly linked to a scene showing a protagonist complaining that the Provisional

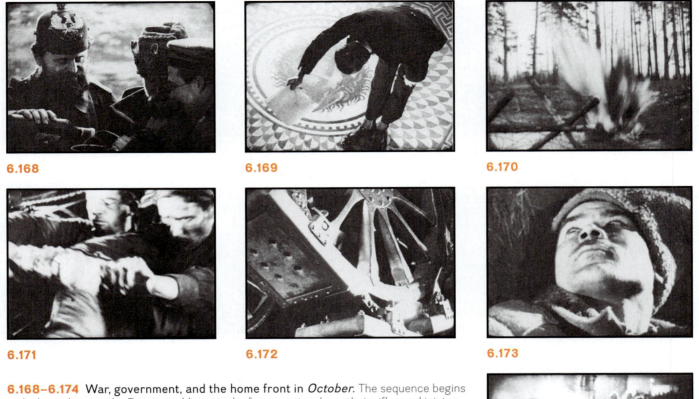

6.168   **6.169**   **6.170**

6.171   **6.172**   **6.173**

6.168–6.174 War, government, and the home front in *October*. The sequence begins with shots showing the Russian soldiers on the front casting down their rifles and joining the German soldiers. Soon the former enemies are drinking and laughing together (6.168). Eisenstein then cuts back to the Provisional Government, where a flunky extends a document to an unseen ruler (6.169); this pledges the government to continue the war. The soldiers' fraternization is suddenly disrupted by a bombardment (6.170). The soldiers run back to the trenches and huddle as dirt and bomb fragments rain down on them. Eisenstein then cuts to a cannon being lowered off an assembly line by factory workers (6.171). For a time, the narration crosscuts the descending cannon (6.172) with the soldiers (6.173). In the last section of the sequence, the shots of the cannon are crosscut with hungry women and children standing in breadlines in the snow (6.174). The sequence ends with two intertitles: "All as before . . . "/ "Hunger and war."

6.174

Government has not solved people's problems. *October*'s protagonist, though, is not one person but the entire Russian people, and the film does not usually use dialogue scenes to present its story points. Rather, *October* seeks to go beyond a straightforward presentation of story events by making the viewer actively connect those events and reflect on their implications. So the film confronts us with a disorienting and disjunctive set of images **(6.168–6.174).**

Not only does *October* lack an individual protagonist; this sequence exploits spatial and temporal discontinuities. Although at times the 180° rule is respected (especially in the shots of women and children), never does Eisenstein introduce his situations with establishing shots. Reestablishing shots are rare, and the major components of the locales are seldom shown together in one shot. On the whole, the Kuleshov effect rules. (No surprise: Eisenstein studied under Kuleshov.)

The organizing principle of the sequence is crosscutting. Eisenstein alternates images of battlefield and government, factory and street. In the continuity system, crosscutting usually indicates that different actions are taking place simultaneously. But *October*'s crosscutting doesn't specify when the events are occurring. The women and children are seen at night, but it's daylight on the military front. Do the battlefield events take place before or after or during the women's vigil? We

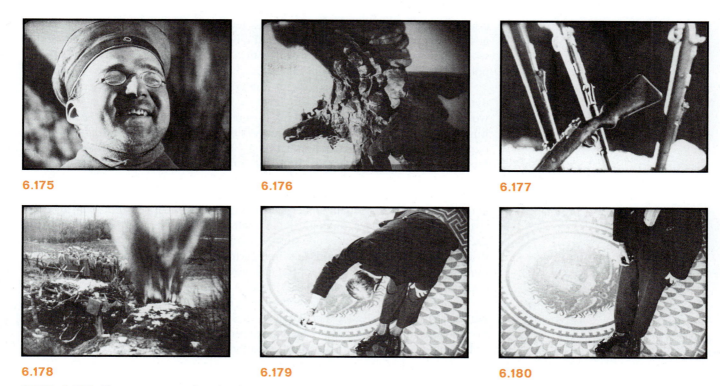

6.175   **6.176**   **6.177**

6.178   **6.179**   **6.180**

6.175–6.180 The government breaks the peace. Eisenstein cuts from a laughing German soldier facing right (6.175) to a menacing eagle statue, facing left, at the government headquarters (6.176). A static shot of rifles thrust into the snow (6.177) cuts to a long shot of a bursting shell (6.178). The impact is enhanced by a bold jump cut: The flunky is bowing (6.179), but suddenly he is standing up (6.180).

can't say. Eisenstein's crosscutting is primarily emotional and conceptual. He's less concerned with presenting a linear story than arousing indignation at government policy and sympathy for its victims.

For example, to dramatize how the government prevents men meeting peaceably, Eisenstein shatters the friendship of the soldiers with disruptive cuts **(6.175–6.180).** The soldiers fraternize in fairly continuous duration, but the Provisional Government's behavior is given in drastic ellipses. This permits Eisenstein to identify the government as the unseen cause of the bombardment that ruptures the peace. This implication is reinforced by the way the first explosions are followed by the jump cut of the government flunky (6.179–6.180). Ellipsis takes on another role when the editing dramatizes the suffering of the women and children waiting in line. Instead of a gradual wasting away, we get abrupt decline: First we see them standing, then later lying pitiably on the ground.

Thinking like a filmmaker: How would you dramatize the idea that the government oppresses its people? Eisenstein does it daringly, by creating a visual metaphor. Once the government orders the bombardment of the front, the soldiers are huddling under the barrage. This already suggests that the government, not the German army, is the real enemy. Eisenstein takes things further by showing men crushed by the war machine. Thanks to editing, shots of the cannon slowly descending are contrasted with shots of the men crouching in the trenches (6.172, 6.173). The graphic clash of directions is reinforced by a false eyeline match. The soldier looks upward, as if he could see the lowering cannon, even though he and the cannon are in entirely separate places. By showing the factory workers lowering the cannon (6.171), the cutting links the captive soldiers to the proletariat. Finally, as the cannon hits the ground, Eisenstein crosscuts images of it with the shots of the starving families of the soldiers and the workers. They, too, are oppressed, literally pressed down, by the government machine. As the cannon wheels hit the floor ponderously, Einstein cuts to the women's feet in the snow. The machine's heaviness is linked by titles ("one pound," "half a pound") to the steady starvation of the women and children. Eisenstein's editing discontinuities encourage us to build up a political commentary on the story events.

Graphic discontinuities recur throughout *October,* especially in scenes of dynamic action, and they hit our eyes more forcefully than neatly matched shots would. To watch an Eisenstein film is to submit oneself to percussive graphic editing. But that editing also gives us powerful images—friendly soldiers, faceless bureaucrats, suffering women and children—that stir our emotions. By refusing to focus on one protagonist, Eisenstein moves masses of people to the fore.

But he did not want to stop with mere sympathy. *October* tries to show the underlying causes of the masses' suffering more directly than the traditional dramatic conflict between individualized heroes and villains could. Eisenstein's editing constructs correspondences, analogies, and contrasts that ask us to *interpret* the story events. The interpretation is not simply handed to the viewer; rather, the editing discontinuities push us to work out implicit meanings. By assembling the shots in our minds, we grasp his idea that the new government is no different from the old one and that ordinary people are sacrificed to an unfeeling political regime.

No one was more aware of the multitude of creative decisions involved in editing than Eisenstein. He saw that classical continuity would not achieve his purposes. So he chose to make a film in which discontinuities of graphic elements, time, and space could prod the spectator into sympathy and thought. In the process he demonstrated that there are powerful alternatives to the principles of continuity editing.

SUMMARY

When any two shots are joined, we can ask several questions:

1. How are the shots graphically continuous or discontinuous?

2. What rhythmic relations are created?

3. Are the shots spatially continuous? If not, what creates the discontinuity? (Crosscutting? Ambiguous cues?) If the shots are spatially continuous, how does the 180° system create the continuity?

4. Are the shots temporally continuous? If so, what creates the continuity? (For example, matches on action?) If not, what creates the discontinuity? (Ellipsis? Overlapping cuts?)

More generally, we can ask the question we ask of every film technique: How does this technique *function* with respect to the film's narrative form? Does the film use editing to lay out the narrative space, time, and cause-effect chain in the manner of classical continuity? How do editing patterns emphasize facial expressions, dialogue, or setting? Do editing patterns withhold narrative information? In general, how does editing contribute to the viewer's experience of the film?

Some practical hints: You can learn to notice editing in several ways. If you are having trouble noticing cuts, try watching a film or video and tapping each time a shot changes. Once you recognize editing easily, watch any film with the sole purpose of observing one editing aspect—say, the way space is presented, or the control of graphics or time. Sensitize yourself to rhythmic editing by noting cutting rates; tapping out the tempo of the cuts can help.

Watching 1930s and 1940s American films can introduce you to classical continuity style; try to predict what shot will come next in a sequence. (You'll be surprised at how often you're right.) When you watch a film on video, try turning off the sound; editing patterns become more apparent this way. When there's a violation of continuity, ask yourself whether it is accidental or serves a purpose. When you see a film that does not obey classical continuity principles, search for its unique editing patterns. Use the slow-motion, freeze, and reverse controls on a video player to analyze a film sequence as this chapter has done. (Almost any film will do.) In such ways as these, you can considerably increase your awareness and understanding of the power of editing.

RECOMMENDED DVD AND BLU-RAY SUPPLEMENTS

Watching people editing is not very exciting, and this technique usually gets short shrift in DVD supplements. There are some exceptions, however.

Each film in the *Lord of the Rings* trilogy contains an "Editorial" section, and *The Fellowship of the Ring* includes an "Editorial Demonstration." This presents an excerpt from the Council of Elrond scene, then displays the raw footage from six cameras before showing how sections from each setup were fitted together. Incidentally, this Elrond scene can give you good practice in noticing continuity. The interactions among many characters are stitched together with correct eyeline matches and occasional matches on action. (Imagine how confusing the conversations could have been if no attention had been paid to eyeline direction.)

The DVD release of Lodge Kerrigan's *Keane* includes not only the theatrical version but a completely recut version of the film by producer Steven Soderbergh. Soderbergh calls his cut his "commentary track" for the disc.

In "Tell Us What You See," the camera operator for *A Hard Day's Night* discusses continuity of screen direction, and in "Every Head She's Had the Pleasure to Know," the film's hairdresser talks about having to keep hair length consistent for continuity.

"15-Minute Film School with Robert Rodriguez," one of the *Sin City* supplements, provides a clear instance of the Kuleshov effect in use. Although Rodriguez does not use that term, he demonstrates how he could cut together shots of characters interacting with one another via eyeline matches even though several of the actors never worked together during the filming. Rodriguez's commentary for *El Mariachi* (Sony "Special Edition") also points out examples of the Kuleshov effect.

A brief section of *Toy Story*'s supplements entitled "Layout Tricks" demonstrates how continuity editing principles govern animation as well as live-action filming. In a shot/reverse-shot sequence involving Buzz and Woody, the filmmakers diagram (as we do on p. 233) where a camera can be placed to maintain the axis of action (or "stage line," as it is termed here). The segment also shows how a camera movement can be used to shift the axis of action just before an important character enters the scene.

"Destination Yuma," a supplement for *3:10 to Yuma*, contains an excellent demonstration of multiple-camera shooting for a scene of a stagecoach flipping over. The short runs the footage from different cameras and then runs the scene as it was finally cut.

7.6–7.7 Subjective silence. In *Babel*, when the deaf teenage girl enters the disco, the club music is about to climax (7.6). Instead, it drops out when we cut to her optical point-of-view on the boy she's following (7.7). Instead of subjective sound, we get subjective silence, and this sharply dramatizes her isolation from what is happening around her.

the introduction of sound cinema, the infinity of visual possibilities was joined by the infinity of acoustic events.

Fundamentals of Film Sound

Film sound can include any mixture of speech, music, and noise. Filmmakers make decisions about the types and density of sounds as well as their properties, including loudness and pitch.

Perceptual Properties

Several aspects of film sound are familiar to us from everyday experience.

Loudness   The sound we hear results from vibrations in the air. The amplitude, or breadth, of the vibrations produces our sense of *loudness,* or volume. Film sound constantly manipulates volume. A dialogue between a soft-spoken character and a blustery one is characterized as much by the difference in volume as by the substance of the talk. In many films, a long shot of a busy street is accompanied by loud traffic noises, but when two people meet and start to speak, the volume of the traffic drops.

While loudness can be measured in precise acoustic terms, for the listener it's relative. A lengthy passage of high-amplitude sound may not sound as loud as a lower burst of sound after a stretch of silence. In *Capote,* a killer's confession is presented in a nearly quiet scene, with only the wind audible. That ambience makes the shotgun blast that follows seem exceptionally loud. As with mise-en-scene and the tonal qualities of the image, the soundtrack seizes our attention through contrast.

Loudness is also related to perceived distance. All other things being equal, the louder the sound, the closer we take it to be. This sort of assumption seems to be at work in the street traffic example already mentioned: the couple's dialogue, being closer to us, is sensed as louder, while the traffic noise recedes to the background. In addition, a film may startle the viewer by exploiting abrupt and extreme shifts in volume (usually called changes in *dynamics*), as when a quiet scene is interrupted by a very loud noise. Changes in loudness may be combined with cutting or camera movement to reinforce our sense of moving toward or away from the source of the noise (**Figs. 7.8–7.10**).

Pitch   The frequency of sound vibrations affects *pitch,* or the perceived highness or lowness of the sound. Certain instruments, such as a tuning fork, can produce

7.8

7.9

7.10

7.8–7.10 Volume as a cue for distance. A hiker is trapped at the bottom of a canyon in *127 Hours*. One shot begins on a high-angle shot of him shouting for help (7.8). As the camera pulls quickly up and away from him, his cries diminish in volume (7.9), until the shot ends on an extreme-long view of the desert, with the canyon a dark line in the landscape and the hiker's voice no longer audible (7.10). Director Danny Boyle uses sound perspective, timed with drastic changes of shot scale, to dramatize how hopeless the young man's plight is.

pure tones, but most sounds, in life and on film, are complex tones, batches of different frequencies. Nevertheless, pitch plays a useful role in helping us pick out distinct sounds in a film. It helps us distinguish music and speech from noises. It also serves to distinguish among objects. Thumps can suggest hollow objects, while higher-pitched sounds, like those of jingle bells, suggest smoother or harder surfaces and denser objects.

Pitch can also serve more specific purposes. When a young boy tries to speak in a man's deep voice and fails, as in *How Green Was My Valley*, the joke is based primarily on pitch. Marlene Dietrich's vocal delivery often depends on a long upward-gliding intonation that makes a statement sound like a question. In the coronation scene of *Ivan the Terrible*, Part I, a court singer with a deep bass voice begins a song of praise to Ivan, and each phrase rises dramatically in pitch **(7.11–7.13)**.

7.11

7.12

7.13

7.11–7.13 Pitch synchronized with cutting. In *Ivan the Terrible*, Eisenstein emphasizes changes in vocal pitch by cutting from a medium-long shot (7.11) to a medium shot (7.12) to a close-up of the singer (7.13).

When Bernard Herrmann obtained the effects of shrill, birdlike shrieking in Hitchcock's *Psycho,* even many musicians could not recognize the source: violins played at extraordinarily high pitch.

As Julianne Moore was planning her performance as the protagonist of Todd Haynes's *Safe,* she took pitch and other vocal qualities into account:

> My first key to her was her voice, her vocal patterns. I started with a very typical Southern California speech pattern. It's almost a sing-song rhythm, you know—it's referred to as the "Valley quality" that travelled across the country and became a universal American vocal pattern. It was important to me that her voice would have that kind of melody to it. And then I would put question marks at the end of the sentence all the time—that way she never makes a statement; it makes her very unsure and very undefined. I also went above my own chords, because I wanted the sensation of her voice not being connected at all to her body—that's why her voice is so high. This is someone who's completely disconnected from any kind of physicality, from any sense of being herself, from really knowing herself. In that sense, I guess the vocal choices are somewhat metaphorical.

Timbre   The harmonic components of sound give it a certain color, or tone quality—what musicians call *timbre.* When we call someone's voice nasal or a musical tone mellow, we're referring to timbre. Timbre is actually a less fundamental acoustic parameter than amplitude or frequency, but it's indispensable in describing the texture or "feel" of a sound. In everyday life, the recognition of a familiar sound is largely a matter of various aspects of timbre.

Filmmakers manipulate timbre continually. Timbre can help articulate portions of the sound track, as when it differentiates musical instruments from one another. Timbre also comes forward on certain occasions, as in the clichéd use of oleaginous saxophone tones behind seduction scenes. More subtly, in the opening sequence of Rouben Mamoulian's *Love Me Tonight,* people starting the day on a street pass a musical rhythm from object to object—a broom, a carpet beater—and the humor of the number springs in part from the very different timbres of the objects. In preparing the sound track for Peter Weir's *Witness,* the editors drew on sounds recorded 20 or more years before, so that the less modern timbre of the older recordings would evoke the rustic seclusion of the Amish community.

Loudness, pitch, and timbre interact to define the overall sonic texture of a film. For example, these qualities enable us to recognize different characters' voices. Both John Wayne and James Stewart speak slowly, but Wayne's voice tends to be deeper and gruffer than Stewart's querulous drawl. This difference works to great advantage in *The Man Who Shot Liberty Valance,* where their characters are sharply contrasted. In *The Wizard of Oz,* the disparity between the public image of the Wizard and the old charlatan who rigs it up is marked by the booming bass of the huge green head and the old man's higher, softer, more quavering voice. During an action sequence, the threshold for loudness is raised, so the film's sound designer may have to introduce noises of different frequencies or textures—a whining bullet during a rumbling car chase, for example—to make sure that certain details aren't drowned out.

These basic sound qualities can also shape our experience of a film as a whole. *Citizen Kane,* for example, offers a wide range of sound manipulations. Echo chambers alter timbre and volume. A motif is formed by the inability of Kane's wife, Susan, to sing pitches accurately. Moreover, in *Citizen Kane,* the plot's shifts between times and places are covered by continuing a sound thread and varying the basic acoustics. A shot of Kane applauding dissolves to a shot of a crowd applauding (a shift in volume and timbre). Leland beginning a sentence in the street cuts to Kane finishing the sentence in an auditorium, his voice magnified by loudspeakers (a shift in volume, timbre, and pitch).

Sound processes create wider ranges of frequency and volume, as well as crisper timbres than filmmakers could achieve in the studio years. Today sound editors can individualize voice or noise to a surprising degree. For *The Thin Red*

> " The Empire spaceship sounded a certain way as compared to the Imperial fleet; that was a deliberate style change. Everybody in the Empire had shrieking, howling, ghostlike, frightening sounds. . . . You hear it—you jump with fear. Whereas the rebel forces had more junky-sounding planes and spaceships. They weren't quite as powerful; they tended to pop and sputter more."
>
> —Ben Burtt, sound editor, *Star Wars*

Line, every character's distinctive breathing sounds were recorded for use as ambient noise. Randy Thoms, sound designer for *Cast Away,* sought to characterize different sorts of wind—breezes from the open sea, winds in a cave. Sound even announces a shift in wind direction crucial to one of the hero's plans. "We can use the wind in a very musical way," Thoms notes.

Choosing, Altering, and Combining Sounds

Sound in the cinema is of three types: speech, music, and noise (usually called *sound effects*). Occasionally, a sound may cross categories—Is a yell speech or noise? Is electronic music noise?—and filmmakers have freely exploited these ambiguities. In *Psycho,* when a woman screams, we expect to hear a voice but instead hear violins. Nevertheless, in most cases, the distinctions hold. Now that we have an idea of some basic acoustic properties, how are speech, music, and noise selected and combined for specific purposes?

Choosing and Manipulating Sounds

A soundtrack, much like the image track, is created through selection and assembly. Just as you can pick the best image from several shots, you can choose what exact bit of sound will best serve the purpose. As we saw in earlier chapters, a shot may be rephotographed or recolored. Similarly, a bit of sound can be processed to change its acoustic qualities. You can link images or superimpose them; you can join any two sounds end to end, or place one over another. The sound track demands as much choice and control as does the visual track.

Sometimes the sound track is conceived before the image track. Animated cartoons typically record music, dialogue, and sound effects before the images are filmed, so the figures will be synchronized with the sound frame by frame. For the adventures of Bugs Bunny and Daffy Duck, Carl Stalling created frantically paced jumbles of familiar tunes, weird noises, and distinctive voices. Experimental films also frequently build their images around a preexisting sound track. Some filmmakers have even thought that abstract form in film is a sort of "visual music" and have tried to create a synthesis of the two media.

Many sound effects are generated by the Foley process, which involves creating noises tailored to the film. In a sonically clean studio, experts record people walking, pouring drinks, splashing in mud, rubbing sandpaper—in short, any events that put human movement in contact with surfaces. Foley artists, who often collect different shoes, fabrics, and car doors, also devise imaginative equivalents. Animated cartoons may have over half their soundtrack created by Foley. But not all the sounds we hear are generated from scratch. Editors tend to build their own collections of sounds that intrigue them, or they reuse music or effects stored in sound libraries. Most famous is the "Wilhelm scream," first heard in a 1951 American film when an alligator bites off a cowboy's arm. The scream was recycled in *Star Wars, Raiders of the Lost Ark, Reservoir Dogs, Transformers,* and over a hundred other films.

At the limit, wholly new sounds may be made of old ones. The noises emitted by the demonically possessed girl in *The Exorcist* blended screams, animal thrashings, and English spoken backward. To create the roar of a *Tyrannosaurus rex* for *Jurassic Park,* sound engineers fused a tiger's roar, a baby elephant's trumpeting at midrange frequencies, and an alligator's growl for the lower tones. To characterize a runaway train as a primal force, *Unstoppable* gave it an auditory identity derived from the sounds of beasts. After smashing another train in its path, the rogue train even lets out a bellow of triumph.

Selection Guides Our Attention

As you read this, you are attending to words on the page and (to various degrees) ignoring certain stimuli that reach your ears. But if you close your eyes and listen keenly, you'll become aware of background sounds—traffic, footsteps, distant voices. You know that if you set up a

> " Too many films seem essentially designed to be heard in the mixing studios. I always fight against recording every single footstep, and would rather lose the sound of people settling into armchairs, etc., and fade out a particular atmosphere sound once the emotional impact has been achieved, even at the cost of realism. You have to know how to play with silence, to treat sound like music."
>
> —Bernard Tavernier, director

> " We're always looking for things that squeak or clank or make springy, sproingy noises. If you go to a swap meet or garage sale, you're always putting your ear up to things and listening. The weirdest thing is when you listen to things in the grocery store—tap on vegetables and rustle them and crunch them a little."
>
> —Marnie Moore, Foley artist, *Boogie Nights, Jarhead*

> "We were going for a documentary feel. We came up with a way for the loop group actors to say lines in a way we called 'nondescript dialogue.' They said lines, but they didn't say the actual words. If you put it behind people speaking, you just think it's people talking offscreen, but your ear isn't drawn to it. It would just lie there as a bed, and you can play it relatively loudly and it just fits in with the scenes."
>
> —Hugh Waddell, ADR supervisor, on *The Thin Red Line*

microphone and recorder in what seems to be a quiet environment, those normally unnoticed sounds can become obtrusive. The microphone is unselective; like the camera lens, it doesn't automatically filter out what's distracting.

As with other film techniques, sound guides the viewer's attention. Normally, the sound track is clarified and simplified so that important material stands out. Dialogue, as a transmitter of story information, is usually recorded and reproduced for maximum clarity. Important lines should not have to compete with music or background noise. Sound effects are usually less important than speech. They supply an overall sense of a realistic environment and are seldom noticed; if they were missing, however, the silence would be distracting. Music is usually subordinate to dialogue as well, entering during pauses in conversation or in passages without dialogue.

Dialogue doesn't always rank highest in importance, though. Sound effects are usually central to action sequences, while music can dominate dance scenes, transitional sequences, or emotion-laden moments without dialogue. And some filmmakers have shifted the weight conventionally assigned to each type of sound. Charlie Chaplin's *City Lights* and *Modern Times* eliminate dialogue, letting sound effects and music come to the fore. The films of Jacques Tati and Jean-Marie Straub retain dialogue but still place great emphasis on sound effects. In Robert Bresson's *A Man Escaped*, music and noise fill out a sparse dialogue track by evoking offscreen space and creating thematic associations.

By choosing only certain sounds, the filmmaker guides our perception of the action. In one scene from Jacques Tati's *Mr. Hulot's Holiday*, vacationers at a resort hotel are relaxing (**7.14**). Early in the scene, the guests in the foreground are murmuring quietly, but Hulot's Ping-Pong game is louder; the sound cues us to watch Hulot. Later in the scene, however, the same Ping-Pong game makes no sound at all, and our attention is drawn to the muttering cardplayers in the foreground. The presence and absence of the sound of the Ping-Pong ball guides our expectations. If you start to notice how such selection of sound shapes our perception, you will also notice that filmmakers often use sound quite unrealistically, to shift our attention to what is narratively or visually important.

Our scene from *Mr. Hulot's Holiday* also points up the importance of how a chosen sound may have its acoustic qualities transformed for a particular purpose. Thanks to a manipulation of volume and timbre, the Ping-Pong game gains in vividness. When two sounds are of the same frequency or loudness, contemporary sound designers freely adjust one to make it stand out more clearly. During the jungle chase in *Indiana Jones and the Kingdom of the Crystal Skull*, the skull's thump was altered. "I changed its pitch so that it would coexist with the music," sound designer Ben Burtt explained.

Nowadays, film sound is normally reprocessed to yield exactly the qualities desired. A *dry recording* of the sound in a fairly nonreflective space will be manipulated electronically to yield the desired effect. For instance, if you chose to present Amanda's dialogue as heard on Jim's phone, her voice would probably have been treated with filters to make it more tinny and muffled. (In Hollywood parlance, this is called "futzing" the sound.) The almost nonstop rock-and-roll music of *American Graffiti* used two recordings of the music. A dry one was prepared for moments when the music was to dominate the scene and had to be of high quality. A more ambient one for background noise was derived from a tape recorder simply playing the tune in a backyard.

7.14 Sound present, then absent. In *Mr. Hulot's Holiday*, in the foreground, guests quietly play cards while in the depth of the shot, Mr. Hulot is frantically playing Ping-Pong. Sometimes we hear the ball, sometimes not.

Sound Mixing   Guiding the viewer's attention, then, depends on selecting and reworking particular sounds. It also depends on **mixing,** or combining them. It is useful to think of the sound track not as a set of discrete sound bits but as an ongoing *stream* of auditory information. Each sound takes its place in a specific pattern. This pattern both links events in time and layers them at any given moment.

The auditory stream goes beyond linking one line of dialogue or bit of noise to another. It involves a constant set of decisions about how it meshes with the image track. For example, there are many fine-grained choices involved in blending the stream of sound with classical principles of continuity editing.

CREATIVE DECISIONS

Editing Dialogue: To Overlap or Not to Overlap?

It helps to think of the soundtrack as a stream, a current carrying auditory elements to the surface or sinking them out of awareness as time rushes on. One decision that faces the filmmaker involves that current: Should it be choppy or smoothly flowing?

Consider dialogue scenes. Thinking like a filmmaker, we can see that there are many choices about the timing of picture editing. You have to decide when to cut from a shot of A to a shot of B. But another choice is involved, too: How do you cut the dialogue? Editor Tom Rolfe puts it well:

> Is it better to say, "I love you," bang, then cut to the reaction? Or is it better to say, "I love you," hang on it a beat to show the emotion of the person delivering the line, then go for the reaction? It's a matter of choice. Either way, there's a different result for the audience looking at it. Are their sympathies with the guy who said the line, or the girl who said the line? Or is the audience saying, "Don't believe him, he's going to screw you over!" . . . If you find the frame to cut on at that right moment, the audience will be totally satisfied.

There's another alternative. Instead of cutting after the line or holding on the speaker for a beat, you might cut away from the speaker before the line is finished ("I love . . .") to anticipate the reaction of the listener to the final syllables (". . . you!"). Since there are plenty of shot/reverse-shot conversation scenes in movies, and a lot of cutting in those scenes, decision points like these emerge hundreds of times in making most films.

In such situations, filmmakers frequently pick the third option just mentioned, the **dialogue overlap.** In this technique, the filmmaker continues a line of dialogue across a cut, smoothing over the change of shot. During a conversation in John McTiernan's *The Hunt for Red October,* we get the following shots and dialogue:

1. (ms) Over the political officer's shoulder, favoring Captain Ramius **(7.15)**

   Officer: "Captain Tupalev's boat."

   Ramius: "You know Tupalev?"

   Officer: "I know he descends . . ."

2. (ms) Reverse angle over Ramius's shoulder, favoring the officer **(7.16)**

   Officer (continuing): ". . . from aristocracy, and that he was your student. It's rumored he has a special . . ."

3. (mcu) Reverse angle on Ramius **(7.17)**

   Officer (continuing): ". . . place in his heart for you."

   Ramius: "There's little room in Tupalev's heart for anyone but Tupalev."

Here the political officer's chatter provides an auditory continuity that distracts from the shot changes. Moreover, by cutting to a closer view of the listener before a sentence is finished, the sound and editing concentrate our attention on Ramius's response. The principle of dialogue overlap can be used with noise as well. In the

7.15 Shot 1

7.16 Shot 2

7.15–7.17 Dialogue overlap in *The Hunt for Red October*

7.17 Shot 3

Hunt for Red October scene, sounds of a spoon clinking in a tea cup and of papers being riffled also carry over certain cuts, providing a continuous stream of sonic information.

Sometimes the filmmaker wants to introduce more tension. In Fritz Lang's *M*, the city is on edge because a child murderer is at large. An unprepossessing little man urges a little girl to go home, but onlookers suspect him of being the killer. One comes up to him challengingly.

1. (ls) The little man is accosted by a huge one, who asks, "What's it to you where she lives?"

   The first man turns **(7.18)**.

2. (ms) High-angle POV on the little man **(7.19)**.

   Little man: "I?" Although intimidated, he starts to speak.

3. (ms): Low angle POV on the big man **(7.20)**.

   Little man (offscreen): "Excuse me?"

   Big man: "What do you want with that kid?" (pause)

4. (ms) as 2 **(7.21)**.

   Little man (pause): "Absolutely nothing!"

Here the cuts accentuate the suspense evoked by the pauses. In shot 2, the little man takes time to register the danger he's in. When he finally summons up a feeble self-defense ("Excuse me?"), it is heard offscreen. Lang forces us to wait for the ominous question from the thug, which is uttered in full. In shot 4, the little man gets to assert himself fully. After another pause, he defends himself, and his line isn't interrupted by a cut. The pattern of cutting has given his denial a greater weight because we didn't see him speak during shot 3, and shot 4 plays out his entire line.

Lang was perfectly capable of overlapping sound across his cuts. *M* does it throughout; in fact, the next line the little man speaks initiates a dialogue overlap. By aligning certain cuts with dramatic pauses in the dialogue, Lang gives special

7.18 Shot 1

7.19 Shot 2

7.20 Shot 3

7.21 Shot 4

7.18–7.21 Cuts emphasize pauses in dialogue in *M*

weight to the lines spoken by the thug in shot 3 and his innocent target in shot 4. As usual, different stylistic choices produce different effects onscreen.

Layers and Contrasts   The sounds flow not only in waves but also in layers. We have already seen that in production, combining sounds is usually done after shooting, in the mixing process. The mixer can precisely control the volume, duration, and tone quality of each sound, weaving them in and out, making them momentarily clear or pushing them out of hearing. For example, in *Jurassic Park,* Steven Spielberg manipulates volume unrealistically for purposes of narrative clarity. After a live cow has been lowered into the velociraptors' pen, the South African hunter gives important information about the habits of these predators, and his voice comes through louder than those of characters closer to the camera (**7.22**).

In modern filmmaking, a dozen or more separate tracks may be layered at any moment. The mix can be quite dense. An airport scene may combine the babble of voices, footsteps, luggage trolleys, Muzak, and plane engines. Or the mix can be very sparse, with an occasional sound emerging against a background of total silence. That's what happens in the *M* scene (7.18–7.21), where no ambient sound distracts from the confrontation of the two men. Most cases will fall somewhere between a thick mix and a thin one. In our *Hunt for Red October* scene

7.22 Selective sound volume. In *Jurassic Park,* Hammond and Ellie are closer to the camera than is anything else in the shot, but their dialogue is an unintelligible murmur. In the background, the hunter supplies important information about velociraptors, and that is clearly audible.

CONNECT TO THE BLOG
www.davidbordwell.net/blog

We've been fortunate enough to sit in on some mixing sessions and learn from people who mix sound. See "Christian Bale picks up a rail," "What does a Water Horse sound like?" and "The Boy in the Black Hole."

"For the last few years—since *Blue Velvet,* I think—I have tried to do most of the music before the shoot. I discuss the story with my composer, Angelo Badalamenti, and record all sorts of music that I listen to as I'm shooting the film, either on headphones during dialogue scenes or on loudspeakers, so that the whole crew gets in the right mood. It's a great tool. It's like a compass helping you find the right direction."
—David Lynch, director

(7.15–7.17), a distant throbbing engine and slight brushings of fabric form a muted background to the conversation.

The filmmaker may create a mix in which each sound blends smoothly with the others. This is commonly the case when music and effects are mixed with speech. In classical Hollywood cinema of the 1930s, the musical score may become prominent in moments in which there is no dialogue, and then it's likely to fade unnoticeably down just as the characters begin to talk. (In studio parlance, this is called *sneaking in* and *sneaking out.*) Sometimes the mix will associate sounds evocatively. In *The English Patient,* when the nurse feeds the patient a plum, a distant church bell rings, suggesting a peaceful refuge from the war.

Alternatively, the acoustic stream may contain much more abrupt contrasts. In *The Godfather,* just as Michael Corleone is steeling himself to shoot the rival gangster Sollozzo, we hear a loud, metallic screech, presumably from a nearby elevated train. The sound suggests impending danger, both for the victim and for Michael: after the murder, Michael's life will change irrevocably (**7.23**). Contemporary Hollywood films often exploit the dynamic range of Dolby technology to fill chase sequences with startling shifts between low, rumbling engines and whining sirens or squealing tires.

Yet another alternative is explored in Alexander Sokurov's *Alexandra.* A soldier's grandmother visits him at his camp and wanders freely among the men preparing for war. The sound track includes naturalistic dialogue and effects. But these conventional elements are wrapped in soft voices, orchestral chords, and snatches of rising and falling soprano singing. The murmuring auditory collage suggests a collective dimension to the old lady's stay, as if she is visiting on behalf of the unseen families of all the men, perhaps all soldiers' families throughout history.

A Dramatic Sound Stream: *Seven Samurai*   Akira Kurosawa was well aware of how sounds can combine to create a stream of information, as we can see from the final battle sequence of his *Seven Samurai.* In a heavy rain, marauding bandits charge into a village defended by the villagers and the samurai. Kurosawa chooses to keep the torrent and wind as a constant background noise. Before the battle, he punctuates the conversation of the waiting men, the tread of footsteps, and the sound of swords being drawn with long pauses in which we hear only the drumming rain. Like the defenders, we're uncertain about when and how the attack will come.

Suddenly distant horses' hooves are heard offscreen. This triggers the expectation that we will soon see the attackers. Kurosawa cuts to a long shot of the bandits; their horses' hooves become abruptly louder. (The scene employs vivid **sound perspective:** The closer the camera is to a source, the louder the sound.) When the bandits burst into the village, yet another sound element appears—the bandits' harsh war cries, which increase steadily in volume as they approach.

The battle begins. The rhythmic cutting and the muddy, storm-swept mise-en-scene gain impact from the way in which the incessant rain and splashing are explosively interrupted by brief noises—the howls of the wounded, the splintering of a fence one bandit crashes through, the whinnies of horses, the twang of a samurai's bowstring, the gurgle of a speared bandit, the screams of women when the bandit chieftain breaks into their hiding place. The sudden intrusion of certain sounds marks abrupt developments in the battle, standing out against the pounding rain. Such frequent surprises heighten our tension, since the narration frequently shifts us from one line of action to another.

The scene climaxes after the main battle has ended. Offscreen the pounding of horses' hooves is cut short by the sharp crack of a bandit's rifle shot, which fells one samurai. A long pause, in which we hear only the rain, emphasizes the moment.

7.23 Harsh sound contrasts: *The Godfather.* As Michael sits opposite Sollozzo, the sudden rumble and whine of an offscreen train sound all the more harsh when compared with the calm expression on Michael's face.

The samurai furiously flings his sword in the direction of the shot and falls dead into the mud. Another samurai splashes toward the bandit chieftain, who has the rifle; another shot cracks out and he falls back, wounded; another pause, in which only the relentless rain is heard. The wounded samurai kills the chieftain. The other samurai gather. At the scene's end, the sobs of a young samurai, the distant whinnies and hoof beats of riderless horses, and the rain all fade slowly out.

Kurosawa's relatively dense mix gradually introduces sounds that turn our attention to new narrative elements (hooves, battle cries) and then modulates these sounds into a harmonious stream. This stream is then punctuated by abrupt sounds of unusual volume or pitch associated with crucial narrative actions (hooves, archery, women's screams, gunshots). Overall, the combination of sounds enhances the unrestricted, objective narration of this sequence, which shows us what happens in various parts of the village rather than confining us to the experience of a single participant.

Sound and Film Form   The choice and combination of sound materials can create patterns that run through the film as a whole. A musical score is perhaps the clearest example of how this can work. A melody or musical phrase can be associated with a particular character, setting, situation, or idea. *Local Hero,* a film about a confused young executive who leaves Texas to close a business deal in a remote Scottish village, uses two major musical themes. A rockabilly tune is heard in the urban Southwest, while a slower, more poignantly folkish melody is associated with the seaside village. In the final scenes, after the young man has returned to Houston, he recalls Scotland with affection, and the film plays the two themes simultaneously.

In contrast, a single musical theme can change its quality when associated with different situations. In *Raising Arizona,* the hapless hero has a terrifying dream in which he envisions a homicidal biker pursuing him, and the accompanying music is appropriately ominous. But at the film's end, the hero dreams of raising dozens of children, and now the same melody, reorchestrated and played at a calm tempo, conveys a sense of peace and comfort.

Musical Motifs in *Jules and Jim*   By reordering and varying musical motifs, the filmmaker can subtly compare scenes, trace patterns of development, and suggest implicit meanings. A convenient example is Georges Delerue's score for François Truffaut's *Jules and Jim.* Overall, the music reflects the Paris of 1912–1933, the years during which the action takes place. Many of the melodies resemble works by Claude Debussy and Erik Satie, two of the most prominent French composers of that era. Virtually the entire score consists of melodies in ¾ meter, many of them in waltz time, and all the main themes are in keys related to A major. These rhythmic and harmonic decisions help unify the film.

More specifically, musical themes are associated with particular aspects of the narrative. For instance, Catherine's search for happiness and freedom outside conventional boundaries is conveyed by her "Tourbillon" ("Whirlwind") song, which says that life is a constant changing of romantic partners. Settings are also evoked in musical terms. One tune is heard every time the characters are in a café. As the years go by, the tune changes from a mechanical player-piano rendition to a jazzier version played by a black pianist.

The characters' relations become more strained and complicated over time, and the score reflects this in its development of major motifs. A lyrical melody is first heard when Jules, Jim, and Catherine visit the countryside and bicycle to the beach **(7.24)**. This "idyll" tune will recur at many points when the characters reunite, but as the years pass, it will become slower in tempo and more somber in instrumentation, and will shift from a major to a minor mode. Another motif that reappears in different guises is a "dangerous love" theme associated with Jim and Catherine. This grave, shimmering waltz is first heard when he visits her apartment and watches her pour a bottle of sulphuric acid down the sink **(7.25)**. (The

> " It's a lot like writing an opera. There's a lot of form and structure. We're very conscious that LOTR is one story that has been broken into three parts. My score is a complex piece that has to be structured carefully, musically and thematically, so that all the parts relate to one another."
> —Howard Shore, composer, *The Lord of the Rings*

7.24

7.25

7.26

7.24–7.26 *Jules and Jim*: **Three musical motifs.** An idyllic bicycle ride in the country introduces the main musical theme associated with the three characters' relations (7.24). Catherine pours out the acid, which she has said is "for lying eyes" (7.25). The camera slowly arcs around the statue as a new musical motif is introduced (7.26).

> ❝ So, given this mood-altering potential of music, it becomes a great source of fun, as well as a chance to make a scene that works OK work a whole lot better—to bring out the point of a scene that you haven't captured in the shooting of it, to excite the audience, to create the impression that something is happening when something isn't, and also to create little emotional touchstones which you can draw upon as the story changes—so that the music that seemed so innocent and sweet earlier, in new circumstances brings on a whole other set of feelings.❞
>
> —Jonathan Demme, director

acid, she says, is "for lying eyes.") Thereafter, this harmonically unstable theme, which resembles one of Satie's *Gymnopédies* for piano, is used to underscore Jim and Catherine's stormy love affair. At times it accompanies scenes of passion, but at other times it accompanies their growing disillusionment and despair.

The most varied theme is a mysterious phrase first heard on the flute when Jules and Jim encounter a striking ancient statue **(7.26)**. Later they meet Catherine and discover that she has the statue's face; a repetition of the musical motif confirms the comparison. Throughout the film, this brief motif is associated with the enigmatic side of Catherine. In the film's later scenes, this motif is developed in an intriguing way. The bass line (played on harpsichord or strings) that softly accompanied the woodwind tune now comes to the fore, creating a relentless, often harsh, pulsation. This "menace" waltz underscores Catherine's fling with Albert and accompanies her final revenge on Jim: driving her car, with him as passenger, off a broken bridge and into the river.

Once musical motifs have been selected, they can be combined to evoke associations. During Jim and Catherine's first intimate talk after the war, the bassline-dominated version of the enigma waltz is followed by the love theme, as if the latter could drown out the menacing side of Catherine's character. The love theme accompanies long tracking shots of Jim and Catherine strolling through the woods. But at the scene's end, as Jim bids Catherine farewell, the original woodwind version of her theme recalls her mystery and the risk he is running by falling in love with her. Similarly, when Jim and Catherine lie in bed, facing the end of their affair, the voice-over narrator says, "It was as if they were already dead" as the dangerous-love theme plays. This sequence associates death with their romance and foreshadows their fate at the film's end.

A similar sort of blending can be found in the film's final scene. Catherine and Jim have drowned, and Jules is overseeing the cremation of their bodies. As shots of the coffins dissolve into detailed shots of the cremation process, the enigma motif segues into its sinister variant, the menace motif. But as Jules leaves the cemetery and the narrator comments that Catherine had wanted her ashes to be cast to the winds, the string instruments glide into a sweeping version of the whirlwind waltz

(7.27). The film's musical score thus concludes by recalling the three sides of Catherine that attracted the men to her: her mystery, her menace, and her vivacious openness to experience. In such ways, a musical score can create, develop, and associate motifs that enter into the film's overall form.

Dimensions of Film Sound

We've seen what sounds consist of and how the filmmaker can select among the different kinds of sounds available. We've also seen how sound can guide the viewer's attention and create patterns across the film. But filmmakers have still more choices when they consider how to connect sounds to images.

7.27 Combining the motifs. The sadness of the ending is undercut by the lilting whirlwind waltz.

First, sound unfolds over time, so it has a *rhythm*. Second, a sound can relate to its perceived source with greater or lesser *fidelity*. Third, sound suggests something about the *spatial* conditions in which it occurs. And fourth, the sound relates to visual events that take place at particular points in time, and this relationship gives sound a *temporal* dimension. These dimensions offer the filmmaker a great many areas of control and choice.

Rhythm

Rhythm is one of the most powerful aspects of sound, for it works on our bodies at deep levels. We have already considered it in relation to mise-en-scene (p. 150) and editing (p. 226). Rhythm involves, minimally, a *beat*, or pulse; a *tempo*, or pace; and a pattern of *accents*, or stronger and weaker beats. In the realm of sound, all of these features are naturally most recognizable in film music, since there beat, tempo, and accent are basic compositional features. In our examples from *Jules and Jim*, the motifs can be characterized as having a 3/4 metrical pulse, putting an accent on the first beat, and displaying variable tempo—sometimes slow, sometimes fast.

We can find rhythmic qualities in sound effects as well. The plodding hooves of a farm horse differ from a cavalry mount galloping at full speed. The reverberating tone of a gong may offer a slowly decaying accent, while a sudden sneeze provides a brief one. In a gangster film, a machine gun's fire creates a regular, rapid beat, while the sporadic reports of pistols may come at irregular intervals.

Speech also has rhythm. People can be identified by voice prints that show not only characteristic frequencies and amplitudes but also distinct patterns of pacing and syllabic stress. In *His Girl Friday*, our impression is of very rapid dialogue, but the scenes actually are rhythmically subtler than that. In the start of each scene, the pace is comparatively slow, but as the action develops, characters talk at a steadily accelerating rate. As the scene winds down, the conversational pace does as well. This rise-and-fall rhythm matches the arc of each scene, giving us a bit of a rest before launching the next comic complication.

Rhythm in Sound and Image: Coordination   Any consideration of the rhythmic uses of sound is complicated by the fact that the movements in the images have a rhythm as well, distinguished by the same principles of beat, tempo, and accent. In addition, the editing has a rhythm. As we have seen, a succession of short shots helps create a rapid tempo, whereas shots held longer tend to slow down the rhythm.

In most cases, the rhythms of editing, of movement within the image, and of sound all cooperate. Possibly the most common tendency is for the filmmaker to match visual and sonic rhythms to each other. In a dance sequence in a musical, the figures move about at a rhythm determined by the music. But variation is always possible. In the "Waltz in Swing Time" number in *Swing Time*, the dancing of Fred Astaire and Ginger Rogers moves quickly in time to the music. Yet no fast cutting accompanies this scene. Indeed, the scene consists of a single long take from a long-shot distance.

Animated films often closely coordinate visible movement and sound. In Walt Disney films of the 1930s, the characters often move in exact synchronization with the music, even when they aren't dancing. (As we've seen, such exactness was possible because the sound track was recorded before the drawings were made.) Tightly matching movement to music came to be known as *Mickey-Mousing.*

It isn't only animated films that exploit correspondences among musical and pictorial rhythms. Michael Mann's *The Last of the Mohicans* culminates in a chase and a fight along a mountain ridge. Alice has been captured by the renegade Magua, and Hawkeye, Uncas, and Chingachgook race up the trail to rescue her. We might expect, then, the standard thunderous action score, but what we hear is a quick, grave Scottish dance, initially played on fiddle, mandolin, and harpsichord. The tune was heard in an earlier dance scene at the fort, so it functions to recall the two couples' romances, but here it gives the scene a propulsive energy. Hand-to-hand struggles stand out against the throbbing music. Eventually, the theme swells to the full orchestra, but the same implacable beat governs the action. When Alice hovers on the cliff edge, about to jump off, somber chords repeat a seesaw pulse, as if time is standing still.

At the scene's climax, Chingachgook sprints into the fray, and faster musical figures played by stringed instruments recall the early dance tune. Chingachgook's attack on Magua consists of four precise blows from his battle-axe; each blow coincides with the third beat in a series of musical measures. In the final moment of combat, the two warriors stand frozen opposite each other. The shot lasts three beats. On the fourth beat, Chingachgook launches the fatal blow. As Magua topples over, the music's pulse is replaced by a sustained string chord. *The Last of the Mohicans* synchronizes dance music with visual rhythms, but the result doesn't feel like Mickey-Mousing. The throbbing 4/4 meter, the accented beats, and the leaping melody give the heroes' precise movements a choreographic grace.

Rhythm in Sound and Image: Disparities   The filmmaker may also choose to create a disparity among the rhythms of sound, editing, and image. One of the most common options is to edit dialogue scenes in ways that cut against natural speech rhythms. In our example of dialogue overlap from *The Hunt for Red October* (7.15–7.17), the editing doesn't coincide with accented beats, cadences, or pauses in the officer's speech. Thus, the editing smoothes over the changes of shot and emphasizes the words and facial expressions of Captain Ramius. If a filmmaker wants to emphasize the speaker and the speech, the cuts usually come at pauses or natural stopping points in the line, as in our example from *M* (7.18–7.21).

The filmmaker may contrast the rhythm of sound and picture in more noticeable ways. For instance, if the source of sound is primarily offscreen, the filmmaker can utilize the behavior of onscreen figures to create an expressive counterrhythm. Toward the end of John Ford's *She Wore a Yellow Ribbon,* the aging cavalry captain, Nathan Brittles, watches his troops ride out of the fort just after he has retired. He regrets leaving the service and longs to go with the patrol. The sound of the scene consists of two elements: the cheerful title song sung by the departing riders, and the quick hoof beats of their horses. Yet only a few of the shots show the horses and singers, who ride at a rhythm matched to the sound. Instead, the scene concentrates our attention on Brittles, standing almost motionless by his horse. The contrast of brisk musical rhythm and the static images of the solitary Brittles expresses his regret at having to stay behind for the first time in many years.

Sometimes the musical accompaniment might even seem rhythmically inappropriate to the images. At intervals in *Four Nights of a Dreamer,* Robert Bresson presents shots of a large, floating nightclub cruising the Seine. The boat's movement is slow and smooth, yet the sound track consists of lively calypso music. (Not until a later scene do we discover that the music comes from a band aboard the boat.) The strange combination of fast sound tempo with the slow passage of the boat creates a languid, mysterious effect.

In Chris Marker's *La Jetée,* the contrast between image and sound rhythms dominates the entire film. *La Jetée* is made up almost entirely of still shots; except for one tiny gesture, all movement within the images is eliminated. Yet the film utilizes voice-over narration, music, and sound effects of a generally rapid, constantly accented rhythm. Despite the absence of movement, the film doesn't seem uncinematic, partly because it offers a dynamic interplay of audio-visual rhythms.

Most films don't follow just one strategy in combining the rhythms of pictures and sounds. A filmmaker may change rhythms in order to reset our expectations. In the famous battle on the ice in *Alexander Nevsky,* Sergei Eisenstein develops the sound from slow tempos to fast and back to slow. The first 12 shots of the scene show the Russian army anticipating the attack of the German knights. The shots are of moderate length, and they contain very little movement. The music is comparably slow, consisting of short, distinctly separated chords. Then, as the German army rides into sight over the horizon, both the visual movement and the tempo of the music increase quickly, and the battle begins. At the end of the battle, Eisenstein creates another contrast: a long passage of slow, lamenting music accompanies majestic tracking shots with little figure movement.

Fidelity

By *fidelity,* we don't mean the quality of recording. In our sense, fidelity refers to the extent to which the sound is faithful to the source as we conceive it. If a film shows us a barking dog and we hear a barking noise, that sound is faithful to its source; the sound maintains fidelity. But if the image of the barking dog is accompanied by the sound of a cat meowing, there enters a disparity between sound and image—a lack of fidelity.

From the filmmaker's standpoint, fidelity has nothing to do with what originally made the sound in production. Even if our dog emits a bark on screen, perhaps in production the bark came from a different dog or was electronically synthesized. We do not know what light sabers really sound like, but we accept the whang they make in *Return of the Jedi* as plausible. (In production, their sound was made by hammering guy wires that anchored a radio tower.) You can make a dog meow as easily as making it bark. If the viewer takes the sound to be coming from its source in the diegetic world of the film, then it is faithful, regardless of its actual source in production. Fidelity is thus purely a matter of expectation.

When we're led to notice that a sound is unfaithful to its source, that awareness is usually used for comic effect, as with our meowing dog. In Jacques Tati's *Mr. Hulot's Holiday,* much humor arises from the opening and closing of a dining room door. Instead of recording a real door, Tati inserts a twanging sound like a plucked cello string each time the door swings. Aside from being amusing in itself, this sound functions to emphasize the rhythmic patterns created by waiters and diners passing through the door. Because many gags in Tati films are based on quirkily unrealistic noises, his films are good specimens for the study of fidelity.

As with low- or high-angle framings, no formula or recipe demands that every manipulation of fidelity be comic. Some non-faithful sounds have serious functions. In Alfred Hitchcock's *The Thirty-Nine Steps,* a landlady discovers a corpse in an apartment. We see her scream but hear a train whistle; then the scene shifts to an actual train. The whistle isn't faithful to its source, but it provides a dramatic transition.

Subjectivity can motivate unrealistic techniques of all sorts, and this holds true for fidelity. Volume can help: A sound may seem unreasonably loud or soft in relation to other sounds in the film. For example, Curtis Bernhardt's *Possessed* centers on a woman gradually falling into mental illness. One rainy night she's alone and highly distraught, and sound devices enable the narration to achieve subjective depth. We begin to hear things as she does; a ticking clock, her heartbeat, and

> " [Sound] doesn't have to be in-your-face, traditional, big sound effects. You can especially say a lot about the film with ambiences—the sounds for things you don't see. You can say a lot about where they are geographically, what time of day it is, what part of the city they're in, what kind of country they're in, the season it is. If you're going to choose a cricket, you can choose a cricket not for strictly geographic reasons. If there's a certain cricket that has a beat and a rhythm to it, it adds to the tension of a scene."
>
> —Gary Rydstrom, sound editor, *Toy Story*

dripping raindrops gradually magnify in volume. Here the shift in fidelity functions to suggest a psychological state, a movement from the character's heightened awareness into sheer hallucination.

Space

Sound has a spatial dimension because it comes from a *source*. Our beliefs about that source have a powerful effect on how we understand the sound.

Diegetic Versus Nondiegetic Sound   When we considered narrative form back in Chapter 3, we described events taking place in the story world as *diegetic* (p. 76). Accordingly, **diegetic sound** is sound that has a source in the story world. The words spoken by the characters, sounds made by objects in the story, and music represented as coming from instruments in the story space are all diegetic sound.

Diegetic sound is often hard to notice as such. It may seem to come naturally from the world of the film. But as we saw when the Ping-Pong game in *Mr. Hulot's Holiday* becomes abruptly quiet to allow us to hear action in the foreground, the filmmaker may manipulate diegetic sound in ways that aren't at all realistic.

Alternatively, there is **nondiegetic sound,** which is represented as coming from a source outside the story world. Music added to enhance the film's action is the most common type of nondiegetic sound. When Roger Thornhill is climbing Mount Rushmore in *North by Northwest* and tense music comes up, we don't expect to see an orchestra perched on the side of the mountain. Viewers understand that movie music is a convention and does not issue from the world of the story. The same holds true for the so-called omniscient narrator, the disembodied voice that gives us information but doesn't belong to any of the characters in the film. An example is *The Magnificent Ambersons,* in which the director, Orson Welles, speaks the nondiegetic narration.

Nondiegetic sound effects are also possible. In *Le Million,* various characters pursue an old coat with a winning lottery ticket in the pocket. The chase converges backstage at the opera, where the characters race and dodge around one another, tossing the coat to their accomplices. What we hear, however, are the sounds of a football game, including a cheering crowd and a referee's whistle **(7.28).**

A film's soundtrack can be completely nondiegetic. Bruce Conner's *A Movie,* Kenneth Anger's *Scorpio Rising,* and Derek Jarman's *War Requiem* use only nondiegetic music. Similarly, many compilation documentaries include no diegetic sound; instead, omniscient voice-over commentary and orchestral music guide our response to the images.

As with fidelity, the distinction between diegetic and nondiegetic sound reflects the conventions of film viewing. Viewers understand that certain sounds seem to come from the story world, while others come from outside the space of the story events. We've learned these conventions so thoroughly that we usually don't have to think about which type of sound we're hearing at any moment. At many times, though, a film's narration deliberately blurs boundaries between different spatial categories. A play with the conventions can be used to puzzle or surprise the audience, to create humor or ambiguity, or to suggest thematic implications. We'll give some examples shortly.

Resources of Diegetic Sound: Offscreen Sound   We know that the space of the narrative action isn't limited to what we can see on the screen at any one moment. The same thing holds true for sound. In the last shot of our *The Hunt for Red October* scene, we hear the officer speaking while we see a shot of just Captain Ramius, listening (7.17). Early in the attack on the village in *The Seven Samurai,* we, along with the samurai, hear the hoof beats of the bandits' horses

7.28 Nondiegetic sound effects. As characters in *Le Million* toss the coat around, director René Clair fades in the sounds of a football game. Because the maneuvers of the chase do look like a scrimmage, this enhances the comedy of the sequence by creating a sort of audio-visual pun.

7.29   **7.30**   **7.31**

7.29–7.31 Offscreen sound implies space. In *His Girl Friday*, Hildy goes into the pressroom to write her final story. As she chats with the other reporters, a loud clunk comes from an offscreen source, and they glance to the left (7.29). Hildy and another reporter walk to the window (7.30) and see a gallows being prepared for a hanging (7.31).

before we see a shot of them. These instances remind us that diegetic sound can be either *onscreen* or *offscreen*, depending on whether its source is inside the frame or outside the frame.

Offscreen sound is crucial to our experience of a film, and filmmakers know that it can save time and money. A shot may show only a couple sitting together in airplane seats, but if we hear a throbbing engine, other passengers chatting, and the creak of a beverage cart, we'll conjure up a plane in flight. Offscreen sound can create the illusion of a bigger space than we actually see, as in the cavernous prison sequences of *The Silence of the Lambs.* It can also shape our sense of how a scene will develop **(7.29–7.31).**

Offscreen sound can fill in information very economically. In *Zodiac,* we see the alcoholic reporter Avery wake up after sleeping in his car. As he abruptly sits up, we hear the clink of bottles on the floor. The sound confirms our suspicion that he has spent another night drinking.

Used with optical point-of-view shots, offscreen sound can create restricted narration, guiding us toward what a character is noticing. In *No Country for Old Men,* Llewelyn Moss is holed up in a hotel room with a bag of cash, hiding from his implacable pursuer Anton Chigurh. When he realizes that a tracking device has been hidden among the bills, the narration is limited solely to what Moss sees and hears. He tries calling the downstairs desk. We dimly hear the distant phone ringing unanswered, so like him we infer that Chigurh has killed the clerk.

The sonic texture is very detailed, highlighting the slight noises of Moss shifting on the bed and switching off the lamp. Then, against a muted background of wind, we hear steadily approaching footsteps in the hall, accompanied by rapid pinging on a homing device. Moss's optical point-of-view confirms Chigurh's arrival: we see the shadows of his feet in the crack under the door. Moss cocks his shotgun, creating a click that seems abnormally loud and close. The shadows move away, and we hear the slight creaking of a light bulb being unscrewed in the hall, eliminating the streak of illumination under the door. The auditory climax of the scene is the metallic burst of the door lock rocketing into the room. *No Country*'s narration has created suspense by restricting both vision and sound to Moss's range of knowledge. For another instance, see "A Closer Look."

Resources of Diegetic Sound: Subjectivity   Diegetic sound harbors other possibilities. It can give us perceptual subjectivity, in a way parallel to an optical POV shot (p. 90). In *The King's Speech,* a therapist treats a man with a bad stammer. He directs the patient to read a text into a microphone while listening to music

7.57

7.58

7.59

7.57–7.59 A character replies to the narrator. We see a group of townswomen gossiping about the marriage of Isabel Amberson, and one predicts that she will have "the worst spoiled lot of children this town will ever see" (7.57). The nondiegetic narrator resumes his description of the family history: "The prophetess proved to be mistaken in a single detail merely; Wilbur and Isabel did not have *children*. They had only one." But at this point, over the shot of the street, we hear the gossiper's voice again: "Only one! But I'd like to know if he isn't spoiled enough for a whole carload" (7.58). The narrator goes on, "Again, she found none to challenge her. George Amberson Minafer, the Major's one grandchild, was a princely terror." While they're talking, a pony cart comes up the street, and we see George for the first time (7.59). In this exchange, the woman seems to reply to the narrator, even though we must assume that she can't hear what he says. (After all, she's a character in the story and he isn't.)

be taken as diegetic and offscreen, since she has been listening to Aimee Mann tunes in an earlier scene. But then Anderson cuts to other characters elsewhere singing along, even though they cannot be hearing the music in Claudia's apartment. It would seem that the sound is now nondiegetic, with the characters accompanying it as they might do in a musical. The sequence underlines the parallels among several suffering characters and conveys an eerie sense of disparate people for once on the same emotional wavelength. The sound also works with the crosscutting to pull the characters together before the climax, when many will meet face to face.

A more disturbing uncertainty about whether a sound is diegetic often crops up in the films of Jean-Luc Godard. He narrates some of his films in nondiegetic voice-over, but in other films, such as *2 or 3 Things I Know About Her,* he seems also to be in the story space, whispering questions or comments whose sound perspective makes them seem close to the camera. Godard does not claim to be a character in the action, yet the characters on the screen sometimes behave as though they hear him. This uncertainty as to diegetic or nondiegetic sound sources enables Godard to stress the conventionality of traditional sound usage.

Sound Perspective   One characteristic of diegetic sound is the possibility of suggesting **sound perspective.** This is a sense of spatial distance and location analogous to the cues for visual depth and volume that we get with visual perspective. "I like to think," remarks sound designer Walter Murch, "that I not only record a sound but the space between me and the sound: The subject that generates the sound is merely what causes the surrounding space to resonate."

Sound perspective can be suggested by volume. A loud sound tends to seem near; a soft one, more distant. The horses' hooves in the *Seven Samurai* battle and the bugle call from *Stagecoach* exemplify how rising volume suggests closer distance. Sound perspective is also created by timbre. The combination of directly registered sounds and sounds reflected from the environment creates a timbre specific to a given distance. Timbre effects are most noticeable with echoes. In *The Magnificent Ambersons,* the conversations that take place on the baroque staircase have a distinct echo, giving the impression of huge, empty spaces around the characters.

Point of View and Expressiveness   As the camera follows a character, the filmmaker may use changes in sound perspective to suggest the character's movement through space, a sort of sonic point of view. But many uses of sound perspective don't try to be realistic. In a long shot, a character's voice will usually be clearer than if we were the same distance from her or him in reality, and when we cut to a close-up, that character's voice will not be significantly louder or crisper. In a conversation with sound overlaps, like the one in *The Hunt for Red October* (p. 275), the speaker's voice doesn't change perspective when the camera shifts to show the listener.

In our hypothetical example presenting Jim and Amanda talking on the phone, one option would involve sound perspective. If we stayed with Jim and only heard Amanda's replies, her voice would be given a different perspective. Generally, when the person on camera is speaking, the lines are clear and enhanced by natural ambient sounds. A voice heard over the receiver is usually more coarsely rendered and more reverberant, carrying lower pitches and providing little ambient sound. Sound editors call this disparity the *telephone split*. It represents the fact that the listener is hearing a voice on the line, but it seldom matches what a phone call sounds like in reality.

Like all conventions, the telephone split can be adjusted for expressive possibilities. In *Phone Booth,* a publicist is trapped in a booth, pinned down by an unseen sniper who keeps him talking on the phone. Here the telephone split takes an unusual form. The publicist is heard normally, with ambient sound, but we don't hear the sniper as a crackling telephone voice. Instead, we hear soft, closely miked speech in a dry sound envelope. It does not change when the camera moves toward or away from the booth. The voice has a slight electronic twang, so it doesn't sound as neutral as a narrator's voice-over, but it remains closer to our perspective than to the protagonist's. Whispering, laughing, making rude remarks about what's happening around the booth, the sniper's voice hovers in a realm somewhere between us and the street. It enhances the sense that the protagonist is being watched by a distant, somewhat ghostly threat.

Sound Perspective in the Theater Space   Multichannel recording and reproduction tremendously increase the filmmaker's ability to suggest sound perspective. In multiplex theaters equipped with multitrack sound systems, three speakers are located behind the screen. The center speaker transmits most of the onscreen dialogue, as well as the most important effects and music. The left and right speakers are stereophonic, adding their sound effects, music, and minor dialogue. These channels can suggest a region of sound within the frame or just offscreen. Surround channels principally carry minor sound effects and some music, and they are divided among several speakers arranged along the sides and in the back of the theater. The "inner dialogue" shots in *Paranoid Park* and *The Iron Lady* are unusual in spreading more important dialogue to subsidiary channels.

By using stereophonic and surround tracks, a film can more strongly imply a sound's distance and placement. In farcical comedies such as *The Naked Gun,* stereophonic sound can suggest collisions and falls outside the frame. Without the greater localization offered by the stereophonic channels, we might scan the frame for sources of the sounds. Even the center channel can be used to localize an off-screen object. In the climactic scene of *The Fugitive,* Richard Kimble is sneaking up on the friend who has betrayed him, and he reaches down past the lower frame line. As he slides his arm to the right, a rolling clank in the center channel tells us that there is an iron pipe at his feet.

In addition, stereo reproduction can specify a moving sound's direction. In David Lean's *Lawrence of Arabia,* for instance, the approach of planes to bomb a camp is first suggested through a rumble occurring only on the right side of the screen. Lawrence and an officer look off right, and their dialogue identifies the source of the sound. Then, when the scene shifts to the besieged camp itself, the sound slides from channel to channel, suggesting the planes swooping overhead.

With stereophonic and surround channels, a remarkably convincing three-dimensional sound environment may be created within the theater. Sound sources can alter in position as the camera pans or tracks through a locale. The *Star Wars*

> ❝ She first hears the music at a bit of a distance, coming from the house, and as she walks in—the music is getting closer, step-by-step—she goes from the entrance way up the stairs—the music is still growing—and she finally passes by a guitarist on the stairs."
> —Tony Volante, re-recording mixer, *Rachel Getting Married*

series uses multiple-channel sound to suggest space vehicles whizzing not only across the screen but also above and behind the spectators.

Like other techniques, sound localization in the theater needn't be used for realistic purposes. *Apocalypse Now* divides its six-track sound among three channels in the rear of the theater and three in the front. In the film's first sequence, mentioned above, the protagonist Ben Willard is seen lying on his bed. Shots of his feverish face are superimposed on shots of U.S. helicopters dropping napalm on the Vietnamese jungle. The sound oscillates between internal and external status, as Willard's mind turns the whoosh of a ceiling fan into the whir of helicopter blades. These subjective sounds issue from both the front and back of the theater, engulfing the audience.

Abruptly, a POV shot tracking toward the window suggests that Willard has gotten to his feet and is walking. As the camera moves, the noises fade from all rear speakers and become concentrated in the front ones at screen left, right, and center. Then, as Willard's hand opens the venetian blinds to reveal his vision of the street outside, the sound fades out of the left and right front speakers and comes only from the center channel. Our attention has been narrowed: As we leave Willard's mind, the sound steers us back to the outside world, which is rendered as unrealistically monophonic. In addition, the disparity in acoustic dimensions suggests that the protagonist's wraparound memory of jungle destruction is more powerful than the pallid environment of Saigon.

Time

Sound also permits the filmmaker to represent time in various ways. Just as the sources we hear need not be in the space we see; the time represented on the sound track need not coincide with the time that the image presents. To capture all the choices the filmmaker faces, we'll need to make some distinctions that require a little patience.

Most often, the filmmaker decides to hear the sound at the same time as we see what makes it. Characters move their lips, and we hear the appropriate words. A gun fires and we hear a blast. These are instances of **synchronous sound.**

When the sound does go out of synchronization during a viewing (often through an error in projection or lab work), the result is quite distracting. Would a filmmaker ever want to put such **asynchronous,** or out-of-sync, **sound** into the film itself? Yes, sometimes. *Singin' in the Rain* creates gags based on asynchronous sound. In the early days of sound filming, a pair of silent screen actors have just made their first talking picture, *The Dueling Cavalier.* Their film company previews the film for an audience, but the technology fails and the picture gets out of synchronization. All the sounds come several seconds before their sources are seen in the image. A line of dialogue begins and *then* the actor's lips move. A woman's voice is heard when a man moves his lips, and vice versa. The humor of this disastrous preview in *Singin' in the Rain* depends on our realization that a film's synchronization of sound and image is simply a mechanical illusion.

A lengthier play with our expectations about synchronization comes in Woody Allen's *What's Up Tiger Lily?* Allen dubbed a new sound track on an Asian spy film, but the English-language dialogue isn't a translation of the original. Instead, it creates a new story. The movie's one-liners and non sequiturs are enhanced by our constant awareness that the words are barely synchronized with the actors' lips. Allen has turned the usual problems of the dubbing of foreign films into the basis of his comedy.

Matters of synchronization are fairly easy to spot. They relate to screen duration, or *viewing* time. As we saw in Chapter 3, though, narrative films can also present *story* and *plot* time. Story time consists of the order, duration, and frequency of all the events pertinent to the narrative, whether they are shown to us or not. Plot time consists of the order, duration, and frequency of the events actually represented in the film. Plot time shows us selected story events but skips over or only suggests others.

TABLE 7.2   Temporal Relations of Sound in Cinema

Time	Space of Source	
	Diegetic (Story Space)	Nondiegetic (Nonstory Space)
1. Nonsimultaneous; sound from *earlier* in story than image	Sound flashback; image flashforward; sound bridge	Sound marked as past put over images (e.g., sound of John Kennedy speech put over images of United States today)
2. Sound simultaneous in story with image	*External:* dialogue, effects, music *Internal:* thoughts of character heard	Sound marked as simultaneous with images put over images (e.g., narrator describing events in present tense)
3. Nonsimultaneous; sound from *later* in story than image	Sound of flash-forward; image flashback with sound continuing in present; character narrates earlier events; sound bridge	Sound marked as later put over images (e.g., reminiscing narrator of *The Magnificent Ambersons*)

Filmmakers have realized that sound can manipulate story and plot time in two basic ways. Does the sound take place at the same time as the image, in terms of the story events? If so, we can call it **simultaneous sound.** This is overwhelmingly the most common usage. We see and hear two characters speaking, or we see a truck driving down the street and hear the truck's sounds. The plot isn't manipulating the order of sound events.

But filmmakers also realize that the sound we hear can occur earlier or later in the story than the events we see in the image. In this manipulation of story order, the sound becomes **nonsimultaneous.** The most common example of this is the sonic flashback. For instance, we might see characters chatting in the present but hear another character's voice from an earlier scene. Or, instead of hearing the truck's engine, we hear gunshots from an earlier scene. By means of nonsimultaneous sound, the film can present earlier story events without showing them.

So filmmakers have a wide range of options about sound and story time. To help to distinguish them, Table 7.2 sums up the possible temporal and spatial relationships that image and sound can display.

Diegetic Sound   The first and third of these possibilities are rare, so let's start with the second, most common, option:

2. *Sound simultaneous in story with image.* As we just mentioned, this is by far the most common temporal relation that sound displays in fiction films. Noise, music, or speech that comes from the space of the story almost invariably occurs at the same time as the image.

   Like any other sort of diegetic sound, simultaneous sound can be either external (objective) or internal (subjective). So instead of a character speaking, we might hear an inner monologue, with the character talking to himself or herself. But that monologue is still presumably simultaneous with the image onscreen.

1. *Sound earlier in story than image.* Here the sound comes from an earlier point in the story than the action we're seeing onscreen. A sonic flashback is

Today's films often replay scenes in order to give us new story information, but sometimes a film does this just on the auditory level. We look at two examples of sound from the story past rerun in the present in "Play it again, Joan."

7.60

7.61

7.60–7.61 A sound bridge between scenes. One scene of *The Silence of the Lambs* ends with Clarice Starling on the telephone, as she mentions a location called the "Your Self Storage facility . . ." (7.60). Her voice continues, ". . . right outside central Baltimore" over the first shot of the next scene, the sign for the Your Self warehouse (7.61).

one example. At the end of Joseph Losey's *Accident,* over a shot of a driveway gate, we hear a car crash. The sound represents the crash that occurred at the beginning of the film. In this film, an unrestricted narration makes an ironic final comment on the action.

More often, sonic flashbacks are subjective, as when a character remembers things said in earlier scenes. Contemporary films often involve sonic replays of dialogue we've heard earlier in the story chronology.

Sound may belong to an earlier time than the image in another way. The sound from the previous scene may linger briefly while the image is already presenting the next scene. This common device is called a **sound bridge.** Sound bridges of this sort may create smooth transitions by setting up expectations that are quickly confirmed (**7.60, 7.61**).

Sound bridges can also make our expectations more uncertain. In Tim Hunter's *The River's Edge,* three high-school boys are standing outside school, and one of them confesses to having killed his girlfriend. When his pals scoff, he says, "They don't believe me." There is a cut to the dead girl lying in the grass by the river, while on the sound track we hear one of his friends call it a crazy story that no one will believe. There's a brief uncertainty. Is a new scene starting, with the friend's response an offscreen one? Or are we are seeing a cutaway to the corpse, which could be followed by a shot returning to the three boys at school? The shot dwells on the dead girl, and after a pause, we hear, with a different sound ambience, "If you brought us . . ." Then there is a cut to a shot of the three youths walking through the woods to the river, as the same character continues, ". . . all the way out here for nothing. . . ." The friend's remark about the crazy story belongs to an earlier, somewhat indeterminate time than the shot of the corpse, and it becomes an unsettling sound bridge to the new scene.

3. *Sound later in story than image.* Sound may also occur at a time later than that depicted by the images. Here we usually tend to take the images as occurring in the past and the sound as occurring in the present or future.

A simple prototype occurs in many trial dramas. The testimony of a witness in the present is heard on the sound track, while the image presents a flashback to an earlier event. The same effect occurs when the film employs a reminiscing narrator, as in John Ford's *How Green Was My Valley.* Aside from a glimpse at the beginning, we don't see the protagonist Huw as a man, only as a boy, but his grown-up voice-over accompanies the bulk of the plot, which is set in the distant past. Huw's present-time voice on the sound track creates a strong sense of nostalgia for the past and constantly reminds us of the pathetic decline that the characters will eventually suffer.

Since the late 1960s, it has become somewhat common for the sound from the next scene to begin while the images of the last one are still on the screen. Like the instances in which the next scene begins when we're hearing sound from the previous one, this transitional device is called a *sound bridge.* In Wim Wenders's *American Friend,* a nighttime shot of a little boy riding in the back seat of a car is accompanied by a harsh clacking. There is a cut to a railroad station, where the timetable board flips through its metal cards listing times and destinations. Since the sound over the shot of the boy comes from the later scene, this portion is nonsimultaneous.

In principle, one could also have a sound *flashforward.* The filmmaker could, say, use the sounds that belong with scene 5 to accompany the images in scene 2. In practice, such a technique is almost unknown. In Godard's *Contempt,* a husband and wife quarrel, and the scene ends with her swimming out to sea while he sits quietly on a rock formation. On the sound track, we hear her voice, closely miked, reciting a letter in which she tells him she has driven back to Rome with another man. Since the husband has not yet received the letter, and perhaps the wife has not yet written it, the letter and its recitation presumably come from a later point in the story. Here the sound flashforward sets up strong expectations that a later scene confirms: We see the wife and the husband's rival stopping for gas on the road to Rome. In fact, we never see a scene in which the husband receives the letter.

Nondiegetic Sound   Most nondiegetic sound has no relevant temporal relationship to the story. When mood music comes up over a tense scene, it would be irrelevant to ask if it is happening at the same time as the images, since the music has no existence in the world of the action. But occasionally, the filmmaker uses a type of nondiegetic sound that does have a defined temporal relationship to the story. Welles's narration in *The Magnificent Ambersons,* for instance, speaks of the action as having happened in a long-vanished era of American history.

An Abundance of Choices   As viewers watch a film, they don't mentally slot each sound into each of these spatial and temporal categories. We offer them here as a way of looking systematically at creative decisions filmmakers have made. Once we've done that, we can use the distinctions to help understand our viewing experience. Tracing out the choices explicitly offer us ways of noticing important aspects of films—especially films that play with our expectations about sounds. By becoming aware of the rich range of possibilities, we're less likely to take a film's sound track for granted and more sensitive to unusual sound strategies.

7.62

At the start of Alain Resnais's *Providence,* we see a wounded old man pursued by other men. This action is crosscut with an interrogation in a courtroom (**7.62–7.66**). At one point, the prosecutor pauses and we hear a man's voice whisper, "A werewolf." The prosecutor then asks, "A werewolf, perhaps?" The whispered words startle us, for we can't immediately account for them. Are they whispered by the witness off-screen? Are they subjective, conveying the thoughts of the prosecutor or the witness? Are they perhaps even nondiegetic, coming from outside the story world, like Godard's whispered side remarks in *2 or 3 Things I Know about Her*? The plot will eventually motivate this eerie interruption; eventually we learn whose voice whispered these words. The entire opening of *Providence* provides an excellent extended case of how a filmmaker can play with conventions involving sound sources.

7.63

In the *Providence* sequence, we are aware of the ambiguity immediately, and it points our expectations forward, arousing curiosity as to how the whisperer can be identified. The filmmaker can also use sound to create a retrospective awareness of how we have *mis*interpreted something earlier. This sort of realization occurs in Francis Ford Coppola's *The Conversation,* a film that is virtually a textbook on the manipulation of sound and image.

7.64

7.65

7.66

7.62–7.66 **Playing with possibilities.** The prosecuting attorney in *Providence* questions a man accused of murder (7.62). The scene returns to the hunt, during which the old man was apparently murdered (7.63). A cut returns us to the courtroom, where the prosecutor continues his sarcastic questioning (7.64). The young man justifies his act by saying that the man was turning into an animal (7.65). The prosecutor pauses, astonished, "Are you suggesting some kind of actual metamorphosis?" A man's voice whispers, "A werewolf." The prosecutor takes his cue: "A werewolf, perhaps?" (7.66).

The plot centers on Harry Caul, a sound engineer specializing in surveillance. Harry is hired by a mysterious corporate executive to tape a conversation between a young man and woman in a noisy park. Harry cleans up the garbled tape, but he starts to suspect foul play and refuses to give it to his client. Now Harry obsessively replays, refilters, and remixes all his tapes of the conversation. Flashback images of the couple—perhaps in his memory, perhaps not—accompany his reworking of the tape. Finally, Harry arrives at a good dub, and we hear the man say, "He'd kill us if he could."

The overall situation is quite mysterious. Harry does not know who the young couple are (is the woman his client's wife or daughter?). Nevertheless, Harry suspects that they are in danger from the executive. Harry's studio is ransacked, the tape is stolen, and he later finds that the executive has it. Now more than ever, Harry feels that he is involved in a murder plot. After a highly ambiguous series of events, including a possible murder, Harry learns that the situation is not as he had thought.

Without giving away the revelation of the mystery, we can say that in *The Conversation* the narration misleads us by suggesting that certain sounds are objective when at the film's end we are inclined to consider them subjective, or at least ambiguous. The film's surprise, and its lingering mysteries, rely on unsignaled shifts between external and internal diegetic sound.

Providence and *The Conversation* show that distinguishing different types of sound can help us analyze filmmakers' creative choices. They and other examples also suggest that our categories correspond pretty well to how viewers understand what they hear. We tacitly learn to distinguish between diegetic and nondiegetic, internal and external, simultaneous and nonsimultaneous sound. That's not surprising. Filmmakers have worked for nearly a century to establish these conventions.

But sometimes they challenge the conventions. We notice when a sound crosses the boundaries between diegetic and nondiegetic, internal and external, simultaneous and nonsimultaneous. Because the distinctions fit with our assumptions about normal cases, the unusual sound in *Providence, The Conversation,* and many other films can undermine our expectations, creating suspense or surprise or ambiguity. The categories we've reviewed point to ways in which sound, often without our awareness, shapes our experience of a film.

Functions of Film Sound: *The Prestige*

In London around 1900, two magicians are locked in desperate competition, each searching for ever more baffling illusions. As they deceive each other and their audiences, the film about them tries to deceive us as well.

A story of crime, professional rivalry, personal jealousy, and grand aspirations, *The Prestige* sets itself a difficult task. The film tries to be as tantalizing as a magic trick, but one that can eventually be explained. As a result, director Christopher Nolan and his screenwriter (and brother) Jonathan Nolan must both reveal and conceal information. The film must present us just enough of the story to keep us engaged, while holding back the answers to the puzzles—and sometimes, like a magician, distracting us from what is really going on. Throughout *The Prestige,* sound is crucial to an elaborate choreography of misdirection.

Transported Men

The conflict between the eager Robert Angier (Hugh Jackman) and the more sinister Alfred Borden (Christian Bale) begins when both are apprentice magicians. Robert's wife, Julia, dies in an immersion tank as a result of Borden's faulty rope-knot. As the two men grow in fame, their feud escalates. Robert shoots off two of Alfred's fingers in a botched "bullet catch." In response, Alfred sabotages one of Robert's illusions. Then Alfred mounts an amazing trick, the Transported Man. Alfred seems to disappear from one end of the stage and reappear instantly at the other. In retaliation, Robert finds a man who resembles him and creates a similar illusion. But Alfred unmasks the stunt, breaking Robert's leg and humiliating him before his audience.

Robert vows to find the secret behind Alfred's Transported Man. After consulting with Nicola Tesla, the great experimenter with electricity, Robert returns to London with a stunning new illusion. He stands onstage in a crackling field of lightning bolts and disappears, reappearing a few seconds later in the balcony. Alfred, usually quick to unravel a trick, is baffled. He resigns himself to quitting the trade. Nonetheless, he shows up in disguise at one of Robert's performances and penetrates the area below stage. At the climax of the trick, Alfred sees Robert fall through a trapdoor into a tank of water below. He watches Robert drown. Alfred is arrested for murder and condemned to death.

At the climax of the film, Alfred's original Transported Man illusion is revealed as a simple trick: There are two Bordens, identical twins. At any moment, one takes the Alfred identity, while the other is disguised as Fallon, Alfred's designer of illusions or *ingénieur*. So when one Borden twin does change his mind about quitting magic, the other obstinately attends Robert's performance. As a result, while one Alfred is hanged, the other can stalk Robert for a final act of revenge.

Somewhat earlier, and more gradually, we learn that Robert's version of the Transported Man is no illusion but rather super-science. Tesla has created a cloning machine, which makes an identical copy of Robert and deposits that at some distance from the original. At every performance, one Robert falls through the trapdoor and into a waiting tank, where he drowns. The reconstituted, identical Robert, dispatched elsewhere in the theater, takes the crowd's applause—only to be sacrificed under the stage the following night.

The rising conflict between Robert and Alfred reveals contrasting aspects of each man's personality. Robert is a smooth showman, one whose highest goal is to amaze an audience. Alfred, less concerned with ornate effects, builds his original Transported Man illusion out of two simple doors and a child's red ball. He believes that a magician has a duty to come up with the most baffling trick possible, one that will puzzle not just the public but other professionals. To achieve that, the magician should be prepared to "live his act," to give up a full personal life if that helps him to purify his art. So when one Borden brother loses two fingers to the bullet catch, his twin must slice off his own fingers to continue their charade.

Gradually, the personalities of Robert and Alfred move closer together, and our sympathies shift. At first Robert's love of magic is sensibly balanced by his love for Julia. Her death increases our sense that Alfred is treacherous and Robert a victim. But as Robert launches an all-out effort to destroy his rival, he comes to seem possessed. Both Tesla and Robert's *ingénieur* Cutter warn him that he is becoming obsessive. At the other pole, one of the Borden twins falls in love with Sarah, a young governess. He risks giving his secret away in order to have something like a normal life with her and their daughter Jess. The other, more cynical twin takes up an affair with Olivia, who becomes the act's assistant. The price of finding a woman to love is that sometimes one twin must stand in for the other. These substitutions create emotional disruptions that each woman detects. To the art of magic, the two Alfreds sacrifice not only themselves but also their loved ones.

The Sounds of Magic

The basic story of *The Prestige* is complicated, but it could have been presented in linear order, letting us in on secrets behind the illusions. The plot might have made Robert the protagonist, withholding the information about Albert's personal and professional life that Robert never learns. Alternatively, the plot could have stuck to Alfred's range of knowledge and shown the Borden twins pulling off their stratagems. (David Cronenberg's *Dead Ringers* provides a rough example.) Instead, *The Prestige* wants to mystify us as much as the illusions mystify the magicians and their audiences. The competing magicians are driven by curiosity about how the tricks are done, and this curiosity is central to our experience as well.

Accordingly, the story is presented via unrestricted narration, but it is manipulated through many techniques of plot construction. The plot shuffles story order, plays with levels of knowledge, replays some scenes, and cuts off others, withholding their consequences. Yet these maneuvers don't confuse us about the basic story progression. They arouse curiosity (what has led up to this turn of events?) and suspense (what will happen next?). At the same time, the plot misdirects our attention, suppressing key information about the magicians' secrets.

The overall dramatic progression is framed by present-time action, that of the climactic performance of Robert's Tesla-driven illusion. This stage spectacle leads to one of the Borden twins being arrested, condemned, and hanged for the death of one Robert in his below-stage tank. The other Alfred faces Robert one last time. Most of the plot consists of layered flashbacks showing different stages of the two men's struggle. Our understanding is eased by the fact that most of the story strands are presented chronologically, as in *Citizen Kane* (pp. 101–102). In addition, the basic conflict is maintained through familiar means—scenes of confrontation, or backstage plotting, or confidences shared between the protagonists and their families and friends. Occasionally, there are personalized flashbacks illustrating what a character is recalling, as when in prison Alfred remembers his romance with Sarah. And when the second Alfred confronts the clone Robert at the climax, a series of more impersonal flashbacks shows us what was really happening in scenes we thought we understood.

Along with visual techniques, sound choices help smooth our understanding of the ongoing action. Characters are differentiated through their voices, especially the contrast between Alfred's London working-class accent and Robert's American accent (which turns out to be fake). A sketchy piano motif in the score is associated with Alfred's life with his wife and child. Each locale has its characteristic ambience—the prison with distant scuffling and slamming, the less cavernous echo of the warehouse that becomes Robert's workshop, the warmer sound of the theaters, the crunching snow surrounding Tesla's compound in Colorado.

The sound track is often expressive as well. David Julyan's score consists largely of prolonged notes shifting slightly up or down the scale, creating a moody, layered drone. Julyan leads into Robert's Real Transported Man by layering string chords and soft booms reminiscent of Tesla's lab. The score even makes use of an electronically generated Shepard tone, which creates an illusory sense of continually rising or falling pitch. The danger inherent in the giant Tesla coils is conveyed through brittle, harsh crackling that often cuts off menacingly, as if it had atomized its target. Indeed, from the very start, abrupt silences jolt the viewer into paying attention to the imagery.

As in most modern films, sound plays an important role in linking scenes. A sustained musical chord links a shot of Robert looking out of his coach with a shot of him already striding along the ground. There are many sound bridges as well. At the close of one performance, we hear Alfred saying, "He's complacent, he's predictable," and this comment carries us to the next scene, in which he continues to complain about the magician who employs the two men. Robert is musing on a name for his act, and we hear him ask, "How about the New Transported Man?" as crowds arrive to see that new show.

Nolan and Nolan also employ the *dialogue hook,* the technique of ending a scene with a line that prepares for the next scene. (This isn't a sound bridge, because the line is completed in the lead-in scene.) A simple instance occurs when Tesla asks Robert, "Have you eaten, Mr. Angier?" Cut to the two men at lunch. More dramatically, at a Colorado Springs hotel, the clerk remarks that Tesla has left a box for Robert. Robert: "What box?" Cut to the crate in the hotel ballroom. Dialogue hooks propel the story briskly and can call the viewer's attention to salient aspects of the scene to come, as the box example does.

Naturally, dialogue can mislead as well. Olivia, Robert's spy in his rival's camp, assures him that Alfred doesn't use a double, because the man onstage is lacking

> "With *The Prestige* I was using electronics to achieve effects I couldn't get with the orchestra. . . . There's a lot of stuff in tracks such as 'Colorado Springs' where in the background there is a Shepard's Tone. That's the audio equivalent of an optical illusion so that it appears to rise constantly. It's a very nice effect that Chris and I settled on. It also allows me to produce a very textural bed to lay under the orchestra."
>
> —David Julyan, composer for *The Prestige*

two fingers; we later learn that one Alfred cut off his fingers so the twins would remain identical. In retrospect, many lines prove to have hinted at the Borden brothers' secret. In a quarrel with Olivia, Alfred assures her that "part of me" had a child with Sarah but "part of me" didn't, "the part that found you, the part that's sitting here right now." At the prison, bidding farewell to Fallon (his disguised twin), Alfred refers to the other's urge to quit. "You were right. I should have left him to his damn trick. . . . You go live your life in full now." Robert's own cloning stratagem is foreshadowed when he tries to hire a double: "I don't need him to be my brother. I need him to be me." Few films contain so many lines of dialogue that can be understood in two equally valid ways.

Echoes, Visual and Auditory

Parallelism, a common narrative strategy, is important for advancing the film's action, tracing character development, and maintaining the mysteries. *The Prestige* is based on parallels: two magicians, each with a double and an *ingénieur*. Each magician wounds his counterpart, and each falls in love with a woman but loses her. Other parallels depend on the show business milieu. Acts are rehearsed and re-performed, each time with variations, as when Robert's double becomes more drunk and heedless. The stage trapdoors that we see so often point toward the gallows trapdoor that will end the life of the brusque Borden twin. Julia's drowning in the tank onstage is mirrored in Robert's drowning below stage, and the motif recurs up to the very last image **(7.67–7.69)**.

7.67

There are auditory motifs as well. The harsh sound of iron, suggesting an age of lumbering mechanical contraptions, is first heard in the opening, when the top of the tank slams down with a shudder. From then on, we frequently hear rasping metal—chains in Alfred's prison, the buzzing shock Robert gets from Tesla's fence, the clank when the Tesla coil is switched off (but not concealing the snick of Robert's trapdoor), and the groaning spring that locks a dove into a trick apparatus. When Sarah hangs herself, some metallic clashing is heard, and later, when Alfred kneels to his daughter behind prison bars, we see little of his gestures but judge from the frantic clanking of his chains that he's desperate. This sound motif informs the final sequence, which crosscuts Alfred's hanging with Robert's disposal of Tesla's machine: while Cutter winds a creaking winch, the prisoner's chains clank and drag as he mounts the gallows.

7.68

A less harsh motif dominates the scenes involving Julia's immersion stunt. When she is first bound and submerged in the tank, a soft snare drum taps out a pulse. Later, when she is tied and can't escape, the tick of Cutter's stopwatch takes over the sound track, as if measuring her heartbeat; the sound stops when she is dead. At the film's climax, when Robert's opening act is replayed, a similar pulsation is heard in the nondiegetic music as he drowns—creating a parallel to Julia like the one we've seen in the images (7.67–7.69).

In many films, parallels are carried by dialogue, and *The Prestige* makes constant use of recurring lines. Julia says that calling the act The Great Danton is "sophisticated," and after her death, Robert honors her by using the name: "It's sophisticated." Tesla's remark that "Man's grasp should exceed his nerve" is modified by Robert as his new tagline: "Man's reach exceeds his imagination." The most vivid dialogue motif is

7.69

7.67–7.69 *The Prestige*: **The drowning motif.** The trauma that sets off Robert's obsession: He watches his wife drown in a failed illusion (7.67). In his own version of the Transported Man, Robert drowns every night, replaced by a clone that appears in the auditorium (7.68). One of the sacrificed Roberts is seen submerged in the last shot (7.69).

probably the one launched by Cutter, when he talks of "getting your hands dirty." At various points, Cutter and Alfred invoke this line to taunt Robert's reluctance to risk everything for his magic. At the end, however, confronting Robert's elaborate revenge scheme, both Alfreds admit that he has finally gotten his hands dirty.

As with other techniques, some of these dialogue motifs not only clarify the story but also drop hints about the mysteries. One striking instance occurs when at the climax we hear the warden intone, "Alfred Borden" during the hanging scene but see the mysterious assistant Fallon making his way to Robert. The juxtaposition prepares us for the unmasking of Fallon as one of the twins. At various points, Robert says that in a disappearing act "no one cares about the man who goes into the box. They care about the man who comes out the other side." The motif points toward his method of callously killing one version of himself in the Tesla machine so that his double can be reborn elsewhere. The line also anticipates the ending, in which Alfred, apparently hanged, returns home to Jessie and Cutter: He has come out the other side.

Two Journals

The Prestige uses Robert's and Alfred's journals to frame certain parts of the past. One man reads the other man's diary, which will lead us into or out of a flashback. In itself, the diary device is quite familiar, but *The Prestige* gives it a special emphasis by embedding one diary within another. In the past, Robert acquired Alfred's notebook, and as he deciphered it, Robert recorded his reactions and memories in his own diary during his trip to Colorado. That diary, which comments on Alfred's journal, is later read by Alfred in his cell during his trial.

This plot pattern sounds complex, but in fact the embedded diaries help keep us oriented in time, guiding us from present to past and back again. Again, sound plays a crucial role in acclimating us to the device. We hear the diarist's voice as the reader scans the lines, and this anchors us in two time frames simultaneously.

After the imprisoned Alfred is given Robert's diary, he starts to read it, and we hear Robert's voice-over, representing what he has written. "A cipher—an enigma—a search." The line leads us into the first of several flashbacks to Robert's trip to Tesla. During that visit to Colorado, Robert begins to decipher Borden's notebook. Robert's diary voice-over describes a passage as taking place "just days after he first met me." This segues into Alfred's voice-over, representing what Robert has just decoded from the notebook: "We were two young men devoted to an illusion." The transition to a flashback within a flashback is made clear through the smooth transfers from one voice-over to the next.

The conflict between the men gets sharpened when even the diary entries seem to quarrel. As we see Alfred double over in pain from the botched bullet catch, we hear his diary voice-over explaining that he didn't really know what knot he had tied to bind Robert's wife. "I told him the truth" is followed by a cut back to Colorado, showing Robert reading Alfred's diary as the voice continues: ". . . that I have fought with myself over that night." Robert looks up from the diary and cries out, "How could he not know?" That external line of dialogue is repeated, but now as a voice-over: "How could he not know?" Cut to Alfred reading the line in his cell. The embedded diaries and blended voice-overs create a tense conversation between the rivals across time and space.

Once the early transitions have established the nested time frames, however, Nolan and Nolan start to shift among them without showing the diaries or employing a voice over. Instead, the voices of Robert and Alfred are used to punctuate certain scenes, supplying private thoughts in the manner of an internal diegetic monologue. For example, on the street, Robert spies on Alfred and his family. Robert's commentary bursts out, "I saw happiness—happiness that should have been mine."

Above all, it is Robert's diary voice-over that helps shift among time frames. His summaries of what he reads in Alfred's diary substitute for Alfred's direct voice-over. This prepares us for a surprise when Robert skips to the end of the diary and Albert's voice-over returns ominously:

> Today Olivia proves her love for me—to you, Angier. Yes, Angier, she gave you this notebook at my request. And Tesla is merely the key to my diary, not to my trick. Did you really think I'd part with my secret so easily, after so much? Good-bye, Angier. May you find solace for your thwarted ambition back in your American home.

But in a film of many parallels, even this mocking challenge is surpassed by another. Alfred, reading Robert's journal in his cell, confronts this on the last page:

> But here, at the turn, I must leave you, Borden. Yes, you, Borden. Sitting there in your cell, reading my diary. Awaiting your death, for my murder.

Alfred is as baffled as we are. How could Robert have known that he would die during the trick and that Alfred would be accused of his murder?

In retrospect, we realize that Robert (the clone who survived that night in the theater but didn't reveal himself) has prepared the final entry, and perhaps the whole journal, after Alfred's arrest as a way of tormenting him. The power of these surprises derives from a subtle shift in the voice-over convention. Going beyond simply giving us information, the diary-driven voices have misled us.

Hinting at Secrets

By weaving parallels and journal entries into the plot, the film propels the action forward while enhancing the mysteries. We are continually confronted with new information that has to be fitted into what we have already seen and heard. Yet the film also hints at what is concealed. Most centrally, the secret of both illusions is substitution of a double, and this is suggested by a visual motif. We learn that, since canaries look alike, magicians make canaries vanish and reappear by killing one and substituting another. This is a prototype of Robert's cloning technique, but it also foreshadows the consequences of the Borden twins' decision to live out their act, with one eventually sacrificed for the other.

As we've seen, hinting occurs throughout the dialogue and the voice-overs. As a single character, Alfred seems contradictory, alternately considerate and brusque. He speaks of having a secret, of being torn in two. His wife, Sarah, says that when he says he loves her, some days he does and some days he doesn't. In the climactic quarrel between the couple, she says she knows "what you really are," which panics the cold twin. Perhaps she suspects that there are two Alfreds? Sarah asks if he loves her. "Not today." She hangs herself.

More subtly, offscreen sound is used to withhold the "Prestige," or the payoff, of each man's greatest trick. (Originally, the word *prestige* meant "illusion," especially one that dazzles the eyes.) Alfred's first, minimal version of the Transported Man is shown only in part. We see the setup with Robert watching avidly and Cutter elsewhere in the audience, skeptical. But we don't see the Prestige phase of the trick. Nolan keeps the camera on Cutter while we hear the second door open and the bouncing ball being caught by the duplicate Alfred. Nolan thereby makes the trick itself vague, to be revealed in full later. Conveying the illusion through offscreen sound also emphasizes the contrasting reactions of Cutter, who is unimpressed, and Robert, who considers it "the greatest magic trick I've ever seen."

Another parallel, then: When Robert demonstrates his Real Transported Man before a world-weary theatrical agent, he vanishes from the stage in jagged blasts of the Tesla coil. The agent protests, "He has to come back. There has to be—" "A Prestige?" says a voice from offscreen. The agent turns automatically to see Robert behind him, stepping down from the back of the balcony. We will see the same stunt presented more fully and with panache in the first performance, but the momentary channeling of story information through the agent emphasizes what Robert values as a performer: watching the viewer's stunned expression when confronted with what appears to be a miracle.

The Opening

The use of sound to both reveal and conceal story information, in conjunction with other film techniques, comes at the very start of the film. Here sound and image must orient us to the narrative world, introducing the main characters and dramatic issues. The opening must also plant details that may seem unimportant or puzzling but that will later play major roles. The opening of *The Prestige* also introduces us to one of the film's major storytelling techniques, that of the voice-over commentary we encounter in the diaries. And some clues tantalize us but become comprehensible once we have penetrated the film's secrets. Once more, we find that sound assists both clear storytelling and bold misdirection.

The most dramatic portions of the opening involve a performance of Robert's Tesla-inspired version of the Transported Man. Alfred, disguised in the audience, goes onstage to inspect the gadget and then dodges into the wings and down under the stage. There he finds the tank awaiting Robert. As the trick is consummated, Robert plummets into the water and starts to drown before Alfred's eyes.

The performance is played with no dialogue, apart from the moment when Alfred assures a stagehand that he's part of the act. There is a soft but ominous drone from the musical score, overridden by fierce crackling as the Tesla coil fires up. As with the other major illusions, the act's payoff takes place offscreen; we see the result when Robert falls through the trapdoor. The coil's crackling and the musical score stop abruptly, in a harsh cutoff that will be typical of the rest of the film, and we hear a splash as Robert is submerged. The top of the tank snaps shut with a whang. Then another long silence, enhancing suspense.

The theater audience stirs restlessly. Where has Robert gone? Meanwhile, below stage, Alfred approaches the drowning Robert, and we hear the heartbeat pulse in the orchestra, foreshadowing Cutter's ticking stopwatch. As Robert thrashes underwater, the nondiegetic music turns into frantic string twitterings. The image fades to black, the music dies, and the next sequence, at Alfred's trial, begins.

But this highly dramatic scene, showing a magic trick apparently gone horribly wrong, is crosscut with a more mundane, even trivial moment, taking place in an unidentified time. We see Cutter stroll past a row of cages, select one canary, put it into a cage, and make it disappear. He then makes it reappear to the delight of a little girl. (We'll later learn that she's Alfred's daughter Jessie.) There is no dialogue from within this scene, only the chirping of the birds and the sound of Cutter performing the trick. The tense, somber music starts in this sequence and continues until the moment of Robert's immersion.

Two magic tricks, one of great simplicity and the other of lethal complexity, are shown in alternation. In three minutes, the film has aroused all manner of questions about what has led up to these events and what will follow. The narration also asks us what connection we are to make between the canary trick and the elaborate stage show. The answer, itself partial and teasing, is provided by a voice-over commentary.

We hear Cutter's voice explaining that every magic trick has three parts, and his layout of the phases corresponds to both crosscut lines of action. His description of the Pledge, the promise that things work in the ordinary way, is heard in his voice-over as he silently shows Jessie the canary and puts it in the cage. Cut to Robert displaying himself and his machine. Spectators, including Alfred, climb onstage to inspect the gadget.

Then, Cutter explains, comes the Turn, the moment when the ordinary becomes extraordinary. Covering the birdcage with a scarf, he flattens it. Cutter's commentary coincides with Robert stepping into the electrical field while Alfred explores the trapdoor area below stage. Finally, after the canary and Robert have disappeared, Cutter's voice-over says:

> But you wouldn't clap yet. Because making something disappear isn't enough. You have to bring it back. That's why every magic trick has a third act—the hardest part. The part we call the Prestige.

As we hear these words, we see him showing Jessie the revived canary—a successful feat of legerdemain—crosscut with Robert's uneasy audience and shots of Alfred staring at Robert struggling underwater.

Cutter's voice has been closely miked in a dry recording, lending it the sort of intimate, direct-address perspective we'll encounter in the diary voice-overs. But now, at the fade-out, in a more hollow timbre, another man's voice repeats, "The Prestige." As the new scene fades up, Cutter is in the witness box. His dialogue now comes from a more reverberant sound field, suitable to a large courtroom. His voice-over explanation of a trick's three acts is now motivated as his testimony at Alfred's trial.

Cutter's voice-over introduces some central themes, such as the idea that a magic trick has an artistic structure that demands both skill and showmanship—the two features that distinguish Alfred (skill) and Robert (showmanship). Cutter also stresses the need to distract the audience, because, he says, the spectator wants to be fooled. This could be taken as a commentary on our own urge to overlook details in watching the film. And Cutter's stress on bringing back the vanished object establishes the motif that when the Prestige arrives, no one cares about the man in the box.

In the plot's overall patterning, Cutter's commentary establishes the death of Robert as a flashback scene from the present time of the court proceedings. At the film's close, we learn that the canary trick that Cutter performs is a sort of flashforward, referring to a still later present time enclosing the whole film. The crosscutting has shuttled us between two moments of story time, while the voice-over has put us in yet a third, the court testimony. That testimony is nonsimultaneous with respect to both lines of visual action; it takes place after the death of Robert but long before the scene with Jessie. This opening not only introduces us to major characters and themes but also establishes the time-juggling shifts that we'll encounter in the film to come.

Cutter's voice-over prepares us for the tight image/sound synchronization that will carry the plot forward. His voice speaks of showing the Pledge object; he shows the canary; cut to Robert displaying his machine. When Cutter says the object probably isn't normal, we see Alfred tear off his false beard to prove he's part of the performance. Cutter explains the second phase, and as his voice says, "The Turn," cut to Robert literally turning to us. Cutter flattens the birdcage as his voice speaks of the "extraordinary"; cut to Robert galvanized by the Tesla coil.

The commentary drops a few hints, too, as when Cutter indirectly introduces the film's protagonists (**7.70, 7.71**). Later, as Alfred prowls in the stage cellar, studying the water tank, Cutter speaks of the audience "not really looking" at what is going on in the trick. Robert plummets into the tank, the lock snaps shut, and Cutter says, "You want to be—" Cut to him snatching the scarf away, showing that the birdcage has vanished as his voice-over finishes: "—fooled." Indeed, Alfred will be fooled, since he does not understand Robert's manipulation of his clones until the end. Cutter's calm delivery about "bringing back" the ordinary object, timed to his presentation of the canary, serves as an upbeat contrast to the stage act. Jessie applauds, but Robert's audience doesn't, because the Prestige ("the hardest part") is missing. Robert, flailing underwater, will not be brought back—at least, not for some time.

This opening could not be as economical and intriguing as it is without Cutter's voice-over narration. The crosscutting and juxtapositions of dialogue will reappear in the climax and be finally explained in the final shots. Yet there is one more element in the opening passage to consider.

The very first shot of the film fades in on a leftward tracking shot across a field of top hats (**7.72**). Later we will learn

7.70

7.71

7.70–7.71 Cutter introduces the protagonists. As Cutter's voice-over talks about a magician showing us something ordinary, his mention of "a man" is synchronized with the first shot of Alfred, disguised in the audience (7.70). But Alfred isn't the man central to the Pledge. That is Robert himself, seen in the next shot (7.71). Along with the editing, the commentary subtly establishes these two as the central antagonists.

7.72

7.73

7.74

7.72–7.74 Opening hints. In the first shot of *The Prestige*, the camera tracks over the scattered top hats (7.72). The next shot continues to move along several parakeet cages (7.73), creating a parallel based on the idea of identical copies. Addressing Jessie, Cutter invites us as well to consider how a magic trick may mislead the audience (7.74).

that those are the hats that Tesla has accidentally cloned in his experiments. The next shot shows a row of canaries in cages **(7.73);** one of these will be the star of Cutter's trick for Jessie **(7.74).** In hindsight, we can see that these two shots hint at how both Alfred and Robert accomplish their magic—by using exact copies. In addition, just as a canary has to die in order to disappear, death will haunt each magician's double. Alfred has given up a great deal for his art, with each twin living only half a life. But Robert has wound up devoting himself to his craft just as passionately. In dying and being reborn every night, he has embraced what Alfred calls "total self-sacrifice."

As usual, sound plays a role, too. At three points in the rest of the film, Alfred will ask someone, "Are you watching closely?" It's his mocking warning that he will practice some deceptive sleight of hand. At the very start, however, as the camera coasts over the top hats, we hear this line for the first time. Shifted out of its story position, spoken by a character we don't yet know, the question becomes a challenge and warning to the viewer. As a film inviting us to unmask its own legerdemain, *The Prestige* could just as easily start with the question "Are you listening closely?"

SUMMARY

As usual, both wide viewing and focused attention will sharpen your awareness of this technique. You can get comfortable with the analytical tools we have suggested by asking several questions about a film's sound:

1. What sounds are present—music, speech, noise? How are loudness, pitch, and timbre used? Is the mixture sparse or dense? Modulated or abruptly changing?

2. Is the sound related rhythmically to the image? If so, how?

3. Is the sound faithful or unfaithful to its perceived source?

4. *Where* is the sound coming from? In the story's space or outside it? Onscreen or offscreen? If offscreen, how is it shaping your response to what you're seeing?

5. *When* is the sound occurring? Simultaneously with the onscreen story action? Before? After?

6. How are the various sorts of sounds organized across a sequence or the entire film? What patterns are formed, and how do they reinforce aspects of the film's overall form?

7. For each of questions 1–6, what *purposes* are fulfilled and what *effects* are achieved by the sonic manipulations?

Practice at answering such questions will familiarize you with the basic uses of film sound.

As always, it isn't enough to name and classify. These categories and terms are most useful when we take the next step and examine how the types of sound chosen by the filmmakers *function* in the total film.

 ## RECOMMENDED DVD AND BLU-RAY SUPPLEMENTS

The section called "Sound Design Suite" (25 minutes) in the *Kingdom of Heaven* supplements is an unusually detailed and wide-ranging discussion of aspects of sound creation. It consists of a set of featurettes on dialogue editing, ADR, Foley recording, and mixing.

ADR, the postdubbing of dialogue, seldom finds its way onto DVD supplements. An exception comes in "Peter Lorre's ADR Tracks" on the *20,000 Leagues Under the Sea* DVD. (The track is well hidden: in the "Bonus Material" section, click right to "Lost Treasures" and then choose "Audio Archives #2.") The opposite technique, recording songs for playback and lip-synching on set during the filming of musical numbers, is demonstrated in "Scoring Stage Sessions" on the *Singin' in the Rain* disc. The short "*Munich*: Editing, Sound and Music," includes a description of how sound in the post-production process can begin during principal photography.

An excellent survey of how sound tracks are built up is "On Sound Design," for *Master and Commander,* where a dense ambient mix had to support the depiction of a crowded ship. This supplement shows why so much dialogue recorded during filming is not usable and must be replaced by ADR. Sound-effects specialists demonstrate the subtleties of re-creating the noises of firing of various types of weapons.

How was sound created in the era before digital multi-track mixing? The documentary "Akira Kurosawa: It Is Wonderful to Create," on the Criterion boxed set of *Seven Samurai,* supplies intriguing insights. At 42 minutes into the documentary, sound-effects recordist Ichiro Minawa discusses being limited to four tracks and creating Foley effects.

The "Sound Design" section of "Music and Sound" on the *Toy Story 2* supplements includes a clear example of how sound functions within scenes. In the scene where the band of toys crosses a street full of traffic, the filmmakers' goal was to create extreme contrasts between movement and stasis. One technique was to stop and start the music as the toys

froze and then moved on. The scene is played through with only sound effects, only music, and the final mix.

Each volume of *The Lord of the Rings* offers a supplement called "The Soundscapes of Middle-earth," with the three adding up to about an hour. The *Fellowship of the Ring* documentary discusses ADR as well as sound effects. Each volume also contains a segment, "Music for Middle-Earth," totaling about an hour. The *Two Towers* DVD set contains a demonstration of sound mixing, with eight versions of the same clip from the Helm's Deep battle: one with the sound recorded on-set during filming, six with selected parts of the sound (music in one, weapon sounds in another, and so on), and the final mix. The six incomplete tracks have already been partially mixed from separate recordings. Originally, each sound was recorded separately. Early in *The Return of the King,* for example, as Gandalf leads the group through the woods to visit Isengard, one track was made just for the clicking of Legolas's arrows in his quiver—a sound barely distinguishable in the final mix.

Discussions of musical scores are among the most common of making-of supplements. In a particularly detailed and systematic discussion, "Scoring *War of the Worlds,*" John Williams comments extensively on the narrative functions of his music. The supplement was directed by Steven Spielberg. In the "Music" supplement for *The Golden Compass,* composer Alexandre Desplat discusses musical motifs; he also talks about the exotic instruments he chose to distinguish the story's ethnic groups. Hans Zimmer, composer for *The Dark Knight,* describes the dissonant music associated with the Joker character in "The Sound of Anarchy" supplement.

Sergio Leone's Westerns are often called operatic, and film music historian Jon Burlingame explains why in "Il Maestro: Ennio Morricone and *The Good, the Bad, and the Ugly.*" Morricone wrote Leone's scores in advance, and this supplement explains how the music guided the director during shooting and editing.

8

Summary: Style and Film Form

I n Part Two, we considered how the parts of a film create its overall *form* and how that form engages the viewer. In this, the third part of the book, we've explored the techniques of the film medium. Just as filmmakers decide how to construct a plot that will shape the viewer's experience, they make choices within each of the areas of technique we've examined—mise-en-scene, cinematography, editing, and sound—and then organizes those choices. The distinctive patterns of technique we find in a film constitute its **style.**

The Concept of Style

From the start of this book, in following Michael Mann's production of *Collateral,* we've seen how artistic decisions govern a film's distinctive style.

The earlier chapters in this part showed how a film's style is coordinated with its overall form. Buster Keaton's use of deep space reinforces the comedy of *Our Hospitality*'s plot, and Jean Renoir's long takes and camera movements create connections and parallels among characters in *Grand Illusion.* John Huston's choices about continuity editing emphasize certain aspects of the opening of *The Maltese Falcon,* while Sergei Eisenstein's discontinuity editing provides thematic commentary on the action of *October.* We've also analyzed how voice-over narration in *The Prestige* both explains the story and half-reveals certain secrets. Our less extended examples have pointed to the same conclusion: Patterns of techniques work within the film's overall form, shaping the effects the movie has on its viewer.

As a start, then, we use the term "style" to talk about particular films. Sometimes, though, critics talk about style in several films by the same filmmaker. We examined how *Our Hospitality* organizes its comic mise-en-scene around long shots; this is part of Buster Keaton's style in other films, too. It's not surprising that we extend the term to talk about a filmmaker's distinctive style across several films. Everyone builds up certain habits in ordinary life, a particular way of dressing or talking or behaving with others, and we often call that his or her personal style.

In art, as in ordinary life, this styling may be done deliberately or without much thought. Either way, it comes down to decisions. Recall a quotation from Chapter 2: "At the point of making the movie," says Ethan Coen, "it's just about making individual choices," and his brother Joel adds: "You make specific choices that you think are appropriate or compelling or interesting for that particular scene. Then, at the end of the day, you put it all together and somebody looks at it and, if there's some consistency to it, they say, 'Well, that's their style.'"

❝ The choices you make push you in a certain direction, and that becomes what people call style."
—Chris Doyle, cinematographer, *Chungking Express*

The term "style" has still other meanings. Sometimes we speak of a *group style*—the consistent use of techniques across the work of several filmmakers. We can speak of a German Expressionist style or a Soviet montage style. In Part Six, we consider some significant group styles that have emerged in film history.

CREATIVE DECISIONS

Style and the Filmmaker

Throughout this book we've suggested that considering a filmmaker's creative options can make you a keener viewer. When it comes to style, as with form, creative choices aren't infinite. The filmmaker is always choosing within limits.

What can limit the choices? For one thing, technology. Before 1928, directors didn't have the option of using synchronized dialogue, and making films in lifelike color was very difficult and expensive. Even today, when the range of technical choices seems far broader, there are limits. Contemporary filmmakers can't use the orthochromatic film stock of the silent era, although in some respects it was superior to today's stocks. As digital grading advances, filmmakers will have to abandon the advantages of photochemical grading.

It isn't only technology that constrains creative choices. So do tastes, fashion, dominant trends, and stylistic norms. D. W. Griffith is acclaimed as a great director, but directors today would be reluctant to let their performers display the sort of acting we find in *Intolerance*. Few directors have the power to make a black-and-white film today, since it's widely believed that audiences will spurn films that aren't in full color. Changes in viewers' tastes eliminate certain options.

Some constraints, as we saw in Chapter 1, stem from the mode of production in which the filmmaker works. The studio mode of production developed a standardized menu of options, such as continuity editing, partly because that makes planning, shooting, and postproduction more efficient. Filmmakers working independently have more freedom to make daring choices about form and style, as is seen in limit cases like Michael Snow's *Wavelength* but also in unusual films like *Memento* and *Run Lola Run*.

Filmmakers know that making one decision doesn't end the matter. One choice leads to further choices—and constraints. If you shoot a conversation in the intensified continuity technique, giving each speaker a tight single shot, you'll probably have to cut more often. You need to remind the audience of the other characters who are present, even if they don't speak. If you choose to play a scene in a long take, your actors' performances must more be carefully timed and executed than if you build the scene out of lots of cuts. Choosing to shoot in 3D enforces a new set of constraints. With a distant convergence point (p. 181), a character in the foreground can't be partly cut off by the left or right frameline, because then the audience sees a bisected body floating out at them. Every choice creates new problems to be solved.

As a result of pressures like these, a filmmaker tends to rely on similar techniques across the film. Once certain choices have been made in one scene, it's easier to replicate them in another. But there are more positive reasons for directors embracing certain possibilities and ruling out others. Most directors feel comfortable with a particular stylistic option because it suits the stories they're telling. Antonioni's complex staging techniques in *L'Avventura* are appropriate for characters whose feelings fluctuate unpredictably from moment to moment (4.120, 4.121). The filmmaker's personality plays a role too. Some directors prefer straightforward, efficient technique, while others, like Alfred Hitchcock and James Cameron, enjoy setting themselves technical problems. And some filmmakers want to find new possibilities in the techniques that appeal to them. Eisenstein plunged into editing because he believed he could force it to do things it had never done before.

Decision Making: Techniques Working Together

Because one choice creates further choices later, filmmakers tend to think out their decisions fairly carefully. Many, for instance, watch for ways to create parallels among situations and characters. Piotr Sobocinski, cinematographer for Krystytof Kieslowski, says that in *Three Colors: Red,* a crane shot down to a fashion show was designed to recall an earlier camera movement, when the camera craned down as a book fell into the street. Similarly, in filming *Viva Zapata!* Elia Kazan tracked in on Zapata, who is ignoring the fact that a crowd of peasants is marching with him. "We had to go close on that shot and dolly [i.e., track] because what I wanted to show was his expression or lack of expression. We later contrasted that with a similar dolly shot on the police chief beginning to notice what was happening. The point was to contrast those two attitudes."

Films setting up narrative or thematic contrasts may recruit several techniques to reinforce them. Jacques Tati's *Mon Oncle* opposes the charm and community spirit of old Parisian neighborhoods to the sterile, enclosed homes that replace them. M. Hulot lives in a ramshackle apartment building on a quiet little square. The Arpel family—Hulot's sister, brother-in-law, and nephew—have just moved into an ultramodern house full of high-tech gadgets and chic but uncomfortable furniture. Scenes in Hulot's neighborhood tend to be accompanied by jaunty music. In this locale, the camera stays outside his apartment, stressing the interactions of the many people living and working around the square **(8.1).** By contrast, the Arpel scenes contain no music. Instead, we hear the tapping of shoes on stone floors and the clicks and whirs of the absurd appliances. There are frequent shots inside the house, and the street is almost invisible behind the family's security wall **(8.2).**

Many filmmakers let stylistic elements cooperate to differentiate locales or story lines. In *Inception,* a complicated science-fiction plot takes its characters into four layers of dreams within dreams. Each dream level involves a distinct fantasy world, and about midway through the film, the action starts shifting abruptly among these levels. Yet settings, costumes, lighting, color schemes, weather, and other aspects of the mise-en-scene allow us to keep track of which level each shot occurs in **(8.3–8.6).** Cinematographer Wally Pfister said of the different levels, "We wanted to have the color palette change quite a bit when we go from one location to another. . . . You immediately know where you are, even if we cut to a tighter shot or to something that is slightly out of context. It's a choice that helps tell the story." Steven Soderbergh's *Traffic* uses color contrasts to help spectators to recognize the three separate plotlines as he crosscuts them. There are washed-out, yellow images for the scenes in Mexico, blue-cast scenes for the story of a newly appointed drug czar and his addicted daughter, and a more conventional range of colors for scenes involving the wealthy wife of an arrested drug smuggler.

When we see techniques lining up and working together this way, it's likely that the patterning has been created more or less consciously by the filmmaker. Perhaps it wasn't done through elaborate storyboarding or deep thought. Often, as the Coens' remarks suggest, a director may shoot one scene fairly spontaneously, then realize that another scene could parallel it through lighting or music or some other technique. That is, the filmmaker may discover significant patterns in the process of making the film. The task then becomes to find ways to enhance those patterns in ways that will give the audience a particular experience.

8.1

8.2

8.1–8.2 Old style community, modern domestic fortress. In *Mon Oncle.* Mr. Hulot chats with a neighbor while others pass (8.1). The Arpels's inconveniently laid-out garden has a metal security door that blots out their view of the street (8.2).

Watching and Listening: Style and the Viewer

During a film, the filmmakers' stylistic choices register on us at every moment. We don't take them in passively; we're alert to them, even though we may not be aware of how sensitive we are.

For example, we tend to have expectations about style. If we see two characters in a long shot, we expect a cut-in to a closer view. If the actor seems about to leave

8.3

8.4

8.5

8.6

8.3–8.6 Differentiating dreams. *Inception*'s first dream level takes place mostly outdoors in a city, with a white, gray, and black color scheme tinged with blue. In this dream, it's raining (8.3). The second dream's action occurs inside a hotel. The characters wear business clothes, and the corridors and bathrooms have warm brown and orange tones (8.4). The next level involves a large gray fortress and white costumes, set against a snowy mountain landscape (8.5). Finally, "Limbo" places the characters in deserted cities and bare seascapes, where high-contrast sunshine creates both glare and deep shadows (8.6).

the frame, we expect the camera to pan or track to keep the person in the shot. If a character speaks, we expect to hear diegetic sound that is faithful to its source. Like other kinds of expectations, stylistic ones derive from both our experience of the world generally (people talk; they don't chirp) and our experience of film and other media. The specific film's style can confirm our expectations, or modify them or challenge them.

The conventions of the classical Hollywood cinema and of specific genres provide a firm basis for reinforcing our prior assumptions. But other films ask us to revise our expectations somewhat. *Our Hospitality* accustoms us to deep-space manipulations of figures and objects, while *Grand Illusion* makes us expect that camera movements will link characters. Still other films make highly unusual technical choices, and to follow them we must construct new stylistic expectations. The editing discontinuities in *October* and the voice-over narration in *The Prestige* in effect teach us how to understand the film's distinctive style.

In other words, a director directs not only the cast and crew. A director also directs us, directs our attention, and thus shapes our reaction. The filmmaker's technical decisions affect what we perceive and how we respond.

Analyzing Style

We usually don't notice style; we're too busy following the story. Suppose, though, we want to notice stylistic patterning—to enhance our appreciation, or to understand how we might also create films. How can we study style?

One suggestion is apparent: *Look and listen carefully*. But what should we watch and listen for? The last four chapters have made plenty of suggestions. We've also urged you: *Think like a filmmaker*. That mindset can coax you into considering the functions of what you're seeing and hearing. In addition, you can try picking a single scene and concentrating on how techniques blend to create particular effects. We'll do that shortly.

First let's consider four general questions we can ask in trying to understand a film's style.

1. What Is the Film's Overall Form?

A good first step is to think about how the film is put together as a whole. If it's a narrative film, it will draw on all the principles discussed in Chapter 3. (Not all films tell stories. We'll discuss other types of form in Chapter 10.) Typically, we'll confront a plot that cues us to construct a story. The film will manipulate causality, time, and space. It will probably give characters goals, motives, thoughts, and feelings, all of which need to be conveyed to the viewer through form and style. The film will use its opening (abrupt or gradual) to introduce a situation. It will have a distinct pattern of development—a search, a journey, an escalating conflict. Characters will change, situations will become emotionally weighted, and parallels will emerge. The film's narration will manipulate what we know and how and when we learn of it, to guide us toward specific responses. And it may play games with conventions by rearranging scenes in time, manipulating degrees of subjectivity, or otherwise challenging us to create a story out of the plot's presentation. Whatever the film's overall form, once you have a grasp on it, you'll find it easier to understand how style works, and works on us.

2. What Are the Primary Techniques Being Used?

CONNECT TO THE BLOG
www.davidbordwell.net/blog

We discuss *Indiana Jones and the Kingdom of the Crystal Skull* and some aspects of Steven Spielberg's editing and use of light in "Reflections in a crystal eye."

Here your analysis can draw on our survey of technical possibilities in Chapters 4–7. You can look for things like color, lighting, framing, cutting, and sound. Once you notice them, you can identify them as creative options: not just music, but nondiegetic music; not just framing, but low-angle framing.

Noting and naming are only the beginning. You should try to identify *salient* techniques. What techniques does the film most rely on? The jerky forward zoom in *Wavelength* and the rapid, discontinuous editing of *October* stand out because they play a central role in the overall effect of each film.

In addition, what is salient depends partly on your interests. If a film's style strikes you as typical of a broader approach to filmmaking, you may focus on how the technique conforms to stylistic expectations. The 180-degree editing of *The Maltese Falcon* isn't obvious or emphasized, but adherence to rules of classical continuity is one characteristic of the film's style. Our purpose in Chapter 6 was to show that the film is typical in this respect.

If you want to explore more unusual stylistic devices, you can concentrate on more original, even puzzling choices. Eisenstein's editing in *October* is unusual, representing choices that few filmmakers would make. It was the originality of these options that we chose to stress in Chapter 6. From the standpoint of originality, costume in *October* isn't as salient a stylistic feature as editing because it isn't as original. Your decision about what techniques are salient will be influenced partly by what the film emphasizes, and partly by what you're interested in knowing more about.

3. What Patterns Are Formed by the Techniques?

Once you've identified salient techniques, you can notice how they are organized. Techniques will be repeated and varied, developed and paralleled, across the whole film or within a single segment. Chapters 4–7 have shown how this occurs in some films.

You can zero in on stylistic patterns in two ways. One way is to reflect on your responses. If a scene begins with a track-in, do you expect that it will end with a track-out? If you see a character looking left, do you assume that someone or

8.7

8.9

8.8

8.10

8.7–8.10 Patterns of camera distance and angle. During the initial conversation in *The Silence of the Lambs*, shooting in depth emphasizes the distance between Clarice and Lecter, and each one looks slightly to the right or left (8.7, 8.8). As their conversations become more intense and intimate, the camera positions move closer to each character and shift subtly toward the axis of action until each person is looking directly into the lens (8.9, 8.10).

something is offscreen and will be revealed in the next shot? If you feel a mounting excitement in an action scene, is that traceable to a quickening tempo in the music or to accelerating editing?

A second strategy is to look for stylistic patterns that reinforce the unfolding narrative. As we've seen throughout this part of the book, filmmakers often deliberately design the film's style to create parallels or underscore developments in the drama. Shifting color schemes reflect three stages of the plot's development in *Women in Love* (4.42–4.44). The repetition of the line "Are you watching closely?" in *The Prestige* gives weight to the way both the magicians and the film's narration lead and mislead us about what is happening (p. 306).

Even within a shorter span, style can create a subtle sense of narrative progression. A scene usually has a dramatic pattern of encounter, conflict, and outcome, and the style often reflects this, with the cutting becoming more marked and the shots coming closer to the characters as the scene progresses. In *The Silence of the Lambs,* for example, the scenes between Clarice Starling and Hannibal Lecter tend to begin with conventional shot/reverse-shot conversations but become more intimate and psychologically revealing **(8.7–8.10)**. In a later chapter, we'll see how style can also reinforce the organization of nonnarrative films.

Occasionally, stylistic patterning doesn't accord neatly with the overall structure of the film. Style can claim our attention in its own right. We saw this happen in such experimental films as *Serene Velocity* and *Wavelength*. It can happen in more straightforward narratives, too. In 6.144 and 6.145, a cut from a washline to a living room acts as a transition between scenes. But the cut is of interest for other reasons, too, since we don't expect a narrative film to treat objects as flat patches of color to be matched across shots. This sort of attention to graphic play is more common in abstract form.

In this passage from Ozu's *Ohayo,* a stylistic choice becomes salient because it goes beyond its narrative function. Even here, though, stylistic patterns continue to call on the viewer's expectations and to draw the spectator into a dynamic process. Anyone who notices the graphic match on red objects in *Ohayo* will most likely be intrigued at such an unconventional way of editing. And, if stylistic patterns do swerve off on their own, we still need a sense of the film's narrative organization to show how and when that happens.

CONNECT TO THE BLOG
www.davidbordwell.net/blog

In "Alignment, allegiance, and murder," we consider how staging, camera position, and cutting blend to create a play of point-of-view in a scene.

CONNECT TO THE BLOG
www.davidbordwell.net/blog

For a discussion of how various techniques of film style can function to call our attention to things, see "Gradation of emphasis, starring Glenn Ford."

❝There's no scene in any movie that 50 different directors couldn't have done 50 different ways."
—Paul Mazursky, director

CONNECT TO THE BLOG
www.davidbordwell.net/blog

Subtle stylistic echoes enrich *The Prestige,* as we show in "Niceties: How classical filmmaking can be at once simple and precise."

4. What Functions Do the Techniques and Patterns Fulfill?

Now we look for the role that style plays in the film's overall form. Does the use of music or noise alter our attitude toward a character? Does the composition of the shot tend to make us concentrate on a particular detail (4.151, the shot of Anne's face in *Day of Wrath*)? Does the use of camera movement hold off story information to create suspense, as in the opening of *Touch of Evil* (pp. 214–216)? Does the use of discontinuous editing cue us to create thematic comparisons, as in the sequence we analyzed in *October* (pp. 261–264)?

A direct route to noticing function is to notice the *effects* of the film on our viewing experience. Style may enhance *emotional* aspects of the film. Rapid cutting in *The Birds* triggers shock, while the fluctuating drone of the score in *The Prestige* creates a tense but melancholy tone. The sadness of Elsa's life with her daughter in *Grand Illusion* is conveyed by the tracking shot to the table that is "too large," especially when we compare that shot with Rauffenstein's conscription of a chapel for his quarters (5.183–5.193). Style is intimately tied to the emotions that the film expresses and that it can engender in the viewer.

Style also shapes *meaning.* Eisenstein clearly wants us to take away a message from the October sequence: The Provisional Government is dictatorial, oppressing both the families at home and the soldiers on the front. We should, however, avoid reading isolated elements atomistically, taking them out of context. As we noted on p. 191, a high angle does not automatically mean "defeat," just as a low angle does not automatically mean "power." Thematic interpretation can be sensitive to contexts—the particular scene, the whole film, the patterns of techniques, and the overall effects.

Meaning is only one type of effect, and there is no reason to expect that every stylistic feature will yield thematic significance. One part of a director's job is to direct our attention, and so style will often function simply *perceptually*—to get us to notice things, to emphasize one thing over another, to clarify, intensify, or complicate our understanding of the action. One shot in *Red Beard* makes the woman patient seem close to the young doctor, but another corrects that impression (5.39, 5.40). Here, as often happens, film style is readjusting the story information we're getting, guiding our uptake moment by moment.

One way to sharpen our sense of the functions of specific techniques is to *imagine alternatives* and reflect on what differences would result. Suppose the director had made a different technical choice. How would this create a different effect?

Our Hospitality creates its gags by putting two elements into the same shot and letting us observe the comic juxtaposition. Suppose Keaton had instead isolated each element in a single shot and then linked the two elements by editing. The basic information might be the same, but our response would be different. Instead of a simultaneous presentation that lets our attention shuttle to and fro, we would have a more step-by-step pattern of building up the gags and paying them off. Or, suppose that John Huston had handled the opening scene of *The Maltese Falcon* as a single take with camera movement. How would he then have drawn our attention to Brigid O'Shaughnessy's and Sam Spade's facial reactions, and how would this have affected our expectations? By focusing on effects and imagining alternatives to the technical choices that were made, the analyst can gain a sharp sense of the particular functions of style in the given film.

The rest of this chapter provides two illustrations of how we can analyze film style. First we concentrate on a single scene, from Alfred Hitchcock's *Shadow of a Doubt*. (See "A Closer Look.") This will show you how all the techniques we've surveyed can work together to create a specific attitude toward a character and a phase of story action. Even though we focus on one scene, our analysis has to take other scenes, and the film's overall narrative form, into account.

Uncle Charlie has come to visit his sister's family in Santa Rosa, California. Charlie is a suave, sophisticated man who flashes money around freely. His sister Emmy adores him and has even named her daughter Charlie in his honor. But as Uncle Charlie lingers in town, Little Charlie begins to suspect that he's a serial killer who preys on rich widows. She can't prove it—she has only the shadow of a doubt—but she now sees his menacing side. In many scenes, Hitchcock organizes film style to link our perception and understanding of events to those of Little Charlie.

A decisive moment in this progression comes in a scene of the family having dinner. Uncle Charlie praises small-town living. Towns like Santa Rosa, he says, keep their women busy, while cities let them sink into self-indulgence. He slips into a venomous monologue:

> "And what do the wives do, these useless women? You see them in the hotels, the best hotels, every day by the thousands. Drinking the money, eating the money, losing the money at bridge, playing all day and all night. Smelling of money. Proud of their jewelry but nothing else. Horrible . . . fat, faded, greedy women."

Reacting to this, Little Charlie blurts out, "But they're alive! They're human beings!" Uncle Charlie replies, "Are they? Are they, Charlie? Are they human or are they fat, wheezing animals?" As if realizing he's gone too far, Uncle Charlie smiles and switches back to his ingratiating manner.

This powerful scene depends on many stylistic decisions about how to affect the audience. The dialogue constitutes a step in the process of strengthening Little Charlie's suspicions that her uncle is a murderer. The scene nudges us closer to the same belief. The scene also suggests that Uncle Charlie is slightly mad; his killing proceeds not only from lust for money but also from a deep-seated hatred of women. His harangue gives us a better understanding of his personality. Our response has an emotional dimension, too, since in his description of the women he dehumanizes them to chilling effect.

Within the context of the film, this scene serves several functions. The development of the story depends on Uncle Charlie's visit to his family and Little Charlie's growing suspicions about his murderous instincts. She can't tell anyone the truth, though, since doing so would devastate her mother. This creates a powerful conflict, not only between Little Charlie and her uncle but also within her mind. Similarly, as she learns the truth, her attitude changes. Initially, she worships her uncle, but eventually, she becomes bitterly aware of his real nature, and her trust in the world starts to crack. The dinner scene, then, contributes to a growth in Little Charlie's character.

Even the fact that the scene occurs at dinner is important. More cheerful scenes have taken place at the same table. At one point, Uncle Charlie gives Emmy restored photographs of their parents, which seems to convey his sincere love for her and their family. Little Charlie is exuberant **(8.11)**. In these early scenes, we're told of a special rapport that uncle and niece share, and he even presents her with an elegant ring **(8.12)**. The ring plays an important role in the plot, since Little Charlie discovers an inscription on it (a clue that it came from one of her uncle's victims). So Uncle Charlie's hate-filled monologue fits into a pattern of other moments we've already seen.

Hitchcock firmly believed in using the medium to arouse the viewer's mind and feelings. So, as Uncle Charlie launches into his monologue, Hitchcock presents us with an establishing shot of the entire table **(8.13)**. We've seen similar shots in earlier scenes, and it orients us to the positions of the scene's major characters. At the same time, Hitchcock stages the scene so that Uncle Charlie rather than Emmy's husband sits at the head of the table. His domination of the household is presented visually. As Charlie starts to talk, after a shot of Emmy we get a brief shot of Little Charlie, eying him anxiously **(8.14)**. When he begins to denounce the "useless women," we see a close view of him as he continues his attack **(8.15)**.

8.11 In *Shadow of a Doubt*, Little Charlie is delighted when Uncle Charlie presents pictures of her grandparents.

8.12 In an eerie parallel to a lovers' engagement, Uncle Charlie presents his niece with a ring.

8.13 A general shot shows the family at table, with the two Charlies most visible.

Joseph Cotten's performance is very important here. He seethes with resentment of the "fat, faded, greedy women." He delivers the speech without blinking, as if musing to himself rather than talking to others. Hitchcock magnifies the effect of Cotten's performance with a tracking shot that eliminates everyone else at the table. The camera comes steadily forward, filling the frame with Uncle Charlie's face as his monologue increases in anger and intensity **(8.16)**.

Hitchcock could have used other techniques. He could have filmed Uncle Charlie from the rear, concealing his face but showing us the reactions of others at the table. He could have interrupted shots of Uncle Charlie with the reactions of Emmy, her husband, and her children. But Hitchcock achieves a very different effect by the slow, riveting movement toward Uncle Charlie's face as his hatred for women surfaces. Even though he's speaking the lines aloud, the relentless forward tracking movement suggests that we're getting a glimpse into his mind.

When Little Charlie objects, "But they're alive! They're human beings!" most directors would have cut to a shot of her. But Hitchcock keeps her outburst offscreen. Then he adds an unexpected and eerie touch. As the tracking shot ends on an extremely tight close-up, Uncle Charlie turns slightly and looks into the camera as he replies, "Are they, Charlie?" **(8.17)**.

Suddenly, we're put in the young woman's place, seeing the full force of her uncle's hatred. (We've just seen Jonathan Demme employing a comparable technique in filming Hannibal Lecter in *The Silence of the Lambs*, 8.7–8.10). Like Little Charlie, we begin to realize that he's a sociopath, made all the more frightening by his steady gaze and controlled speech. Hitchcock's decisions about staging, framing, sound, and editing have intensely engaged our minds and emotions in the story.

Hitchcock's style here is related to technical choices in the movie as a whole. For one thing, the shot of Uncle

8.14 After a shot of Emmy, Hitchcock cuts to Little Charlie looking uneasily at her uncle.

8.15 Uncle Charlie begins his monologue about useless women.

8.16 The camera moves closer to him . . .

Our second example is *Citizen Kane*. Chapter 3 discussed the film's narrative organization, and we'll refer back to that to ground our comments. (You may want to return to reread it as preparation for what follows.) Our analysis will concentrate on identifying some salient techniques, locating stylistic patterns, and proposing some functions for the patterns we detect.

Style in *Citizen Kane*

Orson Welles didn't make *Citizen Kane* alone. He had at his disposal a major Hollywood studio, RKO, and he assembled exceptionally gifted collaborators. Just as the film's narrative organization owes a good deal to the screenplay that Welles wrote with Joseph Mankiewicz, its style is the result of thousands of decisions made by director, cast, and crew.

Several of Welles's actors had worked with him in theater and radio, so he knew what they could bring to the project. Among other talents were cinematographer Gregg Toland, composer Bernard Herrmann, and special-effects supervisor Vernon Walker. All three had distinguished careers before and after *Kane*. Walker

Charlie is the closest we ever come to him, so this tight framing gives the scene particular force. More generally, Hitchcock employs techniques that put us in the position of the characters. Throughout the film, he uses optical point of view, most often allowing us to share Little Charlie's vantage point **(8.18, 8.19)**.

This pattern of stylistic choices is sustained throughout the dinner table monologue. The brief shot of Little Charlie reminds us of her position beside her uncle (8.14). But rather than have Uncle Charlie start his monologue by glancing at her, Hitchcock lets him speak to the others at the table, or perhaps merely to himself (8.15, 8.16). Only after Little Charlie's offscreen outburst does Uncle Charlie turn to her—and us (8.17). Hitchcock has saved the most startling point-of-view moment for the end of the shot.

The style of this scene enhances the film's pattern of restricted narration. After Uncle Charlie arrives in Santa Rosa, we get some private glimpses into his activities, but the scenes concentrate largely on Emmy's family and particularly on Little Charlie. We know a bit more than she knows about her uncle. For example, from the start, we suspect that he's being sought by the police, but we don't know what they're investigating. Later we learn that Uncle Charlie has torn a story out of the newspaper, but not until Little Charlie finds it do we discover what he was trying to conceal. Slowly, along with Little Charlie, we discover that the Merry Widow Murderer is at large and that Uncle Charlie is a prime suspect.

The overall form of the plot and the stylistic presentation in each scene work to put us close to Little Charlie. We know roughly what she knows, and we learn some key information when she does. In the dinner table scene, the developing story line and Hitchcock's style combine to tie us even more tightly to Little Charlie. The moment when Uncle Charlie turns challengingly to the camera becomes a high point of this pattern.

8.17 . . . and is very close when he turns and replies to Little Charlie's protests that these women are human. "Are they, Charlie?"

8.18 Earlier in the film, when Little Charlie has begun to suspect her uncle, she pauses on the front doorstep.

8.19 Hitchcock then gives us an optical point-of-view shot of what makes her hesitate: Uncle Charlie holding her mother spellbound.

created dazzling special effects for 1930s musicals and comedies. Toland's style helped popularize the deep-focus look during the 1940s, while Herrmann worked frequently with Hitchcock, notably on *Psycho.*

Welles had unusual directorial control over the project, so he could ask his colleagues to execute his ideas. At the same time, he could encourage their suggestions. For instance, *Kane* allowed Toland to push further his experiments in deep-focus cinematography. Ultimately, it was Welles's responsibility to decide how to blend all these contributions into the film that became *Citizen Kane.* The result harmonizes the various techniques in ways that sometimes brashly, sometimes subtly, shape our experience as viewers.

Mystery and the Penetration of Space

In analyzing *Citizen Kane*'s narrative, we discovered that the film is organized as a search (p. 102). A detective-like figure, the reporter Thompson, tries to find the significance of Kane's last word, "Rosebud." But even before Thompson appears as a character, the film's narration invites us to ask questions about Kane and to seek the answers.

8.20 The Opening of *Citizen Kane*. At the film's start, dissolving views bring us closer to Xanadu. This sequence depends largely on special effects. The house itself is a series of paintings, combined through matte work with three-dimensional miniatures in the foreground.

The very beginning of the film sets up a mystery. After a fade-in reveals a "No Trespassing" sign, in a series of craning movements upward, the camera travels over a set of fences, all matched graphically in the slow dissolves that link the shots. There follows a series of shots of a huge estate, always with the great house in the distance **(8.20)**. The gloomy lighting, the deserted setting, and the ominous music give the opening of the film the eerie uncertainty that we associate with tales of mystery and horror. These opening shots are connected by dissolves, making the camera seem to draw closer to the house although there is no forward camera movement. From shot to shot, the foreground changes, yet the lighted window remains in almost exactly the same position on the screen. Graphically matching the window from shot to shot already focuses our attention on it; we assume that whatever is in that room will be important in initiating the story.

At several points later in the film, the camera moves toward things that might reveal the secrets of Kane's character. One instance is in the spectacular crane up the side of a nightclub to a skylight as Thompson goes to interview Susan Alexander **(8.21–8.24)**. As the camera reaches the skylight, a dissolve and a crack of lightning shift the scene inside to another craning movement down to Susan's table.

8.21

8.22

8.23

8.24

8.21–8.24 Exploring the mystery, advancing into space. As this scene begins, the camera frames a poster of Susan Alexander on an outside wall of the nightclub (8.21). The camera cranes up the wall toward the roof (8.22). The camera continues its advance through the "El Rancho" sign (8.23) and over to the skylight (8.24). Some of these camera movements were created through laboratory special effects.

The opening scene and the introduction to El Rancho have some striking similarities. Each begins with a sign ("No Trespassing" and the publicity poster), and each moves us into a building to reveal a new character. The first scene uses a series of shots, whereas the second depends more on camera movement, but these different techniques are working to create a consistent pattern of penetration that becomes part of the film's style. Later, Thompson's second visit to Susan at the club repeats the crane shots of the first. The second flashback of Jed Leland's story begins with yet another movement into a scene. The camera is initially pointed at wet cobblestones. Then it tilts up and tracks in toward Susan coming out of a drugstore. Only then does the camera pan right to reveal Kane standing, splashed with mud, on the curb. This pattern of gradual movement into the story space not only suits the narrative's search pattern but also creates curiosity and suspense.

Films' endings often contain variations of their beginnings. Toward the end of *Citizen Kane*, Thompson gives up his search for Rosebud. But after the reporters leave the huge storeroom of Xanadu, the camera begins to move over the great expanse of Kane's collections. It cranes forward high above the crates and piles of objects **(8.25)**, then moves down to center on the sled from Kane's childhood **(8.26)**. After a cut to the furnace, the camera again moves in on the sled as it is tossed into the fire. At last we are able to read the word "Rosebud" on the sled **(8.27)**. The ending continues the pattern set up at the beginning; the film techniques create a penetration into the story space, probing the mystery of the central character.

After our glimpse of the sled, however, the film reverses the pattern. A series of shots linked by dissolves leads us back outside Xanadu, the camera travels down to the "No Trespassing" sign again, and we are left to wonder whether this discovery really provides a resolution to the mystery about Kane's character. Now the beginning and the ending explicitly echo each other.

Style and Narration: Restriction and Objectivity

Our study of *Citizen Kane*'s organization (pp. 108–109) showed that Thompson's search is presented through a fairly complex narrational strategy. At one level, our knowledge is restricted principally to what Kane's acquaintances know about him. Within the flashbacks, the style avoids crosscutting or other techniques that would move toward a more unrestricted range of knowledge. Many of the flashback scenes are shot in fairly static long takes, strictly confining us to what participants could know. When the youthful Kane confronts Thatcher during the *Inquirer* crusade, Welles could have cut away to the reporter in Cuba sending Kane a telegram or could have shown a montage sequence of a day in the life of the paper. Instead, because this is Thatcher's tale, Welles handles the scene in a long take showing Kane and Thatcher in a face-to-face standoff, which is then capped by a close-up of Kane's cocky response.

We've also seen that *Kane*'s narration requires us to take each narrator's version as objective within his or her limited knowledge. Welles reinforces this by avoiding shots that suggest optical

8.25

8.26

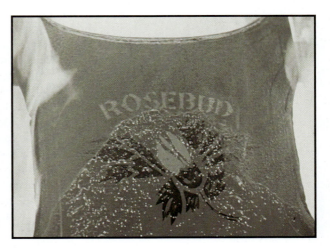

8.27

8.25–8.27 The final camera movement. A crane shot near the end (8.25) moves down to center on Kane's sled (8.26). Another forward camera movement brings the sled into close-up (8.27). Interestingly, the original program booklet for Kane included a section called "Star Orson Welles Makes Fluid Camera the Star of 'Citizen Kane'."

p-focus for objec-
taneous action. The
in *Citizen Kane*'s childhood
s as a long shot of the young
ay in the snow (8.28). This
s an interior view as the camera
s a window, with Kane's mother
earing at the left and calling to him
.29). The camera tracks back with
Mrs. Kane (8.30) and keeps the boy in
extreme long shot throughout the rest of
the scene (8.31). Although the cabin interior is rendered in photographic deep
focus, the image of the boy Charles is a
rear projection, creating another layer
of depth.

8.28

8.29

8.30

8.31

or mental subjectivity. As usual, once a filmmaker commits to one creative option, this excludes other possibilities. By contrast, Hitchcock favors POV cutting in *The Birds* and *Rear Window* (pp. 226–227 and 244–245), which militate against the long-take option Welles pursues.

Welles's commitment to an external perspective on the action is also evident in his choice of deep-focus cinematography. The shot in which Kane's mother signs her son over to Thatcher is a good example. After some shots showing him playing in the snow, we get what at first seems a simple long shot of the boy **(8.28)**. Soon, however, the camera is tracking back and following the adults to a table **(8.29, 8.30)**, where they settle the guardianship. Mrs. Kane and Thatcher sit at a table in the foreground to sign the papers, while Kane's father remains standing farther away at the left, and the boy plays in the distance **(8.31)**.

By eliminating cutting here, Welles captures a complex, developing stretch of the drama, like the opening of *Touch of Evil* discussed on pp. 214–216. Most Hollywood directors would have handled this scene in shot/reverse shot, but Welles keeps all the implications of the action before us throughout. The boy, who is the subject of the discussion, remains framed in the distant window through the whole scene, unaware of what the adults are doing.

The tensions between the father and the mother are conveyed not only by the fact that she excludes him from the discussion at the table but also by the layered sound. Mr. Kane's objections to signing his son away mix in with the dialogue in the foreground, and even the boy's shouts (ironically, "The Union Forever!") can be heard in the distance. The framing also emphasizes the mother in much of the scene. This is her only appearance in the film. Her severity and clamped-down emotions help motivate the many events that follow from her action here. We have had little in-troduction to the family before this scene, but the combination of sound, cinematog-raphy, and mise-en-scene conveys the complicated action with an overall objectivity.

Every director directs our attention, but Welles does so in unusual ways. *Citizen Kane* offers a good example of how a director can choose between stylistic alterna-tives. In the scenes that avoid cutting, Welles cues our attention by using deep-space mise-en-scene (figure behavior, lighting, placement in space) and sound. We can watch expressions because the actors play frontally (8.27). In addition, the framing emphasizes certain figures by putting them in the foreground or in the center **(8.32)**. And, of course, our attention shifts from one character to another as they speak lines, as Tim Smith's eye-tracking study shows (p. 140). Avoiding the classical Hollywood shot/reverse shot, Welles uses other techniques to prompt us to build up the story.

Style and Narration: Omniscience

Citizen Kane's narration also embeds the narrators' objective but restricted versions of events within broader contexts. Thompson's investigation links the various tales, so we learn substantially what he learns. Yet he must not become the protagonist of the film, for that would remove Kane from the center of interest. Welles makes a crucial stylistic choice here. By the use of low-key selective lighting and patterns of staging and framing, Thompson is made virtually unidentifiable. His back is to us, he's tucked into the corner of the frame, and he's usually in darkness. The stylistic handling makes him the neutral investigator, less a character than a channel for information.

8.32 **Depth and centering.** Although Susan is much larger than Kane in this shot, his placement in frame center, as well as his frontal position, assure that we will look at him. The main purpose of the shot seems to be to emphasize that the vast spaces of Xanadu reflect their emotional distance from one another.

More broadly still, we have seen that the film encloses Thompson's search and each narrator's recollection within a more omniscient narration. Our discussion of the opening shots of Xanadu is relevant here. In the gradual approach to Xanadu, film style is used to convey a high degree of knowledge that no character has. When we enter Kane's death chamber, the style suggests even more—that the narration can plumb characters' minds. We see shots of snow covering the frame (for example, **8.33**), which hint at a subjective vision. Later in the film, the camera movements occasionally remind us of the broader range of narrational knowledge, as in the first version of Susan's opera premiere, shown during Leland's story in segment 6. There the camera moves to reveal something neither Leland nor Susan could know about **(8.34–8.36)**. The final sequence, which at least partially solves the mystery of "Rosebud," also uses a vast camera movement to give us an omniscient perspective. The camera cranes over objects from Kane's collection, moving forward in space but backward through Kane's life to concentrate on his earliest memento, the sled. Again a salient technique conforms to pattern by giving us knowledge no character will ever possess.

Narrative Parallels: Settings

In looking at the development of the film's narrative (pp. 108–109), we saw that Kane changes from an idealistic young man to a friendless recluse. The film contrasts Kane's early life as a newspaper publisher and his later withdrawal from public life after Susan's opera career fails. This contrast is most readily apparent in the settings. The *Inquirer* office is initially an efficient but cluttered place. When Kane takes over, he creates a casual atmosphere by moving in his furniture and living in the office. The low camera angles tend to emphasize the office's thin pillars and low ceilings, which are white and evenly, brightly lit. Xanadu, in contrast, is huge and sparsely furnished (8.32). The ceilings are too high to be seen in most shots, and the few furnishings stand far apart. The lighting often strikes figures strongly from the back or side, creating a few patches of hard light in the midst of general darkness. The expanded collection of antiquities and mementos now is housed in colossal storerooms.

The contrast between the *Inquirer* office and Xanadu is also created by the sound techniques associated with each locale. Several scenes at the newspaper office (Kane's initial arrival and his return from Europe) involve a dense sound mix

8.33

8.34

8.35

8.36

8.33–8.36 Wide-ranging narration at work. The snowstorm paperweight is itself bathed in fluttering snowflakes, suggesting a mental vision (8.33). In the film's first opera scene, the camera cranes up from the stage (8.34) and through the rigging above (8.35) to reveal a stagehand indicating that Susan's singing stinks (8.36).

with a babble of overlapping voices. Yet the cramped space is suggested by the relative lack of resonance in timbre. In Xanadu, however, the conversations sound very different. Kane and Susan speak to each other slowly, with pauses between. Moreover, their voices have a booming echo effect that combines with the setting and lighting to suggest huge, empty space.

This transition from Kane's newspaper days to his eventual seclusion at Xanadu is suggested by changes in the mise-en-scene at the *Inquirer.* While Kane is in Europe, the paintings and statues he sends back begin to fill up his small office. The new clutter hints at Kane's growing ambitions and declining interest in working personally on his newspaper. This change culminates in the last scene in the *Inquirer* office—Leland's confrontation with Kane. The office is being used as a campaign headquarters. With the desks pushed aside and the employees gone, the room looks larger and emptier than it had before. Welles emphasizes this by placing the camera at floor level and shooting from a low angle (5.113). The Chicago *Inquirer* office, with its deep, shadowy spaces, pushes this pattern further **(8.37),** as do later conversation scenes in the caverns of Xanadu (8.32).

Contrast these scenes with one near the end of the film. The reporters invade Kane's museum-like storeroom at Xanadu **(8.38).** Although the echoes remind us of the estate's vastness, the reporters transform the setting briefly by the same sort of dense, overlapping dialogue that characterized the early *Inquirer* scenes and the scene after the newsreel. By bringing together these reporters and Kane's final surroundings, the film creates another parallel emphasizing the changes in the protagonist.

Parallels: Other Techniques

Parallels are important throughout *Citizen Kane,* and most of the techniques chosen by Welles, Toland, and their colleagues help create them. For example, deep focus and deep space can pack many characters into the frame in order to summon up similarities and contrasts. Late in Thatcher's account (segment 4), a scene presents Kane's financial losses in the Depression. He is forced to sign over his newspaper to Thatcher's bank. In a single take, a turning point in the plot is created by the arrangement of the figures and the image's depth of field **(8.39, 8.40).** The lowering of the contract recalls the previous scene, when Thatcher puts down the newspaper that has concealed him **(8.41, 8.42).** There Thatcher had been annoyed, but Kane could defy him. Years later in the story, Thatcher has gained control and Kane paces restlessly, still defiant but stripped of his power over the *Inquirer* chain.

Editing patterns can also suggest similarities between scenes, as when Welles compares two moments in which Kane seems to win public support. In the first scene, Kane is running for governor and makes a speech at a mammoth rally. This scene is principally organized around an editing pattern that shows one or two shots of Kane speaking, then one or two close shots of small groups of characters in the audience (Emily and their son, Leland, Bernstein, Gettys), then another shot of Kane. The cutting establishes the characters who are important for their views of Kane. Boss Gettys is the last to be shown in the scene, and we expect him to retaliate against Kane's denunciation.

After his defeat, Kane sets out to make Susan a successful singer, not because she wants it but because she will be an extension of him. "We're going to be a great opera star," he promises a reporter. In Susan's debut, the organization of shots follows the pattern of the campaign rally. Again the figure on the stage, Susan, serves as a pivot for the editing, with shots of her alternating with shots of the listeners (Bernstein, Leland, the singing teacher, and above all Kane) **(8.43, 8.44).** The general narrative parallels are sharpened by specific stylistic techniques. Together they articulate two stages of Kane's power quest: first his own attempt and then with Susan as his proxy.

Parallels can be brought out by music as well. Susan's singing is causally central to the narrative, for it propels her to the limelight with Kane as her backer; her

8.37

8.38

8.37–8.38 Depth and cavernous spaces. In *Citizen Kane,* rear projection exaggerates the depth of the *Inquirer* office. Welles as Kane performed at the foreground typewriter, while wide-angle, deep-focus footage of Joseph Cotten (Leland) and Everett Sloane (Bernstein) was projected behind him (8.37). Extreme deep focus, also possibly enhanced by back projection, is employed in the final scene in Xanadu's warehouse, which is enlivened by rapid dialogue (8.38).

failure becomes another phase of his failure. Musically, Susan's elaborate aria in *Salammbo* contrasts sharply with the other main diegetic music, the party song about "Charlie Kane." But both relate to Kane's ambitions. The lyrics of the "Charlie Kane" ditty show that Kane intends it as his signature song, and it does turn up later as campaign music. In addition, the chorus girls who sing the song wear costumes with boots and Rough Rider hats **(8.45).** Kane's desire for war with Spain has shown up even in this apparently simple farewell party for his departure to Europe.

8.39

8.40

8.39–8.42 Parallel gestures underscored by deep space. The contract scene opens with a close-up of Kane's manager, Bernstein, reading the contract (8.39). He lowers the paper to reveal Thatcher, now much older, seated opposite him. We hear Kane's voice offscreen, and Bernstein moves his head slightly, the camera reframing a little. Now we see Kane pacing beyond them in a huge office or boardroom (8.40). This shot echoes the composition of an earlier scene (8.41), which dramatizes our first real look at Kane as an adult (8.42).

8.41

8.42

8.43

8.44

8.43–8.44 Editing parallels opera and politics. Susan's opera debut repeats the editing pattern of Kane's campaign rally. Shots of Susan onstage (8.43) are followed by shots of listeners, most notably her brooding and domineering puppet master (8.44).

When Kane's political ambitions are dashed, he tries to create a career for his wife instead, but her voice falters in singing grand opera. The songs cooperate with other techniques in creating parallels between phases of Kane's career.

A Convincing Newsreel

The "News on the March" sequence is crucial to the film. It fills us in about Kane's background, and it provides a map of the upcoming plot events (p. 103–104). Also, we need to believe that this is a real newsreel in order to motivate Thompson's search for the key to Kane's life. A plausible-looking newsreel sequence also helps establish Kane's power and wealth, which will be the basis of much of the upcoming action.

Welles sets off this sequence by techniques that don't appear elsewhere in *Citizen Kane*. These techniques imitate the look and sound of documentary footage of the period. The music recalls actual newsreels, and the insert titles, outmoded in fictional films, were still a convention of documentaries. Welles uses several different film stocks to make it appear that the shots have been assembled from widely different sources. Some shots copy the jerkiness of silent film run at sound speed. Welles also scratched and faded this footage to give it the look of old, worn film. This distressing of the footage, combined with the makeup work, creates a remarkable impression that Kane was a historical figure. We see him with major political leaders **(8.46),** and glimpse him wheeled around his estate **(8.47).** The visual conventions are enhanced by the use of a narrator whose booming voice mimics (and mocks) the commentary typical in newsreels of the day.

Plot Time through Editing

One of *Citizen Kane*'s outstanding formal features is the way its plot manipulates story time (pp. 101–102). This process is motivated by Thompson's inquiry and the order in which he interviews Kane's acquaintances (p. 104). Welles and his collaborators selected a variety of techniques to signal shifts from scene to scene, creating both ellipses and rearrangements of story chronology.

Perhaps the most startling transitional device for 1941 audiences was the *shock cut*. A shock cut creates a jarring juxtaposition, usually by means of a sudden shift to a higher sound volume and a considerable graphic discontinuity. *Citizen Kane* offers several instances: the abrupt beginning of the newsreel after the lingering deathbed image, the leap from the quiet conversation in the newsreel projection room to the lightning and thunder outside El Rancho, and the sudden appearance of a screeching cockatoo in the foreground as Raymond's flashback begins **(8.48).** The shock cuts create surprise and sharply mark off certain scenes. Somewhat milder shock cuts occur within scenes as well, creating tension and edginess. The newsreel

8.45

8.46

8.47

8.45–8.47 Kane in history. The chorus girls, bearing hats modeled on Teddy Roosevelt's Rough Riders, clap them on the partying journalists' heads (8.45). In "News on the March," simulated newsreel footage shows Kane visiting world leaders like Hitler (8.46). After Kane becomes a recluse, the handheld camera, the barriers, and the ill-composed framing imitate covertly shot footage (8.47).

comes to an abrupt, skidding halt and during the scene in which Susan berates Kane for sending Leland a $25,000 check, her shrill demands, "What?" "What is it?" are accentuated by abrupt sound cuts and brief shots.

Some transitions that skip over or drastically compress time are less abrupt than the harsh sound and image cuts. Kane's sled is covered by snow through a languid series of dissolves. More extensively, the breakfast table montage (segment 6) shows, with big ellipses, the decline of Kane's first marriage. It starts with the loving couple at their early wedding breakfast, rendered in a track-in and a shot/reverse-shot series. Then the sequence moves through several brief episodes, consisting of shot/reverse-shot exchanges linked by superimpositions of lighted windows whizzing by. (The effect resembles the transitional device of the **whip pan,** a fast panning movement.) In each episode, Kane and Emily become more sharply hostile. The segment ends by tracking away to show the surprising distance between them at the table, using spatial distance to indicate emotional distance in the way that will be developed in scenes with Kane's second wife Susan (8.32).

8.48 **Editing for shock.** After Raymond says, "Like the time his wife left him," a quick dissolve is underscored by a cockatoo's shriek and an abrupt close-up, starting the scene at a high dramatic and auditory pitch.

Composer Bernard Herrmann also guided our experience of the breakfast-table montage. The romantic breakfast is accompanied by a lilting waltz. At each transition to a later time, the music changes. A comic variation of the waltz follows, and then a tense one; then horns and trumpets restate the Kane theme. The payoff of the sequence shows the couple eating in stony silence, with Emily ostentatiously reading a rival newspaper. That passage is accompanied by a slow, eerie variation on the initial theme. The dissolution of the marriage is stressed by this theme-and-variations accompaniment. A similar sort of temporal compression and sonic elaboration can be found in the montage of Susan's opera career (segment 7).

Our brief examination of *Citizen Kane*'s style has pointed out only a few of the major patterns in the film. You can find others. There's the musical motif associated with Kane's power; the "K" motif appearing in Kane's costumes and in Xanadu's settings; the way the decor of Susan's room in Xanadu reveals Kane's attitude toward her; the changes in the actors' performances as the characters age in the course of the story; and the striking photographic devices, such as the photos that become animated or the many superimpositions during montage sequences.

Critics have argued that the film's stylistic richness, along with its complex narrative structure, works somewhat against our feeling much for its protagonist. Kane, seen mostly from the outside by those who knew him, is an object of admiration or dislike, but never real sympathy. (For a more intensely emotional film, we must go to Welles's next film, *The Magnificent Ambersons*.) Is *Citizen Kane* then a cold intellectual exercise? Our analysis of the film's form and style suggests that an emotional distance on Kane is exactly what Welles and his collaborators were aiming at. Through the flashback structure and the omniscient but detached narration, we're asked to judge him from the outside—or rather, given the revelation of the Rosebud sled, to suspend final judgment on a figure we can't fully understand. "I don't think any word can explain a man's life," says Thompson.

Yet one implication of the revelation of Rosebud is that old age leaves one reflecting on what might have been. Bernstein talks of recalling a girl in a white dress, and Leland remembers Kane's first wife Emily from dancing school. The snowstorm paperweight that Kane drops as he dies is a motif recalling not only the Kane family cabin and the boy's games in the snow but also his failure to find new happiness with Susan **(8.49, 8.50).** The film's formal and stylistic dynamics grant some sympathy for an arrogant, self-centered man. Even so forbidding a figure as Charles Foster Kane can cherish a fleeting memory of a moment in childhood just before his world changed forever.

significant ways. Genres also change over time, as filmmakers invent new twists on old formulas. Although we have solid intuitions about what genre a film falls into, defining the precise boundaries between genres can be tricky, as we'll see.

When we think about genre, the examples that come to mind are usually those of fictional live-action films. We'll see in the next chapter that there can be genres of other basic sorts of cinema. There are genres of documentary, such as the compilation film and the concert movie. Experimental films and animated films belong to genres as well.

Defining a Genre

Popular, mass-market cinema rests on genre filmmaking. Most countries have versions of romance stories, action sagas, supernatural tales, and comedies. Some genres are more local in flavor. Germany has its *Heimatfilm,* the tale of small-town life. The Hindi cinema of India has produced *devotionals,* films centering on the lives of saints and religious figures, as well as *mythologicals,* derived from legend and literary classics. Mexican filmmakers developed the *cabaretera,* a type of melodrama centering on prostitutes.

Sometimes reviewers dismiss genre films as shallow and trivial, assuming them to be simply formulaic: It's only a Western; it's just a horror film. Undoubtedly, many films in all genres are cheaply and unimaginatively made. Yet, because genres are central to most filmmaking, a genre picture can be excellent. *Singin' in the Rain* is a musical, as well as one of the best American films. *Grand Illusion* is a war film. *Psycho* is a thriller. *The Godfather* is a gangster film. On the whole, genre is a category best used to describe and analyze films, not to evaluate them.

Audiences know the genres of their culture very well—so well that genres may structure people's ways of seeing the world. Children may grow up pretending to be superheroes or fairy-tale princesses. Patton Oswalt reports that his high-school friends categorized themselves along genre lines: They were Zombies (fans of Goth culture and metal rock), Spaceships (high-tech gadgets, futuristic utopias), or Wastelands (punk rock, apocalyptic fiction). Since the Internet allows everyone to learn as much as they want about anything in popular culture, everyone can be a genre connoisseur, a passionate and knowledgeable fan.

> " I've got news for you—pop culture *is* nerd culture."
> —Patton Oswalt, comedian and actor

What Makes a Genre? Everyone seems reasonably agreed on what genres exist and what films fall into them, but it's not clear how we arrive at that consensus. What makes us think that dozens or hundreds of films belong to the same category?

Most scholars agree that no genre can be defined in a single hard-and-fast way. In some genres the films share subjects or themes. A gangster film centers on urban organized crime. A science-fiction film features a technology beyond the reach of contemporary science. A Western is usually about life on some frontier (not necessarily the American West, as *North to Alaska* and *Drums Along the Mohawk* suggest).

Subject matter or theme isn't so central to defining other genres. Musicals are recognizable chiefly by their manner of presentation: singing, dancing, or both. The detective film is partly defined by the plot pattern of an investigation. And some genres are defined by the distinctive emotional effect they aim for: amusement in comedies, tension in suspense films.

Even when we have a firm sense of what a particular genre is, we may find films that fit the category to different degrees. Typically, we think of a genre as consisting of clear, core cases and fuzzier examples. *Singin' in the Rain* is a prime example of a musical, but David Byrne's *True Stories,* with its ironic presentation of musical numbers, is more of a borderline case. And an audience's sense of the core cases can change over history. For modern audiences, a gory film such as *The Silence of the Lambs* probably exemplifies the thriller, whereas for audiences of the 1950s, a prime example would have been an urbane Hitchcock exercise such as *North by Northwest.*

Sometimes a film seems to straddle two genres. Is *Groundhog Day* a romantic comedy or a fantasy? Is *Psycho* a slasher film or a mystery thriller? Steven Spielberg's *War of the Worlds* combines horror, science fiction, and family melodrama. As we'll see, mixing genres is one important source of change in film history.

Subgenres   You've probably noticed that some genre labels are very broad. The comedy category includes slapstick comedies such as *Animal House,* romantic comedies such as *The Proposal,* parodies such as the Austin Powers series, and raunchy male-oriented comedies such as *The Hangover.* Similarly, melodrama, as thought of today, encompasses stories of crises in marriage (*In the Bedroom*), dysfunctional families (*Magnolia*), and doomed love affairs on the Romeo-and-Juliet model.

For this reason, it's useful to have the idea of *subgenres* to refer to distinct and fairly long-lasting types within a genre. There are science-fiction films involving interplanetary travel (sometimes mockingly called "space opera"), alien invasions of earth, biological experiments (like *Rise of the Planet of the Apes*), or future societies, like the worlds of *Gattaca* and *THX-1138.* These subgenres will have distinct conventions of their own and perhaps appeal to different viewers. Again, sometimes critics call our attention to subgenres. Reviewers have popularized terms like "dystopias" for bleak science-fiction futures and "buddy films" for action movies like *Lethal Weapon* that display male bonding.

The Usefulness of Genre Categories   Everyone who comes into contact with cinema relies on ideas of genre. Genre concepts help producers decide what films to make. Science-fiction and action films are currently popular, and executives would be likelier to green-light projects perceived to fit into those genres. The massive success of young-adult fantasy fiction, crystallized in the Harry Potter franchise, led many studios to finance expensive ventures into the same territory (*Inkheart, The Golden Compass*). By contrast, during the 1960s studios backed *The Sound of Music* and other big-budget musicals because they attracted a wide audience. Such lavish projects are risky today, and many have failed, even when they were based on acclaimed Broadway shows (such as *The Phantom of the Opera* and *Rent*). Contemporary musicals tend to be lower-budget items such as *Mamma Mia!* and the *Step Up* series.

Advertising tends to pinpoint a film's genre. "Vampires. Werewolves. Humans," proclaims the poster for *Twilight: Eclipse.* "It's time to choose a side." Coming-attractions trailers and the film's poster design usually leave no doubt about what genre the film is in, the better to target fans. Critics and entertainment reporters play a role in this promotional process. To call *(500) Days of Summer* "a romantic comedy that remembers that the best romances have a touch of the bittersweet" not only announces what genre the film belongs to but also expresses an evaluation of how well it fulfills certain conventions.

For viewers, genre categories are a part of their tastes. Every moviegoer likes some genres, tolerates others, and loathes still others. Fans may try to see everything in a genre they love and to learn as much as possible about their favorites. They may exchange information via magazines, websites, or conventions. Peter Jackson and Guillermo del Toro started out as passionate genre geeks, and their intimate knowledge of horror and fantasy traditions pervades the films they direct.

Analyzing a Genre

Both filmmakers and film viewers, then, share some general notions about the types of films that compete for our attention. We largely agree on the genre's conventions, the kinds of recurring elements we picked out in romantic comedies. For the filmmaker, the conventions are materials they work with. For the viewer, conventions shape our expectations about what we're likely to see and hear.

9.3

9.4

9.3–9.4 Genre-specific techniques. An aggressive depth composition would usually be out of place in a musical or romantic comedy, but it suits the tension developing in a police interrogation in *The Secret in Their Eyes* (9.3). In *The Exorcist*, a single streetlight picks out the priest as he arrives at night, while light streams from the room where the possessed girl is confined (9.4).

Conventions of Story and Style Genre conventions often center on plot patterns. We anticipate an investigation in a mystery film; revenge plotlines are common in Westerns; a musical finds ways to provide song-and-dance situations. The gangster film usually centers on the gangster's rise and fall as he struggles against police and rival gangs. We expect a biographical film ("biopic") such as *Ray* or *J. Edgar* to trace significant episodes in an actual person's life. In a cop thriller, certain characters are conventional: the shifty informer, the comic sidekick, the exasperated captain who despairs of getting the squad to follow procedure.

Other genre conventions are more thematic, involving broad meanings that are summoned again and again. The Hong Kong martial-arts film commonly celebrates loyalty and obedience to one's teacher. A standard theme of the gangster film has been the price of criminal success, with the gangster's rise to power portrayed as a hardening into egotism and brutality. The screwball comedy traditionally sets up a thematic opposition between a stiff, unyielding social milieu and characters' urges for freedom and innocent zaniness. A melodrama such as *One Day* suggests the cost of failing to recognize your true love.

Still other genre conventions involve stylistic patterns. Techniques that would be jarring in one genre may become common in another **(9.3).** Low-key and high-contrast lighting is rare in a musical or romantic comedy but it's standard in the horror film and the thriller **(9.4).** In an action picture, we expect rapid cutting and slow-motion violence. In the melodrama, an emotional twist may be underscored by a sudden burst of poignant music. That sort of music would be out of place in a horror film, which might instead offer us a grating burst of sound effects.

Genre Iconography As a visual medium, cinema can also define genres through conventional *iconography*. A genre's iconography consists of recurring symbolic images that carry meaning from film to film.

Objects and settings often furnish iconography for a genre. A close-up of a tommy gun lifted out of a 1920s Ford would probably be enough to identify a scene as being from a gangster movie, while a shot of a long, curved sword hanging from a kimono would place us in the world of the samurai. The war film takes place in battle-scarred landscapes, the backstage musical in theaters and nightclubs, the space-travel film in starships and on distant planets. Certain film stars can become iconographic as well—Judy Garland and Barbra Streisand for the musical, John Wayne and Clint Eastwood for the Western, Arnold Schwarzenegger for the action picture, Steve Carrell and Seth Rogan for comedy, Meg Ryan and Sandra Bullock for romantic drama and comedy.

By knowing conventions, viewers have a clear pathway into the film. Our expectations are set, and the film can communicate information economically. When we meet the weak sheriff, we strongly suspect that he will not stand up to the outlaw gang. We can then focus attention on the cowboy hero as he is slowly drawn into helping the townspeople defend themselves.

Audiences expect the genre film to offer something familiar, but they demand something new as well. So a film can revise or even reject the conventions associated with its genre. *Bugsy Malone* is a gangster musical in which children play all the traditional adult roles. *2001: A Space Odyssey* violated several conventions of the science-fiction genre: beginning with a lengthy sequence set in prehistoric times, synchronizing classical music to outer-space action, and ending with an enigmatically symbolic fetus drifting through space. Some reviewers objected to the Tesla machine in *The Prestige,* claiming that it violated the conventions of a historical mystery film. But what one critic called "a sudden, desperate leap into fantasy" can be seen as an effort to update traditional intrigue for an audience fascinated by fantasy and science fiction.

By blending or varying or even rejecting genre conventions, filmmakers force viewers to reset their expectations and engage with the film in fresh ways. (See "Creative Decisions in a Contemporary Genre.") The interplay of convention and innovation, familiarity and novelty, is central to the genre film.

> **"** Fixed forms can yield infinite, ingenious variations."
> —Joyce Carroll Oates, novelist

Genre History

Because filmmakers frequently play with conventions, genres and subgenres change constantly. The broader, blanket genres such as thrillers, romances, and comedies may stay popular for decades, but a comedy from the 1920s is likely to be very different from one in the 1960s. Genres change over history. Their conventions get recast, and by mixing conventions from different genres, filmmakers create new possibilities surprisingly often.

Origins   Many film genres begin by borrowing conventions from other media. The melodrama has clear antecedents in stage plays and novels such as *Uncle Tom's Cabin.* Types of comedy can be traced back to stage farces or comic novels. Musicals draw on both musical comedies and variety shows.

Yet the film medium always reshapes an adopted genre. For example, Western novels were already popular in the 19th century when cinema was invented. Yet Westerns did not become a film genre until after 1908. Why the delay? Westerns need outdoor landscapes. As films got longer (up to roughly 15 minutes) and studios hired actors on contract, filmmakers may have been encouraged to shoot more on location. Using rural American landscapes in turn fostered stories involving the frontier, and the Western quickly became a tremendously popular genre. It was also a uniquely American genre, giving U.S. films a way to compete in the growing international market. In such ways film genres acquire their own history, combining borrowings from other arts and distinctive innovations.

One important pressure on genres is technology. The musical film crystallized with the arrival of synchronized sound, and the development of color processes favored genres of spectacle, for example, Westerns, musicals, and historical dramas. Most recently, computer-generated imagery has made it easy to conjure up unreal creatures and imaginary landscapes. Digital special effects have encouraged the expansion of the fantasy and science-fiction genres, as well as films based on animated cartoons (such as *Speed Racer*) and on comic-book superheroes (1.33, 1.34).

Genres and Cycles   Once a genre and its subgenres are launched, there seems to be no predictable trajectory. We might expect that the earliest films in the genre are the purest instances, with genre mixing coming at a late stage. But genre mixing can take place very soon. *Whoopee!* (1930), a musical from the beginning of talking pictures, is also a Western. *Just Imagine* (1930), one of the first sound science-fiction films, contains a comic song. Some historians have also speculated that a genre inevitably passes from a phase of maturity to one of parody, when it begins to mock its own conventions. Yet an early Western, *The Great K & A Train Robbery* (1926), is an all-out parody of its own genre. Early slapstick comedies often take moviemaking as their subject and ruthlessly poke fun at comic conventions, as in Charlie Chaplin's farcical *His New Job* (1915).

Over history, genres rise and fall in prestige and popularity. The result is the phenomenon known as *cycles.* A cycle is a batch of related genre films that enjoys intense popularity and influence over a fairly short period.

A CLOSER LOOK

Creative Decisions in a Contemporary Genre
The Crime Thriller as Subgenre

The thriller, like the comedy, is a very broad category, with many subgenres. There are supernatural thrillers (*The Sixth Sense*), political thrillers (*Munich*), and spy thrillers (*The Bourne Ultimatum*), but many others revolve around crime—planned, committed, or thwarted.

Using few special effects and set in contemporary urban locations, crime thrillers can be comparatively cheap to produce. They offer showy roles to actors, and they allow writers and directors to display their ingenuity in playing with the audience's expectations. Although the genre has fuzzy edges, we can chart some core cases by considering the ways in which filmmakers have exploited narrative conventions of the genre.

Four Character Roles   A crime is at the center of the thriller plot, and usually four sorts of characters are involved. There are the victims, the more or less innocent bystanders, the forces of justice, and the lawbreakers. Typically, the filmmaker decides to organize the film's narration around one or two of these character roles.

In *Double Jeopardy*, a husband fakes his own death in order to run off with his mistress. His wife is found guilty of his murder, but in prison, she discovers that her husband is alive under a new identity. Released on parole, she sets out to find her son, but she is pursued by her hard-bitten parole officer. Suspense arises from the double chase and the cat-and-mouse game played by the desperate husband and his embittered "widow," who can now murder him with impunity. The plot action and narration are organized around the victimized wife. Her vengeful pursuit propels the action forward, and the narration favors her, restricting us largely to what she believes and eventually learns.

Double Jeopardy concentrates on an innocent person who is the target of the crime, and this is one common pattern in the subgenre. At some point, the victim usually realizes that he or she cannot react passively and must fight back, as in *Duel, The Fugitive, The Net, Breakdown,* and *Panic Room* (**9.5**). In *Ransom*, the father of a kidnapped boy refuses to pay the ransom, offering it as a bounty on the gang holding his son.

Alternatively, the filmmaker can center the plot on an innocent bystander dropped into a struggle between the criminal, the victims, and the forces of justice. In *Die Hard*, an off-duty detective is accidentally trapped in a hostage crisis, so he must fight both police and thieves to rescue the hostages. *The Ghost Writer* thrusts a free-lance biographer into a murderous political conspiracy. In *Cellular*, through an accidental phone call, a beach idler must locate a woman who's been kidnapped.

Thematically, this innocent-bystander plot pattern often emphasizes characters discovering resources within themselves—courage, cleverness, even a capacity for vio-

lence. *Collateral* centers on a taxi driver forced to chauffeur a paid killer from target to target. In the course of the night, Max must abandon his fantasy of a desert island and face the sordid reality of the city he lives in (p. 5).

Instead of spotlighting the victim or an innocent bystander, the filmmaker may build the plot around the forces of justice. The action then typically becomes an investigation, in which police or private detectives seek to capture the criminal or prevent a crime. A classic example is *The Big Heat*, in which a rogue cop seeks to avenge the death of his wife by capturing the mobsters responsible. *Nick of Time, The Bodyguard,* and *In the Line of Fire* present protagonists seeking to forestall a threatened murder. The contemporary serial-killer plot tends to emphasize police pursuit, offering only glimpses of the criminal. *Se7en* follows two policemen in their efforts to untangle a string of murders emblematic of the seven deadly sins. When a plot highlights the investigators, themes of the fallibility of justice tend to come to the fore. In *L.A. Confidential*, three ill-matched detectives join forces to reveal how official corruption has led to the murders of prostitutes.

Alternatively, the maker of a crime thriller can put the criminal center stage. Perhaps the protagonist is a mild-mannered murderer, as in *The Suspect*, or a paid killer, as in Jean-Pierre Melville's *Le Samourai*. Another variant is the heist or caper film, showcasing a tightly orchestrated robbery. This subgenre became a mainstay in the 1950s, with *The Asphalt Jungle, Bob Le Flambeur,* and *Rififi*, and it made a comeback in recent years with the *Ocean's Eleven* series. There is also the avenging outlaw, as in *Payback* and *Drive*, but there's also the dishonor-among-thieves variant, in which criminals betray one another. *A Simple Plan* portrays nervous amateur thieves, whereas *Jackie Brown* traces an expanding web of double-crosses.

Sometimes the filmmaker will devote equal time to the police and the criminal, a strategy which can build up thematic parallels. In John Woo's *The Killer*, a hit man tries to quit the business, aided by his weak mentor. At the same time, we follow the investigation conducted by a police detective, who's also under the sway of an older colleague. Michael Mann's *Heat* creates strong parallels between cop and robber, each having problems with the women in their lives. In both *The Killer* and *Heat*, the opposing characters recognize their kinship. In contrast, *Fargo* plays on the sharp differences between the sunny common sense of the policewoman and an almost pitiably blundering kidnapper.

Narration's Effects   Thrillers obviously aim to thrill us—that is, to startle, shock, and maintain suspense. How do we distinguish them from horror films, which seek similar effects? Horror aims to disgust as well as frighten, but the thriller need not involve disgust. The central character of a horror film is a monster that is both fearsome and repellent, but a thriller villain may be quite attractive (the suave men in *Red Eye* and *Primal Fear*; the enticing women in *Red Rock West* and *The Last Seduction*). While suspense and surprise are important in all cinematic storytelling, these responses dominate the crime thriller. The plots highlight clever plans, still more clever blocking moves, and sudden coincidences that upset carefully timed schemes. Tracing out a plan or following an investigation can yield suspense (Will the criminal succeed? How?), while unexpected twists trigger surprise, forcing us to reconsider the odds of the criminal's success.

More specifically, the thriller's effects depend on which characters are highlighted by the plot and narration. If the protagonist is a victim or a bystander, the suspense we feel comes from the likelihood that he or she will be harmed. If the hero is a figure of justice, we become concerned that she or he will not be able to save the innocents. When the investigator doesn't have the police force as backup, anxiety can intensify: the unauthorized detectives of *The Girl with the Dragon Tattoo* must fight on their own.

When the narration centers on the criminal, how can the filmmaker arouse the viewer's sympathy for him or her? One way is to rank the lawbreakers on a scale of immorality. The most sympathetic criminals will be ones who are trying to give up their crime career (*The Killer*) or ones who oppose even more immoral figures. The heroes of *Out of Sight* are easy-going, good-humored thieves ripping off a white-collar embezzler and a band of crazed killers. Sometimes criminal protagonists can stretch our sympathies in challenging directions. We might admire the bravado of the *Ocean's Eleven* gang, but we aren't so comfortable with the ingratiating psychopath of *The Talented Mr. Ripley*. In *A Simple Plan*, basically good people turn crooked after a momentary weakness, and even though they have done wrong, we may find ourselves hoping that they succeed in their crime. As Dostoevsky showed in *Crime and Punishment*, a crime tale can make us think about what forces drive people to murder **(9.6)**.

Innovations in the Thriller Like any genre or sub-genre, the crime thriller can mix with others. It blends with

9.5

9.6

9.5–9.6 Crime thriller: Victims and victimizer. Innocents in jeopardy: an unusual camera position for a classic thriller situation in *Panic Room* (9.5). In *A History of Violence*, Tom Stall, quiet owner of a small-town diner, is revealed to have a killer's instincts (9.6).

The Social Functions of Genres

The fact that every genre has fluctuated in popularity reminds us that genres are tightly bound to cultural factors. Why do audiences enjoy seeing the same conventions over and over?

Rituals and Ambivalence   Many film scholars believe that genres are ritualized dramas resembling holiday celebrations—ceremonies that are satisfying because they reaffirm cultural values in a predictable way. At the end of *Saving Private Ryan* or *You've Got Mail,* who can resist a surge of reassuring satisfaction that cherished values—self-sacrificing heroism, the desirability of romantic love—have been validated? And just as one can see these ceremonies as helping us forget the more disturbing aspects of the world, the familiar characters and plots of genres may also serve to distract the audience from real social problems.

Some scholars would argue that genres go further and actually exploit ambivalent social values and attitudes. The gangster film, for instance, makes it possible for audiences to relish the mobster's swagger while still feeling satisfied when he receives his punishment. Seen from this standpoint, genre conventions arouse emotion by touching on deep social uncertainties but then channel those emotions into approved attitudes.

Because of the contract between filmmaker and audience, the promise of something new based on something familiar, genres may also respond quickly to broad social trends. During the economic depression of the 1930s, for instance, the Warner Bros.'s musical films introduced social commentary into stage numbers. In *Gold Diggers of 1933,* a singer asks the Depression-era audience to remember "my forgotten man," the unemployed war veteran. More recently, Hollywood producers have tried to suit romantic comedies to the tastes of career women with the *Sex and the City* films and Sandra Bullock vehicles such as *The Proposal* and *Two Weeks Notice.* In Chapter 11, we consider how another musical, *Meet Me in St. Louis,* seems tailored to the home-front audience of World War II.

Genres as Social Reflection   It's one thing to suggest that filmmakers deliberately address their films to current concerns or tastes. But some scholars suggest that at different points in history, the stories, themes, values, or imagery of the genre harmonize with public attitudes in a more involuntary fashion. For instance, don't the science-fiction films of the 1950s, with hydrogen bombs creating Godzilla and other monsters, reveal fears of nuclear technology run amok? Even if the filmmakers didn't knowingly put such messages in their work, perhaps the success of the films reflected what the audiences felt. The hypothesis is that genre conventions, repeated from film to film, reflected the audience's pervasive doubts or anxieties. Many film scholars would argue that this approach helps explain why genres vary in popularity. As the public anxieties change, new genres will reflect more up-to-date concerns.

Social processes can be reflected in genre innovations as well. Ripley, the female protagonist of *Aliens,* is a courageous, even aggressive, warrior who also has a warm, maternal side **(9.8, 9.9).** This was something of a novelty in the science-fiction genre. Many commentators saw Ripley as a product of attitudes derived from the Women's Movement of the 1970s. Feminist groups argued that women could be seen as active and competent without losing positive qualities associated with feminine behavior, such as gentleness and sympathy. As these ideas spread through mainstream media and social opinion, films such as *Aliens* could turn traditionally masculine roles over to female characters. Perhaps the filmmakers didn't intend to send this message, but the attitudes in the films could be seen as harmonizing with new conceptions of gender roles.

Such ways of looking at genre are usually called *reflectionist,* because they assume that genres reflect social attitudes, as if in a mirror. Some critics would object that reflectionist readings can become oversimplified. If we look closely at a genre film, we usually discover complexities that nuance a reflectionist account.

9.8

9.9

9.8–9.9 Genre and gender roles: Warrior and mother. In *Aliens,* Ripley learns how to use a weapon (9.8), but she can also comfort the orphaned girl the soldiers find (9.9).

For instance, if we look beyond Ripley, the protagonist of *Aliens,* we find that all the characters lie along a continuum running between "masculine" and "feminine" values, and the survivors of the adventure, male or female, seem to blend the best of both gender identities. Moreover, often what seems to be social reflection is simply the film industry's effort to exploit the day's headlines. A genre film may reflect not the audience's hopes and fears but the filmmakers' guess about what might sell.

Three Genres

Whether we study a genre's history, its cultural functions, or its representations of social trends, conventions remain our best point of departure. To illustrate how we might analyze conventions and their change across history, we look at three significant genres of American filmmaking.

The Western

The Western is one of the earliest film genres, having become established in the 1910s. It is partly based on historical reality, since in the American West there were cowboys, outlaws, settlers, and tribes of Native Americans. Films also derived their portrayal of the frontier from songs, popular fiction, and Wild West shows. Early actors sometimes mirrored this blend of realism and myth: Cowboy star Tom Mix had been a Texas Ranger, a Wild West performer, and a champion rodeo rider.

Quite early, the central theme of the genre became the conflict between civilized order and the lawless frontier. From the East and the city come the settlers who want to raise families, the schoolteachers who aim to spread learning, and the bankers and government officials. In the vast natural spaces, by contrast, people outside civilization thrive—not only the Native Americans but also outlaws, trappers and traders, and greedy cattle barons.

Iconography reinforces this basic duality. The covered wagon and the railroad are set against the horse and canoe; the schoolhouse and church contrast with the lonely campfire in the hills. As in most genres, costume is iconographically significant, too. The settlers' starched dresses and Sunday suits stand out against American Indians' tribal garb and the cowboys' jeans and Stetsons.

Interestingly, the typical Western hero stands between the two thematic poles. At home in the wilderness but naturally inclined toward justice and kindness, the cowboy is often poised between savagery and civilization. William S. Hart, one of the most popular early Western stars, crystallized the character of the "good bad man" as a common protagonist. In *Hell's Hinges* (1916), a minister's sister tries to reform him; one shot represents the pull between two ways of life **(9.10).**

9.10–9.11 Hero in between. The "good bad" hero of *Hell's Hinges* reads the Bible, a bottle of whiskey at his elbow (9.10). In *Straight Shooting*, the hero stands framed in the farmhouse doorway, halfway between the lure of civilization and the call of the wilderness (9.11).

9.10

9.11

> " I knew Wyatt Earp. In the very early silent days, a couple of times a year he would come up to visit pals, cowboys he knew in Tombstone; a lot of them were in my company. I think I was an assistant prop boy then and I used to give him a chair and a cup of coffee, and he told me about the fight at the O.K. Corral. So in *My Darling Clementine*, we did it exactly the way it had been. They didn't just walk up the street and start banging away at each other; it was a clever military manoeuvre."
>
> —John Ford, director, *Stagecoach*

The in-between position of the hero affects common Western plots. The protagonist may start out on the side of the lawless, or he may simply stand apart from the conflict. In either case, he becomes uneasily attracted to the life offered by the newcomers to the frontier. Eventually, the hero decides to join the forces of order, helping them fight hired gunmen, bandits, or whatever the film presents as a threat to stability and progress.

As the genre developed, a social ideology governed its conventions. White populations' progress westward was considered a historic mission, while the conquered indigenous cultures were usually treated as primitive and savage. Western films are full of racist stereotypes of Native Americans and Hispanics. On a few occasions, filmmakers treated Native American characters as tragic figures, ennobled by their closeness to nature but facing the extinction of their way of life. The best early example is probably *The Last of the Mohicans* (1920).

Nor was the genre always optimistic about taming the wilderness. The hero's eventual commitment to civilization's values was often tinged with regret for his loss of freedom. In John Ford's *Straight Shooting* (1917), Cheyenne Harry (played by Harry Carey) is hired by a villainous rancher to evict a farmer, but he falls in love with the farmer's daughter and vows to reform. Rallying the farmers, Harry helps defeat the rancher. Still, he is reluctant to settle down with Molly (**9.11**).

Within this set of values, a great many conventional scenes became standardized—the Indians' attack on forts or wagon trains, the shy courting of a woman by the rough-hewn hero, the hero's discovery of a burned settler's shack, the outlaws' robbery of a bank or stagecoach, the climactic gunfight on dusty town streets. Writers and directors could distinguish their films by novel handlings of these elements. In Sergio Leone's flamboyant Italian Westerns, conventions are stretched out in minute detail and amplified to a huge scale (**9.12**).

9.12 Showdown in an arena. The three-way shootout at the climax of *The Good, the Bad, and the Ugly* (1966) is filmed to resemble a bullfight.

9.13

9.14

9.13–9.14 **The solitary hero.** During the closing shot of *The Searchers* (9.13), John Wayne repeats Harry Carey's characteristic gripping of his forearm in *Straight Shooting* (9.14).

There were narrative and thematic innovations as well. After such liberal Westerns of the 1950s as *Broken Arrow* (1950), indigenous cultures began to be treated with more respect. In *Little Big Man* (1970) and *Soldier Blue* (1970), the conventional thematic values were reversed, depicting Indian life as civilized and white society as marauding. Some films played up the hero's uncivilized side, showing him perilously out of control (*Winchester 73,* 1950), or even psychopathic (*The Left-Handed Gun,* 1958). The heroes of *The Wild Bunch* (1969) would have been considered unvarnished villains in early Westerns.

The new complexity of the protagonist is evident in John Ford's *The Searchers* (1956). After a Comanche raid on his brother's homestead, Ethan Edwards sets out to find his kidnapped niece Debbie. He is driven primarily by family loyalty but also by his secret love for his brother's wife, who has been raped and killed by the raiders. Ethan's sidekick, a young man who is part Cherokee, realizes that Ethan plans not to rescue Debbie but to kill her for becoming a Comanche wife. Ethan's fierce racism and raging vengeance culminate in a raid on the Comanche village. At the film's close, Ethan returns to civilization but pauses on the cabin's threshold before turning back to the desert **(9.13).**

The shot eerily recalls the doorway compositions of Ford's *Straight Shooting* (9.11); John Wayne even repeats Harry Carey's characteristic gripping of his forearm **(9.14).** Now, however, it seems that the drifting cowboy is condemned to live outside civilization because he cannot tame his grief and hatred. More savage than citizen, he seems condemned, as he says of the souls of dead Comanches, "to wander forever between the winds." This bitter treatment of a perennial theme illustrates how drastically a genre's conventions can change across history.

The Horror Film

While the Western is most clearly defined by subject, theme, and iconography, the horror genre is most recognizable by the emotional effect it tries to arouse. The horror film aims to shock, disgust, repel—in short, to horrify. This impulse is what shapes the genre's other conventions.

What can horrify us? Typically, a monster. In the horror film, the monster is a dangerous breach of nature, a violation of our normal sense of what's possible. The monster might be unnaturally large, as King Kong is. The monster might violate the boundary between the dead and the living, as ghosts, vampires, and zombies do. The monster might be an ordinary human who is transformed, as when Dr. Jekyll drinks his potion and becomes the evil Mr. Hyde. Or the monster might be something wholly unknown to science, as with the creature in the *Alien* films. The

9.15

2:29:45 AM

9.16

9.15–9.16 Horror implied, not shown. A shadow and a character's reaction suggest an offscreen menace in *Cat People* (9.15). Video surveillance in *Paranormal Activity*: The readout indicates that the heroine, who has mysteriously risen from her sleep, stands transfixed for nearly two hours (9.16).

CONNECT TO THE BLOG
www.davidbordwell.net/blog

Director Joe Dante specializes in comic horror films. We discuss his work in "Dante's Cheerful Purgatorio."

genre's horrifying emotional effect, then, is usually created by a character convention: a menacing, unnatural monster.

Other conventions follow from this one. Our reaction to the monster may be guided by other characters who react to it in the properly horrified way. In *Cat People* (1942), a mysterious woman can, apparently, turn into a panther. Our revulsion and fear are confirmed by the reaction of the woman's husband and his coworker **(9.15).** By contrast, we know that *E.T.* is not a horror film because, although the alien is unnatural, he isn't threatening, and the children don't react to him as if he is.

The horror plot will often start with the monster's attack on normal life. In response, the other characters must discover that the monster is at large and try to destroy it. This plot can be developed in various ways: by having the monster launch a series of attacks, by having people in authority resist believing that the monster exists, or by blocking the characters' efforts to destroy it. In *The Exorcist,* the characters only gradually discover that Regan is possessed; after they realize this, they still must struggle to drive the demon out.

The genre's characteristic themes also stem from the response the filmmakers aim to arouse. If the monster horrifies us because it violates the laws of nature that we know, the genre is well suited to suggest the limits of human knowledge. It's probably significant that the skeptical authorities who must be convinced of the monster's existence are often scientists. In other cases, the scientists themselves unintentionally unleash monsters through their risky experiments. A common convention of this type of plot has the characters concluding that there are some things that humans are not meant to know. Another thematic pattern of the horror film plays on fears about the environment, as when nuclear accidents and other human-made disasters create mutant monsters like the giant ants in *Them!*

Not surprisingly, the iconography of the horror film includes settings where monsters might lurk. The old dark house in which a group of potential victims gather was popularized by *The Cat and the Canary* in 1927 and was re-used for *The Haunting* (1999) and *The Others* (2001). A more modern version of the haunted house is seen in *Paranormal Activity* (2008; **9.16**). Cemeteries can yield the walking dead; scientists' laboratories, an artificial human (as in *Frankenstein*). Filmmakers have played off these conventions cleverly, as when Hitchcock juxtaposed a mundane motel with a sinister, decaying mansion in *Psycho,* or when George Romero had humans battle zombies in a shopping mall in *Dawn of the Dead.* The slasher subgenre has made superhuman killers invade everyday settings such as summer camps and suburban neighborhoods.

Heavy makeup is unusually prominent in the iconography of horror. A furry face and hands can signal transformation into a werewolf, while shriveled skin indicates a mummy. Some actors have specialized in transforming themselves into many frightening figures. Lon Chaney, who played the original Phantom in *The Phantom of the Opera* (1925), was known as "the man of a thousand faces." Boris Karloff's makeup as Frankenstein's monster in *Frankenstein* (1930) rendered him so unrecognizable that the credits of his next film informed viewers that it featured the same actor. More recently, computer special effects and motion capture have supplemented makeup in transforming actors into beastly creatures.

Like the Western, the horror film emerged in the era of silent moviemaking. Some of the most important early works in the genre were German, notably *The Cabinet of Dr. Caligari* (1920) and *Nosferatu* (1922), the first adaptation of the novel *Dracula*. The angular performances, heavy makeup, and distorted settings characteristic of German Expressionist cinema conveyed an ominous, supernatural atmosphere **(9.17)**.

Because a horror film can create its emotional impact with grisly makeup and other low-technology special effects, the horror genre has been favored by filmmakers on tight budgets. During the 1930s, a second-rank Hollywood studio, Universal, launched a cycle of horror films. The popularity of *Dracula* (1931), *Frankenstein* (1931), and *The Mummy* (1932; **9.18**) helped the studio become a major company. A decade later, RKO's B-picture unit under Val Lewton produced a cycle of literate, somber films on minuscule budgets. Lewton's directors proceeded by hints, keeping the monster offscreen and cloaking the sets in darkness. In *Cat People,* for instance, we never see the heroine transform herself into a panther, and we only glimpse the creature in certain scenes. The film achieves its effects through shadows, offscreen sound, and character reaction (9.15).

In later decades, horror became a staple of 1960s low-budget independent production, with many American entries targeted at the youth market. George Romero's *Night of the Living Dead* (1968) was budgeted at only $114,000, but it found wide success on college campuses. At the other end of the budgetary scale, the genre acquired a new respectability, chiefly because of the prestige of *Rosemary's Baby* (1968) and *The Exorcist* (1973). These films innovated by presenting violent and disgusting actions with unprecedented explicitness. When the possessed Regan vomited in the face of the priest bending over her, a new standard for horrific imagery was set.

The horror film entered into a period of popularity that has not yet ended. Many major Hollywood directors have worked in the genre, and several horror films—from *Jaws* (1975) and *Carrie* (1976) to installments in the *Twilight* saga (2008 on)—have become huge hits. Low-budget horror has flourished as well. *The Blair Witch Project* (1999), shot for a reputed $35,000, found a huge audience internationally. A decade later, *Paranormal Activity,* shot for $11,000, earned a spectacular $200 million at worldwide box offices.

More broadly, the genre's iconography pervades contemporary culture, decorating lunch boxes and theme park rides. Horror novels by Stephen King and Stephenie Meyer have been adapted for films and TV series, while genre classics such as *The Mummy* and *Frankenstein* have been remade for modern audiences. The interest in producing horror films is global, with Europe and Asia adding to the repertory with *Anatomy* (Germany), *28 Days Later* (UK), *Nightwatch* (Russia), *The*

9.17 German Expressionist horror. In *Nosferatu,* Max Schreck's makeup and acting make his Count Orlock eerily resemble a rat or a bat.

❝ Our formula is simple. A love story, three scenes of suggested horror and one of actual violence. Fade-out. It's all over in less than 70 minutes."
—Val Lewton, producer, *Cat People*

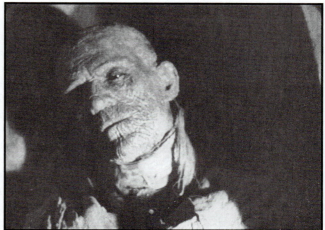

9.18 Subtle horror on a low budget. A tiny gleam reflected in Boris Karloff's eye signals the moment when the monster revives in *The Mummy.*

Host (South Korea), *The Ring* (Japan), *The Devil's Backbone* (Spain), *Let the Right One In* (Sweden), and many more titles.

The centrality of horror to modern American cinema has set scholars looking for cultural explanations. Many critics suggest that the 1970s subgenre of family horror films, such as *The Exorcist* and *Poltergeist,* reflects social concerns about the breakup of American families. Others propose that the genre's questioning of traditional categories of normality is in tune with both the post-Vietnam and the post–Cold War eras: viewers may be uncertain of their fundamental beliefs about the world and their identity. The continuing popularity of the teen-oriented slasher films might reflect young people's anxieties about sexual identity. Fans are also drawn by the imaginative special effects and makeup, so filmmakers compete to show ever gorier and more grotesque imagery. For all these reasons, horror-film conventions grew so familiar that parodies such as the *Scary Movie* franchise and *Shaun of the Dead* became as popular as the films they mocked. Through genre mixing and the give-and-take between audience tastes and filmmakers' ambitions, the horror film has displayed the interplay of convention and innovation that's basic to any genre.

The Musical

The Western is largely based on the subject matter of the American frontier, and the horror film is characterized by the emotional effect it wants to arouse. By contrast, the musical came into being in response to a technological innovation. Although there had been attempts to synchronize music and song with moving images during the silent era, the notion of basing a feature-length film on a series of musical numbers did not emerge until the late 1920s with the successful introduction of recorded sound tracks. One of the earliest features to include the human voice extensively was *The Jazz Singer* (1927), which contained almost no recorded dialogue but had several songs.

At first, many musicals were *revues,* programs of numbers with little or no narrative linkage between them. Such revue musicals aided in selling these early sound films in foreign-language markets, where spectators could enjoy the performances even if they could not understand the dialogue and lyrics. As subtitles and dubbing solved the problem of the language barrier, musicals featured more complicated story lines. Filmmakers devised plots that could motivate the introduction of musical numbers.

Two major subgenres of the musical emerged during the 1930s and are still with us. One of these was the *backstage musical,* with the action centering on singers and dancers who perform for an audience within the story world. Warner Bros.'s successful early musical, *42nd Street* (1933), set the classic pattern for backstage musicals by casting dancer Ruby Keeler as the understudy for a star who breaks her leg just before the big opening. The director tells Keeler, "You're going out a youngster, but you've *got* to come back a star!" and indeed she wins the audience's cheers **(9.19).** During the decade, Warner's elaborately choreographed Busby Berkeley musicals, MGM's pairing of the youthful Judy Garland and Mickey Rooney in a series of "Let's put on a show!" plots, and RKO's elegant cycle of films starring the dance team of Fred Astaire and Ginger Rogers established the conventions of the backstage musical. Later examples included musicals in which the characters are film performers, as in *Singin' in the Rain* (1952). More recent backstage musicals are *The Commitments, That Thing You Do!, What's Love Got to Do with It, Music and Lyrics,* and *Dreamgirls.* In some cases, dance competitions become the equivalent of stage shows, as in *You Got Served* and *Stomp the Yard.*

Not all musicals take place in a show-business situation, however. There is also the *straight musical,* where people may sing and dance in situations of everyday life. Even in backstage musicals, the characters occasionally break into song in an everyday setting. Straight musicals tend to be romantic comedies as well, so that

> ❝ [Producer Arthur Freed] came to me and said, 'What are you going to do with it?' I said, 'Well, Arthur, I don't know yet. But I do know I've gotta be singing and it's gotta be raining.' There was no rain in that picture up to then."
>
> —Gene Kelly, actor/choreographer, on *Singin' in the Rain*

9.19   **9.20**

9.19–9.20 Backstage musical vs. straight musical. Ruby Keeler hoofs her way to stardom in *42nd Street*'s title number (9.19). The citizens of a whole town are drawn into the dance in Jaques Demy's *Young Girls of Rochefort* (9.20).

songs and dances express the characters' fears, longings, and joys. We analyze one such film, *Meet Me in St. Louis,* in Chapter 11. In 1968, *The Young Girls of Rochefort* took the romantic musical to extremes by having its characters sing most of the dialogue in the film, with dozens of passersby joining in dance numbers in the town's streets **(9.20).** Straight musicals are rare today, but Julie Taymor made an effort to revive the subgenre in *Across the Universe,* basing the score entirely on Beatles songs and adding social commentary in the spirit of the 1960s **(9.21).**

In both backstage and straight musicals, the numbers often reflect a couple's courtship. Often the hero and heroine realize that they are an ideal couple because they perform beautifully together. In *Top Hat* the Ginger Rogers character sheds her original annoyance with Fred Astaire during the "Isn't It a Wonderful Day" number, and by the end, they have clearly fallen in love. This plot device has remained a staple of the genre. Astaire again charms his reluctant partner, this time Cyd Charisse, in the "Dancing in the Dark" number in *The Band Wagon* (1953), and John Travolta meets his romantic match on the disco dance floor in *Saturday Night Fever* (1977). In *Moulin Rouge!* the lovers serenade each other, both onstage and off, with classic pop and rock songs **(9.22),** and the dance interludes in the *House Party* and *Step Up* films become courtship rituals.

Musicals have long been associated with children's stories, from *The Wizard of Oz* to recent films such as *Lilo & Stitch.* Many animated features contain musical numbers, a practice going back to Disney's *Snow White and the Seven Dwarfs.*

9.21 A musical evoking 1960s counterculture. In *Across the Universe,* a young man taking his army draft physical is greeted by the Beatles song "I Want You." The film was released at the height of the U.S. occupation of Iraq.

9.22 Performance as courtship. A flamboyant onstage musical number in *Moulin Rouge!* centers on the rapturous lovers.

But adult-oriented musicals have taken on more serious material. *West Side Story* portrays a romance that tragically crosses ethnic lines, and *Pennies from Heaven* evokes the bleak atmosphere of the Depression through characters who lip-synch to recordings from that era. Biopics of performers, such as *Lady Sings the Blues, Ray,* and *Walk the Line,* become somber backstage musicals.

Still, while the Western and the horror film may explore the darker side of human nature, Hollywood musicals tend to accentuate the positive. High ambitions are rewarded when the show is a hit, and lovers are united in song and dance. In *The Pajama Game,* a strike is averted when the leaders of the union and management become a romantic couple. Some of these conventions persist today. *The School of Rock* and today's hip-hop and stepping musicals rework the backstage musical's theme that talent and hard work will eventually win out. Even the grittier *8 Mile* follows the traditional plot pattern of showing a gifted young performer overcoming disadvantages and finding success.

The range of subject matter in musicals is so broad that it may be hard to pin down specific iconography associated with the genre. The backstage musical had its characteristic settings: the dressing rooms and wings of a theater, the flats and backdrops of the stage (as in 9.19), and the nightclub with orchestra and dance floor. Similarly, performers in these musicals are often recognizable by their distinctive stage costumes. During the 1930s, Fred Astaire wore the most famous top hat in the cinema, a hat so closely associated with his musicals that the beginning of *The Band Wagon*—where Astaire plays a washed-up movie actor—could make a joke about it. Similarly, Travolta's white suit in *Saturday Night Fever* became an icon of the disco era. Opportunities for novelty have always been present in the musical, however, as the musical numbers set in a factory (*The Pajama Game*) or on the prairie (*Oklahoma!*) indicate.

The characteristic techniques of the musical are similarly diverse. Musicals tend to be brightly lit, to set off the cheerful costumes and sets and to keep the choreography of the dance numbers clearly visible. For similar reasons, color film stock was applied quite early to musicals, including Eddie Cantor's *Whoopee!* and, as we saw in Chapter 2, *The Wizard of Oz.* While classic musicals tend to rely on long takes, contemporary musicals tend to be cut very quickly, partly because of the influence of MTV videos. Still, to show off the patterns formed by the dancers in musical numbers, crane shots and high angles remain common **(9.23).** One technique widely used in the musical is not usually evident to viewers: lip-synching to prerecorded songs. On the set, performers move their lips in synchronization to a playback of the recording. This technique allows the singers to move about freely and to concentrate on their acting.

9.23 Genre motivation for stylistic choices. Swooping crane shots emphasize the geometry and coordination of an ensemble in *Stomp the Yard*.

The 1935 RKO Astaire–Rogers musical *Swing Time* is one of the exemplary backstage musicals. Early in the film, the hero, a gambler and tap dancer nicknamed Lucky, is trying to quit his stage act and get married. At once, we sense that his fiancée is not right for him. She isn't a dancer, and she isn't even seen during the early scenes in which his colleagues try to trick him into missing the wedding. The opening scenes take place in the conventional settings of the stage, wings, and dressing room of a theater. Later, when Lucky goes to the city and meets the heroine, Penny (a name that echoes Lucky's precious lucky quarter), she quickly takes a strong dislike to him. An amusing scene in the dance school where she works shows Lucky pretending to be hopelessly clumsy. Yet when the school's owner fires Penny, Lucky saves her job by suddenly launching into a graceful, virtuoso, and unrehearsed dance with her. By the end, her animosity has disappeared, and the school owner arranges for the couple to audition at a fashionable club.

Obstacles ensue, primarily in the form of a romantic rivalry between Lucky and the orchestra leader at the club. Further complications result from the sort of Big Misunderstanding characteristic of romantic comedies: Penny thinks that Lucky intends to return to his fiancée. Near the end, Penny seems ready to marry the conductor. She and Lucky meet, apparently for the last time, and their talk at cross-purposes reveals the link between performance and romance:

9.24

PENNY: "Does she dance very beautifully?"

LUCKY: "Who?"

PENNY: "The girl you're in love with?"

LUCKY: "Yes—very."

PENNY: "The girl you're going to marry."

LUCKY: "Oh, I don't know. I've danced with you. I'm never going to dance again."

That Fred Astaire will never dance again is the ultimate threat, and his song "Never Gonna Dance" leads into a duet that reconfirms that they are meant for each other. In the end, Lucky and Penny reconcile.

The film calls on the newly established conventions of the genre. Lucky wears Astaire's classic top hat and formal clothes **(9.24)**. Astaire and Rogers dance in the Art Deco–style sets that were typical of musical design in the 1930s **(9.25)**. The film departs from convention, however, in a remarkable number, "Bojangles of Harlem," where Astaire pays tribute to the great African-American dancers who had influenced him during his New York stage career in the 1920s. When he appears in

9.25

9.24–9.25 *Swing Time* as musical. After losing his suit in a card game, Lucky still wears Astaire's signature top hat (9.24). Penny and Lucky dance in the Art Deco nightclub set (9.25).

CONNECT TO THE BLOG
www.davidbordwell.net/blog

We discuss other genres on our blog. For the relationship between fantasy and sci-fi films in recent years, see "Swords vs. lightsabers," and for movies based on superhero comic books, see "Superheroes for sale." We discuss spy-thriller conventions in "*Tinker Tailor Soldier Spy*: A guide for the perplexed" and our entries on the *Bourne* franchise.

blackface here, it is not to exploit a demeaning stereotype but to impersonate Bill "Bojangles" Robinson, the most famous black tap dancer of the era. (The tribute is all the more unusual because Robinson was then costarring in Shirley Temple musicals for a rival studio, Twentieth Century Fox.)

Despite its backstage settings and show business plot, *Swing Time* sets some numbers in an everyday environment. When Lucky visits Penny's apartment, he sings "The Way You Look Tonight" as she shampoos her hair—using a convenient piano in her apartment to accompany himself (though a nondiegetic orchestra plays along as well). When the couple visits the snowy countryside and sings "A Fine Romance," there is no diegetic accompaniment at all, only an unseen orchestra. The world of the musical makes it possible for people, at any time and in any place, to express their feelings through song and dance.

In studying film, we often need to make explicit some things we ordinarily take for granted—those assumptions so fundamental that we no longer even notice them. Genres are examples of such taken-for-granted categories. At the back of our minds whenever we watch a film, these categories shape what we expect to see and hear. They guide our reactions. They press us to make sense of a movie in certain ways. Shared by filmmakers and viewers alike, these categories are a condition for film art as we most often experience it.

Yet other kinds of categories shape our assumptions about films. If we look beyond live-action fictional features, we find other modes of filmmaking. These depend on ways in which the films are made and the intentions of the filmmakers, and they often have distinctive approaches to form and style. The most common modes are documentary, experimental, and animated cinema, and we examine these in the next chapter.

SUMMARY

One of the most common ways in which we approach films is by type, or genre. Genres are categories that are largely shared across society, by filmmakers, critics, and viewers. Films are most commonly grouped into genres by virtue of similar plot patterns, similar thematic implications, characteristic filmic techniques, and recognizable iconography.

When trying to characterize a film genre, you can ask such questions as these:

1. Before you saw the film, did you know what genre or subgenre it belonged to? What factors in advance publicity or conversation gave you hints?

2. What conventions in the film signal its genre? How do those conventions function? Do they allow storytelling to be more rapid and economical? Do they aim to arouse strong emotional responses?

3. What genre innovations can you find in the film? A good way to determine these is to ask if your expectations were thrown off at certain points.

4. Does this film seem to be combining conventions from more than one genre? If so, how does it make the genre elements compatible? Do innovative aspects of the film depend on the genre mixing, and if so, how?

RECOMMENDED DVD AND BLU-RAY SUPPLEMENTS

Genre Studies

The 55-minutes documentary, "*Seven Samurai*: Origins and influences," presents an excellent study of the enduring swordplay genre. The first 14 minutes are devoted to a history of samurai and their place in Japanese culture. A second section, "Early Samurai Film Influences" defines the subgenres of swordplay films and discusses the early era of their making, stopping at the end of the Occupation. At about 26 minutes in, "The Samurai Film Reinvented" surveys Kurosawa's impact on the genre, mainly in relation to *Seven Samurai*.

Westerns

"The Making of *Silverado*" is in some ways a conventional making-of documentary, with sections on rehearsal, storyboards, editing, cinematography, set design, and so on. Yet the overall emphasis is on the film as a Western. Director Lawrence Kasdan tried to revive the classic Western and to pay homage to it at the same time. Cast and crew discuss how form and style supported the retro-Western's conventions. "The Making of *Butch Cassidy and the Sundance Kid*" contains an amount of footage unusual for a late 1960s promotional documentary. Director George Roy Hill provides a warts-and-all account of the production of this classic Western.

"A Turning of the Earth: John Ford, John Wayne, and *The Searchers*" combines accounts by the participants, contemporary footage of the production, and expert analysis of the film. A biographical overview of one of the major directors of Westerns is "Budd Boetticher—an American Original," on the DVD of one of his classic films, *Seven Men from Now.* Other interesting discussions of Westerns include "Sir Christopher Frayling on *The Magnificent Seven*" and "Leone's West" (*The Good, the Bad, and the Ugly*).

In "An Epic Explored," director James Mangold talks about making *3:10 to Yuma* in an era when Westerns are rare. The same disc has a short but information-packed documentary on the film's production, including rarely discussed topics like a gun that fires dust pellets to simulate bullet strikes. In the three documentaries about *Once upon a Time in the West* directors analyze Leone's style and discuss the film's place in the Western genre.

Horror Films

"Inside the Labyrinth," though primarily a making-of for *The Silence of the Lambs,* includes considerable discussion of it as a horror or thriller film. Similarly, the making-of "Behind the Scream," on *Scream,* discusses horror-film conventions. A brief making-of featurette on *Rosemary's Baby* discusses it as "the great horror film without any horror in it," stressing its lack of special effects and its dependence on suggestion rather than explicit displays of the film's monstrous elements.

Quite possibly the most extensive DVD supplement dealing with a horror film is "The Making of *The Frighteners,*" a 4½-hour documentary directed by Peter Jackson that deals with every aspect of the production—including a tour of the tiny Weta Digital facility that would later expand for *The Lord of the Rings.*

Both *Hellboy* and *Hellboy II: The Golden Army* have making-of documentaries that emphasize the monsters used in each. The second movie famously featured 32 types of monsters, created through a wide range of means, from elaborate puppets and costumes to computer-generated creatures.

Musicals

"Musicals Great Musicals: The Arthur Freed Unit at MGM," included on the *Singin' in the Rain* DVD, chronicles the golden era of musical production at the studio that also produced *The Wizard of Oz, The Band Wagon, Meet Me in St. Louis,* and other classics. Excerpts from MGM musicals made in the early years of sound make this an exemplary historical survey. The DVD also includes a charming supplement, "What a Glorious Feeling," on the making of *Singin' in the Rain.*

"More Loverly Than Ever: *My Fair Lady* Then and Now," a 1994 documentary dealing not only with the film's history but also with its restoration, points out that the film came at the end of a cycle of big-budget adaptations of Broadway musicals.

The "Behind the Music" supplement for *Saturday Night Fever* discusses that enormously popular film's innovations, including central characters who dance but don't sing. It traces how the disco cycle of the 1970s underwent sudden success and abrupt decline.

In "The Nightclub of Your Dreams: The Making of *Moulin Rouge!*" Nicole Kidman talks about singing live during filming rather than the usual lip-synching to a song's playback. There's also a segment on the choreography.

Documentary, Experimental, and Animated Films

S tudying genres shows that categories shape our experience of films. Our sense of genre guides our expectations: We anticipate one sort of thing from a comedy, something quite different from a horror film. Our knowledge of the genre's conventions shapes what we think is likely to happen from moment to moment.

There are still other ways to categorize films. Viewers and filmmakers distinguish documentary from fiction, experimental films from mainstream fare, and animation from live-action filming. Each of these types of film leads us to different sorts of expectations about form, style, and theme.

In a way, these types are more basic categories than genres. Most of our familiar genres are fiction films; it would be odd to call a documentary about witchcraft a horror movie. A cartoon can be a musical or a comedy, but more basically it's an animated movie. Chapter 3, on narrative form, drew its examples principally from fictional, live-action, non-experimental cinema. Now we explore these other important types of films.

Documentary

Before we see a film, we nearly always have some sense whether it is a documentary or a piece of fiction. Moviegoers entering theaters to view *March of the Penguins* expected to see real birds in nature, not the wisecracking penguins of *Madagascar*. A filmmaker launching a project will keep in mind the fiction/nonfiction distinction, although sometimes the project will change directions. Errol Morris began what became the documentary *Vernon, Florida* as a fictional film set in that city. And the same incident can be treated in the two modes. Werner Herzog remade his documentary on a Vietnam-era fighter pilot, *Little Dieter Needs to Fly,* as a fiction film, *Rescue Dawn.*

What Is a Documentary?

What justifies viewers assuming that this or that film is a documentary? With two films titled *Spellbound,* how do we know that one is a Hitchcock thriller and the other is about children's spelling contests? For one thing, a documentary typically comes labeled as such. The filmmakers tell us through publicity, and press coverage reinforces the message. (The *New York Times* review of *Spellbound* called it a documentary in the first paragraph.) In turn, the documentary label leads us to expect that the persons, places, and events shown to us exist or have existed. We'd feel cheated if the kids in *Spellbound*, struggling to spell "logorrhea," were in fact actors. A documentary claims to present factual information about the world.

This information can be presented in a variety of ways. In some cases, the filmmakers are able to record events as they actually occur **(10.1)**. This is what happened in *Spellbound*, with filmmaker Jeff Blitz filming the 1999 National Spelling Bee. In making *Primary*, an account of John Kennedy and Hubert Humphrey campaigning for the 1960 Democratic presidential nomination, the camera operator and sound recordist were able to closely follow the candidates through crowds at rallies (5.145).

But a documentary may also convey information without photographing events as they're spontaneously occurring. The filmmaker might present charts, maps, or other visual aids **(10.2)**, even using animation. In addition, the filmmaker might stage certain events for the camera to record.

Staging Events for the Camera

It's worth pausing on that last point. Some viewers suspect that a documentary is unreliable if it manipulates the events that are filmed. It is true that, very often, the documentary filmmaker records an event without scripting or staging it. For example, in interviewing an eyewitness, the documentarist typically controls where the camera is placed, what is in focus, and so on. The filmmaker likewise controls the final editing of the images. But the filmmaker doesn't tell the witness what to say or how to act. The filmmaker may also have no choice about setting or lighting.

Still, viewers and filmmakers regard some staging as legitimate in a documentary if the staging serves the larger purpose of presenting accurate information. Suppose you are filming a farmer's daily routines. You might ask him or her to walk toward a field in order to frame a shot showing the whole farm. After all, walking into the field is something the farmer does when the camera isn't there. Similarly, the title performer in Dziga Vertov's documentary *Man with a Movie Camera* is clearly performing for Vertov's camera, but he's not doing things he wouldn't do ordinarily **(10.3)**.

Some documentaries make extensive use of staging. For *Man on Wire*, director James Marsh had very little footage of acrobat Philippe Petit's astounding wire-walking between New York's World Trade Center towers. To clarify how Petit and his associates sneaked into the buildings and set up the stunt, Marsh assigned actors to reenact their tactics. In some cases, staging may intensify the documentary value of the film. Humphrey Jennings made *Fires Were Started* during the German bombardment of London in World War II. Unable to film during the air raids, Jennings found a group of bombed-out buildings and set them afire. He then filmed the fire patrol battling the blaze **(10.4)**. Similarly, after Allied troops liberated the Auschwitz concentration camp near the end of World War II, a newsreel cameraman assembled a group of children and had them roll up their sleeves to display the prisoner numbers tattooed on their arms. This staging of the action arguably enhanced the film's reliability.

Staging events for the camera, then, need not make the film fictional or fake. Regardless of the details of its production, the documentary filmmaker asks us to

10.1

10.2

10.1–10.2 On the scene or after the fact. For *The War Tapes*, lightweight digital video equipment allowed National Guard fighters to present their perspective on their tours of duty in Iraq. Here a U.S. serviceman, filming from a military vehicle, captures the explosion of a roadside bomb (10.1). But some things can't be directly filmed, so *Inside Job* includes animated charts to illustrate causes of the 2007–2008 financial collapse (10.2).

> " There are lots of in-between stages from shooting to public projection—developing, printing, editing, commentary, sound effects, music. At each stage the effect of the shot can be changed but the basic content must be in the shot to begin with."
>
> —Joris Ivens, documentary filmmaker

10.3

10.4

10.3–10.4 Staging in documentary. Although the central figure of *Man with a Movie Camera* is an actual cinematographer, his actions were staged (10.3). Blazes like this in *Fires Were Started* were staged, but the firefighters judged the film to be an accurate depiction of their challenges under real bombing (10.4).

assume that the film presents trustworthy information about its subject. Even if the filmmaker asks the farmer to wait a moment while the camera operator frames the shot, the film suggests that the farmer's morning visit to the field is part of the day's routine. It's this suggestion that is set forth as reliable information.

Truth and Opinion in Documentary   As a type of film, documentaries present themselves as factually trustworthy, but across film history many documentaries have been challenged as inaccurate. *An Inconvenient Truth,* Vice-President Al Gore's film about global warming, was accused in some quarters of presenting weak arguments and skewed data. Even if its claims proved false, however, *An Inconvenient Truth* would not then turn into a fiction film. An unreliable documentary is still a documentary. Just as there are inaccurate or misleading news stories, so there are inaccurate or misleading documentaries.

A documentary may take a stand, state an opinion, or advocate a solution to a problem. As we'll see shortly, documentaries often use rhetoric to persuade an audience. But simply mounting an argument does not turn the documentary into fiction. To persuade us, the filmmaker marshals evidence, and this evidence is put forth as being factual and reliable. A documentary may be strongly partisan in its viewpoint, but as a documentary, it presents itself as providing trustworthy, factual information about its subject.

The Boundaries between Documentary and Fiction

Fictional Films and Actuality   Shown a fictional film, we assume that it presents imaginary beings, places, or events. We take it for granted that Don Vito Corleone and his family never existed, and that their activities, as depicted in *The Godfather,* never took place. Yet just because a film is fictional, that doesn't mean that it's completely unrelated to actuality.

For one thing, not everything shown or implied by a fiction film need be imaginary. *The Godfather* alludes to World War II and the building of Las Vegas, both historical events; it takes place in New York City and in Sicily, both real locales. Nonetheless, the characters and their activities remain fictional, with history and geography providing a context for the made-up elements.

Fictional films are tied to actuality in another way. They often comment on the real world. *Dave,* about an imaginary U.S. president and his corrupt administration, criticizes contemporary political conduct. In 1943, some viewers took Carl Dreyer's *Day of Wrath,* a film about witch-hunts and prejudice in 17th-century Denmark, as a covert protest against the Nazis currently occupying the country. Through theme, subject, characterization, and other means, a fictional film can directly or obliquely present ideas about the world outside the film.

Sometimes our response to a fictional film is shaped by our assumptions about how it was made. The typical fictional film stages all or nearly all its events; they are designed, planned, rehearsed, filmed, and refilmed. The studio mode of production is well suited to creating fiction films, since it allows stories to be scripted and action to be staged until what is captured on film satisfies the decision makers. As a result, in a fictional film, the characters are portrayed by actors. The camera films not Vito Corleone but Marlon Brando portraying the Don.

This assumption about how the film was made typically comes into play when we consider historical films or biographies. *Apollo 13, Schindler's List,* and *Margin Call* base themselves on actual events, while *Malcolm X, Walk the Line, W., Milk, The Iron Lady,* and other *biopics* trace episodes in the lives of people who really existed. Should we call these documentaries or fictional films?

In practice, most such films add purely make-believe characters, speeches, or actions. But even if the films didn't tamper with the record at all, they would remain fictional according to our assumptions about how they were produced. The events we see aren't taking place at the time of the actual events. More important, the films don't present themselves as documentaries. They come to us labeled as historical re-creations or reenactments. Like plays and novels based on actual events, films can use historical settings and real people for fictional storytelling.

Blurring the Boundaries   As you might expect, filmmakers have sometimes tried to test our ability to distinguish documentary from fiction. A notorious example is Mitchell Block's *No Lies,* which purports to present an interview with a woman who has been raped. Audiences are usually disturbed by the woman's emotional account and by the callousness of the offscreen filmmaker questioning her. A final title, however, reveals that the film was scripted and that the woman was an actor. Part of Block's purpose was to show how presenting a film as a documentary can induce viewers to believe in the reality of what they see.

Most fake documentaries, or "mockumentaries," are not this serious. Often mock documentaries imitate documentary conventions but don't pretend to portray actual people or events. This strategy turns the film into fiction. A classic case is Rob Reiner's *This Is Spinal Tap,* which uses documentary conventions to satirize rock bands and their followers.

A filmmaker may fuse documentary and fiction in other ways. For *JFK,* Oliver Stone inserted documentary footage into scenes in which actors played historical figures such as Lee Harvey Oswald. Stone also staged and filmed the assassination of Kennedy in a pseudo-documentary manner. This material was then intercut with genuine archival footage, creating constant uncertainty about what was staged and what was authentic.

Errol Morris's *The Thin Blue Line,* a documentary investigation into a murder, mixes interviews and archival material with episodes performed by actors. The sequences, far from being the jittery reenactments of television true-crime shows, are shot with smooth camera work, dramatic lighting, and vibrant color **(10.5).** The result is a film that not only seeks to identify the real killer but also raises questions about how fact and fiction may intermingle (see pp. 433–438).

10.5 Signaling manipulation. Carefully composed shots such as this from *The Thin Blue Line* emphasize the fact that some events have been reenacted. Several of these staged sequences dramatize witnesses' alternative versions of the crime.

Genres of Documentary

As with fiction films, the documentary filmmaker faces choices about genre. One common documentary genre is the *compilation* film, produced by assembling images from archival sources. *The Atomic Cafe* compiles newsreel footage and instructional films to suggest how 1950s American culture reacted to the proliferation of nuclear weapons **(10.6).** The *interview,* or *talking-heads,* documentary records testimony about events or social movements. *Word Is Out* consists largely of interviews with lesbians and gay men discussing their lives.

The *direct-cinema* documentary characteristically records an ongoing event as it happens, with minimal interference by the filmmaker. Direct cinema emerged in the 1950s and 1960s, when portable camera and sound equipment became available and allowed films such as *Primary* to follow an event as it unfolds. For this reason, such documentaries are also known as *cinéma-vérité,* French for "cinema-truth." *Hoop Dreams* traces two aspiring basketball players moving through high school and into college, while *Spellbound* focuses on six young competitors vying to win a national spelling bee. The deceptiveness of *No Lies* owed something to its being shot in the style of *cinéma-vérité.*

Another common type is the *nature* documentary such as *Winged Migration,* which used in-flight cameras to soar and float along with birds. A *portrait* documentary centers on aspects of the life of a compelling person. Terry Zwigoff's *Crumb* captures the eccentricities of underground cartoonist Robert Crumb and his family. *American Movie* presents a Milwaukee filmmaker struggling with budgetary problems and amateur actors to make a horror film **(10.7).**

10.6

10.7

10.8

10.6–10.8 Documentary genres: Compilation, portraiture, and synthesis. Old footage of protective radiation gear was incorporated into *The Atomic Café* (10.6). Filmmaker Mark Borchardt and his friend Mike (on left) freely discussed their lives and projects with Chris Smith for *American Movie* (10.7). Ten days before his death, the protagonist of *Grizzly Man* displays his intimacy with the bears he loves (10.8).

 **CONNECT TO THE BLOG**
www.davidbordwell.net/blog

Documentary films often explore unusual formal and stylistic options. We look at films by Wim Wenders and Ben Rivers that mix the two modes in "Ponds and performers: two experimental documentaries."

Very often a documentary pursues several of these genre options at once. A film may mix archival footage, interviews, and material shot on the fly, as do *Fahrenheit 9/11, The Fog of War,* and *An Unreasonable Man,* a portrait documentary centering on Ralph Nader. *Wordplay,* a study of crossword-puzzle fans, interweaves portraits of makers and solvers along with the drama of the annual American crossword competition. This *synthetic* documentary format is also common in television journalism.

Werner Herzog makes memorable use of the synthetic approach in the portrait film *Grizzly Man.* An adventurous young man, Timothy Treadwell, became convinced that he had made friends with the bears in a national park. But he was wrong: He and his girlfriend were killed and partially eaten by a bear. Herzog combines his own present-day inquiry into Treadwell's life, consisting of interviews and explorations of the park sites, with still photos and letters that cover Treadwell's efforts to protect the bears. Most vivid are the extracts from Treadwell's own video footage showing his encounters with grizzlies **(10.8).**

Form in Documentary Films

Back in Chapter 3, we mentioned that stories offer a major lens through which people understand their world and their lives. So we shouldn't be surprised that many documentarists organize their films as narratives, just as makers of fiction films do. William Wyler's World War II–era *Memphis Belle* follows the course of a single raid over Germany, seen largely from inside a B-17 bomber. Eugene Jarecki's *Why We Fight* traces how what President Eisenhower called "the military-industrial complex" achieved greater power over U.S. policies after the 9/11 attacks. On a more intimate level, the portrait documentary *Rivers and Tides* explains how an artist makes his unique natural-landscape sculptures (**10.9**).

The filmmaker can choose to employ *non*narrative types of form as well. The film might be designed to convey categorized information, so we can call this formal patterning **categorical form.** Or the filmmaker may want to make an argument that will convince the spectator of something. In this case, the film draws on **rhetorical form.** Given the attractiveness of stories, narrative principles sometimes mix with these other sorts of form. One section of a categorical or rhetorical documentary may tell a story, thus following principles of chronology and cause-and-effect. In these other types, however, the narrative sections fulfill the larger purpose of exploring a category or building an argument.

As we consider each formal option, we'll analyze one film as a prime example. To get a sense of each film's overall form, we'll break it into segments, as we did with *Citizen Kane* in Chapter 3. Along the way, we'll discuss how particular stylistic choices support the film's large-scale development.

10.9 Narrative documentary. In Nova Scotia, environmental artist Andy Goldsworthy creates a delicate sculpture out of stones and icicles. It will eventually be carried away by the tides.

> " To deprive the audience entirely of narrative in a long film is a real risk."
> —Pat O'Neill, experimental filmmaker

Categorical Form: Introduction

Categories are groupings that individuals or societies create to organize their knowledge of the world. Some categories are based on scientific research, and these often attempt to account exhaustively for all the data in question. For example, scientists have developed an elaborate system to classify every known animal and plant into genus and species.

Most of the categories we use in our daily life are less strict, less neat, and less exhaustive. Ordinarily, for example, we do not sort animals we see by genus and species. We use rough categories such as "pets," "wild animals," "farm animals," and "zoo animals." Such groupings are not clear-cut; at one time or another, some animals might fit into most or all of these categories. Yet they suffice for our usual purposes. Similarly, we may employ ideologically based categories such as distinctions between "primitive" and "advanced" societies. These are groupings that have been developed out of clusters of beliefs, and they may not stand up to scrutiny.

If you're a documentary filmmaker and you want to convey some information about the world to audiences, you can organize the movie around categories. Suppose the Discovery cable television channel hires you to make a film about butterflies. You might organize it according to scientific classification, showing one type of butterfly and giving information about its habits, then showing another, with more information, and so on. Alternatively, a travelogue about Switzerland might offer a sampling of local sights and customs, using more commonsensical categories (windmills, chocolates) that your audience can easily recognize.

Leni Riefenstahl's *Olympia,* Part 2, was made in 1936 as a record of the Berlin Olympics. Its basic category is the Games as an event, which Riefenstahl had to condense and arrange into two feature-length films. Within these films, the games are broken down into subcategories—sailing events, sprinting events, and so on. Beyond this, Riefenstahl creates an overall tone, stressing the games' grandeur and the international cooperation implicit in the gathering.

A categorical film often begins by identifying its subject. Our clichéd travelogue might start with a map of Switzerland. Riefenstahl begins *Olympia*'s second part with athletes jogging and then fraternizing in their clubhouse. They aren't identified by the sport each specializes in but are presented simply as participants in the Olympics. Later the individual sequences assign the athletes to various events.

CREATIVE DECISIONS

Engaging Viewers Using Categorical Form

The filmmaker using categorical form tends to use simple patterns of development. The film might move from small to large, local to national, personal to public, and so on. Your film on butterflies, for example, might begin with smaller species and work up to large ones, or it might go from drab to colorful types.

Riefenstahl organizes *Olympia* according to a large-scale ABA pattern. The early part of the film concentrates on the games as such, rather than on the competition among athletes and countries. Later she shifts to setting up more dramatic tension by focusing on some of the individual athletes and asking whether they will be successful in their events. Finally, in the diving sequence at the end, there is again no differentiation among participants, and the sheer beauty of the event dominates. Thus Riefenstahl achieves her thematic goal of stressing the international cooperation inherent in the Olympics.

Because categorical form tends to develop in fairly simple ways, it risks boring the spectator. If the progression from segment to segment depends too much on repetition ("And here's another example . . ."), our expectations are too easily satisfied. If you were to make a categorical film, you'd be challenged to introduce variations and make us adjust our expectations. For example, you might choose a category that is exciting or unusual enough to present many ways of stirring the viewer's interest. Riefenstahl realized that the Olympics have an innate drama based on competition and a potential for beauty in the display of physical grace. In *Cinemania,* a portrait documentary, we meet five passionate New York City film lovers who schedule their lives around screenings, sometimes four or five each day. But the film maintains our interest by contrasting its subjects in age, gender, and tastes. What might seem an obsessive lifestyle becomes a small community that accommodates people with varying personalities.

You might also engage a viewer by showing how the category and subcategories connect to broader matters. What designers think about a typeface might seem of pretty narrow interest, but Gary Hustwit made *Helvetica* into an engrossing film. He showed that those who love or hate Helvetica often belong to different generations and hold contrasting views about modern life. For the film that provides our main example, *Gap-Toothed Women,* Les Blank chose an offbeat category that turns out to be broad enough to encompass many sorts of women. As a result, the film's interviews cover a range of varying viewpoints, and Blank livens things up by inserting unexpected images that prove relevant to his subject.

Another way in which the filmmaker can maintain our interest across a categorical film is through patterned use of film techniques. Your film about butterflies might concentrate on conveying information about species, but it could also exploit colors and shapes to add abstract visual interest. The diving sequence at the end of *Olympia* is famous for its dazzling succession of images of divers filmed from many angles **(10.10),** while *Helvetica* seeks out varieties of the typeface in public places, suggesting that it's a pervasive part of the modern city **(10.11).**

Finally, the categorical film can maintain interest by mixing in other kinds of form. Although overall a film might be organized around categories, it can include small-scale narratives. At one point, *Olympia* singles out track-and-field athlete Glenn Morris and follows him through the stages of his event, because he unexpectedly won the decathlon. Similarly, a filmmaker might try to make an ideological point about the category, injecting a bit of rhetorical form into the film. We'll see

10.10

10.11

10.10–10.11 Striking visual values in categorical form. Filmed against the sky, the divers at the end of *Olympia,* Part 2 become soaring shapes rather than individual competitors (10.10), while *Helvetica* often presents examples of the typeface straight-on, as if a building were a page in a book (10.11).

that Les Blank hints that treating gapped teeth as a flaw reflects a society's bias about what constitutes beauty.

Categorical form is simple in principle, but it can create surprising effects. In *The Sweetest Sound*, Alan Berliner surveys the category of people's names. He investigates the origins of his name, tracks down other Alan Berliners, and asks strangers how they feel about their names. His compilation of newsreel footage, home movies, interviews, voice-over narration, and sound bites yields some diverting gags ("Every Tom, Dick, and Harry is called John") and neurotic reflections on identity ("Are they better Alan Berliners than I am?").

> "The whole history of movie making has been to portray extraordinary things, and no one has felt that much confidence in looking at life itself and finding the extraordinary in the ordinary."
> —Albert Maysles, documentary filmmaker

An Example of Categorical Form: *Gap-Toothed Women*

Les Blank has been making modest personal documentaries since the 1960s. His *Garlic Is as Good as Ten Mothers* captures different people's attitudes toward the popular condiment. Blank has employed categorical organization in original ways, showing that this formal approach can be entertaining and thought-provoking.

Gap-Toothed Women was conceived, directed, and filmed by Blank, in collaboration with Maureen Gosling (editor), Chris Simon (associate producer), and Susan Kell (assistant director). The film consists largely of brief interviews with women who have spaces between their front teeth. Why make a film on this unusual, maybe inconsequential subject?

The film's organization suggests a larger theme: Sometimes society has rather narrow notions of what counts as beauty. After introducing the category, the film examines social attitudes, both positive and negative, toward gap-toothed women. If gapped teeth seem to be flaws at the beginning of the film, by the end, being gap-toothed is identified with attractiveness, energy, and creativity.

We can break *Gap-Toothed Women* into these segments:

1. A pretitle sequence introducing a few gap-toothed women.
2. A title segment with a quotation from Chaucer.
3. Some genetic and cultural explanations for gaps.
4. Ways American culture stigmatizes gap-teeth, and efforts to correct or adjust to them.
5. Careers and creativity.
6. An epilogue: gaps and life.
C. Credits.

These segments are punctuated with songs, as well as with still images from magazine covers and photographs that comment on the subject matter of the interviews.

The Opening The first image is a startlingly close view of a woman's mouth (**10.12**) as she recalls baby-sitting for her brothers. Somehow her parents knew when she had stolen bites from forbidden sweets. She has a wide gap between her teeth, and Blank cuts to a close view of an apple, the clue that tipped off her parents (**10.13**). Blank sets up the film's category humorously, making the tooth gap a wry mark of a woman's individuality. A quick series of closer views of six smiling gap-toothed mouths follows, culminating in a shot of a woman's entire head. All are accompanied by folksy harp music that enhances the cheerful tone.

While quickly establishing the category governing the film, this sequence also sets up a recurring stylistic choice. Usually, documentary talking heads are framed in medium shots or medium close-ups, but Blank also includes many extreme close-ups centering on the subjects' mouths, as in the opening view of gapped teeth (**10.14**).

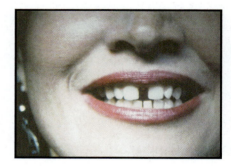

10.12

10.13

10.12–10.13 The opening. In *Gap-Toothed Women*, a close view of a woman's mouth with a large gap (10.12) leads to the telltale apple—"My signature, which was my teeth marks" (10.13).

10.14

10.15

10.14–10.15 Emphasizing the gaps. "My father has a gap, about as wide as mine is; my mom has a gap that's a little smaller" (10.14). Later, we strain to see a woman's gap as she smiles at the camera (10.15).

Blank zooms in on the woman's mouth, and presents the face against a neutral background; both choices reappear often in the film. Once we've learned to notice tooth gaps, we'll concentrate on the speaker's mouth even in the more normally composed head shots. Later Blank (in one of his few offscreen comments) coaxes an elderly woman to grin more broadly to show off her gap **(10.15).** As we start to notice the gaps, we register their differences. Some are wide, some narrow, and we're invited to compare them. By a certain point, the speakers no longer mention them, and the filmmakers seem confident that by then we'll pay attention to them as a visual motif.

The next segment switches to slower shots of a woman playing a harp in a garden. The pleasant tone of this opening is echoed at the end by another, more buoyant, musical performance. In between, the film explores its subjects' attitudes toward being gap-toothed.

During the harpist's performance, the film's title appears in white longhand **(10.16).** This writing recalls the initial woman's reference to her gap-teeth as "my signature." The title leads to a superimposed epigraph: "'The Wife of Bath knew much about wandering by the way. She was gap-toothed, to tell the truth.'—Geoffrey Chaucer, The Canterbury Tales, 1386 A.D." This epigraph suggests that the film's central category originated long ago. Moreover, Chaucer's Wife of Bath is traditionally associated with erotic playfulness, and this element becomes a motif in the film as a whole.

Gaps: Truth and Myth

The film's third segment deals with where gaps come from and what they are thought to mean. In a cluster of brief interviews, three women mention that other members of their family had gap-teeth as well, so we infer that this feature might be inherited genetically. All three women speak in a neutral way about gapped teeth, but the first, mentioning that her mother had worn braces, drops the hint that some people take gapped teeth to be undesirable.

This segment then shifts its focus to consider how various cultures—specifically, non-white societies—have interpreted gap-teeth. A young Asian woman with a gap speculates on a "stupid" myth that gap-toothed women "are supposed to be sexier." Blank then cuts to a brief clip from the fiction film *Swann in Love,* with the protagonist making love to a beautiful gap-toothed woman in a carriage. Does this confirm the myth? Or only suggest that the myth has been applied to gap-toothed women in general, since the actress is not Asian? This clip from another film introduces Blank's tactic of intercutting images from art and popular culture with the interview footage. This other material tests the comments and reminds us of how pervasive the image of the gap-toothed woman is.

The erotic motif brings back the Wife of Bath, now in an engraving showing her riding at the head of a group of pilgrims **(10.17).** A scholarly male voice-over explains that in medieval times being gap-toothed was associated with a love of travel and an amorous nature. There follows a string of interviews developing positive interpretations of the motif. A gap-toothed woman explains, in sign language, that she dreamed of kissing her instructor and having their gaps interlock. An African-American woman describes how, in places like Senegal, gaps are seen as lucky or beautiful **(10.18).** An Indian woman asserts that in her culture gaps are so normal as not to require comment. Abruptly, Blank cuts to a modern copy of a sphinx, and we hear a woman's voice claiming that ancient Egyptian women believed that gaps were associated with beautiful singing. Overall, the segment shows that cultures have interpreted gap-teeth very differently. Most don't consider them flaws, and many treat them as signs of beauty.

Segment 4 tries to show that, in contrast to these cultures, modern Western society stigmatizes gaps. Several more interviews, intercut with other material, show that women have felt that their own teeth were unattractive. One tells of a dentist who tried to convince her to fix her gap (mocked in a song about "filling your mouth with wires, your head with lies"). But the idea that gapped teeth are ugly is immediately counterbalanced by vigorous editing. Two magazine images of models

10.16   10.17   10.18

10.16–10.18 Gaps and femininity. The film's title is superimposed on a garden scene (10.16). The image of the Wife of Bath stands out incongruously from the dignified group, with her low-cut dress and broad grin (10.17). Blank follows this with imagery from cultures in which gaps are valued (10.18).

without gaps are followed by a pretty little African-American girl with a gap; then a photo of Madonna, a gap-toothed glamour icon; and then a *Vogue* cover (**10.19**). As if in reply to these images, a woman says she's worried about her height and weight, as well as her teeth, although she herself is conventionally attractive (**10.20**). Her comment is then countered by other opinions, as one woman talks about how in magazines "you never see a person with gapped teeth," and a mother with a gap-toothed toddler recalls that she had hated her own teeth until Lauren Hutton became a successful model. By intercutting the woman's comments with illustrations of what she mentions (**10.21–10.24**), Blank achieves an intellectual comparison somewhat akin to Sergei Eisenstein's intellectual montage (pp. 261–264). Overall, the editing drives home conflicting attitudes toward what is beautiful.

10.19   10.20   10.21

10.22   10.23   10.24

10.19–10.24 Western attitudes toward gaps. Images from popular culture reveal attitudes: Les Blank shows Lauren Hutton, the first major gap-toothed fashion model (10.19). By contrast, a beautiful woman worries that her gap makes her unattractive (10.20). Another young woman recalls being teased and compared to Howdy Doody (10.21–10.22). This comparison is followed by a shot of the woman praising Lauren Hutton (10.23), which leads to a glamorous cover photo of Hutton revealing her gap (10.24; compare 10.19).

10.25

10.26

10.25–10.26 Satirizing the media. In an echo of traditional documentary, Blank uses a TV-style handheld camera to follow Lauren Hutton's search for gap-toothed women (10.25). Later Blank includes a fake commercial demonstrating a device designed to fill in gaps (10.26).

These interviews have been less playful than the opening sequence, but now the film lightens again. Lauren Hutton herself roams through city streets in a vain attempt to find gap-toothed people to interview. The scene turns the usual show-business interview upside-down by having celebrity pursue and question ordinary people **(10.25).** Hutton is then interviewed in her home, saying that if a person finds herself attractive on the inside, she can be satisfied with her appearance.

The same playfulness is sustained in another musical interlude, folk singer Claudia Schmidt's "I'm a Little Cookie," a song accompanied by 10 photos of gap-toothed girls and teenagers, all smiling. This segues into a series of testimonies about how women have tried to correct their teeth with homemade devices, followed by a mock commercial for an actual device designed to fill in gaps **(10.26).** This segment of the film ends with the interview with the elderly woman who is proud to still have her own teeth, gap and all (10.15).

Women Glorying in the Gap Segment 5, which we've labeled "Careers and Creativity," begins with another Schmidt song about gaps. As we see images of more gap-toothed women, including Whoopi Goldberg, the song reintroduces the Wife of Bath motif ("old Chaucer knew where the score was at") and leads into an interview with Schmidt herself. She recalls that she used to be defiant about having a gap and extolled "gap power." There follows an interview with the cartoonist Dori Seda, standing beside a poster for the film we're watching and explaining that recognizing her gap helped her link herself to a tradition of unusual women **(10.27).** The film is moving toward associating gapped teeth with pride, comradeship, and creativity.

The next string of interviews reinforces this theme—oddly, by not mentioning gapped teeth at all. The emphasis now falls on women's activities **(10.28).** The Indian woman seen earlier draws rice-paint patterns on her threshold; a Hispanic woman trucker describes a long, difficult trip through a storm. The editing contrasts these stories with one, told by Catherine de Santis, about Arab women who remove body hair with a hot-wax concoction. This tale recalls the theme that it can be dangerous to conform to external standards of beauty.

More positive instances follow, as a heavy-metal singer explains that she quit her band because of its violent messages, and a gap-toothed woman displays the symbols for "woman" and "peace" painted on her face. A sudden sound bridge plays a dual role here. Over the woman's face, we hear a chorus singing, "They'll be marching, marching, marching when the Army comes to town," as if referring to her antiwar slogans. A cut to a new sequence reveals the music to be diegetic, played by a Salvation Army band before a speech is given by Sandra Day O'Connor **(10.29).**

Why is this Supreme Court Justice in the movie? For one thing, she's gap-toothed. For another, her speech emphasizes "creativity, work, and love" as things

10.27

10.28

10.29

10.27–10.29 Gaps and creative energy. Cartoonist Dori Seda discusses active women (10.27). A sculptor talks of how her work helps communities (10.28). Sandra Day O'Connor extols "creativity, work, and love" (10.29).

that make life worthwhile. Since we've just seen several working and creative women, the thematic connection becomes stronger.

The Epilogue   O'Connor also says that when creativity is gone, "the will to live seems to go with it." Her remark leads to the final summarizing segment of the film. In a tight shot, a woman's midriff gyrates in a belly dance. We glimpse other costumed women looking on and musicians accompanying the dancer. The dancer's voice-over commentary explains that she is in remission from acute cancer. A cut moves us to a quiet interview with her, identified as Sharlyn Sawyer, in everyday clothes against a simple board fence. After facing death, she explains, physical flaws no longer bother her. "You get stepped on by a horse, fine, you know, you've got a scar on your leg. Oh, well, you know, you've got a gap between your teeth, hey, no problem!" To underscore the comment, the film freezes on her cheerful face **(10.30)**. Sawyer's spontaneity and commonsense acceptance of physical flaws and aging help put the anxieties of some of the earlier women in perspective.

Another sound bridge—this time, applause that seems to approve of what Sawyer has said—takes us back to the Middle Eastern dance class, where Sawyer performs another lively dance **(10.31)**. The credits begin to roll, revealing a very close photo of a smiling gap-toothed mouth, an image that echoes the first shot. A final acknowledgment maintains the film's exuberant tone: "Many thanks to all the wonderful Gap-Toothed women who made this film possible!"

10.31

10.30–10.31 Putting gaps in perspective. The frame freezes on a leukemia survivor's gap-toothed smile, underscoring the fact that in the larger scheme of things, gaps are insignificant (10.30). Soon she is leaping and spinning to great applause (10.31).

Categorical Form and Interpretation   *Gap-Toothed Women* shows that category-based form need not be a dry recitation of similarities and differences. A filmmaker choosing this method of organizing can take a stance on a subject, play off contrasting attitudes, and entertain an audience. By choosing an unusual category and using simple but vivid film techniques, Blank and his collaborators have created a light film with a serious point.

The filmmakers also show that categorical form can create the four levels of meaning that we described in Chapter 2 (pp. 57–60). On the referential level, *Gap-Toothed Women* presents a series of gap-toothed women from different races and different cultural and class backgrounds. We may know some of their faces and names from previous experience (Madonna and Whoopi Goldberg most obviously, Claudia Schmidt and Dori Seda to fans of folk music and underground comics). We also know that *Vogue* is a fashion magazine and assume that the magazines with Russian or other foreign writing are those countries' equivalents of *Vogue*.

Moving to the level of explicit meaning, the interviewees display a range of reactions to gapped teeth. Some are obviously proud, some embarrassed, others more ambivalent. Some express quite directly the idea that mass media often stigmatize people with gaps, while others reveal that gaps are admired in some cultures. At one point, the sculptor compares the lack of gap-toothed models in magazines to the notion of black people seeing only white faces in media images. This explicitly links stereotyped attitudes about feminine beauty to racism. In most cases, the filmmakers' voices are not heard; they let their interviewees make these points.

The film's form is not organized as an explicit argument in favor of gap-teeth being a natural, even attractive, trait. Yet on the level of implicit meaning, the music and photographs of smiling, gap-toothed women tend to suggest just that. The choice of beautiful women who are worried about their gaps cues us to interpret their fears as unnecessary. Certain women's comments signal the ideas that the filmmakers wish to convey. Dori Seda's discussion of how important it is for women to do things helps define the film's segment on careers and creativity, and the cancer survivor's speech at the end makes anxieties about gapped teeth trivial in relation to the potential joys of life.

Beyond these three levels of meaning, we can also discern symptomatic meanings. Blank began making films in the 1960s, when a counterculture based on distrust of authority emerged. More specifically, it was an era of women's liberation, with its demands for gender equality and the breaking down of feminine stereotypes. By 1987, when Blank's film appeared, the counterculture of the 1960s and 1970s had waned, but many people preserved its ideals. Several of the women interviewed in Blank's film are clearly of this generation and sensibility. Moreover, one legacy of the counterculture has been widespread attention paid to society's pressures on women to conform to limiting ideals of beauty. *Gap-Toothed Women* could be interpreted as an example of how radical attitudes of the 1960s slipped into the mainstream—a situation that persists and makes Blank's 1987 film still relevant today.

Rhetorical Form: Introduction

Another type of documentary film uses *rhetorical* form, in which the filmmaker presents a persuasive argument. The goal in such a film is to persuade the audience to adopt an opinion about the subject matter and perhaps to act on that opinion. This type of film goes beyond the categorical type in that it tries to make an explicit argument.

Rhetorical form is common in all the media, most obviously in televised political speeches. We encounter rhetoric in daily life too, whenever people try to persuade each other. Salespeople try to get you to buy something, and over lunch you may try to convince a skeptical friend of the virtues of a band or athlete you like. Television bombards us with one of the most pervasive uses of rhetorical form in film—commercials, which try to compel viewers to buy products or vote for candidates.

Factors in Rhetorical Form We can define rhetorical form in film by four basic attributes. First, it addresses the viewer openly, trying to move him or her to a new intellectual conviction, to a new emotional attitude, or to action.

Second, the subject of the film is usually not an issue of scientific truth but a matter of opinion, an issue you can take many plausible attitudes toward. The filmmaker tries to make the particular position convincing by presenting different types of arguments and evidence. Because rhetorical films deal with beliefs and arguments, they involve the expression of ideology; indeed, perhaps no type of film form centers so consistently on explicit meaning and ideological implications.

A third aspect of rhetorical form follows from the emphasis on opinion. If the conclusion cannot be proved beyond question, the filmmaker often appeals to our emotions, rather than presenting only factual evidence. And fourth, the film often attempts to persuade the viewer to make a choice. That may be big or small, but rhetorical form asks you to take a side, and perhaps take action. Which shampoo to buy? What candidate to vote for? Should my country go to war?

Types of Rhetorical Argument Filmmakers can use all sorts of arguments to shape our choices. Often, however, they don't present these arguments *as* arguments. A rhetorical film frequently presents arguments as if they were simply observations or factual conclusions. Nor does the film tend to point out other opinions. The filmmaker using rhetorical form tries to get the audience to accept debatable arguments as plausible on their face. Here are some types of arguments a filmmaker may use: relating to the source, to the subject, and to the viewer.

Arguments from Source Some of the film's arguments will rely on what are taken to be reliable sources of information. The film may present firsthand accounts of events, expert testimony at a hearing, or interviews with people assumed to be knowledgeable on the subject. Most political documentaries include talking-head footage of investigators, scholars, or insiders. At the same time, the filmmakers will try to show that they themselves are well informed and trustworthy. They may insert themselves into the interview situation, as Michael Moore does in his documentaries, or they may use a voice-over narrator speaking in tones of crisp conviction.

Subject-Centered Arguments   The film also employs arguments about its subject matter. Sometimes the film appeals to beliefs common at the time in a given culture. For example, many contemporary Americans suspect that most politicians are cynical and corrupt. Accordingly, a candidate may invoke that belief and tell potential voters that he or she will bring a new honesty to government.

Typically, a subject-centered approach relies on *evidence* to support the film's argument. Evidence could consist of statistics, research findings, poll results, eye-witness testimony, expert judgment, and the like—the sort of evidence you would use in a research paper. But often the documentarist will select vivid examples that stand in for a body of data. Instead of a poll chart showing citizens' resistance to going to war, you the filmmaker might supply shots of a demonstration, with placards and footage of speakers. This footage is more vivid than a chart, but it may suggest that the demonstrators' position is widely held, even if it's a minority view. In other words, evidence may be more or less strong, and dramatic examples may not be typical of wider trends.

Further, filmmakers can back up an argument by exploiting familiar, easily accepted argumentative patterns. Students of rhetoric call such patterns *enthymemes,* arguments that rely on widespread opinion and usually conceal some crucial assumptions. "He must favor low taxes. After all, he's a millionaire" is a common political claim. The implicit argument runs: *He's a millionaire; all millionaires favor low taxes; he must favor low taxes.* But the middle premise is questionable. There are many millionaires and billionaires who claim that out of a sense of social obligation they would support raising tax rates.

Enthymemes allow an easy but slippery movement from problems to a solution. Suppose you're making a film about your city's problem with graffiti. You find that in some cities, after strict vandalism laws were enacted, the incidents of tagging dropped. So you could argue that stiffer punishment is the best solution for your town. This sort of inference is so familiar that we tend to accept it as reasonable. But in this case you'd be assuming that your town is like the other cities in respects that are relevant to graffiti. That might not be true. In some cities, tagging is a casual pastime that could be cut by stronger penalties. In other cities, it's a strong tradition among youth gangs and artistic subcultures and resists policing. At the same time, the stiffer-punishment solution that your film proposes might overlook other solutions, such as providing approved areas for graffiti. (In some cities graffiti zones have become tourist attractions.)

Often the problem-then-solution enthymeme isn't as well justified as we'd like to think. Solutions to human problems are hard, and sometimes we're not sure why certain policies have succeeded or failed. It's easy to assume that solutions fit problems perfectly. Shortly, we'll see taken-for-granted enthymematic patterns at work in *The River.*

Viewer-Centered Arguments   Beyond appeals to authority and subject-centered appeals like enthymemes, the film may make an argument that taps into the emotions of the viewer. Politicians seek out photo ops that show them with flag, family, and ordinary folks. Appeals to patriotism, family sentiments, and other emotions are common in rhetorical films. Sometimes emotional appeals can disguise the weakness of other arguments of the film.

A viewer-centered appeal need not be heavy-handed. *Darwin's Nightmare* argues that Lake Victoria in Tanzania exemplifies basic problems facing Africa as a whole. The area has been colonized by an industry that impoverishes the locals, and it is a prime drop-off point for armaments that fuel civil wars. But the film's point is not introduced explicitly. Instead, we get vignettes showing a wasp being swatted, mysterious men getting off planes and carousing with local women, looming shots of giant fish, images of desolate poverty, and scenes of street musicians and brawling youths. This opening relies on unusual viewer-centered appeals. It arouses curiosity about how all these disparate elements will coalesce into an overall argument. The problem at the core of *Darwin's Nightmare* emerges gradually from the evidence that the filmmaker accumulates after whetting our interest with vivid, perplexing scenes.

If you were to make a rhetorical documentary about a problem, you could organize the types of argumentative appeals in various ways. You could start by introducing the problem explicitly, perhaps dramatizing it with strong emotion. Then you could review some supporting evidence before proposing a solution. You might end your film with a scene that bathes the solution in an affirmative tone. *The River,* our main example of rhetorical form, adheres to this pattern.

An Example of Rhetorical Form: *The River*

Pare Lorentz made *The River* for the U.S. government's Farm Security Administration. In 1937, the country was making progress toward pulling out of the Great Depression. Under the administration of Franklin Delano Roosevelt, the federal government used its powers to create public works programs. These programs sought to provide jobs for the large numbers of unemployed workers, as well as to correct various social problems. Although many people tend now to think of Roosevelt's policies as the right ones and to credit him with bringing America out of the Depression, he faced strong political opposition at the time.

The River hails the Tennessee Valley Authority (TVA) as the solution to the region's problems of flooding, agricultural depletion, and non-electrification. The argument had a definite ideological slant: it sought to promote Roosevelt's controversial policies. Let's look at how this film sets out to persuade its audience that the TVA is a good program.

The River can be broken into eleven segments.

C. Credits.

1. A prologue title setting forth the subject of the film.

2. A description of the rivers that flow into the Mississippi and then into the Gulf of Mexico.

3. A history of the early agricultural use of the river.

4. The problems caused in the South by the Civil War.

5. A section on lumbering and steel mills in the North, and the building of urban areas.

6. The floods caused by careless exploitation of the land.

7. The current effects of these cumulative problems on people: poverty and ignorance.

8. A map and description of the TVA project.

9. The dams of the TVA and the benefits they bring.

E. An end title.

At first the film seems merely to be giving us information about the Mississippi. It proceeds for quite a while before its argument becomes apparent. Slowly, by careful repetition, variation, and development, Lorentz builds up a case that depends on all the segments working together.

Prelude and Premises The opening credits of the film appear over an old-fashioned picture of steamboats on the Mississippi and then over a map of the United States **(10.32).** The film immediately suggests to the audience that its makers are reliable and knowledgeable and that it is based on historical and geographical facts. The same map returns under the prologue in the brief opening segment, which states: "This is the story of a river." Such a statement disguises the rhetorical purpose of the film, implying that the film will be an objectively told story, drawing on narrative form.

Segment 2 continues the introduction with shots of the sky, mountains, and rivers. This motif of the majestic beauty of the Mississippi valley will be repeated at the start of later sections and then contrasted with the bleak landscapes that dominate the middle parts of the film. As we see the beauty of the river (**10.33**), a resonant male voice tells us how water flows into the Mississippi from as far away as Idaho and Pennsylvania. The narrator's rich voice accords with conventional notions of a trustworthy person. The narrator, Thomas Chalmers, was an opera baritone whose voice resonates with calm assurance.

Lorentz uses the sound track to arouse emotion. While we see rivers swelling as they join, the narrator's commentary avoids the dry, factual tone of most documentaries. The sentences rush in an urgent rhythm: "Down the Yellowstone, the Milk, the White, and Cheyenne . . . the Cannonball, the Musselshell, the James, and the Sioux." This famous roll call of the rivers, recalling the teeming catalogues of Walt Whitman's poetry, evokes the power and the grandeur of the Mississippi valley. No less emotional is the spacious folk-song score composed by Virgil Thomson. The film identifies itself with American tradition, appealing to the viewer's patriotic sentiments and implying that the whole country should face up to a regional problem.

The River in History   Segment 2 has established an idyllic situation, with its beautiful images of mountain and river landscapes. The overall development of the film is toward a restoration of this beauty, but with a difference. Segment 3 begins to fit the Mississippi into one version of American history.

The new section begins much as segment 2 did, with a view of clouds. But now, instead of the mountains we saw earlier, we see mule teams and drivers. Again the narrator launches a list: "New Orleans to Baton Rouge . . . Baton Rouge to Natchez . . . Natchez to Vicksburg." The narrator tells of the dikes built along the Mississippi to control flooding in pre–Civil War days. The facts and dates he provides present him as a credible source, trustworthy and knowledgeable. We see cotton bales loaded onto steamboats, giving a sense of the country's early strength as an exporter of goods. The brisk cutting here, as elsewhere in the film, evokes American enterprise and energy. Graphic discontinuities suggest both change and continuity (**10.34, 10.35**). Dynamic compositions suggest the exhilaration of a growing nation (**10.36**).

In segments 1–3, Lorentz has seemed simply to be telling a story of the river. But in segment 4, the film begins to introduce the problems that the TVA will eventually solve. Bleak images show the results of the Civil War: destroyed houses, the land worn out by the cultivation of cotton, and people forced to move west. The tone

10.32

10.33

10.32–10.33 **Winning the viewer's trust.** While we hear a resonant, assuring voice-over narrator, *The River* shows the Mississippi River and its tributaries exaggerated in size (10.32). Soon we have an idyllic image of nature (10.33).

10.34

10.36

10.34–10.36 **Dynamic visuals present energetic growth.** Lorentz uses graphic contrast in cutting from a mud-filled sledge (10.34) to a plow thrusting in the opposite direction (10.35). The clashing movements suggest a shift in technology, but their similarities suggest a connection between building a dike and farming cotton. Later, a canted framing shows workers loading cotton bales onto a steamboat (10.36). The composition, accompanied by sprightly banjo music, makes the bales seem to roll downhill almost effortlessly.

10.37

10.38

10.37–10.38 Before and after. *The River* returns to the motifs of pines and clouds seen in the beginning (10.37), but soon the pines become stumps, the clouds an ominous fog (10.38).

of concern becomes apparent, and it appeals to emotion. Over images of impoverished people, somber music plays. It is based on a familiar folk tune, "Go Tell Aunt Rhody," which, with its line "The old gray goose is dead," underscores the farmers' losses. The narrator's voice expresses compassion as he speaks of the South's "tragedy of land impoverished." This attitude of sympathy may incline us to accept as true other things that the film tells us. The narrator also refers to the people of the period as "we": "We mined the soil for cotton until it would yield no more." Here the film's persuasive intent becomes evident. It was not literally *we*—you and I and the narrator—who grew this cotton. The use of *we* is a rhetorical strategy to make us feel that all Americans share a responsibility for this problem and for finding a solution.

The narrator resumes his story, moving outside the impoverished South to arouse our pride in the growth of other regions. In segment 5, poetically repetitious narration describes the lumber industry's growth after the Civil War, listing "black spruce and Norway pine" and other trees. In the images, we see evergreens against the sky, echoing the cloud motif that opened segments 2 and 3 (**10.37**). This creates a parallel between the riches of the agricultural areas and the industrial ones. A sprightly sequence of logging, accompanied by music based on the tune "Hot Time in the Old Town Tonight," again gives us a sense of America's vigor. A section on coal mining and steel mills follows, enhancing this impression. This segment ends with references to the growing urban centers: "We built a hundred cities and a thousand towns," and a roll call invokes many of their names.

Up to this point, we have seen the strengths of America associated with the river valley, with just a hint of problems that growth has sparked. But segment 6 switches tactics and creates a lengthy series of contrasts to the earlier parts. It begins with the same list of trees—"black spruce and Norway pine"—but now, instead of seeing trees against clouds, we see stumps against fog (**10.38**). Another line returns, but with a new phrase added: "We built a hundred cities and a thousand towns . . . but at what a cost." Beginning with the barren hilltops, we are shown how melting ice runs off, and how the runoff gradually erodes hillsides and swells rivers into torrential floods. Once more we hear the list of rivers from segment 2, but now the music is somber and the rivers are no longer idyllic. Again we get a parallel, this time between the soil erosion here and the soil depletion in the South after the Civil War.

Style Arousing Emotion   It's worth pausing to comment on Lorentz's use of film style, because he reinforces the film's argument through techniques that arouse the audience's emotions. The contrast of segment 6 with the lively logging segment that precedes it could hardly be stronger. The sequence begins with lingering shots of the fog-shrouded stumps (10.38). There is little movement. The music consists of threatening, pulsing chords. The narrator speaks more deliberately. Dissolves, rather than straight cuts, connect the shots. The segment slowly builds up tension. One shot shows a stump draped with icicles, and an abrupt cut-in emphasizes the steady drip from them (**10.39**). A sudden, highly dissonant chord signals us to expect danger.

Then, in a series of close-ups of the earth, water gathers, first in trickles (**10.40**), then in streams washing the soil away. By now the music presents soft, tom-tom-like beats punctuating a plaintive and rising orchestral melody. As the narrator intones dates, we see streams turning into creeks, and creeks into waterfalls, and eventually rivers overflowing their banks (**10.41–10.43**). Lorentz uses rhythmic editing and music to sweep us along with the mounting tragedy.

As the flooding intensifies, brief shots of lightning bolts are intercut with shots of raging water. The dramatic musical score is overwhelmed by sirens and whistles. From a situation of natural beauty, the film has taken us to a disaster for which humans were responsible. Lorentz's stylistic choices have blended to convey a sense of rising tension, convincing us of the flood's menace. The film's overall argument becomes more compelling because we're made to grasp that threat emotionally

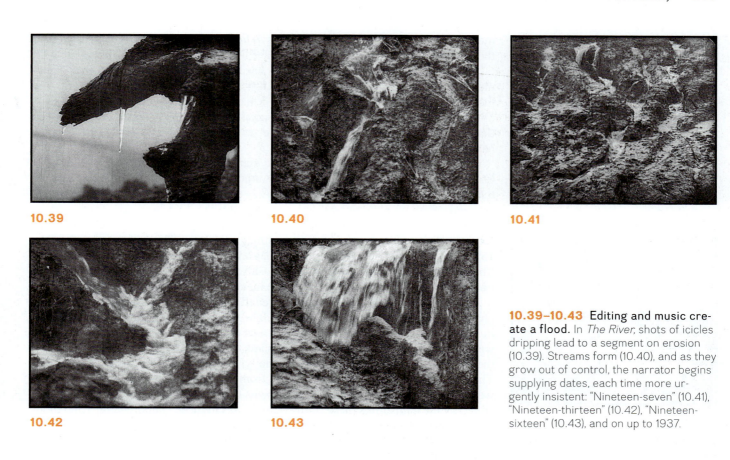

10.39   **10.40**   **10.41**

10.42   **10.43**

10.39–10.43 **Editing and music create a flood.** In *The River,* shots of icicles dripping lead to a segment on erosion (10.39). Streams form (10.40), and as they grow out of control, the narrator begins supplying dates, each time more urgently insistent: "Nineteen-seven" (10.41), "Nineteen-thirteen" (10.42), "Nineteen-sixteen" (10.43), and on up to 1937.

as well as factually. Throughout *The River,* voice, music, editing, and movement within the shot combine to create a rhythm for such rhetorical purposes.

By this point, we understand the information the film is presenting about flooding and erosion. Still, the film withholds the solution and presents the effects of the floods on people's lives in contemporary America. Segment 7 describes government aid to flood victims in 1937 but points out that the basic problem remains. The narrator employs a striking enthymeme here: "And poor land makes poor people— poor people make poor land." This sounds reasonable on the surface, but how did the poor people deplete the land? Didn't the southern plantation owners whose ruined mansions we saw in segment 4 have a lot to do with the impoverishment of the soil? Such statements are employed more for their poetic neatness and emotional appeal than for any rigorous reasoning they may contain. Scenes of tenant farmer families appeal directly to our emotional response to such poverty **(10.44)**. This segment picks up on motifs introduced in segment 4, on the Civil War. Now, the film tells us, these people cannot go west, because there is no more open land there.

Solving the Problem   The core problem has been introduced and discussed, and emotional appeals have prepared the audience to accept a solution. Segment 8 presents that solution and begins the part of the film devoted to the proofs that this solution is an effective one.

In segment 8, the map of the opening titles returns, and the narrator becomes analytical. "There is no such thing as an ideal river in nature, but the Mississippi River is out of joint." Here we have another example of an enthymeme—an inference assumed to be logically valid and factually accurate. The Mississippi may be "out of joint" for certain uses, but would it present a problem to the animals and plants in its ecosystem? This statement assumes that an "ideal" river would be one perfectly suited to *our* needs and purposes. The narrator goes on to give the film's

10.44 **The human cost.** After delineating the environmental dangers, Lorentz gives them a human face.

10.45

10.46

10.45–10.46 Problem solved. The idyllic imagery of the beginning returns, but now the lakes are human-made (10.45). The new economy of the Valley allows men to work again, heroically framed in low angle against the sky (10.46).

most clear-cut statement of its argument: "The old River *can* be controlled. We had the power to take the Valley apart. We have the power to put it together again."

Now we can see why the film's form has been organized as it has. In early segments, especially 3 and 5, we saw how America developed great agricultural and industrial strength. At the time, we might have taken these events as simple facts of history. But now they turn out to be crucial to the film's argument. We have seen that the American people have the power to build and to destroy; therefore, they have the power to build again.

The narrator continues: "In 1933 we started . . . ," going on to describe how Congress formed the Tennessee Valley Authority, an agency tasked with restoring the region. This segment presents the TVA as an already settled solution to the problem and offers no alternative solutions. Although the TVA was very controversial, it's presented as a matter of straightforward implementation. Nor does *The River* show the dislocations caused by the building of the dams. There is no mention of the 15,000 people who had to leave their homes and be resettled elsewhere. Nor does the film attempt to rebut the alternative proposals that arose at the time. In all, the solution that was adopted is assumed to be the inevitable one, without risks or drawbacks.

Segment 9 introduces features that recall several earlier parts, but with an emphasis on the future rather than the past. It begins with a list of dams, which we see in progress or finished. This echoes the lists of rivers, trees, towns, and so on that we have heard at intervals. The serene shots of the artificial lakes that follow link the ending to the beginning, recalling the lyrical river shots of segment 2 **(10.45)**. The flooded-out and unemployed people from segment 6 seem now to be happily at work **(10.46)**, building planned model towns on government loans. Electricity generated by the dams links these rural communities to those "hundred cities and thousand towns" we heard about earlier, bringing to the countryside "the advantages of urban life." Many motifs planted in a simple fashion are now picked up and woven together to act as proofs of the TVA's benefits.

Nature and Humans in Harmony   The ending shows life as being parallel to the way it was in the beginning—beautiful nature, productive people—but enhanced by modern government planning. The film's middle segments have denied us the picturesque views of mountains and sky we saw at the beginning. But after the introduction of the TVA, such shots return **(10.47, 10.48)**. Tying the ending back to the beginning, the imagery shows a return to idyllic nature, under the auspices of government planning.

An upswell of music and a series of images of the dams and rushing water create a brief epilogue summarizing the force that has wrought the change—the TVA. Under the ending titles and credits, we see the U.S. map again. A list tells us the names

10.47

10.48

10.47–10.48 Nature regained. The hillsides celebrated in the beginning now shelter modern, model towns.

of the various government agencies that sponsored the film or assisted in its making. These again seem to lend authority to the source of the arguments in the film.

The River achieved its purpose. Favorable initial response led a major American studio, Paramount, to agree to distribute the film, a rare opportunity for a government-sponsored short documentary at that time. Reviewers and public alike greeted the film enthusiastically. A contemporary critic's review testifies to the power of the film's rhetorical form. After describing the early portions, Gilbert Seldes wrote: "And so, without you knowing it, you arrive at the Tennessee Valley— and if this is propaganda, make the most of it, because it is masterly. It is as if the pictures which Mr. Lorentz took arranged themselves in such an order that they supplied their own argument, not as if an argument conceived in advance dictated the order of the pictures."

President Roosevelt was pleased with *The River*. He helped get congressional support to start a separate government agency, the U.S. Film Service, to make other documentaries like it. But not everyone was in favor of Roosevelt's policies or believed that the government should set itself up to make films that espoused the views of the current administration. By 1940, the Congress had taken away the U.S. Film Service's funding, and documentary films were once again made only within other government agencies. In such ways, rhetorical form can lead both to direct action and to controversy.

Experimental Film

Another basic type of filmmaking is willfully nonconformist. In opposition to dominant or mainstream cinema, some filmmakers set out to create films that challenge normal notions of what a movie can show and how it can show it. These filmmakers work independently of commercial production, distribution, and exhibition, and often they work alone. Their films are hard to classify, but usually they are called *experimental* or *avant-garde.*

Experimental films are made for many reasons. The filmmaker may wish to express personal experiences or viewpoints in ways that would seem eccentric in a mainstream context. In *Mass for the Dakota Sioux,* Bruce Baillie suggests his despair at the failure of America's optimistic vision of history. Su Friedrich's *Damned If You Don't,* a story of a nun who discovers her sexuality, presents the theme of release from religious commitment. Alternatively, the filmmaker may seek to convey a mood or a physical quality (**10.49, 10.50**).

The filmmaker may also wish to explore some possibilities of the medium itself. Experimental filmmakers have tinkered with cinema in myriad ways. They have presented cosmic allegories, such as Stan Brakhage's *Dog Star Man,* and highly private japes, as in Ken Jacobs's *Little Stabs at Happiness.* Robert Breer's *Fist Fight* experiments with shots only one or two frames long (6.141); by contrast, the shots in Andy Warhol's *Eat* last until the camera runs out of film. You can make an experimental film through improvisation, or a mathematical plan, or just letting nature take its course. For *Eiga-zuke (Pickled Film),* Japanese-American Sean Morijiro Sunada O'Gara applied pickling agents to negative film and then handprinted the blotchy abstractions onto positive stock.

The experimental filmmaker may tell no story, creating poetic reveries (**10.51**) or pulsating visual collages such as *Ballet mécanique,* which serves as one of our main examples here. Alternatively, the filmmaker may create a fictional story, but it's likely to challenge the viewer. Yvonne Rainer's *Film About a Woman Who . . .* presents its narrative partly through a series of slides that a group of men and women are watching. At the same time, on the sound track, we hear anonymous voices carrying on a conversation, but we cannot confidently assign any voice to an individual onscreen. Rainer thus forces us to weigh everything we see and hear on its own terms, apart from any involvement with characters (**10.52**).

> " One of the things that goes on in *Critical Mass* (this is also true of much of the rest of my work and of the work by others I admire) is a process of training the spectator to watch the film."
>
> —Hollis Frampton, experimental filmmaker

10.49

10.50

10.49–10.50 Kinetic grace in the experimental film. Maya Deren's *Choreography for Camera* shows a dancer lifting his leg in a forest (10.49) and bringing it down in a studio (10.50). The match on action yields smooth movement across different times and places.

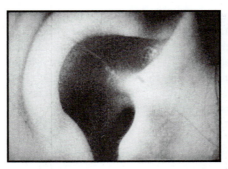

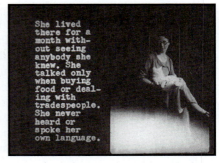

10.51

10.52

10.51–10.52 Nonnarrative and narrative form in experimental film. In Willard Maas's *Geography of the Body,* an ear creates an abstract, lyrical composition (10.51). Thanks to Rainer's combination of images, sounds, and captions in *Film About a Woman Who . . . ,* the viewer is encouraged to imagine several possible stories (10.52).

10.53

10.54

10.53–10.54 The found-footage film. *A Movie* cuts from a low-angle shot of a stagecoach (10.53) to a similar one of a hurtling tank (10.54), mixing staged footage and newsreel footage to create a graphic match.

A Range of Technical Choices

Any sort of footage may be used for an avant-garde film. Images that a documentarist might take as fragments of actuality can be mobilized for quite different purposes. For the aptly titled *A Movie,* Bruce Conner pulls footage from Hollywood Westerns, travelogues, and newsreels to create a sweeping image of the destruction of civilization (**10.53–10.54**). Within the experimental mode, such scavenged works are often called *found-footage films.* Found-footage films rely on editing, but experimentalists have also expressed distinct feelings or ideas through staging (**10.55, 10.56**). There is avant-garde animation as well, as we'll see later in this chapter.

The freedom available to experimental film is on flamboyant display in Kenneth Anger's *Scorpio Rising.* Anger takes as his subject the motorcycle culture of the 1960s, and he includes scenes of bikers working on their machines, dressing, partying, and racing. Alongside footage of bikers glimpsed on the streets or in parties, there are many staged incidents—chiefly around Scorpio, a James Dean–like figure. Anger also cuts in still photos, comic strips, found footage from old movies, and Nazi posters. In addition, each segment is accompanied by a rock-and-roll song that adds an ironic or ominous tone to the images (**10.57**). Throughout the film, Anger links biking to a death wish. *Scorpio Rising* creates elusive but powerful associations, suggesting the homoerotic dimensions of bike culture, comparing its rituals to fascism and Christianity, and evoking the possibility that people often model their behavior on images supplied by mass media.

10.55

10.56

10.55–10.56 Staging in experimental film. James Broughton's *Mother's Day* offers carefully composed arrays of adults playing children's games (10.55). By superimposing different phases of a kitchen scene, Ivan Galeta's *Two Times in One Space* creates cycles of people splitting or drifting like phantoms (10.56). Mysteriously, the action on the distant balcony unfolds in normal duration.

Impossible to capture in a neat formula, avant-garde cinema is recognizable by its efforts at self-expression or experimentation outside mainstream cinema. Yet the boundary lines can be breached. Techniques associated with the avant-garde have been deployed in music videos by Michel Gondry and Chris Cunningham. In fact, Conner, Anger, Derek Jarman, and other experimentalists were early pioneers of music video. Meanwhile, mainstream features have been continually drawing on the avant-garde for ideas and techniques, just as experimentalists have plundered mainstream films for ideas to push in unexpected directions.

Types of Form in Experimental Films

Like documentaries, experimental films sometimes use narrative form. James Sibley Watson, Jr., and Melville Webber's 1928 film *The Fall of the House of Usher* evokes the atmosphere of the Edgar Allan Poe story through expressionistic sets and lighting. Occasionally, we find an experimental film organized by categories. Peter Greenaway's *The Falls* traces, in alphabetical order, information about an imaginary group of people with the surname Fall. Christian Marclay's 24-hour *The Clock* is organized by times of day, as illustrated in shots from fiction films.

Two other types of form are characteristic of experimental films: abstract form and associational form.

Abstract Form: Introduction

When we watch a film that tells a story, or surveys categories, or makes an argument, we usually pay little attention to the sheer pictorial qualities of the shots. Yet it's possible to organize an entire film around colors, shapes, sizes, and movements in the images.

How could you do this? Consider *Railroad Turnbridge,* by the sculptor Richard Serra. A turnbridge allows a section of railroad tracks to swivel on a central column, clearing space for tall boats passing along a river. Serra set up a camera at the center of a turnbridge and filmed the bridge's movement. The result onscreen is surprising. The bridge is swiveling, but because the camera is anchored to it, the crossed girders and powerful uprights seem monumentally static, and the landscape rotates majestically **(10.58).** There is no argument here, no survey of categories. A narrative film might have used the bridge for an exciting chase or fight, but Serra invites us to contemplate the bridge as a geometrical sculpture, all grids and angles, in relation to the curves and sweeps of nature beyond. Serra asks us to notice and enjoy the slowly changing pictorial qualities of line, shape, tonalities, and movement.

Of course, all films contain pictorial qualities like these; we noticed them when we studied mise-en-scene, frame composition, and editing. In this chapter, we've seen how the lyrical beauty of the river and lake shots in *The River* functions to create parallels, and the rhythm of its musical score enhances our emotional involvement in the argument being made. But in *The River,* an abstract pattern becomes a means to an end, always furthering Lorentz's rhetorical purposes. *The River* isn't organized around abstract qualities but rather emphasizes such qualities only occasionally. In **abstract form,** the *whole* film's patterning will be determined by such qualities.

10.57 *Scorpio Rising.* As a young man fetishistically tunes up his bike, the figure of death looms above him. On the soundtrack we hear, "My boyfriend's back . . . and he's coming after you."

CONNECT TO THE BLOG
www.davidbordwell.net/blog

Christian Marclay's *The Clock* is both an epic experimental film and a clock itself, because the times shown on-screen correspond to the time that the audience is living. See our entry "Time piece."

10.58 **Abstracting a real object.** The slowly changing background emphasizes the symmetrical geometry of the bridge's design in *Railroad Turnbridge.*

▪▪▪▪▪▪▪▪▪▪▪▪▪▪▪▪▪▪▪▪▪▪▪▪▪▪▪▪▪▪▪▪▪▪▪▪
CREATIVE DECISIONS

Designing Form in an Abstract Film

How can you organize a film based on visual qualities? A common option is a pattern of *theme and variations.* This term usually applies to music, where a melody or other type of motif is introduced, and then a series of different versions of that same melody follows—often with such extreme differences of key and rhythm that the original melody becomes difficult to recognize.

You can design an abstract film's form in a similar fashion. An introductory section typically shows us the kinds of relationships the film used as its basic material. Then other segments go on to present similar kinds of relationships but with changes. The changes may be slight, but soon they will differ sharply from the introductory material. Bigger contrasts emerge, and sudden variations can help us to sense when a new segment has started. If the film's formal organization has been created with care, the similarities and differences won't be random. There will be some underlying principle that runs through the film.

The theme-and-variations principle is clearly evident in J. J. Murphy's *Print Generation*. Murphy selected 60 shots from home movies, then rephotographed them over and over on a contact printer. Each succeeding duplication lost photographic quality, until the final images became unrecognizable. *Print Generation* presents the footage 25 times, starting with the most abstract images and moving to the most recognizable ones. Then the process is reversed, and the images gradually move back toward abstraction (**10.59, 10.60**). On the sound track, the progression is exactly the opposite. Murphy rerecorded the sound 25 times, but the film begins with the most clearly audible version. As the image clarifies, the sound deteriorates; as the image slips back into abstraction, the sound clarifies. Part of the fascination of this experimental film derives from seeing blobs and sparkles of abstract color become slowly defined as people and landscapes before passing back into abstraction. The film also teases us to discover its overall formal pattern.

As *Railroad Turnbridge* and *Print Generation* indicate, by calling a film's form abstract, we don't mean that the film has no recognizable objects in it. True, you could make an abstract film out of pure shapes and colors, created by painting, drawing, cutting out pieces of colored paper, or playing with computer-generated shapes. But you could also film real objects in such a way that their abstract qualities come forward. After all, every abstract quality you might explore exists both in nature and in human-made objects. Bird songs, cloud formations, the markings on fur or feathers—natural phenomena like these attract us because they seem beautiful or unusual. They are some of the same qualities that we look for in artworks. Moreover, even those objects that we create for very practical uses may have pleasing contours or textures. Chairs are made to sit on, but we will usually try to furnish our home with chairs that also look attractive to us.

So experimental filmmakers often start by photographing real objects. But the filmmakers then juxtapose the images to emphasize relations of shape, color, movement, and so on. As a result, the film is still using abstract organization in spite of the fact that we can recognize the object as a bird, a face, or a spoon.

The result often pushes us to use our senses in an unusual way. Normally, there's a practical purpose to noticing abstract qualities. Driving a car, we use colors and shapes to spot traffic signs and signals. Picking out a new shirt or dress, we often ask whether it makes us look fashionable or will cost too much. In watching

> ❝Thematic interpretation comes from literature: it's been carried over to conventional narrative films, but it shouldn't be grafted onto experimental films, which are often a reaction against such conventions."
>
> —J. J. Murphy, experimental filmmaker

10.59–10.60 Theme and variations in *Print Generation*. In early portions of the film, each one-second shot is more or less identifiable (10.59). After many generations of reprinting, the same image becomes abstract, with hot highlights remaining (10.60). The color is biased toward red because that is the last layer of the emulsion to fade in rephotography.

10.59

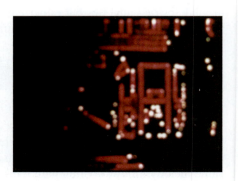

10.60

an abstract film, though, we don't need to use our eyes for practical purposes. The abstract side of the world becomes interesting for its own sake.

This "impractical" interest has led some critics and viewers to think of abstract films as frivolous. Critics may call them "art for art's sake," since all they seem to do is present us with a series of interesting patterns. Yet these films make us more aware of such patterns. No one who has watched *Railroad Turnbridge* can see bridges in quite the same way afterward. In talking about abstract films, we might amend the phrase to "art for life's sake," because such films can enhance our lives as much as do films of other formal types.

An Example of Abstract Form: *Ballet Mécanique*

Ballet mécanique ("*Mechanical Ballet*"), one of the earliest abstract films, was also one of the most influential. It remains a highly enjoyable avant-garde film and a classic example of how mundane objects can be transformed when their abstract qualities become the basis for a film's form.

Two filmmakers collaborated on *Ballet mécanique* during 1923–1924. They were Dudley Murphy, a young American journalist and aspiring film producer, and Fernand Léger, a major French painter. Léger had developed his own distinctive version of Cubism in his paintings, often using stylized machine parts. His interest in machines transferred well into the cinema, and it contributed to the central formal principles of *Ballet mécanique*.

This title suggests the paradox that the filmmakers employ in creating their film's pictorial theme and variations. We expect a ballet to be flowing, with human dancers performing it. Here, however, we have a mechanical dance. Few of the many objects in the film are actually machines; it mostly uses hats, faces, bottles, kitchen utensils, and the like. But the context trains us to see even a woman's moving eyes and mouth as being like machine parts.

Film style plays a crucial role in most films using abstract form. In keeping with its overall formal design, *Ballet mécanique* uses film techniques to stress the geometric qualities of ordinary things. Close framing, masks, unusual camera angles, and neutral backgrounds isolate objects' shapes and textures **(10.61)**. Through overall form and selected techniques, Leger and Murphy reverse our normal expectations about the nature of movement, making objects dance and turning human action into machine motion.

We can't segment *Ballet mécanique* by tracing its arguments or dividing it into scenes of narrative action. Instead, we must look for changes in abstract qualities being used at different points in the film. Going by this principle, we can find nine segments in *Ballet mécanique*:

C. A credits sequence with a stylized, animated figure of Charlie Chaplin ("Charlot" in France) introducing the film's title.
1. The introduction of the film's rhythmic elements.
2. A treatment of objects viewed through prisms.
3. Rhythmic movements.
4. A comparison of people and machines.
5. Rhythmic movements of intertitles and pictures.
6. More rhythmic movements, mostly of circular objects.
7. Quick dances of objects.
8. A return to Charlot and the opening elements.

Ballet mécanique uses the theme-and-variations approach in a complex way. The film throws a great deal of material at us in a short time, and we must actively seek to make connections among motifs. Léger and Murphy introduce many individual motifs in rapid succession, then bring them back at intervals and in different combinations. Each new segment picks up on a limited number of the abstract qualities from the

10.61 Abstracting ordinary objects. A horse collar in *Ballet mécanique*.

10.72

10.73

10.72–10.73 Repetitive machine, repetitive shot. A throbbing machine part gives way to many repetitions of the same shot of the laundry woman.

Segment 4 closes with one of *Ballet mécanique*'s most famous and daring moments. After a shot of a rotating machine part, we see 7 identically repeated shots of a laundry woman climbing a stair and gesturing (**10.72, 10.73**). After more glimpses of the smiling mouth, we get 11 more repetitions of the same shot of the laundry woman, then a shot of a large piston, and 5 more repetitions of the laundry woman shot. Instead of the woman on the swing, who moves to a rhythm she creates, the film endows the laundry woman with rhythm by repeating the same shot again and again. Again, even though she is a real woman in a real place, we must notice her movements' rhythms.

Word and Number Machines   Segment 4 has been the culmination of the film's comparison of mechanical objects with people. Although some motifs, such as the masked eye, reappear in segment 5, this portion of the film will introduce a new set of elements. The clue is given at the opening. Unlike other segments, this one begins with a black screen, which is gradually revealed to be a dark card on which a white zero is painted.

Unexpectedly, an intertitle appears: "ON A VOLÉ UN COLLIER DE PERLES DE 5 MILLIONS" ("A pearl necklace worth 5 million has been stolen"). In a narrative film, this might give us story information, but the filmmakers are now starting to use printed language as one more visual motif for rhythmic variation. We're now peppered with quick shots showing large zeros, sometimes one, sometimes three, appearing and disappearing, shrinking and growing. Parts of the intertitle appear in isolation (*on a volé*), participating in this dance of letters. The film plays with an ambiguity: Is the zero really an "O," the first letter of the sentence? Or is it part of the number 5,000,000? Or is it a geometric representation of the pearl necklace itself? Beyond this sort of play with a visual pun, the zero recalls and varies the circle motif that has been so prominent in the film.

More punning occurs as the zero gives way to a picture of a horse collar—which resembles the zero visually but also refers to the word *collier* (which in French can mean either "necklace" or "collar"). Editing makes the collar execute a hopping dance (10.58). The collar images alternate with moving zeros and parts of the intertitle sentence, sometimes printed backward—to emphasize their graphic, rather than informative, function.

Returning to the Beginning   After its efforts to mechanize words and numbers, the film moves toward variations that are closer to the opening segments. Segment 6 shows us rhythmic movements involving mostly circular shapes (**10.74, 10.75**). Once again we're asked to compare persons and objects. An abstract circular shape grows. A woman's face appears in a prismed view; she passes a piece of cardboard with holes cut in it before her face, with her expression continually changing in a mechanical fashion. We see the circles and triangles alternate again, but this time in four different sizes. A quick series of shots of rows of shiny kitchen utensils follows (**10.76**), with short bursts of black film interspersed. This blackness picks up and varies the dark backgrounds of the intertitles in segment 5, and the shiny pots and other utensils reintroduce a motif that has appeared in every segment *except* 5. The motif of rows of objects had come in segment 3, while the swinging motion of the utensils in many of these shots echoes the swinging of the woman and the shiny ball from segment 1.

Segment 7 continues the turn back to the beginning. It begins with a shot of a display window dominated by a corkscrew shape (**10.77**). The circle motif returns, leading into a set of dances that vary key motifs. Very rapid editing makes a pair of mannequin legs dance (**10.78**); then the legs start to spin within the shots. The shiny ball motif returns, but now two balls spin in opposite directions. Then a hat and a shoe alternate quickly (**10.79**), and the editing creates a startlingly abstract effect. At first, we see the different shapes distinctly, but as the brief shots continue

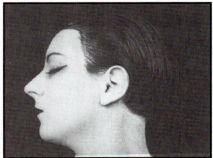

10.74   **10.75**

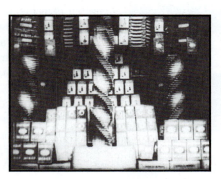

10.76   **10.77**

10.74–10.77 Circles. A new series of circular shapes begins with a woman's head, eyes closed (10.74). She turns, and then we see a statue swing toward and away from the camera (10.75). Soon there are circular kitchen utensils (10.76). In a shop window, spiral shapes seem to freeze the gyrating motions that have made up so much of the film (10.77).

to alternate, we notice variations. The hat changes position, and sometimes the shoe points in one direction, sometimes the other. The cutting rhythm accelerates, and the shots become so short that we see only a single white object pulsating, morphing from circle to lozenge and back again. The filmmakers use the graphic contrasts they've created to make us aware of apparent motion, our tendency to see movement in a series of slightly different still pictures. This is one process that makes cinema itself possible (see Chapter 1).

After the shoe-and-hat duet, more shots of the woman follow, again making her face execute artificial shifts **(10.80).** Finally, quick shots of bottles make them seem to change position in a dancelike rhythm. Here, where the mechanical ballet becomes most explicit, the film draws together elements from its beginning and from the previous segment, where the recapitulation of the earlier segments had begun. Segment 7 avoids motifs from the center of the film—segments 3–5—and thus gives us a sense both that the film is continuing to develop and that it is coming full circle.

The final segment makes this return more obvious by showing us the Chaplin figure again. Now its movements are even less human, and at the end, most of its parts seem to fall away, leaving the head alone on the screen. The spinning head may remind us of the woman's profile (10.74) seen earlier. But the film is not quite over. Its last shot brings back the woman from the swing in segment 1, now standing in the same garden smelling a flower and looking casually around her **(10.81).**

Seen in another context, the woman's gestures might seem ordinary to us. But as Hollis Frampton puts it (p. 55), *Ballet mécanique* has taught us to look at this image in the light of everything that has come before it. By now we're so accustomed to seeing rhythmic, mechanical movement that we're invited to see her smiles and head gestures as *un*natural, like other motifs we have seen in the film. Léger and

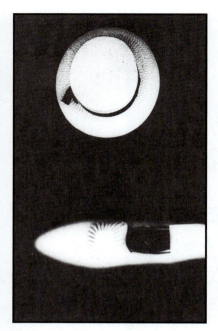

10.79

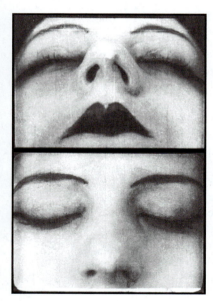

10.78   **10.80**

10.78–10.80 Artificial motion. The mannequin legs seem to move when they're presented in short shots (10.78). At silent film speed, the three-frame shot in the center would flash by in less than a third of a second. (Recall the short shots we described in *The Birds*, pp. 224–226.) Similarly, rapidly alternating shots make a hat seem to squash into a shoe (10.79), and a woman seem to nod her head (10.80).

Murphy end their abstract film by emphasizing how much they have altered our perception of ordinary objects and people.

Abstract form isn't only a matter of older cinema. Apart from earlier examples in this chapter, we could point to *Tape Generations* (p. 42), a recent film that creates geometric patterns out of ordinary transparent tape. Abstract form will always be attractive to filmmakers who want us to see the world around us with fresh, sharpened vision.

Associational Form: Introduction

Abstract form, then, is one option for the experimental filmmaker. Another is **associational form.** Associational form suggests ideas and emotions to the viewer by assembling images and sounds that may not have any logical connection. But the very fact that the images and sounds are put together prods us to look for some connection—an *association* that binds them together.

Bruce Conner's compilation *A Movie* is a vivid example of associational form. The 12-minute film pulls together shots of widely different things—blimps and stagecoaches, auto races and undersea exploration. Early on, shots of stagecoaches and cavalry from old Westerns are followed by shots of a charging elephant and locomotive wheels. The shots ask us to build up associations. Galloping horses are like rampaging elephants and locomotives, and all evoke motion across a landscape. Soon that association will embrace armored tanks and race cars. Eventually we'll see car crashes and vehicles hurtling off cliffs, as if the frantic race that started with cowboys has led to mass suicide.

A Movie doesn't tell a story in the manner of narrative filmmaking. It offers no characters, no specific causal connections, and no temporal order among the scenes. The film suggests that humans enjoy dangerous excitement and that other films encourage that (hence the title *A Movie*). But it doesn't try to persuade us that humans are by nature reckless by giving reasons and offering evidence. There is no voice-over narrator as in *The River* to define problems, assemble evidence, and point to a conclusion. Nor does the film explore a clear-cut set of categories. And yet *A Movie* is not purely a pictorial exercise either, in the manner of abstract form. It employs patterns of imagery and music (Respighi's classical piece *The Pines of Rome*) in order to conjure up ideas and emotions.

Poetic Film   We can think of associational form as working somewhat as poetry does. When Robert Burns says, "My love is like a red, red rose," we don't assume that his love is prickly to the touch, glowing red, or vulnerable to aphids. Rather, we look for the possible associations: Her beauty is the most likely reason for the comparison. A similar process goes on in associational films. Here the metaphorical implications that poetry conveys through language are presented in images and sounds. A director could film a woman he loved in a garden and suggest that she is like the flowers that surround her. (This might be an implicit meaning that viewers could assign to *Ballet mécanique*'s last shot, if it were taken out of context.)

Associational form offers the filmmaker a rich array of choices. You could pick very conventional images or more original ones, and you can create both simple and complicated linkages. Again, poetry offers examples. In "America the Beautiful," the images of "spacious skies," "purple mountains' majesty," and "fruited plain" add up to suggest the patriotic fervor expressed in the chorus, "God shed his grace on thee." Another poem might be more elusive in its effect, giving us less explicit statements of the associative qualities of its imagery. The Japanese poetic form called *haiku* usually juxtaposes two images in a brief three-line form, in order to express a mood. Here is a haiku by the Japanese poet Kakei:

> The eleventh moon—
> Storks listlessly
> Standing in a row

Kakei's images are very sparse, but if we fill them in with our imaginations, we can feel a mood of autumnal stillness, with perhaps a little melancholy. This tone isn't present in the moon or the storks alone but emerges from the juxtaposition of the two images—something akin to the Kuleshov effect in film (pp. 227–228).

Basic Principles of Associational Form

An entire film can be made along associational lines. But imaginative links are unpredictable, so it's impossible to generalize about this formal pattern as clearly as we can with narrative or rhetorical patterns. Still, if you were to make an associational film, you would probably follow some basic principles.

First, you would probably assemble your images into distinct parts. This principle of grouping is also seen in abstract form, as our *Ballet mécanique* analysis shows. Second, your film would likely create variations from part to part. Many filmmakers achieve this by changing tempo, following a fast section by a slow one. In one section of *A Movie*, disasters result from the frantic chase we've already mentioned; later in the film, the disasters are shown in much less energetic imagery, such as acrobats balancing above a city street. Third, as with other types of form, you would probably use repeated motifs to reinforce associations. *A Movie* constantly invokes images of catastrophe, created by man or nature. Finally, associational form strongly invites interpretation, the assigning of general meanings to the film. Watching *A Movie*, we're tempted to conclude that Conner is suggesting that if a society keeps over-stimulating itself, it will collapse.

Associational form tends to shy away from explicit statement, however. Very often the filmmaker won't necessarily give us obvious cues to the appropriate expressive qualities or concepts. He or she may simply create a series of unusual and striking combinations and let our imaginations tease out their relations. Kenneth Anger's *Scorpio Rising*, for instance, strongly associates motorcycle gangs with traditional religious groups and with Nazi violence, while implying that gang regalia and rituals have homoerotic aspects.

Because associational form can be demanding for an audience, it's often confined to shorter films like *A Movie* and *Scorpio Rising*, as well as music videos like Björk's *Joga*. David Byrne's feature-length *True Stories* includes some song sequences, notably "Puzzling Evidence," that work by association. Making a lengthy film based on these principles is more of a challenge, but it can be done, as the feature-length *Koyaanisqatsi* shows.

An Example of Associational Form: *Koyaanisqatsi*

With its breathtaking desert vistas and vast cityscapes, *Koyaanisqatsi* might seem a ripe example of a *National Geographic* documentary aiming to explore different environments, perhaps through a trip taken by a friendly narrator. It might also seem ready-made for rhetorical form, perhaps pressing an argument about the problems of urban sprawl and mechanized lifestyles. Yet Godfrey Reggio, the principal filmmaker behind *Koyaanisqatsi*, has claimed something quite different. The film,

10.81 Back to normal? The final shot of *Ballet mécanique*, with ordinary human movement now seeming a little mechanical.

> " That shot [of a puppy in *Winter*] is preceded by a series of car headlights. So then with the dog's two black eyes, which are like negative headlights, there's something interesting to me there. . . . The nature of the human mind is such that it tries to build concepts out of each moment, and so, therefore, if I think the concept it can build is interesting and poignant, then I'll stick with it."
>
> —Nathanial Dorsky, experimental filmmaker

he says, is "meant to provoke, to offer an experience rather than an idea or information or a story about a knowable or fictional subject."

The experience Reggio refers to, we think, stems from associational form. Because of its worldwide success as a theatrical feature, *Koyaanisqatsi* is probably the most famous example of the associational strategy. The film does suggest some ideas about technology and modern life, but it does so without appeal to narrative or rhetoric. Both large-scale parts and shot-by-shot connections are linked by principles of analogy, metaphor, and implication, the sort of principles we find in poetry. Reggio and his collaborators guide us to follow certain motifs, to make comparisons, and to register the sheer impact of images combined with expressive music, all focusing on the differences between a natural environment and a human-made one.

The appeal to our imagination starts at the title, which will be unintelligible to most audience members. The subtitle given in some versions is "Life out of Balance," but not until the end of the film will we learn that this phrase is one of several possible translations of *koyaanisqatsi,* a word from the Hopi Native-American language. Reggio could have called the film *Life out of Balance,* but the unfamiliar word creates an aura of mystery, along with echoes of a society very different from that of the modern America on display in much of the film.

Koyaanisqatsi can be segmented into 10 distinct parts, signaled by changes in both imagery and Philip Glass's virtually nonstop musical score. Our titles are less precise than the ones we've seen in earlier segmentations in this chapter, as you might expect in a film based on imaginative associations. We'll try to specify them more as we move through the film.

10.82

10.83

10.82–10.83 *Koyaanisqatsi:* From ancient to modern. The age and simplicity of the drawings evoke an ancient culture, while the figures convey a certain mystery (10.82). The fact that they're painted on stone may indicate an enduring authority lacking in the modern culture we see almost immediately, in the exploding rocket (10.83).

1. Prologue
2. Drifting
3. Flowing
4. Taming the Land
5. Man-Made Majesty
6. Collapse
7. Inhabitants
8. The Frenzy of Daily Life
9. Dirge
10. Epilogue

The film is framed by a Prologue (Part 1) and an Epilogue (Part 10), both of which center on human-like figures painted on stone. The film doesn't tell us that these pictographs were created hundreds of years ago by Native Americans in Horseshoe Canyon in Utah's Canyonlands National Park. As with the title, this lack of explanation encourages us to build our own associations **(10.82).**

Primal Beginnings   In the Prologue, this image dissolves to blazing shots of a NASA rocket being launched, the fire from the blast eventually wiping across the screen. More associations accrue. The painted figures resemble rockets, and the juxtaposition of an ancient culture with a modern one marks a strong contrast between eternal calm and furious mechanical movement. On liftoff, the rocket emits a blizzard of metal fragments, a bursting motif we'll see later in the film **(10.83).** The effect is to suggest that the drawings have been incinerated.

To a large extent, the Prologue gives us the film in miniature form, because many upcoming segments will end with explosions that seem to demolish natural surroundings or the human-built environment. Likewise, the Prologue establishes the power of the film's score, a central factor in guiding us to make certain associations. The pictographs are accompanied by a male chorus chanting, "Koyaanisqatsi," accompanied by thunderous organ chords. The effect is of primal, monumental solemnity, as if the figures on the wall are chanting and the organ is providing a cavernous echo. Throughout, Glass's rhythmic and repetitive score provides a firm base for the imagery, with changes in instrumentation often signaling a shift within a section.

Drifting and Flowing   The next two sequences give us much more placid imagery, returning to the sense of serenity summoned up by the canyon drawings. Prolonged aerial shots drift over desert buttes and huge wrinkles of rock winding to the horizon. Droning chords on the soundtrack suggest that time is suspended. Soon things get more energetic, when the camera shows steaming and smoking craters. There follows a passage of associations based on wind **(10.84–10.85).** There is plenty of movement, underlined by a fast tempo in the score, but the movement is gentler and less mechanical than what we saw in the rocket launch. A final shot of this "Drifting" part includes smoke, dripping water, and the natural movement of birds and insects **(10.86).** This is organic, free movement, very different from the harshness of the rocket launch.

The third sequence, which we call "Flowing," accentuates the quality of organic movement. Now undercranking, the camera yields fast-motion shots of clouds racing through the frame. Soon they are intercut with rushing water, inviting us to associate streams and rivers with clouds as another form of water (which, after all, they are; **10.87**). The movement of flowing is intensified when aerial shots race along the landscape, sort of a "cloud POV shot" as the music becomes livelier.

10.84

10.85

10.86

10.87

10.84–10.87 Wind and water. An analogical link among shots: The drifting smoke (10.84) leads to blowing sand (10.85), then the shifting shadows of clouds (10.86). As if to confirm the likeness between different aspects of nature, the film gives us a "cloud waterfall" (10.87).

10.88 **Webs of metal.** In the Epilogue, a title will cite a Hopi prophecy that "there will be cobwebs spun back and forth in the sky," but this metaphor is already suggested in the electric pylons standing like giants.

10.89

10.90

10.89–10.90 **Artificial nature.** Skyscrapers seem to become windows onto the sky (10.89), and thanks to a telephoto lens jet planes emit heat ripples that recall streams of clouds and water (10.90).

The unity of water, air, and land is now evident, but the terrain has changed. Instead of the desert vistas of Part 2, we have lush landscapes teeming with crops. Have the clouds and water of the early images fertilized the desert? This new blend of the elements is affirmed by a majestic aerial shot moving toward a butte surrounded by sky and water. Suddenly organic harmony is shattered by quick shots of explosions, as if the butte were under assault.

Machines Invade and Build A shift in the musical score announces Part 4, which we call "Taming the Land." To ominously pulsing chords, trucks arrive wrapped in black smoke, contrasting with the white and gray clouds we've seen in earlier sections. We glimpse some humans, but they're swallowed up by the haze and the vast machines they manipulate. (We won't be able to identify individuals until later in the film.) Colossal pipelines cut across the landscape, and geometrical forms like wheels and grids are laid across more organic shapes (**10.88**). A fast-paced passage of mining the earth leads quickly to a string of fires and explosions, culminating in a nearly sixty-second shot of an atomic bomb test. The rush of imagery suggests that taming nature has led to a cataclysm. This implication will again be tied down in the Epilogue, with a prophecy: "If we dig precious things from the land, we will invite disaster."

"Man-Made Majesty," our title for Part 5, begins with an image of a power plant looming over a beach where people sunbathe. Early portions of this sequence suggest that humans have created a vast environment on a scale like the buttes and canyons of the desert. The score, a warbling chorus, has a quality of awe, while the cinematography suggests a new, human-made harmony of elements (**10.89–10.90**). The same sort of achievement is seen in traffic, with aerial angles showing highways forming beautiful spirals and the bubbling pulse of the music suggesting elation at this splendid human accomplishment.

But technology again turns destructive. The natural flowing we saw in Part 3 is evoked, but negatively, when military images emerge. Fighter jets whoosh over the desert and missiles are launched. Again the atomic bomb is evoked, and we get another montage of explosions—this time not related to construction and mining, but wartime bombardment. The imagery reinforces the implication of the nuclear blast at the end of Part 4: the technology that built this awe-inspiring world can destroy it.

Collapse and Survivors Part 6 probes the built environment more closely, suggesting that it is vulnerable to decay, or what we'll dub "Collapse." The sequence starts with shining buildings, as the shadows of clouds wipe across them in the manner of the desert vistas of Parts 2 and 3. Likewise, the streets are filmed to resemble canyons (**10.91**). So far, so successful: Humans have created their own massive landscape to live in. Yet it's an eerie place, with the sound of wind rising and fretful string chords in the score.

Gradually the cityscape becomes desolate. To the accompaniment of slowly rising and falling musical phrases, the camera takes us to decaying neighborhoods, hollowed-out buildings, and glimpses of misery. Instead of the springs and rivers seen earlier, water now sprays out of a fire hydrant. Now the wind no longer blows across sand dunes but instead ruffles dead grass and flaps a strip of canvas in a wrecked building.

10.91

10.92

10.91–1.92 Monuments built and destroyed. City canyons echo the rugged desert landscapes (10.91). The destruction of failed housing projects (10.92) recalls the slowly floating debris seen in the opening rocket launch (10.83).

After swooping aerial shots of massive housing blocks, as bare of human presence as the buttes of Monument Valley, the sequence ends in more explosions. This time the assault stems from humans' recognition that they have failed to create a new world. To the sound of frantically wailing choruses, we see housing projects, skyscrapers, derricks, and bridges blasted apart, melting back to earth, and the sequence ends with floating debris choking the frame **(10.92).**

The ending of "Collapse" is bleak enough, but the next part, which we call "Inhabitants," heightens this quality with a view of lowering clouds and thunderstorms striking a city. What follows is our first extended view of human-scale life in this built world. In contrast to the extreme wide-angle imagery that surveyed the desert vistas, urban spaces here and in other sections are shot with very long lenses **(10.93).** Fast- and slow-motion imagery, reinforced by plodding, electronically tinged music, offer glimpses of people **(10.94).** Are they enjoying their lives? Are they unhappy? We're allowed to come to our own conclusions, as a few seem quite cheerful, while others—notably the fighter pilot toward whom the camera tracks—are severe and impassive.

Life at Warp Speed

Most of the film's parts have run seven or eight minutes, but the one we call "The Frenzy of Daily Life" lasts over 20 minutes. It's hypnotic and exhausting. The pace of the cutting and the action in the shot (given in hyper-fast motion) rises relentlessly with the dizzying pace of multiple rhythms in Glass's score. The sequence is tied together by the images of work and play, transportation and recreation. In this respect, the sequence recalls "city symphonies" like Vertov's *Man with a Movie Camera* (pp. 429–433).

At first things are calm enough. Long, static shots show skyscrapers at dusk. Earlier we've seen clouds reflected in buildings, and now we see the sun set in reflection; it's as if such natural occurrences can no longer be seen directly, only through our artificial environment. The pace picks up, and night traffic streams in accelerated motion **(10.95, 10.96).** The music becomes exhilarating and the city seems to pulse with energy. People rush down escalators and bustle through the streets.

As the film starts to mix daytime shots with night ones, fast-motion filming makes all human activity part of a gigantic machine. People process meat, sort letters, sew jeans, assemble

10.93

10.94

10.93–10.94 The new world. Shadows sweep in fast motion across skyscrapers (10.93), as they had moved across the buttes (Fig. 10.85). Meanwhile, citizens walk the streets, captured against ironic signs (10.94).

10.95

10.96

10.95–10.96 Electrical flows. In Part 4, water was shown captured (10.95); now traffic, flowing in fast motion, creates similar patterns of channeled energy (10.96).

TV sets. In the film's most famous sequence, frankfurters pumped out of machines are compared to the flow of traffic and people hurtling up escalators **(10.97–10.98).** This might be the moment of the film's most explicit meaning: Mechanization has ground humans into identical sausages. These images of production are followed by shots of consumption: video games, bowling, film viewing, and above all eating **(10.99–10.100).** Still building the pace, the sequence shows people leaving work, commuting home, and reveling in consumption **(10.101–10.102).** The sequence climaxes in a flurry of TV images, with talking heads and commercials bombarding us. A reprise of people stalking to the camera as in the "Portraits" section seems to remind us that the frantic robots we've seen are really human, but this passage is interrupted by another string of explosions. Now it's TV sets that are blown up, suggesting that the new built environment includes the media world, and it, too, is self-destructive.

We call Part 9 "Dirge" because it changes tempo drastically from the furious movement of its predecessor. Slow, nearly silent shots gliding over the city suggest a weary giant at rest. Urban grids are now compared to the patches on a microprocessor **(10.103–10.104),** as if the city were no longer a machine but a repository of information.

The bits, we might think, are the people, and immediately we see them in a rather different way than we do in "Inhabitants." To plaintive organ chords and an almost funereal chorus, people haunt the streets. A woman can't light her cigarette; a policeman lifts a man off the sidewalk. Most faces are blank, puzzled, or suspicious **(10.105).** These wraiths might be the exhausted survivors of all the hectic rush of the previous section. Are they zombies or ghosts **(10.106)**? Abruptly, a rocket is launched, and (as in *Ballet mécanique*) the film starts to circle back to its opening imagery.

Several sections of *Koyaanisqatsi* have included extremely lengthy shots. The image of the passenger jet nosing its way through traffic runs about two and a half minutes. Arguably, however, the nearly four-minute slow-motion shot of the rocket rising and exploding and falling to earth forms the climax of the film **(10.107).** A briefer shot shows the rocket as it continues to spin endlessly in its descent, and Glass's repetitive score, replaying the hollow chanting of the title that we heard at the start, gives no hint about when the rocket will hit the earth. The image fuses many motifs: air and fire and smoke, as well as the bright particles that have showered other scenes. More broadly, the rocket that was launched in the Prologue has now apparently self-destructed, and along with it the overambitious hopes of man-made technology.

The Epilogue, a very brief sequence, returns to the canyon pictures and zooms back to a fuller view before the shot fades out. Appended titles give the word *koyaanisqatsi* several definitions, including "a state of life that calls for another way

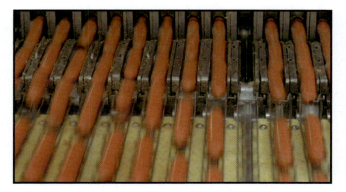

10.97

10.98

10.99

10.100

10.101

10.102

10.97–10.102 People as products. Juxtaposing commuters and frankfurters, both shoved through rigid pathways, implies that mechanization has turned people into standardized units (10.97, 10.98). Fast food becomes very fast food in this rapid footage of mass-produced snacks and people eating identical items (10.99, 10.100). Shot hurtling through the streets (10.101) is followed by a Twinkie's-eye view (10.102), as if the people hurrying home had become another assembly-line product.

of living." A film using rhetorical form would have spelled out that new way, but this film doesn't do that. Indeed, by opening out the title onto a range of meanings, Reggio encourages us to create various interpretations of the film we have seen.

Yet we can't avoid building some implicit meanings out of the associations the film calls up. We might say, for instance, that the film implies that technological progress is too often pursued without thinking about its consequences for both nature and human beings. This theme would tie together a lot of what we've seen, especially the final contrast between the rocket's death spiral and the solemn humanoids on the walls. We have already quoted two of the three closing Hopi prophecies that sum up certain motifs, and the third one recalls the plummeting rocket:

10.103

10.104

10.103–10.104 **Grids.** The city as microchip.

10.105

10.106

10.105–10.106 **Faces of the city.** Glimpses of life on the street (10.105). On the Stock Exchange, ghosts trade shares (10.106).

10.107 **Epilogue.** The final piece of debris: The exploded rocket spins endlessly.

"A container of ashes might one day be thrown from the sky, which could burn the land and boil the oceans."

Like other associational films, *Koyaanisqatsi* invites us to tease out implications from its combination of images and sounds. That invitation doesn't end with the epilogue. There is no spoken language in the film until now, but as the final credits roll, we hear a babble of voices. It's a mix of TV commercials, newscasts, and stock-market reports. This sound montage reenacts the associational patterning we've seen onscreen throughout the film, but it also reminds us of the overwhelming media environment in which we live. Having exercised our eyes and ears and imaginations, this final sequence suggests, we might return to our everyday world more sensitive to the costs of the modern American way of life.

The Animated Film

Most fiction and documentary films photograph people and objects in full-sized, three-dimensional spaces. As we have seen, the standard shooting speed for such *live-action* filmmaking is usually 24 or 25 frames per second.

Animated films are distinguished from live-action ones by the kinds of work done at the production stage. Instead of continuously filming an ongoing action in real time, animators create a series of images by shooting one frame at a time. Between the exposure of each frame, the animator changes the subject being

> "Animation is not a genre, it's a medium. And it can express any genre. I think people often sell it short. But 'because it's animated, it must be for kids.' You can't name another medium where people do."
> —Brad Bird, director, *The Incredibles*

photographed. Daffy Duck isn't a tangible creature you can film, but you can film a series of slightly different images of Daffy as single frames. When projected, the images create illusory motion comparable to that of live-action filmmaking. Anything in the world can be animated by means of two-dimensional drawings, three-dimensional objects, or information stored in software. As we shall see, digitally created films usually imitate the various traditional methods of animation.

Because animation is the counterpart to live action, any sort of film that can be shot live can be made using animation. We're most familiar with animated fiction films, both short and feature-length. There are animated documentaries, usually instructional ones. Animation provides a convenient way of showing things that are normally not visible, such as the internal workings of machines or the extremely slow changes of geological formations. We've already seen animation used for charts and graphs in documentaries such as *Inside Job* (10.2). More daringly, after interviewing Israeli army veterans, Ari Folman sought to represent their lives and recollections in hallucinatory animated imagery (**10.108**).

With its potential for stylized imagery, animation lends itself readily to experimental filmmaking as well. Many classic experimental animated films employ either abstract or associational form. For example, both Oskar Fischinger and Norman McLaren made films by choosing a piece of music and arranging abstract shapes to move in rhythm to the sound track.

Types of Traditional Animation

The oldest type of animated film is *drawn* animation. From almost the start of cinema, animators drew and photographed long series of cartoon images. At first, they drew on paper, but copying the entire image, including the setting, over and over proved too time-consuming. During the 1910s, animators started using clear rectangular sheets of celluloid, nicknamed **cels.** Characters and objects could be drawn on different cels, and these could then be layered like a sandwich on top of an opaque painted setting. The whole stack of cels would then be photographed. New cels showing the characters and objects in slightly different positions could then be placed over the same background, creating the illusion of movement (**10.109**).

The cel process allowed animators to save time and to split up the labor among assembly lines of people doing drawing, coloring, photography, and other jobs. The most famous cartoon shorts made during the 1930s to the 1950s were made with cels. Warner Bros. created characters such as Bugs Bunny, Daffy Duck, and Tweety Bird; Paramount had Betty Boop and Popeye; Disney made both short films (starring Mickey Mouse, Pluto, Goofy) and, beginning with *Snow White and the Seven Dwarfs* in 1937, feature-length cartoons.

Cel animation continued well into the 1990s, with big-budget studio cartoons employing *full* animation. This approach renders figures in fine detail and supplies them with tiny, nonrepetitive movements. (See 4.144, as well as 5.138–5.140.) Cheaper productions use *limited* animation, with only small sections of the image moving from frame to frame. Limited animation is mainly used on television, although Japanese theatrical features also exploit it (**10.110**).

Cels and drawings are photographed, but you can create animation without a camera. You might draw directly on the film, scratch on it, even attach flat objects to it. Stan Brakhage taped moths' wings to film stock in order to create *Mothlight*. The innovative animator Norman McLaren made *Blinkety Blank* by engraving the images frame by frame, using knives, needles, and razor blades (**10.111**).

Another type of traditional animation working with two-dimensional images involves *cut-outs.* Sometimes filmmakers make flat puppets with movable joints

10.108 The animated documentary. A recurring memory image in *Waltz with Bashir* shows soldiers wading toward an eerily beautiful bombardment.

CONNECT TO THE BLOG
www.davidbordwell.net/blog

For a discussion of how animation can be used in documentaries, see "Showing what can't be filmed."

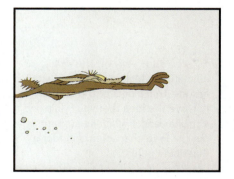

10.109

10.110

10.109–10.110 Cel animation. Two layered cels from a Road Runner cartoon, with Wile E. Coyote on one cel and the patches of flying dust on another (10.109). Limited animation in *Silent Möbius* creates fairly static images recalling comic-book panels (10.110).

10.111

10.112

10.113

10.111–10.113 Varieties of animation. A nearly abstract but recognizable bird is etched directly into the black emulsion in *Blinkety Blank* (10.111). Lotte Reiniger specialized in lighting her cut-outs in silhouette to create delicate, intricate fairy tales, as in *The Adventures of Prince Achmed* (1926; 10.112). It was the first feature-length animated film. Frank Mouris's exuberant *Frank Film* presents a flickering dance of popular-culture imagery (10.113).

> " You don't very often see model animation which is well lit, do you? For me, that's part of the comedy of it; I love the idea that you're making a thriller and it all looks authentic, but the lead character is in fact a Plasticine penguin."
>
> —Nick Park, director and animator, *The Wrong Trousers*

(**10.112**). Animators can also manipulate cut-out images frame by frame to create moving collage (**10.113**). A very simple form of cut-out animation involves combining flat shapes of paper or other materials to create pictures or patterns. *South Park: Bigger, Longer & Uncut* employs computer animation to mimic the rudimentary shapes and unshaded colors of crude cut-out animation.

Three-dimensional objects can also be manipulated frame by frame to create apparent movement. Animation of objects falls into three closely related categories: clay, model, and pixillation. *Clay animation,* often termed *claymation,* sometimes actually does involve modeling clay. But more often, flexible Plasticine is used, since it is cleaner to work with and is available in a wider range of colors. Sculptors create objects and characters of Plasticine, and the animator then bends, twists, or stretches them slightly between exposures.

Although clay animation has been used occasionally since the early years of the 20th century, it has grown in popularity since the mid-1970s. Nick Park's *Creature Comforts* parodies the talking-heads documentary by creating droll interviews with the inhabitants of a zoo. His "Wallace and Gromit" series (including *The Wrong Trousers* and *A Close Shave*) and *Chicken Run* (codirected with Peter Lord; **10.114**) contain complex lighting and camera movement.

Model or *puppet animation* is often similar to clay animation. As the name implies, it employs figures with bendable wires or joints. Historically, the master of this form of animation was Ladislav Starevich, who as early as 1910 baffled Russian audiences with realistic insect models acting out human dramas and comedies (**10.115**). Starevich's puppets display intricate movements and detailed facial expressions (4.89). Some of the main characters in his films had up to 150 separate interchangeable faces to render different expressions. Perhaps the most famous animated puppet was the star of the original 1933 version of *King Kong,* a small, flexible doll. If you watch *King Kong* closely, you can see his fur rippling—the traces of the animator's touch as he shifted the puppet between exposures. Recent feature-length puppet films include *The Nightmare Before Christmas, Coraline,* and *Fantastic Mr. Fox* (**10.116**).

Pixillation is a term applied to frame-by-frame manipulation of people and ordinary objects (**10.117**). Although actors ordinarily move freely and are filmed in real time, occasionally an animator pixillates them. That is, the actor freezes in a pose for the exposure of one frame, then moves slightly and freezes again for another frame, and so on. The result is a jerky, unnatural motion quite different from ordinary performance. The innovative animator Norman McLaren uses this approach to tell the story of a feud in *Neighbours* and to show a man struggling to tame a rebellious piece of furniture in *A Chairy Tale.* Dave Borthwick's *The Secret Adventures of Tom Thumb* animates a tiny Plasticine figure of Tom as well as eerie giants played by real actors. The humans are pixillated even in scenes without Tom.

10.114

10.115

10.116

10.117

10.114–10.117 Animating objects. A flock of Plasticine hens in *Chicken Run* receives Hollywood-style lighting (10.114). In 1912, *A Cameraman's Revenge* used realistic insect puppets to enact a comic melodrama of infidelity, jealousy, and revenge (10.115). In *Fantastic Mr. Fox,* the hero endangers his family and neighbors when he can't resist his urge to steal from local farmers (10.116). In 1908, Arthur Melbourne-Cooper animated toys in a miniature set to create dense layers of movement in *Dreams of Toyland* (10.117), an early example of pixillation.

Traditional animation has sometimes been mixed with live-action filming. Walt Disney's earliest success came with a 1920s series, "Alice in Cartoonland," which embedded an actress in a black-and-white drawn world. Gene Kelly entered a world of cels to dance with Jerry the Mouse in *Anchors Aweigh*. Perhaps the most elaborate combination of cel animation and live action has been *Who Framed Roger Rabbit* (5.58).

Types of Computer Animation

Computer imaging has revolutionized animation. Software can quickly generate the thousands of slightly altered images that will supply the illusion of movement. On a creative level, software can be devised that enables filmmakers to create images of things that could not be filmed in the real world.

CGI (computer-generated imagery) was used occasionally for special effects scenes in the 1970s and 1980s. In the next decade, George Lucas's Industrial Light

& Magic, Steve Jobs's Pixar Animation, and other firms developed powerful computers and complex programs for creating animated imagery. Images generated in computers were transferred to film either by filming directly off a high-resolution monitor or by using a laser to imprint individual pixels onto each frame. In 1995, Pixar's *Toy Story,* the first animated feature created entirely via computer, was released through Disney. It presented a compelling three-dimensional world peopled by figures that resembled Plasticine models (**10.118**). Pixar's programs steadily improved the rendition of fur (*Monsters, Inc.*), water (*Finding Nemo*), reflective metal (*Cars*), and other surface textures.

Toy Story's illusion of solid, sculptural cartoon figures helped establish the conventions of **3D computer animation.** (The term "3D" is also applied to movies giving a stereoscopic impression of depth when viewed through special glasses, as indicated in Chapter 5. Things get confusing when some animated films are released in stereoscopic 3D, so we can have "3D animation" that isn't presented in 3D projection. Usually only the context indicates which type of 3D is being referred to.) By contrast, **2D computer animation** uses digital imaging to simulate the look of traditional cel animation, as in *The Prince of Egypt* and *My Dog Tulip.*

"Computer animation" doesn't mean that the filmmaker just makes a few mouse clicks and the computer generates a movie. The software can work only with what the filmmaker puts into it. If you were to make a computer-animated film, your input might be a scanned image (**10.119**) of a three-dimensional model. You might draw on a digital tablet (**10.120–10.121**) or build up a wire-frame image and

10.118

10.119

10.120

10.121

10.118–10.121 Computer animation. *Toy Story*'s computer-generated world (10.118). Nina Paley created all the images for her feature *Sita Sings the Blues* herself. Here she combines scans from printed images in a collage fashion, placing a scanned silhouette in the foreground, and placing a computer-generated sunburst shape as a background (10.119). Compare her image with *Frank Film,* 10.113. Paul and Sandra Fierlinger worked on their own to draw and color the 2D images for *My Dog Tulip.* Here Paul draws on a digital tablet (10.120). The result resembles traditional cel animation (10.121).

10.122

10.123

10.122–10.123 Digital animation mimics traditional animation. The digital characters in *A Bug's Life* resemble puppets (10.122). Ben Hibon designed digital silhouettes for the three-minute animated segment of *Harry Potter and the Deathly Hallows: Part 1* (10.123). Hibon, a fan of Lotte Reiniger, deliberately recalled the effects she achieved with paper cut-outs (10.112).

then render a surface onto it. Increasingly, visual material is fed into the computer using motion capture, as we saw in Chapter 4 (pp. 137–139). Once the basic visual material is digitized, you would create the most important bits of the figures' movements (called "keyframing"). The software fills in the frames between those poses, saving you the effort of creating every frame yourself. Other programs add color, texture, and lighting.

The kinds of films made with computer animation are similar to the traditional ones we surveyed above. 3D animation frequently resembles puppet films. *A Bug's Life* was Pixar's second feature, and the filmmakers chose insects as their characters because they were made of simple, smooth shapes that were relatively easy to render (**10.122**). The result echoes Starevich's early insect films like *A Cameraman's Revenge* (10.115). Similarly, the short segment, "The Tale of the Three Brothers," an animated scene in *Harry Potter and the Deathly Hallows: Part 1,* imitated the look of a traditional silhouette film (**10.123**).

Some animators, most famously Hiyao Miyazaki, combine analog and digital imaging (**Fig. 10.124**). They may draw the pictures but use a paint program to add the color. Or a complicated camera movement may be rendered using computer animation, while the rest of the film is hand-drawn. This tactic was also used in *The Illusionist,* where a shot flying over a cityscape was created via computer while the other shots used traditional cel drawings.

CONNECT TO THE BLOG
www.davidbordwell.net/blog

For more on Ben Hibon's animated segment of *Harry Potter and the Deathly Hallows: Part 1,* see "Three minutes of 'Three Brothers.'"

10.124 Merging cel and computer animation. In *Princess Mononoke,* five portions of the image (the grass and forest, the path and motion lines, the body of the Demon God, the shading of the Demon God, and Ashitaka riding away) were joined by computer. That yielded smoother, more complex motions than regular cel animation could achieve.

CONNECT TO THE BLOG
www.davidbordwell.net/blog

We comment on the Oscar-nominated animated shorts for 2007 in "Do sell us shorts," and the ones for 2008 in "Do sell us shorts, the sequel." The rise of computer animation led to an expansion of the Best Animated feature Oscar category. We discuss the trend in "The other expanded Oscar category."

❝ As the six-year-old boy protested when I was introduced to him as the man who draws Bugs Bunny, 'He does not! He draws pictures of Bugs Bunny.'"
—Chuck Jones, animator

❝ Animators have only one thing in common. We are all control freaks. And what is more controllable than the inanimate? You can control every frame, but at a cost. The cost is the chunks of your life that the time consuming process devours. It is as if the objects suck your time and energy away to feed their own life."
—Simon Pummell, animator

Traditional animation was so labor-intensive that for decades only the extensive Disney studio could regularly turn out full-length animated features. The lower cost of computer animation has led to an explosion of feature-length cartoons. Moreover, as Nina Paley's *Sita Sings the Blues* and Paul and Sandra Fierlinger's *My Dog Tulip* show, an individual or small team can make professional-level features that play in theaters and at festivals. Thanks to digital technology, animation has moved into the mainstream of commercial filmmaking.

An Example of Traditional Animation: *Duck Amuck*

During the golden age of Hollywood short cartoons, from the 1930s to the 1950s, Disney and Warner Bros. were rivals. Disney animators had far greater resources at their disposal, and their animation was more elaborate and detailed than the simpler Warner product. Warner cartoonists fought back by exploiting the comic fantasy possible in animated films and playing with the medium in imaginative ways.

Warner Bros. cartoons reveled in fast, violent action. In *Rabbit Seasoning,* shotgun blasts keep rearranging Daffy Duck's features. The Warner team exploited an impudent tone as well, making Daffy and Bugs Bunny wisecracking cynics far removed from the sweet altruism of Mickey Mouse. Warner's comedy was often surreal, letting characters speak to the audience or mock studio executives. The unit's producer Leon Schlesinger appeared in *You Ought to Be in Pictures,* letting Porky Pig out of his contract so that he could move up to live-action features.

Of the many Warner experiments, none went further than *Duck Amuck,* directed by Charles M. (Chuck) Jones in 1953. It is now recognized as one of the masterpieces of American animation. Although it was made within the Hollywood system and uses narrative form, it has an experimental feel because it asks the audience to take part in an exploration of techniques of cel animation.

As the film begins, it seems to be a swashbuckler of the sort Daffy Duck had appeared in before, such as *The Scarlet Pumpernickel* (1950), itself a parody of one of Errol Flynn's most famous Warner Bros. films. When Daffy is first seen, he is a dueling musketeer. But when he moves to the left, he passes the edge of the painted background **(10.125).** He's baffled, calls for scenery, and exits. A giant animated brush appears from outside the frame and paints in a barnyard **(10.126).** When Daffy enters, still in musketeer costume, he is annoyed but changes into a farmer's outfit. Such quick switches continue throughout the film, with the paintbrush and a pencil eraser adding and removing scenery, costumes, props, and even Daffy himself, with dizzying illogic. At times the sound cuts out, or the film seems to slip in the projector, so that we see the frame line in the middle of the screen **(10.127).**

10.125   **10.126**   **10.127**

10.125–10.127 The breakdown of cartoon space. Early in *Duck Amuck*, the background tapers off into white blankness (10.125). An inappropriate background for a swashbuckler appears in the blank space (10.126). In *Duck Amuck*, as the image apparently slips in the projector, Daffy splits in two and converses with himself (10.127).

All these tricks result in a peculiar narrative. Daffy repeatedly tries to get a plot, any plot, going, and the unseen animator constantly thwarts him. As a result, the film's principles of narrative progression are unusual. We begin to realize that the film is creating comedy by frankly acknowledging various techniques of animation: painted backgrounds, sound effects, framing, music, and so on. Meanwhile, the outrages perpetrated against Daffy escalate, and his frustration builds accordingly. Soon a mystery surfaces. Who is this perverse animator? Why is he tormenting Daffy?

At the end, the mystery is solved when the animator blasts Daffy with a bomb and then closes a door in his face **(10.128).** The next shot moves us to the animation desk itself, where we see Bugs Bunny, who has been the animator all along. He grins at us: "Ain't I a stinker?" **(10.129).** To a spectator who has never seen a Warner Bros. cartoon before, this ending would be puzzling. The narrative logic of *Duck Amuck* depends largely on knowing that Bugs and Daffy often costarred in other cartoons. Invariably the calm, ruthless Bugs would get the better of the manic, dim-witted Daffy.

Duck Amuck's use of animation techniques is just as unconventional as its narrative form. Because the action moves so quickly, we might fail on first viewing to note that aside from the credit title and the familiar "That's All, Folks!" logo, the film contains only four separate shots, three of which come in quick succession at

10.128   **10.129**

10.128–10.129 Who's in charge here? A pencil protruding into the frame finally begins to reveal *Duck Amuck*'s fiendish animator (10.128). As in many other Warner Bros. cartoons, Bugs turns and speaks to the audience after he triumphs over Daffy (10.129).

10.130

10.131

10.130–10.131 Daffy beseiged. Daffy is trapped without background or sound track (10.130). Daffy struggles to preserve his personal space as the frame collapses on him like syrup (10.131).

the end. The bulk of the cartoon consists of a single lengthy and continuous shot—animation's equivalent of a long take. Yet the settings and situations change quickly as the paintbrush and pencil re-create the image, and Daffy moves in and out of the frame. Often he appears against a stark white background. Such moments emphasize the fact that in cel animation, the figures and background are layers that can be photographed separately. In *Duck Amuck,* the only certain space is that of the frame itself—a quality quite different from the clearly established settings provided in more conventional cartoons.

Similarly, the time frame becomes warped as Daffy moves into and out of diegetic situations, launching into one possible plotline only to find it cut short by the mystery animator. Daffy keeps assuming that the cartoon is just beginning, but time is flowing inexorably by in the outer cartoon, *Duck Amuck* itself. (Traditionally, cartoons were around seven minutes long to fit into the shorts section of movie theater programs.) At one point more than halfway through, Daffy shouts, "All right! Let's get this picture started!" Immediately a "The End" title appears, but Daffy pushes it aside and tries to take charge: "Ladies and gentlemen, there will be no further delays, so I shall attempt to entertain you in my own inimitable fashion," going into a soft-shoe routine against the blank background.

Duck Amuck also plays with onscreen and offscreen space. Many of the startling transformations we witness come from outside the limits of the frame. Most important, the unknown animator is in the space from which the camera photographs the scene, with the brush and pencil sliding in from under the camera. Daffy enters and exits frequently, and the frame often moves to reveal or conceal new portions of the scenery. When the sound cuts out entirely, Daffy asks to get it back **(10.130),** and then we hear a scratchy sound, as if from a phonograph somewhere outside the frame playing a worn record. This unseen phonograph provides inappropriate noises—a machine gun when Daffy strums the guitar, a donkey's bray when he breaks it—an elaborate joke on the fact that in animated films, the sound is never really produced by the characters and objects we see on the screen.

The most spectacular gag involving the space outside the edges of the image comes when the top of the frame sags, dripping down onto Daffy **(10.131).** For a moment, what we can't see—the areas outside the frame—invade what goes on inside it.

The inventiveness of *Duck Amuck* sets it apart from typical Hollywood animated films. Yet Chuck Jones also motivates its play with the medium by using narrative form, situating it in the genre of comedy, and presenting familiar characters (Bugs mistreating Daffy, as usual). It's possible to go further, however. Other filmmakers have created experimental animation more surprising and disturbing than the antics of the Warner Bros. stars.

An Example of Experimental Animation: *Dimensions of Dialogue*

Jan Švankmajer, a Czech animator, is probably best known for the feature-length narrative films *Alice* and *Faust.* But he has also explored several daring formal options. His short film *Game of Stones* utilizes abstract form in the manner of *Ballet mécanique.* Another short, *Historia Naturae, Suita,* is organized by ancient biological categories (Reptiles, Birds, Sea-dwelling, and others) and whimsically correlates each one with a different musical form (tango, minuet, and so on). This film, incidentally, reminds us that categorical form isn't found only in documentaries. Švankmajer is probably best known for the feature-length narrative films *Alice* and *Faust.*

Short or long, Švankmajer's films display a striking individual style. Most of his work relies on pixillation, which creates movement by shifting the positions of humans or objects frame by frame. His shots often look like still-life paintings, but they are seldom still. Stones, skulls, stuffed animals, and slabs of meat scuttle around Švankmajer's frames. In giving life to our everyday tools and furnishings, Švankmajer reawakens the sense of magic that we find in the earliest pixillated films.

But his approach to pixillation is sinister. Švankmajer's world is on the verge of decay or annihilation. Everything seems to crumble, collapse, or be crushed. Thanks to fast editing and high-key lighting, close-ups of familiar objects being maimed or pulled apart yield an almost horrifying effect. We expect to be repelled by a decaying zombie, but why should we feel the same sort of qualm when see vegetables hammered to pulp, or scissors snipping apart a peach? Švankmajer's films arouse the sense of touch by dwelling on images that a child would call icky and that a grownup might find disgusting.

Dimensions of Dialogue displays the aggressive alchemy that is Švankmajer's hallmark. Its overall structure depends on an odd trio of categories: "Factual Dialogue," "Passionate Dialogue," and "Exhausting Dialogue." The titles are important clues to interpretation, but initially they serve to mark off three narrative encounters between vaguely human characters made of clay or assembled out of household objects.

Dialogue as Aggression   The first episode is populated by vaguely human profiles. One is made out of common food items, another out of kitchen utensils, a third out of office supplies. The action consists of a simple theme-and-variations pattern. Two of the profiles lumber along and meet **(10.132).** In each "dialogue," one profile devours the other, chops and mashes its components mercilessly, and spews out the bits **(10.133).** After several such ravenous encounters, the profiles are reduced to mush, metal shards, and paper scraps. Finally the profiles emulsify into smooth rounded heads **(10.134).** This shift into identical heads is puzzling but becomes coherent in retrospect. We'll see the process of reducing differences among the "speakers" conclude later parts.

"Passionate Dialogue" gives us a more familiar story. Human figures made of smooth clay, reminiscent of the busts at the end of "Factual Dialogue," face each other across a table. One is male, the other female. They share a kiss, and this leads to a complete merger of their forms, an analogy to copulation **(10.135).** Once they have split apart, a lump of clay is left over. It tries to get their attention, but both mistreat it. When the man tries to mash the "baby" into the woman's face, she scratches his face, and soon they are tearing each other apart. In the end both dribble into a mass of clay.

CONNECT TO THE BLOG
www.davidbordwell.net/blog

We look at a very creepy version of *Alice in Wonderland* made by Švankmajer in "That reminds me . . ."

"We have been seeking the feeling of emotional security in touch from the day we were born, in our tactile experiences with our own mother. This was our first contact with the world, before we could see it, smell it, hear it, or taste it."
—Jan Švankmajer, animator

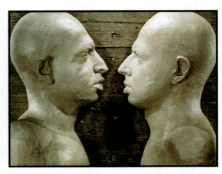

10.132

10.133

10.134

10.132–10.134 "Factual Dialogue." Food profile meets Utensil profile in *Dimensions of Dialogue* (10.132). Office-Supply profile spits out Utensil profile (10.133). Throughout the film, the minced items are heaped together or whipped into a sludge that condenses into smooth heads (10.134).

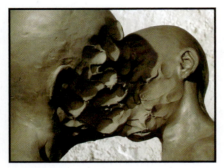

10.135 "Passionate Dialogue." Male and female figures kiss and merge into one another.

The final episode, "Exhausting Dialogue," revives motifs from the first two parts. Two clay busts of men's heads echo the end of Part 2 (10.134), though these middle-aged fellows aren't identical, as the heads were earlier. The heads spring up from a mass of clay and rest on a table, recalling the end of the second part. As in the first part, household objects are brought into play in a cycle of turn-taking that resembles conversation. Each man sticks out his tongue and reveals an object resting on it **(10.136)**. Returning to a theme-and-variations structure that sets up clear expectations, this "Exhausting Dialogue" is also an exhaustive one, running through humorous but also disturbing combinations of familiar things.

In the first round, each man's proffered object complements the other man's. One offers a toothbrush, the other toothpaste. One offers bread, the other butter. After four turns in which each pair of objects harmonizes, the men switch positions. Now the process breaks down crazily. Toothpaste is spread on bread, butter drips onto a pencil, and a pencil sharpener grinds away at a toothpaste tube. Every possible mismatch is tried, always with disastrous results **(10.137)**.

The heads, now starting to crack, swap places again. Each man's tongue offers his counterpart an identical object—shoe to shoe, laces to laces, and so on. But this apparent harmony is actually undercut because the objects always start fighting. Slices of bread become jaws; shoelaces wrestle one another. When all of the possibilities have been exhausted, the heads sag like fallen soufflés **(10.138)**.

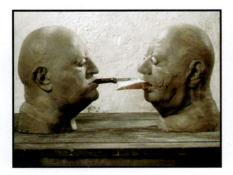

10.136

10.137

10.138

10.136–10.138 "Exhausting Dialogue." Butter knife and bread meet in the third section (10.136). The opening passage suggests cooperation, with each man's object appropriate to his partner's. In the second round of exchanges, however, the objects don't suit one another, and the encounters turn violent (10.137). The dialogue ends with deflated heads (10.138).

10.139

10.140

10.141

10.142

Formal Patterning: Theme and Variations   The simplicity of each episode highlights some subtle variations. Part 1's profiles are flat, while the figures in the following sections are three-dimensional. Švankmajer has filmed each set of conversationalists differently, with Part 2 introducing head-on views and shot/reverse shot angles. The couple in Part 2 have blank eyes, but the men in Part 3 have realistic and expressive eyes of different colors. Parts 1 and 3 assemble kitchen and office implements. The profile figures are collaged from familiar tools, while the tongue sequence brings mismatched objects into harsh conflict. Švankmajer was affiliated with the Czech branch of the Surrealist movement, reminding us that artists in this vein often used bizarre juxtapositions to evoke the mystery and irrationality of life. (See pp. 474–476.)

The force of these juxtapositions is greater because the objects have vivid textures. The smooth clay figures in Part 2 eventually become a mass of smudges, while the poor offspring of the mating ceremony gets mashed against the table and its parents. The brutal chopping and shredding of items in Part 1 are shown in high-key lighting more appropriate to food photography, while Part 3's punishing tongue close-ups could make any viewer squirm **(10.139, 10.140).** The film would be much less harsh without all the glimpses of unassuming objects pulped and shredded, accompanied by whacks and crunches on the soundtrack.

Each episode features violent confrontation. Part 2's erotic encounter gives conflict a more or less human face, but the other sections are just as disquieting. We're not used to seeing tools and vegetables maiming each other, or tongues flexing like fists. Although the assaults have a dark humor, the imagery and abrupt, grating noises suggest a mechanized massacre **(10.141, 10.142).** In making us feel the pain of these inanimate objects, Švankmajer has made a shocking, violent movie without gore.

Conversation as Annihilation   In about 11 minutes, *Dimensions of Dialogue* surveys different sorts of interactions, and it cries out for thematic interpretation.

Here, instead of being a civil exchange of ideas and opinions, dialogue consists of unbridled attack and retaliation. In the "Factual Dialogue," even before views are exchanged, one head minces another. But nobody wins: Eventually all three speakers are reduced to particles and then identical busts. Is the film suggesting that inducing someone to agree with you eventually creates a bland uniformity of opinion?

Švankmajer made the film during a period of severe political repression in Czechoslovakia, and some critics see the first episode as an implied protest against state-imposed conformity. From this perspective, the "factual" side of the conversation wouldn't be a matter of arguing about facts but rather recognizing the basic fact that under tyranny dialogue is nonexistent. Opinions get crushed, and everyone winds up looking and thinking the same. Significantly, the film was banned by the Communist government.

Part 2 doesn't start with the violence that opens the first dialogue. Here the couple's mutual attraction seems to hold out the possibility of harmony. But soon they attack their offspring and eventually one another. Again, the individuals are reduced to uniformity, a heap of clay, but this time in a family setting.

Harmony and cooperation are again seen at the start of Part 3. When butter meets bread and laces wind their way onto shoes, both parties seem to be in agreement. Yet the tongue game spirals into an exchange of mismatched objects, as if the two heads are talking past one another, and violence is the result. During the third round of Part 3, the heads thrust out identical objects, in effect "saying the same thing." Yet even the identical objects attack one another. This might imply that each person isn't really responding to the other, that dialogue has become two monologues. In the end, both partners have collapsed, becoming, like the characters at the end of the previous parts, indistinguishable.

Throughout the film, face-to-face interactions are brutally aggressive and self-destructive, and they usually end in exhaustion. This is a fairly bleak view of human relationships, but delivered with arresting imagery and black humor.

Like *Duck Amuck, Dimensions of Dialogue* summons up bizarre transformations and creates comedy by violating our expectations. But Daffy's dislocated adventures are eventually explained by Bugs's prankishness. The Švankmajer flavor is more elusive. Setting a trio of narratives within the frame of categorical form, he takes us through sharply etched formal variations. These present motifs that are more disturbing, even queasy, than the slapstick offered by Chuck Jones. The very different experiences provided by the two films illustrate the range of expressive choices available to the film animator.

CONNECT TO THE BLOG
www.davidbordwell.net/blog

We profile another great experimental animator in "Len Lye, Renaissance Kiwi."

⏭ SUMMARY

In most situations, when we watch a film, we have some idea of what type it will be, and this shapes our expectations. If we're seeing a documentary, we expect to learn something, perhaps in a way that will entertain or move us in the process. An experimental film, however, will probably challenge us, rather like a game, to figure out its patterns and strategies. Animated films that we encounter in theaters will most likely amuse and entertain us.

In watching a documentary film, we can ask ourselves what it claims to be true about the world. Does it present

one or more categories of things? If so, how are these organized? Is the filmmaker trying to convey an attitude about the topic? Are there abstract or narrative portions that lend interest to its subject? Or is the topic organized as an argument? If so, is the argument convincing?

As we have seen, experimental films often employ abstract or associational formal patterns. From moment to moment, we can try to understand the connections among shots or small-scale segments. Is there a similarity in shapes on the screen, in directions of movement, or in colors? If so, the film probably uses abstract form. But if you detect linkages that shift in evocative ways as the film progresses, associational form is probably at work.

Animated films can present narratives, convey documentary information, or experiment with the medium. In most cases, however, you should be able to detect gener-ally what techniques were used in making the film. Is the movement on the screen based on drawings or on moving puppets, clay figures, flat cut-outs, or computer-generated images? If you're attentive to how these techniques are employed, you should be able to enjoy the freedom from reality that animation offers the filmmaker.

RECOMMENDED DVD AND BLU-RAY SUPPLEMENTS

There are at least three different versions of *Ballet mé-canique,* and at least two of those are available on DVD. Our analysis in this chapter is based on the version in Kino Video's two-disc set, "Avant-Garde: Experimental Cinema of the 1920s and '30s." (The version included in the set "Unseen Cinema" is distinctly different, with the sequences in a different order.)

DVDs of documentaries and experimental films sel-dom include supplements, so for these two types of films, we list some major films that are available.

Documentary

Feature-length documentary films on DVD include *4 Little Girls* (HBO Home Video), *The Wild Parrots of Telegraph Hill* (New Video Group), *The Story of the Weeping Camel* (New Line Home Video), *Enron—The Smartest Guys in the Room* (Magnolia; this disc includes a making-of supplement), *The Cruise* (Live/Artisan), *Control Room* (Lions Gate), *Winged Migration* (Sony), *The War Room* (MCA Home Video), *Born into Brothels* (Thinkfilm), *The Gleaners and I* (Zeitgeist), *The UP Series* (1964 onward, First Run Features), *Super Size Me* (Hart Sharp Video), *Burden of Dreams* (Criterion), *Sans soleil* (Criterion), *An Inconvenient Truth* (Paramount), *Inside Job* (Sony Pictures Classics), and *Restrepo* (Virgil Films and Entertainment). Short films are collected in *Full Frame Documentary Shorts,* vols. 1–5 (New Video Group).

Classic documentaries on DVD include *Why We Fight* (1943, Edi Video), *Memphis Belle* (1944, Aircraft Films), *Triumph of the Will* (1934, Synapse), *Kon-Tiki* (1951, Image Entertainment), *In the Year of the Pig* (1969, Homevision), *Point of Order!* (1964, New Yorker Video), and *Salesman* (1969, Criterion). Pioneering documentary maker Robert Flaherty is represented by *Nanook of the North* (Criterion) and *Man of Aran* (Homevision). *Listen to Britain and Other Films by Humphrey Jennings* (Image) collects works by the great British filmmaker.

Experimental

A seven-disc, 155-film survey of experimental cinema is *Unseen Cinema: Early American Avant-Garde Film 1894–1941* (Image Entertainment; a book of the same name, published by the Anthology Film Archives, was printed separately). There is some overlap in contents between this and *Avant-garde: Experimental Cinema of the 1920s and '30s, Avant-Garde 2: Experimental Cinema 1928–1954,* and *Avant-Garde 3: Experimental Cinema 1922–1954* (Kino Video). *American Treasures IV: Avant-garde Film 1947–1986* (Image) contains many classic experimental films from the postwar era. Luis Buñuel's *Un Chien andalou* (1928, Transflux Films) and *L'Age d'or* (1930, Kino video) are Surrealist classics.

Full-length experimental films available include *Berlin: Symphony of a Great City* (Image Entertainment), *Water and Power* (Lookout Mountain), and *Man with a Movie Camera* (Image Entertainment).

Collections of individual experimentalists' work include *By Brakhage: An Anthology, Volumes 1 and 2* (Criterion; these collections includes interviews with the filmmaker), *Maya Deren: Experimental Films* (Mystic Fire Video), *Pat O'Neill: Five Films* (Lookout Mountain), *The Guy Maddin Collection* (Zeitgeist), *The Brothers Quay Collection* (Zeitgeist), and *The Films of Kenneth Anger,* vols. 1 and 2, and *The Complete Magic Lantern Cycle* (Fantoma). Ken Jacobs' feature-length *Tom, Tom, The Piper's Son* has been issued on DVD by the artist. Documentaries about experi-mental filmmakers include *In the Mirror of Maya Deren* (Zeitgeist Films) and *Brakhage* (Zeitgeist Films).

Animation

Several animators whose work we mention are repre-sented on DVD. Lotte Reiniger's silhouette feature, *The Adventures of Prince Achmed,* is available from Milestone. A collection of twenty shorter films has been issued by the British Film Institute in a Region 2 two-disc set; it includes a documentary, *The Art of Lotte Reiniger.* Two separate DVDs, "The Collected Shorts of Jan Švankmajer" (Image) contain both live-action and animated experimental shorts, including *Dimensions of Dialogue.* The *Dimensions* disc includes a BBC documentary, *Animator of Prague.*

The DVD releases of many feature-length animated films contain supplements. Disney films often contain infor-mative making-of extras for its classic films. "The Making of *Bambi:* A Prince Is Born" discusses the technique and style of the design. The "Art Design: Impressions of the Forest" section includes an excellent explanation of the multiplane camera that was used to create depth effects in this and other Disney films. The "Tricks of the Trade" excerpt has more on the multiplane camera, discussing depth cues and demonstrating the use of the technique in the opening of *Bambi*. "Inside the Disney Archive" shows examples of both cels and backgrounds, including lengthy backgrounds used to simulate camera movement. "*Bambi: Inside Walt's Story Meetings*" has actors reading transcriptions of meetings from the period of the film's production, discussing a wide variety of narrative and stylistic possibilities as scenes from the film play. "No Strings Attached: The Making of *Pinocchio*" is another excellent documentary on a Disney classic.

Walt & el Grupo (Walt Disney Studios Home Entertainment) is a fascinating feature-length documentary (2008) about a trip to South America made by Disney and several of his animators and designers during World War II. The visit was part of the Good Neighbor Policy and resulted in two films, *Saludos Amigos* and *The Three Caballeros.* The former, with its classic "Aquarela do Brasil" number, is included in its original 1943 version. (Later prints removed a brief section showing Goofy smoking.)

"The Hatching of *Chicken Run*" has a little background information on Aardman animation, also responsible for the "Wallace and Gromit" and "Creature Comforts" series. It deals with the specifics of animation, including how three-point lighting works on a very small scale. (The "Poultry in Motion" supplement, aimed at children, is far less informative.) The DVD of *Wallace & Gromit: The Curse of the Were-rabbit* includes several informative and entertaining pieces: "How Wallace and Gromit Went to Hollywood," a history of director Nick Park's career with Aardman; "Behind the Scenes of 'Wallace & Gromit: The Curse of the Were-rabbit'"; "A Day in the Life of Aardman: Studio Tour"; and "How to Make a Bunny," a demonstration of how Plasticine figures are created.

The DVD of *The Incredibles* contains two making-of supplements. The first, "Making of *The Incredibles*," is only mildly informative, focusing on how wacky and eccentric the Pixar team is. The second, "More Making of *The Incredibles*," is an excellent overview of the basic techniques for making a complex CGI film, from character design and three-point lighting to sound effects.

The DVD of *My Dog Tulip* (New Yorker) includes a 20-minute featurette, *Making Tulip,* that demonstrates how 2D animated films can be made digitally by drawing and painting on tablets.

Some major animators have been profiled in DVD supplements. "Jiří Trnka: Puppet Animation Master" *(The Puppet Films of Jiří Trnka)* offers a sketch of the great Czech animator's career. The DVD set *Norman McLaren: The Collector's Edition* contains a feature-length biography, "Creative Process: Norman McLaren," including many clips. McLaren used so many imaginative filmmaking methods that "Creative Process" constitutes a good survey of the vast range of possibilities offered by animation.

PART 5

Throughout this book we've asked you to think like a filmmaker, to consider how the things we see and hear in a film result from creative decision making. This perspective can give us a healthy respect for the demanding craft of making any film. More broadly, we've suggested that putting yourself in the filmmaker's place yields a keener sensitivity to film artistry—how form works, how techniques are utilized, and how a film taps into wider categories such as genres.

As viewers, we don't have access to all the filmmakers' options. True, we may learn of some through interviews or the sort of explanations we've quoted throughout the book. Often we can reconstruct the logic of choice, by imagining alternative ways of lighting or staging or cutting a sequence. Normally, however, we concentrate on the result: the finished film.

Everything we've considered in this book prepares you to think critically about the films you encounter. Doing film criticism means thinking and talking in an informed way about a movie. As we try to get to know the film better and to understand our responses to it, we're inclined to share our opinions and ideas with others. We might talk with friends, or write a comment on a website. These are all informal kinds of film criticism.

Critical Analysis of Films

You may want to pursue film criticism more systematically. Your project might be an extended web essay or blog entry, a paper for a course, or an article for a newspaper or magazine. At this point, you're moving toward film analysis, the activity of looking closely at how the movie works. This chapter provides you some sample essays in film analysis, as well as some suggestions for how to do it.

An analyst is usually driven by some purpose. Perhaps something in the film puzzles you and you want to understand why. Or perhaps you want to find out what gave you a certain emotional response. Or maybe you want to convince others that this film is worthwhile. We prepared the analyses in this part with two other purposes. First, we want to illustrate how form and style work together in a variety of films. Second, we provide models of short critical analyses that might illuminate some aspects of a film's workings.

These analyses don't drain the films dry. You might study any one of the films and find many more points of interest than we've presented here. Entire books have been written about single films, and there still remains much to say. Cinema, like other art forms, is inexhaustible.

11

Film Criticism: Sample Analyses

CONNECT TO THE BLOG
www.davidbordwell.net/blog

For a consideration of what film critics do, including evaluation, and what part the Internet now plays, see "In critical condition."

The four sections of this chapter emphasize different aspects of various films. We begin by discussing three classical narrative films: *His Girl Friday, North by Northwest,* and *Do The Right Thing.* Since classically constructed films are familiar to most viewers, it's important to study closely how they work.

We move to three films that represent alternatives to classical norms. *Breathless* relies on ambiguity of character motivation and on stretches of rambling action, all presented through loose, casual techniques. In contrast, *Tokyo Story* departs from classical norms to create a highly rigorous style. In *Chungking Express,* the viewer is prompted to concentrate on narrative parallels.

The first two sections are concerned with fictional films, but documentaries can be no less carefully constructed. This section considers two examples of how formal and stylistic processes can give a documentary a wide range of implications. The first, *Man with a Movie Camera,* documents a day in the life of the Soviet Union, but it also celebrates the power of cinema to transform reality. *The Thin Blue Line* tells the story of a miscarriage of justice; at the same time, it invites us to reflect on the difficulties of responsibly investigating any crime.

Finally, we move to analyses that emphasize social ideology. Our first example, *Meet Me in St. Louis,* is a film that accepts a dominant ideology and reinforces the audience's belief in that ideology. In contrast, *Raging Bull* shows how a film's ideological implications can be less clear-cut.

We could have emphasized different aspects of any of these films. *Meet Me in St. Louis,* for example, is a classical narrative film and could be considered from that perspective. Similarly, *Man with a Movie Camera* could be seen as offering an alternative to classical continuity editing. And any of the films represents an ideological position that could be analyzed. Our choices suggest only certain angles of approach; your own analyses will discover many more.

Your critical activities are the focus of the Appendix to this chapter. There we suggest some ways in which you can prepare, organize, and write a critical analysis of a film.

You can find analyses that have appeared in earlier editions of *Film Art* at http: //davidbordwell.net/filmart10/. The blog on the site also contains many analyses of sequences and entire films.

CONNECT TO THE BLOG
www.davidbordwell.net/blog

We offer some thoughts on the history and purposes of film criticism in "Love isn't all you need."

The Classical Narrative Cinema

His Girl Friday

1940. Columbia. Directed by Howard Hawks. Script by Charles Lederer from the play *The Front Page* by Ben Hecht and Charles MacArthur. Photographed by Joseph Walker. Edited by Gene Havlick. Music by Morris W. Stoloff. With Cary Grant, Rosalind Russell, Ralph Bellamy, Gene Lockhart, Porter Hall.

His Girl Friday is often said to be the fastest sound comedy ever made, largely because most of the dialogue is delivered at a machine-gun pace. A contemporary analogy would be *The Social Network,* another movie driven by quick thinkers and fast talkers. To speed up the dialogue, director Howard Hawks encouraged his actors to allow few pauses and to start talking before the previous actor had finished. In *His Girl Friday,* however, dialogue isn't the only factor creating a sense of speed. Conventions of classical narrative form, along with particular film techniques, play important parts in this whirlwind experience.

Lines of Action and Character Goals   Classical Hollywood narrative is well suited to give the impression of speed. Its tradition of concise exposition and tightly woven plotting can carry us along swiftly. For example, *His Girl Friday* contains only 13 major scenes, so the filmmakers haven't chosen to create the pace through a series of very brief sequences. Moreover, the action takes place in only a handful of settings, so there's a sense of greater pressure as people rush in and out of the same locale and new groups of characters collide with one another in pursuit of their own purposes.

Those purposes fit into broader patterns of development. As we saw in Chapter 3 (pp. 85–86), classical Hollywood cinema often centers stories on characters with definite traits who want to achieve specific goals. These characters' contrasting traits and conflicting goals propel *His Girl Friday*'s plot forward along two primary lines of action.

1. *The romance.* Hildy Johnson wants to quit newspaper reporting and settle down with Bruce Baldwin. But Hildy's editor and ex-husband, Walter Burns, has a different goal: He wants her to continue as his reporter and to remarry him. Given these two goals, the characters enter into a conflict in several stages. First, Walter lures Hildy by promising a nest egg for the couple in exchange for her writing one last story. But Walter also arranges to have Bruce robbed. Learning of Walter's scheme, Hildy tears up her story. Walter continues to delay Bruce, however, and eventually wins Hildy through her renewed interest in reporting. She changes her mind about marrying Bruce and stays with Walter.

2. *Crime and politics.* Earl Williams is to be hanged for shooting a policeman. The city's political bosses are relying on the execution to ensure their reelection. This is the goal shared by the mayor and the sheriff. But Walter's goal is to induce the governor to reprieve Williams and thus unseat the mayor's party at the polls. Through the sheriff's stupidity, Williams escapes and is concealed by Hildy and Walter. In the meantime, a reprieve does arrive from the governor; the mayor bribes the messenger into leaving. Williams is discovered, but the messenger returns with the reprieve in time to save Williams from death and Walter and Hildy from jail. Presumably, the mayor's political allies will be defeated at the election.

> " If you'll ever listen to some people who are talking, especially in a scene of any excitement, they all talk at the same time. All it needs is a little extra work on the dialogue. You put a few words in front of somebody's speech and put a few words at the end, and they can overlap it. It gives you a sense of speed that actually doesn't exist. And you can make the people talk a little faster."
>
> —Howard Hawks, director

The crime-and-politics line of action is tied tightly to the romance line. Walter uses the Williams case to lure Hildy back to him, Hildy chases the Williams story instead of returning to Bruce, Bruce's mother reveals to the police that Walter has concealed Williams, and so on. More specifically, the interplay of the two lines of action alters the characters' goals. By inducing Hildy to write the story, Walter fulfills his goals of embarrassing the politicos and of tempting Hildy back into his life. Hildy's goals are more greatly changed. After she destroys her article, her abrupt decision to report on Earl Williams's jailbreak marks her acceptance of Walter's scheme. Her later willingness to hide Williams and her indifference to Bruce's pleas firmly establish her goals as linked to Walter's.

As the two goal-oriented plotlines interconnect, the actions start to multiply and expand. For example, Walter's delaying tactics (involving his confederates Duffy, Louie, and Angie) set up short-term bursts of cause and effect. At the same time, Bruce is shouldered out of the romance plot as he is shuttled in and out of precinct jails. Earl Williams undergoes a parallel experience as he is manipulated by Hildy, the sheriff, the psychologist, and Walter. Swiftly, the tangle of romance and politics pulls in secondary characters, such as Mollie Malloy (Williams's sweetheart), Bruce's mother, the other reporters, and Pettibone, the delightful emissary from the governor. All these characters aren't simply pawns of the larger plotlines, however. They can affect those plotlines by their actions, as when Earl Williams escapes or Mrs. Baldwin bursts in to denounce Walter as a kidnapper. With so many characters pulled in, swerving the action this way or that, the plot twists can become rapid and unpredictable.

Picking up the Pace: Time Pressures   Classical narrative not only tries to tie all the characters to a broader momentum; it also ties one scene to another. In *His Girl Friday,* an event at the end of one scene becomes a cause leading to an effect— the event that begins the next scene. For example, at the end of the first scene, Walter offers to take Bruce and Hildy to lunch; scene 2 starts with the three of them arriving at the restaurant. In *His Girl Friday,* this linear pattern helps keep the plot action hurtling, setting up each new scene quickly at the end of the previous one.

One of the most common ways in which Hollywood storytelling dials up the pace involves setting a deadline for the action. The deadline is a convention of the newspaper genre, adding a built-in suspense factor. But in *His Girl Friday,* each line of action has its own deadlines. The mayor and the sheriff face an obvious deadline: Earl Williams must be hanged before the governor can reprieve him. In his political strategizing, Walter Burns faces the other side of the same deadline: he wants Williams reprieved. What we might not expect is that the romance plot has deadlines as well.

Bruce and Hildy are set to leave on a train bound for Albany and eventual marriage at four o'clock that very day. Walter's machinations keep forcing the couple to postpone their departure. Add to this the fact that when Bruce comes to confront Hildy and Walter, he exits with the defiant ultimatum "I'm leaving on the nine o'clock train!" (Hildy misses that train as well.) The film's sense of mounting tension depends on the tight deadlines. If Earl Williams were to be hanged next month, or if the election were two years off, or if Bruce and Hildy were planning a marriage at some distant future date, the sense of dramatic pressure would be lacking. The piled-up deadlines squeeze together all the lines of action and sustain the breathless pace of the film.

His Girl Friday finds another, more unusual way to drive that pace. The plot presents events in straightforward chronological order, but it takes remarkable liberties with story duration. Of course, since the primary story action consumes about nine hours (from around 12:30 P.M. to around 9:30 P.M.), we expect that certain portions of time *between* scenes will be eliminated. What's unusual is that the time *within* scenes has been accelerated as well.

At the start of the very first scene, for example, the clock in the *Post* office reads 12:36; after 12 minutes of screen time have passed, the same clock reads 12:57.

Yet there have been no editing ellipses in the scene; the story duration has simply been compressed. If you time the film's longest scene (33 minutes!), you will find even more remarkable acceleration. People leave on long trips and return less than 10 minutes later. Again, the editing presents continuity of duration: It's story time that goes faster than screen time. This temporal compression combines with everything we've surveyed so far—tight causal connections, unexpected entrances and exits, and frenetically rushed dialogue—to create the film's breakneck pace.

With so much talk and turmoil, you might expect that the cutting would be quick. But actually the film's editing rhythm is much slower than we'd find in today's intensified continuity approach. The average shot in the film runs 15 seconds, four to five times slower than what we'd get in a comedy now. Instead, by sustaining the shot, Hawks can let the dialogue move more quickly, without distracting cuts, and can shift his actors around the frame in expressive patterns. Many shots let staging and the actors' performances define the comedy (**11.1, 11.2**). And for simultaneous dialogue, it's preferable to keep the actors in the same shot rather than trying to cut between them (**11.3**).

When Hawks does cut, he often uses continuity tactics to anticipate or underline a dramatic point. He will smoothly match on action during a comic climax (**11.4, 11.5**). Virtually every scene, especially the early restaurant lunch and the dizzying final scene in the courthouse pressroom, offers many subtle examples of classical editing. Hawks's aim is clearly to enhance the dialogue and the plot twists.

The film increases the tension of these rapid scenes through one device that involves both sound and mise-en-scene. We'd expect that newspapermen in 1939 use telephones, but *His Girl Friday* makes the phone integral to the narrative. Walter's subterfuges demand phones. At the restaurant, he pretends to be summoned away to a call; he makes and breaks promises to Hildy via phones; he directs Duffy and other minions by phone. More generally, the pressroom is equipped with a veritable flotilla of phones, enabling the reporters to contact their editors. And, of course, Bruce keeps calling Hildy from the various police stations in which he continually

CONNECT TO THE BLOG
www.davidbordwell.net/blog

How did *His Girl Friday* go from obscurity to being hailed as a masterpiece? See "Creating a classic, with a little help from your pirate friends."

11.1

11.2

11.4

11.5

11.3

11.1–11.5 Long takes and cutting for comic flow. In *His Girl Friday*, Walter and Hildy pace in a complete circuit around the desk (11.1). Cutting would distract from Walter's dynamic and comic postures (11.2). Several long takes employ deep-space staging and deep-focus cinematography (11.3). In the opening scene, Hildy's action of throwing her purse at Walter (11.4) is matched at the cut to a more distant framing (11.5). The mismatch in his arm positions goes unnoticed in projection, probably because we tend to focus on Hildy's broader gestures.

finds himself. The telephones become a communications network that relays story action from point to point.

Given the prominence of phones, Hawks visually and sonically orchestrates the characters' use of them. There are many variations. One person may be talking on the phone, or several may be talking in turn on different phones, or several may be talking at once on different phones, or a phone conversation may take place during a conversation elsewhere in the room. When several reporters race in to phone their editors, the cutting accentuates single lines or words. Later, while Hildy frantically phones hospitals, Walter hollers into another phone (11.3). When Bruce returns for Hildy, a confused din arises that eventually sorts itself into three sonic lines: Bruce begging Hildy to listen, Hildy obsessively typing her story, and Walter yelling into the phone for Duffy to clear page one ("No, no, leave the rooster story! That's human interest!"). (See 5.31.) Like much in *His Girl Friday,* the telephones are pulled into the unfolding action in ways that boost the rapid tempo.

North by Northwest

1959. MGM. Directed by Alfred Hitchcock. Script by Ernest Lehman. Photographed by Robert Burks. Edited by George Tomasini. Music composed by Bernard Herrmann. With Cary Grant, Eva Marie Saint, James Mason, Leo G. Carroll, Jessie Royce Landis.

Hitchcock long insisted that he made thrillers, not mystery films. For him, creating a puzzle was less important than generating suspense and surprise. While there are mystery elements in films such as *Notorious* (1946), *Stage Fright* (1950), and *Psycho* (1960), *North by Northwest* shows that the mystery element can serve as merely a pretext for intriguing the audience. The film's tight causal unity enables Hitchcock to create an engrossing plot that fulfills the norms of classical filmmaking. This plot is presented through a narration that continually emphasizes suspense and surprise. (For more on thrillers, see pp. 334–336.)

Plot and Counterplot   Like most spy films, *North by Northwest* has a complex plot. There are two main lines of action. In one, a gang of spies mistakes advertising agency executive Roger Thornhill for a secret agent, George Kaplan. Although the spies fail to kill Thornhill, he becomes the chief suspect in a murder that the gang commits. He must flee the police while trying to track down the real George Kaplan. Unfortunately, Kaplan does not exist; he is merely a decoy invented by the United States Intelligence Agency (USIA). Thornhill's pursuit of Kaplan leads to the second line of action: his meeting and falling in love with Eve Kendall, who is the mistress of Philip Van Damm, the spies' leader. The spy-chase line and the romance line further connect when Thornhill learns that Eve is actually a double agent, secretly working for the USIA. He must then rescue her from Van Damm, who has discovered her identity and has resolved to kill her. In the course of all this, Thornhill also discovers that the spies are smuggling government secrets out of the country in pieces of sculpture.

From even so bare an outline, it should be evident that the film's plot presents many conventional patterns to the viewer. There's the search pattern, seen when Thornhill sets out to find Kaplan. There's also a journey pattern: Thornhill and his pursuers travel from New York to Chicago and then to Rapid City, South Dakota, with side excursions as well. In addition, the last two-thirds of the plot is organized around the romance between Thornhill and Eve. Moreover, each pattern develops markedly in the course of the film. In the course of his search, Thornhill must sometimes assume the identity of Kaplan, the man he is trailing. The journey pattern gets varied by all the vehicles Thornhill uses—cabs, train, pickup truck, police car, bus, ambulance, and airplane.

Most subtly, the romance line of action is constantly modified by Thornhill's changing awareness of the situation. Believing that Eve wants to help him, he falls

> " He (Hitchcock) was fairly universal, he made people shiver everywhere. And he made thrillers that are also equivalent to works of literature."
>
> —Jean-Luc Godard, director, *Breathless*

in love with her. But then he learns that she sent him to the murderous appointment at Prairie Stop, and he becomes cold and suspicious. When he discovers her at the auction with Van Damm, his anger and bitterness impel him to humiliate her and make Van Damm doubt her loyalty. Only after the USIA chief, the "Professor," tells him that Eve is really an agent does Thornhill realize that he has misjudged and endangered her. Each step in his growing awareness alters his romantic relation to Eve.

This intricate plot is unified and made comprehensible by other strategies of classical Hollywood storytelling. *North by Northwest* has a strict time scheme, comprising four days and nights (followed by a brief epilogue on a later night). The first day and a half take place in New York; the second night on the train to Chicago; the third day in Chicago and at Prairie Stop; and the fourth day at Mount Rushmore. The timetable is neatly established early in the film. Van Damm, having abducted Roger as Kaplan, announces: "In two days you're due at the Ambassador East in Chicago, and then at the Sheraton-Johnson Hotel in Rapid City, South Dakota." This itinerary prepares the spectator for the shifts in action that will occur in the rest of the film.

Apart from the time scheme, the film also gives Thornhill specific traits of character. He's initially presented as a resourceful liar when he grabs a cab from another pedestrian. Later, he will have to lie in many circumstances to evade capture. Similarly, Roger is established as a heavy drinker, and his ability to hold his liquor will enable him to survive Van Damm's attempt to force him to kill himself when driving while drunk.

A great many motifs are repeated and help make the film cohere. Roger is constantly in danger from heights: his car hangs over a cliff; he must sneak out on the ledge of a hospital; he has to clamber up Van Damm's modernistic cliff-top house; and he and Eve wind up dangling from the faces on Mount Rushmore. Thornhill's constant changing of vehicles also constitutes a motif that Hitchcock varies. A subtler example is the motif that conveys Thornhill's growing suspicion of Eve **(11.6, 11.7).**

Narration and Knowledge, Suspense and Surprise

Still, narrative unity alone can't explain the film's strong emotional appeal. In Chapter 3's discussion of narration, we used *North by Northwest* as an example of a hierarchy of knowledge (p. 88). We suggested that as the film progresses, sometimes we're restricted to what Roger knows, but at other times, we know significantly more than he does. At still other moments, our range of knowledge, while greater than Roger's, is not as great as that of other characters. Now we're in a position to see how Hitchcock's decision to create this pattern of narration helps create suspense and surprise across the whole film.

The most straightforward way in which the film's narration controls our knowledge is through the numerous optical point-of-view (POV) shots Hitchcock employs. This device yields a degree of subjective depth: we see what a character sees more or less as she or he sees it. More important here, the optical POV shot restricts us to what that character learns at that moment. Hitchcock gives almost every major character a shot of this sort. The very first optical POV we see in the film is taken from the position of the two spies who are watching Roger apparently respond to the paging of George Kaplan. Later, we view events through the eyes of Eve, of Van Damm, of his henchman Leonard, and even of a clerk at a ticket counter.

By far the greatest number of POV shots are attached to Thornhill. Through his eyes, we see his approach to the Townsend mansion, the mail he finds in the library, his drunken drive along the cliff, and the airplane that is "crop dusting where there ain't no crops." Some of the most extreme uses of optical POV give us Roger's experience directly, as when he's punched by a state trooper or caught in the path of a fuel truck.

Thornhill's optical POV shots function within a narration that is often restricted not only to what he *sees* but also to what he *knows*. The plane attack at Prairie Stop, for example, is confined wholly to Roger's range of knowledge. Hitch-

11.6

11.7

11.6–11.7 Gesture motifs for psychological revelation. On the train, when Thornhill and Eve kiss, his hands close tenderly around her hair (11.6). But later, when he believes she has sent him to be murdered, his hands freeze in place, as if he fears touching her (11.7).

cock could have cut away from Roger waiting by the road in order to show us the villains spotting him from their plane, but he doesn't. Similarly, when Roger is searching for George Kaplan's room and gets a phone call from the two hench-men, Hitchcock could have used crosscutting to show the villains phoning from the lobby. (Telephone calls, as we mention on p. 266, are always notable decision points for directors.) Instead, we learn that the thugs are in the hotel when Roger does. And when Thornhill and his mother hurry out of the room, Hitchcock does not use crosscutting to show the villains in pursuit. This makes it more startling when Roger and his mother get on the elevator and discover the two men there already. In scenes like these, confining us to Thornhill's range of knowledge sharpens the effect of surprise.

Sometimes the same effect comes from the film's restricting us to Roger's range of knowledge and then giving us information that he does not at the moment have. On p. 88, we suggested that this sort of surprise occurs when the plot shifts us from Roger's escape from the United Nations murder to the scene at the USIA office, where the staff discusses the case. At this point, we learn that there is no George Kaplan—something that Roger won't discover for many more scenes to come.

The abrupt shifts from Roger's range of knowledge yield a similar effect during the train trip from New York to Chicago. During several scenes, Eve Kendall helps Thornhill evade the police. Finally, they are alone and relatively safe in her com-partment. At this point, the narration shifts the range of knowledge. We see a mes-sage delivered to another compartment. Hands unfold a note: "What do I do with him in the morning?" The camera tracks back to show us Leonard and Van Damm reading the message. We realize that Eve is not merely a sympathetic stranger but someone working for the spy ring. Again, Roger will learn this much later.

Such moments evoke surprise, but we have already noted that Hitchcock claimed in general to prefer to generate suspense (p. 89). Suspense is created by giving the spectator *more* information than the character has. In the scenes we've just mentioned, once the short-term surprise has been achieved, the narration can use our superior knowledge to build suspense across several sequences. After the audience learns that there is no George Kaplan, every attempt by Thornhill to find him builds up suspense about whether he will discover the truth. Once we learn that Eve is working for Van Damm, her message to Roger on behalf of Kaplan will make us worry that Roger will fall into the trap.

In these examples, suspense arises across a series of scenes. Hitchcock also uses unrestricted narration to build up suspense within a single scene. His handling of the UN murder differs sharply from his treatment of the scene showing Roger and his mother in Kaplan's hotel room. In the hotel scene, Hitchcock refused to employ crosscutting to show the spies' pursuit. At the United Nations, however, he crosscuts between Roger, who is searching for Townsend, and Valerian, one of the thugs following him. Just before the murder, a rightward tracking shot establishes Valerian's position in the doorway (something of which Roger is wholly unaware). Here crosscutting and camera movement widen our frame of knowledge and create suspense about the scene's outcome.

The sequence in Chicago's Union Station is handled similarly. Here crosscut-ting moves us from Roger shaving in the men's room to Eve talking on the phone. Another lateral tracking shot reveals that she is talking to Leonard, who is giving her orders from an adjacent phone booth. We now are certain that the message she will give Roger will endanger him, and the suspense is increased accordingly. Note, however, that the narration does not reveal the conversation itself. As often happens, Hitchcock conceals certain information for the sake of further surprises.

The Climax on Mount Rushmore Thornhill's knowledge expands as the lines of action develop. On the third day, he discovers that Eve is Van Damm's mistress, that she is a double agent, and that Kaplan doesn't exist. He agrees to help the Professor in a scheme to clear Eve of any suspicion in Van Damm's eyes. When

11.8

11.9

11.10

11.11

11.8–11.11 Embedded POV patterns. In *North by Northwest,* Thornhill watches in dismay as Leonard betrays Eve to Van Damm (11.8, 11.9). When Van Damm reacts by punching Leonard, he is seen from Leonard's POV (11.10). Then Leonard is seen from his POV (11.11). This POV exchange is enclosed within a broader pattern presenting the entire scene through Thornhill's range of knowledge.

the scheme (a faked shooting in the Mount Rushmore restaurant) succeeds, Roger believes that Eve will leave Van Damm. Once more, however, he has been duped (as we have). The Professor insists that she must go off to Europe that night on Van Damm's private flight. Roger resists, but he is knocked out and held captive in a hospital. His escape leads to the final major sequence of the film.

Here the plot resolves all its lines of action, and the narration continues to expand and contract our knowledge for the sake of suspense and surprise. This climactic sequence comprises almost 300 shots and runs for several minutes, but we can conveniently divide it into three sections.

In the first section, Roger arrives at Van Damm's house and reconnoiters. He clambers up to the window and learns from a conversation between Leonard and Van Damm that the piece of sculpture they bought at the auction contains microfilm. More important, he watches Leonard inform Van Damm that Eve is an American agent. This action is conveyed largely through optical POV (**11.8, 11.9**; also 3.20–3.22). At two moments, as Leonard and Van Damm face each other, the narration gives us optical POV shots from each man's standpoint (**11.10, 11.11**), but these are enclosed within Roger's ongoing witnessing of the situation. For the first time in the film, Roger has more knowledge of the situation than any other character. He knows how the smuggling has been done, and he discovers that the villains intend to murder Eve.

The second phase of the sequence begins when Roger enters Eve's bedroom. She has gone back downstairs and is sitting on a couch. Again, Hitchcock emphasizes the restriction to Thornhill's knowledge through optical POV shots (**11.12, 11.13**). This time, however, he doesn't show us what the other character sees and instead only suggests Eve's reaction (**11.14**). Roger's range of knowledge remains the broadest, and his optical POV encloses another character's experience. On a pretext, Eve returns to her room, and Roger warns her not to get on the plane.

As the spies make their way to the landing field outside, Roger starts to follow. Now Hitchcock's narration shifts again to show Van Damm's housekeeper spotting Roger's reflection in a television set. As earlier in the film, we know more than Roger does, and this generates suspense when she walks out . . . and returns with a pistol aimed at him.

The third section of the climax takes place outdoors. Eve is about to get in the plane when a pistol shot distracts the spies' attention long enough for her to grab the statuette and race to the car Roger has stolen. This portion of the sequence confines

11.12

11.13

11.14

11.12–11.14 Suppressing characters' POVs. To warn Eve, Roger uses his ROT monogrammed matchbook (a motif set up on the train as a joke). He tosses the matchbook down toward her (11.12, 11.13). This initiates suspense when Leonard sees it, but he unconcernedly puts it in an ashtray on the coffee table. Earlier Hitchcock shifted optical POV to present the face-off between Van Damm and Leonard (11.10, 11.11). Now he does not show us Eve's face or what she sees. Instead, through Roger's eyes, we see her back stiffen; we *infer* that she is looking at the matchbook (11.14).

> In *North by Northwest* during the scene on Mount Rushmore I wanted Cary Grant to hide in Lincoln's nostril and have a fit of sneezing. The Parks Commission of the Department of Interior was rather upset at this thought. I argued until one of their number asked me how I would like it if they had Lincoln play the scene in Cary Grant's nose. I saw their point at once."
>
> —Alfred Hitchcock, director

us to Eve's range of knowledge, accentuating it with shots from her optical POV. The pattern of surprise interrupting a period of suspense—here, Roger's escape from the house interrupting Eve's tense walk to the plane—will dominate the rest of the sequence.

There follows a chase across the presidents' faces on Mount Rushmore. Some crosscutting informs us of the spies' progress in following the couple, but on the whole, the narration restricts us to what Eve and Thornhill know. As usual, some moments are heightened by optical POV shots, as when Eve watches Roger and Valerian roll down what seems to be a sheer drop. At the climax, Eve is dangling over the edge while Roger is clutching one of her hands and Leonard grinds his foot into Roger's other hand. It is a classic, not to say clichéd, situation of suspense. Again, however, the narration reveals the limits of our knowledge. A rifle shot cracks out and Leonard falls to the ground. The Professor has arrived and captured Van Damm, and a marksman has shot Leonard. Once more, a restricted range of knowledge has enabled the narration to spring a surprise on the audience.

The same effect gets magnified at the very end. In a series of optical POV shots, Roger pulls Eve up from the brink. But this gesture is made continuous, in both sound and image, with that of him pulling her up to a train bunk. The narration ignores the details of their rescue in order to cut short the suspense of Eve's plight. Such a self-conscious transition isn't completely out of place in a film that has taken time for offhand jokes. (During the opening credits, Hitchcock himself is shown being shut out of a bus. As Roger strides into the Plaza Hotel, about to be plunged into his adventure, the Muzak is playing "It's a Most Unusual Day.") This final twist shows once again that Hitchcock's moment-by-moment manipulation of our knowledge yields a constantly shifting play between the probable and the unexpected, between suspense and surprise.

Do The Right Thing

1989. Forty Acres and a Mule Filmworks (distributed by Universal). Directed and scripted by Spike Lee. Photographed by Ernest Dickerson. Edited by Barry Alexander Brown. Music by Bill Lee et al. With Danny Aiello, Ossie Davis, Ruby Dee, Giancarlo Esposito, Spike Lee, Bill Nunn, John Turturro, Rosie Perez.

At first viewing, Spike Lee's *Do The Right Thing,* with its many brief, disconnected scenes, restlessly wandering camera, and large number of characters without goals might not seem a classical narrative film. And, indeed, in some ways, it does depart from classical usage. Yet it has the redundantly clear action and strong forward impetus that we associate with classical filmmaking. It also fits into a familiar genre of American cinema—the social problem film. Moreover, closer analysis reveals that Lee has also drawn on many traits of classicism to give an underlying unity to this apparently loosely constructed plot.

A Day in the Life of a Community

Do The Right Thing takes place in the predominantly African-American Bedford–Stuyvesant section of Brooklyn during a heat wave. Sexual and racial tensions rise as Mookie, an irresponsible pizza delivery man, tries to get along with his Puerto Rican girlfriend, Tina, and with his Italian-American boss, Sal. An elderly drunk, Da Mayor, sets out to ingratiate himself with his sharp-tongued neighbor, Mother Sister. An escalating quarrel between Sal and two customers, Buggin' Out and Radio Raheem, leads to a fight in which Radio Raheem is killed by police. A riot ensues, and Sal's pizzeria is burned.

Do The Right Thing has many more individual sequences than *His Girl Friday* or *North by Northwest.* Even if we lump together some of the very briefest scenes, there are at least 42 segments. Laying out a detailed segmentation of *Do The Right Thing* might be useful for another analysis, but here we want to concentrate on how Lee weaves his many scenes into a whole.

Setting helps the characters and their actions together. The entire narrative is played out on one block in Bedford–Stuyvesant. Sal's Famous Pizzeria and the Korean market opposite lie at one end of the block, where much of the action takes place. Other scenes are played out in or in front of the brownstone buildings that line the rest of the street. The plot is driven forward by encounters between members of the neighborhood.

In accord with the limited setting, the action consumes a short time span, running from one morning to the next. Structuring a film around a brief stretch in the lives of several major characters isn't unknown in American filmmaking, as with *Street Scene, Dead End, American Graffiti, Car Wash, Nashville,* and *Magnolia.*

The radio DJ Mister Señor Love Daddy provides a running motif that also binds the film's events together. He appears in close-up in the first shot of the opening scene, and this initial broadcast provides important information about the setting and the weather, a heat wave that ratchets up the characters' tensions and contributes to the final burst of violence. As the DJ speaks, the camera tracks slowly out and cranes up to reveal the street, still empty in the early morning. At intervals throughout the film, Mister Señor Love Daddy provides commentary on the action, as when he tells a group of characters spewing racist diatribes to "chill out." The music he plays creates sound bridges between otherwise unconnected scenes, since the radios in different locations are often tuned to his station. The end of the film echoes the beginning, as the camera tracks with Mookie in the street and we hear the DJ's voice giving a spiel similar to the one on the previous morning, then dedicating the final song to the dead Radio Raheem.

As the setting and the neighborhood radio station suggest, *Do The Right Thing* centers more on the community as a whole than on a few central characters. The need to respect community, it seems, is a central theme of the film. On the one hand, there are older traditions that are worth preserving, represented by the elderly characters: the moral strength of the matriarch Mother Sister, the decency and courage of Da Mayor, the wit and common sense of the three chatting men, M. L., Sweet Dick Willie, and Coconut Sid. On the other hand, the younger people need to create a new community spirit by overcoming sexual and racial conflict. The women are portrayed as trying to make the angry young African-American men more responsible. Tina pressures Mookie to pay more attention to her and to their son; Jade lectures both her brother Mookie and the excitable Buggin' Out, telling the latter he should direct his energies toward doing "something positive in the community." The emphasis on community is underscored by the fact that most of the characters address one another by their nicknames.

One of the main conflicts in the film arises when Sal refuses to add some pictures of African-American heroes to his "Hall of Fame" photo gallery of Italian

Americans. Sal might have become a sort of elder statesman in the community, where he has run his pizzeria for 25 years. He seems to like the kids who eat his pizza, but he also views the restaurant as entirely his domain, emphatically declaring that he's the boss. He reveals his lack of real integration into the community and ends by goading the more hot-headed elements into attacking him.

In creating its community, *Do The Right Thing* includes an unusually large number of characters for a classical film. Eight of them provide the main causal action: Mookie, Tina, Sal, Sal's son Pino, Mother Sister, Da Mayor, Buggin' Out, and Radio Raheem. The others, intriguing or amusing as they may be, are more peripheral, mainly reacting to the action set in motion by these characters' conflicts and goals. (Some modern American screenwriting manuals recommend seven to eight important characters as the maximum for a clearly comprehensible film, so Lee is not departing from tradition here.) Moreover, the main causal action falls into two related lines, as in traditional Hollywood films: One involves the community's relations to Sal and his sons; the other deals with Mookie's personal life. Mookie becomes the pivotal figure, linking the two lines of action.

Revising Classical Conventions

Do The Right Thing also departs from classical narrative conventions in some ways. Consider the characters' goals. Usually, the main characters of a film formulate clear-cut, long-range goals that bring them into conflict with one another. In *Do The Right Thing,* most of the eight main characters create goals only sporadically; the goals are sometimes introduced fairly late in the film, and some are vague.

Buggin' Out, for example, demands that Sal put up pictures of some black heroes on the pizzeria wall. When Sal refuses and throws him out, Buggin' Out shouts to the customers to boycott Sal's. Yet a little while later, when he tries to persuade his neighbors to participate in the boycott, they all refuse, and his project seems to sputter out. Then, later in the film, Radio Raheem and the mentally retarded Smiley agree to join him. Their visit to the pizzeria to threaten Sal then precipitates the climactic action. Ironically, Buggin' Out's goal is briefly achieved when Smiley puts a photograph of Malcolm X and Martin Luther King Jr. on the wall of the burning pizzeria—but by that point, Buggin' Out is on his way to jail.

Mookie's goal is hinted at when we first see him. He is counting money, and he constantly emphasizes that he just wants to work and get paid. His repeated reference to the fact that he is due to be paid in the evening creates the film's only appointment, helping to emphasize the compressed time scheme. Yet his purpose remains unclear. Does he simply want the money so that he can move out of his sister's apartment, as she demands? Or does he also plan to help Tina care for their son?

Some characters have goals, but they are vague and long-range. Da Mayor tells Mother Sister that someday she will be nice to him. After he persistently acts courteously and bravely, she does in fact relent and become his friend. Sal's goal is similarly open-ended. He wants simply to keep operating his pizzeria in the face of rising tensions. This puts him in conflict with his son Pino, who has the long-range goal of convincing Sal to sell the pizzeria and leave the neighborhood. Perhaps he will get his desire at the end, although the narrative leaves open the question of whether Sal will rebuild.

In traditional classical films, clear-cut goals generate conflict, since the characters' desires often clash. Lee neatly reverses this pattern by making character goals less sharply defined, but creating a community that is full of conflict from the very beginning of the film. Racial and sexual arguments break out frequently, and insults fly. Such conflict is tied to the fact that *Do The Right Thing* is a social-problem film. Its didactic message gives it much of its overall unity. Everything that happens relates to a central question: With the community riven with such tensions, what can be done to heal it?

The characters' goals and actions suggest some of the possible ways of reacting to the situation. Some of the characters desire simply to avoid or escape this tense

> ❝ It's funny how the script is evolving into a film about race relations. This is America's biggest problem, always has been (since we got off the boat), always will be. I've touched upon it in my earlier works, but I haven't yet dealt with it head on as a primary subject.❞
>
> —Spike Lee, from the production journal of *Do The Right Thing*

atmosphere—Pino by leaving the neighborhood, Da Mayor by overcoming Mother Sister's animosity. Mookie attempts to stay out of trouble by not siding with either Sal or his black friends in their escalating quarrel. Only the death of Radio Raheem drives him to join in, and indeed initiate, the attack on Sal's pizzeria.

Other characters attempt to solve their problems. One central goal is Tina's desire to induce Mookie to behave like a responsible father and spend time with her and with their child. There is a suggestion at the end that she may be succeeding to some extent. Mookie gets his pay from Sal and says that he will get another job and that he's going to see his son. The last shot shows him walking down the now-quiet street, hinting that he may become a better father.

The central question in the film, however, is not whether any one character will achieve his or her goals. It is whether the pervasive conflicts can be resolved peacefully or violently. As the DJ says on the morning after the riot, "Are we gonna live together—together are we gonna live?"

Do The Right Thing leaves questions unanswered at the end. Will Sal rebuild? Is Mookie really going back to see his son? Most important, though the conflict that flared up has died down, the tension is still present in the community, waiting to resurface. The old problem of how to tame it remains, and so the film does not achieve complete closure. Indeed, such an ending is typical of the social-problem genre. While the immediate conflict may be resolved, the underlying dilemma that caused it remains.

That's also why there is a deliberate ambiguity at the end. Just as we are left at the end of *Citizen Kane* to wonder whether the revelation of the meaning of "Rosebud" explains Kane's character, in *Do The Right Thing* we are left to ponder what "the right thing" is. The film continues after the final story action, with two non-diegetic quotations from Martin Luther King, Jr., and Malcolm X. The King passage advocates a nonviolent approach to the struggle for civil rights, while Malcolm X condones violence in self-defense.

Do The Right Thing refuses to suggest which leader is right—although the overall action and use of the phrase "by any means necessary" at the end of the credits seem to weight the film's position in favor of Malcolm X. Still, the juxtaposition of the two quotations, in combination with the open-ended narrative, also seems calculated to spur debate. Perhaps the implication is that each position is viable under certain circumstances. The line of action involving Sal's pizzeria ends in violence; yet at the same time, Da Mayor is able to win Mother Sister's friendship through kindness.

Lee's Technical Choices

Like its narrative structure, the style of *Do The Right Thing* stretches the traditional techniques of classical filmmaking. The film begins with a credits sequence during which Rosie Perez performs a vigorous and aggressive dance to the rap song "Fight the Power." The editing here is strongly discontinuous; sometimes she wears a red dress, sometimes a boxer's outfit, and sometimes a jacket and pants. This brief sequence, which is not part of the narrative, employs the flashy style made familiar by MTV and by television commercials. But stylization during a credits sequence is itself a convention of classical Hollywood film, as we've already seen in Chapter 3 (pp. 94–95).

Throughout *Do The Right Thing,* Lee employs the continuity system. As we saw in Chapter 6, he is adept at handling complicated scenes without breaking the axis of action (6.81–6.86, from *She's Gotta Have It,* pp. 239–241). Most scenes use standard shot/reverse shots and eyeline matching **(11.15, 11.16),** but other moments are marked by different handling. The lengthy conversation in which Pino asks Sal to sell the pizzeria is rendered in one solemn, somewhat suspenseful long take **(11.17–11.19).** At two moments, Lee cuts together two takes of the same action, so that the plot presents a single important story event twice: when Mookie first kisses Tina and when the garbage can hits Sal's window. These instants of discontinuity gain special emphasis, highlighting Mookie's genuine love for Tina and the decisive moment when he turns on Sal, the employer he's defended in earlier scenes.

11.15

11.16

11.17

11.18

11.19

11.15–11.19 **Classical cutting and camera movement.** *Do The Right Thing* often employs classic shot/reverse-shot editing, as in this conversation between Jade and Buggin' Out (11.15–11.6). At another point Lee uses an exceptionally long take to give weight to the serious father-son exchange at the window (11.17). When Smiley appears, the forward tracking movement accumulates suspense (11.18). His interruption of their talk seems to prove Pino's point about the neighborhood, and Pino chases Smiley away while Sal slumps despondently (11.19).

Just as continuous is the soundtrack, which gives us the flavor of the neighborhood in a smooth sound stream. As Mookie walks past a row of houses, we hear radios tuned to different stations fade up and down, giving us audio perspective but also reminding us that the neighborhood's ethnic groups have differing tastes in music. The DJ's radio show helps pull the brief scenes together, with the same song carrying over various exchanges of dialogue.

At certain points, Lee's choices of form and style emphasize the community as a whole. The narration is largely unrestricted, flitting from one batch of characters to another, seldom lingering with any individual. Similarly, complex camera movements follow characters through the street, catching glimpses of other activities going on in the background. As in *Grand Illusion,* camera movements link characters to one another **(11.20–11.22).** Stylistic patterning also stresses the underlying problems in the community **(11.23, 11.24).**

The vagueness about goals, the treatment of the community as the central protagonist, and the moments of unusual style exemplify how Lee, like other

11.20

11.21

11.22

11.20–11.22 **Camera movement ties together lines of action.** On the morning after the riot, Da Mayor wakes up in Mother Sister's apartment. Da Mayor and Mother Sister talk and then move out into her front room, the camera tracking with them (11.20). The camera moves backward through the window as they reach it and starts to crane down (11.21). The camera movement ends on a close view of Mookie, on his way to the pizzeria (11.22).

11.23 **11.24**

11.23–11.24 Style emphasizing community problems. Radio Raheem's threatening demeanor is emphasized in some scenes by his direct address into a wide-angle lens (11.23). Mookie's self-absorption is suggested in a visual motif of high-angle views showing him stepping unheedingly on a cheerful chalk picture of a house that a little girl is drawing on the pavement (11.24).

contemporary filmmakers, has reshaped some conventions of classical filmmaking. (See pp. 488–494.) Overall, however, *Do The Right Thing* adheres to the formal and stylistic traditions of Hollywood cinema. Its multiple-threaded plot builds to a climax that is causally motivated by what went before, and our responses to the characters are built out of a concise, clear narration. Lee's approach to storytelling helps his film fulfill one convention of the social-problem genre: to raise questions and to stir debate.

Narrative Alternatives to Classical Filmmaking

Breathless (À bout de souffle)

1960. Les Films Georges de Beauregard, Impéria Films and Société Nouvelle de Cinéma. Directed by Jean-Luc Godard. Story outline by François Truffaut, dialogue by Godard. Photographed by Raoul Coutard. Edited by Cécile Decugis. Music by Martial Solal. With Jean-Paul Belmondo, Jean Seberg, Daniel Boulanger, Henri-Jacques Huet, Van Doude, Jean-Pierre Melville.

In some ways, *Breathless* imitates a 1940s Hollywood staple, the **film noir,** or "dark film." Such films dealt with hard-boiled detectives, gangsters, or ordinary people tempted into crime. Often a seductive femme fatale would lure the protagonist into a dangerous scheme (for example, *The Maltese Falcon*). *Breathless*'s plot links it to a common noir vehicle: the outlaw movie involving young criminals on the run, such as *They Live by Night* and *Gun Crazy*.

An Outlaw Couple?   The bare-bones story could serve as the basis of a Hollywood script. A car thief, Michel, kills a motorcycle cop and flees to Paris to get money to escape to Italy. He also tries to convince Patricia, an American art student writer with whom he had a brief affair, to leave with him. After equivocating for nearly two days, she agrees. Just as Michel is about to receive the cash he needs, Patricia calls the police, and they kill him.

Yet Godard's presentation of this story could never pass for a polished studio product. For one thing, Michel's behavior is presented as driven *by* the very movies that *Breathless* imitates. He rubs his thumb across his lips in imitation of his idol Humphrey Bogart. Yet he is a petty thief whose life spins out of control. He can only fantasize himself as a Hollywood tough guy.

The film's ambivalent attitude toward classical American cinema also pervades form and technique. As we've seen, the norms of classical style and storytelling promote narrative clarity and unity. In contrast, *Breathless* appears awkward and casual, almost amateurish. It makes character motivations ambiguous and lingers over incidental dialogue. Its editing jumps about frenetically. And, whereas films noirs were made largely in the studio, where selective lighting could swathe the characters in a brooding atmosphere, *Breathless* utilizes location shooting with available lighting.

These strategies make Michel's story quirky, uncertain, and deglamorized. They also ask the audience to enjoy the film's rough-edged reworking of Hollywood formulas. An opening title dedicates the film to Monogram Pictures, a Poverty Row studio that churned out B-movies. The title seems to announce a film that is indebted to Hollywood but not wholly bound by its norms.

Goals, Delays, and Puzzles   Like many protagonists in classical Hollywood films, Michel has two main goals. To leave France, he must search for his friend Antonio, the only one who can cash a check for him. Michel also hopes to persuade Patricia to go with him. As the plot progresses, it becomes apparent that, despite his flippant attitude, Michel's attraction to her outweighs his desire to escape.

In a classical film, these goals would drive the action along fairly steadily. Yet in *Breathless,* the plot moves in fits and starts. Brief scenes, some largely unconnected to the goals, alternate with long stretches of seemingly irrelevant dialogue. Most of *Breathless*'s 22 separate segments run four minutes or less. One 43-second scene consists simply of Michel pausing in front of a theater and looking at a picture of Bogart.

Scenes containing crucial action are sometimes brief and confusing. The murder of the traffic cop, an event that makes Michel a hunted man, is handled in a very elliptical fashion. In long shot, we see the officer approaching Michel's car, parked in a side road. In medium long shot, Michel reaches into the car for the gun. After that, the action becomes fragmentary **(11.25–11.28).** So much has been left out that we can barely comprehend what is happening, let alone judge whether Michel shot deliberately or by accident.

In contrast to the whirlwind presentation of this key action, a lengthy conversation in the middle of the film brings the narrative progression almost to a standstill.

11.25–11.28 Temporal discontinuity for a murder scene. In *Breathless,* Michel's shooting of the cop is fractured by abrupt cuts and camera movements. We see a close shot of his head, as the cop's voice is heard saying, "Don't move or I'll drill you" (11.25). Two very brief close-ups pan along Michel's arm and along the gun (11.26, 11.27), accompanied by the sound of a gunshot (though the pistol doesn't seem to be firing). We then get a glimpse of the cop falling into some underbrush (11.28), followed by an extreme long shot of Michel, running far across a field.

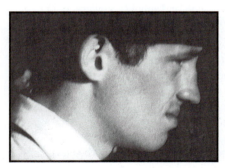

11.25

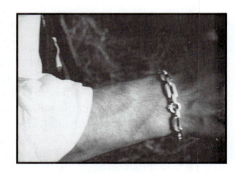

11.26

11.27

11.28

For nearly 25 minutes, Michel and Patricia chat in her bedroom. At some points, Michel attempts to further his goals, trying vainly to phone Antonio and to persuade Patricia to come to Rome. As for Patricia's response, she suggests that she will not run off with him, because she does not know if she loves him. Michel: "When will you know?" Patricia: "Soon." Michel: "What does that mean—soon? In a month, in a year?" Patricia: "Soon means soon." So although the pair make love, by the end of the long scene (which occupies nearly a third of this 89-minute film), we still do not have a definite step forward or backward in Michel's courting of Patricia, and he has made no progress toward escaping. Such scenes make him seem more like a wandering, easily distracted delinquent than the desperate, driven hero of a film noir.

You could argue that the bedroom scene functions not to advance the plot but to characterize the couple. Yet here, too, nothing definite emerges. Most of the conversation is trivial, as when Michel criticizes the way Patricia puts on lipstick or when she asks whether he prefers records or the radio. The pair try to outstare each other, and they discuss Patricia's new poster. So rambling is their exchange that some critics have assumed that the dialogue was improvised (although Godard attests that it was all scripted).

It's not until the scene outside the *Tribune* office that another decisive action occurs. A passerby (played by Godard) recognizes Michel and tells the police. This triggers a chain of events that lead to Michel's death. Yet now the plot meanders once more. In the next scene, Patricia participates in a news conference with a famous novelist, a character unrelated to the main action. Most of the questions asked by the reporters deal with the differences between men and women, but the novelist's responses seem more playful than meaningful. Finally, Patricia asks him his greatest ambition, and he replies enigmatically: "To become immortal and then to die." Patricia's puzzled glance into the camera at the close of the scene prepares us for the ambiguity that will linger at the film's end.

After Detective Vital questions Patricia at the *Tribune* office, she and Michel realize that the police are on his trail. Now *Breathless* begins to progress in a somewhat more conventional way. In the next scene, Patricia says that she loves Michel "enormously," and they steal a car. Here Michel seems to reach his romantic goal, as Patricia commits herself to fleeing with him. When Antonio agrees to bring the cash the next morning, Michel moves toward his second goal. We might anticipate possible outcomes: the pair will escape, or one or both will be killed in the attempt. The next morning, however, Patricia confounds our expectations by betraying Michel to Vital. Even then Michel has a last chance. Antonio arrives just before the police, with money and a getaway car—yet Michel cannot bring himself to leave Patricia.

More Questions   The ending is particularly enigmatic. As Michel lies bleeding to death, Patricia looks down at him. He slowly makes the same playful faces at her that he had made during their bedroom conversation. Muttering, "That's really disgusting" ("*C'est vraiment dégueulasse*"), he dies. Patricia asks Detective Vital what he said, and Vital misreports Michel's last words: "He said, 'You are really a bitch'" ("*Il a dit, 'Vous êtes vraiment une dégueulasse'*"). We are left to ponder what Michel thought was disgusting—Patricia's betrayal, his own last-minute failure to flee, or simply his death. In the final shot, Patricia looks out at the camera, asks what *dégueulasse* means, rubs her lips with the Bogart-inspired gesture that Michel has used throughout the film **(11.29),** and abruptly turns her back on us as the image fades out.

Breathless achieves a degree of closure: Michel fails to achieve his goals. But we are left with many questions. Although Michel and Patricia talk constantly about themselves, we learn remarkably little about why they act as they do. Unlike characters in classical films, they do not have a set of clearly defined traits. The film begins with Michel saying, "All in all, I'm a dumb bastard," and in a way, his actions bear this out. Yet we never learn background information that would explain his decisions. Why did he become a car thief? Since he abandons his female accomplice

11.29 Gesture as motif. Patricia's enigmatic gesture at the end of *Breathless* mimics the way Michel copies Humphrey Bogart.

early in the film, what makes him willing to risk death to stay with Patricia, a woman whom he has known only briefly? Because dying for an unworthy woman is what a would-be Hollywood hero is supposed to do?

Patricia's traits and goals are even more uncertain. When Michel first finds her selling newspapers on the Champs Elysées, she is far from welcoming. Yet at the scene's end, she runs back to give him a kiss. She keeps saying she wants to get a job as a *Tribune* reporter and to write a novel, yet she seems to throw these ambitions away when she thinks she loves Michel. Patricia also tells Michel she is pregnant by him, but she has not received the final test results, and she never raises this as a reason she should stay in Paris. She often says that she is scared, yet after she and Michel steal a car, she remarks: "It's too late now to be scared." This hints that she has resolved her own doubts and has thrown in her lot with Michel. When she suddenly betrays him, she does not intend that he should be killed but simply wants to force him to leave her. Still, her speech about why she informed on Michel seems not really to explain her abrupt change of heart. Just as Michel is ill-suited to be a tough guy, Patricia is too naive and indecisive to play the role of the classic femme fatale.

In the outlaw film noir, the characters are intensely committed to each other, but Michel and Patricia seem to have few strong feelings about what they do. When the treacherous woman deceives the noir hero, he often becomes bitterly disillusioned; but Michel apparently does not blame Patricia for betraying him. It is as if these ambivalent, diffident, confused characters are unable to play out the desperately passionate roles that the Hollywood tradition has assigned to them.

Breaking with Tradition *Breathless*'s elliptical, occasionally opaque narrative is presented through techniques that are equally unconventional. As we have seen, Hollywood films use a three-point system of key light, fill light, and backlight, carefully controlled in a film studio (pp. 127–128). *Breathless* was shot entirely on location, even the interiors. Godard and cinematographer Raoul Coutard often decided not to add any artificial light in the settings. As a result, the characters' faces sometimes fall into shadow **(11.30)**.

Filming on location, especially in small apartments, would ordinarily make it difficult to obtain a variety of camera angles and movements. But taking advantage of new portable equipment, Coutard was able to film while hand-holding the camera. Several lengthy tracking shots follow the characters **(11.31)**. Coutard apparently rode in a wheelchair to film this shot, as well as more elaborate movements that follow the characters in interiors **(11.32)**. Such shots recall the location shooting of many films noirs, such as the final airport scenes of Stanley Kubrick's *The Killing,* but the low camera position and the passersby who turn to look at the actors (as with the man at the right in 11.31) call attention to the technique in a way that departs from Hollywood usage.

Even more striking than the mise-en-scene is Godard's editing. Again he sometimes follows tradition, but at other points, he breaks away. Standard shot/reverse-shot cutting organizes several scenes **(11.33, 11.34)**. Similarly, when Michel spots the man examining the telltale photo in the newspaper, Godard supplies correctly matched glances. Since this is a turning point in the plot, it was important that the audience understand that the man may recognize Michel, and so Godard adheres to the 180° line.

Yet the film also violates continuity editing, and in ways that are still jolting today. In the opening scene, as Michel's accomplice points out a car he wants to steal, the eyelines are quite unclear, and we get little sense of where the two are in relation to each other. Nor does Godard feel an obligation to respect screen direction **(11.35, 11.36)**. Most original of all are his jump cuts. During the classic studio years, Hollywood editors avoided the jump cut, in which a segment of time is eliminated without the camera being moved to a new vantage point (p. 258). By contrast, *Breathless* employs the technique throughout. In an early scene, when Michel visits an old girlfriend, jump cuts shift their positions abruptly **(11.37, 11.38)**.

11.30

11.31

11.32

11.30–11.32 Available lighting and flexible camerawork. When Patricia sits against a window and lights a cigarette, the natural light of the scene illuminates her only from behind (11.30). Michel's first meeting with Patricia as she strolls along the Champs Elysées selling papers occurs in a three-minute take (11.31). Later, when Michel visits a travel agent trying to claim his check, the framing glides with ease as he moves through offices and corridors (11.32).

11.33

11.34

11.35

11.36

11.33–11.36 **Editing, normal and disruptive.** When Michel pauses in front of a movie theater and looks at a photo on display (11.33), Bogart seems to look back at him in reverse shot (11.34). At other times, Godard breaks the 180° rule. In the first shot, Patricia moves from left to right (11.35), but in the next, she is walking right to left (11.36). This cut flagrantly violates conventional screen direction.

Even when Godard shifts the camera position between cuts, he may drop out a bit of time or mismatch the actors' positions. At many cuts, the action seems to jerk forward. One effect of this jumpy editing is to enliven the rhythm. At times, as during the murder of the police officer, we have to be very alert to follow the action. The elliptical editing also makes other scenes stand out by contrast, particularly the single-take scenes with moving camera and the rambling 25-minute conversation in Patricia's apartment.

The film's sound often reinforces these editing discontinuities. When the characters' dialogue and other diegetic sounds continue over the jump cuts, we are forced to notice the contradiction: Time drops out of the visual track but not the sound track. The location shooting also created situations in which ambient noises intrude on the dialogue. A passing siren outside Patricia's apartment nearly overwhelms her

> On *À Bout de souffle,* he'd [Godard] ask the script-girl what kind of shot was required next to fulfill the requirements of traditional continuity. She'd tell him, and then he'd do the exact opposite."
> —Raoul Coutard, cinematographer

11.37

11.38

11.37, 11.38 **The jump cut.** During Michel's visit to an old girlfriend, we get several jump cuts. Compare the last frame of one shot (11.37) with the first of the next shot (11.38). We've seen another example earlier, when jump cuts show Patricia riding in a car (6.51, 6.52, again the last and first frames of adjacent shots).

conversation with Michel during the long central scene. Later the press conference with Parvulesco inexplicably takes place on an airport observation platform, where the whines of nearby planes drown out the dialogue. Such scenes lack the balance of volumes of the well-mixed Hollywood sound track.

Godard's avoidance of the rules of smooth sound and picture steers *Breathless* away from the glamorous portrayals seen in the Hollywood crime film. The stylistic awkwardness suits the pseudo-documentary roughness of filming in an actual, hectic Paris. The discontinuities are also consistent with other nontraditional techniques, like the motif of the characters' mysterious glances into the camera. In addition, the jolts in picture and sound create a self-conscious narration that makes the viewer aware of its stylistic choices. In making the director's hand more apparent, the film presents itself as a deliberately unpolished revision of tradition.

Godard did not set out to criticize Hollywood films. Instead, he took genre conventions identified with 1940s America and gave them a contemporary Parisian setting and a modern, self-conscious treatment. He thereby created a new type of hero and heroine. Aimless, somewhat banal lovers on the run became central to later outlaw movies such as *Bonnie and Clyde, Badlands,* and *True Romance.* More broadly, Godard's film became a model for directors who wished to create exuberantly offhand homages to, and reworkings of, Hollywood tradition. This attitude would be central to the stylistic movement that *Breathless* helped launch, the French New Wave. (See Chapter 12, pp. 485–488.)

Tokyo Story (Tokyo Monogatari)

1953. Shochiku/Ofuna, Japan. Directed by Yasujiro Ozu. Script by Ozu and Kogo Noda. Photographed by Yuharu Atsuta. With Chishu Ryu, Chieko Higashiyama, So Yamamura, Haruko Sugimura, Setsuko Hara.

We've seen that the classical Hollywood approach to filmmaking tends to let story action dominate. The plot is constructed to encourage us to build the story in our minds in a certain way. What do you show and when do you show it? The answer to these questions is usually based on how the filmmaker wants us to experience the story's action. With so much emphasis on the story, we seldom pay particular attention to the space in which it occurs. The setting, and the manner of showing it to us, functions chiefly as an arena for character conflict and change. Spade's office in *The Maltese Falcon* (pp. 235–239) isn't explored as a locale, it's merely a nondescript area for initiating the mystery plot. *North by Northwest* doesn't want us to study Mount Rushmore as a piece of mammoth sculpture; it's rather a dramatic backdrop for a chase and cliff-hanging.

What, however, if a filmmaker wanted to change the way we thought about the space around a story? You wouldn't have to go as far as Michael Snow in *Wavelength* and almost obliterate a story altogether (pp. 208–209). You might try to tell a story, in fact a rather emotional one, but allow the locales in which the story takes place to gain more prominence, to claim our attention in their own right. Patterns of space could enrich the story while at the same time having a certain independence.

This all sounds a little abstract, so let's look at a famous example. The Japanese director Yasujiro Ozu has sought to tell gripping stories while also making narrative space more than a container for action. We've given you a preview of Ozu's unique style of exploring space through graphic matching (6.142–6.145) and using an area of space to condense story time (5.207, 5.208). Through such choices, Ozu created a systematic alternative to classical continuity filming (p. 257). Our analysis here tries to show how his strategies operate across an entire film.

Oblique Storytelling *Tokyo Story,* Ozu's first film to make an impression on Western audiences, presents a simple narrative. An elderly provincial couple visit their grown children in Tokyo, only to be treated as nuisances. As the couple return home, the wife falls ill, and she dies after reaching their house. Now the children come to visit the parents, and though some are sorrowful, others continue to be emotionally distant. The plot lacks the goals, conflicts, crises, and climaxes that we associate with Hollywood cinema. Told this succinctly, it seems little more than a sad anecdote.

What makes this tale more complex, and our responses more nuanced, is Ozu's handling. *Tokyo Story*'s narration is, by classical standards, rather oblique. Sometimes we learn of important narrative events only after they have occurred. For example, although the grandparents are the film's central characters, we do not see the grandmother falling ill. We hear about it only when her son and daughter get telegrams with the news. Similarly, the grandmother's death occurs between scenes. In one scene, her children are gathered by her bedside; in the next scene, they are mourning her.

Yet these ellipses are not evidence of a fast-paced film such as *His Girl Friday,* which tries to cover a lot of narrative ground in a hurry. On the contrary, the sequences of *Tokyo Story* often linger over details: the melancholy conversation between the grandfather and his friends in a bar as they discuss their disappointment in their children, or the grandmother's walk on a Sunday with her grandchild. The result is a shift in narrative balance. Key narrative events are deemphasized by means of ellipses, whereas narrative events that we do see in the plot are ones that would be considered minor.

Transitional Spaces   As Ozu shifts our attention away from the most dramatic events, he often steers us away from dramatically significant space. Scenes don't begin and end with shots showing the most important elements in the mise-en-scene. Instead of the usual transitional devices, such as dissolves and fades, Ozu typically employs a series of separate transitional shots linked by cuts. A landscape or object becomes the pivot to a new scene. In effect, Ozu makes bits of setting fill in the time gaps between scenes. This already gives greater weight to the space around the story action.

Moreover, these transitional shots often show spaces not directly connected with the action of the scene; the spaces are usually *near* where that action will take place. The opening of the film, for example, has five shots of the port town of Onomichi—the bay, schoolchildren, a passing train—before the sixth shot reveals the grandparents packing for their trip to Tokyo. Although a couple of important motifs make their first appearances in these first five shots, no narrative causes occur to get the action underway. (Compare the openings of *His Girl Friday* and *North by Northwest.*)

These transitions have only a minimal function as establishing shots. In fact, sometimes they mislead us about what's coming next. At a crucial moment in the drama, the narration moves from the daughter-in-law Noriko to the clinic of the eldest son, yet Ozu can extend the transition with shots of a construction site (**11.39–11.42**). But the shots of the building under construction aren't necessary to the action, and we get no hint of where the building is. We might assume that it is outside Noriko's office, but the riveting sound we hear in the transitional shots isn't audible in the interior shots before and after.

What are the functions of these stylistic patterns? It's hard to assign them explicit or implicit meanings. For example, someone might propose that the transitional shots symbolize the new Tokyo that is alien to the visiting grandparents from a village reminiscent of the old Japan. But often the transitional spaces don't present outdoor locales, and some shots are within the characters' homes. Moreover, why insert these shots here rather than anywhere else in the film, where the same thematic opposition would be just as appropriate? And finally, if the shots reiterate the old/new theme, they would be quite redundant, because the contrast between the grandparents' tradition and their children's urban lives is already stressed in the story action.

A more systematic function, we suggest, is narrational, having to do with the flow of story information. Ozu's narration alternates between scenes of story action and inserted portions that lead us to or away from them. As we watch the film, we start to form expectations about these wedged-in shots. Ozu emphasizes stylistic patterning

> " I don't think the film has a grammar. I don't think film has but one form. If a good film results, then that film has created its own grammar."
> —Yasujiro Ozu, director

11.39

11.40

11.41

11.42

11.39–11.42 Ambivalent transitions in *Tokyo Story.* After the daughter-in-law, Noriko, gets a phone call at work telling her of the grandmother's illness, the scene ends in a medium shot of her sitting pensively at her desk. The only diegetic sound is the loud clack of typewriters (11.39). A nondiegetic musical transition comes up in this shot. Then there is a cut to a low-angle long shot of a building under construction (11.40). Riveting noises replace the typewriters, with the music continuing. The next shot is another low angle of the construction site (11.41). A cut changes the locale to the clinic belonging to the eldest son, Dr. Hirayama. The sister, Shige, is present. The music ends and the new scene begins (11.42).

by creating anticipation about when a transition will come and what it will show. The patterning may delay our expectations and even create some surprises.

For example, early in the film, Mrs. Hirayama, the doctor's wife, argues with her son, Minoru, over where to move his desk to make room for the grandparents. This issue is dropped, and there follows a scene of the grandparents' arrival. This ends on a conversation in an upstairs room. Transitional music comes up over the end of the scene. The next shot frames an empty hallway downstairs that contains Minoru's school desk, but no one is in the shot. There follows an exterior long shot of children running along a ridge near the house; these children are not characters in the action. Finally, a cut back inside reveals Minoru at his father's desk in the clinic portion of the house, studying.

Here the editing creates a very indirect route between two scenes, going first to a place where we expect a character to be (at his own desk) but isn't. Then the scene moves completely away from the action, outdoors. Not until the third shot does a character reappear and the action continue. Likewise, after we leave Noriko at her typewriter (11.39) and see the building under construction, we might expect to move to another office building. Instead, the next shot takes us to the family's suburban home. The construction site is neither fully urban (the building is unfinished), nor rural either. In its in-between status we can see it, in retrospect, as a conceptual link between Noriko and the clinic. In these transitional passages, a kind of game emerges. Ozu asks us to form expectations not only about story action but about editing and setting. Just as Ozu's plotting is unpredictable, leaving major actions offscreen and elevating minor ones, so too is his film's movement through space and time.

11.43

11.44

11.45

11.43–11.45 **360° editing space.** At the beginning of a scene in Shige's beauty salon, the initial interior medium shot frames Shige from opposite the front door (11.43). A 180° cut reveals a medium long shot of a woman under a hair dryer; the camera now faces the rear of the salon (11.44). Another 180° cut presents a new long shot of the room, again oriented toward the door, and the grandparents come into the salon (11.45).

The Space around the Characters

Ozu finds another way to activate the space his characters inhabit. We mentioned in Chapter 6 (p. 256) that he creates a 360° space for many of his scenes. He will cut across the 180° line to frame the scene's space from the opposite direction. This, of course, violates rules of screen direction, since characters or objects on the right in the first shot will appear on the left in the second, and vice versa. He's not doing this occasionally, as Ford does in our *Stagecoach* example (6.94, 6.95), but consistently. The editing in Shige's beauty salon exemplifies Ozu's typical approach to framing and editing a scene **(11.43–11.45)**.

When we look closely, we find that Ozu has his own rules for staging, shooting, and cutting, and these revise the continuity guidelines. He relies on eyeline cuts, but these are often "wrong" by Hollywood standards, since both characters are looking in the same direction **(11.46, 11.47)**. He matches on action but shifts back and forth across the axis of action, as when Noriko and her grandmother walk toward the door of Noriko's apartment **(11.48, 11.49)**. Instead of restricting his camera

11.46

11.47

11.46–11.49 **360° space breaks the axis of action.** The grandfather and his old friend converse, but they look in the same direction (11.46, 11.47). Adherents of classical continuity would say that this cut implies that the two men are looking off at something else, yet we aren't confused by it. Similarly, Noriko and her grandmother advance to the camera, then away from it (11.48, 11.49). The women's movements are closely matched, and normally head-on and tail-on shots of action can cut together. (See 6.89–6.94.) But here the similar framings make the characters seem to bump into themselves. Their screen positions, left and right, are also abruptly reversed, something that is usually considered an error in the continuity style.

11.48

11.49

positions to one side of the axis of action, Ozu cuts in a full circle around the action, usually in segments of 90° or 180°. This means that backgrounds change drastically, as in our examples. In a Hollywood film, the camera rarely crosses the axis of action to look at the fourth wall. Because surroundings change more frequently in *Tokyo Story*, they become more prominent in relation to the action; the viewer must pay attention to setting or become confused.

This 360° space works together with the transitional shots that prolong or thwart the viewer's expectations. One of the most famous scenes in the film shows the grandparents visiting a spa at Atami, sent there because they inconvenience their offspring. Even though they enjoy looking at the sea, their nights are disturbed by partyers around them. Ozu introduces us to their unhappiness gradually and without sentimental pathos. For seven shots, the film slowly explores the space of the scene, gradually letting us discover the situation **(11.50–11.57)**. The presence

11.50

11.51

11.52

11.53

11.54

11.55

11.56

11.57

11.50–11.57 Sidling into a scene. The Atami spa scene begins with a long shot along a hallway (11.50). Latin-style dance music plays offscreen, and several people walk through the hall. The next shot (11.51) is a long shot of another hallway upstairs, with a maid carrying a tray; two pairs of slippers are just visible by a doorway at the lower left. But instead of taking us into the room with the grandparents, Ozu takes us to a hallway (11.52) and then a mah-jongg game nearby (11.53). Ozu cuts 180° across the axis, framing another mah-jongg table (11.54). The first table is now in the background, viewed from the opposite side. So will the scene's action take place here among the mah-jongg players? The next cut returns to the medium long shot along the courtyard hallway (11.55). Finally, there is a medium shot of the two pairs of slippers by the door in the upper hallway (11.56), suggesting that this is the grandparents' room. A medium shot of the Hirayamas in bed, trying to sleep through the noise, finally reveals the narrative situation (11.57). Only now do the Hirayamas start to talk.

of the couple's slippers in the second shot (11.51) is almost unnoticeable. It hints that the grandparents are there, but the revelation of their whereabouts is then put off for several more shots as the shots sidle through other rooms in the spa. The unpredictability of the scene's unfolding is created through the transitional shots and the 360° shifts.

In these ways, Ozu draws our attention away from the strictly causal functions of space and makes space important in its own right. He does the same with the flat space of the screen by cutting to highlight graphic configurations. Now we can see that his strategy of 360° cutting also functions to create strong graphic matches between shots. (Look back at 11.46 and 11.47, and you'll see the same sort of graphic matching we pointed out in 6.142–6.145.) The stylistic device is characteristic of Ozu, who seldom uses the graphic match for any narrative purpose. In this respect, Ozu's style owes something to abstract form (see Chapter 10, pp. 371–378). It's as if he sought to make a narrative film that would make graphic similarities as evident as they are in an abstract film like *Ballet mécanique*.

Ozu's narration may not seem as suspenseful as Hitchcock's or as eccentric as Godard's. His dwelling on the spaces around the characters may seem less economical than Spike Lee's concise creation of a city block in *Do The Right Thing*. What Ozu does, more quietly, is to suggest that around his characters, behind them, alongside them, exist places and people that have their own integrity and interest. Moreover, by asking us to form expectations about what areas of the setting we will see next, he draws us into an experience that involves more than building up the story. Just as when we read a novel we can appreciate a lyrical paragraph of description as well as a conflict among characters, Ozu takes us beyond the immediate action and shows that unusual patterns of cinematic space can be enjoyed in their own right.

Chungking Express (Chung Hing sam lam)

1994. Jet Tone, Hong Kong. Directed by Wong Kar-wai. Script by Wong Kar-wai. Photographed by Andrew Lau Wai-keung and Christopher Doyle. With Brigitte Lin Ching-hsia, Takeshi Kaneshiro, Tony Leung Chiu-wai, Faye Wong Jingwen.

Filmmakers in many countries have sometimes explored what has been called the *web-of-life plot* or the *network narrative*. Instead of two primary lines of action, as in *His Girl Friday* or *North by Northwest*, some recent films weave together a large number of plotlines, often involving many characters. American precedents for this can be found in *Grand Hotel* (1932) and *Nashville* (1976), but in the 1990s, such films as *Short Cuts*, *Pulp Fiction*, *Magnolia*, *Traffic*, *Babel*, and *Love Actually* made this sort of plotting more common. Unlike the characters of *Do The Right Thing*, who all live in the same neighborhood, the characters in a web-of-life plot are largely at first unknown to one another. Eventually, however, they are likely to converge, revealing unexpected causal connections. In *Magnolia*, disparate as the characters are, they are connected either to the television producer Earl Partridge or through chance encounters, as when the police patrolman meets Partridge's unhappy daughter.

The audience expects a network narrative to reveal unforeseen relations among the disparate characters. Seen from this standpoint, *Chungking Express* constitutes an intriguing experiment in nonclassical form. It is broken into two distinct stories, each organized around a different batch of characters. The two stories aren't crosscut but simply set side by side. One question that viewers commonly ask is, What has director Wong Kar-wai accomplished by putting these two stories in the same film? Our analysis will try to find an answer.

Two Sad Policemen In the first tale, Officer 223 (for ease of recall, we'll call him Officer 1) has just broken up with his girlfriend and lives in hope that she'll take him back before May 1, his 25th birthday. Wandering the city at night, he runs into a mysterious woman in dark glasses and a blonde wig. He doesn't know that

> " [Financiers in Asia] always ask, 'Is it a cop story or a gangster story?' So you have to choose. One or the other. . . . So with *Chungking Express*, I said it is a cop and a gangster story. We have gangsters, and we have cops. But it is not a gangster/cop story. It's just about their lives, and that's it."
> —Wong Kar-wai, director

11.58 Passing unawares. In *Chungking Express,* while the mysterious blonde woman lounges outside a shop, Faye (whom we do not meet until part two) leaves with a stuffed toy (perhaps destined for Officer 2's apartment). Each of the three main characters of part 2 is glimpsed during the first story.

she is part of a drug-smuggling outfit. She has hired some Indian down-and-outs to carry bags of cocaine out of the country, but they have defected with the drugs. She must recover the shipment or face the wrath of her boss, who runs a bar. Officer 1 meets her in a bar and takes her to a cheap hotel, where she sleeps off her drinking and he eats snacks. In the morning, he leaves her. She posts an affectionate message on his pager before returning to the bar and shooting her boss dead.

The second and longer tale introduces Officer 633 (Officer 2), who is happy with his girlfriend, a flight attendant. But one day she leaves him. He is still trying to get over their affair when Faye, a counterwoman at his favorite fast-food spot, the Midnight Express, takes an interest in him. The flight attendant leaves Officer 2's keys at the Midnight Express for him to pick up, and Faye uses them to explore his apartment while he's out. She tidies it up and redecorates it, leaving fresh soap and towels and filling his aquarium with fish. After catching her in the apartment, he realizes she's flirting with him. They make a date. But she stands him up, leaving for California—the place she had always hoped to visit. A year later, Officer 2 has bought the Midnight Express and is renovating it when Faye returns. Now *she's* a flight attendant, and there is a hint that their romance might finally begin.

What links the two parts? Both employ handheld camera work, moody music, and voice-over commentaries drifting in and out. But a common style is normally not enough to justify putting two stories together. Since both protagonists are policemen, we might expect them to encounter one another, but they never do; the first is a plainclothes detective, while the second pounds a beat. Nor does the mysterious blonde's drug smuggling ever impinge on the cops' activities. Officer 1 is ignorant of her racket, and Officer 2 doesn't investigate the murder of the bar owner, as he might in another kind of plot. The two strands do share one locale: Both Officer 1 and Officer 2 hang out at the Midnight Express. Nonetheless, this doesn't connect the parts causally, since Officer 1 meets Faye only once, and he never becomes a rival for her affections. As if to tease sharp-eyed repeat viewers, Wong inserts into the first part a brief, distant shot of each main character who will appear in the *second* part—Officer 2, the flight attendant, and Faye **(11.58).** But they are unknown to us on the initial viewing, and they aren't presented as shaping the story action in the first part.

It is as if Wong has juxtaposed the two stories in such a way to demand that we find our own connections between them. By analyzing narrative form and style, we can bring to light some intriguing similarities and differences, which in turn point to a set of themes that unify the film.

Two Times, Two Places   In broad narrative terms, the two parts stand in sharp contrast. The first takes place on the Kowloon peninsula of Hong Kong, in and around Chungking Mansions, a decaying block of cheap guest quarters, shops, and Indian restaurants. (The Cantonese title of the film translates as "Chungking Jungle," and it may tease the local viewer into believing that eventually the second story will return to this neighborhood.) The second part takes place on Hong Kong Island, across the bay from Kowloon, in the vicinity of the Midnight Express. The Kowloon of part one teems with crime; Officer 1 chases suspects down at gunpoint, while the blonde works for a drug cartel. Part two presents a far less threatening world, where romance can blossom and the cop on the beat drops in for snacks. The English-language title of the film fuses the basic locales of each part, balancing Chungking Mansions with Midnight Express in a single phrase.

The two parts offer very different time schemes as well. The first part takes place over a short span, about four days, and the action labors under deadlines. Officer 1 has given May, his ex-girlfriend, the month of April to come back to him. The blonde's deadline for the smuggling operation has been set by her boss, and she meets it by shooting him and escaping from Hong Kong on May 1. The second part has a much looser time frame and no strong deadlines. Over a period of weeks, Officer 2's girlfriend leaves him, Faye invades his apartment, he transfers his beat, and after a series of casual encounters they finally make a date. Faye stands up Officer 2 and, like the blonde woman, departs. The action concludes a year later when she flies back to Hong Kong.

Yet within these broad contrasts, some echoes do emerge. Each man is coming out of a love affair; each meets a woman by chance; quickly or slowly, each becomes attached to her; the woman abruptly departs. The characters' goals are also revealing. Officer 1 seeks a new woman to love, and although Officer 2 is content to drift, Faye seems to try to ease his bruised heart. These goals are presented more vaguely and pursued more erratically than in a Hollywood film, but the parallels suggest that *Chungking Express* revolves around romance. The more closely we look at cause–effect chains, motifs, and visual style, the more evidence we find that the film is comparing ways in which people try to find love.

The two policemen's romantic problems shape their attitudes toward time. Neither man realizes that love affairs must adjust to change. In part one, ruled by fast pace and deadlines, Officer 1 has been pining for a month and now wants to find a new girlfriend immediately. Officer 2, suddenly dumped by his flight-attendant girlfriend, can't summon up the energy to restart his love life. Both men fill their stretches of waiting with cycles of repetitive behavior. Officer 1 badgers May's family and then calls old girlfriends to ask for a date. Officer 2 repeatedly visits the Midnight Express, first to pick up snacks for himself and his girlfriend, then simply to brood. Although one wants a sudden adventure and the other falls back on routine, both are caught in spirals of inactivity. Wong emphasizes this through parallel images of each man moping in his apartment **(11.59, 11.60).**

11.59

11.60

11.59–11.60 **Policemen wounded by romance.** Wong uses parallel images to show Officer 1 and Officer 2 moping in their apartments.

Food and Flight   The two cops need a change—according to the film's most pervasive motif, a change of menu. Food is central to both stories, announced at the start in the headlong tracking shots through Chungking Mansions, where the snack stalls are filled with eaters. May loved pineapple, so Officer 1 measures the time he waits for her in pineapple cans, each day buying one with a May 1 expiration date. On the last day, when she hasn't returned to him, he gorges himself on the 30 cans he has saved. When he meets the blonde, he asks if she likes pineapple. Similarly, Officer 2 always orders chef's salads at the Midnight Express.

The men stick with one food, but the women crave varied menus. As the blonde studies Officer 1 in the bar, her voice-over commentary remarks, "Knowing someone doesn't mean keeping them. People change. A person may like pineapple today and something else tomorrow." When Officer 2 brings home pizza and fish and chips, his girlfriend leaves him. He muses that she realized that she had a choice of lovers as well as dinners.

The food motif goes on to define the men's attitudes toward change. While the blonde sleeps in a Chungking Mansions hotel room, Officer 1 stuffs himself with hamburgers, salads, and fries. Once outside, he thinks that she has forgotten him, but her pager message ("Happy birthday") leads him to wish that the expiration date on his memory of her will last forever. No longer treating a girlfriend as a fast-food snack, Officer 1's sense of time has expanded. Instead of seeking a new future, he treasures a moment in the past **(11.61).**

11.75 The glamor of the machine.
Framing and lighting enhance the dynamism of throbbing, gleaming machine parts.

Vertov also points out weak spots in contemporary life, such as lingering class inequalities. Shots in a beauty shop suggest that some bourgeois values have survived the Revolution, and the leisure-time sequence near the end contrasts workers involved in outdoors sports with chubby women exercising in a weight-loss gym.

Vertov also takes pains to criticize drunkenness, a major social problem in the USSR. One of the first shots within the inner film shows a derelict sleeping outdoors, juxtaposed with a huge bottle advertising a café. A shop front that we repeatedly see advertises wine and vodka, and later there is a scene where the cameraman visits this bar. When he leaves, we see shots of workers' clubs, converted from former churches. Associational crosscutting contrasts these two places where workers can spend their leisure time: A woman shooting at targets in one of the clubs seems to be shooting away bottles of beer that, thanks to stop-motion, disappear from a crate in the bar.

During the 1920s, government officials sought to steer Soviet citizens away from taverns and churches and toward film theaters and workers' clubs. (Since the government's biggest source of income came from its monopoly on vodka sales, the policy also aimed at making film a major alternative source of revenue.) *Man with a Movie Camera* seems to be subtly promoting this policy by using playful camera techniques to make both movie houses and clubs seem attractive.

Implicitly, *Man with a Movie Camera* can be seen as an argument for Vertov's approach to filmmaking. He opposed narrative form and the use of professional actors, preferring that films use camera technique and editing to create their effects on the audience. He was not, however, entirely against controlling the mise-en-scene, and several scenes, particularly the woman waking up and washing, clearly were staged. On the whole, the film is a sort of demonstration of what path Vertov thought cinema should take.

Vertov strengthens his case by associating making a film with other sorts of productive labor. The camera operator goes to his job in the morning, like other workers. Like them, he uses a machine; editing compares the camera's crank with the crank on a cash register and with moving parts on factory equipment. And the filmmaker is dedicated. He accepts dangerous missions, climbing up a huge smokestack, crouching on the tracks to film an oncoming train, riding a motorcycle one-handed as he cranks the camera to capture a race. Even when other workers are relaxing at the beach or at sporting events, the cameraman is on the job.

As the cameraman's work is compared with running factory machines or taking on hazardous missions, editing is seen as a patient craft. The editor whom we see cutting the footage is Elizaveta Svilova, Vertov's wife and the actual editor of *Man with a Movie Camera*. Her gestures of scraping the film and dabbing cement to make a splice are crosscut with shots of a manicure in a beauty parlor. More generally, across the film we see the same shots in different contexts: on our screen, on the screen within the movie theater, in fast-motion, or in freeze frame. We see shots filmed, snipped apart, spliced together. We must therefore view these images not only as moments of recorded reality but also as pieces of a whole put together through the painstaking efforts of film workers like Svilova. The film becomes a sort of machine to be assembled and tuned to perfection by expert hands. Filmmaking is a job, not an elite-oriented art, and it has a useful role in building the new society.

Judging from the delighted reactions of the audience we see in the theater, Vertov hoped that the Soviet public would find his celebration of filmmaking educational and entertaining. This hope went unfulfilled. During the late 1920s, Soviet authorities wanted films that would be easily understandable and would convey propagandistic messages to a far-flung, often illiterate, populace. Policy makers were increasingly critical of filmmakers such as Sergei Eisenstein and Vertov, whose films, though celebrating revolutionary ideology, were extremely complex. In Chapter 6, we saw how Eisenstein adopted a dense, discontinuous style of editing. While Vertov disagreed with Eisenstein, particularly over the latter's reliance on narrative form, both belonged to a larger stylistic movement called Soviet Montage, whose history we examine in Chapter 12 (pp. 476–479). Both used very complex editing that they hoped to teach audiences to follow.

With its contradictory time scheme and rapid editing (it contains over 1,700 shots, more than twice what most Hollywood films of the same period had), *Man with a Movie Camera* is a difficult film, especially for an audience unaccustomed to the conventions of Montage filmmaking. Over the next few years, Soviet authorities increasingly criticized Vertov and his colleagues, limiting their ability to experiment with concepts like the kino-eye. Vertov was constrained in his later projects, but *Man with a Movie Camera* eventually came to be recognized around the world as a sophisticated documentary, a classic experiment in associational form, and an uninhibited display of the power of cinematic technique.

The Thin Blue Line

1988. An American Playhouse production (PBS). Directed by Errol Morris. Photographed by Stefan Czapsky, Robert Chappell. Edited by Paul Barnes. Music by Philip Glass.

On a west Dallas highway one night in 1976, a police officer named Robert Wood was fatally shot by a driver he had pulled over. Wood's partner, officer Teresa Turko, saw the killer drive off, but it took months of investigation for the police to discover that the car had been stolen by David Harris. Harris, a 16-year-old from the small town of Vidor, admitted to being in the car but said that the killer was Randall Adams, a man with whom he had hung around that day. Adams was tried for murder, found guilty, and sentenced to death. Eventually, through an appeal process, his sentence was commuted to life imprisonment. Harris, because of his age and his cooperation with the police, was given a suspended sentence.

In 1985, documentary filmmaker Errol Morris met Randall Adams while he was researching another project. Morris became convinced that Adams had been unjustly convicted, and over the next three years, he prepared a film based on his investigation of the case.

The Thin Blue Line employs narrative form, telling the story of events leading up to and following the murder of Officer Wood. Yet the film's narration enriches that basic story. By juggling time, inserting many details, developing the reenactments of the killing into a powerful pattern, and subtly engaging our sympathy for Randall Adams, Morris not only takes us through a criminal case but also suggests how difficult the search for truth can be.

Parts and Wholes   The overall plot guides us through the story events, but not in a wholly linear way. For this reason, it's useful to compose a segmentation of the film. We can find 31 fairly distinct sequences, although many contain brief flashbacks to the interrogation and the crime. Some also contain fairly lengthy reenactments, which are signaled here by italics.

C. Opening credits
 1. Dallas, Randall Adams, and David Harris are introduced.
 2. Officer Wood is shot. *First shooting reenactment*
 3. Adams is arrested and interrogated. *First interrogation reenactment*
 4. Police describe the interrogation and the beginning of the investigation. *Second interrogation reenactment*
 5. Police describe the two officers' states of mind. *Second shooting reenactment*
 6. Police search for the car, even using hypnotism. *Third shooting reenactment*
 7. Big break: David Harris is discovered in Vidor, Texas.
 8. Harris accuses Randall Adams of the shooting.
 9. Adams responds to Harris's charge.

10. Adams is interrogated. *Third interrogation reenactment*
11. Police explain the mistaken auto identification.
12. Adams's two lawyers are introduced and describe their inquiry into Harris's hometown.
13. Adams's lawyers discuss Harris as a criminal; the judge describes his attitude toward police.
14. Adams recounts Harris's version of events. *Fourth shooting reenactment*
15. Adams explains his alibi.
16. Trial: Officer Turko testifies, implicating Adams. *Fifth shooting reenactment*
17. Trial: New witnesses emerge. Mr. and Mrs. Miller claim to have seen Adams shoot Wood. *Sixth shooting reenactment*
18. Adams's lawyers and Mrs. Carr rebut the Miller couple's testimony.
19. Trial: Third new witness, Michael Randell, claims to have seen Adams shoot Wood. *Seventh shooting reenactment*
20. Trial: Jury declares Adams guilty.
21. Trial: Judge sentences Adams to death.
22. Adams reacts to the death sentence.
23. Adams's lawyers petition for a retrial and lose.
24. Adams's appeal is supported by the U.S. Supreme Court; his sentence is commuted to life in prison.
25. Vidor detective explains: Harris is arrested again.
26. Rethinking the case: Witnesses reflect, and Harris hints that he has lied. *Eighth shooting reenactment*
27. Vidor detective explains: Harris has committed a murder in town.
28. Adams: "The kid scares me"; he reflects on the mistake of letting Harris go free.
29. Harris, now on death row, reflects on his childhood.
30. Final interview on audiotape: Harris calls Adams a "scapegoat" and virtually confesses.
31. Title: Current situation of the two men.
E. Closing credits.

Segments 1–3 form a prologue, introducing the essential information and arousing our curiosity and concern. The opening sequence presents the city of Dallas; the two main characters, Randall Adams and David Harris; and their current situation: both men are in jail. What has brought them there? They tell of meeting each other and spending the day drinking, smoking marijuana, and going to a drive-in movie. Segment 2 is the first of many shocking reenactments of the shooting of Officer Wood at the dark roadside. Here, as in all the others, actors play the participants, and the framing often conceals their faces, concentrating instead on details of action or setting. The third sequence depicts Adams's arrest and interrogation (**11.76**).

Then the film's plot flashes back to explain events leading up to Adams's arrest, concentrating on the police investigation (segments 4–11). In the course of this, David Harris names Randall Adams as the killer (8), and Adams is arrested and interrogated (10). Eventually, the confusion about the make of the car is cleared up, though Morris hints that the police investigation was muddled (11). These sequences are interrupted by two more reenactments of Adams's questioning and two reenactments of the death of Officer Wood.

The longest stretch of the film (segments 12–24) centers on Randall Adams's confrontation with the courts. After his lawyers and the judge are introduced (12–13), we're given two conflicting versions of events—Adams's and Harris's (14–15).

11.76 Staging in documentary. *The Thin Blue Line:* The questioning of Randall Adams, staged so that its status as a reenactment is unmistakable.

Three surprise witnesses identify Adams as the shooter (16–19), although some of the testimony is undercut by a woman who claims that two witnesses bragged to her about trying to earn a reward (18). Again, at certain moments the crime is reenacted to illustrate witnesses' testimony. The jury finds Adams guilty (20), and he's sentenced to death (21–22). The legal maneuvers that follow put Adams in prison for life without parole (23–24).

The film has answered one question posed at the outset. Now we know how Randall Adams got to prison. But what of David Harris, who is also serving time? The final stretch of the film continues the story after the trial, concentrating on Harris's criminal career. Harris is arrested for other crimes (25), and Morris inserts a sequence (26) designed to suggest his guilt in the Wood case. The surprise eyewitnesses are shown to be unreliable and confused, and as having things to hide. Most tellingly, Harris explains, "Of course I picked out Randall Adams." In the next sequence, a detective in Harris's hometown of Vidor explains how Harris invaded a man's home, violently abducted his girlfriend, and fatally shot the man (27). Harris, now revealed as a polite, easygoing sociopath, reflects on his childhood, when his brother drowned and his father seemed to become more distant (29). But whatever sympathy he might arouse is undercut by his final acknowledgment, captured by Morris on audiotape, that Randall Adams is innocent (30). A title explains that Adams is still serving his life sentence, while Harris is on death row (31).

Complicating the Plot

In outline, then, this is a straightforward tale of crime and injustice. The film's explicit meaning was compelling enough to trigger a new inquiry into the case, and Adams was freed in 1989. But Morris's film is more than a brief for the defense. It demands a great deal of the viewer; it does not spell out its message in the manner of most documentaries. We tend to side with Randall Adams and to distrust the police, prosecutors, and "eyewitnesses" aligned against him, but Morris does not explicitly favor Adams and criticize the others. The film's form and style shape our sympathies rather subtly. At another level, the film denies the viewer many of the usual aids for determining what happened on that night in 1976. Instead, it asks us to heighten our attention, to concentrate on details, and to weigh the incompatible information we are given. Morris's detective story asks us to reflect on the obstacles to arriving at the truth about any crime.

The film's materials are for the most part the stuff of any true-crime report. Morris uses talking-head interviews, newspaper headlines, maps, archival photos, and other documents to present information about the crime. He also includes reenactments of key events, signaled as such. Nonetheless, other documentary conventions are missing. There is no voice-over narrator explaining the situation, and no captions identify the speakers or provide dates. The reenactments don't carry the "Dramatization" caption seen in television documentaries. As a result, we're forced to evaluate what we see and hear without help. This extra responsibility is intensified by a framing that is rare in most documentary interviews: several of the speakers look straight out at the camera, a tactic that forces us to weigh the testimony we hear **(11.77)**.

Moreover, the use of paper documents is fairly cryptic: The film doesn't always specify their source, and the extreme close-ups often show only fragments of text. (One shot of a news article frames these partial phrases: ". . . ved to be a 1973 . . . earing Texas licens . . . with the letters H . . .") Likewise, Philip Glass's repetitive score is hardly conventional documentary music, especially for a true-crime story. With its mournful, unresolved harmonies and nervously oscillating figures, the music arouses tension, but it also creates an eerie distance from the action: it throbs on, unchanged whether it accompanies an empty city landscape or a violent murder.

Other formal and stylistic qualities complicate the plot. For example, when an interviewee mentions a particular place, Morris tends to insert a quick shot of that locale **(11.78)**. So many abrupt interruptions wouldn't appear in a normal documentary, since they don't really give us much extra information. It's as if Morris

❝ I wanted to make a film about how truth was difficult to know, not impossible to know."

—Errol Morris, director

11.77 Address to the viewer. A police detective gives his version of Adams's interrogation in a somewhat unnerving direct address.

11.78

11.79

11.80

11.78–11.80 Minor details as motifs. Morris cuts away to the motel where Adams stayed; in light of Adams's fate, the billboard in the background becomes ironic (11.78). A popcorn machine at the drive-in ominously fills the foreground, while the clock serves as the basis for David Harris's testimony (11.79). While Harris the teenager is associated with popcorn, Adams the panicked victim is associated with an ashtray full of cigarettes (11.80).

11.81 An echo of film noir. In a reenactment, Officer Wood is shown approaching the car.

wants to suggest the vast number of tiny pieces of information that an investigator must process. Similarly, during most reenactments, the participants' faces aren't shown. Instead, the scenes are built out of many close-ups: fingers resting on a steering wheel, a milkshake flying through the air in slow motion, a popcorn machine (**11.79**). Again, Morris stresses the apparently trivial details that can affect our sense of what really happened on the highway.

By amplifying apparently minor details he also invites us to see some of these shots metaphorically. Carefully composed and lit in high-key, the details become evocative motifs. Some inserts comment ironically on the situation (11.78). Others, such as the ever-present clocks and watches, indicate the ominous passing of time. Even the slowly shattering flashlight and the milkshake dribbling onto the pavement suggest the life pumping out of the fatally wounded officer Wood.

Reenactments and Revelations   Morris subtly orchestrates our attitudes toward the people presented in the film. By and large, the plot is shaped to create sympathy for Randall Adams. He is the first person we see, and Morris immediately makes him appealing by letting him explain that he was grateful to find a good job immediately after coming to Dallas. "It's as if I was meant to be here." Morris presents him as a decent, hardworking man railroaded by the justice system. The interrogation of Adams is associated with filled ashtrays, making him seem nervous and vulnerable (**11.80**), as do the repeated close-ups of newspaper photos of his frightened eyes. When the accusers state their case, Morris keeps us on Adams's side by letting him rebut them. In segment 9, Adams replies to Harris's charge that he was the shooter; in segment 15, Adams presents his alibi in reply to Harris's claims about the time frame of events. By the end, Adams becomes the authoritative commentator. In segment 28, after Harris has committed another murder, Adams reminds us that a life could have been saved if the Dallas police hadn't released Harris. At this point, our sympathies for Adams are strong, and we understand why he reverses his initial judgment on Dallas: It's now "hell on earth."

Our acceptance of Adams's account is subtly reinforced by the many reenactments of the murder. They are clearly set off as reconstructions by their use of techniques more closely associated with the fiction film, particularly film noir (**11.81**; also 4.61). They also distinguish themselves from the restagings shown on true-crime television shows, which tend to include the faces of actors and which are usually shot in a loose, hand-held style suggesting that we are witnessing the real event.

The reenactments present different versions of the crime in accord with different witnesses' recollections. By presenting contradictory versions of what happened that night, Morris may seem to be suggesting that everyone involved saw things from his or her own perspective, and so there is no final fact of the matter. But the overall progression of the film leads us to a likely conclusion: that David Harris, on his own, killed Wood. Rather than suggesting that truth is relative, the incompatible reconstructions dramatize the conflicting testimony. Like jurors or courtroom spectators, we have to decide on the most plausible version, and the plot develops the reenactments in a strongly suggestive pattern.

In the segments devoted to the police investigation, the restagings emphasize matters of procedure. Did Officer Turko identify the car correctly? No, the police detectives eventually decide; but both before and after they arrive at this conclusion, Morris shows us two different cars, making the options visually concrete. Another question is just as important: Did Turko back up Officer Wood according to procedure, or did she remain in the car? Morris dramatizes both possibilities, but he leads us to infer that she probably was inside the car drinking her milkshake, since in the crime scene sketch, spilled chocolate liquid was found near the car. It is a matter of probabilities, and we can never be certain; but on the evidence we are given, we infer that she probably did not back up Wood.

The reenactments of Officer Wood's murder in the investigation section concentrate on police procedure, but during the trial section, the reenactments suggest different versions of what was happening in the killer's car. Was David Harris ducking down in the front seat? Was Adams's bushy silhouette confused with a fur-lined coat collar? When the surprise witnesses are introduced, Morris shows reenactments that present their cars passing the murder scene. Again, the reconstructions present the alternatives neutrally, but some become more plausible than others, especially once the eyewitnesses are rebutted by other testimony or betrayed by their own evasive answers.

The last reenactment, presented in the section devoted to David Harris, shows how Harris could have committed the murder, and significantly, it is accompanied by his voice virtually confessing to it. Now, after many other reenactments, this one is presented as most worthy of our belief. Morris carefully refrains from saying explicitly that Harris was the killer. But the development of the reconstructions, eliminating the most questionable versions and focusing more and more on the identity of the driver, pushes us toward accepting this as the likeliest account.

Digressions and Motifs   As in any narrative film, then, the manner of storytelling, the play with narration and knowledge, shapes our attitudes toward the characters. By letting Adams comment on other characters, and by arranging the reenactments so as to point eventually toward David Harris's guilt, the film aligns us with Randall Adams, the innocent victim. Correspondingly, Morris uses other stylistic devices to make us mistrust the forces set against Adams. The film doesn't present the Dallas law officers as brutal villains, though. All are soft-spoken and articulate, and Judge Metcalfe comes across as calm and patient. But Morris's editing decisions give prominence to Adams's account and allow him to answer their charges, so we're inclined to appraise their words cautiously.

Morris comes closest to criticizing the authorities at two points. Both are semicomic digressions relying on the sort of associational form exploited by *Koyanisqaatsi* (pp. 379–386). Judge Metcalfe reminisces about the death of John Dillinger (**11.82, 11.83**) and supplies background trivia about the woman who betrayed Dillinger. When he says she was sent back to her native Romania, Morris cuts to a map of Bucharest, as if that were as relevant to Adams's case as the Texas maps used elsewhere in the film. A similar bit of mocking humor appears when one eyewitness says that she always imagined herself as a girl detective in 1950s TV shows. Morris lets her voice-over commentary run during a clip from a B-film in which a young

CONNECT TO THE BLOG
www.davidbordwell.net/blog

For more on Errol Morris's approach to documentary, see the entry, "Errol Morris, boy detective."

11.82

11.83

11.82–11.83 Romanticizing the war on crime. Judge Metcalfe recalls that he grew up with a great respect for law and order because his father was present when FBI agents shot the gangster John Dillinger (11.82). Morris cuts to a scene from a Hollywood crime movie that presents Dillinger's death, an ancestor of the reenactments in *The Thin Blue Line* (11.83).

11.95 Comfort food as motif. A framing in depth stresses the family as a group, with a plate of cake prominent on the piano in the foreground.

which Rose's boyfriend fails to propose to her by phone, the tensions are reconciled, and the maid serves large slices of corned beef.

In the Halloween scene, the connection between plentiful food and family unity becomes even more explicit. At first, the children gather around to eat cake and ice cream, but the father arrives home and makes his announcement about moving to New York. The family members depart without touching their food. Only when they hear the mother and father singing at the piano do they gradually drift back to eat **(11.95).** The words of the song—"Time may pass, but we'll be together"—accompany them. The use of food as a motif associates the family's life in the house with plenty and with the individual's place as part of a group. At the fair in the last sequence, the family decide to visit a restaurant together. The food motif returns at the moment of their reaffirmation of their life together in St. Louis.

Light and Family Life Another motif of family unity involves light. The house is ablaze much of the time. As the family sits together at dinner, the low evening sun sends bright yellow rays through the white curtains. Later, one of the loveliest scenes involves Esther's request that John accompany her through the downstairs to help her turn out the lights **(11.96).** As the rooms darken and the couple moves out to the hall, the camera cranes down to a height level with their faces. The shot contains a remarkable shift of tone. It begins with Esther's comically contrived excuse ("I'm afraid of mice") to keep John with her and develops gradually toward a genuinely romantic mood.

The Halloween sequence takes place entirely at night and makes light a central motif. The camera initially moves in toward the house's glowing yellow windows. Tense, slightly eerie music makes the house seem an island of safety in the darkness. As Tootie and Agnes go out to join the other children in playing tricks, they are silhouetted against the flames of the bonfire the group has gathered around. At first the fire seems threatening, contradicting the earlier associations of light with safety and unity, but this scene actually harmonizes with the previous uses of light. Tootie is excluded from the group activities because she is "too little." After she proves herself worthy, she is allowed to help feed the flames along with the others. Note particularly the long track-back as Tootie leaves the fire to play her trick; the fire remains in the background of the shot, appearing as a haven she has left behind **(11.97).** Indeed, the first sequence of the Halloween section of the film becomes a sort of miniature working out of the entire narrative structure. Tootie's position as a part of the group is abandoned as she moves away from the fire and then triumphantly affirmed as she returns to it.

Similarly, light plays an important part in the resolution of the threat to the family's unity. Late on Christmas Eve, Esther finds Tootie awake. They look out the window at the snow people standing in the yard below. A strip of yellow light falls across the snow, suggesting the warmth and safety of the house they plan to leave (11.94). Tootie's hysterical crying, however, leads Mr. Smith to reconsider his decision. As he sits thinking, he holds the match, with which he was about to light his cigar, unnoticed in his hand until it burns his fingers. Combined with the slow playing of the "Meet Me in St. Louis" theme, the flame serves to emphasize his distraction and his gradual change of mind.

As he calls his family down to announce his decision not to move, he turns up all the lights. The dim, bleak halls full of packing boxes become again the scene of busy activity as the family gathers. The lamps' glass shades are red and green, identifying the house with the appropriate Christmas colors and recalling Esther's and Rose's party dresses. The announcement of the decision leads directly to the opening of the presents, as if to emphasize that staying in St. Louis will not create any financial hardship for the family.

11.96

11.97

11.98

11.96–11.98 Light as motif. As Esther and John turn out the downstairs lights one by one, a long-take crane shot follows the characters from room to room (11.96). At each pause, the chandelier is framed in the upper portion of the screen. During the Halloween sequence, a terrified Tootie moves into the darkness to play her trick (11.97). The motif of light culminates in the revelation of the fairgrounds (11.98).

As night falls in the final fair sequence, the many lights of the buildings come on, dazzlingly reflected in lakes and canals **(11.98).** Here the film ends, with the family gazing in awe at the view. Once more light signifies safety and family enjoyment. These lights also bring the other motifs of the film together. Alonzo Smith had originally wanted to move to New York as a provision for his family's future. In deciding to stay in St. Louis, he had told them: "New York hasn't got a copyright on opportunity. Why, St. Louis is headed for a boom that'll make your head swim. This is a great town." The fair solves the problems of the future and family unity. The family is able to go to a French restaurant without going away from home. The ending also restores the father's position as at least the titular head of the family. Only he is able to remember how to get to the restaurant and prepares to guide the group there.

By the end, St. Louis allows the family to retain its unity, comfort, and safety and yet have all the benefits of progress. The film ends with this dialogue:

MOTHER: There's never been anything like it in the whole world.

ROSE: We don't have to come here in a train or stay in a hotel. It's right in our own hometown.

TOOTIE: Grandpa, they'll never tear it down, will they?

11.99 **Resolution through the couple.** The film's final shot, with Esther's dazzled reaction to the fair.

GRANDPA: Well, they'd better not.

ESTHER: I can't believe it. Right here where we live. Right here in St. Louis (**11.99**).

These lines do not *create* the film's ideology, which has been present in the narrative and stylistic devices throughout. The dialogue puts into words what has been presented through narrative and stylistic patterning all along.

Ideology and Broader Meanings   Understanding a film's ideology typically involves analyzing how form and style create meaning. As Chapter 2 suggested, meaning can be of four general types: referential, explicit, implicit, and symptomatic. Our analysis of *Meet Me in St. Louis* has shown how all four types work to reinforce a social ideology—in this case, the values of tradition, home life, and family unity. The referential aspects of the film presuppose that the audience can grasp the difference between St. Louis and New York, and that it knows about international expositions, American family customs, national holidays, and so on. These address the film to a specifically American audience. The explicit meaning of the film is formulated by the final exchange we have just considered, in which the small city is discussed as the perfect fusion of progress and tradition.

We have also traced out one major implicit meaning: the family and home as creating a "haven in a heartless world," the central reference point for the individual's life. What, then, of symptomatic meanings?

Chapter 2 mentioned that systems of values and beliefs may seem unquestionable to the social groups that hold them. One way that groups maintain such systems is to assume that certain things are beyond human choice or control, that they are simply natural. Historically, this habit of thought has often been used to justify oppression and injustice, as when women, minority groups, or the poor are thought to be naturally inferior. *Meet Me in St. Louis* participates in this general tendency, not only in its characterization of the Smith women (Esther and Rose are simply presumed to want husbands) but also in the very choice of a white, upper-middle-class household as an emblem of American life. More subtly, the natural cycle of the seasons is harmonized with the family's life, and the conclusion of the plot takes place in the spring, the time of renewal.

We can also consider more historically specific symptomatic meanings. The film was released in November 1944 (just in time for Christmas). World War II was still raging, although some countries had already been liberated from the Nazis. The audience for this film would have consisted largely of women and children whose male relatives had been absent for extended periods, often overseas. Families were often forced apart, and the people who remained behind had to make considerable sacrifices for the war effort. In a time when women were required to work in defense plants, factories, and offices (and many were enjoying the experience), there appeared a film that restricted the range of women's experiences to home and family, and yearned for a simpler time when they ruled only the kitchen.

Meet Me in St. Louis can thus be seen as a symptom of a nostalgia for a distant America. In a 1944 audience, parents of young fighting men would remember the 1903–1904 period as part of their own childhoods. All of the formal and stylistic choices—narrative construction, seasonal segmentation, songs, color, and visual motifs—can be seen as reassuring the viewers. If the women and others left at home can be strong and hold their families together, domestic harmony will eventually return. From this perspective, *Meet Me in St. Louis* upholds dominant conceptions of American life and may even propose an ideal of family unity for the postwar future.

Raging Bull

1980. United Artists. Directed by Martin Scorsese. Script by Paul Schrader and
Mardik Martin. From the book *Raging Bull* by Jake La Motta, with Joseph Carter and
Peter Savage. Photographed by Michael Chapman. Edited by Thelma Schoonmaker.
With Robert De Niro, Cathy Moriarty, Joe Pesci, Frank Vincent, Nicholas Colasanto,
Theresa Saldana.

In analyzing *Meet Me in St. Louis,* we argued that the film upholds a characteristically American ideology. It's also possible for a film made in Hollywood to take a
more ambivalent attitude toward ideological issues. Martin Scorsese's *Raging Bull*
does so by making violence its central theme.

Violence is widespread in American cinema, often serving as the basis for
entertainment. Extreme violence has become central to many genres, from crime
films to science-fiction and horror films. Such genres often make their violence
very stylized, usually thanks to special effects, and thus not fundamentally disturbing. *Raging Bull* uses a different tactic, drawing on conventions of cinematic
realism to make violence visceral. Not only the brutal boxing matches but also the
harsh quarrels in everyday life bring violence to the fore.

Scorsese's film is loosely based on the career of boxer Jake La Motta, who became the world middleweight champion in 1949. *Raging Bull* uses the scenes based
on actual prizefights as emblematic of the violence that pervades Jake's life. He
seems incapable of dealing with people without picking quarrels, making threats,
or exploding in fury. His marriages, especially his second one to Vickie, are full of
bickering and domestic abuse. Although his closest relationship is apparently with
his brother Joey, who initially manages his career, Jake eventually thrashes Joey in
a jealous rage and permanently alienates him. Moreover, while Jake's actions hurt
others, he also wreaks havoc on himself. He drives away everyone he loves and
ends up as an overweight stand-up comic, then as an actor reciting speeches from
famous plays and films.

How are we to understand the ideology of a film that makes such a vicious
bully its hero? We might be tempted to posit either/or interpretations. Either the film
celebrates Jake's murderous rage, or it condemns him as a pathological case. Yet in
settling on one of these simple notions, we would fail to confront the film's uneasy
balance of sympathy for and revulsion toward its central character. We suggest that
Raging Bull uses a variety of strategies, both of narrative and style, to make Jake a
case study in the role of violence in American life. By balancing repulsion with a
degree of compassion, Scorsese thus creates a complex context within which Jake's
actions must be judged.

Narrative Progression   As usual, it helps to start an analysis by mapping the
film's formal structure. If we were to segment *Raging Bull,* we would come up with
about 46 distinct scenes, including the opening credits and the closing quotation
title. To make things manageable, we group them into 12 major parts:

1. The opening credits, shown over a lengthy shot of Jake warming up alone in
   a boxing ring.
2. Backstage in a nightclub, 1964. Jake practices a poem he will recite.

   Flashback begins:
3. 1941. Expository scenes of Jake losing a match, fighting with his wife, seeing
   Vickie, and having his first date with her.
4. 1943. Two matches with Sugar Ray Robinson, separated by a love scene between Jake and Vickie.
5. A montage sequence alternating a series of fights, 1944 to 1947, and home
   movies of Jake's private life.

11.100 The isolated fighter. The slow-motion opening shot of *Raging Bull.* Unspecified in time and place, it presents a lyrical, idealized image of prizefighting very different from the bouts we'll see.

6. A lengthy series of scenes in 1947, including three in the Copacabana night-club, establishing Jake's jealousy over Vickie and hatred of the mob. He ends by throwing a fight for them.

7. 1949. An argument with Vickie, followed by Jake's winning the middle-weight champion bout.

8. 1950. Jake beats up Vickie and his brother Joey in an unjustified jealous rage. He defends his title and fights Robinson again.

9. 1956. Jake retires and buys a nightclub in which he does comedy routines. Vickie leaves him, and he is arrested on a morals charge.

10. 1958. Jake does his comedy act in a cheap strip joint; he fails to persuade Joey to reconcile with him.

    Flashback ends.

11. 1964. Jake prepares to go onstage to perform his recital.

12. A black title with a biblical quotation and the film's dedication.

The beginning and ending of the film are vital in shaping our attitude toward Jake's career. The first image shows him warming up in the ring before an un-specified fight **(11.100).** Several filmic devices create our initial impressions of the protagonist. He bounces up and down in place, in slow motion. This slow tempo is accompanied by languid classical music, suggesting that his boxing warm-up is like a dance. The deep-space staging places the ring's ropes prominently in the foreground and makes the ring seem huge, emphasizing Jake's solitude. This long take continues through the main credits, establishing boxing as both a beautiful and a lonely sport. The image remains abstract and remote: it is the only scene in the narrative that does not take place in a year specified by a superimposed title.

A straight cut to segment 2 shows Jake, suddenly fat and old. He's practicing, but now it's rehearsal for a one-man show of readings and recitations. He tries out a poem he has written about himself: "So give me a stage / Where this bull here can rage / And though I can fight / I'd much rather recite—That's entertainment!" The opening image has given him a bare stage, but the comedown from his glory days is apparent. This backstage episode takes place quite late in the story chronol-ogy, after the long struggles of his boxing career. Not until segment 11 will the plot return to this moment, with Jake continuing to rehearse his lines. In segment 11, as the manager summons him onstage, he executes some warm-up punches to build his confidence, muttering rapidly over and over, "I'm the boss, I'm the boss."

By framing most of the story action as a flashback, Scorsese links violence with entertainment, in the ring or in a nightclub. Jake's gesture of spreading his arms as he says, "That's entertainment!" in segment 2 resembles the triumphant raising of his glove-clad hands whenever he wins a fight in the lengthy central flashback. Cor-respondingly, *Raging Bull* ignores Jake's early life and concentrates on two periods: his boxing career and his turn to stand-up comedy and literary performances. Both periods present him as trying to control his life and the people around him. "I'm the boss," the last line spoken in the film, sums up Jake's attitude in every phase.

The plot structure we've outlined also traces a rise-and-fall pattern of develop-ment. After segment 7, Jake's high point, his life runs downhill, and his violence appears more and more savagely self-destructive. In addition, certain motifs high-light the role of violence in his life and the lives of those around him. During a rest period in his first bout (segment 3), a fistfight breaks out in the stands, suggesting at the outset that violence spills beyond the ring. Domestic relations are expressed through aggression, as in the tough-guy shoving between Jake and Joey and in Joey's disciplining his son by threatening to stab him.

Most vividly, violence is turned against women. Both Jake and Joey insult and threaten their wives, and Jake's beating of both his wives forms a grim counterpoint to his battles in the ring. During the first scene at the Copacabana, women emerge as targets of abuse. Jake accuses Vickie of flirting with other men; he insults a boxer and a mob member by suggesting that both are like women; and even the comedian onstage mocks women in the audience. Scene by scene, the organization of incidents and motifs suggests that male aggression pervades American life.

Violence: Realism and Stylization   The film's presentation of violence draws on particular conventions of realism. A series of superimposed titles identify each boxing match by date, locale, and participants. This narrational tactic yields a quasi-documentary quality. The most important factor creating realism, however, is probably the acting. Aside from Robert De Niro, the cast was chosen from virtually unknown actors or nonactors. As a result, they did not bring glamorous star associations to the film. De Niro was known mainly for his grittily realistic performances in Scorsese's *Mean Streets* and *Taxi Driver,* as well as Michael Cimino's *The Deer Hunter.* In *Raging Bull,* the actors speak with thick Bronx accents, repeat or mumble many of their lines, and make no attempt to create likable characters. In the publicity surrounding the film, much was also made of the fact that De Niro gained 60 pounds in order to play Jake as an older man. The film emphasizes De Niro's transformation at various points **(11.101, 11.102).** Such realism in the acting and other techniques makes it difficult for us to accept the film's violence casually, as we might in a conventional horror or crime film.

Film techniques also make violence disturbing. Outside the ring, domestic violence is presented harshly, but usually in long shots and without extravagant sound effects. More aggressive stylistically are the prizefight scenes, which arouse visceral shock in the viewer. Many of the fights are filmed with the camera on a Steadicam brace, which yields ominous tracking movements or close shots of grimaces. Backlighting, motivated by the spotlights around the ring, highlight droplets of sweat or blood that spray off the boxers **(11.103).** Punches are intensified with loud, stinging cracks on the soundtrack and rapid editing, often with abrupt ellipses from shot to shot. Special makeup shows facial blood vessels spurting grotesquely.

Through its narrative structure and its use of the stylistic conventions of realism, the film offers a criticism of violence in American life, both in the ring and in the home. Yet the film doesn't permit us to condemn Jake as merely a raging bull. It also presents violence as fascinating and ambiguous. Although the fight scenes favor brutal realism, aspects of them are distorted in mesmerizing ways. The sounds of punches assault our ears with shuddering impact. The sound mix for the fights blended animal cries, airplane motors, whizzing arrows, and even music, but the sources are unrecognizable because they are slowed down or played backward. For all their bloodiness, the fight scenes have their own beauty, partly thanks to slow-motion shooting and stylized lighting.

Narrational Restriction and Masculine Aggression   Violence is made disturbingly attractive even in the scenes outside the ring. This is partly because the narration concentrates far more on the perpetrators of the violence than on the victims. In particular, the three important female characters—Jake's first wife, Joey's wife Lenore, and Vickie—have little to do in the action except take abuse or rail ineffectually against it. We never learn why they are initially attracted to the violent men they marry or why they stay with them so long. At first Vickie seems to admire Jake for his fame and his flashy car, but her willingness to sustain their marriage for so long is not explained. Indeed, her sudden decision to leave him after 11 years has no specific motivation.

The victims of Jake's violence serve chiefly to provoke him to respond. One portion of the action focuses on his pummeling of a "pretty" fighter to whom he thinks Vickie is attracted. Another deals with Jake's violent reaction to his irrational belief that Joey and Vickie have had an affair. It is notable that after this crisis, when Jake beats Joey up, Joey becomes as peripheral a figure as Vickie. We

11.101

11.102

11.101–11.102 Contrast for realistic impact. A graphic match cuts straight from a medium close-up of Jake at the end of segment 2, in 1964 (11.101), to a similar framing of him in the ring in 1941 (11.102).

11.103 Visceral impact. Realistic violence in the boxing scenes.

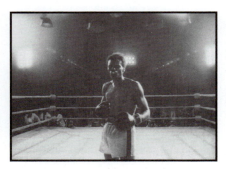

11.104

11.105

11.104–11.105 Violence as entertainment and as psychological drive. Jake's point of view during a fight (11.104). At home, a close-up links violence and sexuality as Jake asks Vickie to kiss his bruises (11.105).

glimpse him briefly watching Jake's bloody title defeat and then see a short scene of him resisting Jake's offer of reconciliation. The film thus offers no positive counterweight to Jake's excesses.

The film's restriction to a male perspective is even more apparent when the narration shifts into subjective presentation. Several scenes show events from Jake's point of view, using slow motion to suggest that we are seeing not just what he sees but how he responds to it. This technique becomes especially vivid when Jake notices Vickie with other men and becomes jealous. Similarly, in the final fight with Robinson, Jake's vision of his opponent is shown via a markedly subjective point-of-view framing. The POV imagery also incorporates a combined track-forward and zoom-out to make the ring seem to stretch far into the distance, while a decrease in the frontal light makes Robinson appear even more menacing **(11.104).** Other deviations from realism, such as the thunderous throbbing on the sound track during Jake's major victory bout, also suggest that we're entering Jake's mind.

Moments of perceptual and mental subjectivity don't necessarily make us forgive Jake's brutality, but they do make us understand him better. Along similar lines, Scorsese includes scenes that suggest that Jake can at moments tame his aggressiveness. However much he hurts other people, he injures himself, too. He sometimes regrets having hurt people, as several parallel scenes show. In segment 3, Jake has a vicious argument with his first wife in which he threatens to kill her but then immediately says, "Come on, honey, let's be—let's be friends. Truce, all right?" Later, after he has beaten Vickie up for her imagined infidelities, he apologizes and persuades her to stay with him. These domestic reconciliations are echoed in the big title fight where he defeats the current champion, Marcel Cerdan, then walks to his opponent's corner and magnanimously embraces him.

A degree of compassion for Jake is reinforced by other means. *Raging Bull* suggests that he is strongly masochistic, inducing others to inflict pain on him. This notion is emphasized in the love scene in segment 4, when he childishly asks Vickie to caress and kiss the wounds from his triumph over Sugar Ray Robinson **(11.105).** Soon Jake denies himself sexual gratification by pouring ice water into his shorts. The scene then leads directly into a fight in which Robinson defeats Jake. This defeat is paralleled in segment 8, another boxing scene, when Jake simply stands and goads Robinson into beating him to a pulp. The motif of masochism comes to a climax in segment 9, when Jake is thrown into solitary confinement in a Dade County jail. A long, disturbing take has Jake beating his head and fists against the prison wall, as he asserts that he is not an animal and berates himself as stupid.

More implicitly, the film suggests that some of Jake's aggressiveness can be traced to repressed homosexuality. His embrace of the defeated opponent, Cerdan, in his title fight, as well as his urging of Robinson to attack him in his final bout, suggest such an interpretation. In segment 6, when Jake sits down at a nightclub table and jokes about how pretty his upcoming opponent is, he tauntingly offers him as a sex partner to a mobster he suspects of being in love with Vickie. In segment 8, one scene begins with an erotically suggestive slow-motion shot of seconds' hands massaging Jake's torso. There are hints that Jake's fascination with boxing and his refusal to deal with his domestic life stem from an unacknowledged homosexual urge. Such an implication goes against the usual ideology of Hollywood, which assumes that a heterosexual romance is the basis for most narratives.

Ultimately, the ideological stance that *Raging Bull* offers is far from being as straightforward as that of *Meet Me in St. Louis.* Instead of displaying an idealized image of American society, the film criticizes one pervasive aspect of that society: its penchant for violence, as public entertainment and private conduct. Yet it also displays a considerable fascination with that violence, acknowledging its visceral force and considerable beauty. Similarly, Jake is admirable as a dedicated gladiator, but he's also a brute. The film doesn't make us like Jake or even sympathize with him, but it does suggest ways of understanding him—with even a degree of compassion.

A man who does not know why he does what he does, who slams his head against the wall shouting that he's not an animal, is perhaps more to be pitied than despised.

Closing on an Uncertain Note
The film's ambiguity intensifies at the end. In segment 12, a biblical quotation appears: "So, for the second time, [the Pharisees] summoned the man who had been blind and said: 'Speak the truth before God. We know this fellow is a sinner.' 'Whether or not he is a sinner, I do not know,' the man replied. 'All I know is this: once I was blind and now I can see.'"

As this quotation emerges line by line, we are cued to relate it to the protagonist. Has Jake achieved some sort of enlightenment through his experiences? Several factors suggest not. Despite being a poor actor, he continues to perform literary recitals, trying to regain his public ("I'm the boss"). Furthermore, the speech he practices at the end is the famous "I could have been a contender" passage from *On the Waterfront*. In that film, a failed boxer blamed his brother for his lack of a chance to succeed. Is Jake now blaming Joey or someone else for his decline? Or is it possible that he has become aware enough of his faults to ironically recall a film in which the hero admits his mistakes?

After the biblical quotation, there appears Scorsese's dedication of the film: "Remembering Haig R. Manoogian, teacher, May 23, 1916–May 26, 1980, with love and resolution, Marty." Now the biblical quotation may apply to Scorsese, also from the tough Italian neighborhoods of New York. Were it not for people like this teacher, he might have ended up somewhat like Jake. And perhaps the film professor, who helped him "to see," enabled Scorsese to present Jake with a mixture of detachment and sympathy. Like the two taglines at the close of *Do The Right Thing*, these final inscriptions invite us to weigh alternative interpretations of the action we've seen.

As a cinema student, Scorsese was well aware of innovative foreign films such as *Breathless* and *Tokyo Story*, so it's not surprising that his own work invites a range of interpretations. The film's ending places *Raging Bull* in a tradition of Hollywood films, such as *Citizen Kane*, that keep us at some distance from their protagonist so that we can judge him objectively. Like *Kane*, Scorsese's film avoids complete closure and opts for a degree of ambiguity, a denial of either/or answers. This ambiguity can render the film's ideology equivocal, generating contrasting and even conflicting implicit meanings.

> "I was fascinated by the self-destructive side of Jake La Motta's character, by his very basic emotions. What could be more basic than making a living by hitting another person on the head until one of you falls or stops? . . . . I put everything I knew and felt into that film, and I thought it would be the end of my career. It was what I call a kamikaze way of making movies: pour everything in, then forget about it and go find another way of life."
> —Martin Scorsese, director

learn what counts as a good performance. A tradition, in effect, favors certain creative choices over others.

One of the best examples of a filmmaking tradition is American studio cinema, so at various points in the chapter we'll examine how that tradition emerged and changed. In many respects, the Hollywood tradition influenced filmmaking around the world. A more limited tradition is that of Hong Kong action cinema of the 1980s and 1990s. That too, as we'll see, proved quite influential.

Traditions nudge a filmmaker toward certain choices and away from others. But sometimes filmmakers want to explore those others. In instances like these, we get the shorter-lived trends we call *movements*. In a movement, filmmakers typically operate within a common production structure and share certain assumptions about filmmaking. Above all, they favor a common approach to form, style, and theme that sets them somewhat apart from the usual practices. They innovate. Movements, then, are *un*traditional in some ways. They press filmmakers to make unusual formal and stylistic choices.

Sometimes the filmmakers in a movement know one another well and respond to one another's projects. This situation occurred with the Soviet Montage filmmakers of the 1920s, the Surrealists of the period, and the French New Wave of the 1950s–1960s. Here we find young people cooperating and competing because they wanted to explore some new ideas about what cinema could be. To clarify those ideas, they often wrote books and articles. Other movements are more diffuse, with unconnected filmmakers gravitating toward a common approach to form and style.

Most movements don't last more than a few years, but they can exercise a far-reaching effect. Some movements of the silent and early sound era have affected filmmaking for decades afterward. As we'll see, many movements have been selectively absorbed into broader traditions, particularly Hollywood's. The films of our time reenact creative decisions made by filmmakers in the past.

You should already have a sense of this, because our examples from both recent films and older ones show that today's films often accept or rework choices that were made in much earlier work. In several sections that follow, we mention how some contemporary filmmakers have found inspiration in the choices favored by film movements.

Because we're exploring historical contexts, we'll go beyond noting stylistic and formal qualities. For each tradition and movement, we'll point to relevant factors that affect the filmmakers' options—factors such as the state of the industry, artistic theories held by the filmmakers themselves, technological features, and cultural and economic forces. These factors help explain how a particular trend began and developed. This material will also provide a context for particular films we've already discussed. For example, we introduced you to Georges Méliès in Chapter 4 and Louis Lumière in Chapter 5. In the previous chapter, we analyzed a Soviet Montage film (*The Man with a Movie Camera*) and a French New Wave one (*Breathless*). Now you have a chance to see this work in a broader context.

In the sections that follow, we haven't tried to characterize other important traditions, such as that of Japanese cinema, or other movements, such as French populist cinema of the 1930s and Brazil's Cinema Nôvo of the early 1960s. Readers interested in knowing more can consult our *Film History: An Introduction*. Here we simply trace how certain possibilities of film form and style were explored in a few typical and well-known historical traditions and movements. The first section sets the stage for them by examining the origins of cinema itself.

Early Cinema (1893–1903)

In Chapter 1, we saw that film is a technology-driven medium. To create the illusion of movement, still pictures must appear in rapid succession. To prepare them and display them at the right rate, certain technologies are necessary.

Photography and Cinema

Most basically, there must be a way of recording a long series of images on some sort of support. In principle, one could simply draw a string of images on a strip of paper or a disc. But photography offered the cheapest and most efficient way to generate the thousands of images needed for a reasonably lengthy show. Thus the invention of photography in 1826 launched a series of discoveries that made cinema possible.

Early photographs required lengthy exposures (initially hours, later minutes) for a single image; this made photographed motion pictures, which need 12 or more frames per second, impossible. Faster exposures, of about 1/25th of a second, became possible by the 1870s, but only on glass plates. Glass plates weren't usable for motion pictures since there was no practical way to move them through a camera or projector. In 1878, Eadweard Muybridge, an American photographer, did make a series of photographs of a running horse by using a series of cameras with glass plate film and fast exposure, but he was primarily interested in freezing phases of an action, not re-creating the movement by projecting the images in succession.

In 1882, another scientist interested in analyzing animal movement, the Frenchman Étienne-Jules Marey, invented a camera that recorded 12 separate images on the edge of a revolving disc of film on glass. This constituted a step toward the motion picture camera. In 1888, Marey built the first camera to use a strip of flexible film, this time on paper. Again, the purpose was only to break down movement into a series of stills, and the movements photographed lasted a second or less. In 1889, George Eastman introduced a crude flexible film base, celluloid. After this base was improved and camera mechanisms had been devised to draw the film past the lens and expose it to light, the creation of long strips of frames became possible.

Projectors had existed for many years and had been used to show slides and shadow entertainments. These magic lanterns were modified by the addition of shutters, cranks, and other devices to become early motion picture projectors.

One final device was needed if films were to be projected. Since the film stops briefly while the light shines through each individual frame, there had to be a mechanism to create an *intermittent* motion of the film. Marey used a Maltese cross gear on his 1888 camera, and this became a standard part of early cameras and projectors.

A flexible and transparent film base, a fast exposure time, a mechanism to pull the film through the camera, an intermittent device to stop the film, and a shutter to block off light—all these innovations had been achieved by the early 1890s. After several years, inventors working independently in many countries had developed film cameras and projection devices. The two most important firms were the Edison Manufacturing Company in America, owned by inventor Thomas A. Edison, and Lumière Frères in France, the family firm of Louis and Auguste Lumière.

Edison vs. Lumière

By 1893, Thomas A. Edison's assistant, W. K. L. Dickson, had developed a camera that made short 35mm films. Interested in exploiting these films as a novelty, Edison hoped to combine them with his phonograph to show sound movies. He had Dickson develop a peep-show machine, the *Kinetoscope* (**12.7**), to display these films to individual viewers.

But Edison believed that movies were a passing fad, so he didn't develop a system to project films onto a screen. This task was left to the Lumière brothers. They invented their own camera independently; it exposed a short roll of 35mm film and also served as a projector (**12.8**). On December 28, 1895, the Lumière brothers presented motion pictures on a screen, at the Grand Café in Paris.

There had been several earlier public screenings, but the Lumières found the most practical method for projecting films, and their format largely determined the direction in which the new medium developed. Edison was obliged to follow their example, abandoning the Kinetoscope and creating his own production company to make films for public projection.

CONNECT TO THE BLOG
www.davidbordwell.net/blog

Early cinema was influenced by other media of its day, including narrative painting. We suggest some similarities in "Professor sees more parallels between things, other things."

12.7–12.9 Alternative approaches to early filmmaking. Edison's Kinetoscope threaded film in a continuous loop around a series of bobbins (12.7). The film was watched by one viewer at a time. The Lumière brothers aimed for public screenings, so they put a magic-lantern projector behind their camera so the images could be displayed to several viewers (12.8). In Edison's rotating film studio, the Black Maria, a hinged central portion of the roof swung open for filming (12.9).

12.7

12.8

12.9

> "In conjuring you work under the attentive gaze of the public, who never fail to spot a suspicious movement. You are alone, their eyes never leave you. Failure would not be tolerated. . . . While in the cinema . . . you can do your confecting quietly, far from those profane gazes, and you can do things thirty-six times if necessary until they are right. This allows you to travel further in the domain of the marvellous."
>
> —George Méliès, magician and filmmaker

Early Form and Style

The first films usually consisted of a single shot framing an action, usually at long-shot distance. In the first film studio, Edison's Black Maria **(12.9),** vaudeville entertainers, famous sports figures, and celebrities such as Annie Oakley performed for the camera. A hinged portion of the roof opened to admit a patch of sunlight, and the entire building turned on a circular rail (visible in 12.9) to follow the sun's motion. The Lumières, however, took their cameras out to parks, gardens, beaches, and other public places to film everyday activities or news events, as in their *Arrival of a Train at La Ciotat* (5.64).

Until about 1903, most films showed scenic places or noteworthy events, so these can be considered early documentaries. The Lumières sent camera operators all over the world to photograph important events and exotic locales. Staged narratives, brief skits or gags, were also popular. Edison's staff played out comic scenes, such as one copyrighted 1893 in which a drunken man struggles briefly with a policeman. The Lumières made a popular short, *L'Arroseur arrosé* (*The Waterer Watered*, 1895), also a comic scene, in which a boy tricks a gardener into squirting himself with a hose (4.8).

The earliest films may look crude to us today. This is partly because we seldom see good copies. In properly preserved prints, shown at the right projection speed, the films have a photographic richness that has seldom been equaled since. But because they were so short—before 1905, running only a few minutes—the first films couldn't develop complex stories or rhetorical arguments. Relying on unusual events, cute animals, and other brief attractions, they look forward to the amateur videos that show up on YouTube today (**12.10**). Early films have inspired avant-garde filmmakers to explore movement and abstract photographic qualities (**12.11**).

Méliès, Magic, and Fictional Narrative

In 1896, Georges Méliès built his own camera, based on a projector he had bought. His first films resembled the Lumières' shots of everyday activities. But as we have seen (pp. 113–114), Méliès was a stage magician, and he discovered the possibilities of simple special effects. In 1897, Méliès built his own studio, filled with flats and trapdoors. These allowed him to control his effects very precisely (**12.12**).

Méliès built elaborate settings to create fantasy worlds within which his magical transformations could occur. As we've already seen, this care in manipulating setting, lighting, costume, and staging made Méliès the first master of mise-en-scène (4.3–4.6). He was also an important innovator in editing. For one thing, he found that he could create magical transformations by stopping the camera, adjusting elements in the scene, and then resuming filming. Inspecting the original material, historians have found that Méliès trimmed a few frames at each special effect. Stopping and restarting the camera created light bursts on the first few frames, and these had to be snipped out. Moreover, Méliès progressed to longer narratives, with each scene played out in a single camera position, and he used cuts to link them. The most famous of these was *A Trip to the Moon* (1902). Méliès's Star Film company was associated with magic tricks and fairy stories, but it turned out an astonishing variety of films, including scenes from the Bible and a series based on the Dreyfus case. The dazzling special effects, the impressive settings and costumes, and the expansive fantasies and historical narratives made Méliès's films popular and widely imitated. They still exercise a powerful hold, having been painstakingly collected and restored, released on DVD, and given a central role in Martin Scorsese's *Hugo* (2011), which pays homage to Méliès by restaging some of the films.

The work of Lumière, Méliès, and other early filmmakers gained worldwide fame because films circulated freely from country to country. The French phonograph company Pathé Frères moved into filmmaking from 1901 on, establishing production and distribution branches in many countries. Soon Pathé was the largest film concern in the world, a position it retained until 1914, when the beginning of World War I forced it to cut back. In England, several entrepreneurs managed to invent or obtain equipment and made scenics, narratives, and trick films from 1895 into the early years of the 20th century. Members of the Brighton School (primarily G. Albert Smith and James Williamson), as well as others such as Cecil Hepworth, shot their films on location or in simple open-air studios (as in **12.13**). Their innovative films circulated abroad and influenced other filmmakers. Pioneers in other countries invented or bought equipment and were soon making their own films of everyday scenes or fantasy transformations.

As films became longer, narrative form became the most prominent type of filmmaking in the commercial industry, and the popularity of cinema continued to grow. French, Italian, and American films ruled world markets. Later, World War I was to restrict the international flow of films, and Hollywood emerged as the dominant

12.10

12.11

12.10–12.11 Early film and later interests. A Lumière film from 1900, *La petite fille et son chat* (*The Little Girl and Her Cat*), centers on a perennial attraction of today's online videos (12.10). In *Tom, Tom the Piper's Son* (1969), avant-garde filmmaker Ken Jacobs uses an optical printer to dissect and stylize a 1905 film of the same name, creating what Jacobs calls "a dream within a dream" (12.11).

12.12

12.13

12.12–12.13 Early studio shooting. Unlike Edison's Black Maria, Méliès's studio was glass-sided, like a greenhouse, and admitted sunlight from many directions (12.12). G. Albert Smith's *Santa Claus* (1898) was filmed in the open air, with a false backdrop (12.13). It displays typical traits of the first fictional narratives: distant camera position, flat lighting, and a rear wall placed perpendicular to the camera lens.

CONNECT TO THE BLOG
www.davidbordwell.net/blog

Hollywood wasn't the only place where film form and style were developing in the 1910s. For an international survey of the important year 1913, see "Lucky '13," and for a look at alternatives to continuity editing, see "Looking different today?" We examine the work of two early French masters in "Capellani trionfante" and "How to watch *Fantômas,* and why."

> The cinema knows so well how to tell a story that perhaps there is an impression that it has always known how."
> —André Gaudreault, film historian

industrial force in film production. In some countries, filmmakers responded by creating movements that differed sharply from the look and feel of the American product.

The Development of the Classical Hollywood Cinema (1908–1927)

Edison, determined to make money from his invention, brought patent-violation suits against competing moviemaking firms. When he failed to stamp out his rivals, he allied with several of them in 1908 to establish the Motion Picture Patents Company (MPPC). Edison and the American Mutoscope and Biograph company were the only stockholders and patent owners. They licensed other members to make, distribute, and exhibit films, and they standardized film lengths at one reel (running about 15 minutes). But this move didn't eliminate the other production companies, who sprang up quickly. In 1912 the U.S. government sued the MPPC, and three years later it was declared a monopoly and forced to break up.

Hollywood and the Studio System of Production

At the same period, both MPPC companies and independents began to relocate from New York and Chicago to California. Los Angeles offered a climate that permitted shooting year-round, and a great variety of locations—mountains, ocean, desert, city. Soon Hollywood and other small towns on the outskirts of Los Angeles hosted film production.

Through the 1910s and 1920s, the smaller firms merged to form the large film corporations that still exist today. Famous Players joined with Jesse L. Lasky and then formed a distribution wing, Paramount. By the late 1920s, most of the major companies—MGM (a merger of Metro, Goldwyn, and Mayer), Fox Film Corporation (merged with 20th Century in 1935), Warner Bros., Universal, and Paramount—had been created. Though in competition with one another, the companies cooperated to some degree, because they realized that the demand for films was so great that no one firm could satisfy the market.

By the early 1920s, the American industry had created a structure that would continue for decades. A few large firms with individual artists under contract were supplemented by small independent producing companies. Within a company, filmmaking tasks were carefully divided among specialists, and each project was overseen by a producer, who kept an eye on budget and schedule. Thomas Ince, a major producer, pioneered the use of detailed shooting scripts and time sheets so that the shooting could be cost-efficient. The stages of production we surveyed in Chapter 1 (pp. 16–28) were systematized by the Hollywood companies of the late 1910s. This business model came to be known as the studio system. Aiming to turn out narrative films in large quantities, the American cinema became oriented toward narrative form.

Narrative Continuity: Early Prototypes

One of Edison's directors, Edwin S. Porter, made some of the first films to use principles of narrative continuity and development. Among these was *The Life of an American Fireman* (1903), which showed the race of the firefighters to rescue a mother and a child from a burning house. Although this film used several striking narrative elements (a fireman's premonition of the disaster, a series of shots of the horse-drawn engine racing to the house), the cutting presents an odd time scheme. We see the rescue of a mother and her child twice, from both inside and outside the house. Porter had not realized the possibility of intercutting the two locales to sustain simultaneous action.

In 1903, Porter made *The Great Train Robbery,* in some ways a prototype for the classical American film. Here the action develops with a linear time, space, and cause-effect logic. We follow each stage of the robbery **(12.14),** the pursuit, and the final defeat of the robbers. In 1905, Porter also created a simple parallel narrative in *The Kleptomaniac,* contrasting the fates of a rich woman and a starving woman who are both caught stealing.

British filmmakers were working along similar lines. Indeed, many historians now believe that Porter derived some of his editing techniques from films such as James Williamson's *Fire!* (1901) and G. A. Smith's *Mary Jane's Mishap* (1903). The most famous British film of this era was Lewin Fitzhamon's 1905 film *Rescued by Rover* (produced by a major British firm, Cecil Hepworth), which treated a kidnapping in a linear fashion similar to that of *The Great Train Robbery.* After the kidnapping, we see each stage of Rover's journey to find the child, his return to fetch the child's father, and their retracing of the route to the kidnapper's lair. All the shots make the geography of the action completely intelligible **(12.15, 12.16).**

In 1908, D. W. Griffith began his directing career. Over the next five years, he would make hundreds of one- and two-reelers (running about 15 and 30 minutes, respectively). These films created relatively complex plots in short spans. Griffith certainly didn't invent all the devices with which he has been credited, but he did give many techniques strong narrative motivation. For example, a few other filmmakers had used simple last-minute rescues with crosscutting between the rescuers and victims, but Griffith developed and popularized this technique (6.111–6.114). By the time he made *The Birth of a Nation* (1915) and *Intolerance* (1916), Griffith was creating lengthy sequences by cutting among several different locales.

Griffith made another creative choice that was unusual for the early 1910s: he concentrated on subtle changes in facial expression (4.33). To catch such nuances, he set up his camera closer to the action than did many of his contemporaries, framing his actors in medium long shot or medium shot.

Griffith's films were widely influential. In addition, his dynamic, rapid editing in the final chase scenes of *Intolerance* was to have a considerable impact on the Soviet Montage style of the 1920s. But he wasn't alone in refining technique. Supervising production at his company, Thomas Ince demanded tight narratives, with no digressions or loose ends, and his request for detailed shooting scripts favored breaking scenes up into several camera positions. Films made under Ince's control, such as *Civilization* (1915), *The Italian* (1915), and the Westerns of William S. Hart (p. 339), helped stabilize the emerging continuity conventions.

Cecil B. De Mille, a director who was to have a much longer career than Griffith and Ince, made several feature-length dramas and comedies. His *The Cheat* (1915) reflects important changes occurring in the studio style between 1914 and 1917.

12.14 An early effort at narrative continuity. The robbers in the telegraph office in *The Great Train Robbery*, preparing to board the train seen through the window. The train portion of the image is an early matte shot.

12.15

12.16

12.15–12.16 Matching screen direction. In *Rescued by Rover,* the heroic dog leads his master along a street from the right rear moving toward the left foreground (12.15). The pair is moving from right to left as they reach their destination (12.16).

CONNECT TO THE BLOG
www.davidbordwell.net/blog

A Spanish filmmaking student created a revealing video analyzing a 1912 Griffith Biograph short. We talk about the analysis and link to it in "A Variation on a Sunbeam."

12.17

12.18

12.17–12.18 **Narrative coherence.** The opening scene of *The Cheat* introduces the branding motif (12.17). It returns later when the villain brands the heroine as another item of property (12.18). Both use the "Rembrandt lighting" that made De Mille famous.

CONNECT TO THE BLOG
www.davidbordwell.net/blog

On two of the most important filmmakers of the early classical period, see our entries on William S. Hart in "Rio Jim, in discrete fragments," and Douglas Fairbanks in "His Majesty the American."

" That evening I tried to increase my knowledge of motion-picture technique by going to the movies. I sat with a stop watch and notebook and tried to estimate the number of cuts or scenes in a thousand-foot reel, the length of individual scenes, the distance of the subject from the camera, and various other technical details."

—King Vidor, director, recalling the night before he began directing his first film, c. 1912

During that period, the glass-roofed studios of the earlier period began to give way to studios dependent on artificial lighting rather than mixed daylight and electric lighting. *The Cheat* used spectacular effects of chiaroscuro, with only one or two bright sources of light and no fill light. According to legend, De Mille justified this effect to nervous exhibitors by calling it "Rembrandt lighting." This north lighting was to become part of the classical repertoire of lighting techniques.

Like many American films of the teens, *The Cheat* uses a linear pattern of narrative. The first scene **(12.17)** introduces the hard lighting but also quickly establishes the Japanese businessman as a ruthless collector of objects; we see him burning his brand onto a small statue. The initial action motivates a later scene in which the businessman brands the heroine, who has fallen into his power by borrowing money from him **(12.18).** *The Cheat* was one of several 1915 films that showed that Hollywood films were moving toward greater complexity in their storytelling.

The 180° system of staging, shooting, and editing (pp. 233–235) was developing as well. Eyeline matches became more common from 1910 on, and the match on action was in common use by 1916, appearing in such Douglas Fairbanks films as *The Americano* (1916) and *Wild and Woolly* (1917). Shot/reverse shot cutting became widespread as well, as seen in *The Cheat* (1915), Hart's Western *The Narrow Trail* (1917), and Griffith's *A Romance of Happy Valley* (1919).

Classical Form and Style in Place

By the early 1920s, the continuity system had become a standardized style that directors in the Hollywood studios used to create coherent, gripping storytelling. Screen direction was usually respected. A match on action could provide a cut to a closer view in a scene **(12.19, 12.20).** A conversation around a table would no longer be handled in a single frontal shot **(12.21–12.25).** When an awkward match might have resulted from the joining of two shots, the filmmakers could cover it by inserting a dialogue title.

Filmmakers conceived ways to handle large-scale narrative form as well. By 1923, Buster Keaton could construct a perfectly balanced plot for *Our Hospitality.* As we saw in Chapter 4, the action develops logically from the death of Willie McKay's father to Willie's final resolution of the feud. Along the way, motifs like the railroad tracks, water, and pistols are carefully motivated and ingeniously varied.

In only a decade or so, Hollywood cinema had developed into a sophisticated cinematic tradition. As we've indicated (p. 232), classical continuity became a kind of universal language of fictional moviemaking that's still in force today. Yet no sooner had the tradition crystallized than alternatives began to appear. Filmmakers

12.19

12.20

12.19–12.20 Smooth action matching in the early 1920s. In Fred Niblo's *The Three Musketeers* (1921), a long shot of the group (12.19) leads to a cut-in to the central character, played by Douglas Fairbanks (12.20).

12.21

12.22

12.23

12.24

12.25

12.21–12.25 Consistent eyelines around a table. In an establishing shot from *Are Parents People?* (Malcolm St. Clair, 1925), the daughter sits down at the table (12.21). In the medium shot she looks leftward toward her father (12.22). He responds to her by looking rightward in the reverse shot (12.23). The daughter then turns to look to the right at her mother (12.24). Her mother returns her gaze in reverse shot (12.25).

in other countries pushed in directions that American cinema had not explored. After examining these alternative movements, in the silent era, we'll return to consider the classical Hollywood cinema after the coming of sound.

CONNECT TO THE BLOG
www.davidbordwell.net/blog

For more on the emergence of Hollywood film style in the late 1910s, see "Happy birthday, classical cinema!"

German Expressionism (1919–1926)

The worldwide success of American films in the late 1910s and through the 1920s confronted filmmakers with a harsh choice. Should you try to imitate Hollywood? The big budgets of the American studios were hard to match in the aftermath of a war that had devastated the European continent. Or should you try to offer a type of cinema markedly different from the Hollywood standard? Most filmmakers took the first option and adopted American techniques of lighting, staging, and editing. (Principles of story construction took longer to be adopted.) But a few filmmakers sought to be more original, and some of them formed movements that had an enduring effect on world cinema.

In 1914, although some impressive pictures had been made in Germany, the industry's output was relatively small. The nation's 2000 movie theaters were playing

12.26 The UFA historical epic.
Madame Dubarry: A crowd scene in the Tribunal of the French Revolution.

> **"**Everything is composition; any image whatsoever could be stopped on the screen and would be a marvellously balanced painting of forms and lights. Also, it is one of the films which leaves in our memories the clearest visions—precise and of a slightly static beauty. But even more than painting, it is animated architecture."
>
> —François Berge, French critic, on Fritz Lang's *The Nibelungen*

mostly French, American, Italian, and Danish films. When the war began, America and France banned German films from their screens immediately, but Germany couldn't afford to ban French and American films, for then the theaters would have had little to show.

To combat imported competition, as well as to create its own propaganda films, the German government began to support the film industry. In 1916, film imports were banned except from neutral Denmark. Production increased rapidly; from a dozen small companies in 1911, the number grew to 131 by 1918. But government policy encouraged these companies to band together into cartels.

The war was unpopular with many in Germany, and rebellious tendencies increased after the success of the Russian Revolution in 1917. To promote pro-war films, the government, the Deutsche Bank, and large industrial concerns combined several small film firms to create the large company UFA (short for Universum Film Aktiengesellschaft) in late 1917. Backed by these conservative interests, UFA was a move toward control of the German market and, its backers hoped, the postwar international market as well. With this huge financial backing, UFA was able to gather superb technicians and build the best-equipped studios in Europe.

In late 1918, with the end of the war, the need for overt militarist propaganda disappeared. But now German films were unwelcome abroad. Although mainstream dramas and comedies continued to be made, filmmakers concentrated on three genres. One was the adventure serial, featuring spy rings, clever detectives, and exotic settings. These films from America, Denmark, and France had proven internationally popular, but the German films failed overseas. Another genre consisted of a sex exploitation cycle, which dealt "educationally" with such topics as homosexuality and prostitution. UFA's third option was to create big-budget historical spectacles like those that Italy had made popular in the prewar period.

This strategy proved successful. Ernst Lubitsch's *Madame Dubarry* (1919; **12.26**), a historical epic of the French Revolution, broke down international opposition to German films. Although the French authorities treated it as propaganda, it proved extremely popular elsewhere and helped reopen the world market for local films. Other Lubitsch historical films were soon exported, and in 1923, he became the first German director to be hired by Hollywood.

A more unusual strategy of differentiation emerged at the same time. Despite UFA's expansion, some small companies remained independent. Among these was Erich Pommer's Decla (later Decla-Bioscop). In 1919, the firm undertook to produce an unconventional script by two unknowns, Carl Mayer and Hans Janowitz. These young writers wanted their story to be told in an unusually stylized way. The three designers assigned to the film—Hermann Warm, Walter Reimann, and Walter Röhrig—suggested that it be done in an Expressionist style. As an avant-garde movement, Expressionism had first been important in painting (starting about 1910) and had been quickly taken up in theater, then in literature and architecture. Now company officials consented to try it in the cinema, apparently believing that this might be a selling point in the international market. This belief was vindicated in 1920 when Decla's inexpensive film *The Cabinet of Dr. Caligari* (1920) created a sensation in Berlin and then in the United States, France, and other countries.

A few German directors made abstract films—for example, Viking Eggeling's *Diagonal-symphonie* (1923)—or Dada films influenced by the international art movement—such as Hans Richter's *Ghosts Before Breakfast* (1928). But thanks to the success of *Caligari* most filmmakers who wanted to explore new paths in form and style stayed within the industry. UFA, along with smaller companies, invested in Expressionist films because these could compete with those of America.

The first film of the movement, *Caligari,* is a powerful example of the Expressionist style. One of its designers, Warm, claimed, "The film image must become graphic art." With its extreme stylization, *Caligari* was like a moving Expressionist painting or woodcut print. In contrast to French Impressionism, which based its style primarily on cinematography and editing, German Expressionism depended heavily

12.27   **12.28**   **12.29**

12.27–12.29 Actors as part of setting. In Robert Wiene's *Genuine,* the bedroom is flamboyantly Expressionist. As the heroine leans backwards, she blends in with the curved, spiky shapes behind her (12.27). *The Cabinet of Dr. Caligari:* Dr. Caligari totters along a corridor that suggests a madman's vision of the world (12.28). When the hero arrives at Caligari's asylum, he steps into the center of a pattern of black-and-white lines that radiate across the floor and up the walls (12.29).

on mise-en-scene. Shapes are distorted and exaggerated to suggest emotional states. Actors often wear heavy makeup and move in jerky or slow, sinuous patterns. Most important, all of the elements of the mise-en-scene interact graphically to create an overall composition. We have already seen an example of this in 4.115, where the character Cesare collapses in a stylized forest, his body and outstretched arms echoing the shapes of the trees' trunks and branches. Characters do not simply exist within a setting but rather form visual elements that *merge with* the setting **(12.27).**

Such a departure from realism demands motivation, which *Caligari* provides through mental subjectivity. We see the world as the mad hero imagines it to be **(12.28).** This narrative function of the settings becomes explicit at one point, when the hero enters an asylum in his pursuit of Caligari. As he pauses to look around, the world of the film is literally a projection of the hero's mind **(12.29).** Later, as Expressionism became an accepted style, filmmakers didn't motivate the style as the subjective state of mad characters. Instead, genre conventions were invoked. Expressionist design could create stylized imagery for fantasy and horror stories, as with *Waxworks* (1924) and *Nosferatu* (1922; see 9.17). *The Nibelungen* (1923–1924) showed that abstract patterning of costume, sets, and crowds could be applied to historical epics as well. All these genres depended greatly on their set designers. In the German studios, a film's designer received a relatively high salary and was often featured in publicity.

By the mid-1920s, German films were widely regarded as among the best in the world. UFA's rich studio facilities attracted foreign filmmakers, including the young Alfred Hitchcock. During the 1920s, Germany coproduced many films with companies in other countries, thus helping to spread its stylistic influence abroad. The rampant inflation of the early 1920s actually favored Expressionist filmmaking, partly by making it easy for exporters to sell German films cheaply abroad. Inflation discouraged imports as well, because the tumbling exchange rate of the mark made foreign purchases too expensive.

In 1924, the U.S. Dawes Plan helped to stabilize the German economy, and foreign films came in more frequently, offering a degree of competition unknown in Germany for nearly a decade. Expressionist film budgets, meanwhile, were climbing. The last major films of the movement, F. W. Murnau's *Faust* (1926) and Fritz Lang's *Metropolis* (1927; see **12.30**), were costly epics that drove UFA deeper into financial difficulty, leading Erich Pommer to quit and try his luck briefly in America. Other personnel were lured away to Hollywood as well. Trying to counter the stiffer competition, the Germans began to imitate the American product. The resulting films, though sometimes impressive, diluted the unique qualities of the Expressionist style.

CONNECT TO THE BLOG
www.davidbordwell.net/blog

For many years, incomplete versions of *Metropolis* circulated. In 2008 nearly all the long-lost footage was finally discovered. We tell the story and assess how the new scenes changed the film in "*Metropolis* unbound."

12.30

12.31

12.30–12.31 Lang sustains Expressionism. *Metropolis* contained many large, Expressionistic sets, including this garden, with pillars that appear to be made of melting clay (12.30). In *M*, reflections and a display of knives in a shop window create a semi-abstract composition that mirrors the murderer's obsession (12.31).

12.32 Expressionism for horror-comedy. Joe Dante's episode of *Twilight Zone: The Movie* (1983) refers to the contorted décor of *Caligari* (12.28).

By 1927, Expressionism as a movement had died out. But as Georges Sadoul has pointed out, an expressionist (spelled with a lowercase "e" to distinguish it from the Expressionist movement proper) tradition lingered on in many of the German films of the late 1920s and even into such 1930s films as Fritz Lang's *M* (1930; see **12.31**) and *Testament of Dr. Mabuse* (1932). Some set designers came to the United States and applied their techniques there. Hollywood horror and crime films sometimes displayed expressionist tendencies in their settings and lighting. Although the movement lasted only about seven years, expressionism has never entirely died out as one approach to film style, and even today directors may refer to the original German version of it **(12.32).**

French Impressionism and Surrealism (1918–1930)

During the silent era, a number of film movements in France posed major alternatives to the emerging Hollywood tradition. Some of these alternatives, such as abstract cinema and Dada filmmaking, weren't specifically French and constituted instead a part of the growing international avant-garde. But two alternatives to the American mode remained quite localized.

Impressionism was an avant-garde style that operated largely within the film industry. Most of the Impressionist filmmakers started out working for major French companies, and some of their avant-garde works proved financially successful. In the mid-1920s, most formed their own independent companies but remained within the mainstream commercial industry by renting studio facilities and releasing their films through established firms. The other alternative movement, Surrealism, lay largely outside the film industry. Allied with the Surrealist movement in other arts, these filmmakers relied on their own means and private patronage. France in the 1920s offers a striking instance of how different film movements may flourish in the same time and place.

Impressionism

World War I struck a serious blow to the French film industry. Personnel were conscripted, studios were shifted to wartime uses, and much export was halted. The two major firms, Pathé Frères and Léon Gaumont, also controlled circuits of theaters and they needed to fill vacant screens. As a result, in 1915 American films began to flood into France. Represented by De Mille's *The Cheat* and films featuring Douglas Fairbanks, Charlie Chaplin, William S. Hart, and other popular stars, the Hollywood cinema dominated the market by the end of 1917. After the war, French filmmaking never fully recovered. The industry tried in several ways to recapture the audience, mostly through imitation of Hollywood production methods and genres. Alternatively, there emerged a movement consisting of younger directors: Abel Gance, Louis Delluc, Germaine Dulac, Marcel L'Herbier, and Jean Epstein.

Films and Feelings The previous generation had regarded filmmaking as a commercial craft, but the younger filmmakers wrote essays proclaiming cinema to be an art comparable to poetry, painting, and music. Astonished by the verve and energy of the American cinema, the young theorists compared Chaplin to a ballet dancer and the films of Hart to *The Song of Roland*. Cinema should, the young filmmakers argued, be what other arts were: a vehicle for feelings. Gance, Delluc, Dulac, L'Herbier, Epstein, and other, more tangential members of the movement sought to put this idea into practice as filmmakers. Between 1918 and 1928, the younger directors experimented with cinema in ways that posed an alternative to the emerging Hollywood tradition.

The movement gained the name "Impressionist" because filmmakers wanted to give their narration subjective depth, to capture the momentary impressions that flit through a character's mind. Believing that cinema should project heightened and subtle emotional states, the directors concentrated on intimate psychological stories. They favored situations with a small number of characters, often caught up in a love triangle, as in Gance's *La Dixième symphonie* (1918), Delluc's *L'Inondation* (1924), and Epstein's *Coeur fidèle* (1923) and *La Belle nivernaise* (1923). These charged situations created fleeting moods and shifting sensations.

An Impressionist film replaces external action with an exploration of the characters' inner life. Flashbacks depict memories; sometimes the bulk of a film will be one flashback or a series of them. The films register characters' dreams, fantasies, and mental states. Dulac's *The Smiling Mme. Beudet* (1923) consists almost entirely of the main character's imaginary escape from a dull marriage. Despite its epic length (over five hours), Gance's *La Roue* (1922) rests essentially on the erotic relations among only four people, and the director seeks to trace the development of each character's feelings in great detail.

Subjective Style The movement earned its name as well for its distinctive film style. *The Cabinet of Dr. Caligari* had evoked its protagonist's mental states through mise-en-scene, but the French relied more on cinematography and editing. In Impressionist films, optical effects such as superimpositions imply characters' thoughts and moods **(12.33)**. In *La Roue,* the image of Norma is laid over the smoke from a locomotive, representing the fantasy of the engine driver, who is in love with her. Going beyond mental subjectivity, the filmmakers try to register characters' optical impressions as well. POV cutting is common, and so are shots suggesting altered states of perception. When a character in an Impressionist film gets drunk or dizzy, that experience is rendered in vertiginous camera movements, or slow motion, or distorted or filtered shots **(12.34)**.

> "Another period arrived, that of the psychological and impressionist film. It would seem stupid to place a character in a given situation without penetrating into the secret realm of his inner life, and the actor's performance is explained by the play of thoughts and of visualized sensations."
> —Germaine Dulac, director

12.33

12.34

12.33, 12.34 Cinematography for subjectivity. In *Coeur fidèle,* the barmaid looks out a window, and a superimposition of the flotsam of the waterfront conveys her dejection at working in a dockside tavern (12.33). In *El Dorado,* a man's tipsiness in a cabaret is conveyed by means of a curved mirror that stretches his body sideways (12.34).

CONNECT TO THE BLOG
www.davidbordwell.net/blog

We consider the heritage of Expressionism and Impressionism in the work of Martin Scorsese, including *Taxi Driver* and *Shutter Island*, in "Scorsese, 'pressionist."

The Impressionists also experimented with pronounced rhythmic editing to suggest the pace of an experience as a character feels it, moment by moment. During scenes of violence or emotional turmoil, the rhythm accelerates—the shots get shorter and shorter, building to a climax, sometimes with images only a few frames long. In *Coeur fidèle,* lovers at a fair ride in whirling swings, and Epstein presents their giddiness in a series of shots 4 frames, then 2 frames, long. In *La Roue,* a train crash is presented in accelerating shots ranging from 13 frames down to 2, and a man's last thoughts before he falls from a cliff are rendered in a hail of single-frame shots. We've seen this pattern of accelerated editing in *The Birds* (p. 224), but these passages from *La Roue* are the first known instances of it.

Impressionist form and style put demands on film technology. Abel Gance, the boldest innovator in this respect, used his epic *Napoléon* (1927) as a chance to try new lenses (even a 275mm telephoto), multiple frame images (called Polyvision), and widescreen ratio (the celebrated triptychs; see 5.70). Impressionists were especially interested in frame mobility. After all, if the camera was to represent a character's eyes, it should be able to move with the ease of a person. Impressionists strapped their cameras to cars, carousels, and locomotives. For Gance's *Napoléon,* the camera manufacturer Debrie perfected a handheld model that let the operator move on roller skates. Gance lashed the machine to wheels, cables, pendulums, and bobsleds. In *L'Argent* (1928), L'Herbier sent his camera gliding through huge rooms and plummeting down from the dome of the Paris stock exchange **(12.35).**

Such innovations had given French filmmakers the hope that their films could be as popular as Hollywood's product. Some Impressionist films did appeal to the French public, but foreign audiences weren't attracted. Moreover, although production costs were rising, Impressionists such as Gance and L'Herbier became more free-spending. As a result, filmmakers' companies either went out of business or were absorbed by the big firms. Two behemoth productions of the decade, *Napoléon* and *L'Argent,* failed and were reedited by the producers; they were among the last Impressionist films released. With the arrival of the sound film, the French film industry tightened its belt and had no money to risk on experiments.

Impressionism as a distinct movement may be said to have ceased by 1929. But the filmmakers' explorations of psychological narrative and subjective style became a legacy to future generations. These innovations continued in the work of Alfred Hitchcock and Maya Deren, in Hollywood montage sequences, and in certain American genres and styles (the horror film, film noir). Even today, when a director wants to convey what a character is sensing or feeling in some abnormal state of mind, Impressionist techniques of camerawork and editing—blurred imagery, superimposition, slow motion, accelerating cutting—prove to be common choices **(12.36**; see also 3.42, from *The Road Warrior*).

Surrealism

The French Impressionist filmmakers worked within the commercial film industry, but Surrealist filmmakers relied on private patronage and screened their work in small artists' gatherings. Not surprisingly, Surrealist cinema was a more radical movement, producing films that would perplex and shock ordinary audiences.

Surrealist cinema was directly linked to Surrealism in literature and painting. According to its spokesperson, André Breton, "Surrealism [was] based on the belief in the superior reality of certain forms of association, heretofore neglected, in the omnipotence of dreams, in the undirected play of thought." The Impressionist filmmakers sought to catch the flow of consciousness as a tumble of sensations and memories. But Surrealist art, influenced by Freudian psychology, wanted to go deeper. Surrealists wanted to plumb the hidden currents of the unconscious.

Automatic writing and painting, the search for bizarre or evocative imagery, the deliberate avoidance of rationally explicable form or style: these became features of

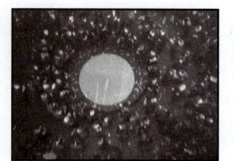

12.35 The dizzying crane shot. In *L'Argent,* the camera drops toward the floor of the stock exchange in an effort to convey the traders's frenzied excitement.

12.36 Camerawork for hallucination. Impressionists would probably have admired the opening of *Apocalypse Now*. Superimpositions, striking compositions, and the mixing of sounds and images of battle with the whirring of the overhead fan—all take us into Willard's mind.

Surrealism as it developed in the period 1924–1929. From the start, the Surrealists were attracted to the cinema, especially films that presented untamed desire or the fantastic and marvelous. They admired slapstick comedies, *Nosferatu,* and serials about mysterious super-criminals. In due time, painters such as Man Ray and Salvador Dalí and writers such as Antonin Artaud began dabbling in cinema, while the young Spaniard Luis Buñuel, drawn to Surrealism, became its most famous filmmaker.

Hollywood filmmakers, the Expressionists, and the Impressionists were all committed to storytelling, even if their methods differed. But Surrealist cinema was anti-narrative, attacking causality and coherence. If rationality is to be fought, connections among events must be dissolved, as in *The Seashell and the Clergyman* (1928—scripted by Artaud, filmed by the Impressionist Germaine Dulac (**12.37**). In Dalí and Buñuel's *Un Chien andalou (An Andalusian Dog,* 1928), the hero drags two pianos, stuffed with dead donkeys, across a parlor. In Buñuel's *L'Age d'or* (1930), a woman begins obsessively sucking the toes of a statue.

But even while banishing causality, many Surrealist films tease us to find it. It becomes as evasive as in a dream. Instead, we find events juxtaposed for their disturbing effect. The hero gratuitously shoots a child (*L'Age d'or*), a woman closes her eyes only to reveal eyes painted on her eyelids (Ray's *Emak Bakia,* 1927), and—most horrifying of all—a man strops a razor and deliberately slits the eyeball of an unprotesting woman (**12.38**). An Impressionist film would motivate such events as a character's dreams or hallucinations, but in these films, character psychology can't be determined. Sexual desire and ecstasy, violence, blasphemy, and bizarre humor take the place of conventional narrative. The hope was that the free form of the film would arouse the deepest impulses of the viewer, even if those impulses were unsavory. Buñuel called *Un Chien andalou* "a passionate call to murder."

The style of Surrealist cinema is eclectic. Mise-en-scene is often influenced by Surrealist painting. The ants in *Un Chien andalou* come from Dalí's pictures; the pillars and city squares of *The Seashell and the Clergyman* hark back to the Italian painter Giorgio de Chirico. Surrealist editing is an amalgam of some Impressionist devices (many dissolves and superimpositions) and some devices of the dominant cinema. The shocking eyeball slitting at the start of *Un Chien andalou* relies on continuity editing as well as the Kuleshov effect. However, discontinuous editing is also commonly used to fracture any coherence of space and time. In *Un Chien*

12.37

12.38

12.37–12.38 Surrealists' irrational imagery. *The Seashell and the Clergyman:* the clergyman's distorted view of a threatening military officer, inexplicably dressed in baby's clothes (12.37). A shocking eye-slitting scene opens *Un Chien andalou* (12.38).

12.39 **Surrealism's heritage.** The mysterious ear, discolored and covered with ants, discovered at the opening of *Blue Velvet* (1986) recalls the heritage of *Un Chien andalou*.

andalou, a woman locks a man out of a room only to turn and find him inexplicably behind her. On the whole, Surrealist film style refused to define itself by any particular techniques, since that would order and rationalize what had to be an "undirected play of thought."

The fortunes of Surrealist cinema shifted with changes in the art movement as a whole. By late 1929, when Breton joined the Communist Party, Surrealists were embroiled in internal dissension about whether communism was a political equivalent of Surrealism. Buñuel left France for a brief stay in Hollywood and then returned to Spain. The chief patron of Surrealist filmmaking, the Vicomte de Noailles, supported Jean Vigo's *Zéro de Conduite* (1933), a film of Surrealist ambitions, but then stopped sponsoring the avant-garde. Thus, as a unified movement, French Surrealism was no longer viable after 1930. Individual Surrealists continued to work, however. The most famous was Buñuel, who continued to work in his own brand of the Surrealist style for 50 years, in works such as *Belle de Jour* (1967) and *The Discreet Charm of the Bourgeoisie* (1972). He was followed by other filmmakers, including the avant-gardist Kenneth Anger. Similarly, David Lynch's *Blue Velvet, Lost Highway,* and *Mulholland Dr.* owe a good deal to Breton's demand to plumb the unconscious mind "in the absence of any control exercised by reason, and beyond any aesthetic and moral preoccupation" **(12.39).**

Soviet Montage (1924–1930)

Few artists were as determined to innovate as the men and women who came of age during the Russian Revolution of October 1917. In all the arts, the call went out for a new way of seeing, and the creation of an art that would reflect new social ideals. The film world was galvanized by young people who scorned the current customs. They wanted to forge a cinema that would be revolutionary in subject, theme, form, and style. They wanted to provide filmmakers with brand-new tools.

Most Russian films made before the revolution were somber, slow-paced melodramas featuring bravura performances by popular stars **(12.40).** The dominant style favored long takes and intricate staging. One master of the period was Yevgenii Bauer, who brought pictorial elegance to tales of flirtation and betrayal among the upper classes. (See 4.129–4.132.) The young filmmakers, fascinated by continuity editing and the extroverted, athletic performance style in westerns and comedies, saw the Hollywood style as the cutting-edge approach that would sweep away the previous generation's work. But the aspiring directors didn't simply copy the American methods. They pushed them to the limit, in the process creating a new and distinctive set of filmmaking tools.

Artists and the State

The government aimed to remake all sectors of life. At first, policy makers tried to nationalize all private property. In response, film companies simply refused to supply films to theaters operating under the government control. In July 1918, the State Commission of Education put strict controls on the existing supplies of raw film stock. As a result, producers began hoarding their stock; the largest firms took all the equipment they could and fled to other countries. Some companies made films commissioned by the government, while hoping that the Reds would lose the Civil War and that things would return to pre-Revolutionary conditions.

CONNECT TO THE BLOG
www.davidbordwell.net/blog

We analyze Bauer's masterful staging in his upper-class melodramas in "Watching movies very, very slowly."

12.40 **The tsarist style.** In Yakov Protazanov's 1916 *The Queen of Spades,* the gambling-addicted hero, played by the popular Ivan Mozhukin, imagines himself winning at cards, with his vision superimposed at the right.

Like other Soviet industries, film production and distribution took years to build up a substantial output. To fill the void in theaters, American films, particularly those of D. W. Griffith, Douglas Fairbanks, and Mary Pickford, kept circulating. They became a tremendous influence on young filmmakers.

Faced with little equipment and difficult living conditions, a few young filmmakers made tentative moves that would result in the development of a national cinema movement. Dziga Vertov began working on documentary footage of the war; at age 20, he was placed in charge of all newsreels. Lev Kuleshov, also in his early 20s, was teaching in the newly founded State School on Cinema Art. There he performed a series of experiments by editing footage from different sources into a whole that creates an impression of continuity (pp. 227–228). Kuleshov, perhaps the most conservative of the young Soviet filmmakers, tried to systematize principles of editing based on the emerging Hollywood style. Even before they were able to make films, Kuleshov and his young pupils were working at the first film school in the world and writing theoretical essays on the new art form. This grounding in theory would be the basis of the Montage style.

Other young people moved into cinema, often from scientific backgrounds. The engineer Sergei Eisenstein, after work during the Civil War, began directing plays in a workers' theater in Moscow. For one 1923 production he made a short film, and soon he was directing a feature. Vsevolod Pudovkin, trained in chemistry, made his acting debut in a play presented by Kuleshov's State Film School. He had been inspired to go into filmmaking by seeing Griffith's *Intolerance,* and he would make his first feature a few years later. Some tsarist-era directors, Protozanov, for example, would continue to work under the Soviet regime, but the breakthroughs came from newcomers.

NEP Cinema

Circumstances favored their rise. By 1921, the country was facing tremendous problems, not least a widespread famine. To facilitate the production and distribution of goods, Lenin instituted the New Economic Policy (NEP), which for several years permitted private management of business and a measure of free enterprise. For film, the NEP meant a sudden reappearance of film stock and equipment. Slowly, Soviet production began to grow as private firms made more films.

"Of all the arts, for us the cinema is the most important," Lenin stated in 1922. Since Lenin saw film as a powerful tool for education, the first films encouraged by the government were documentaries such as Vertov's newsreel series *Kino-Pravda.* Soviet fictional films were being made from 1917 on, but it was not until 1923 that a Georgian feature, *Red Imps,* became the first Soviet film to compete successfully with the foreign films dominating local screens. And not until 1927 did the industry's income from its own films top that of the films it imported.

The NEP brought forth a burst of fresh, daring films from the youngsters. From Kuleshov's class at the State Film School came *The Extraordinary Adventures of Mr. West in the Land of the Bolsheviks* (1924; **12.41**). This satiric comedy, along with Kuleshov's next project, *The Death Ray* (1925), were stunningly different from the tsarist cinema—fast-paced, full of stunts, chases, and fights, and cut with the freedom of an American film. Kuleshov showed that a Soviet film could generate something as entertaining as the Hollywood product. Eisenstein's first feature, *Strike* (1925) mixed cartoonish satire with violent action, including a workers' massacre intercut with the slaughter of a bull. Although it wasn't seen outside the USSR until decades later, historians now consider it the first full-blown exercise in the Montage style. Eisenstein's next film, *The Battleship Potemkin* (1925), came to epitomize the new movement. Stupendously successful abroad, it was praised as a masterpiece. Over the next few years, as silent cinema was coming to an end, Eisenstein, Pudovkin, Vertov, Alexander Dovzhenko, and other directors created a series of films that became classics.

> " Everyone who has had in his hands a piece of film to be edited knows by experience how neutral it remains, even though a part of a planned sequence, until it is joined with another piece, when it suddenly acquires and conveys a sharper and quite different meaning than that planned for it at the time of filming."
> —Sergei Eisenstein, director

12.41 Soviet satire. *The Extraordinary Adventures of Mr. West in the Land of the Bolsheviks:* a gang of thieves terrifies the naive American, Mr. West, by presenting him with clichéd caricatures of fierce Soviet revolutionaries.

The Priority of Editing

What was the basis of the Montage movement? In their writings and films, these directors championed editing over all other film techniques. This was a clear attack on the long-take style that had dominated earlier Russian film. Bauer and other tsarist directors used analytical editing occasionally, but usually to accentuate an actor's face after a sustained long shot, the better to register the nuances of performance. Inspired by viewings of American and French Impressionist films, the young Soviet directors declared that a film's power arose not from the delicate performances of expert actors, but from the combination of shots. Through editing, they maintained, two shots give birth to a feeling or idea not present in either one. This is the insight behind Kuleshov's experiments. If you intercut different images with impassive shots of a man's face, or show a couple looking offscreen and then a shot of a building, the editing is what endows the performance with meaning. Here the Soviets went beyond their Hollywood peers, who counted on star actors to help carry the story.

"Montage," the Russian word for cutting, seemed to show the way forward for modern cinema. But not all of the young theoreticians agreed on exactly what the Montage approach to editing should be. Pudovkin, for example, believed that shots were like bricks, to be joined together to build a sequence. Eisenstein disagreed, saying that the maximum effect would be gained if the shots did not fit together perfectly, if they created a jolt for the spectator. Many filmmakers tried out discontinuities of this sort (**12.42**). Eisenstein also favored juxtaposing shots to create an abstract theme, as we've already seen with his use of conceptual editing in *October* (pp. 261–264). Vertov disagreed with both theorists. He disapproved of the fiction film altogether and promoted montage-based documentary cinema, as in *The Man with a Movie Camera* (pp. 429–433).

However the filmmakers might have disagreed in debate, they often converged in practice. Pudovkin's *Storm over Asia* makes use of conceptual editing similar to that of Eisenstein's *October*. Shots of a military officer and his wife being dressed in their accessories are intercut with shots of the preparation at the temple. Pudovkin's parallel montage points up the absurdity of both rituals (**12.43–12.46**). Elsewhere *Storm over Asia* employs many jump cuts, breaking spatial and temporal coherence for the sake of stirring the spectator's senses. American continuity style taught the Montagists the power of editing, but once they learned the lesson, they pushed the technique in radical directions that would have shocked Hollywood filmmakers.

The Montage movement went even farther beyond Hollywood in their approach to narrative. Soviet films tended to downplay character psychology as a trigger for plots; instead, social forces provided the major causes. Characters were interesting not as individuals but as examples of how large-scale processes affected people's lives. As a result, Soviet Montage films didn't always have a single protagonist. Social groups could form a collective hero, as in several of Eisenstein's films. In the *October* sequence (pp. 262–263), his editing shows how social groups, such as the soldiers at the front or the women and children on the breadlines, are victimized by brutal government policies.

In keeping with this downplaying of individual personalities, Soviet filmmakers often preferred to cast non-actors. This practice was called **typage,** since the filmmakers would often choose an individual whose appearance seemed directly to convey the type of character in the role. Except for the hero, Pudovkin used non-actors to play all the Mongols in *Storm over Asia*.

The Movement Ends

By the late 1920s, each of the major directors of this movement had made about four important films. The decline of the movement was not caused primarily by industrial and economic factors, as in Germany and France. Instead, the Communist

CONNECT TO THE BLOG
www.davidbordwell.net/blog

For more on Eisenstein's approach to editing, see "Seed-beds of style."

12.42 Discontinuity for shock. In *House on Trubnoi Square,* Montage director Boris Barnet uses a jump cut to convey the heroine's sudden realization that a streetcar is headed straight for her.

12.43

12.44

12.45

12.46

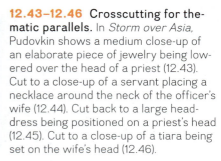

12.43–12.46 Crosscutting for thematic parallels. In *Storm over Asia,* Pudovkin shows a medium close-up of an elaborate piece of jewelry being lowered over the head of a priest (12.43). Cut to a close-up of a servant placing a necklace around the neck of the officer's wife (12.44). Cut back to a large headdress being positioned on a priest's head (12.45). Cut to a close-up of a tiara being set on the wife's head (12.46).

government came to disapprove of the Montage style. Vertov, Eisenstein, and Dovzhenko were criticized for their excessively formal and esoteric approaches. In 1929, Eisenstein went to Hollywood to study the new technique of sound; by the time he returned in 1932, the attitude of the film industry had changed. While he was away, a few filmmakers carried their Montage experiments into sound cinema. But the Soviet authorities, under Stalin's direction, encouraged filmmakers to create simple films that would be readily understandable to all audiences. Stylistic experimentation and nonrealistic subject matter were condemned.

This trend culminated in 1934, when the government instituted a new artistic policy called Socialist Realism. This policy dictated that all artworks must depict revolutionary development while being firmly grounded in realism. The great Soviet directors continued to make films, occasionally masterpieces, but the Montage theories of the 1920s had to be discarded or modified. Eisenstein continued experimenting with editing and occasionally incurred the wrath of the authorities until his death in 1948. As a movement, the Soviet Montage style can be said to have ended by 1933, with the release of such films as Vertov's *Enthusiasm* (1931) and Pudovkin's *Deserter* (1933).

Yet like other silent film movements, its legacy proved enormous. As Kuleshov and his pupils imitated American films, Hollywood borrowed Soviet strategies by creating the "montage sequences" (p. 254) that became common in the 1930s and are still used today. American filmmakers have paid homage to *The Battleship Potemkin* in movies as different as *Bananas* and *The Untouchables.* The films of Resnais, especially *Hiroshima mon amour, Muriel,* and *La Guerre est finie,* rework Soviet Montage principles. Even more pervasive were Montage influences on avant-garde filmmaking. Makers of found-footage films such as *A Movie* owe a good deal to Vertov's Kino-Eye, and Eisenstein's idea that discontinuity in editing was one creative option underwrote many modern experiments **(12.47).** Not least, the writings of the Montage directors, with their passionate call for breaking with the past, have inspired young filmmakers to make daring creative choices.

12.47 Discontinuity multiplied. Panels from old comic books, panned over jerkily and cut together disjunctively, are glimpsed in Lewis Klahr's *Two Minutes to Zero Trilogy* (2003–2004). In a test of Soviet Montage theories, we're invited to assemble the fragmentary shots into an ominous story of crime and panic.

The Classical Hollywood Cinema after the Coming of Sound (1926–1950)

The arrival of synchronized sound filming in the late 1920s dramatically shows how technological change can widen a filmmaker's creative choices. Before that, nearly all music heard in cinema was played on the spot, provided by a piano, organ, or an orchestra. Sound effects might be added; some organs could mimic pistol shots. But there would be no spoken dialogue. The silent cinema had written language in its intertitles, but not speech.

You can argue that film form and style would have been very different if cinema could have recorded spoken dialogue when movies began. Wouldn't the line of least resistance have been to simply photograph stage performances? If cinema had not been condemned to silence, would actors like Chaplin and Fairbanks have developed such a visually expressive performance style? Would Griffith and other directors have developed crosscutting and continuity editing? Would the Impressionists have tried to render the fluidity of thought, or the Soviet Montagists sought to make conceptual points through their cutting patterns? More likely, as many writers thought at the time, cinema would have become primarily a recording medium, and films would have been canned theater, like the opera performances on public television.

From this perspective, the absence of recorded speech was a great gift. It drastically constrained filmmakers' choices. It pushed them to find ways of telling stories visually, and the results yielded a new art form.

With the advent of synchronized sound, filmmakers faced perhaps the most important decision point in film history. Should they give up all the resources of film form and style developed over 30 years of silent moviemaking? Should they simply turn movies into photographed stage plays? Or should filmmakers try to integrate spoken language, along with music and effects, into the sophisticated visual storytelling of the late silent era? Or were there still other options? The decision would shape the future of a medium that was already still very young compared to the other arts.

Converting to Sound

Like many media technologies, synchronized sound was born from a business decision. During the mid-1920s, Warner Bros. was expanding its facilities and holdings. One of these expansions was the investment in a sound system using records in synchronization with film images. By releasing *Don Juan* (1926) with orchestral accompaniment and sound effects on disc, along with a series of vaudeville shorts with singing and talking, Warner Bros. began to popularize the idea of sound films. In 1927, *The Jazz Singer* (a part-talkie with some scenes accompanied only by music) was a tremendous success, and the Warner Bros. investment began to pay off.

The success of *Don Juan, The Jazz Singer,* and the shorts convinced other studios that sound contributed to profitable filmmaking. Unlike the era of the Motion Picture Patents Company, there was now no fierce competition within the industry. Firms realized that whatever sound system the studios finally adopted, it would have to be compatible with the projection machinery of any theater. Eventually, the sound-on-disc system was rejected and a sound-on-film one became the standard up to the present. As we saw in Chapter 1, the sound track was printed on the strip of film alongside the image. By 1930, most theaters in America were wired for sound. The question for filmmakers was: What to do with this new technology?

Problems and Solutions

It seemed for a few years that much of the visual storytelling of the silent era would be lost. Camera positions were more limited, because the camera had to be put inside a sound booth so that its motor noise would not be picked up by the microphone **(12.48).** The camera operator could hear only through his earphones, and

> "You know, when talkies first came in they were fascinated by sound—they had frying eggs and they had this and that—and then people became infatuated with the movement of the camera; I believe, the big thing right now is to move a handheld camera. I think the director and his camerawork should not intrude on the story."
> —George Cukor, director

the camera could not move except for short pans to reframe. The bulky microphone, on the table at the right, also did not move. Complicated staging was ruled out because the actors had to stay close to the microphone. Often several cameras in their booths were filming from different angles, so lighting had to be rather broad and flat; it could not be tailored to a particular shot. Such restrictions seemed to confirm critics and filmmakers' worst fears: movies would now be static and stagey.

Still, from the very beginning of sound filming, problems were solved. When several cameras recorded the scene from different angles, the footage could be cut together to provide continuity editing patterns, complete with close-ups. A booth might be mounted on wheels to create camera movements, or a scene might be shot silent and a sound track added later. Early sound films such as Rouben Mamoulian's *Applause* (1929) showed that the camera could regain considerable flexibility of movement. Later, equipment manufacturers came up with smaller enclosures that replaced the cumbersome booths. These *blimps* (**12.49**) permitted cinematographers to place the camera on movable supports. Similarly, microphones mounted on booms and hanging over the heads of the actors could also follow moving action and maintain recording quality.

It became clear that instead of wiping out all the options of classical Hollywood form and style, recorded sound would be integrated into that system. Once cutting, camera movement, and fluid staging were restored, filmmakers returned to many of the stylistic characteristics developed in Hollywood during the silent period. Diegetic sound provided a powerful addition to the system of continuity editing. A line of dialogue could continue over a cut, creating smooth temporal continuity. (See pp. 275–277.) In addition, music could be more precisely timed to the action than was possible in live accompaniment. Max Steiner's scores for *The Most Dangerous Game* (1932) and *King Kong* (1933) showed that music could powerfully enhance both the image and spoken dialogue—sometimes amplifying frenzied action, sometimes quietly stressing a single sentence.

12.48

12.49

12.48–12.49 **From booth to blimp.** A posed publicity still demonstrated the limitations of early sound filming (12.48). A blimped camera during the early 1930s allowed more freedom of camera placement (12.49).

Studios, Genres, and Spectacle

Within the overall tradition of continuity style and classical narrative form, each of the large studios developed a distinctive approach of its own. Thus MGM, for example, became the prestige studio, with a huge number of stars and technicians under long-term contract. MGM lavished money on settings, costumes, and special effects, as in *The Good Earth* (1937), with its locust attack, and *San Francisco* (1936), in which the great earthquake of 1906 is spectacularly re-created. Warner Bros., in spite of its success with sound, was still a relatively small studio and specialized in less expensive genre pictures. Its series of gangster films (*Little Caesar, Public Enemy*) and musicals (*42nd Street, Gold Diggers of 1933, Dames*) were

CONNECT TO THE BLOG
www.davidbordwell.net/blog

Some of these early sound and color films can be hard to find, but we look at some DVD collections that provide lots of information and clips in "All singing! All dancing! All teaching!"

12.50 Studios specialize in genres. Heavy shadows, spiky shapes, and eccentric performances mix a menacing atmosphere with a touch of humor in Universal's *The Old Dark House.*

among the studio's most successful products. Even lower on the ladder of prestige was Universal, which depended on imaginative filmmaking rather than established stars or expensive sets in its atmospheric horror films, such as *Frankenstein* (1931) and *The Old Dark House* (1932; **12.50**).

One major genre, the musical, became possible only with the introduction of sound. Indeed, the original intention of the Warners when they began their investment in sound equipment was to circulate vaudeville acts on film. Most musicals presented a linear plot with separate numbers inserted, although a few revue musicals simply strung together a series of numbers. One of the major studios, RKO, made a series of musicals starring Fred Astaire and Ginger Rogers: *Swing Time* (George Stevens, 1936) illustrates how a musical can be a classically constructed narrative (see pp. 347–348).

During the 1930s, color film stocks became widely used for the first time. In the 1920s, a small number of films had Technicolor sequences, but the process was crude, using only two colors in combination to create all other hues. The result tended to emphasize greenish-blue and pink tones; it was also too costly to use extensively (**12.51**). By the early 1930s, however, Technicolor had been improved. It now used three primary colors and thus could reproduce a large range of hues. Though still expensive, it was soon proved to add hugely to the appeal of many films. After *Becky Sharp* (1935), the first feature-length film to use the new Technicolor, and *The Trail of the Lonesome Pine* (1936), studios began using Technicolor extensively. The Technicolor process was used, for either camera originals or release prints, until the early 1970s. (For examples of Technicolor, see 2.14–2.24, 4.2, 4.144, 5.7, and 11.87–11.99.)

Deep Focus and Narrative Innovations

Technicolor needed a great deal of light on the set, so more powerful lighting units were introduced. Some cinematographers began to use the new units for black-and-white filming. These more powerful lamps, combined with faster film stocks, made it easier to achieve greater depth of field in the image. Many cinematographers stuck to the standard soft-focus style of the 1920s and 1930s, but others began to experiment.

By the late 1930s, there was a definite trend toward a deep-focus style. It was *Citizen Kane* that in 1941 brought deep focus strongly to the attention of spectators and filmmakers. Orson Welles's compositions placed the foreground figures close to the camera and the background figures deep in the space of the shot, and all were kept in sharp focus (5.48; 8.28–8.32, 8.37–8.42). In some cases, the image was achieved through matte work and rear projection, not cinematography on the set.

Overall, *Citizen Kane* helped make deep focus a major creative option within classical Hollywood style.

Directors found that depth staging and deep-focus filming allowed them to create striking compositions and to sustain scenes in longer takes (**12.52**). The light necessary for deep focus tended to lend a hard-edged appearance to objects, a look well-suited to the stories of crime and pursuit that would eventually be called *film noir*. But like every creative choice, the new technique forced fresh decisions. If an object or a face was placed close to the foreground, cinematographers found it hard to keep the composition balanced and in focus when actors moved around the shot. The most famous deep-focus shots in *Citizen Kane* and other films tend to be fixed long takes with simple staging. As a result, many deep-focus images seem more static and enclosed than the fluid performances and framings of films like *His Girl Friday* (pp. 403–406).

During the same period, Hollywood was also broadening its narrative options. Flashbacks had been used since the 1910s, but

12.51 Two-strip Technicolor. *Under a Texas Moon* (1930) captures mostly reddish-orange and green hues.

they gained a new prominence in the 1940s. Films such as *The Long Night* (1947) and *The Big Clock* (1948) start from a point of crisis and go back in time to trace how events led up to it. Or there might be several flashbacks, perhaps threaded together by an investigation as in *Citizen Kane* or *The Killers* (1946). The flashback might replay an earlier scene, but now revealing unexpected information, as in the climax of *Mildred Pierce* (1945). Along with flashbacks, screenwriters began experimenting with voice-over narration, already well-established on radio but given a new power with the accompanying images. Both flashbacks and voice-over narration fed into a new emphasis on mental subjectivity, so more than in the 1930s, films rendered dreams, hallucinations, and drunken or drug-induced visions. There are moments in *Murder, My Sweet* (1944) and *Possessed* (1947) that hark back to German Expressionism and French Impressionism, with subjective sound enhancing the imagery.

All these narrative strategies could have broken with classical narrative principles. Instead, screenwriters strove to sort out their scrambled time-schemes and firmly mark the division between objective reality and subjective states of mind. The principles of classical construction—goal-oriented characters, motivated conflict, clarity of time and space and character traits—remained paramount.

By assimilating sound and color to its system of visual storytelling, the Hollywood cinema laid the foundation of the popular film as we know it today. Later changes in technology, such as widescreen filming, multiple-track sound, computer-driven special effects, and digital capture, would build on this solid tradition (12.53). For decades to follow, the formal and stylistic conventions elaborated in the Hollywood studios of the 1930s and 1940s would guide the creative choices of filmmakers. Those conventions would also become targets for filmmakers who wanted to try something different.

12.52 The spread of deep-focus cinematography. Many films using the technique soon appeared. *Citizen Kane*'s cinematographer, Gregg Toland, worked on some of them, such as William Wyler's *The Little Foxes*.

CONNECT TO THE BLOG
www.davidbordwell.net/blog

We examine deep-focus cinematography and staging in the 1930s and 1940s in "Foreground, background, playground."

Italian Neorealism (1942–1951)

One of the most influential movements in film history, Neorealism has somewhat diffuse origins. The label first appeared in the writings of Italian critics of the 1940s. From one perspective, the term represented a younger generation's desire to break free of the conventions of ordinary Italian cinema. Under dictator Benito Mussolini, the motion picture industry had created colossal historical epics and sentimental upper-class melodramas (nicknamed *white-telephone films*), and many critics felt these to be artificial and decadent. Something closer to real life was needed. Some critics found that quality in French films of the 1930s, especially works by Jean Renoir. Other critics turned closer to home to praise films like Luchino Visconti's *Ossessione* (1942).

Today most historians believe that Neorealist filmmaking was not a complete break with Italian cinema under Mussolini. Pseudo-documentaries such as Roberto Rossellini's *White Ship* (1941), even though propagandistic, prepared the way for more forthright handling of contemporary events. Other current trends, such as regional dialect comedy and urban melodrama, encouraged directors and scriptwriters to turn toward realism. Overall, spurred by both foreign influences and indigenous traditions, the postwar period saw several filmmakers aiming

12.53 Neo-noir pays homage to the past. A deep-focus composition in *The Usual Suspects* adapts Welles-Toland deep focus to the widescreen format.

12.54

12.55

12.56

12.54–12.56 **Filming in the streets.**
In one scene in *Open City*, Francesco
is thrown into a truck by Nazi soldiers
(12.54). His common-law wife Pina
breaks through the guards (12.55), and a
rough, bumpy shot taken from the truck
shows her running after him (12.56).

to reveal contemporary social conditions. This trend became known as the Neoreal-ist movement.

Leaving the Studio

Economic, political, and cultural factors helped Neorealism survive. Unlike the young Soviet filmmakers, nearly all the major Neorealists—Rossellini, Vittorio De Sica, Visconti, and others—came to the movement as experienced filmmakers. They had absorbed lessons from Hollywood and European film traditions. They knew one another, frequently shared scriptwriters and personnel, and gained public attention in the journals *Cinema* and *Bianco e Nero*. Before 1948, the Neorealist movement had enough friends in the government to be relatively free of censorship. There was as well an affinity between Neorealism and an Italian literary movement of the same period modeled on the *verismo* of the previous century. The result was an array of Italian films that gained worldwide recognition: Visconti's *La Terra Trema* (1947); Rossellini's *Rome Open City* (1945), *Paisan* (1946), and *Germany Year Zero* (1947); and De Sica's *Shoeshine* (1946) and *Bicycle Thieves* (1948).

Neorealism created a somewhat distinctive approach to film style. By 1945, the fighting had destroyed most of Cinecittà, the large Roman studio complex, so sets were in short supply and sound equipment was rare. As a result, Neorealist mise-en-scene relied on actual locales, and its photographic work tended toward the raw roughness of documentaries. Rossellini has told of buying bits of negative stock from street photographers, so that much of *Rome Open City* was shot on film with varying photographic qualities.

Shooting on the streets and in private buildings made Italian camera operators adept at cinematography that often avoided the three-point lighting system of Holly-wood (4.69–4.70). Although Neorealist films often featured famous stage or film actors, non-actors were also recruited for their realistic looks and behavior. For the adult "star" of *Bicycle Thieves,* De Sica chose a factory worker: "The way he moved, the way he sat down, his gestures with those hands of a working man and not of an actor . . . everything about him was perfect." The Italian cinema had a long tradition of dubbing, so sound didn't have to be recorded on site. The ability to postsynchro-nize dialogue permitted the filmmakers to work on location with smaller crews and to move the camera freely. With a degree of improvisational freedom in the acting and setting went a certain flexibility of framing, well displayed in the death of Pina in *Rome Open City* **(12.54–12.56)** and the final sequence of *Germany Year Zero*. The tracking shots through the open-air bicycle market in *Bicycle Thieves* illustrate the possibilities that the Neorealist director found in returning to location filming.

A New Model of Storytelling

Just as influential was the Neorealist sense of narrative form. Reacting against the intricately plotted white-telephone dramas, the Neorealists tended to loosen up nar-rative relations. The earliest major films of the movement, such as *Ossessione, Rome Open City,* and *Shoeshine,* contain relatively conventionally organized plots (albeit with unhappy endings). But the most formally innovative Neorealist films allow the intrusion of scenes that aren't motivated causally—that seem, in fact, to be accidents **(12.57).** The director may dwell on moments that are worth savoring for their own sake. A famous scene in De Sica's *Umberto D* (1951) records a pregnant housemaid grinding morning coffee. Her daily routine yields its own fascination, but the effect is very different from Hollywood's conception of what counts as drama.

Although the causes of characters' actions are usually seen as concretely eco-nomic and political (poverty, unemployment, exploitation), the effects are often fragmentary and inconclusive. Rossellini's *Paisan* is frankly episodic, presenting six anecdotes of life in Italy during the Allied invasion. Often we are not told the outcome of an event, the consequence of a cause. In a harsh break with mainstream storytelling, Rossellini abruptly kills off one of his protagonists in *Rome Open City,* wiping out the film's romance plot.

Both the porous plot structure and the narration often refuses to provide an omniscient knowledge of events. The film seems to admit that the totality of reality is simply unknowable. This is especially evident in the films' endings. *Bicycle Thieves* concludes with the worker and his son wandering down the street, their stolen bicycle still missing, their future uncertain. *La Terra Trema* concludes with the suppression of the Sicilian fishermen's revolt against the merchants, but it hints that a future revolt might succeed. Neorealism's tendency toward slice-of-life plot construction gave many films of the movement an open-ended quality quite opposed to the tidy wrapup favored by American studio cinema.

The Movement's End and Its Legacy

As economic and cultural forces had sustained the Neorealist movement, so they helped bring it to an end. When Italy began to prosper after the war, the government looked askance at films so critical of contemporary society. After 1949, censorship and state pressures began to constrain the movement. Large-scale Italian film production began to reappear, and Neorealism no longer had the freedom permitted by small production companies. Neorealist directors, now famous, began to pursue more individualized concerns: Rossellini's investigation of Christian humanism and Western history, De Sica's sentimental romances, and Visconti's examination of upper-class milieus. Most historians date the end of the Neorealist movement with the public attacks on De Sica's *Umberto D* (1951). Nevertheless, Neorealist elements are still quite visible in the early works of Federico Fellini (*I Vitelloni,* 1954, is a good example) and Michelangelo Antonioni (*Cronaca di un amore,* 1951); both directors had worked on Neorealist films. Neorealist impulses periodically returned to Italian cinema, notably in the long career of Ermanno Olmi (*Il Posto, The Tree of the Wooden Clogs*).

The production strategies and artistic goals of this movement opened up a vast realm of creative choices. Throughout Latin America, the Middle East, and Asia, filmmakers followed the Neorealist model in rejecting polished studio production values. They realized that they could cast non-actors and let them perform in actual settings. They could rely on available light for shooting. Their screenplays didn't need intricate plotting and could incorporate the accidents and digressions of everyday life. The plot could even leave the story action unresolved at the end, the better to provoke the audience to weigh possible outcomes. The tenets of Neorealist theory and practice have formed a robust tradition for decades of non-Hollywood cinema. Today, filmmakers in many places continue to devise their own versions of Neorealism **(12.58)**.

The French New Wave (1959–1964)

The late 1950s and early 1960s saw the rise of a new generation of filmmakers around the world. In country after country, there emerged directors born before World War II but grown to adulthood in the postwar era of reconstruction and rising prosperity. Japan, Canada, England, Italy, Spain, Brazil, and the United States all had their new waves or young cinema groups—some trained in film schools, many allied with specialized film magazines, most in revolt against their elders in the industry. The most influential of these groups appeared in France.

12.57 The drama of accident. In *Bicycle Thieves,* the hero takes shelter along with a group of priests during a rain shower. The incident doesn't affect the plot and seems as casual as any moment in daily life.

> **❝** The sentiment of [*Bicycle Thieves*] is expressed overtly. The feelings invoked are a natural consequence of the themes of the story and the point of view it is told from. It is a politically committed film, fueled by a quiet but burning passion. But it never lectures. It observes rather than explains."
> —Sally Potter, director, *Orlando*

12.58 Neorealism's legacy. Contemporary Iranian filmmakers continue the Neorealist impulse: casual, anecdotal plots using non-actors to present social criticism. In Jafar Panahi's *Offside* (2006), female soccer fans, trying to attend a match disguising themselves as men, are held under guard.

> "We were all critics before beginning to make films, and I loved all kinds of cinema—the Russians, the Americans, the Neorealists. It was the cinema that made us—or me, at least—want to make films. I knew nothing of life except through the cinema."
>
> —Jean-Luc Godard, director

Critics Become Moviemakers

In the mid-1950s, a group of young men who wrote for the Paris film journal *Cahiers du cinéma* made a habit of attacking the most artistically respected French filmmakers of the day. "I consider an adaptation of value," wrote François Truffaut, "only when written by a *man of the cinema*. Aurenche and Bost [the leading scriptwriters of the time] are essentially literary men and I reproach them here for being contemptuous of the cinema by underestimating it." Addressing 21 major directors, Jean-Luc Godard was more insulting: "Your camera movements are ugly because your subjects are bad, your casts act badly because your dialogue is worthless; in a word, you don't know how to create cinema because you no longer even know what it is." Truffaut and Godard, along with Claude Chabrol, Eric Rohmer, and Jacques Rivette, also praised directors considered somewhat outdated (Jean Renoir, Max Ophuls) or eccentric (Robert Bresson, Jacques Tati).

More important, the young men saw no contradiction in rejecting the French filmmaking establishment while loving blatantly commercial Hollywood. The young rebels of *Cahiers* claimed that in the works of certain directors—certain *auteurs* (authors)—artistry existed in the American cinema. An **auteur** usually did not literally write scripts but managed nonetheless to stamp his or her personality on studio products, transcending the constraints of Hollywood's standardized system. Howard Hawks, Otto Preminger, Samuel Fuller, Vincente Minnelli, Nicholas Ray, Alfred Hitchcock—these were more than craftsmen. Each director's total output constituted a coherent world. Truffaut quoted Giraudoux: "There are no works, there are only auteurs." Godard remarked later, "We won the day in having it acknowledged in principle that a film by Hitchcock, for example, is as important as a book by Aragon. Film auteurs, thanks to us, have finally entered the history of art." And indeed, many of the Hollywood directors these critics and filmmakers championed have become recognized as great artists.

Writing criticism didn't satisfy these young men. They itched to make movies. Borrowing money from friends and filming on location, each started to shoot short films. By 1959, they had become a force to be reckoned with. In that year, Rivette filmed *Paris nous appartient* (*Paris Belongs to Us*); Godard made *À Bout de souffle* (*Breathless*); Chabrol made his second feature, *Les Cousins;* and in April, Truffaut's *Les Quatre cent coups* (*The 400 Blows*) won the Grand Prize at the Cannes Festival.

The novelty and youthful vigor of these directors led journalists to nickname them *la nouvelle vague*—the *New Wave*. Their output was staggering. All told, the five central directors made 32 feature films between 1959 and 1966; Godard and Chabrol made 11 apiece. So many films must of course be highly disparate, but there are enough similarities for us to identify a broadly distinctive New Wave approach to style and form.

12.59 Location filming. *Les Bonnes femmes:* While a serial killer stalks them, two of the heroines sit idly at work. Like many New Wave directors, Claude Chabrol followed the Neorealists in shooting on locations like this drab appliance shop.

A New Wave Style

The most obviously revolutionary quality of the New Wave films was their casual look. To proponents of the carefully polished French "cinema of quality," the young directors must have seemed hopelessly sloppy. The New Wave directors had admired the Neorealists (especially Rossellini) and, in opposition to studio filmmaking, took as their settings actual locales in and around Paris. Shooting on location became the norm **(12.59)**. Similarly, glossy studio lighting was replaced by available light and simple supplemental sources. Few postwar French films would have shown the dim apartments and grimy corridors featured in *Paris Belongs to Us*.

Cinematography changed, too. The New Wave camera moves a great deal, panning and tracking to follow characters or to explore a locale. To make mobile shots cheaply on location demanded flexible, portable equipment. Fortunately, Eclair had recently developed a lightweight camera that could be handheld. (That the Eclair had been used primarily for documentary work accorded perfectly with the realistic mise-en-scene of the New Wave.) New Wave filmmakers were intoxicated with the new freedom offered by the handheld camera. In *The 400 Blows,* the camera explores a cramped apartment and rides a carnival centrifuge. In *Breathless,* the cinematographer held the camera while seated in a wheelchair to follow the hero's winding path through a travel agency (11.32).

One of the most salient features of New Wave films is their casual humor. These young men deliberately played with the medium. In Godard's *Band of Outsiders,* the three main characters resolve to be silent for a minute, and Godard dutifully shuts off *all* the sound. In Truffaut's *Shoot the Piano Player,* a character swears that he's not lying: "May my mother drop dead if I'm not telling the truth." Cut to a shot of an old lady keeling over.

Along with humor came esoteric references to other films, Hollywood or European. There are homages to admired auteurs: Godard characters allude to *Johnny Guitar* (Ray), *Some Came Running* (Minnelli), and "Arizona Jim" (from Renoir's *Crime of M. Lange*). In *Les Carabiniers,* Godard parodies Lumière, and in *Vivre sa vie,* he visually quotes *La Passion de Jeanne d'Arc* (**12.60, 12.61**). Hitchcock is frequently cited in Chabrol's films, and Truffaut's *Les Mistons* re-creates a shot from a Lumière short. Such citations, the New Wave directors felt, acknowledged that cinema, like literature and painting, had lofty traditions that could be honored.

Neorealism Recast

New Wave films also pushed further the Neorealist experimentation with plot construction. In general, causal connections became quite loose. Is there actually a political conspiracy going on in *Paris Belongs to Us?* Why is Nana shot at the end of *Vivre sa vie?* In *Shoot the Piano Player,* the first sequence consists mainly of a conversation between the hero's brother and a man he accidentally meets on the street. The passerby laments his marital problems at some length. In a Hollywood film, he would become a major character, but here he departs and never appears.

The films often lack goal-oriented protagonists. The heroes may drift aimlessly, engage in actions on the spur of the moment, or pass the time chatting in a café or going to movies. New Wave narratives also introduce startling shifts in tone, jolting our expectations. When two gangsters kidnap the hero and his girlfriend in *Shoot the Piano Player,* the whole group begins a comic discussion of sex. Discontinuous editing further disturbs narrative continuity; this tendency reaches its limit in Godard's jump cuts (6.151, 6.152, 11.37, 11.38).

Perhaps most important, the New Wave film typically ends ambiguously. Antoine in *The 400 Blows* reaches the sea in the last shot, but as he moves forward, Truffaut zooms in and freezes the frame, ending the film with the question of where Antoine will go from there (3.10). We've seen a similar lack of resolution in the final scene of *Breathless* (p. 417). In Chabrol's *Les Bonnes Femmes* and *Ophelia,* in Rivette's *Paris Belongs to Us,* and in nearly all the work of Godard and Truffaut in this period, the looseness of the causal chain leads to endings that remain defiantly open and uncertain.

Into the Mainstream and Beyond

The filmmakers were often bad-mannered, and the films placed strong demands on the viewer, but the French film industry wasn't hostile to the New Wave. The decade 1947–1957 had been good to film production: The government supported the industry through enforced quotas, banks had invested heavily, and there was a flourishing business of international coproductions. But in 1957, cinema attendance fell off drastically, chiefly because television became more widespread. By 1959,

12.60

12.61

12.60–12.61 Classic film as a reference point. In Godard's *Vivre sa vie,* a clip from Dreyer's *The Passion of Joan of Arc* (12.60) provokes Nana's sympathy as she watches it (12.61). It also equates her with one of the great suffering heroines of silent cinema (see 4.41).

12.62 Borrowing from, and fighting, the New Wave. In spring 1995, a group of Danish directors founded a movement they called Dogme, to continue the impulse of the French New Wave. The group's manifesto laid down a series of rules, demanding that people shoot on location with a handheld camera and use no postproduction sound editing. One result was the second Dogme film, *The Idiots* (1998). It centered on a gang of young people who practice "spazzing"—going to public places and pretending to be physically or mentally handicapped, chiefly to test ordinary citizens' tolerance.

the industry was in a crisis. One solution was to encourage the independent financing of low-budget projects. New Wave directors shot films much more quickly and cheaply than did reigning directors. Moreover, the young directors helped one another out and reduced financial risk. By 1964, each New Wave director had his or her own production company, and the group had become absorbed into the film industry. By that time as well, the characteristic New Wave form and style had already become diffused and imitated (by, for instance, Tony Richardson in his 1963 English film *Tom Jones*). Most historians would argue that the movement, as a group initiative, had come to an end. Certainly, after 1968, the political upheavals in France drastically altered the personal relations among the directors.

New Wave figures remained powerful filmmakers for decades. Chabrol, Truffaut, and Rohmer became firmly entrenched in the French film industry, whereas Godard set up a facility in Switzerland, and Rivette began to create narratives of staggering complexity and length (such as *Out One,* originally about 12 hours long). Their films, though seldom popular, continued to be supported by government subsidies, international agencies, and private financing. They had, in a sense, become the sort of Old Guard that they had rebelled against. Yet many continued to produce provocative and influential films. Godard in particular attracted notoriety with his controversial retelling of the Old and New Testaments, *Hail Mary* (1983). He was one of the first filmmakers to embrace video as a medium, and in 2010 he released an HD feature, *Film Socialisme,* that remains as defiantly nonconformist as all his work.

The New Wave not only created several original and valuable films but also demonstrated that a stodgy film industry could gain new energy from talented, aggressive young people inspired by the sheer love of cinema. It has become the prototype of the fully self-conscious movement—aware of its place in film history, able to work with low budgets, and shrewd in its realization that media culture is always looking for the next big thing. The journalists-turned-filmmakers understood the power of publicity, a lesson that later film movements learned. The Danish Dogme 95 group attacked the French New Wave (it "proved to be a ripple that washed ashore and turned to muck"), but they followed the earlier generation in demanding a break with conformity **(12.62).** And the New Wave was not mere bluff. Like the Neorealists they admired, these young filmmakers showed that making unusual creative decisions could reveal new possibilities in the art of cinema.

The New Hollywood and Independent Filmmaking, 1970s–1980s

Hollywood filmmakers sustained their tradition during the 1930s and 1940s by assimilating the technological demands of sound and color. In the 1950s and 1960s, they faced greater difficulties. There were new technologies, such as widescreen and stereophonic sound, to master, but the real problems lay elsewhere. By government decree, the vertically integrated studios had been broken up in the late 1940s. Distributors could no longer own theaters or demand that exhibitors take weak films. This breakup coincided with a sharp drop in attendance as Americans turned to television and other leisure activities. Filmmakers responded by targeting certain market segments, like young people, and exploring previously forbidden content, like sex and drug use.

The Sound of Music (1965), *Dr. Zhivago* (1965), and a few other big films yielded huge profits, but these could not shore up the declining industry. Television networks, which had paid high prices to broadcast films after theatrical release, stopped bidding for pictures. American movie attendance flattened out at around 1 billion tickets per year. By 1969, Hollywood companies were losing over $200 million annually.

Blockbusters and Indie Pictures

The industry was saved by what has been called the blockbuster mentality. Along with the predictable favorites, like Disney animation, the top-ranking films of the period included some surprises: *The Godfather* (1972), *The Exorcist* (1973), *American Graffiti* (1973), *Jaws* (1975), *Star Wars* (1977), *Close Encounters of the Third Kind* (1977), and *Superman* (1978). Unlike most hits, these lacked established stars. They weren't based on Broadway musicals. They were in recognizable, even slightly down-market genres such as horror and science fiction, but they were enhanced by high production values and state-of-the-art special effects. Aimed at young audiences, they became "must-see" events, and many viewers returned again and again to their favorites. The 1970s blockbusters weren't usually designed to be colossal successes, but their box-office triumph convinced producers that a blockbuster could be engineered. In the process, Hollywood could be reinvented.

The studio-designed blockbusters came to be known as "tentpole" pictures because their profits sheltered other, smaller films. Studios spread their investment to star-driven romantic comedies, dramas, and adventure films. They continued to support, often by simply acquiring distribution rights, cheaper genre pictures likely to turn a profit. The studios also encouraged riskier fare that might win critical attention and awards. These might be prestige pictures like *Sleuth* (1972), or more controversial items like *Taxi Driver* (1976).

This division among blockbusters, program genre fare, Oscar bait, edgy experiments, and niche independents would roughly hold good from the 1970s through the 2000s. Tastes and trends would vary; *The Matrix* (1999) and *Inception* (2010) tell more complex stories than *The Empire Strikes Back* (1980), but all show that science fiction, garlanded with top-flight special effects, was a steady source of blockbusters. Filmmakers might hop from one category to another. Spike Lee went from being a niche independent (*She's Gotta Have It,* 1986) to directing a prestige picture (*Malcolm X,* 1992), and then to more mainstream genre pictures (*Clockers,* 1995; *Inside Man,* 2006). Few would have predicted on the basis of *Mean Streets* (1973) and *Raging Bull* (1980) that Martin Scorsese would someday direct a children's 3D film budgeted at $150 million (*Hugo,* 2011). Regardless of such mixing and matching, the strategy of designing projects at different budget levels and for different tastes sustained the Hollywood tradition in the modern era.

The Rise of the Movie Brats

Nearly all the directors of Hollywood's golden age were dead or retired by 1975, so many major trends of that era sprang from young talent. A crucial feature set them apart from earlier American directors. Instead of coming up through the ranks of the studio system, most had gone to film schools. At New York University, the University of Southern California, and the University of California at Los Angeles, they had not only mastered the mechanics of production but also learned about film aesthetics and history. Like the French New Wave directors, the newcomers often had an encyclopedic knowledge of great movies and directors. As a result, they came to be known as the "movie brats." Whatever level of production they worked in, they were quite aware of the traditions that they inherited, and they set out to both extend the traditions and try something new.

> " I love the idea of not being an independent filmmaker. I've liked working within the system. And I've admired a lot of the older directors who were sort of 'directors for hire.' Like Victor Fleming was in a contract all those years to Metro and Selznick and Mayer . . . he made *Captains Courageous.* And you know, his most famous films: *Wizard of Oz* and *Gone with the Wind."*
> —Steven Spielberg, producer/director

> " To a whole generation, these [Hollywood classics] were more than just commodities. It was a part of who we are."
> —Martin Scorsese, director

12.63 **Staging for multiple points of interest.** In *Jaws*, Steven Spielberg displayed a flair for depth staging that has been a hallmark of his work ever since.

So, for instance, when Steven Spielberg and George Lucas revived the science-fiction genre, they did so in full awareness of film history. With *Close Encounters* and *E. T.: The Extraterrestrial* (1982), Spielberg defied the tradition of predatory alien invaders by presenting his creatures as lovable. With *Star Wars* and its sequels, George Lucas consciously revived the disreputable "rocket opera" of Flash Gordon serials and Saturday-matinee kiddie shows. Collaborating on *Raiders of the Lost Ark* (1981), Spielberg and Lucas updated the B-movie serial, giving preposterous plots the dazzle of modern action choreography. Spielberg also tried his hand at Oscar bait, with *The Color Purple* (1985), *Schindler's List* (1993), and other prestige projects. His Amblin company produced lively genre pictures such as *Poltergeist* (1982) and *Gremlins* (1984).

For the studio-oriented movie brats, it wasn't all nostalgia. To turn B-movie material into blockbusters and A-pictures, they called on sophisticated technique. Lucas developed motion-control techniques for filming miniatures for *Star Wars,* and his firm Industrial Light and Magic (ILM) became the leader in new special-effects technology. From *Jaws* onward, Spielberg used deep-focus tactics reminiscent of *Citizen Kane* (5.48, **12.63**). Spielberg and Lucas also led the move toward digital sound and high-quality theater reproduction technology. They wanted the modern equivalent of the showmanship that had characterized such 1950s innovations as Cinerama and 3D.

Other filmmakers sought to revive the old Hollywood at a lower budget level. Brian De Palma's admiration for Hitchcock led him to a series of horror films (*Carrie,* 1976) and thrillers (*Obsession,* 1976). *Dressed to Kill* (1980) was an overt redoing of *Psycho.* Peter Bogdanovich's *What's Up, Doc?* (1972) was an updating of screwball comedy, with particular reference to Howard Hawks's *Bringing Up Baby.* John Carpenter's *Assault on Precinct 13* (1976) derived partly from Hawks's *Rio Bravo;* the editing is credited to "John T. Chance," the character played by John Wayne in Hawks's Western.

Other Paths

For many critics, what made the 1970s an era of rejuvenation was the presence of *anti*-blockbusters, intimate dramas of ordinary people leading more or less recognizable lives. In *Five Easy Pieces* (1970), *The Last Picture Show* (1972), *The Last Detail* (1973), *Alice Doesn't Live Here Anymore* (1974), and other films, everyday crises and psychological tensions came to the fore. They gave American cinema a dose of social realism that had been missing from both old Hollywood and the "New Hollywood" of Spielberg, Lucas, and other movie brats. Some of these films traced their impulse to the work of John Cassavetes, who presented immediate and visceral confrontations in *Faces* (1968), *Husbands* (1970), and *A Woman under the Influence* (1974).

Small-scale dramas might be backed by a studio or financed and distributed independently. Although they lacked the splashy technique of the blockbusters, they showed that American cinema could adapt the slice-of-life approach to narrative construction seen in Italian Neorealism. But the rationale wasn't wholly formal. Part of these films' appeal came from a sexual frankness that was made possible by the establishing of the film ratings system in 1968. Curses and obscenities, nudity, adulterous affairs, and simulated sex came into the mainstream, and these were motivated as elements of a cinema that dared to shatter classic Hollywood conventions of romance.

Narrative experiments were even more marked in other films of the 1970s. Some directors dreamed of making complex art films in the European mold. The best-known effort is probably Coppola's *The Conversation* (1974), a mystery-story reworking of Antonioni's *Blow-Up* (1966) that plays ambiguously between reality and hallucination (p. 302). Ventures into subjectivity, less clear-cut than the flashbacks and fantasies of the 1940s, were also seen in Robert Altman's *Images* (1972), Bob Fosse's *All That Jazz* (1979), and the opening of Coppola's *Apocalypse Now* (1979; 12.36). Echoing the New Wave were films in which the directors' love of cinema emerged as self-conscious reminders that the audience was watching a film. Dennis Hopper's *The Last Movie* (1971) interrupted its flow with a title, "SCENE MISSING." In Altman's *The Long Goodbye* (1973), Los Angeles detective Philip Marlowe seems aware that he's playing a hard-boiled detective but is not quite up to the part; the last shot shows him tap-dancing down a road to the tune of "Hooray for Hollywood."

Altman gave currency to another storytelling strategy, one we might call the "network narrative." "All-star" movies such as *Grand Hotel* (1932) had occasionally been made in the studio era, but *Nashville* (1975) and *A Wedding* (1978) took the principle of multiple protagonists and interwoven story lines to a new level. In these films, many characters converge in a single locale, such as a city or a social occasion, and then cross each others' paths, each one with individual concerns and no one emerging as a clear-cut hero or heroine. For Altman, the emphasis fell on chance encounters and incidents that might reveal character, rather than on a forward-moving, goal-driven plot.

Stylistically, the films in all these registers didn't challenge the core of the classic continuity system. Most filmmakers were content to employ it but inflect it in certain directions. It's in this period that we start to find that variant of the traditional 180° system we called intensified continuity in Chapter 6 (p. 248). Many filmmakers exploited the new resources of Dolby sound, which allowed for much greater dynamic range and permitted fine-grain detailing of the soundtrack. Altman pioneered a multiple-microphone recording technique that let him record, during a crowded scene, different conversations on different tracks and merge them into a dense mix that could stress or muffle certain lines.

The 1980s and After

With the colossal failure of *Heaven's Gate* (1980), studios lost faith in the auteur-driven blockbuster and turned control of such projects over to more tractable hands. More personal cinema survived, however, in the emerging realm of independent filmmaking. As usual, technology and money had a good deal to do with it.

During the 1980s, both cable television and home video, in the form of the videocassette tape, grew more popular. Small-budget filmmakers learned that they could finance a film by preselling the rights to video companies. In addition, European television channels were eager for American films that were more affordable than Hollywood blockbusters. Films could find funding through the so-called mini-majors, firms that had access to private capital and had solid distribution prospects.

12.64

12.65

12.64–12.65 **1980s independents.** Wide-angle tracking shots follow crawling babies along the floor and under furniture in *Raising Arizona* (12.64) and Eva and Willie, the listless protagonists of *Stranger Than Paradise* (12.65): "These characters," Jarmusch explains, "move through the world of the film in a kind of random, aimless way, like looking for the next card game or something."

For these and other reasons, the 1980s saw a wave of independently made films that achieved fairly wide distribution.

This was the period that launched novelist John Sayles on a directing career that led to his exploration of U.S. social and political history (*The Return of the Secaucus Seven*, 1980; *Matewan*, 1987). Joel and Ethan Coen established their comic-grotesque vision of America and its film genres with *Blood Simple* (1984) and *Raising Arizona* (1987; **12.64**). In *Stranger Than Paradise* (1984) and *Down by Law* (1986), Jim Jarmusch presented quirky, decentered narratives peopled by drifting losers **(12.65)**. Susan Seidelman's *Desperately Seeking Susan* (1985) featured a not-yet-famous Madonna in a romantic comedy of mistaken identities. For many observers, this trend crystallized when Steven Soderbergh's *sex, lies, and videotape* (1989) won the top prize at the Sundance Film Festival, already emerging as a showcase for off-Hollywood work. By the late 1980s there were 200–250 independent releases per year.

Several directors from independent film managed to shift into the mainstream, making medium-budget pictures with widely known stars. David Lynch moved from the midnight movie *Eraserhead* (1978) to the cult classic *Blue Velvet* (1986), and Canadian David Cronenberg, a specialist in low-budget horror films such as *Shivers* (1975), won wider recognition with *The Dead Zone* (1983) and *The Fly* (1986). Oliver Stone won Academy Awards for *Platoon* (1986), which propelled him into the bigger-budget realm. *She's Gotta Have It* gave Spike Lee access to studio financing for *Do The Right Thing* (1989) and other films. Lee's success paved the way for other African-American directors during the 1990s, a period that saw several minority and women directors starting careers in Hollywood or the independent realm.

Formally and stylistically, many 1980s films extended tendencies of the 1970s. David Lynch created disturbing, phantasmagoric narration in *Blue Velvet*, and his explorations of subjectivity would become a hallmark of his career up through *Mulholland Dr.* (2001). *Stranger Than Paradise* presented a plot full of hesitations and down time, filmed in a rigorous fashion: one shot per scene, nearly always with the camera anchored to one spot. Jarmusch's later *Mystery Train* (1989) experimented with multiple stories playing out simultaneously in different areas of Memphis, all linked by the moment of a gunshot. Playwright David Mamet, always fascinated with mind games and power trips, brought his sensibility to the world of gambling in *House of Games* (1987), in which restricted narration conceals a cascade of deceptions.

Hollywood and Independents, To Be Continued

Much has happened since the 1980s, with studios sometimes courting independents and sometimes discouraging them, and animated features coming to play a bigger role at the box office. But many of the trends established in the 1970s persist. The major studios finance tentpole films, support star-driven comedies such as *Date Night* (2010), acquire genre projects as program filler, and occasionally turn a prestige picture such as *Brokeback Mountain* (2005) into a popular hit. Independent companies, or some "dependent" boutique branches of the studios, aim at ambitious genre pictures such as *Hanna* (2011) and *Drive* (2011), along with Oscar bait. Still smaller independents, such as Charlie Kaufman (*Synecdoche, New York,* 2008) and Miranda July (*You and Me and Everyone We Know,* 2005), survive on critics' accolades and foreign distribution.

As usual, every opportunity demands decisions. James Cameron, with *Titanic* (1997) and *Avatar* (2009), personifies the director who sees his future bound up with blockbusters. The movie brats' fondness for retooling genre pictures reappears in a younger generation's *Cloverfield* (2008) and *Source Code* (2011). *Old Joy* (2006), *Rachel Getting Married* (2008), *Frozen River* (2008), *The Kids Are All Right* (2010), and many other films continue the 1970s impulse toward friends-and-family dramas with social implications (**12.66**). At the microbudget level is the trend called Mumblecore, low-tech exercises in psychological observation, with loose plotting and performances that give off an air of improvisation.

At all these levels of production, reworking narrative strategies has become a commanding trend over the last decades. We see it in mainstream romances, science fiction tales, and crime thrillers (p. 334), and even in blockbusters such as *Inception.* M. Night Shyamalan followed Hitchcock in turning narrative subterfuge into a personal signature (**12.67**). Storytelling experiments are a hallmark of the independent realm as well. The 1990s and 2000s saw a burst of network narratives such as *200 Cigarettes* (1999), *Thirteen Conversations about One Thing* (2001), and *Love Actually* (2003), with *Babel* (2006) taking the format to a global scale. Explorations of subjectivity continued as well. Two films of 2011, *Take Shelter* (Jeff Nichols) and *Martha Marcy May Marlene* (Sean Durkin), showed that ambiguous plunges into memories, dreams, and hallucinations still offered powerful resources to enterprising directors.

CONNECT TO THE BLOG
www.davidbordwell.net/blog

Some independent filmmakers use sensationalism to call attention to their work. See "Visionary Outlaw Mavericks on the dark edge; or, Indie Guignol."

12.66

12.67

12.66–12.67 **Narrative explorations.** The first shot of Ramin Bahrani's *Goodbye Solo* (2008) avoids traditional exposition and plunges us into a scene that is already at a turning point: Solo is laughing at what his grizzled passenger has just asked him to do (12.66). Many viewers went back to see Shyamalan's mystery story *The Sixth Sense* (1999) a second time in order to detect how the narration had misled them. His smooth use of intensified continuity techniques, as in the arcing traveling shot here, helped conceal the plot's secret (12.67).

CONNECT TO THE BLOG
www.davidbordwell.net/blog

The 50-year career of one director offers us a chance to survey changes in Hollywood and the independent scene in our entry, "Endurance: Survival Lessons from Lumet."

It's perhaps no coincidence that the 2000s saw network and cable television experimenting with narrative as well. *The Wire, Six Feet Under, Damages,* and other ambitious series attracted admirers of independent cinema. Independent distributors began producing television shows, and directors often wound up working on high-profile cable series. With most low-budget films finding their core audience on DVD and video on demand, the boundaries among theatrical film, cable television, and the Internet as exhibition platforms were dissolving. The changes generated more constraints, more opportunities, and more hard decisions for directors who wanted to tell stories in unexpected ways.

Hong Kong Cinema, 1980s–1990s

While independent directors were revamping American films in the 1980s, a young generation of directors in Hong Kong found footing in their industry and recast its traditional genres and creative methods. The result was a vigorous local tradition. Hong Kong's innovations in cinematic style and storytelling strongly influenced world filmmaking well into the 21st century.

A Local Tradition Goes Global

Although Hong Kong produced films in the silent era and during the 1930s, World War II halted production. When the industry revived in the 1950s, Shaw Brothers became the most powerful studio. Shaws owned theaters throughout East Asia and used Hong Kong as a production base for films in several languages, chiefly Mandarin Chinese. Shaws made films in many genres, but among its biggest successes were dynamic, gory swordfighting films (*wuxia pian,* or "tales of martial chivalry"). In the 1970s, another studio, Golden Harvest, triumphed with kung-fu films starring Bruce Lee. Although Lee completed only four martial-arts films before his death in 1973, he became the most famous Chinese actor of all time. Lee's graceful, almost feral presence brought Hong Kong cinema to worldwide attention and forever identified it with films of acrobatic and violent action.

Several major directors worked in this period. Most famous is King Hu, who started as a Shaws director. In films such as *Dragon Gate Inn* (1967) and *The Valiant Ones* (1975; 5.76), Hu reinvigorated the *wuxia pian* through graceful airborne swordplay and inventive cutting. Chang Cheh, another Shaws director, turned the swordplay film toward violent male melodrama (such as *The One-Armed Swordsman,* 1967) before specializing in flamboyant kung-fu films such as *Crippled Avengers* (also called *Mortal Combat,* 1978). Neither King Hu nor Chang Cheh was a practitioner of martial arts, but Lau Kar-leung was a fight choreographer before becoming a full-fledged director. Lau created a string of inventive films (such as *36th Chamber of Shaolin,* 1978, and *The Eight-Diagram Pole Fighter,* 1983) that showcased a range of dazzling martial-arts techniques.

The New Generation: Two Schools

By the early 1980s, traditional kung-fu was fading in popularity, and Shaws turned from moviemaking to its lucrative television business. At the same time, a new generation of directors came forward. One group had little formal education but had grown up in the film industry, working as stuntmen and martial artists. Among those who became directors were choreographers Yuen Wo-ping and Yuen Kuei (*Yes, Madam!,* 1985). Sammo Hung choreographed, directed, and starred in many lively action films (such as *Eastern Condors,* 1987).

The most famous graduate of the studio system was Jackie Chan, who labored as a copy of Bruce Lee before finding his feet in comic kung-fu. With *Drunken Master* (1978, directed by Yuen Wo-ping), he became a star throughout Asia and gained the power to direct his own films. In the early 1980s, Chan and his

CONNECT TO THE BLOG
www.davidbordwell.net/blog

We examine Hong Kong filmmaking style, and especially the work of Jackie Chan, in "Bond vs. Chan: Jackie shows how it's done."

colleagues realized that kung-fu could be incorporated into action movies in the Hollywood mold. Chan made the historical adventure *Project A* (1983, also starring Hung) and the contemporary cop drama *Police Story* (1985). These and others were huge hits across Asia, partly because of Chan's lovably goofy star persona and partly because of his resourceful and dangerous stunt scenes (6.49–6.51).

A second group of directors had more formal training, with many attending film schools in the United States or Britain. When Ann Hui, Allen Fong, and others returned to Hong Kong, they found work in television before moving on to feature filmmaking. For a time, they constituted a local art cinema, attracting attention at festivals with such films as Hui's *Boat People* (1982). But most of this group gravitated toward independent companies turning out comedies, dramas, and action films. Tsui Hark was the leader of this trend. As both director and producer, Tsui revived and reworked a range of genres: swordplay fantasy (*Zu: Warriors of the Magic Mountain,* 1979), romantic comedy (*Shanghai Blues,* 1984), historical adventure (*Peking Opera Blues,* 1986; **12.68**), supernatural romance (*A Chinese Ghost Story,* 1987, directed by Ching Siu-tung), and classic kung-fu (*Once upon a Time in China,* 1990).

Seeing the success that urban crime films were enjoying, Tsui partnered with John Woo on *A Better Tomorrow* (1986), a remake of a 1960s movie (**12.69**). Woo was something of an in-between figure, having been a successful studio comedy director during the 1970s. With Tsui as producer, *A Better Tomorrow* became Woo's comeback effort, one of the most successful Hong Kong films of the 1980s and a star-making vehicle for the charismatic Chow Yun-fat. Tsui, Woo, and Chow teamed again for a sequel and for the film that made Woo famous in the West, *The Killer* (1989), a lush and baroque story of the unexpected alliance between a hitman and a detective (**12.70**).

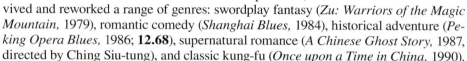

12.68 **Rhythmic staging.** Abrupt movements into and out of the frame are characteristic of Hong Kong film style. In this shot from *Peking Opera Blues,* the sheriff and his captive rise into the foreground as the three heroines watch from the rear.

Story and Style

Hong Kong cinema of the 1980s and early 1990s simmered with almost reckless energy. The rushed production schedules didn't allow much time to prepare scripts, so the plots, borrowing freely from Chinese legend and Hollywood genres, tended to be less tightly unified than those in U.S. films. They avoided tight linkage of cause and effect in favor of a more casual, episodic construction—not, as in Italian

12.69

12.70

12.69–12.70 **John Woo, influential stylist.** A striking long shot as a hero walks to meet his fate in *A Better Tomorrow* suggests Woo's debt to the Western (12.69). The urban crime thriller often parallels cop and crook—a convention that *The Killer* boldly fulfills in presenting detective and hitman as mirror images (12.70).

12.71 **Hong Kong stylization.** Blocks of colored light enhance a gun battle in *The Longest Nite* (1998).

Neorealism, to suggest the randomness of everyday life but rather to permit chases and fights to be inserted easily. Whereas action sequences were meticulously choreographed, connecting scenes were often improvised and shot quickly. Similarly, the kung-fu films had often bounced between pathos and almost silly comedy, and this tendency to mix tones continued through the 1980s. Because of rushed shooting, the plots often end abruptly, with a big action set-piece but little in the nature of a mood-setting epilogue. One of Tsui's innovations was to provide more satisfying conclusions, as in the lilting railroad station finale of *Shanghai Blues*.

At the level of visual style, Hong Kong directors brought the action film to a new pitch of excitement. Gunmen (and gunwomen) leaped and fired in slow motion, hovering in midair like 1970s swordfighters and kung-fu warriors. John Woo, who had been an assistant director for Chang Cheh, pushed such shots to extravagant limits. Directors also developed florid color designs, with rich reds, blues, and yellows glowing out of smoky nightclubs or narrow alleyways. Well into the 2000s, unrealistically tinted mood lighting was a trademark of Hong Kong cinema **(12.71).** Above all, everything was sacrificed to constant motion; even in dialogue scenes, the camera and the characters seldom stood still.

Aiming to energize the viewer, the new action directors built on the innovations of King Hu and his contemporaries. They developed a staccato cutting technique based on the tempo of martial-arts routines and Peking Opera displays, alternating rapid movement with sudden pauses. If shot composition was kept simple, an action could be cut to flow across shots very rapidly, while one shot could accentuate a moment of stillness **(12.72–12.74).** Most Hong Kong directors were unaware of the Soviet Montage movement, but in their efforts to arouse viewers through expressive movement and editing, they were reviving ideas of concern to those 1920s filmmakers.

Legacy Overseas

The 1990s brought the golden age of Hong Kong action cinema to a close. Jackie Chan, John Woo, Chow Yun-fat, Sammo Hung, and action star Jet Li began working in Hollywood, with Yuen Wo-ping designing the action choreography for *The Matrix* (1999) and *Crouching Tiger, Hidden Dragon* (2000). A recession after Hong Kong's 1997 handover to China depressed the local film industry. As Hollywood began imitating Hong Kong movies (as in *The Replacement Killers,* 1998), local audiences developed a taste for U.S. films. At the same time, the art-cinema wing became more ambitious, and festivals rewarded the offbeat works of Wong Kar-wai (see the analysis of *Chungking Express,* pp. 425–429). The action tradition was maintained by only a few directors such as Johnnie To, whose laconic film noir *The Mission* (1999) brought a leanness and pictorial abstraction to the gangster genre.

CONNECT TO THE BLOG
www.davidbordwell.net/blog

A week-long series of blog entries devoted to Hong Kong film starts with "PLANET HONG KONG now in cyberspace." "PLANET HONG KONG: The dragon dances" is devoted to analyzing Hong Kong action scenes.

12.72

12.73

12.74

12.72–12.74 Rhythmic editing and movement. During a fight scene in *Yes, Madam!* Michele Yeoh swings swiftly around, in a shot only 7 frames long (12.72). In two more shots, 12.73 and 12.74, she knocks the villain spinning (15 frames), and drops smoothly into a relaxed posture on the rail (17 frames). Her stillness at the end of the shot provides a pause before she launches another assault.

Hong Kong filmmakers had created a new set of creative options for staging and cutting physical action, and some directors took advantage of them. The legions of American fans included Quentin Tarantino, who paid homage to the Asian action cinema in *Kill Bill, Volumes 1 and 2* (2003–2004). He mixed together elements of Japanese swordplay, anime, and low-budget European thrillers, but his allegiance to Hong Kong's tradition shone through **(12.75).** Just as other countries' cinemas borrow from Hollywood, Hollywood selectively absorbs cutting-edge innovations from overseas.

12.75 *Kill Bill* **and Hong Kong cinema.** Although the weaponry in this fight consists mostly of samurai swords, director Tarantino pays tribute to the Hong Kong tradition: Yuen Woo-ping serves as martial-arts choreographer and the heroine wears Bruce Lee's signature yellow track suit.

Tarantino was a film fan from childhood. He watched old movies on TV, recent releases in theatres, and anything that caught his fancy on VHS. Like every filmmaker, he started as a film viewer; like many filmmakers, he was keen to explore the entire range of film history. Asked what he does in his spare time, he replied, "What you'd expect—read, listen to music, hang out with friends, watch my video and DVD collection. Get obsessions about this or that. I'm a film historian so I'm always trying to feed my brain."

Just as anyone who thinks, talks, and writes analytically about movies is doing film criticism, Tarantino is right to suggest that seeking out older films and letting them feed your brain is a step toward doing film history. The films he sees nourish his passion to create films himself. Even if you don't follow that career path, thinking like a filmmaker includes opening yourself up to the vast variety of films made in different times and places. By considering what artistic choices were available, by recognizing the creative decisions made by filmmakers who have come before us, we become more sensitive to every movie we see. To fully appreciate the films we watch now, we need to be aware that their makers are struggling with the same problems and decisions that appear at every moment of film history. Technology, tastes, and received traditions offer both opportunities and constraints—sometimes opportunities *within* constraints.

By looking at films from a historical angle, we realize that filmmakers have always been as fascinated by the power of movies as we are today. As Wölfflin says, not everything may be possible at all times. Still, some filmmakers always try to push the boundaries of what *is* possible, and others show us new possibilities in what seems familiar. Their hard work and imaginative energies have given us richer experiences of the art of cinema.

 ## RECOMMENDED DVD AND BLU-RAY DISCS

Many of the films mentioned in this chapter, especially the ones from recent decades, are available on DVD. So are classics from the silent era, but they're sometimes hard to find or buried in a big compilation. Below we offer information about the best editions of some silent-era titles.

Several DVD companies specialize in releasing historically important films: The Criterion Collection (www.criterion.com), Flicker Alley (www.flickeralley.com), Gartenberg Media (www.gartenbergmedia.com), Image Entertainment (www.image-entertainment.com), Kino Video (www.kino.com), Milestone (www.milestonefilms.com), and in the United Kingdom (coded for Region 2), Eureka!'s "Masters of Cinema" series (www.mastersofcinema.org). Edition Filmmuseum (www.edition-filmmuseum.com/) is a website that sells DVDs issued by several major archives and restoration companies; the website is in German and English, and the offerings all have optional English subtitles and are non-region-coded (Region All). It's an invaluable source for the best prints of classics from around the world. It is as easy to register with Filmmuseum and purchase from the site as it is to buy from Amazon.

Collections of Historically Important Films

Some collections of early films offer an easy way to get a quick overview of a period, filmmaker, or genre. For a brief introduction to the period up to 1913, *Landmarks of Early Film* (1 disc, Image Entertainment) offers 40 shorts. *Edison: The Invention of the Movies* (4 discs, Kino Video and the Museum of Modern Art) collects 140 films from the Thomas A. Edison Company, including *The Great Train Robbery*. It contains interviews with film historians and archivists, as well as program notes and documents. *The Movies Begin: A Treasury of Early Cinema 1894–1913* (5 discs, Kino Video) gathers 133 films arranged thematically: Volume 1, "*The Great Train Robbery* and Other Primary works"; Volume 2, "The European Pioneers" (including films by the Lumières and early British filmmakers); Volume 3, "Experimentation and Discovery" (mostly early British and French films); Volume 4, "The Magic of Méliès"; and Volume 5, "Comedy, Spectacle and New Horizons."

Slapstick Encyclopedia (5 discs, Image Entertainment) surveys the golden age of comedy shorts—the 1910s and early 1920s. *The Harold Lloyd Comedy Collection* (7 discs,

New Line) provides an extensive program of films with one of the masters of silent comedy, as well as a disc of bonus material.

A broad range of types of films is collected in *Treasures from American Film Archives: 50 Preserved Films* (4 discs), *More Treasures from American Film Archives, 1894–1931* (3 discs, Image Entertainment), and *Treasures III: Social Issues in American Film 1900–1934* (4 discs, Image Entertainment). These include documentaries, home movies, animation, experimental cinema, and fiction films such as D. W. Griffith's 1911 one-reeler *The Lonedale Operator* (illustrating his command of early intercutting), Cecil B. De Mille's The *Godless Girl* (1928), and Ernst Lubitsch's masterpiece of continuity filmmaking, *Lady Windermere's Fan* (1925). Each boxed set includes a book of detailed program notes.

Early Cinema

The boxed set "Pioneer Georges Méliès: First Wizard of Cinema (1896–1913)" (Flicker Alley) offers 173 films covering the early director's career; Flicker Alley followed this release with "George Méliès Encore," which includes newly discovered prints. One of the chief early French production firms is represented by "Gaumont Treasures 1897–1913" (Kino). Flicker Alley assembled a collection of restored films from the 1896–1944 era as "Saved from the Flames." It offers a variety of genres, including travelogues and animated films, as well as such classics as Lois Weber's *Suspense*.

The Development of Classical Hollywood Cinema

Many films from the 1910s and 1920s by D. W. Griffith, Cecil B. De Mille, and other major directors are available on DVD. Some notable releases: "Chaplin at Keystone" (Flicker Alley), "The Chaplin Mutual Comedies" (Image), "Douglas Fairbanks: A Modern Pioneer" (Flicker Alley), and "Three Silent Classics by Josef von Sternberg" (Criterion Collection). A little-known but important film from 1915 is Raoul Walsh's *Regeneration* (Image).

German Expressionism

The best collection of Ernst Lubitsch's silent German films is Kino's "Lubitsch in Berlin," with a mixture of his comedies and historical dramas. Kino has also released restored versions of *The Cabinet of Dr. Caligari, The Golem,* and *Metropolis.*

French Impressionism and Surrealism

The French Impressionist movement is not as familiar as the German and Soviet movements of the same era. Its important films are only gradually becoming available on DVD. Two of Abel Gance's most important Impressionist films, *J'accuse* (1919 version) and *La Roue* have been issued by Flicker Alley. (See our review of the *La Roue* disc on our blog, "An old-fashioned, sentimental avant-garde film.") One of the finest films of the movement, Jean Epstein's *Cœur fidèle,* is available from Eureka! in a dual Blu-ray/DVD set. Epstein's *The Fall of the House of Usher* was released by Image.

Gaumont released two early Impressionist films by Marcel L'Herbier, *L'homme du large* and *El Dorado,* in a boxed set, that lacks English subtitles and is coded for Region 2. L'Herbier's late masterpiece of the movement, *L'Argent,* is available from Eureka!, also Region 2 but with English subtitles. This set includes valuable supplements, including a 40-minute making-of and a 45-minute documentary on L'Herbier's silent career.

The first volume of Kino's "Avant-garde" series, mentioned above, contains Epstein's important film, *La glace à trios faces,* as well as Dimitri Kirsanoff's Impressionist short feature, *Ménilmontant* and Germaine Dulac's Surrealist short, *La coquille et le clergyman.*

Soviet Montage

The films of the best-known Montage directors are available on DVD. Sergei Eisenstein's films are available in so many versions that recommendations are in order: Kino's versions of the restored *Strike* and *Potemkin,* and Image's disc of *October. Old and New* is available in Flicker Alley's set, "Landmarks of Early Soviet Cinema," which also includes important but less familiar films such as Lev Kuleshov's *The Extraordinary Adventures of Mr. West in the Land of the Bolsheviks* and Boris Barnet's *House on Trubnoya.*

On our blog, we occasionally review groups of new releases of historical films on DVD, particularly those from the silent era. Also our annual roundup of the 10 best films made 90 years before gives the DVD availability (if any) of the films on the list.

GLOSSARY

abstract form   A type of filmic organization in which the parts relate to one another through repetition and variation of such visual qualities as shape, color, rhythm, and direction of movement.

Academy ratio   The standardized shape of the film frame established by the Academy of Motion Picture Arts and Sciences. In the original ratio, the frame was 1⅓ times as wide as it was high (1.33:1); later the width was normalized at 1.85 times the height (1.85:1).

aerial perspective   A cue for suggesting depth in the image by presenting objects in the distance less distinctly than those in the foreground.

anamorphic lens   A lens for making widescreen films using regular *Academy ratio* frame size. The camera lens takes in a wide field of view and squeezes it onto the frame, and a similar projector lens unsqueezes the image onto a wide theater screen.

angle of framing   The position of the frame in relation to the subject it shows: above it, looking down (a high angle); horizontal, on the same level (a straight-on angle); below it, looking up (a low angle). Also called *camera angle*.

animation   Any process whereby artificial movement is created by photographing a series of drawings (see also *cel animation*), objects, or computer images one by one. Small changes in position, recorded frame by frame, create the illusion of movement.

aspect ratio   The relationship of the frame's width to its height. The standard *Academy ratio* is currently 1.85:1.

associational form   A type of organization in which the film's parts are juxtaposed to suggest similarities, contrasts, concepts, emotions, and expressive qualities.

asynchronous sound   Sound that is not matched temporally with the movements occurring in the image, as when dialogue is out of synchronization with lip movements.

auteur   The presumed or actual author of a film, usually identified as the director; also sometimes used in an evaluative sense to distinguish good filmmakers (*auteurs*) from bad ones.

axis of action   In the *continuity editing* system, the imaginary line that passes through the main actors or the principal movement. The axis of action defines the spatial relations of all the elements of the scene as being to the right or left. The camera is not supposed to cross the axis at a cut and thus reverse those spatial relations. The axis of action is also called the 180° line. See also *180° system, screen direction*.

backlighting   Illumination cast onto the figures in the scene from the side opposite the camera, usually creating a thin outline of highlighting on those figures.

Blu-Ray Disc (or BD)   A high-definition digital medium for home video, similar to a DVD but having a higher storage capacity and producing a higher-resolution image.

boom   A pole on which a microphone can be suspended above the scene being filmed and that is used to change the microphone's position as the action shifts.

camera angle   See *angle of framing*.

canted framing   A view in which the frame is not level; either the right or the left side is lower than the other, causing objects in the scene to appear slanted out of an upright position.

categorical form   A type of filmic organization in which the parts treat distinct subsets of a topic. For example, a film about the United States might be organized into 50 parts, each devoted to a state.

cel animation   Animation that uses a series of drawings on pieces of celluloid, called *cels* for short. Slight changes between the drawings combine to create an illusion of movement.

CGI   Computer-generated imagery: using digital software systems to create figures, settings, or other material in the frame.

cheat cut   In the *continuity editing* system, a cut that presents continuous time from shot to shot but that mismatches the positions of figures or objects.

cinematography   A general term for all the manipulations of the film strip by the camera in the shooting phase and by the laboratory in the developing phase.

close-up   A framing in which the scale of the object shown is relatively large; most commonly, a person's head seen from the neck up, or an object of a comparable size that fills most of the screen.

closure   The degree to which the ending of a narrative film reveals the effects of all the causal events and resolves (or "closes off") all lines of action.

continuity editing   A system of cutting to maintain continuous and clear narrative action. Continuity editing relies on matching screen direction, position, and temporal relations from shot to shot. For specific techniques of continuity editing, see *axis of action, crosscutting, cut-in, establishing shot, eyeline match, match on action, reestablishing shot, screen direction, shot/reverse shot*.

contrast   In cinematography, the difference between the brightest and the darkest areas within the frame.

crane shot   A shot with a change in framing accomplished by placing the camera above the subject and moving through the air in any direction.

crosscutting   Editing that alternates shots of two or more lines of action occurring in different places, usually simultaneously.

cut   (1) In filmmaking, the joining of two strips of film together with a splice. (2) In the finished film, an instantaneous change from one framing to another. See also *jump cut*.

cut-in   An instantaneous shift from a distant framing to a closer view of some portion of the same space.

deep focus   A use of the camera lens and lighting that keeps objects in both close and distant planes in sharp focus.

deep space   An arrangement of mise-en-scene elements so that there is a considerable distance between the plane closest to the camera and the one farthest away. Any or all of these planes may be in focus. See also *shallow space*.

depth of field   The measurements of the closest and farthest planes in front of the camera lens between which everything will be in sharp focus. A depth of field from 5 to 16 feet, for example, would mean everything closer than 5 feet and farther than 16 feet would be out of focus.

dialogue overlap   In editing a scene, arranging the cut so that a bit of dialogue coming from shot A is heard under a shot that shows another character or another element in the scene.

diegesis   In a narrative film, the world of the film's story. The diegesis includes events that are presumed to have occurred and actions and spaces not shown onscreen. See also *diegetic sound, nondiegetic insert, nondiegetic sound*.

diegetic sound   Any voice, musical passage, or sound effect presented as originating from a source within the film's world. See also *nondiegetic sound*.

digital intermediate   A strip of film is developed and scanned, frame by frame, to create a digital copy of sequence or a whole movie. The digital copy is manipulated with software. When finished, it is scanned frame by frame onto a strip of negative film, which will be used to make prints to send to theaters.

digital resolution   The detailed clarity of a digital image, typically measured by the number or density of pixels. The common professional image resolutions are measured at horizontal resolutions of 1280, 2K, and 4K.

direct sound   Music, noise, and speech recorded from the event at the moment of filming; opposite of *postsynchronization*.

discontinuity editing   Any alternative system of joining shots together using techniques unacceptable within *continuity editing* principles. Possibilities include mismatching of temporal and spatial relations, violations of the *axis of action*, and concentration on graphic relationships. See also *elliptical editing, graphic match, intellectual montage, jump cut, nondiegetic insert, overlapping editing*.

dissolve   A transition between two shots during which the first image gradually disappears while the second image gradually appears; for a moment, the two images blend in *superimposition*.

distance of framing   The apparent distance of the frame from the mise-en-scene elements; also called camera distance and shot scale. See also *close-up, extreme close-up, extreme long shot, medium close-up, medium shot, plan américain*.

distribution   One of the three branches of the film industry; the process of marketing the film and supplying copies to exhibition venues. See also *exhibition, production*.

dolly   A camera support with wheels, used in making *tracking shots*.

dubbing   The process of replacing part or all of the voices on the sound track in order to correct mistakes or rerecord dialogue. See also *postsynchronization*.

duration   In a narrative film, the aspect of temporal manipulation that involves the time span presented in the *plot* and assumed to operate in the *story*. See also *frequency, order*.

DVD   Short for digital versatile disc or digital video disc, a home-video device containing moving-image content and played on a dedicated player or a game console or computer.

editing   (1) In filmmaking, the task of selecting and joining camera takes. (2) In the finished film, the set of techniques that governs the relations among shots.

ellipsis   In a narrative film, the shortening of *plot* duration achieved by omitting some *story* duration. See also *elliptical editing, viewing time*.

elliptical editing   Shot transitions that omit parts of an event, causing an *ellipsis* in plot duration.

establishing shot   A shot, usually involving a distant framing, that shows the spatial relations among the important figures, objects, and setting in a scene.

exhibition   One of the three branches of the film industry; the process of showing the finished film to audiences. See also *distribution, production*.

exposure   The adjustment of the camera mechanism in order to control how much light strikes each frame of film passing through the aperture.

external diegetic sound   Sound represented as coming from a physical source within the story space that we assume characters in the scene also hear. See also *internal diegetic sound*.

extreme close-up   A framing in which the scale of the object shown is very large; most commonly, a small object or a part of the body.

extreme long shot   A framing in which the scale of the object shown is very small; a building, landscape, or crowd of people will fill the screen.

eyeline match   A cut obeying the *axis of action* principle, in which the first shot shows a person looking off in one direction and the second shows a nearby space containing what he or she sees. If the person looks left, the following shot should imply that the looker is offscreen right.

fade   (1) *Fade-in:* a dark screen that gradually brightens as a shot appears. (2) *Fade-out:* a shot that gradually disappears as the screen darkens. Occasionally, fade-outs brighten to pure white or to a color.

fill light   Illumination from a source less bright than the *key light,* used to soften deep shadows in a scene. See also *three-point lighting*.

film noir   "Dark film," a term applied by French critics to a type of American film, usually in the detective or thriller genres, with low-key lighting and a somber mood.

film stock   The strip of material on which a series of still photographs is registered; it consists of a clear base coated on one side with a light-sensitive emulsion.

filter   A piece of glass or gelatin placed in front of the camera or printer lens to alter the quality or quantity of light striking the film in the aperture.

flashback   An alteration of *story* order in which the *plot* moves back to show events that have taken place earlier than ones already shown.

flashforward   An alteration of story order in which the plot presentation moves forward to future events and then returns to the present.

focal length   The distance from the center of the lens to the point at which the light rays meet in sharp focus. The focal length determines the perspective relations of the space represented on the flat screen. See also *normal lens, telephoto lens, wide-angle lens*.

focus   The degree to which light rays coming from the same part of an object through different parts of the lens reconverge at the same point on the film frame, creating sharp outlines and distinct textures.

following shot   A shot with framing that shifts to keep a moving figure onscreen.

form   The overall system of relationships among the parts of a film.

frame   A single image on the strip of film. When a series of frames is projected onto a screen in quick succession, an illusion of movement is created.

frame rate   In shooting, the number of frames exposed per second; in projection, the number of frames thrown on the screen per second. If the two are the same, the speed of the action appears normal, whereas a disparity creates slow or fast motion. The standard rate in sound cinema is 24 frames per second (fps) for both shooting and projection, although some European films aiming at television broadcast are shot at 25 fps. In video, common frame rates are 23.98 fps, 24 fps, 25 fps, 30 fps, and 60 fps.

framing   The use of the edges of the film frame to select and to compose what will be visible onscreen.

frequency   In a narrative film, the aspect of temporal manipulation that involves the number of times any *story* event is shown in the *plot*. See also *duration, order*.

front projection   A composite process whereby footage meant to appear as the background of a shot is projected from the front onto a screen; figures in the foreground are filmed in front of the screen as well. This is the opposite of *rear projection*.

frontal lighting   Illumination directed into the scene from a position near the camera.

frontality   In staging, the positioning of figures so that they face the viewer.

function   The role or effect of any element within the film's form.

gauge   The width of the film strip, measured in millimeters.

genres   Types of films that audiences and filmmakers recognize by their familiar narrative conventions. Common genres are musical, gangster, and science fiction films.

graphic match   Two successive shots joined so as to create a strong similarity of compositional elements (e.g., color, shape).

handheld camera   The use of the camera operator's body as a camera support, either holding it by hand or using a harness.

hard lighting   Illumination that creates sharp-edged shadows.

height of framing   The distance of the camera above the ground, regardless of the *angle of framing*.

high-key lighting   Illumination that creates comparatively little contrast between the light and dark areas of the shot. Shadows are fairly transparent and brightened by *fill light*.

ideology   A relatively coherent system of values, beliefs, or ideas shared by some social group and often taken for granted as natural or inherently true.

intellectual montage   The juxtaposition of a series of images to create an abstract idea not present in any one image.

internal diegetic sound   Sound represented as coming from the mind of a character within the story space. Although we and the character can hear it, we assume that the other characters cannot. See also *external diegetic sound*.

interpretation   The viewer's activity of analyzing the implicit and symptomatic meanings suggested in a film. See also *meaning*.

iris   A round, moving *mask* that can close down to end a scene (iris-out) or emphasize a detail, or that can open to begin a scene (iris-in) or to reveal more space around a detail.

jump cut   An elliptical cut that appears to be an interruption of a single shot. Either the figures seem to change instantly against a constant background, or the background changes instantly while the figures remain constant. See also *ellipsis*.

key light   In the three-point lighting system, the brightest illumination coming into the scene. See also *backlighting, fill light, three-point lighting*.

lens   A shaped piece of transparent material (usually glass) with either or both sides curved to gather and focus light rays. Most camera and projector lenses place a series of lenses within a metal tube to form a compound lens.

linearity   In a narrative, the clear motivation of a series of causes and effects that progress without significant digressions, delays, or irrelevant actions.

long shot   A framing in which the scale of the object shown is small; a standing human figure would appear nearly the height of the screen.

long take   A shot that continues for an unusually lengthy time before the transition to the next shot.

low-key lighting   Illumination that creates strong contrast between light and dark areas of the shot, with deep shadows and little *fill light*.

mask   An opaque screen placed in the camera or printer that blocks part of the frame off and changes the shape of the photographed image, leaving part of the frame a solid color. As seen on the screen, most masks are black, although they can be white or colored.

masking   In exhibition, stretches of black fabric that frame the theater screen. Masking can be adjusted according to the *aspect ratio* of the film to be projected.

match on action   A continuity cut that splices two different views of the same action together at the same moment in the movement, making it seem to continue uninterrupted.

matte work   A type of *process shot* in which different areas of the image (usually actors and setting) are photographed separately and combined in laboratory work.

meaning   (1) Referential meaning: allusion to particular items of knowledge outside the film that the viewer is expected to recognize. (2) Explicit meaning: significance presented overtly, usually in language and often near the film's beginning or end. (3) Implicit meaning: significance left tacit, for the viewer to discover upon analysis or reflection. (4) Symptomatic meaning: significance that the film divulges, often against its will, by virtue of its historical or social context.

medium close-up   A framing in which the scale of the object shown is fairly large; a human figure seen from the chest up would fill most of the screen.

medium long shot   A framing at a distance that makes an object about 4 or 5 feet high appear to fill most of the screen vertically. See also *plan américain,* the special term for a medium long shot depicting human figures.

medium shot   A framing in which the scale of the object shown is of moderate size; a human figure seen from the waist up would fill most of the screen.

mise-en-scene   All of the elements placed in front of the camera to be photographed: the settings and props, lighting, costumes and makeup, and figure behavior.

mixing   Combining two or more sound tracks by recording them onto a single one.

mobile frame   The effect on the screen of the moving camera, a *zoom lens,* or certain *special effects*; the framing shifts in relation to the scene being photographed. See also *crane shot, pan, tilt, tracking shot.*

monochromatic color design   Color design that emphasizes a narrow set of shades of a single color.

montage   (1) A synonym for *editing.* (2) An approach to editing developed by the Soviet filmmakers of the 1920s; it emphasizes dynamic, often discontinuous, relationships between shots and the juxtaposition of images to create ideas not present in either shot by itself. See also *discontinuity editing, intellectual montage.*

montage sequence   A segment of a film that summarizes a topic or compresses a passage of time into brief symbolic or typical images. Frequently, *dissolves, fades, superimpositions,* and *wipes* are used to link the images in a montage sequence.

motif   An element in a film that is repeated in a significant way.

motion capture   In digital filmmaking, the recording of patterns of movement of a figure. Small reflective markers are placed at key points on a person, animal, or object. These are recorded by a special camera and provide a record of the motion but not the appearance of the subject. From that record, animation software can imbue other creatures with the same patterns of motion. When the markers are placed on an actor's face, the recording is often called *performance capture.*

motion control   A computerized method of planning and repeating camera movements on miniatures, models, and process work.

motivation   The justification given in the film for the presence of an element. This may be an appeal to the viewer's knowledge of the real world, to *genre* conventions, to narrative causality, or to a stylistic pattern within the film.

narration   The process through which the *plot* conveys or withholds *story* information. The narration can be more or less restricted to character knowledge and more or less deep in presenting characters' perceptions and thoughts.

narrative form   A type of filmic organization in which the parts relate to one another through a series of causally related events taking place in time and space.

nondiegetic insert   A shot or series of shots cut into a sequence, showing objects that are represented as being outside the world of the narrative.

nondiegetic sound   Sound, such as mood music or a narrator's commentary, represented as coming from a source outside the space of the narrative.

nonsimultaneous sound   Diegetic sound that comes from a source in time either earlier or later than the images it accompanies.

normal lens   A lens that shows objects without severely exaggerating or reducing the depth of the scene's planes. In 35mm filming, a normal lens has a *focal length* between 35 and 50mm. See also *telephoto lens, wide-angle lens.*

offscreen sound   Simultaneous sound from a source assumed to be in the space of the scene but outside what is visible onscreen.

offscreen space   The six areas blocked from being visible on the screen but still part of the space of the scene: to each side and above and below the frame, behind the set, and behind the camera. See also *space.*

180° system   The continuity approach to editing dictates that the camera should stay on one side of the action to ensure consistent left-right spatial relations between elements from shot to shot. The 180° line is the same as the *axis of action.* See also *continuity editing, screen direction.*

order   In a narrative film, the aspect of temporal manipulation that involves the sequence in which the chronological events of the *story* are arranged in the *plot.* See also *duration, frequency.*

overlap   A cue for suggesting represented depth in the film image by placing objects partly in front of more distant ones.

overlapping editing   Cuts that repeat part or all of an action, thus expanding its viewing time and plot duration.

pan   A camera movement with the camera body turning to the right or left. On the screen, it produces a mobile framing that scans the space horizontally.

performance capture   See *motion capture.*

pixels   Short for "picture elements." The small glowing dots that make up the image on a television monitor or computer screen; also visible in digital theatrical projection. Changes in color and brightness of the array of pixels create moving images on these devices.

pixillation   A form of single-frame animation in which three-dimensional objects, often people, are made to move in staccato bursts through the use of stop-action cinematography.

plan américain   A framing in which the scale of the object shown is moderately small; the human figure seen from the shins to the head would fill most of the screen. This is sometimes referred to as a *medium long shot,* especially when human figures are not shown.

plan-séquence   A French term for a scene handled in a single shot, usually a *long take.*

plot   In a narrative film, all the events that are directly presented to us, including their causal relations, chronological order, duration, frequency, and spatial locations; opposed to *story,* which is the viewer's imaginary construction of all the events in the narrative. See also *duration, ellipsis, flashback, flashforward, frequency, order, viewing time.*

point-of-view shot (POV shot)   A shot taken with the camera placed approximately where the character's eyes would be, showing what the character would see; usually cut in before or after a shot of the character looking.

postproduction   The phase of film production that assembles the images and sounds into the finished film.

postsynchronization   The process of adding sound to images after they have been shot and assembled. This can include *dubbing* of voices, as well as inserting diegetic music or sound effects. It is the opposite of *direct sound*.

preproduction   The phase of filmmaking that prepares for production on the basis of a screenplay, design, and financing.

process shot   Any shot involving rephotography to combine two or more images into one or to create a special effect; also called composite shot. See also *matte work, rear projection, special effects*.

production   One of the three branches of the film industry; the process of creating the film. See also *distribution, exhibition*.

racking focus   Shifting the area of sharp focus from one plane to another during a shot; the effect on the screen is called rack-focus.

rate   In shooting, the number of frames exposed per second; in projection, the number of frames thrown on the screen per second. If the two are the same, the speed of the action will appear normal, whereas a disparity will create slow or fast motion. The standard rate in sound cinema is 24 frames per second for both shooting and projection.

rear projection   A technique for combining a foreground action with a background action filmed earlier. The foreground is filmed in a studio, against a screen; the background imagery is projected from behind the screen. The opposite of *front projection*.

reestablishing shot   A return to a view of an entire space after a series of closer shots following the *establishing shot*.

reframing   Short panning or tilting movements to adjust for the figures' movements, keeping them onscreen or centered.

rhetorical form   A type of filmic organization in which the parts create and support an argument.

rhythm   The perceived rate and regularity of sounds, series of shots, and movements within the shots. Rhythmic factors include beat (or pulse), accent (or stress), and tempo (or pace).

rotoscope   A machine that projects live-action motion picture frames one by one onto a drawing pad so that an animator can trace the figures in each frame. The aim is to achieve more realistic movement in an animated film.

scene   A segment in a narrative film that takes place in one time and space or that uses crosscutting to show two or more simultaneous actions.

screen direction   The right-left relationships in a scene, set up in an establishing shot and determined by the position of characters and objects in the frame, by the directions of movement, and by the characters' eyelines. *Continuity editing* will attempt to keep screen direction consistent between shots. See also *axis of action, eyeline match, 180° system*.

segmentation   The process of dividing a film into parts for analysis.

sensor   A chip designed to capture visual information in digital form. It is located behind the lens in a digital motion-picture camera.

sequence   Term commonly used for a moderately large segment of film, involving one complete stretch of action; in a narrative film, often equivalent to a *scene*.

shallow focus   A restricted *depth of field*, which keeps only one plane in sharp focus; the opposite of *deep focus*.

shallow space   Staging the action in relatively few planes of depth; the opposite of *deep space*.

shot   (1) In shooting, one uninterrupted run of the camera to expose a series of frames; also called a *take*. (2) In the finished film, one uninterrupted image, whether or not there is mobile framing.

shot/reverse shot   Two or more shots edited together that alternate characters, typically in a conversation situation. In *continuity editing*, characters in one framing usually look left; in the other framing, right. Over-the-shoulder framings are common in shot/reverse-shot editing.

side lighting (sidelight)   Lighting coming from one side of a person or an object, usually to create a sense of volume, to bring out surface tensions, or to fill in areas left shadowed by light from another source.

simultaneous sound   Diegetic sound that is represented as occurring at the same time in the story as the image it accompanies.

size diminution   A cue for suggesting represented depth in the image by showing objects that are farther away as smaller than foreground objects.

soft lighting   Illumination that avoids harsh bright and dark areas, creating a gradual transition from highlights to shadows.

sound bridge   (1) At the beginning of one scene, the sound from the previous scene carries over briefly before the sound from the new scene begins. (2) At the end of one scene, the sound from the next scene is heard, leading into that scene.

sound over   Any sound that is not represented as coming from the space and time of the images on the screen. This includes both nondiegetic sounds and nonsimultaneous diegetic sound. See also *nondiegetic sound, nonsimultaneous sound*.

sound perspective   The sense of a sound's position in space, yielded by volume, timbre, pitch, and, in stereophonic reproduction systems, binaural information.

space   Any film displays a two-dimensional graphic space, the flat composition of the image. In films that depict recognizable objects, figures, and locales, a three-dimensional space is represented as well. At any moment, three-dimensional space may be directly depicted, as onscreen space or suggested, as *offscreen space*. In narrative film, we can also distinguish between story space—the locale of the totality of the action (whether shown or not)—and plot space—the locales visibly and audibly represented in the scenes.

special effects   A general term for various photographic manipulations that create fictitious spatial relations in the shot, such as *superimposition, matte work,* and *rear projection*.

story   In a narrative film, all the events that we see and hear, plus all those that we infer or assume to have occurred, arranged in their presumed causal relations, chronological order, duration, frequency, and spatial locations; opposed to *plot,* which is the film's actual presentation of events in the story. See also *duration, ellipsis, frequency, order, space, viewing time.*

storyboard   A tool used in planning film production, consisting of comic-strip-like drawings of individual shots or phases of shots with descriptions written below each drawing.

style   The repeated and salient uses of film techniques characteristic of a single film or a group of films (for example, a filmmaker's work or a national movement).

superimposition   The exposure of more than one image on the same film strip or in the same shot.

synchronous sound   Sound that is matched temporally with the movements occurring in the images, as when dialogue corresponds to lip movements.

take   In filmmaking, the shot produced by one uninterrupted run of the camera. One shot in the final film may be chosen from among several takes of the same action.

technique   Any aspect of the film medium that can be chosen and manipulated in making a film.

telephoto lens   A lens of long focal length that affects a scene's perspective by enlarging distant planes and making them seem close to the foreground planes; in 35mm filming, a lens with a *focal length* of 75mm or more. See also *normal lens, wide-angle lens.*

3D computer animation   Digitally generated series of images that imitate the rounded look of people, puppets, or models (not to be confused with stereoscopic 3D images viewed through glasses).

three-point lighting   A common arrangement using three directions of light on a scene: from behind the subjects (*backlighting*), from one bright source (*key light*), and from a less bright source balancing the key light (*fill light*).

tilt   A camera movement with the camera body swiveling upward or downward on a stationary support. It produces a mobile framing that scans the space vertically.

top lighting   Lighting coming from above a person or an object, usually in order to outline the upper areas of the figure or to separate it more clearly from the background.

tracking shot   A mobile framing that travels through space forward, backward, or laterally. See also *crane shot, pan,* and *tilt.*

2D computer animation   Digitally generated series of images that give the appearance of flat drawings or paintings.

typage   A performance technique of Soviet Montage cinema. The actor's appearance and behavior are presented as typical of a social class or other group.

underlighting   Illumination from a point below the figures in the scene.

unity   The degree to which a film's parts relate systematically to one another and provide motivations for all the elements included.

variation   In film form, the return of an element with notable changes.

viewing time   The length of time it takes to watch a film when it is projected at the appropriate speed.

whip pan   An extremely fast movement of the camera from side to side, which briefly causes the image to blur into a set of indistinct horizontal streaks. Often an imperceptible cut joins two whip pans to create a trick transition between scenes.

wide-angle lens   A lens of short focal length that affects a scene's perspective by distorting straight lines near the edges of the frame and by exaggerating the distance between foreground and background planes. In 35mm filming, a wide-angle lens has a *focal length* of 35mm or less. See also *normal lens, telephoto lens.*

wipe   A transition between shots in which a line passes across the screen, eliminating one shot as it goes and replacing it with the next one.

zoom lens   A lens with a focal length that can be changed during a shot. A shift toward the *telephoto-lens* range enlarges the image and flattens its planes together, giving an impression of magnifying the scene's space; a shift toward the *wide-angle* range does the opposite.

CREDITS

Figures 1.10, 1.11: Wisconsin Center for Film and Theater Research; 1.14: Courtesy Scott Sklenar, Rocky Gersbach, and Matt Rockwell of AMC Star Cinema Fitchburg, Wisconsin; 1.25, 1.26: Courtesy Rick Reavey and Adam Hasz of AMC Star Cinema Fitchburg, Wisconsin; 1.29, 1.30: The Museum of Modern Art Film Stills Archive; 1.36: Wisconsin Center for Film and Theater Research; 1.44: Courtesy Keith Stern, mckellen.com; 1.48: Wisconsin Center for Film and Theater Research. Figure 4.142: Courtesy Norman McLaren with permission of the National Film Board of Canada. **Figure 5.44:** Courtesy Ernie Gehr; 5.204–5.206 Courtesy Michael Snow. **Figures 6.38, 6.39:** Courtesy Bruce Conner. **Figures 10.53, 10.54:** Courtesy Bruce Conner; 10.59, 10.60: Courtesy J. J. Murphy; 10.78: The Museum of Modern Art Film Stills Archive; 10.111: Courtesy Norman McLaren with permission of the National Film Board of Canada. **Figure 12.7:** George Eastman House; 12.48, 12.49: Wisconsin Center for Film and Theater Research.

RECOMMENDED DVD AND BLU-RAY SUPPLEMENTS

Alien (20th Century Fox Home Entertainment), "Collector's Edition," 2 discs

Amadeus: Director's Cut (Warner Bros.), "Two-Disc Special Edition"

American Graffiti (Universal), "Collector's Edition," 1 disc

Armageddon (The Criterion Collection), 2 discs

Avatar (20th Century Fox) Three Disc Extended Collector's Edition and Extended Blu-ray Collector's Edition

Bambi (Disney), "Platinum Edition," 2 discs

Black Narcissus (The Criterion Collection), 1 disc

Blade Runner (Warner Bros.) Five-disc Complete Collector's Edition (also on Blu-ray) and Five-disc Ultimate Collector's Edition

Butch Cassidy and the Sundance Kid (20th Century Fox), "Special Edition," 1 disc

Charlie and the Chocolate Factory (Warner Bros.), "Two-Disc Deluxe Edition"

Che (The Criterion Collection) #496 Also on Blu-ray.

Chicken Run (Dreamworks Home Entertainment), "Special Edition," 1 disc

Cold Mountain (Miramax) 2-Disc Collector's Edition (The supplements are not on the Blu-ray disc)

Contempt (The Criterion Collection), 2 discs

Dancer in the Dark (New Line Home Video), 1 disc

Darby O'Gill and the Little People (Disney)

The Da Vinci Code (Sony) (supplements appear on all editions)

The Dark Knight (Warner Home Video), "Two-Disc Special Edition + Digital Copy"

Days of Heaven (The Criterion Collection) #409

Far from Heaven (Universal)

The Frighteners (Universal), "Peter Jackson's Director's Cut," 1 disc

The Girl with the Dragon Tattoo (Columbia), "3-Disc Combo Pack"

The Godfather (Paramount), "The Godfather DVD Collection," 5 discs

The Golden Compass (New Line Home Entertainment), "New Line Two-Disc Platinum Series"

The Good, the Bad, and the Ugly (MGM), "Special Edition," 2 discs

A Hard Day's Night (Miramax), 2 discs

Hellboy (Columbia Tristar Home Entertainment), "Two-Disc Special Edition"

Hellboy II: The Golden Army (Universal Studios Home Entertainment), "Three-Disc Special Edition"

The Ice Storm (The Criterion Collection) #426

The Incredibles (Disney), "Two-Disc Collector's Edition"

Iron Man (Paramount) "Two-Disc Special Collectors' Edition"

Jaws (Universal), "Anniversary Collector's Edition," 1 disc

Jurassic Park (Universal), "Collector's Edition," 1 disc

King Kong (Warner Bros.), "Two-Disc Special Edition"

King Kong: Peter Jackson's Production Diaries (Universal), 2 discs

Kingdom of Heaven (20th Century Fox) 4-disc Director's Cut

The Lord of the Rings 3 volumes (New Line Home Entertainment), "Special Extended DVD Edition," 4 discs each

The Magnificent Seven (Metro-Goldwyn-Mayer), "Collector's Edition," 2 discs

Magnolia (New Line Home Video), 2 discs

Master and Commander (20th Century Fox Home Entertainment), "Collector's Edition," 2 discs

Miller's Crossing (20th Century Fox) Also on Blu-ray.

Moulin Rouge! (20th Century Fox Home Entertainment), 2 discs

Munich (Universal Studios) Two-Disc Collector's Edition

My Fair Lady (Warner Bros.), "Two-Disc Special Edition"

My Own Private Idaho (The Criterion Collection), 2 discs

The Night of the Hunter (The Criterion Collection) #541

Norman McLaren: The Collector's Edition (Milestone), 2 discs

North by Northwest (Warner Bros.), 1 disc

Oklahoma! (20th Century Fox Home Entertainment), "50th Anniversary Edition," 2 discs

Once upon a Time in the West (Paramount), "Special Collector's Edition," 2 discs

Pickpocket (The Criterion Collection), 1 disc

Pinocchio (Walt Disney Studios Home Entertainment), Platinum Edition

Pirates of the Caribbean: Dead Man's Chest (Disney), "Two-disc Special Edition"

Pulp Fiction (Miramax Home Entertainment), "Collector's Edition," 2 discs

Rosemary's Baby (Paramount), 1 disc

Russian Ark (Wellspring), 1 disc

Saturday Night Fever (Paramount), "25th Anniversary DVD Edition," 1 disc

Scream (Dimension Home Video), "The Ultimate Scream Collection," 4 discs

The Searchers (Warner Home Video), "Ultimate Collector's Edition," 2 discs

A Serious Man (Universal Home Video) Same supplements on DVD and Blu-ray

Seven Men from Now (Paramount), "Special Collector's Edition," 1 disc

The Silence of the Lambs (Metro-Goldwyn-Mayer), "Special Edition," 1 disc

Silverado (Sony Pictures Home Entertainment), 2 discs

Sin City (Dimension), 2 discs

Singin' in the Rain (Warner Bros.), "Two-Disc Special Edition"

The Social Network (Sony Pictures Home Entertainment) Two-disc Collector's Edition, both DVD and Blu-ray

Speed (20th Century Fox Home Entertainment), "Five Star Collection," 2 discs

The Sweet Smell of Success (The Criterion Collection) #555

Take Shelter (Sony Pictures Classics), 1 disc

Terminator 2: Judgment Day (Artisan), "Extreme DVD," 2 discs

3:10 to Yuma (Lionsgate), 1 disc

Titus (20th Century Fox Home Entertainment), 2 discs

Toy Story/Toy Story 2 (Disney/Pixar), "Collector's Edition: The Ultimate Toy Box," 3 discs

20,000 Leagues Under the Sea (Disney), "Special Edition," 2 discs

Wallace & Gromit: The Curse of the Were-Rabbit (DreamWorks), 1 disc

War of the Worlds (2005) (DreamWorks Home Entertainment), "Two-Disc Limited Edition"

Who's Afraid of Virginia Woolf ? (Warner Home Video) Two-Disc Special Edition

The Wizard of Oz (Warner Home Video), "Two-Disc Special Edition"

Zodiac (Paramount), "Two-Disc Special Collector's Edition" (Director's Cut)